LIFE IN ANCIENT EGYPT

LIFE IN ANCIENT EGYPT

Adolf Erman

TRANSLATED BY H. M. TIRARD

WITH A
NEW INTRODUCTION BY
JON MANCHIP WHITE

DOVER PUBLICATIONS, INC.
NEW YORK

Published in Canada by General Publishing Company, Ltd., 30 Lesmill Road, Don Mills, Toronto, Ontario.
Published in the United Kingdom by Constable and Company, Ltd., 10 Orange Street, London WC 2.

This Dover edition, first published in 1971, is an unabridged and unaltered republication of the English translation originally published in 1894 by Macmillan and Company, London. This reprint also contains a new introductory essay by Jon Manchip White.

International Standard Book Number: 0-486-22632-8
Library of Congress Catalog Card Number: 79-115749

Manufactured in the United States of America
Dover Publications, Inc.
180 Varick Street
New York, N.Y. 10014

INTRODUCTION TO THE DOVER EDITION

Georg Adolf Erman was the son of one of Germany's outstanding mathematicians and physicists, a pioneer in the field of electrodynamics. Born in 1854, he passed the whole of his long life in Berlin. While still a young man he was appointed Director of the Egyptian Museum, and was largely responsible for bringing together its famous collections and establishing its international reputation. He died in 1937, at the age of eighty-two.

He was fortunate in finding his vocation early. He was twenty-three when he published the first of his many works on ancient Egypt, and twenty-five when the first edition of his celebrated *New Egyptian Grammar* appeared; this grammar at once secured for him a high position in the world of scholarship and held its place as the standard work on the subject for half a century. The philological studies that remain the basis of his enduring fame culminated between 1926 and 1935 with the publication of his massive five-volume *Dictionary of the Egyptian Language.* His *Literature of the Ancient Egyptians*, published in 1923 and translated into English in 1927 by A. M. Blackman, is still the most useful compendium of its kind. He remained energetic and productive to the end of his long life, publishing a valuable account of Egyptian religion at the age of eighty and a lively summary of his life's work, *The World of the Nile*, at eighty-one. He is one of the revered patriarchs of Egyptology.

The present book, *Life in Ancient Egypt*, appeared in 1886 and went through many editions. It is once more worth noting that Erman was a young man of only thirty-two when he made this significant contribution to the study of ancient Egypt. Several attempts to write synoptic histories of Egyptian civilization had been made prior to that date, including Wilkinson's *Manners and Customs of the Ancient Egyptians* (1847) and Kenrick's *Ancient Egypt under the Pharaohs* (1850), but Erman's book crystallized and consolidated in a masterly manner the advances made by Egyptology to that time, and provided a solid structure for future essays in the genre. The general reader could still not ask for a more compact or informative introductory volume; its clarity of conception and briskness of execution have ensured for it a lasting appeal. It inspired a passion for ancient Egypt among successive generations of educated German youth. Thomas Mann, for example, states in his *A Sketch of My Life* that, when he began to gather materials for his Joseph tetralogy, he was "only going back to a reading beloved in youth and an early passion for the land of the pyramids—childish conquests which had once in the fifth form made me confuse a teacher who had asked me the name of the sacred bull of the Egyptians and was answered with the original instead of the Graecized form of the name." Who would have introduced the young Thomas Mann to "the land of the pyramids" if not Adolf Erman?

Erman's own youth matched the entrancing high noon of his chosen subject. His book evokes the excitement of the era when the physical and intellectual exploration of Egyptian civilization was approaching its peak. Even before the opening of the Suez Canal in 1869 opened Egypt itself to the tourist and dilettante, the foundations of Egyptology had been laid by a generation of scholars—one might better say explorers—whose exploits were to become almost as legendary as those of the pharaohs. First among them was the towering figure of Richard Lepsius, the indomitable and indefatigable German who was despatched to Egypt by the King of Prussia in 1842. Lepsius' classic twelve-volume *Monuments of Egypt and Nubia* (1849–59), which helped to establish Egyptology as a systematic discipline, had a profound effect on the mind of his youthful compatriot in Berlin. Lepsius, who investigated the Step Pyramid and the Pyramids of Gizeh, also sent back to Berlin fifteen thousand choice objects, including three entire tombs, which became the nucleus of the Egyptian Museum over which Erman presided for so many years. It was fitting that the *Monuments* should serve in turn as the prime source of *Life in Ancient Egypt.*

The labours of Lepsius were continued by Auguste Mariette, a Frenchman who in 1858 became the first Director of the Service of Antiquities in Egypt, a post held by Frenchmen for almost a hundred years. In 1859 he founded at Boulaq the original Egyptian Museum, which in 1902 was moved to its present location in Cairo. Mariette's energies were prodigious. He excavated extensively at nearly forty sites in Upper and Lower Egypt and even travelled as far afield as Abu Simbel. With all his faults and lapses, he may perhaps be considered the true founding-father of modern Egyptology. His work as Director was carried on by Sir Gaston Maspero and by Maspero's assistant Emil Brugsch, whose joint discoveries astonished the world at large; while the Swiss Edouard Naville was soon to engage himself upon a series of startling revelations at Deir el-Bahri and elsewhere.

It is against this buoyant pioneering background, when spectacular additions to knowledge were occurring month by month, that Erman's bold attempt to present a coherent synthesis must be seen. The breadth and extent of Egyptian civilization were at last being appreciated, and the moment had arrived to try to estimate its place in world history. Young Erman, with his methodical and analytical mind, was exactly the man for this task.

No doubt it was his upbringing in a scientific household, allied to a systematic training in a Prussian school and university, that made him determined to treat Egyptian civilization in a rigorous and somewhat clinical spirit. He speaks of "the progress of Egyptological science" (p. 3), and although he felt a warm affection for his subject he was resolved not to allow that affection to influence his sense of objectivity. He did not want love to blind him to the beloved's blemishes. This scientific approach was of the highest value at the time, when the prevailing attitude to Egyptology tended to be excessively high-flown and romantic. In spite of the unearthing of the Rosetta Stone in 1799 and the decipherment of the language by Young, Akerblad and Champollion half a century before the appearance of Erman's book, the fundamentally pragmatic and down-to-earth temper of the ancient Egyptians was not yet understood. It was still popularly believed that such works as *The Book of the Dead*, with its evocative title, were of a rare mystical and philosophical character, instead of being somewhat prosaic and matter-of-fact. The ancient Egyptians continued to be glamorous and mysterious, in the tradition of Schikaneder's libretto to *The Magic Flute* and the venerable and indulgent mumbo-jumbo of Masonic lore.

It was Erman's concern to set the record straight. Thus he characterizes the ancient Egyptians as "intelligent, practical, and very energetic, but lacking poetical imagination" (p. 34). This view, which must have come as a shock at the time, served as an excellent corrective to more overblown notions. The terms in which Erman describes the royal inscriptions, then being excavated in such numbers, are particularly sharp and entertaining. He castigates poems that describe in long-winded measures the triumphs of the king (p. 106), and speaks elsewhere of "the wearisome lists of empty titles" (p. 79), "the exaggerated, senseless style" of addressing the pharaoh (p. 72), and "the stupefying clatter of these empty phrases" (p. 57). Such critical pronouncements, just if severe, were a stiff dose of medicine for the more starry-eyed enthusiasts of his epoch.

This cool and detached approach enabled Erman to write matchless chapters on such formal topics as ancient Egyptian administration, government, architecture, trade and warfare. His chapter on Egyptian law, pointing out that this was a people "long past the time of judicial infancy" (p. 147), is especially brilliant. Again, one must emphasize that this book was an amazing performance when one recalls the date at which it was written. The chapters on lighter matters, such as dress and recreation, are correspondingly thorough and systematic, and offer the modern reader a guide that cannot be surpassed.

However, it is possible to argue that Erman, the product of a Prussian environment, sometimes becomes a trifle too censorious with regard to this ancient Eastern people. At times he indulges his desire for impartiality somewhat too severely. Thus one cannot endorse his repeated assertions that the Egyptians were altogether "unimaginative" (p. 385), or that where they showed any imagination it was "joyless" (p. 318); or that their great myths were empty and "devoid of spirituality" (p. 2); or that the ancient Egyptian labourer was "a creature with little pleasure in his life" (p. 13) who had become "selfish and hardened in the severe work of life" (p. 34). This, surely, was to lean too far in the other direction. Modern scholarship would certainly not uphold these views. One suspects that Erman was influenced by the strict ethos of his own age, an age where furthermore it was an article of faith that the civilization of classical Greece was "youthful" and "joyous" (p. 13), and that other civilizations could only be compared to Greece to their detriment. Erman was here falling into the over-romantic frame of mind against which he cogently warned his readers in the case of Egypt. One wonders whether he had read Nietzsche's *Birth of Tragedy*, published fourteen years earlier, which presented a radically different view of Greek thought and activity. However, one must remember that even the morose Mr. Gladstone responded to the supposedly warm and cheerful light of Hellas. In his notion that the ancient Egyptians had been to some degree a gloomy and downtrodden breed, it is likely that Erman, in common with other enlightened Europeans, had been moved by the spectacle of Ottoman rule in Egypt during the nineteenth century. The Egypt of Mohammed Ali, Ibrahim Pasha, Abbas Pasha and Ismail Pasha was often a cruel, bloody and degenerate place. The miseries of the Egyptian fellah as he existed in the days of the viceroys of the Sublime Porte were extrapolated into the pharaonic past. The popular legend of the brutality of the pyramid-builders is still with us and is a legacy from the days of the Ottoman pashas. Elsewhere Erman shows another hint of Bismarck's Germany when he says, for example, that the ancient Egyptians "never experienced the invigorating influence of a great national war" (no doubt he had in mind the Franco-Prussian War) (p. 15); and he is nothing less than Victorian in the manner in which he refers to the "lax" social principles of the Egyptians (p. 155). In comparison with his Greeks, the Egyptians appear to have been marvels of uxoriousness and respectability. Their reputation to the contrary is based on nothing more than a handful of puerile *graffiti* and a few innocent and indeed wholesome frescoes, and also on a single papyrus now at Turin, a casual production which has gained a schoolboyish notoriety (it is amusing to note that, like the magistrates who condemn salacious novels, Erman appears to have studied it). One wonders with what astonishment and dismay the ancient Egyptians would regard the present world-wide traffic in pornography. The Egyptian civilization was fundamentally too religious, too dignified and too responsible to stoop to the lowest kinds of depravity.

When one considers the wholly unfamiliar ethos of ancient Egyptian culture, one is struck by Erman's ability to project himself so completely into the world of Egyptian antiquity. He was one of the first scholars to appreciate the stature of Egyptian art, in spite of its strange idiom, and to pay tribute to it, and his exposition of the remote and obscure problems of Egyptian religion is superb—although once more he could not resist demonstrating his spirit of objectivity by stigmatizing Egyptian religion as "an unparalleled confusion" (p. 261), "confused" and "lifeless," filled with "lifeless, characterless figures" and "meaningless puppets of gods" (p. 263). It is curious that he should express such an opinion when later in the book he gives a perceptive and compelling account of Egyptian magic (pp. 351–

356), the all-pervasive fluid that animated the whole religious structure and gave it coherence. He makes amends, however, by referring to the beautiful and largely vanished body of esoteric mythology that provided the tissue from which Egyptian religion was woven (pp. 263ff.), and acknowledges that "it is entirely erroneous to maintain that the Egyptian divinities were merely abstract phantoms, such as they seem to us; we only know too little of them" (p. 272). The chapters devoted to religion abound in original and often unexpected insights—for example, when he suggests that the tomb robberies were actually carried on with the knowledge of the rulers of the state (p. 325), or that the staggering amount of daily offerings listed in the temple inventories represented the number of priests who were eligible to be fed every day (p. 278). Nevertheless, it is rather a pity that he should have given currency to the idea that Egyptian religion is essentially unfathomable, for it is an impression that has persisted. In point of fact later research has demonstrated that Egyptian religion, though it undoubtedly possesses many baffling features, is neither as inconsistent nor inexplicable as was once supposed, and might actually be a good deal easier to explain to a total stranger than, say, the dogma and ritual of Roman Catholicism.

Since the publication of *Life in Ancient Egypt* in 1886 there have naturally occurred many important developments in the field of "Egyptological science." One cannot begin to list all the major excavations that have taken place since that date. Erman was writing in ignorance of the unearthing of Tell el-Amarna and the Amarna letters, or of the existence of such rich tombs and troves as those of Tutankhamon, Hetephras, Yuaa and Tuiu, or those at Hawara, Lahun, Dahshur or Tanis, to mention a few at random. The careers of a host of famous excavators had yet to open—one thinks of Amélineau, Peet, Garstang, Hall, Junker, Reisner, Borchardt, Lauer, Quibell, Mace, Winlock, Brunton, Grenfell, Hunt, Hogarth, Carter, Pendlebury, Frankfort, Emery—to name a very small number of a distinguished band. And one gigantic figure should perhaps be mentioned above the rest—that of Sir Flinders Petrie, who in the early '80's had only just embarked on the forty-year career of excavation in Egypt that was to transform the entire face of Egyptology and the technical character of archaeology in general. Petrie contributed to every department of Egyptology, and particularly to a department of which Erman, in 1886, confessed frank and utter ignorance. "Preceding this first period of Egyptian history," he writes, "a long time of peaceful development must have elapsed, about which we have no information" (p. 34). Petrie was the first man to establish the existence of the predynastic cultures of the Amratians, Gerzeans and Semainians—and not only to establish them but, by the application of inspired and original methods, to arrange them in sequence. Later the predynastic picture was fleshed out by further discoveries in the Fayum, at Maadi, Merimde, Badari, Naquada, Deir Tasa and other sites. The general outline of the two to three-thousand-year prehistoric and protohistoric age that preceded the First Dynasty has finally emerged, and even though it has not been as yet too firmly limned the modern reader should be aware of it. Ancient Egypt has been shown to possess a more august lineage than the author of *Life in Ancient Egypt* may have suspected. Similarly, Erman was necessarily ignorant of inscriptions and papyri that came to light after his book was finished. Thus his rather perfunctory account of Egyptian medicine, for example, would have been altogether more complete had he been able to draw on the remarkable surgical compilation known as the Edwin Smith Papyrus, which though it had been discovered in 1862 was not published until 1930.

One could multiply such instances and carp about individual details. It would be ungrateful to do so. It is a matter for astonishment to learn how essentially complete a picture of ancient Egypt Erman was able to present almost a century ago. From first to last, *Life in Ancient Egypt* is a superb performance, a book which thoroughly deserves its present revival and which is particularly welcome in its original format. It is in the best tradition of Victorian publishing—clearly printed, lavishly presented, soundly translated, generously illustrated. In fact, it can be commended for the sake of its illustrations alone.

In conclusion, two minor considerations might be mentioned for the sake of the general reader. First, there is the perennial problem of the rendering of proper names from the Egyptian. In some instances Erman has employed forms that are now out of date. However, a small number of such old-fashioned usages no more invalidates his book than they do another important reprint in this Dover series, Wallis Budge's classic edition of *The Book of the Dead* (1895). Among the more important differences between Erman's usages and the current ones the following may be listed (Erman's version first):

Cheta	=	Hittites
Chetasar	=	Hattushilish III
Chnum	=	Khnum
Chnemtamun	=	Hatshepsut
Chuen'eten	=	Akhenaton (Amenophis IV)
'Ersu	=	Yarsu
Mutenr	=	Muwattalish
Nechebt	=	Nekhbet
Subk	=	Sebek
Usertsen	=	Sesostris

(Erman, by the way, supposed that Hatshepsut was Tuthmosis III's sister [p. 163]. In fact she was his aunt).

Finally, Erman's division of dynastic history into a triple division of "Old Empire," "Middle Empire" and "New Empire" (see p. 37), together with the dates for each division that he employs, are still roughly acceptable; but perhaps it would be useful to put forward a somewhat more modern scheme:

Predynastic Period	5000–3300 B.C.
Archaic Period (DYNASTIES I–II)	3300–2778 B.C.
OLD KINGDOM (DYNASTIES III–VI)	2778–2300 B.C.
First Intermediate Period (DYNASTIES VII–XI)	2300–2065 B.C.
MIDDLE KINGDOM (DYNASTIES XI–XII)	2065–1785 B.C.
Second Intermediate Period (DYNASTIES XIII–XVII)	1785–1580 B.C.
NEW KINGDOM (DYNASTIES XVIII–XX)	1580–1085 B.C.
Late Period (DYNASTIES XXI–XXX)	1085–332 B.C.

JON MANCHIP WHITE

PREFACE

THE need of a popular work on the manners and customs of Ancient Egypt has long been felt by the English public. Herr Erman supplied this need in Germany by the publication of his *Aegypten*, but no English scholar has attempted to fill this gap in Egyptian literature since the time of Wilkinson.

In the light of modern discoveries Wilkinson's valuable book, as far as the letterpress is concerned, has now long become obsolete; the illustrations on the other hand will always remain a mine of wealth to every writer on this subject. In the present work, for instance, the low price of the German edition forbade the introduction of many original drawings, and Herr Erman, who chose the illustrations specially to amplify and explain the text, found that the three works most useful to him for this purpose were the *Manners and Customs*, by Wilkinson, the *Denkmäler*, by Lepsius, and *L'Histoire de l'Art*, by Perrot-Chipiez.

With regard to the text, finding little to help him in the work of previous scholars, Herr Erman for several years devoted all the time he could spare from his official duties to original research on the subject. The two works he mentions as having been of special service to him are Lepsius' *Denkmäler* and *The London Select Papyri;* in fact he would almost regard the present work as a commentary on those great publications. A list of quotations from these works is given at the end of this edition. The author has confined himself to the treatment of those periods of ancient Egyptian history which have been styled the "Old Empire," the "Middle Empire," and the "New Empire"; these terms have become so familiar that they have been retained; they are fully explained on p. 37. After the time of the 20th dynasty, the subject becomes too complicated for a work of this size, and too much mixed with foreign elements to be termed purely Egyptian. The orthography of the Egyptian names was decided upon by the author after much thought and consideration; it has therefore been retained in the English edition, with the exception of the name "Thothmes," which, on account of its familiarity to English readers, has been substituted (with Herr Erman's approval) for its more correct form. In the same way the forms Osiris, Isis, and Horus, were retained by the author in the German edition.

In the present English edition there have been but few alterations; a few notes have been added referring to English Egyptological works, or to the more recent research of foreign scholars, as in the case of the translation of (p. 85), giving the result of Borchardt's later work on the subject, with which Herr Erman is in full agreement.

Herr Erman wishes to inform his English readers that he is fully aware that many alterations might be introduced into his work to bring it into accord with the results of later research, but he feels that these alterations would only affect details, and not the general scope of the book. Students of any special branch of Egyptology must consult other text-books dealing with their particular subject in more full and exact detail. For instance, those who desire to study the plans of the houses, the arts and crafts of these ancient workmen, the tools they used, the methods of workmanship they employed, will find far more exact and technical information in the publications of Prof. Petrie, which have appeared since this book was written—details which it would be impossible to incorporate in this work without greatly enlarging its extent.

The valuable work of the Mission Archéologique Française, as well as the excavations of the Egypt Exploration Fund, carried on under the direction of M. Naville, have also added largely to our knowledge in many particulars. Thus, the great altar with its outside staircase, discovered last year in the great temple of Queen Chnemtamun (Hatasu) at Dêr el Bahri, corresponds in many respects with the great altar of the "House of the Sun," depicted on the walls of the tomb of the high priest Meryrê' at Tell el Amarna, described in the twelfth chapter of this work. Neither altar can claim to be unique. The important papers on the Rhind Mathematical Papyrus by F. L. Griffith in the April and May numbers of the *Proceedings of the Bib. Archaeology* throw further light on the subject of Egyptian mathematics, treated at the close of the fourteenth chapter, pp. 364-368; and the paper on Hat Nub by G. W. Fraser in the January number of the Proceedings of the same society ought certainly to be read in connection with the account of the transport of stone at the close of the eighteenth chapter. The latter paper refers not only to the transport of alabaster across the desert from the great quarries of Hat Nub, but also to the important scene found last season by M. Naville at Dêr el Bahri, depicting the transport by boat of the great obelisks of Queen Chnemtamun.

My thanks are especially due to Prof. Stuart Poole, who has most kindly read through the sheets in proof, and to Herr Erman for his help and courtesy in facilitating the appearance of the "child of his brain in a new dress." The German work has already received a warm welcome; my hope is that the *Aegypten*, in its new form of *Life in Ancient Egypt*, may give pleasure and help to many who, in their busy life, prefer to read books in their mother tongue.

HELEN MARY TIRARD.

June 1894,
74 HARLEY STREET, W.

CONTENTS

CHAPTER VI

Political Conditions in Egypt under the New Empire

CHAPTER VII

The Police and the Courts of Justice

CHAPTER VIII

Family Life

CHAPTER IX

The House

CHAPTER X

Dress

CHAPTER XI

Recreation

CHAPTER XII

Religion

CHAPTER XIII

The Dead

CHAPTER XIV

Learning

CHAPTER XV

Literature

CHAPTER XVI

The Plastic Arts

CHAPTER XVII

Agriculture

CHAPTER XVIII

Arts and Crafts

CHAPTER XIX

Traffic and Trade

CHAPTER XX

War

LIST OF PLATES

TABLE OF ABBREVIATIONS

Abb.—Papyrus Abbott, published in the "Select Papyri in the Hieratic Character from the collections of the British Museum." London, 1844-1860.

An.—The Anastasi Papyri, in the Select Papyri.

Ä. Z.—Zeitschrift für ägyptische Sprache und Altertumskunde.

Bol.—die Papyrus von Bologna, published by Lincke, Korrespondenzen aus der Zeit der Ramessiden. Leipzig, 1878.

Br. Wb.—Brugsch, Hieroglyphisch-Demotisches Wörterbuch. Leipzig, 1867-1880.

Br. Gr. W.—Brugsch, die ägyptische Gräberwelt. Leipzig, 1868.

Champ. mon.—Champollion, monuments de l'Egypte et de la Nubie. Paris, 1835, bis 1845.

Düm. Flotte—Dümichen, die Flotte einer ägyptischen Königin. Leipzig, 1868.

Düm. Res.—Dümichen, Resultate der . . . 1868 nach Aegypten entsendeten . . . Expedition. Berlin, 1869.

Ebers—Papyrus Ebers. Das hermetische Buch über die Arzneimittel. Herausgegeben von G. Ebers. Leipzig, 1875.

Harris (I.)—Facsimile of an Egyptian Hieratic Papyrus of the reign of Rameses III. London, 1876.

Harris 500—Papyrus, published in Maspero's Études égyptiennes. Vol. I. Paris, 1886.

Insc. in the hier. char.—Inscriptions in the hieratic character from the collections of the British Museum. London, 1868.

L. A.—From Lepsius' Abklat collection in the Berlin Museum.

L. D.—Lepsius' Denkmäler aus Aegypten und Aethiopien. 1849-1858.

Lee—Papyrus Lee, see below, P. j. T.

Leyden—Papyrus, published in *Leemans*, Aegyptische Monumenten van het Nederlandsche Museum van Oudheden te Leiden. Leyden, 1839-1882.

Lieblein—Lieblein, dictionnaire de noms hiéroglyphiques. Leipzig, 1871.

Mar. Cat. d'Ab.—Mariette, catalogue général des monuments d'Abydos. Paris, 1880.

Mar. Karn.—Mariette, Karnak. Leipzig, 1875.

Mar. Mast.—Mariette, les Mastabas de l'ancien empire. Paris, 1881-1887.

Mar. mon. div.—Mariette, monuments divers recueillis en Egypte. Paris, 1872, bis 1877.

M. E.—Middle Empire.

N. E.—New Empire.

O. E.—Old Empire.

d'Orb.—Papyrus d'Orbiney, published in the Select Papyri.

Pap. de Boul.—Mariette, les papyrus égyptiens de Boulaq. Paris, 1872-1877.

Perrot—Perrot et Chipiez, histoire de l'art dans l'antiquité. Tome I. l'Egypte. Paris, 1882.

P. j. T.—Devéria, le papyrus judiciaire de Turin et les papyrus Lee et Rollin. Paris, 1868 (from the Journal asiatique).

Prisse—Prisse, facsimile d'un papyrus égyptien en caractères hiératiques. Paris, 1847.

Prisse mon.—Prisse, monuments égyptiens. Paris, 1847.

R. J. H.—Rougé, inscriptions hiéroglyphiques. Paris, 1877-1879.

Rollin—Papyrus, see above, P. j. T.

Ros. M. C.—Rosellini, monumenti dell' Egitto e della Nubia. Pisa, 1842-1844. Part entitled "Monumenti civili."

Ros. M. stor.—Ditto. Part entitled "Monumenti storici."

Sall.—The Sallier Papyri, published in the Select Papyri.

Tur.—Pleyte et Rossi, les papyrus de Turin. Leyde, 1869-1876.

W.—Wilkinson, the manners and customs of the ancient Egyptians. New Edition by S. Birch. London, 1878.

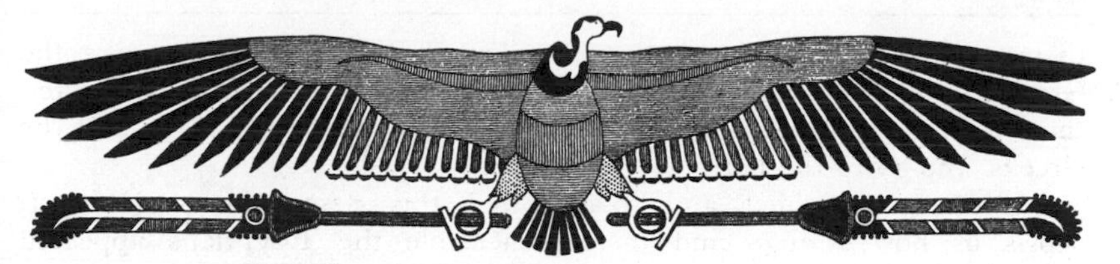

INTRODUCTION

THE Greeks, who from the seventh century B.C. were frequent visitors to the Nile Valley, marvelled to find there a civilisation which, though more ancient, was at least the equal of their own. They saw to their astonishment powerful populous towns, strange gigantic temples, and a people who in no wise resembled the inhabitants of Ionia and the Greek islands. This people honoured as gods oxen and crocodiles, which were served by bald linen-clad priests; and not only in their worship did they differ from other nations, but also in their daily life they seemed to do everything in a way contrary to that usual in other countries.

"Concerning Egypt," says the wise Herodotos, "I shall extend my remarks to a great length, because there is no country that possesses so many wonders, nor any that has such a number of works which defy description. Not only is the climate different from that of the rest of the world, and the rivers unlike any other rivers, but the people also, in most of their manners and customs, exactly reverse the common practice of mankind. The women attend the markets and trade, while the men sit at home at the loom; and here, while the rest of the world works the woof up the warp, the Egyptians work it down; the women likewise carry burthens upon their shoulders, while the men carry them upon their heads. A woman cannot serve the priestly office either for god or goddess, but men are priests to both; sons need not support their parents unless they choose, but daughters must, whether they choose or no. In other countries the priests have long hair, in Egypt their heads are shaven; elsewhere it is customary, in mourning, for near relatives to cut their hair close; the Egyptians, who wear no hair at any other time, when they lose a relative let their beards and the hair of their heads grow long. All other men pass their lives separate from animals, the Egyptians have animals always living with them; others make barley and wheat their food, it is a disgrace to do so in Egypt, where the grain they live on is spelt, which some call *zea*. Dough they knead with their feet, but they mix mud with their hands. Their men wear two garments apiece, their women but one. They put on the rings and fasten the ropes to sails inside, others put them outside. When they write or calculate, instead of going like the Greeks, from left to right, they move their hand from right to left; and they insist, notwithstanding, that it is they who go to the right, and the Greeks who go to the left."

However one-sided and exaggerated this description may be, it shows us how strange and incomprehensible the Egyptians appeared even to the educated among the Greeks, who really tried to understand this ancient people. The Greek populace regarded them with the same timid wonder which our people feel for the pig-tailed Chinese or Japanese. To them they were a subject for cheap wit, and they made jokes about their worshipping oxen instead of sacrificing them, revering eels instead of eating them, and mourning for dead cats instead of skinning them. Yet in spite of their mockery, they had a feeling of respect for this people, who with their ancient civilisation looked upon the Greeks as children; there might be a deep hidden meaning in those strange deities and temples, and it was possible that those bald-headed priests possessed a secret wisdom unknown to the ordinary human understanding. Many a Greek scholar made a pilgrimage to the Nile Valley in the hope that these priests might help to solve the great riddle of the world; undaunted by the timid suspicious way in which they were received, they tried eagerly to grasp the meaning of the old religion, which was so carefully shrouded in mystery. We now know that these mysteries had no deep signification, and that the Greek philosopher was of far higher mental standing than the Egyptian priest. The Greeks, however, never really understood this, and the more taciturn and reserved was the behaviour of the priests, the more did the Greeks believe that they possessed wonderful secrets; and when in time they learned these mysteries and understood what was contained in the sacred writings concerning Osiris and Isis, Typhon and Horus, their faith in the wisdom of the Egyptians was so deeply rooted that they were unable to look with unprejudiced eyes at those myths, so devoid of spirituality. They interpreted them according to their own philosophic ideas, instead of perceiving their emptiness.

The reverence for old Egypt increased as centuries passed by, and at last Isis and even the jackal-headed Anubis were admitted into the circle of the Olympian gods, and under the Romans their mysteries were solemnised everywhere with the noise of the sistrum and with secret ceremonies.

This simple faith of the Graeco-Roman world in the unknown wisdom of the Egyptians has lasted seventeen centuries; not long since pyramids and obelisks were regarded with wonder and dread, mummy-cases with their foolish daemonic representations were looked upon with unfeigned awe, and rosicrucians and freemasons used hieroglyphs and Egyptian symbols as talismans.

Now that we have learned to understand the monuments, to read the inscriptions, and to study the literature of ancient Egypt, the old glamour has departed, and in place of the "dim religious light" of past time, the pitiless sun of science has risen, and we see the old Egyptians as they really were, neither better nor worse than other folk. Their old "wisdom" appears in some respects less wonderful, in others it even grows repulsive, while their customs are not more peculiar than those of other nations, and merit neither our ridicule nor our reverence. In one point only, a point little thought of by the ancients themselves, do we of the modern world regard the Egyptians with the greatest admiration, viz. in their art, which rose to a greatness and individuality shared by few other nations.

The romantic interest of old time has now given place to more serious study awakened by the progress of Egyptological science. The history of Egypt probably goes back to a more remote age than that of any other country, with the exception perhaps of Babylonia. We know the appearance of the country, the language, literature, religion, and art of as early a date as 3000 B.C., while of European countries nothing is known till much later, for at the time when the heroes of Homer were fighting before Troy, ancient Egypt had already passed her zenith and had reached her period of decadence. The civilisation of other countries, though perhaps as ancient, has left no traces, while in Egypt the number of monuments which have come down to us seems inexhaustible.

This happy circumstance is due to the Egyptian climate; for centuries the dry air and the sand have preserved to us even such delicate objects as clothes and papyrus rolls. Moreover, under the influence of their strange religious conceptions the Egyptians paid particular regard to the lasting character and rich adornment of their tombs. Whilst most people of similar standing in civilisation have been content with perishable graves, the Egyptians prepared for their mummies vast enduring monuments, the rich decoration of which gives us full details of their manner of life. Thus in Egypt we learn to know those centuries of the remote past which in other countries are covered with a thick veil.

This glimpse into the old world teaches us much; it dissipates the false notion that men of the last two centuries are different from those of the more ancient past. The Egyptians of 3000 B.C. would resemble modern people were they in the same stage of civilisation and if they had the same surroundings. Their language, religion, and government developed in a similar way to those of later nations. The world was the same in that old time; those eternal laws which ruled them are still in force. The progress of civilisation, the inventions of mankind, have changed but little; the old kingdoms were founded by wars similar to those by which are founded the kingdoms of modern times; ancient art flourished or declined under the identical circumstances which influence the art of to-day.

In one other respect Egypt is full of instruction for us; in no other country are there so few gaps in the historic sequence of events. From the time of King Snofru to the conquest of Alexander the Great, and from the Greek time to the Arab invasion, we have an almost unbroken chain of monuments and writings. In this country alone we can observe the same people for five thousand years: the language changed once, the religion twice, the nationality of the ruling class many times, but the natural conditions of life remained steadfast. How far this people maintained their old ideas and their old customs, in spite of all these changes, is a question of the highest scientific interest. Though in the present state of our knowledge we are not able to answer this question, there is another point, more simple and scarcely less interesting, to which an answer is forthcoming. Doubtless the Egyptians of later times (1500 B.C.) had much intercourse with their northern neighbours; and it has been supposed that these ruder nations learned much from the Egyptians, and that the Greeks especially borrowed from them the first principles of their art. We now know that the classical nations received little direct from Egypt, but that the Phoenicians at a certain period were entirely under Egyptian influence, and that this busy commercial nation spread Egyptian civilisation throughout Greece and Italy.

Three sources of information are within our reach, and from these we can learn particulars of the civilisation of ancient Egypt. 1. The monuments of the country; the temples and tombs with their endless series of inscriptions and pictures; the papyrus rolls from the old libraries and archives, and the numerous objects of daily life buried with the mummies. 2. The Hebrew books giving us the stories of Moses and Joseph, and relating much of Egyptian life. 3. The accounts given by Greek travellers.

The chain of history which we link together from the monuments has naturally many gaps, but if we ourselves are not guilty of misapprehensions, and if we take care not to confuse the monuments of different periods, we shall obtain from them a very fair and comparatively true view of the development of Egyptian civilisation.

It is difficult to say how much we can learn from the "Books of Moses;" much may have been re-edited in later times, and must be accepted with caution as representing Egyptian life of an earlier period.

As to the Greek writers, the most important is Herodotos. What Herodotos learnt, by hearsay from the priests, of early Egyptian history is mostly legendary and unsafe; but what he himself observed gives us as trustworthy an account as is possible to obtain from a tourist who, ignorant of the language, travels for a few months in a foreign country. Herodotos describes the Egypt of more than five hundred years later than the period with which we are now concerned; and what is true of his time is not always so of the time of the Ramessides, and still less so of that of the pyramid age.

Therefore for the solution of our problem we turn to the monuments alone, and at first sight these seem to be quite inexhaustible. The translations of inscriptions and papyri, which have been already published, would fill folios; a great number of Egyptian texts are waiting to be deciphered both in Egypt and in our museums; while no one can say how much still lies hidden under Egyptian soil, for as yet few of the old cities and cemeteries have been thoroughly excavated. We must also add the immense number of pictured representations covering the walls and pillars of the gigantic temples and of the tombs. Yet when we come to sift our materials much has to be put aside as useless. The great towns and the palaces of the kings were built of wood and unburnt brick ; and in the mounds where they formerly stood we can find little to tell us of the life of their inhabitants.

The temples with their inscriptions and wall pictures are still standing, but these inscriptions and representations refer almost solely to the worship of the gods, to sacrifices and processions, or they give us bombastic hymns to the gods, or they may perhaps contain the information that such and such a king built this sanctuary of eternal stones for his father the god, who rewarded him for this pious act by granting him a life of millions of years. If, as an exception, we find an inscription telling us of the warlike feats of a ruler, these are related in such official style and stereotyped formulae, that little can be gained towards the knowledge of Egyptian life.

The tombs are much more satisfactory, for though unfortunately even in them religious inscriptions and religious pictures outweigh all else, yet most of the tombs of the oldest period show us scenes of the home life of the deceased, or tell us of his deeds and of the honours he won. Besides which, the tombs contain objects of all kinds, which the deceased used in his official or home life, and which were intended to serve him also in the under-world—weapons, articles of adornment, a draught-board, or perhaps letters from his relatives, or an important legal document. Yet these tombs and their contents, important as they are, do not give us an unbiassed nor a complete picture of Egyptian life. The deceased sees fit to relate the bright points of his biography, his promotion in office, his rewards from the king, etc., but how he was brought up, how he lived at home—in fact all his private circumstances, he passes over as uninteresting for posterity. Neither must we trust too implicitly to all that we find in the tombs, for in order to give us a high idea of the riches and virtues of the deceased, the pictures and inscriptions may not only be exaggerated and brightly coloured, but also in many cases they have been simply copied from older tombs and therefore do not answer to the truth. The objects also found in these tombs were often kept ready-made for the purpose, and may not exactly resemble those used by the deceased in his lifetime.

As to the papyri, the greater number are of no use for our purpose, as their contents are purely magical or religious. The secular ones are chiefly school books, and are intended to incite youthful students to virtue and knowledge. In these papyri the happiness of the learned profession is so obviously glorified to the prejudice of all others that implicit faith cannot be placed in them. The romances are also not to be relied upon ; the country which they describe is not Egypt but fairyland.

On the other hand, there are a great number of private business letters, inventories, note-books, and legal documents, which are of the greatest importance in the study of the Egyptian nation. In them we see the people as they really were, with all their weak points, and without the pomp and ceremony which surround the life depicted for us on the monuments. Unfortunately these are exceptionally difficult to read—in fact, with their incomprehensible puns on the events of private daily life, and their strange expressions, it is doubtful whether they can ever be completely deciphered.

Thus our sources of information, which seem at first sight so rich, become gradually reduced in number, and those that are left to us are very one-sided, often representing or relating the same thing over and over again, *e.g.* the feeding or care of cattle is depicted a hundred times more frequently than weaving or the making of pottery; probably many industries and customs were considered too unimportant to be represented at all. We must not deny to the Egyptians the possession of some object merely because we can find no representation of it on the monuments.

One other point must be added which tends to render our task of describing the civilisation of ancient Egypt more difficult. The tombs which depict the agriculture, farming, and different industries belong mostly to the period of the "Old Empire"; the papyri, which teach us the customs of social and political life, are nearly all of the later time of the "New Empire." Therefore we know, for instance, exactly how boats were built, furniture was made, birds were snared, three thousand years before our era; but whether the workmen were free labourers or vassals we know not. On the other hand, the papyri of the thirteenth and twelfth centuries teach us the social position of many artisans and workmen, but how they followed their various callings we can rarely tell. In order to draw a picture of life in Egypt during any one period, our imagination must aid in filling in the details of one or another portion of it, as it is never complete in itself.

There is no prospect that this state of things will ever be altered; we have therefore endeavoured in the following pages to give a sketch of the manners and customs of ancient Egypt: more than a sketch is impossible at the present time, and even in the future we can scarcely hope to fill in all the particulars.

HIEROGLYPHIC PORTION OF THE ROSETTA STONE.

CHAPTER I

THE LAND OF EGYPT

THE Nile receives its last great tributary, the Blue Nile, near Khartum, in about the 17th degree of north latitude. Above the town the river flows quietly through grassy plains; below, the stream changes its peaceful character, as it makes its way through the great table-land of the north of Africa, and in an immense bend of over 950 miles forces a passage through the Nubian sandstone. In some places where the harder stone emerges through the sandstone, the river, even after thousands of years, has not succeeded in completely breaking through the barrier, and the water finds its way in rapids between the hard rocks.

There are ten of these so-called cataracts, and they play an important and sometimes an unhappy part in the development of Egypt and the Sudan. It is owing to them that intercourse by boats is rendered almost impossible between the Upper and Lower Nile except during high Nile, and even then there is risk of accidents happening to larger boats passing through these rapids. The last of these cataracts is 7 miles long, and forms the natural boundary of Egypt proper; close to it is situated the town of Assuan, the old Syene.

Below Assuan the character of the country again changes, and the valley, which in Nubia never exceeded 5 to 9 miles in width, broadens out, its greatest extent being, in one place, as much as 33 miles from side to side. The reason of this change is that at Gebel Silsileh, some way below Assuan, the sandstone (found throughout Nubia) gives way to limestone, which forms cliffs bounding the river for nearly 475 miles. When the Nile reaches the Delta the limestone again gives place to later geological formations.

Thus Egypt in its entire length is framed in rocky walls, which sometimes reach a height of 600 to 800 feet; they form the stereotyped horizon of all landscape views in this country. These limestone hills are not mountains in our sense of the word. Instead of rising to peaks, they form the edge of a large table-land with higher plateaus here and there. This table-land is entirely without water, and is covered with the sand of the desert, which is continually trying to trickle down into the Nile, by channels grooved in the steep monotonous wall. On

THE SACRED ISLAND OF PHILAE (after Langl).

the west this barren plateau joins the shifting sand-dunes of the Sahara, which have never been thoroughly explored. About 95 miles from the river, and running parallel with it, are some remarkable dips in this table-land. These "oases" are well watered and very fruitful, but with these exceptions there is no vegetation in this desolate waste, which from old times has been called the Libyan desert. To the east of the Nile is a similar limestone plateau called the Arabian desert. Further inland it changes into a high mountainous country with bold peaks of granite, porphyry, gneiss, and other crystalline rocks rising sometimes to the height of 6000 feet. This magnificent range of mountains stretches along the Red Sea, and though very barren owing to the lack of rain, yet the country presents a more cheerful aspect than the Libyan desert. Springs of water are rare, but a dampness arises from the proximity of the sea, so that hardy desert plants grow everywhere, and in many places small oases are found which provide food for the wild animals and for the cattle of

THE FIRST CATARACT, BETWEEN ASSUAN AND PHILAE, THE BOUNDARY OF EGYPT AND NUBIA.
(After L. Libay.)

the nomadic tribes. The heat, however, and the want of water, make it most difficult to live in these mountains on the east of the Nile, and we cannot help admiring the courage and perseverance of the ancient Egyptians, who maintained hundreds of labourers working the large stone-pits and quarries in this vast rocky waste.

To return to the Nile valley:—had the river merely forced its way through the Nubian sandstone and the Egyptian limestone, the valley could never have attained its wonderful fertility under the rainless glowing sky of Egypt, where decomposition of all vegetation is so rapid. But the Nile is not solely the outflow of the great lakes of tropical Africa; it also receives from the west all the waterflow from the high mountains of Abyssinia; and the mountain torrents, laden with rocky débris, dash down the sides of the hills in the rainy season, and form the two great streams of the Blue Nile and the Atbara which flow into the Nile near Khartum and Berber. Thus in the middle of the summer the river gradually rises so high that the banks can no longer contain the vast quantity of water and mud. The river overflows slowly, and after some months slowly retreats again into its bed. While the water of the inundation covers the valley the mud in the water is of course deposited, and when the stream has retreated, the country is left covered with a thin coating of this mud composed of the finest stone dust from the Abyssinian mountains; it is this black Nile mud which has caused, and which renews each year, the fertility of Egypt. It now forms the soil of Egypt; and from Khartum to the sea the deposit of mud in the valley has reached the height of 30 feet, and in this mud the Nile has hollowed its present bed.

In another respect also the Nile is the life-blood of Egypt; it provides water for the country, for, as in the neighbouring deserts, there is no rainfall. On the coast of the Delta and for some miles southwards rain falls in the same way as in the other coast lands of the Mediterranean; but, with the exception of rare storms, this is never the case in Upper Egypt. There are also no springs nor brooks, so that for water the country depends entirely on the great river from the far south.

The climate of Egypt is more uniform than that of other Mediterranean countries, owing to the absence of the rainy season, which corresponds to our winter. From December to March the air is cool, and at night sometimes the temperature may almost go down to freezing point, but during eight months of the year it is very hot, and in July the thermometer rises to 110° Fahr. in the shade. Several causes combine to produce this difference of temperature. The hot south-east wind blows only from the middle of February to the middle of June, but this wind often rises to a hurricane, filling the air and covering the plants with dust; during the rest of the year even in the hottest season the north-west wind mitigates the intense heat of the day; the ancient Egyptians thought it one of the best things in life to "breathe its sweet breath."[1] The inundation has still more effect on the climate than the wind. The

[1] L. D., iii. 114 i, and many other instances.

stream begins to rise in the beginning of June ; it becomes a mighty torrent by the end of July ; from the end of September to the end of October the water reaches its highest level, after which time it retreats more and more rapidly. In January the stream is back once more in its old bed, but it goes on subsiding till the summer. This inundation, which we must not imagine to overflow the whole country, spreads abroad coolness, dampness, and fertility ; the country revives from the oppression of the summer heat, and we easily understand why the old Egyptians should fix their New Year's Day on the 15th of September, the time of highest Nile.

DATE PALMS AND DÔM PALMS (del. by Stieler).

The days of inundation were, however, days of anxiety and care. The fate of the whole country hung in the balance, for if the water rose insufficiently but one-tenth part, the canals carrying the water to the higher level did not fill, and the result was the failure of the crops and famine. Again, if the inundation rose even slightly too high, sad devastation ensued ; embankments and dykes were thrown down, and freshly cultivated fields, supposed to be beyond the reach of the water, were covered by the inundation. From the earliest times therefore, the rise of the Nile was closely watched and controlled by government officials, who regulated the yearly taxes by the result of the inundation. Nilometers were also constructed,—these were wells in which the height of the water was marked as in a measure or water-gauge; they were under the special protection of the State. In old times as now, the height of the inundation was officially notified; and then also, as at the present day, suspicions were often aroused that the official statement was exaggerated. An old Nilometer still exists on the island of Elephantine, on the southern frontier of Egypt. In Greek times the height of a good inundation at Memphis was said to be 16 ells, and in the beautiful statue of the Nile in the Vatican the boy who represents the 16th ell looks down with great content from the cornucopia, up which he has clambered. This genius of the 16th ell is also to be seen on a coin of Alexandria, presenting his cornucopia to his

SYCAMORES—A FEW PAPYRUS REEDS IN THE FOREGROUND (del. by Stieler).

father Nile. At the present day, on account of the ground level of Egypt having been raised by the mud deposit, a yet higher inundation is needed to ensure a good harvest to the country.

From the fertility of the Egyptian soil we might expect a specially rich flora, but notwithstanding the luxuriant vegetation, no country in the same latitude has so poor a variety of plants. There are very few trees. The sycamore or wild fig and the acacia are the only common forest trees, and these grow in an isolated fashion somewhat as the lime or chestnut tree grows with us. Besides these there are fruit trees, such as the date and dôm palms, the fig tree, and others. The scarcity of wood is quite a calamity for Egypt. It is the same with plants; herbs and vegetables reign in this land of cultivation, and wild flowers are scarcely to be found.

Klunzinger, who knows Egypt most thoroughly, says: "In this country, wherever a spot exists where wild plants could grow (*i.e.* irrigated ground), the agriculturist comes, sows his seed and weeds out the wild flowers. There are also no alpine nor forest plants, no heather, no plants common to ruins, bogs, or lakes, partly because there are no such places in Egypt, partly also for want of water and shade. The ploughed and the fallow land, the banks and hedges, the river and the bed of the inundation canals alone remain. Here a certain number of plants are found, but they are isolated, they never cover a plot of ground, even the grasses, of which there are a good many varieties, never form a green sward; there are no meadows such as charm the eye in other countries, though the clover fields which serve for pasture, and the cornfields as long as they are green, compensate to some extent." Even the streams, the numerous watercourses and canals, are poorer in vegetation than one would expect under this southern sky.

The present aspect of Egypt is pleasant though monotonous; the gleaming water of the broad river flows peacefully through the green fields, and the Delta also, intersected by numerous canals, looks very much like a rich well-cultivated European plain. We scarcely realise that we are on African soil, and on the banks of a river flowing from the heart of the tropics. In prehistoric times, however, the aspect of Egypt was doubtless very different, and probably resembled that of the present valley of the Nile in the interior of Africa.[1] The banks were covered by primaeval forests, the river changed its bed from time to time, leaving behind stagnant branches; the surface of the water was covered with luxuriant weeds, the gigantic papyrus rushes made an impenetrable undergrowth, until the stream broke through them and carried them as a floating island to another spot. These swamps and forests, inhabited by the crocodile, buffalo, and hippopotamus, have been changed into peaceful fields, not so much by an alteration in the climate, as by the hand of man working for thousands of years. The land has been cleared by the inhabitants, each foot has been won with difficulty from the swamp, until at last the wild plants and the mighty animals which possessed the country have been completely exterminated. The hippopotamus is not to be seen south of Nubia, and the papyrus reeds are first met with in the 9th degree of latitude.

In the first historical period, 3000-2500 B.C., this clearing of the land had been in part accomplished. The forests had long ago disappeared, and the acacias of Nubia had to furnish the wood for boat-building;[2] the papyrus, however, was still abundant. The "backwaters," in which these rushes grew, were the favourite resorts for sport, and the reed itself was used in all kinds of useful ways. The same state of things existed in the time of Herodotos. In the time of which we shall treat, Egypt was not so over-cultivated as now, though the buildings were no less extensive.

[1] See *Ueber den afrikanischen Ursprung aegyptischer Kulturpflanzen*, by Schweinfurth, translated by Thiselton Dyer.

[2] Inscription of Une' (Ä. Z., 1882, 25).

SIUT DURING THE INUNDATION.

(After L. D., I. 62.)

The climate of Egypt would seem to make life easy to mankind, the weather provides him with no grievance, the fields bear rich crops throughout the year, the cattle are never in want of pasture, the river is stocked with fish in abundance. We should therefore expect to find a people spending their lives cheerfully and brightly, somewhat after the fashion of the Homeric heroes. Yet the Egyptian labourer, both of the present and of the past, has always been a creature with little pleasure in his life, who does his work in a serious and indeed listless way, rather like his ox or his ass. The Egyptian nation has not the light-heartedness of the Greek, though the sky of Egypt smiles more brightly than that of Hellas. There is good reason for this difference of character. However easy the life of the Egyptian labourer may appear, it is really a hard one, and each day has its toil. He must never neglect his field, he must ever work hard—above all, before and during the time of inundation. The general opinion that the Nile overflows to right and left, making the country like a lake, in which the mounds of villages appear like islands, is not the truth, at least not in the case of the inundation of average height. Earnest work is needed to regulate the irrigation of the fields. The water is drawn off first into large canals, and thence into small trenches, in order to obtain the full benefit of the inundation. Dams are constructed to divide the land to be flooded into large or small parts, these are opened to the water at the right time, and the water is retained at will, or allowed to flow back into the canals by means of sluices. Some fields, completely out of the reach of the inundation, have to be irrigated entirely by means of hydraulic works.

All this labour, which falls now to the lot of the modern fellah, had also to be done in the old time, and doubtless must have been a heavy burden to the Egyptian people. The making of the canals, dykes, and sluices taxed the ingenuity of the nation, and accustomed the people to systematic work. As this system could only be carried out by large bodies of men, it was impossible that the old inhabitants of the Nile valley should consist of free peasants like those of Germany in the old time. The hard logic of facts teaches us that an autocratic government is always necessary in order to control and regulate irrigation. In fact, the earliest knowledge we have of the conditions of life in Egypt shows us a strict administration of political and agrarian relations; a state in which the individual was of little account, but in which much help was given by the government in the establishment of works for the public good, and in the superintendence of practical details.

The Greeks may have enjoyed a richer and more happy civilisation than the Egyptians, but the practical work of the latter people stands higher than that of the former. In making comparisons between the youthful joyous art of Greece and the severe sober art of Egypt we must remember that the latter sprang to life on the sad soil of the Nile valley, where hard work is required of every one. We must also, if we would avoid being unjust to the Egyptian people, make allowance for one other feature of their life, the landscape which surrounded them. The Greek, with his mountains, round which the sea foamed and the winds blew, with his green forests and his flower-decked meadows, created for himself the joyous forms of the youthful gods of Olympus, with their human feelings and sufferings. The horrors and the grandeur of the desert influenced the Semitic nomads, and deepened in them the religious feeling which permeates the purest form of religion. The landscape of Egypt on the contrary was monotonous; everywhere the fertile green fields were intersected by numerous watercourses, here and there grew clumps of palms; and ever the same horizon, the wall of the limestone mountains, bounded the view.

This is not a landscape calculated to awaken the inspiration of the soul; unconsciously the dweller in this country will become sober and prosaic, and his gods will be pale forms with whom he has no sympathy. In fact, the Egyptian peasant could scarcely understand a living personal relationship between the individual and the deity. If fancy were here allowed free course, the spirits and ghosts she would create would not resemble such forms as the friendly angel leading the people through the wilderness, nor the avenging angel stretching his hand over the sinful town to strike it with the plague, nor the ghost of the night, luring the wanderer to his destruction; but they would be frog-headed fiends, fiends with heads twisted awry, human-faced birds, snakes with four legs, repulsive childish forms, which can awaken neither pleasure nor fear.

Thus the Egyptian grew up under conditions unfavourable to the development of his spiritual life, but such as would fortify his understanding and practical industry. Foreign influence affected him little, for he lived secluded from the rest of mankind. On the east and on the west was the desert, on the north were the swamps of the Delta, on the south the rapids of the Nile and the narrow passes of Nubia. The Beduins of the Syrian desert and the Libyans of the eastern Sahara visited Egypt, and drove their flocks into the Delta, but it was only in later times that they gained any political power there, and the predatory incursions of early ages were much like those of the present day. There was little opportunity for friendly intercourse with foreign nations, for the neighbouring countries were far less fertile than Egypt, and their civilisation developed much later. It was only in the time of the New Empire that the people of Syria, Asia Minor, and Nubia attained a civilisation at all resembling that of Egypt; before that time they were barbarians despised by the Egyptians; the Chaldaeans, whose civilisation was as old and at the same time equalled that of the Nile valley, were too far off.

The undisturbed repose in which life in Egypt developed was in many respects happy for the nation; yet there is the reverse side to the picture. The Egyptians were the least warlike of all the nations of the ancient East. Their contests with the Beduins can scarcely be called warfare, and the internal struggles were always of a subordinate character, owing to the curious long form of the country. The Egyptians therefore had no heroes of war whom they could celebrate in song; their heroes, like those of the Chinese, were wise kings and princes of old time; they never experienced the invigorating influence of a great national war.

Equally unfortunate was the fact that they never learnt to carry on commerce with foreign nations. There were no harbours on the north of the Delta, and the currents off the coast made it very dangerous for ships, while the harbours of the Red Sea could only be reached by four days of desert travelling. The cataracts made it difficult to visit the countries of the Upper Nile. Thus commerce was always somewhat strange to the Egyptians, who gladly left it to the Phoenicians; and the "Great Green One," *i.e.* the ocean, was at all times a horror to them. Compared with the Phoenicians, their naval expeditions were insignificant, while in their agriculture, their arts and manufactures, they rose to true greatness.

Egypt played such an important part in the history of the world that involuntarily we are apt to consider the country as one of considerable size. Yet it is a small state, for notwithstanding its length of 570 miles, it only contains about 12,500 square miles, and is therefore somewhat smaller than Belgium. Even including the 1000 miles between the first cataract and Khartum, this would only increase the kingdom of Egypt by about 1125 square miles, the upper valley being very narrow. It was the exceeding fertility of the country which made Egypt so important. This small country is naturally divided into two very different parts. The larger division, the Delta, is a broad swamp intersected with canals, the climate is influenced by the sea, and there is a regular rainy season in the winter. The smaller part, the Nile valley, is as a rule without rain, and it has one great waterway, the stagnant branches and canals being scarcely worth consideration.

This is the present aspect of the country, and in past times it differed little, except that both divisions were more swampy than now. It follows naturally that the dry climate of the south was more favourable to cultivation than the swamps of the north. When the primaeval forest was once cleared, there was little left in Upper Egypt to interfere with the tillage of the soil. In the Delta, on the contrary, thousands of years passed before the swamps were converted into arable land. This work is not yet completed, and indeed many parts of the Delta which were formerly under cultivation are now lost. The brackish waters of Lake Menzaleh now cover a surface of over 1000 square miles, but in old times part of this district was one of the most productive in the country.

Scholars have surmised from the foregoing facts that Upper Egypt was the home of Egyptian civilisation, and that agriculture, the industrial crafts, and art flourished there while the Delta was still a forest swamp, the dwelling-place only of the hunter and the shepherd. Traces are not wanting to confirm this view. Herodotos (ii. 4) tells us a legend which he heard when travelling in Egypt, according to which "the Theban nome" in Upper Egypt was alone inhabited in the time of Menes the first king. All the rest of the country was a swamp, and the Delta was not even in existence. Though this can scarcely have been true of the time of Menes (about 3200 B.C.), yet this legend contains the truth that Lower Egypt remained a land of swamps far later than was the case with Upper Egypt. We learn the same from the fact that it was in comparatively late times that Lower Egypt played an important part in the history of the country.

In the time of the Old Empire (3000-2500 *circa*) we read that the flocks of the rich were driven at times into the Delta, which was therefore considered to be pasture land as compared with the corn lands of Upper Egypt. The name also by which the Delta is known, "the northern country," stamps it as an annexation to Egypt proper, which at Memphis was called "the south" without the addition of the word country. Upper Egypt was also always put first before the larger Delta; the south was said to be in front, the north lay behind. From these facts we conclude, that in the time of the Old Empire the Delta was far behind the southern part of the country in civilisation. The civilisation of Lower Egypt progressed but slowly. We find traces of this process in the names of the towns, many of which were named after some of the old famous places in Upper Egypt, *e.g.* Thebes and Edfu. Colonists from the south carried the names of their old homes to their new settlements, in the same way as our colonists have done in America.

Under the New Empire (about 1300 B.C.) much progress seems to have been made in the east of the Delta, which rose to importance, through being the highway to Syria; the old town of Tanis became the capital, and other towns were founded at different places. The west of the Delta was in a great measure in the hands of the Libyan nomads till the seventh century B.C., when the chief town Sais became the seat of government under the family of Psammetichus, and after the foundation of Alexandria this new city assumed the lead for a thousand years. Even as late as the Middle Ages the "Bushmur," a swampy district, was scarcely accessible; it was inhabited by an early non-Egyptian race, with whom neither the Greek nor the Arab rulers had much to do.

Throughout the ages of antiquity there existed, between Upper and Lower Egypt, a certain rivalry which probably arose in the time when the one was so far behind the other in civilisation. In old times also they were separated politically; they spoke two different dialects; and though they honoured several identical gods under different names, others were peculiar to one half of the kingdom. This contrast between Upper and Lower Egypt was emphasised in many ways by the people. The "two countries" were under the protection of different goddesses; the Delta under that of the snake goddess Uad't, while Upper Egypt was ruled by the snake goddess Nechebt. In mythical ages the land was given to different gods as a possession; the Delta to Set, Upper Egypt to Horus.

Different plants were characteristic of each part of the country: the papyrus grew thickly in the Delta, the flowering rush in Upper Egypt;

and these two plants were used for armorial bearings, a flowering rush for Upper Egypt, and a papyrus plant for the Lower Country. The flowers of these two plants became emblematic of the north and south, and in decorative representations the captives of the north were bound with a rope ending in the blossom of a papyrus, those of the south with one whose end was formed of the flowering rush.

I have already said that the historical importance of Egypt was owing to its fertility ; the dense population of the country was also due to the same cause. The population is now somewhat over five million (exact statistics are not to be obtained), and in the old time it is supposed to have been higher. Only countries as highly developed as Belgium or Saxony are so thickly populated.

We should expect the inhabitants, when so closely crowded together, to be essentially welded into one nation, but the length of Egypt prevented this result ; the inhabitants of one district had neighbours on two sides only, and the people of the Delta had a wearisome journey before reaching Upper Egypt. Therefore we find in Egypt the development of individual townships, reminding us strongly of early conditions of life in Germany.

Each district or province had its chief god and its own traditions ; the inhabitants were often at war with their neighbours, and when the central government was weak, the kingdom became subdivided into small principalities.

The districts were of very small extent, the average size of those of Upper Egypt about 270 square miles ; those of the Delta were rather larger, yet these provinces were of more importance than their size would indicate, as the population of each would probably average 300,000 souls.

Upper Egypt was divided in old times into about twenty provinces or *nomes* as they were called by the Greeks ; the division of the Delta into the same number is an artificial one of later date, as is proved by there being the same number for a country a quarter as large again. The official list of these provinces varied at different times, sometimes the same tract of land is represented as an independent province, and sometimes as a subdivision of that next to it. The provinces were government districts, and these might change either with a change of government or for political reasons, but the basis of this division of the country was always the same, and was part of the flesh and blood of the nation. The names of the nomes are very various—some are such as would naturally occur to the mind of a primitive people ; thus in Upper Egypt we find : the province of the "hare," of the "gazelle," two of the "sycamore," two of the "palm," one of the "knife," whilst the most southern portion was called simply the "land in front." In the Delta (the home of cattle-breeding) we find the province of the "black ox," of the "calf," etc. Other names were derived from the religion ; thus the second nome of Upper Egypt was called "the seat of Horus," the sixth "his mountain," and the twelfth in the Delta was named after the god Thoth.

Each province possessed its coat-of-arms, derived either from its name or its religious myths; this was borne on a pole before the chieftain on solemn occasions. The shield of the hare province explains itself  ; that of the eighth nome was  , the little chest in which the head of Osiris, the sacred relic of the district, was kept. The twelfth province had for a coat-of-arms  , signs which signify "his mountain"; and many others might be quoted.

In the following pages I intend to give a short account of the most important places of ancient Egypt, not as a complete sketch of the geography of the country, but in order to help the reader to recognise the position of those places which most frequently occur in this work. (See the accompanying map.)

The natural boundary of Egypt on the south was always the so-called first cataract, those rapids 7 miles long, in the 24th degree of latitude, where the Nile breaks through the mighty granite barrier. The district of the cataract was inhabited in old times as at present by Nubians, a non-Egyptian race, and the sacred island of Philae at the southern end of the cataract, where the later Egyptians revered one of the graves of Osiris, is in fact Nubian soil. These rapids were of the highest importance for strategic purposes, and the early Egyptians strongly fortified the town of Syene on the east bank so as to be able to blockade the way into Egypt by land, as well as to protect the quarries where from the earliest ages they obtained all their splendid red granite for obelisks and other monuments. The buildings in Egypt occupied so much of the attention of the state that immense importance was attached to the unobstructed working of these quarries.

The capital of this first province of Egypt was not Syene, but the neighbouring town of *'Abu*, which name signifies "ivory town" (Greek Elephantine). To the island on which this town was situated the Nubians of old brought the ivory obtained in their elephant-hunts, in order to exchange it for the products of Egypt. Even in Roman times this town was important for commerce, as the place where the custom duties were paid.

Twenty-eight miles farther to the north on the east bank was the town of *Nubit* (Ombos), where stood the sanctuary of the crocodile god Subk, and 14 miles beyond lay Chenu, the old Silsilis, the modern Silsileh, at the point where the sandstone hills narrow the bed of the river before giving place to the limestone. Like Syene, Silsilis was important because of the great quarries close to the town. Silsilis was the easiest point from Memphis or Thebes, where hard stone was to be obtained; and here were quarried those gigantic blocks of sandstone which we still admire in the ruins of the Egyptian temples.

Whilst the "land in front," or the first province, owed its importance

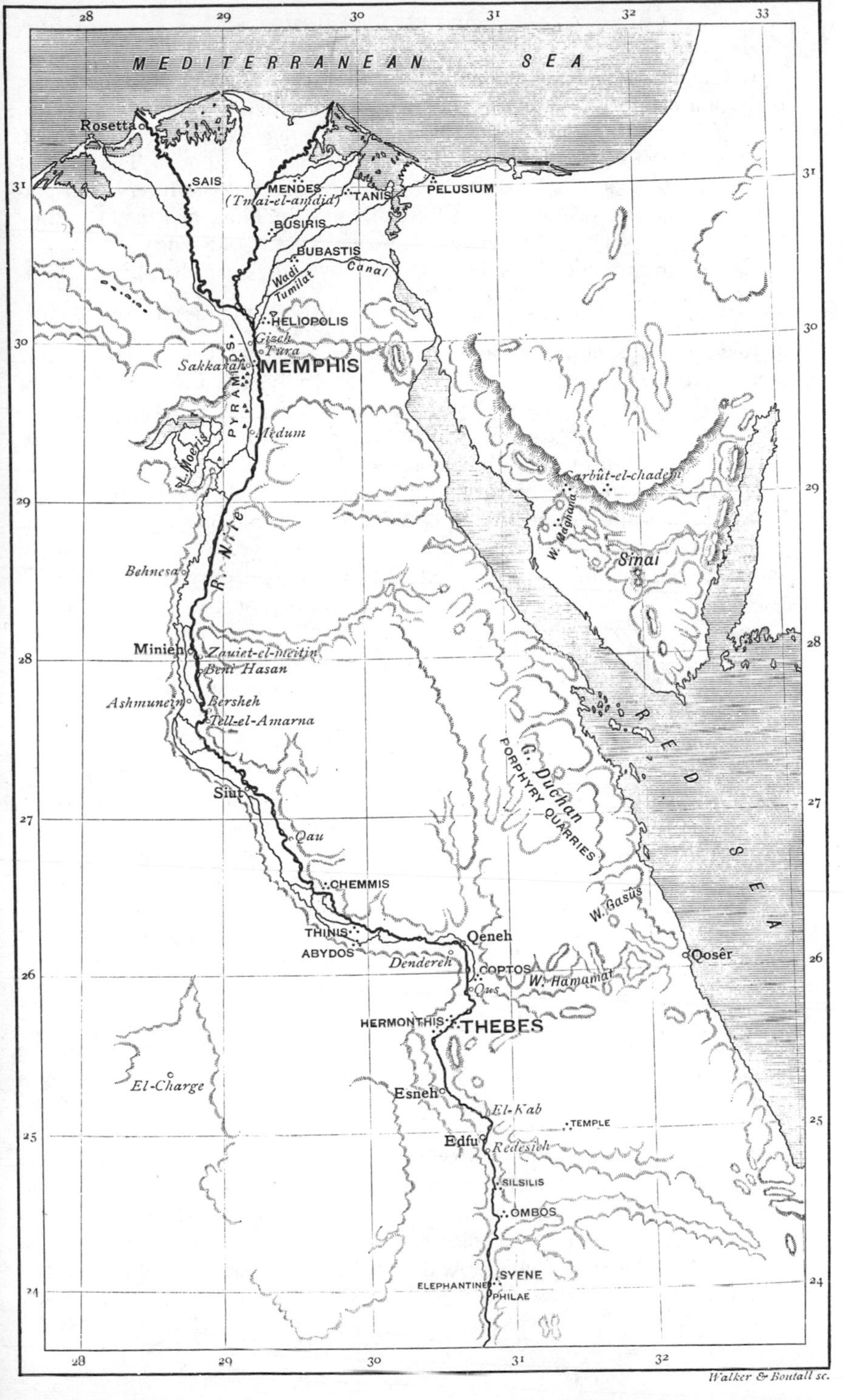
MEDITERRANEAN SEA
Rosetta
SAIS
MENDES
(Tmai-el-amdid)
TANIS
PELUSIUM
BUSIRIS
BUBASTIS
Canal
Wadi
Tumilat
HELIOPOLIS
Gizeh
Tura
Sakkarah
MEMPHIS
PYRAMIDS
Medum
L. Moeris
R. Nile
Behnesa
Minieh
Zauiet-el-meitin
Beni Hasan
Ashmunein
Bersheh
Tell-el-Amarna
Siut
Qau
CHEMMIS
THINIS
ABYDOS
Qeneh
Dendereh
COPTOS
Qus
W. Hamamat
HERMONTHIS
THEBES
El-Charge
Esneh
El-Kab
TEMPLE
Edfu
Redesieh
SILSILIS
OMBOS
SYENE
ELEPHANTINE
PHILAE
Sarbût-el-chadem
W. Maghara
Sinai
G. Duchan
PORPHYRY QUARRIES
W. Gasus
Qosêr
RED SEA
Walker & Boutall sc.

to the quarries and to trade, that of the second province, called "the exaltation of Horus," was, as the name signifies, purely religious. Horus, in the form of the winged disk, here obtained his first victory over Set, and here therefore was built the chief sanctuary of this god. The present temple of Edfu is still dedicated to him; it is in good preservation and stands on the site of the ancient Debḥot, but a building of Ptolemaic time has taken the place of the sanctuary erected by the old kings.

In the third nome, the shield of which bore the head-dress of the ram-headed god Chnum, , three towns are worthy of mention: first, the old *'Enit* (Esneh), the religious centre, where, as at Edfu, a late temple occupies the site of the old building; secondly, the town of Nechebt (El Kab); few towns have played such a leading part in Egypt as this great fortress, the governors of which during their time of office were equal in rank with the princes of the blood. El Kab was also important for the worship of the patron goddess of the south, Nechebt, sometimes represented as a vulture, sometimes as a snake. Numerous inscriptions by pilgrims testify to the honour in which this goddess was held in old times, and even the Greeks resorted to El Kab in order to pray to "Eileithyia."

NECHEBT IN THE FORM OF A VULTURE.

Thirdly, on the northern border of the nome, on the west bank, lay the very ancient town of On, distinguished from other places of the same name, as "On of the god Mont." On suffered the same fate as many other towns in all countries. Owing to political circumstances, the neighbouring town of Thebes rose from a country town to be the "town of the Hundred Gates," the capital of the whole kingdom. On then lost all her power, and it was only when, after a thousand years of splendour, Thebes fell into decay, that On of Mont rose again to importance as the Hermonthis of the Greeks. Erment is now a flourishing town, while the site of her great rival is occupied only by villages.

We now come to that town whose ruins form the greatest of all the wonders of Egypt, and whose buildings seem to have been erected by a race of giants. Thebes cannot boast of the age of Memphis, nor of the sacred character of Abydos or Heliopolis, but she had the good fortune to be the capital of the country during those centuries when Egypt was a mighty power in the world. Therefore she herself became the ruler of the world, the Rome of the ancient east, of which the Hebrew prophet cried in astonishment:[1] "Ethiopia and Egypt were her strength, and it was infinite; Put and Lubim (Arabia and Libya) were thy helpers." The political power of Thebes was also shown by the buildings of the town,

[1] Nahum iii. 9.

which surpassed in magnificence all those of ancient or modern capitals. Thebes attained this splendour at a comparatively late date, being at first only an obscure provincial town devoted to the worship of Amon; neither the town nor the god is mentioned in the older sacred books. About 2000 B.C. we first find a royal residence established here from time to time; but it was not till 1500 B.C. that the town began to flourish, and nearly all the antiquities found at Thebes belong to this later period.

The old town of Thebes, called *Uĕset*, was on the eastern bank, and stretched inland from the present ruins of Karnak. The harbour quarter of the town was close to the modern Luxor. When the town became the seat of government, the kings turned their energies to the building of the temple of the Theban god Amon, in order to make the simple dwelling-place of this comparatively obscure god worthy of the principal deity of the kingdom. One generation after another added to the buildings of *'Epet* (the name of the temple), and in the course of centuries a gigantic sanctuary arose, the ruins of which, near the village of Karnak, stretch for more than half a mile in length. The central of the three great temple enclosures measures about 1500 ft. in width, and about the same in length; the building itself being about 1000 ft. by 300 ft. wide. A second great temple was erected to the same god on the river-bank at Luxor, and smaller temples were built for the other gods of the town. In the midst of these various sanctuaries stood "the town of the Hundred Gates," that great city which, like all other Egyptian towns, has disappeared. The gigantic ruins of the temples alone remain to mark the site of the old capital of the world, of which even the "barbarians" in far-off Ionia sang:[1]

> "Royal Thebes,
> Egyptian treasure-house of countless wealth,
> Who boasts her hundred gates, through each of which,
> With horse and car two hundred warriors march."

During the course of centuries there arose on the western side of the river a strange city with which we shall have much to do in the course of this book. This "west end" was very different in character from that of London or Berlin; it was not the quarter of the rich, but the dwelling-place of the dead.

The steep sides of the strangely-formed western mountains are hollowed out into vaults for the dead, and so numerous did they become that a modern traveller has compared them to the holes in a sponge. In the valley, now called the Bibân el Molûk, were the graves of the kings; immense galleries excavated in the rocks, planned with a boldness and grandeur unlike anything else in Egypt, and which, ever since the time of the Greek travellers, have constituted one of the great sights of Thebes. In Egypt the deceased was honoured as a demigod, and therefore a chapel for his worship was a necessary adjunct of the Egyptian

[1] Iliad, 9, 381 ff., Derby.

tomb. These chapels were as a rule either close to the tomb or they formed part of it; but in the narrow desert valley of Bibân el Molûk, there was no space to erect funeral temples worthy of the kings, and they therefore stood in the plain. Thus on the edge of the western mountains a series of great buildings arose—the funeral temple of Abt el Qurna (Sety I.); Der-el-Baḥri (Queen Chnemtamun); Medinet Habu (Ramses III.); the Ramesseum (Ramses II.), and others to which we shall often refer. It follows, of course, that these colossal erections, with their dependencies, their gardens, their cattle-yards and storehouses, must have given employment to a great number of officials and workmen. If we add to these the crowd of embalmers, coffin manufacturers, and priests of the dead, employed in the numberless private tombs, as well as the stonemasons, builders, and other artisans always required for the building of new tombs, we shall understand how this realm of the dead gradually became a real city. The tract between the river on the edge of the western hills was doubtless more or less covered with houses, at least along the high roads which led down from each great funeral temple to the Nile.

Strabo reckoned the extent of Thebes, including the western side, as nine miles; and even if parts of this gigantic town were taken up with country houses and gardens, yet it may well compare with the great towns of the world of modern times.

Thebes fell like Rome and Nineveh. When the seat of government was removed to Lower Egypt the heart of the city was destroyed and her importance lost, and she became more and more deserted. Those parts of the town which could be used for arable land were cultivated, and gradually the inhabitants who remained withdrew to the sites occupied by the great buildings; and thus the villages of Karnak, Luxor, and Medinet Habu nestled round those vast temples, and now constitute the last remains of the great city.

Sailing down the stream from Thebes, we come on the eastern bank to the "Nome of the two Hawks," important in old and modern days for the same reason. The river here makes a deep bend towards the Red Sea, and is met by a transverse valley of the Arabian desert which forms a natural road from Egypt to the coast. The Egyptian expeditions to the incense country of Punt, the Greek merchantmen travelling to South Arabia, the Indian navigators of the Middle Ages, the modern pilgrims to Mecca, all have used this road; and it is only since the opening of the Suez Canal that traffic has been wholly diverted into another channel. The starting-points for the desert, and the harbours, have changed from time to time; Koptos (Qobte) was the usual starting-point in old times; Qus in the Middle Ages; and at the present time it is Keneh, which lies farther to the north.

In old times this road was also important for the great quarries of Rehanu, the modern Ḥammamat, situated where the limestone meets the older formations. With the exception of granite, all the hard dark-coloured stone used by the Egyptian sculptors came from these quarries;

and those who know how much the Egyptians valued these "eternal stones" can estimate the importance of the road by which alone they could obtain these treasures. Soldiers protected it from the Beduins of the *'Ente*, who, like their successors the Troglodytes and the Ababde, would suddenly attack travellers. A higher protection than the soldiers was also at hand, for Koptos was the abode of the great god Min, the Pan of the Egyptians, who, although he was peculiarly the god of nature, took the travellers of the desert under his special protection. The same god had another famous temple in the town of Chemnis, in the 9th nome, which adjoined the 5th nome on the north.

This part of Egypt is the true home of the great gods. In the 6th nome, about fourteen miles from Koptos, there lay on the western bank the temple of Denderah, the sacred abode of Ḥatḥor, the goddess of joy and love. The old sanctuary is now replaced by a Graeco-Roman building Then again, thirty-eight miles down the stream in the 8th nome, was the most holy place in Egypt, Abydos, with the grave of Osiris. A blessing was supposed to rest on those buried here, and many who preferred to be interred near their homes put up gravestones here, so that "Osiris, the lord of Abydos," should receive them into the underworld. Thus Abydos became in the first place a city of the dead, in which, as in western Thebes, the living only dwelt for the sake of the tombs. Politically, the neighbouring town of Thinis, which lay rather nearer to the river, was the more important, at any rate in old times.

The 10th and 11th nomes both lay on the western bank; they played but a small part in history; the district belonging to them on the eastern bank, the "Nome of the two Gods," was of more importance. The chief town of the latter, *Du qau* (high mountain), the modern Qau, lay at the entrance of one of the great desert roads which led to the porphyry quarries in the northern part of the Arabian desert. Traffic also passed along this road, and across the Gulf of Aqabah to the quarries in the peninsula of Sinai; this was an easier route than that by sea from Lower Egypt.

The 12th nome, "his Mountain," lay on the eastern bank, and was the chief seat of the worship of Anubis, the jackal-headed god of the dead; the same great god was revered in the opposite nome, the "first sycamore nome," with its chief town of Siut (Saut). This latter fact is significant, for this nome with the two following was governed by a powerful race of rulers during the so-called Middle Empire (about 2100-1900 B.C.), and the interesting representations and inscriptions in their rocky tombs are almost all that is left to show us the civilisation of this period. In nearly every section of this work we shall have to refer to these tombs of Siut, Bersheh, and Beni Hasan.

We next come to the 15th province, probably called the "Nome of the Hare," with its famous capital of Chmunu (now Ashmunên, the Greek Hermopolis). This town "of the eight," as Chmunu signifies, was so named from the eight elementary beings of the world, who were honoured here. The chief god of the town was Thoth, the god of wisdom, who was considered to be the guide of these eight elementary beings. The tombs of the princes of this old town lie on the opposite (eastern) side of the river near the modern Bersheh. A little to the south of Bersheh, at a point where the eastern chain of hills retreats somewhat, we find some most remarkable ruins, the remains of the city and tombs of Tell el Amarna. This town was founded (about 1340 B.C.) in a peremptory fashion by the so-called heretic king, the strange creature Amenḥotep IV. He had broken with the old religion, which had been evolved in the course

ROCK TOMBS OF BENI HASAN (see L.D., i. 61).

of centuries, and he wished that the reformation introduced by him should remain untouched by the associations which were bound up with the capital of his fathers. He therefore left Thebes and built a new capital at Tell el Amarna, but this town enjoyed only a short existence, as a few years after the death of this great heretic it was razed to the ground.

We shall often have to speak of Meḥ, the 16th nome, with the antelope as its coat-of-arms, and of the "eastern country," connected with that province, and of the town of Men'at Chufu (the nurse of king Chufu). The tombs of the governors of this part of the country are on the east bank, the celebrated tombs of Beni Hasan; they are most precious for the light they throw on the history of Egyptian manners and customs. At other points also in the eastern hills, *e.g.* at Zawijet el Meïtin and at Qum el aḥmar, we find important tombs in the rocks.

The two provinces No. 5 and No. 9, which were contiguous, both served the god Min; No. 12 and No. 13 the jackal-headed god Anubis;

the latter god was also worshipped on the opposite side of the Nile in the 17th and 18th nomes. These provinces played little part in political history, least of all the 18th, where there was little arable land, but to which belonged the celebrated alabaster quarries lying in the mountains at the distance of about a day's journey. The 19th nome to the west of the Nile, was one of the few parts of Egypt in which Set or Typhon was revered. The worship of this god, the enemy of all fruitfulness, may have been connected with the calling followed by the inhabitants, who were most of them guides to the desert caravans.[1] The road to the northern oasis, both in old and in more modern times, started from this province.

On the west side there follow the anterior and posterior Nomes of the Date Palm (the 20th and the 21st), both famous in old Egypt. The former for religious reasons, for the sun-god Rê' first appeared, bringing light and order into the world, on the hill of its ancient capital Chenensuten or Chenensu (Herakleopolis, the present Ahnas).

The fertile Feyum belonged to the posterior nome, and the water reservoirs here were most important for the whole country of Egypt. Whilst the other oases lie 20 or 30 miles from the Nile, and are watered by springs, the Feyum is connected with the Nile by a canal, and is close to the edge of the western valley, the traveller in fact can cross the intervening mountainous district in little more than an hour.

A little to the south of the above-mentioned Bersheh, the great canal (the modern Baḥr Yusuf, Joseph's river) makes a bend away from the Nile, and flows northwards to the western side of the valley. This is not an artificial canal, as is proved by its many curves and bends, but an old branch of the river like that of Abydos; it is connected with the Baḥr Yusuf by a dry watercourse, the remains of the old bed of the Nile, which can easily be traced farther north into the Delta. Herodotos relates that the present eastern channel of the Nile was not the ancient one; the latter formerly flowed close to the western edge of the valley. This great change was probably due to no sudden convulsion of nature; it is well known that a stream left to itself, with no rocky walls to stop it, will slowly shift its bed, and sometimes, after forming a new branch may even for centuries allow its waters to flow through both branches equally before it entirely gives up the old channel, in which the water gradually subsides till the watercourse is left dry.

Thus in ancient Egypt there was probably an older channel to the west of the valley in addition to the present one on the east side; the former, as was related by the priests to Herodotos, was dammed up above Memphis by Menes, the first Egyptian king of human race, in order to make a site for his new capital. It may be that another work as daring was undertaken at the same time that this dam was constructed,—that a gorge in the rocks between the Nile valley and the Feyum was deepened and the branch of the river allowed to flow into the Feyum. By these means this barren depression in the ground was changed into one of the

[1] Düm. Gesch. des alt. Aeg. 202.

most fertile parts of Egypt, and a province of about 900 square miles of arable land added to the little country. This was not all. An enterprising king (probably Amenemḥe't III. about 2000 B.C.) built dykes some miles in length in order to change the south-eastern corner of the Feyum into an immense reservoir in which the water could be regulated by sluices. By this great basin, 66 square miles in area (the Lake Moeris, the wonder of the Greeks), the inundation in the Feyum and in Lower Egypt was regulated; for if the water rose too high, part was retained in this deep lake, if too low, some of the reserve water could be used from it. It was natural that in this *lakeland*, the ancient name of the Feyum, men should revere the crocodile-headed god Subk, whose temple was to be found in the capital Shedet, called in later times Arsinoe. The two nomes of the Date Palm, and the unimportant nome opposite (the 23rd), complete the provinces of "the South" or Upper Egypt.

We now turn to the discussion of the "North Land," to which the northernmost part of the Nile valley belonged. We shall be able to be the more brief as, with the exception of its southern division, Lower Egypt was of little importance in ancient times. During the course of centuries, in no part of the Nile valley has the river undergone so many changes as in the Delta. There are now but two mouths to the Nile—that of Rosetta and that of Damietta; in Greek times we know there were seven, and of the course of the river in yet earlier periods we really know nothing.

The north of the Delta, as has been said above, was covered with swamps, and our knowledge of the southern part is very scanty. It is therefore difficult to determine the position of individual provinces; indeed it is doubtful whether in the Delta this division was the old national one. We will therefore waive that question entirely, and confine ourselves to the description of certain important towns.

The old capital of Egypt, Memphis (Mennufer), naturally stands first; it was situated a little above the modern Cairo on the west bank of the river. It has entirely disappeared; the mounds overgrown with palms close to the village of Mitrahine alone denote the spot where stood the great temple of Ptaḥ. The famous citadel of the town, the "White Wall," as well as the other buildings, have utterly vanished, evidently owing to the fact that the inhabitants of the neighbouring Cairo used the ruins of Memphis as a convenient quarry. The long line of pyramids, stretching for miles along the western ridge of hills, alone betrays what a powerful city once stood here. Groups of these royal tombs rise from the plateau, which extends past Gizeh, Zawijet el Aryan, Abusir, Sakkarah, Dahshur, and Lisht, to Medum, not far from the entrance to the Feyum (see Plate IV.). Grouped round each pyramid are the smaller tombs of courtiers; these are the so-called mastabahs,—those ancient tombs which teach us so much about the life of the ancient Egyptians in the earliest period, in the same way as those of Thebes picture to us the later times, and those of Beni Hasan the time of the "Middle Empire." We are indebted to the private tombs of this Memphite necropolis for almost all contained in this book concerning the "Old Empire."

About 19 miles to the north of Memphis, north-east of the bend of the river, was the ancient sacred city of On [hieroglyphs], better known to us by its Greek name, Heliopolis. This name, "City of the Sun," shows us which god was revered here; the temple was one of the most splendid in the country, and, according to Herodotos, the priests were considered the wisest in Egypt. A great part of the ancient Egyptian religious literature appears to have been written in this town.[1] At the present day fields cover the sites both of town and temples, and one obelisk stands alone to point out the spot to visitors.

The west of the Delta was probably inhabited chiefly by Libyans, one town only being frequently mentioned in ancient times, Sais (Sau), the city of the goddess of war, Neith. In the eighth century B.C. this town first became of historical importance, the Libyan family reigning there, certain chiefs of the names of Psammetichus and Necho having raised themselves to be kings of Egypt.

The east of the Delta was more thickly populated; at Mendes (*Ded*) the sacred ram was revered; at Busiris was a famous tomb of Osiris; at Bubastis were held the Dionysiac festivals of the cat-headed goddess of pleasure, Bast. To the north-east, on the edge of the swamps, was Tanis (Zoan), an important town even in early ages. Non-Egyptian rulers seem to have reigned there in old times; later kings also resided here and built a great temple to the warrior god Set. Mariette excavated the vast ruins here thirty years ago, and further work has since been carried on by the Egypt Exploration Fund, the results of which have been published by that society.[2]

The isthmus now cut through by the Suez Canal between the Red Sea and the Mediterranean is intersected by a number of lakes, the remains of the strait which formerly separated Africa from Asia. These lakes are connected with the Delta by a narrow valley, the modern Wadi Tumilat. In old times there was a canal from the Nile into this valley, which fertilised the whole district. This is the well-known Land of Goshen, in which, according to the Hebrew account, the ancestors of the Jews fed their cattle. The towns of Ramses and Pithom, built by the Hebrews when in bondage, must have been situated here. The same king Ramses II., who caused these towns to be built, seems to have undertaken another great work here, the continuation of the canal of the Wadi Tumilat to the Bitter Lakes, and the cutting through of the rising ground between them and the Red Sea. This connection between the Nile and the Red Sea was the true precursor of the Suez Canal. However, this great work seems soon to have been rendered useless by the silting up of the sand; King Pharaoh Necho and King Darius re-opened

[1] Ed. Meyer, Set. Typhon, p. 7 ff.; ditto, History of the East, § 93.

[2] See Tanis, i., 1884-85; and ii., 1887-88. Published by the Egypt Exploration Fund.

it, but it was soon filled up again with sand; afterwards Trajan and Hadrian undertook the work, and later the conqueror Amr made the canal navigable for some time. The old course of the canal can still be distinctly traced by the side of the modern one.

The isthmus of Suez was of the greatest consequence also from a military point of view—it was doubtless fortified in very early times. Probably here stood the great fortress T'aru, often spoken of as the starting-point for the expeditions into Syria, and also the strongly fortified town of Pelusium, which was situated at the mouth of the eastern branch of the Nile. Close by we must place Ḥat-uar (Avaris), the fortress which for centuries served as a protection to the power of the barbarian conquerors of Egypt, the Hyksos.

ONE OF THE PATRON GODDESSES OF BOTH DIVISIONS OF THE KINGDOM, IN THE FORM OF A SERPENT.

ORNAMENTATION COMPOSED OF CARTOUCHES GUARDED BY URÆUS SNAKES.

CHAPTER II

THE PEOPLE OF EGYPT

THE people who inhabited ancient Egypt still survive in their descendants the modern Egyptians. The vicissitudes of history have changed both language and religion, but invasions and conquests have not been able to alter the features of this ancient people. The hundreds and thousands of Greeks and Arabs who have settled in the country seem to have been absorbed into it; they may have modified the race in the great towns, where their numbers were considerable, but in the open country they scarcely produced any effect. The modern fellah resembles his forefather of four thousand years ago, except that he speaks Arabic, and has become a Mohammedan. In a modern Egyptian village, figures meet one which might have walked out of the pictures in an ancient Egyptian tomb. We must not deny that this resemblance is partly due to another reason besides the continuance of the old race. Each country and condition of life stamps the inhabitants with certain characteristics. The nomad of the desert has the same features, whether he wanders through the Sahara or the interior of Arabia; and the Copt, who has maintained his religion through centuries of oppression, might be mistaken at first sight for a Polish Jew, who has suffered in the same way. The Egyptian soil therefore, with its ever-constant conditions of life, has always stamped the population of the Nile valley with the same seal.

The question of the race-origin of the Egyptians has long been a matter of dispute between ethnologists and philologists, the former maintaining the African theory of descent, the latter the Asiatic. Ethnologists assert that nothing exists in the physical structure of the Egyptian to distinguish him from the native African, and that from the Egyptian to the negro population of tropical Africa, a series of links exist which do not admit of a break. The Egyptians, they maintain, cannot be separated from the Berbers, nor the latter from the Kelowi or the Tibbu, nor these again from the inhabitants round Lake Tsad; all form one race in the mind of the ethnologist, differentiated only by the influence of a dissimilar manner of life and climate. Therefore, they say, many old customs of the ancient Egyptians are now found amongst the people of the Upper Nile. I will only instance the curious head-rest still used in the east of the Sudan to protect the wig, and the peculiar sickle-shaped sword, still carried by the Monbuttu princes with the same dignity as it was of old by the Pharaohs. On the other side philologists maintain that the language of the ancient Egyptians has distinct kinship with that of the so-called Semitic nations.

PORTRAIT OF AN UNKNOWN MAN OF THE FOURTH DYNASTY. Mistaken by Mariette's workmen for the present Sheik-el-Beled (Mayor) of Sakkarah (Perrot-Chipiez).

Spread over anterior Asia, and the east and north of Africa, is found a great root-language, which has been called after its chief representatives, the Egypto-Semitic. The Semitic languages of Arabia, Syria, and Mesopotamia belong to this group, as well as the allied Ethiopian dialects of east Africa, the languages of the Besharis, Gallas, and Somalis. Further removed is the Libyan, spoken by the people of Berber in north Africa, as far as the Atlantic; and still more peculiarly constituted is the ancient Egyptian. Nothing certain has been or probably will be ascertained, for the Libyan and Ethiopian languages are only known to us in their present much-changed forms. But the fact remains that philologists consider that the people who speak these languages belong to one and the same race. Other reasons tend to show us that the Semitic races migrated from one part of Asia to the districts in which they afterwards settled, and therefore the theory has been accepted that the Ethiopian, Libyan, and Egyptian people all forsook their Asiatic homes during the dim ages of the past, and seized possession of north and east Africa. This theory is directly opposed to that of the ethnologists, according to whom these races are purely African. If we free ourselves, however, from the prejudices which have so long held unlimited sway over this domain of science, we shall be able to reconcile these two theories. It seems a very doubtful hypothesis that ancient races should dwell quietly in one inhospitable region until the idea should suddenly seize them to forsake their homes and, with their children and their goods, to seek a better country. Such migrations have certainly taken place amongst the hordes of barbarians (*e.g.* the old migrations of the Teuton or Scythian races), but they never had much effect. After a few generations all traces of them have disappeared in the countries they conquered, and no one would imagine from the appearance of the inhabitants of modern Italy, Spain, or Tunis, that whole tribes of Germanic race had overrun those countries. Neither the language nor the race of the subject nation suffers permanent change from such violent incursions.

On the other hand, if but a few adventurers conquer a country and thus make it possible for their kindred to settle there, the constant influx

FELLAH FROM EL KAB. (From a photograph by Ebers.)

of immigrants even in small numbers has an immense influence on the people. In the first place, the conquerors succeed in introducing their language to be used officially; the upper classes of the subject race, desiring to belong to the ruling class, then begin ostentatiously to use foreign idioms; at last, perhaps only after a thousand years, the lower classes begin also to adopt the new language. Thus in our own days we have seen nations extend their nationality, *e.g.* a few Spaniards and Portuguese in South America, a few Arabs amongst the Copts and Berbers, a few Anglo-Saxons amongst the Celts in England. In each case we see that in this process the language only of the subject people is changed, the race itself remains unaltered.

In like manner probably ancient nations underwent transformations.

The inhabitants of Libya, Egypt, and Ethiopia have probably belonged to the same race since prehistoric times; in physical structure they are still Africans, though in later times they have adopted an Asiatic language. No one can say how long they have used kindred dialects. It may be these proceeded from the one language they originally possessed, or it is quite possible that one of these races imposed their tongue on the others, or they may have been derived from a tribe of which we have never heard. Considering how little we know of the Egypto-Semitic speech, we may suppose that it was to a Libyan invasion that the valley of the Nile owed in the first place its later language; that a similar incursion endowed the inhabitants of Syria and Arabia with the Semitic tongue; and that the latter nations gave the same to the dwellers in east Africa. This is of course pure hypothesis, for the same process may have taken place in many other ways. Probably we shall never have any certainty on the matter, for these events occurred more than five thousand years ago, which is the length of the period we hope to survey. *How* it happened is of small consequence, it is only important to remember that there is no necessity for a great immigration of the Egyptians from some distant corner of Asia. We may conscientiously believe them to be natives of their own country, children of their own soil, even if it should be proved that their old language, like their modern one, was imported from other countries.

It is well known that the Egyptians considered themselves an indigenous people, free from any foreign taint. Were they not the peculiar people, specially loved by the gods? Did not the great gods first manifest themselves in Egypt, where the sun-god ruled and fought as a king, and where his descendants still sat on the throne? Therefore the Egyptians alone were termed "*men*" (romet); other nations were negroes, Asiatics, or Libyans, but not *men*.[1] According to the myth, these nations were descended from the enemies of the gods, for when the sun-god Rê' overthrew his opponents at Edfu, a few succeeded in making their escape; those who fled to the south became the Ethiopians, those to the north Asiatics; from the fugitives of the west sprang the Libyans, and from those of the east, the Beduins.[2]

The Egyptians named their country from the colour of the soil "the black country" (Qêmet), and thus distinguished it from the *red country* of the barbarians: they also believed themselves to be superior to foreigners by the colour of their skin. The Syrians were light brown, the Libyans white, the negroes black, but the Egyptians had received from the gods their beautiful colour, a deep dark brown for the men, a light yellow for the women.[3]

Circumcision was also practised from early times by the Egyptians,

[1] L.D., iii. 136, where the names of the nations are explained by puns on the name of the god Horus. The word *Retu*, which appears in ethnological works for Egyptians, is incorrect, the word reads *Romet*.

[2] Naville, Myth of Horus, 21, 2.

[3] Stele of Kuban, line 3.

yet probably they did not attach so much importance to this curious custom as the Jews and Mohammedans. It first became a religious token amongst the Jews, who zealously tried to distinguish themselves in all ways from the surrounding heathen ; had the Egyptians also regarded it as a divine institution they would have mentioned it more frequently.

The reader will be able to judge of the physical form of the ancient Egyptians from the illustrations of this book. It must be noticed that the faces of the distinguished men of the Old Empire have as a rule little that is aristocratic about them. These ancient grandees have robust

STATUE OF AN UNKNOWN SCRIBE IN THE LOUVRE (Perrot-Chipiez).

bony features with the clever witty expression that we are accustomed to associate with the faces of knowing old peasants. The expression of the face becomes more refined in the great men of the New Empire, showing the usual effect exercised on the higher class by long intellectual civilisation.

Many contrary opinions have been expressed touching the character of the Egyptian people, and their mental faculties. While Herodotos praises the wisdom and the good memory of the Egyptians, and Diodorus declares them to be the most grateful people in the world, the Emperor Hadrian says that, when travelling in Egypt, he found them to be utterly frivolous, vacillating, credulous of every idle tale, hostile, good-for-nothing, and slanderous. In the same way many modern scholars represent them as pious folk, who thought more of the future world than of the present, while others praise their cheerful childlike pleasure in the things of this world. The exponents of each of these theories regard the matter too exclusively from one point of view; in truth the question is one admitting only of a subjective answer. If the character of an individual is complex, that of a nation is still more so, and what Faust says of the "spirit of the times" is equally true of the "spirit of the nations," for after all, it is a well-known fact that the mind of the man himself is mirrored in that of the people.

We have already indicated in the preceding chapter what we think of the character of the ancient Egyptians. As a nation they appear to us to have been intelligent, practical, and very energetic, but lacking poetical imagination: this is exactly what we should expect from a nation of peasants living in this country of toilsome agriculture. We will quote the words of one, profoundly acquainted with Egypt, referring to the modern lower classes, *i.e.* to those in whom the characteristics of the nation find their natural expression. He says, "In his youth the Egyptian peasant is wonderfully docile, sensible, and active; in his riper years, owing to want and care, and the continual work of drawing water, he loses the cheerfulness, freshness, and elasticity of mind which made him appear so amiable and promising as a boy. He sows and reaps, he works and earns money, but his piastres rarely remain in his own possession, and he sees the fruits of his labour pass into the hands of those above him. His character is therefore like that of a gifted child who has been harshly brought up, and who realises as he grows older that others are taking advantage of his work."[1] This picture of a race, cheerful by nature, but losing the happy temperament and becoming selfish and hardened in the severe work of life, represents also the ancient people, as they appear to the eyes of an unprejudiced observer.

The earliest monuments that have come down to us represent the Egyptians as possessing, even then, an ancient civilisation, also a complete system of writing, a literature, a highly-developed art, and a well-ordered government. Preceding this first period of Egyptian history a long time of peaceful development must have elapsed, about which we have no information. The learned men of Egypt imagined the time before their first king Menes to have been a sort of golden age, in which the gods reigned; the learned men of modern times call the same period "the stone age;" both theories are certainly ingenious, but both are alike difficult to prove. It is but seldom that we can draw any conclusion, as to the life in Egypt in prehistoric times, from customs existing amongst the Egyptians during the historical periods. We may conclude however, from the form of the royal robes, that the dignity of *king* existed in Egypt at a time when the people, like the negroes of to-day, wore nothing but a kirtle. The royal attire was formerly an apron and a lion's tail, whilst the grandees distinguished themselves from the people by a panther's skin,

[1] See Baedeker's Lower Egypt, p. 47.

which they threw over their shoulders. The sportsmen made their way through the swamps on boats made of reeds, and hunted there with throw-sticks. Their knives, in part at least, as well as the tips of their arrows, were made of flint, yet we must not conclude from this fact that they were ignorant of the use of metals. They reckoned their years by notches, reminding us of a time when the art of writing was unknown.

All these customs, which were dying out even in the earliest historical times, are a heritage from that ancient period when the Egyptian civilisation may perhaps have equalled that of the modern Somalis or Gallas. How many hundreds or thousands of years were necessary to evolve the civilised subjects of King Snofru from these simple savages we cannot even conjecture.

In many parts of Egypt, where nature was unfavourable, the people doubtless were far behind their compatriots in civilisation, *e.g.* the people of the swamps (*sochete*), who are represented on the monuments of the Old Empire as shepherds or bird-snarers. Their clothing of rush-mats, and the manner in which they wear their hair and their beard, make them appear very barbaric. These dwellers in the swamps may possibly belong to a different race from the native Egyptians. We know that the north-west of the Delta was inhabited by Libyans and that at one time a foreign element existed also in the north-east. By the latter we refer to that people whose remarkable features we recognise on the so-called Hyksos Sphinxes of Tanis, whose descendants were the Bashmurites of the Middle Ages.

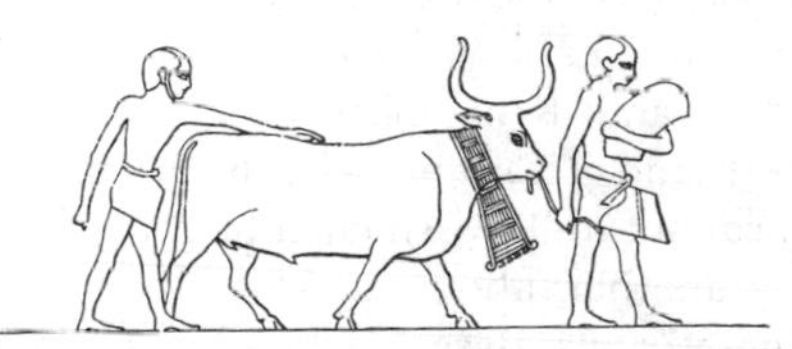

DWELLERS IN THE MARSHES (see L. D., ii. 69).

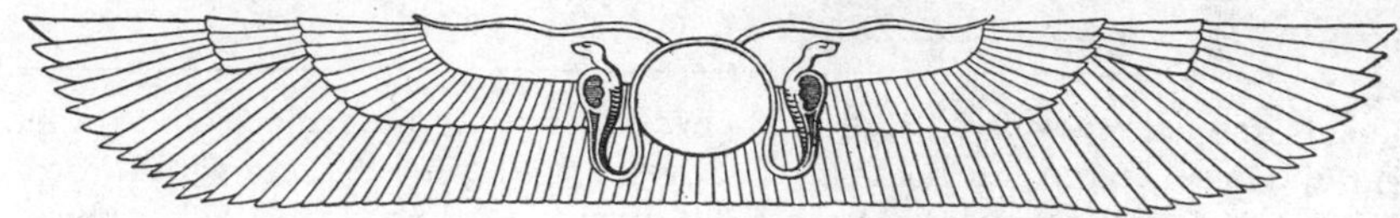

THE SUN'S DISC, WITH BRIGHTLY COLOURED WINGS, THE EMBLEM OF A VICTORIOUS KING.

CHAPTER III

HISTORY OF ANCIENT EGYPT

In the foregoing chapter, we were unfortunately obliged to concern ourselves chiefly with prehistoric conditions, of which we can only form hypotheses. With the first inscriptions we pass on to firmer historical ground. The reader must not expect too much from the short sketch of Egyptian history which follows: to a great degree our knowledge consists merely of the names of the kings and their order of succession, and in several periods even these are not certainly determined. As a rule but few facts can be gleaned from the inscriptions, which mostly contain foolish exaggerations of the glory of the monarch; a hundred texts will tell us that the Pharaoh was the "friend of the gods," and that he "overthrew all the barbarians," while one solitary inscription may inform us which temple he built, or against what nation he sent his soldiers. Civil wars and disputes about the succession are always passed over in silence, that posterity might only know that "the gods have established their son the Pharaoh on the throne, that the world may rejoice."

Chronology also fails us. We can say for certain that King Necho reigned from 609-595, and King Sheshonk about 930, that Ramses II. lived in the thirteenth and Thothmes III.[1] in the fifteenth century B.C., but more than this we cannot tell. Amenemḥê't I. is placed by one scholar about 2130 B.C., by another about 2380 B.C., and by yet another about 2466 B.C.; and the various dates suggested for King Snofru and his successors are quite endless. Whether we follow the date given by Edward Meyer, 2830 B.C., or that of Lepsius, 3124 B.C., or that of Brugsch, 3766 B.C., one is as impossible to prove as another. We should have been able to draw up an approximately correct chronology had we possessed the whole of the Turin Papyrus instead of a few fragments, for this document contained a list of the kings, with the length of their reigns, or again had the Greek history of Egypt by Manetho been preserved to us intact, instead of in a few scanty quotations. Even then our dates would not have been quite trustworthy, for we know that neither the compiler of the

[1] The form Thothmes will be used in the English edition instead of Dḥutmose, the former being more familiar to English readers.

Turin Papyrus nor Manetho was always correctly informed as to the more ancient kings.

Lepsius has collected together all that can be gathered from these two sources, and on the whole his chronology gives us an accurate idea of Egyptian history, especially for the later periods. As it would be impossible to give exact data, I prefer to state the chronology in this book in round numbers, which the reader will at first sight understand to be only approximate. I shall follow the chronology of Edward Meyer in his excellent history of the ancient east, and the numbers given may be accounted as nearly correct from about 1530 B.C.; earlier than that they are only minima data, that is, they indicate the lowest date which can be accepted for the individual ruler, *e.g.* Amenemḥē‘t I. is said to have reigned 2130 B.C., and this signifies that probably his reign was not later than that date, though it may have been one or even two hundred years earlier. This uncertainty is of course greater in the earliest periods, and when we state the latest date for King Snofru to be 2830 B.C., we may be placing him five hundred years too late. As a simple and practical way out of the difficulties which arise from this uncertain chronology, Egyptologists, following the example of Manetho, have divided the kings of Egypt into dynasties, which they have numbered. Historically, this division is often not quite accurate, but it is useful in practice, and enables us to maintain the ancient familiar terms for the different periods of Egyptian history. Otherwise we have little to do with the 30 dynasties, into which the time before the conquest of Alexander has been divided, and of which the following are the principal :—

Dynasty	IV. and V.	At latest from 2830 B.C.	}	The so-called "Old Empire."
"	VI.	" " 2530 "		
"	XII.	About " 2130 "	}	The "Middle Empire."
"	XIII.	" " 1930 "		
"	XVIII.	" 1530-1320 "	}	The "New Empire."
"	XIX.	" 1320-1180 "		
"	XX.	" 1180-1050 "		

We have only to take into serious consideration these three periods, and the reader is requested to remember them carefully, and to note the following facts: there are no monuments belonging to the first three dynasties; from the 7th to the 11th, and from the 14th to the 17th, are periods of political confusion, and after the 20th, inscriptions and papyri are too rare to yield satisfactory results for our object.

Before the time of the 4th dynasty Egypt had already been united into one kingdom, but we may feel sure that this was not the original political state of the country. It was doubtless formerly divided into two parts, the frontier being a little above Memphis. We know not under which king these "two countries" were united (they were not really merged into one country), probably it was under one of the rulers of Upper Egypt, whose titles were used alone by the later kings of the whole country. It may have been Menes, of whom the Egyptian legend tells that he was the first king of human race, that he came from Thinis in Upper Egypt, and that he founded Memphis. In this case Egypt, at the time of the 4th dynasty, would, for about the space of three centuries, have been united into one kingdom, but however powerful this united kingdom

KING CHA'FRÊ' (Gizeh Museum, from Perrot-Chipiez).

may have been, there is no trace of any wish to claim power outside Egypt. We hear of no great wars or conquests, perhaps because the rulers had, as they thought, more important work for the resources of the country. They had to build their gigantic tombs, those pyramids,

THE PYRAMIDS OF GIZEH, SEEN FROM THE SOUTH.

(After L. D., I. 19.)

standing on the Memphite plateau, which have become symbolic of Egypt. All the kings of the Old Empire indulged in this luxury, and this epoch has been rightly termed the Pyramid Age, for apparently the whole life of the nation revolved round the building of those royal tombs.

Three kings of the 4th dynasty have gained special renown for the building of their tombs, Chufu (Cheops), Cha'frê' (Chephren), and Menkerê' (Mykerinos): to them we owe the three famous pyramids of Gizeh. Their successors also built magnificent tombs, and if none of them vie with those of Chufu and Cha'frê', it may have been that the later kings could not devote so much time to their tombs as those two monarchs, whose reigns were so long. At the same time other works were carried on, temples were restored or enlarged, the mines were worked in the Peninsula of Sinai, and numberless private tombs were erected for the courtiers, partly at the public cost.

The mania for building, which is so characteristic of the Egyptians, was thus actively pursued under the Old Empire, and princes were proud to bear the title—"Superintendent of the works of the King." We must be grateful to those old architects; for were it not for the non-religious reliefs which decorate the private tombs surrounding each pyramid, we should be almost entirely ignorant of the cheerful pleasant life of this ancient period.

It is interesting to note how the time of the Old Empire appeared to the later Egyptians. Under the New Empire men looked back to it as to the dim past, a time long before the classical age, and if they wished to represent anything as having happened very long ago, e.g. the discovery of a sacred book, they preferred to ascribe it to one of those ancient rulers. On the contrary, to the men of the time of Psammetichus, the Old Empire appeared to be the finest period of Egyptian history; they delighted to imitate the customs of that time, even in undesirable ways, such as the difficult orthography. Then, again, the populace of late date, and the Greek travellers informed by them, looked back to the pyramid age as to a time when the lower orders were greatly oppressed by forced labour. Lastly, to the modern world, the Old Empire appears to have been a period of youthful power and undisturbed development; for not only do the tomb-pictures show no dislike of this world, but also art itself is fresher than in any subsequent period. Later artists were never able to achieve works like the statues of the scribe of the Louvre or of King Cha'frê'.

The duration of the 4th and 5th dynasties is reckoned as about 300 years, during which time perhaps fifteen kings may have reigned. In the meantime the nation did not remain stationary, and if we compare a monument of the time of Snofru, one of the first kings of the 4th dynasty, with one of the time of 'Ess'e or of Un'es, who reigned at the close of the 5th dynasty, we see at once that the old simplicity has given place to greater luxury.

Pepy, the third king of the 6th dynasty, is worthy of special attention.

He must have been a mighty monarch, for memorials of him are found throughout Egypt, as well as in various mines and quarries. He erected buildings both at Denderah and at Tanis, and yet it appears that in his time there was a decentralisation of the government; this may have been owing to political events at the time of the rise of the 6th dynasty. Formerly the great men, although they can scarcely all have resided in the capital, were buried together in the Memphite city of the dead, but at this time other burial-places in the country began to be used. Many princely families were laid to rest near their homes (*e.g.* the tombs of Zawijet el Meitin), and others of exceptional piety erected their tombs on the sacred soil of Abydos near the grave of Osiris. An inscription tells us of a great campaign, which Pepy carried on against the Syrian Beduins,

SPHINX FROM TANIS.

who had overrun the country. Of the kings who immediately succeeded Pepy we know little, though their tombs and names yet remain with us; after them ensues a period of historical darkness. We know not what happened to the kingdom of Pepy, and though we conjecture that it was afterwards divided into small principalities, history is silent on the subject. Neither can we tell how long the country was split up in this way,—probably for a long time, for under the Middle Empire Egypt has acquired an entirely different aspect.

The east of the Delta was probably governed at this time by a mighty race of rulers, the first king of whom, according to Manetho, was more powerful and more wicked than any preceding monarch. These barbarians were probably the old inhabitants of this part of the Delta; and it is to them I believe that we owe those remarkable unegyptian statues and sphinxes, generally considered as belonging to the later time of the Hyksos invasion.

In Thebes, meanwhile, there ruled another dynasty called the 11th, whose princes bore the names of 'Entef and Ment'uḥôtep. The last of their race seem again to have gained possession of the whole kingdom. There was probably great confusion in the land in their time, and when the first king of the 12th dynasty, Amenemḥê't I., marched through the country "to overthrow the evil, he who shone as the god Atum was obliged to restore what he found destroyed. He divided one town from another, he fixed the frontier of each township, and placed the boundary stones as firm as the sky." He proceeded in this matter not according to his own will, but "he sought information from the books as to the irrigated district belonging to each town, and this was drawn up according to the old writings, because he loved truth so much."[1] Thus the first kings of the 12th dynasty tried to reorganise the country, and the result was that they succeeded in raising the kingdom to a higher level of civilisation than it had reached before.

These kings (who all bore the names of Amenemḥê't and Usertsen) built much in the interior of the country, not temples and tombs alone, but also constructions for general utility. Amenemḥê't III. planned the great reservoir in the Feyum, generally called Lake Moeris, of which we spoke in the first chapter. Literature and art also flourished.

The effect of this prosperity at home was a development of foreign power. For the first time as far as we know the Egyptians planned foreign conquests, and naturally enough they turned their arms first against Nubia. It was not the narrow arable valley of this country which attracted them, but the gold mines in the desert. The rulers of the 12th dynasty fought again and again in Nubia for their possession, until at last Usertsen III. erected a great frontier fortress at Semneh. He was considered therefore to be the real conqueror of Nubia, and five hundred years later, when Thothmes III. carried on the same wars, he thought it his duty to erect a temple to his great predecessor. The kings of the 12th dynasty had constant intercourse also with Syria and South Arabia, but this always seems to have been of a peaceful nature. In short, the two hundred years of the 12th dynasty formed a period of such prosperity, that it is easy to understand how the later Egyptians looked back to it as to a national classical epoch. The kings of the 12th dynasty were considered to be ideal wise rulers, and the language of that time the standard for good writing.

A long line of obscure kings followed, of whom we have few monuments or buildings. Probably a period of political confusion again ensued, and the kingdom was shaken and divided by disputes about the succession. During these years of disorder, we must place the famous invasion of the Shepherd Kings, the Hyksos of the Greeks. A foreign race of nomads broke into the Delta from the north-east, and conquered Egypt. We have no certainty as to their nationality, nor as to the details of their history nor the duration of their invasion. We know that their seat of government was at the city of Ḥatu'ar (Avaris), in the eastern swamps of the Delta, and that they served the native god of this district, Sutech.

[1] Inscription of Chuemḥôtep at Beni Hasan, L. D., ii. 124, ll. 36-46.

Events probably followed the same course as in similar barbaric invasions. The kingdom, weakened by internal strife, was overthrown with terrific force, and when peace ensued, the Hyksos probably found that though they could conquer, they could not govern Egypt. The old form of government was then revived, and the barbarian garrisons alone remained to show that the country was in the hands of foreigners. The strength of the Hyksos lay in their fortress on the Syrian frontier; the rulers resided here, and were contented if the provincial princes sent them rich tribute. After some generations they naturally became civilised, and the later Hyksos were perhaps as good Egyptians as the descendants of Dshingis-khan and Hulagu were good Mohammedans. Like the latter too they forfeited their power, for civilisation will kill a rough nation of nomads as surely as the plants from the desert die in a good soil. Had they remained long enough in Egypt they would no doubt have been absorbed into the Egyptian nation and have left no traces. But it happened otherwise, and they were driven out of Egypt by force.

Thebes was the birthplace of the new kingdom. There ruled here, tributary to the Hyksos, a dynasty who may have been the descendants of the old kings. One of these princes called Ta'a had a quarrel with one of the Hyksos kings Apopi (the same perhaps whose name is cut on a number of older statues in Tanis); this may have been the beginning of the war of liberation. When 'Aḥmose, the grandson of Ta'a, came to the throne, nearly the whole of the country was free, and the country about Ḥatu'ar alone remained in the hands of the Hyksos. Here they made a desperate stand, and it was only in the third campaign that Ḥatu'ar was taken by storm. 'Aḥmose made good use of his victory, and immediately advanced eastwards as far as Sharuhen in the south of Palestine. This advance is important as the first step in the direction afterwards pursued during some centuries by the Egyptian policy. The time of conquest, the "New Empire," begins with 'Aḥmose. Egypt seems to have gained strength like a field that has lain fallow; she now rose to such great prosperity and power as she had neither experienced before nor has since. Her strength showed itself, not in gigantic buildings as in the earlier days of her glory, but in foreign conquest, for these Pharaohs carried their arms as far as the Euphrates and into the distant Sudan. Out of darkness, as it were, the Egyptians rose to be a power in the world, and the results of this new position were soon seen.

The Egyptians came in contact with foreign nations whom they had looked down upon as barbarians; they then found out to their astonishment that their northern neighbours possessed a civilisation nearly equal to their own. They began to admire this civilisation, and soon it was considered permissible to serve Ba'al and Astarte, and it became fashionable to coquet with foreign Canaanitish words, much in the same way as the Germans of the last century did with scraps of French.

The wars of the 18th dynasty were next directed against Nubia, which had to be reconquered. 'Aḥmose fought again and again for the possession of Nubia, and his grandson, Thothmes I., subdued the country as far as the third cataract. From this time the "vile country of Cush" was formed into an Egyptian province, and gradually became civilised; yet at the same time it was always under a separate government, and the governor bore the title of "royal Son of Cush," and was one of the most important officers in the court of the New Empire. Amenḥôtep I. fought against the Libyans only, but his son, Thothmes I., besides his conquest of Nubia, undertook a second great campaign in the north. He overthrew the whole of Palestine and Syria, penetrated into Mesopotamia, and erected a stela east of the Euphrates to tell posterity of his conquests. Yet this great war had no permanent results, for, after the king's death, Thothmes II. and his sister-consort, Queen Ḥa'tshepsu, who succeeded him, preferred to abandon a possession so difficult to maintain. According to their father's will this king and queen reigned conjointly, but for how long we do not know, probably only for a short time. When Thothmes II. died, Ḥa'tshepsu began her reign as sole ruler by erasing her brother's name from all the monuments, and the suspicion of being concerned in the guilt of her brother's death probably does her no injustice. She had a nominal co-regent, a brother who was a minor, who later became Thothmes III.

The reign of this lady, the Egyptian Catherine II., was a peaceful one; her foreign achievements seem to have been limited to the great expedition to the incense countries of the Red Sea, to which we shall frequently have occasion to refer later. Her buildings were also very extensive; we must mention specially her temple of Dêr-el-Baḥri in western Thebes. There is always a powerful favourite to be found under similar queenly governments; in this case he seems to have been a certain Senmut, who was originally an official in the temple of Amon. In the inscription on his statue in the Berlin Museum he boasts that his lady-ruler had made him "great in both countries," and "chief of the chiefs" in the whole of Egypt."[1]

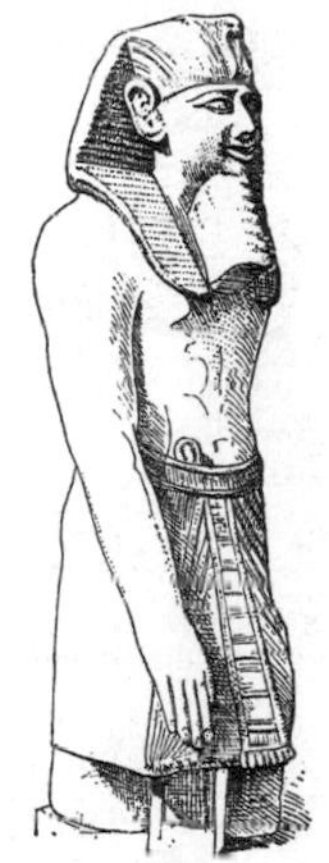

THOTHMES III.
(Granite Statue in the Gizeh Museum.)

Ḥa'tshepsu died after a reign of twenty years, and Thothmes III. retaliated on her the wrong she had done to her elder brother; he ordered her name to be effaced from all the monuments, and again we cannot help suspecting violence to have been the cause of the change of government. However that may be, the reign of Thothmes III. forms a great epoch in Egyptian history, for this young ruler followed the steps of his fathers in the path of conquest. In the twenty-second year of his nominal regency, that is in the first year of his actual government, he marched into Syria. He found no difficulties in the south of Palestine, but at Megiddo to the east of Carmel he first met with serious resistance, viz. a confederate army

[1] L. D., iii. 25 i.

of all the Syrio-Palestinian towns under the command of the prince of Kadesh. A battle ensued; the Egyptians gained the victory, which was so decisive that Megiddo surrendered, and the whole country submitted to the conqueror. After this first campaign the unwearied victor carried on at least fourteen others, by which he finally secured the sovereignty of the whole country southwards from the Amanus, as well as west of the Euphrates, which stream he crossed with his army. The countries yet beyond, *e.g.* Sangara (east of the Euphrates, the modern Sinjar), Assyria, Cilicia, and Cyprus, never belonged to him, and the supposed tributes he received from them were really voluntary presents which they sent to their mighty neighbour. In the annals of Thothmes III. we first find mention of the king of the Cheta, whose capital Kadesh was conquered by the Egyptian monarch in his sixth campaign; about a century later this same people succeeded to the political position in anterior Asia which Egypt had formerly occupied.

Wars seem to have been carried on in the south at the same time as in Syria, and the frontiers of the kingdom were extended southwards into the Sudan. Thothmes III. also erected great buildings, upon which he employed his prisoners of war, and we can easily understand what a mighty hero he appeared to posterity. More than *one* later king esteemed it an honour to assume his prenomen [cartouche] Ra'-men-choper, and it was also thought to be a lucky device, and used as a seal[1] by private individuals during the 19th dynasty. A happy chance has preserved to us the body of this great conqueror, and we see that, like Napoleon, he was of small stature.

AMENḤÔTEP III. FROM HIS TOMB. (From Champollion.)

His son Amenḥôtep II. and his grandson, Thothmes IV., who neither of them reigned long, kept the kingdom together, energetically repressing any attempts at foreign rebellion. Amenḥôtep III., his great-grandson, ruled over all the countries from Ethiopia to the Euphrates, and in time this vast empire might have become a compact kingdom had not disorders broken out in Egypt after the death of Amenḥôtep III., which made it impossible to keep up the Syrian possessions. This confusion was not due to disputes about the succession, which is the usual cause of political trouble in the east, but to an attempt to reform the Egyptian religion.

The old religion of Egypt consisted, broadly speaking, of the worship of the great solar gods. Rê', Horus, Atum, Osiris, were all different conceptions of the sun-god, either as the giver of life, or as the disperser of

[1] Three letters of a certain Mery'etf (Leyden, i. 365-367) are sealed in this way, and the number of scarabæi engraved with this name are countless.

darkness, or as a being dying to-day but rising again on the morrow. In one locality the people preferred to call their god Rê', in another Horus, in a third Osiris ; different customs were developed in the various temples, and different legends were connected with the individual forms of the deity. In this way the sun-god in the Egyptian religion had been divided into various parts, and these became separate gods in the eyes of the people. It could scarcely be otherwise, for the myths relating to Horus differed entirely from those of Rê' or of Osiris. Yet even in early times the educated class believed these deities to be essentially identical, and the priests did not shut their eyes to this doctrine, but strove to grasp the idea of the one god, divided into different persons by poesy and myth. Under the New Empire Re', Atum, Horus, and Osiris were but varying names for the one god. In order to perfect their religious system, they even carried these ideas yet further, and identified with the Sun-god, gods who had really nothing in common with him, *e.g.* Amon the god of the harvest, or Sobk the water-god. As is usual in the decadence of all religions, the boundary lines between the divinities were removed, and the deity was addressed by his worshippers in the same breath as Rê' or as Amon, as Atum or as Horus. The priesthood, however, had not the courage to take the final step, to do away with those distinctions, which they declared to be immaterial, and to adore the one god under one name. They went on in a conventional way, keeping up the worship of all the individual gods as well as the most trivial customs of ruder ages. It is easy to imagine how many were the contradictions which arose.

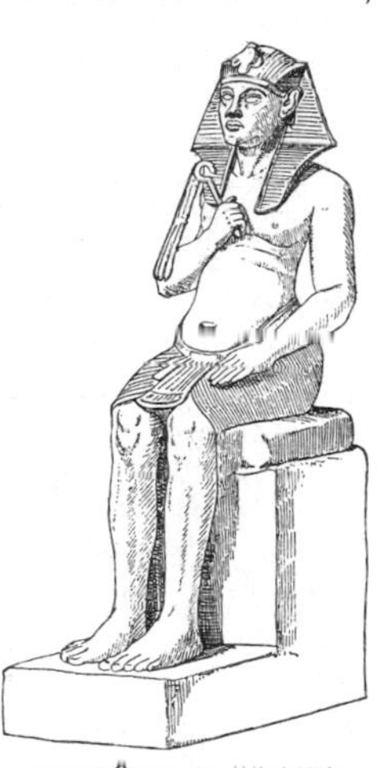
AMENḤÔTEP IV. (Statue in Louvre—from Chipiez).

An Egyptian king, Amenḥôtep IV., the son of Amenḥôtep III. and of Queen Tye, who seems to have played an important part at her son's court, now attempted to take the final step, and, in place of the confusion of the numerous gods of a bygone age, he tried to set up the Sun-god as the one really living god. How the young king extricated himself from the superstitious reverence for the faith of his fathers we know not, his portrait shows us that he had not good health, and it may be that the fanaticism with which he set to work on this meritorious reformation was due to bodily weakness. He introduced the worship of the sun as the one god, and following probably the teaching of Heliopolis, he called this god Rê' Harmachis, or more commonly 'Eten, the "Sun disk." Had he been content to establish this worship officially only, to introduce it gradually, and to let time do its work, his efforts might have been crowned with success ; but he tried violence, and therefore his innovation, in spite of momentary results, had no duration. He endeavoured to exterminate all remembrance of the old gods, and especially he declared war against the great god of his ancestors, Amon, whose name he erased from all the monuments. He changed his old name containing the name of Amon to Chu-en-'eten, the "splendour of the disk," and as the capital, where his famous forefathers had lived, was filled with memorials in honour of Amon, the puritan king resolved to live no longer in such an idolatrous place; he therefore forsook Thebes, and built a new town, the "Horizon of the Sun's disk," near the modern Tell el Amarna. We know not how long he resided here with his mother Tye, his consort Neferteyte, and

CHU-EN-'ETEN, HIS CONSORT, AND HIS SIX DAUGHTERS MAKE OFFERINGS TO THE SUN'S DISK.

Rays of light ending in hands descend to the king. The inscriptions give the names and titles of the god, and of the royal family.

his seven daughters. The representations in the tombs there (to which we shall often refer) show us that splendid buildings were erected, and a brilliant court was held in the new capital.

When Chu-en-'eten died, he was succeeded in the first place by his son-in-law, S'aanacht, and then by his favourite, the priest 'Ey, who had been a zealous adherent of the new religion. The latter, on ascending the throne, thought it wiser to retire from the conflict with the priesthood; he therefore returned to Thebes and made his peace with the old gods; notwithstanding this he was overthrown, and another son-in-law of Chu-en-'eten, Tuet'anchamun, a proselyte, succeeded to the throne, only however, soon to be set aside for a yet more powerful ruler, the great king Ḥar-em-ḥêb, who energetically put down the reformation, and razed to the ground the buildings erected by the heretic. We shall always lament the sad end to Chu-en-'eten's reformation; for though it was a good thing for the country that the state of disorder should cease, yet this victory of the old orthodox party sealed the fate of the Egyptian religion,—no one again attempted a reformation, and the religious conceptions of the nation were narrowed.

The successors of Ḥar-em-ḥêb, the kings of the 19th dynasty, sought to re-establish the Egyptian power in the north, but they encountered much greater difficulties than their predecessors of the 18th dynasty. It appears that during the time of the religious disturbances, whilst Egypt was unable to maintain her possessions in Syria, the Cheta had made good use of the favourable moment, and had succeeded there to the political heritage of the Pharaohs. The Cheta at this time must have been an important nation, for they had gained possession of Syria, the north of Mesopotamia, and the greater part of Asia Minor. We know little for certain about them; their name appears to indicate that their language was not Semitic, but their religion seems to have been that dominant in Syria. They are the Chatti of Assyrian lore, who had their capital in later times on the Euphrates; the semi-legendary Chittim of the Old Testament also probably signify the Cheta. At the time of which we are now speaking they were a highly civilised nation, and it is to be hoped that systematic excavations in north Syria may add greatly to our number of monuments and inscriptions of the Cheta kings. The few that have been found show us that this nation wrote in hieroglyphics something like the Egyptian, but that their art was influenced rather by the Assyrio-Babylonian. Thus the Egyptians found at this time a powerful kingdom opposed to them, instead of a number of small states, and we are therefore not surprised to learn that these wars were far less successful than those of Thothmes III.

SETIY I. (relief at Abydos).

Sety I., the second king of the 19th dynasty, began the campaign; in the first year of his reign he fought against the Beduins dwelling between Egypt and Canaan, and thus opened the way to north Palestine, which submitted to him. Here Mutenr, the king of the Cheta, met him, and it is doubtful whether, as the results were so insignificant, the war actually ended in such great victories as are described by the Egyptian inscriptions. The Egyptian king also seems to have made little way in the south of

Palestine. Later in his reign he had to fight for the western frontier of Egypt against the Libyans, who with the barbaric tribes of the islands and the coast-lands of the Mediterranean, the Shardana, the Shakarusha, etc., had made an incursion into the west of the Delta. Sety beat them, and thus the danger was averted, though only for a time. His son Ramses II., on his accession, again led his forces against the Cheta kingdom. He spent the first years of his reign in subjecting Palestine, and then turned his arms against the Cheta themselves. Their king had collected together all the forces of his kingdom and a powerful army of confederates; he made a stand at Kadesh on the Orontes. In the fifth year of Ramses II. there was a great battle, which, although at first unlucky for the Egyptians, was finally won by the personal bravery of the young ruler. At the same time it was not a decisive victory, for the war was continued several years longer with varying success. At one time we find the Egyptian king in Mesopotamia, but at another time he is fighting close to his own frontier and storming Askelon. At last, in the twenty-first year of his reign, he concluded not merely a peace, but a treaty, with Chetasar the king of the Cheta. Egypt kept the south of Palestine, but the kingdom of the Cheta was treated as an equal power. This *entente cordiale* was maintained, and thirteen years later Chetasar visited his Egyptian ally, and his daughter became one of the principal consorts of the Pharaoh. A busy peaceful intercourse soon developed between the two kingdoms; Egyptian civilisation was brought closer to the tribes of anterior Asia, whilst the Egyptians themselves were influenced more and more by their Canaanite neighbours.

Ramses II. reigned forty-six years after this conclusion of peace, and he made great and good use of his time. No king of Egypt built as much as he did; from Tanis to the deserts of Nubia numberless temples were erected by him, and it is said (it is difficult to say with how much truth) that half of all the Egyptian buildings that remain to us may be ascribed to him. He seems specially to have loved building in the east of the Delta, at the town called after him, "the house of Ramses," or, according to the official title, "the house of Ramses, the beloved of Amon, the great image of the sun-god." Here he had his seat of government close to the Syrian frontier; this change of residence is easily explained by the new political conditions of the kingdom.

When Ramses II. died, he had not only outlived thirteen of his sons, but also, as it would appear, the glory of his kingdom. The country was, however, still able to withstand one blow from without. In the fifth year of Merenptaḥ, his fourteenth son, who succeeded him, hordes of the above-mentioned Mediterranean tribes broke into the east of the Delta, and at the same time Maraju, the king of the Libyans, marched into Egypt. Merenptaḥ beat both armies, which had joined forces near the town of Per-'er-shepes.

Soon afterwards the Egyptian king died; his son, Sety II., not being able to withstand his internal foes, there followed a time of confusion and conflict about the throne. Several pretenders were set up, but not one

RAMSES II. STATUE AT TURIN.

AFTER PERROT-CHIPIEZ. DRAWN BY WILKE.

was able to maintain the upper hand ; therefore, as so frequently happened in Egypt, there ensued "many years in which the country of Egypt was governed by princes who killed each other in pride and arrogance, and did after their own pleasure, for they had no chief." 'Ersu, a prince of Syrian descent, succeeded, "in the years of famine," in subjecting the other rulers, and in making the whole country pay tribute. The son of his opponent tells us with pious horror that under him one joined with another in making piratical incursions, and "they treated the gods as they treated men, no one brought any offerings into the temples."[1] 'Ersu in fact, relying on his strength, had ventured to touch the temple revenues, and had in that way fallen under the displeasure of the priesthood, who now supported one of his rivals named Setnacht. In official language we read : "the gods placed their son, born of the gods, on their great throne as prince of the whole country. He was as the god Chepr'e-Set, when he is angry. He organised the whole country, which had been in confusion. He slew the enemies who had been in the country ;" and when he had attained to power, he "provided the temples with sacred revenues," and thus attached the priesthood to his cause.

SETY II. (Statue in the Louvre). From Perrot-Chipiez.

Ramses III., the first king of the 20th dynasty, reaped the reward of the work of his father Setnacht ; his reign, which lasted thirty-three years, was apparently equalled by few in splendour. His own wish was to emulate the fame of Ramses II. ; he therefore named all his sons after those of his great predecessor, and gave to each the same office in the state which those had held before. A prince Cha'emuêse was again high priest of Memphis, and a prince Meryatum high priest of Heliopolis.[2] He won over the priesthood by endowing them with large presents and immense buildings ; he re-established the old worship everywhere, "he created truth and abolished lies." He reorganised the mining operations in the Peninsula of Sinai, as well as the expeditions to the incense countries. He was also a great warrior. In the same way as under Sety I. and Merenptah II., the Libyans, during the late time of confusion, had taken possession of the west of the Delta, and at this time they occupied the country as far as the neighbourhood of Memphis. Ramses III. attacked them in the fifth and eleventh years of his reign, and subdued them. In the interval between these two wars a yet more serious danger threatened the country.

The pirates of the sea, who had already made several descents into Egypt, the Shardana, the Turusha, and the Shakarusha, with some other tribes, were again in a disturbed state ; they had overrun North Syria in a real national migration. They travelled with their wives and their

[1] Harris, I. 75.

[2] Ä. Z., 1883, pp. 60, 61.

goods partly by land in bullock waggons, and partly by water in stately ships. They seem to have overthrown the kingdom of the Cheta, which from this time disappears from Egyptian history, but in Palestine they were met by Ramses III. in the eighth year of his reign, and vanquished both by land and by sea. This is the last time that we hear of incursions made by the Libyans and the seafolk ; they probably never again renewed their attempts on Egypt. They had already obtained a footing in the country in another way, for since the time of Ramses II. the Egyptian army consisted in great part of mercenary Shardana and Libyan soldiers, whose leaders gradually became a power in the state.

We know very little of the nine kings who succeeded Ramses III. They all bore the name of Ramses, and were some of them his sons. Most of them were but tools in the hands of the two existing powers, the mighty priesthood and the foreign mercenaries. The former were the first to gain the supremacy, for about a century after the time of Ramses III., Ḥriḥor, the high priest of Amon of Thebes, forced the last of the Ramessides to abdicate in his favour. The priest-kings maintained themselves on the throne for about a century, after which, under the great king Sheshonk, the government passed into the hands of the Libyans, whose chiefs had already played a powerful part in the state. From this time Egypt became completely Libyanised, Libyan governors ruled in all the towns, and even the high priests of Thebes and Memphis were Libyans.

The adherents of the old priest-kings seem to have fled into Ethiopia, where about this time there arose an independent kingdom with Egyptian civilisation, in which the priestly power was so supreme that the king himself was obliged to bow to it. Two hundred years later, 728 B.C., king Shabaka left his capital Napata, situated in the 19th degree of latitude, and completed the conquest of the whole of Egypt, the southern part of which had been for centuries in the possession of the Ethiopians. Shabaka would gladly have advanced still further, and have penetrated into Syria, but the power of the Assyrians, which was then pre-eminent there, caused his schemes to miscarry.

There now began the conflict between the Assyrian and the Egypto-Ethiopian kingdom. The campaigns were at first fought with varying success in Syria, but at last the Assyrians, under Asarhaddon, marched into Egypt and conquered the country as far as Thebes, and the governors of the towns became the vassals of the great king of Assyria. Twice the Assyrians were driven out by the Ethiopians, but they again succeeded in re-entering the country, and in the year 662 B.C. Egypt became an Assyrian province. Their power, however, did not last long, for in 654 B.C. prince Psammetichus, who was descended from the Libyan chiefs of Sais, succeeded, with the help of his Greek mercenaries, in driving the Assyrians out of Egypt.

Psammetichus was the founder of the famous 26th dynasty, under which Egypt rose again to prosperity after the troubles she had suffered during the last centuries. The illustrious names of Psammetichus, Necho, and Amasis, are known to every reader of Herodotos. On one hand these kings favoured the settlements of the Greeks, and on the other they endeavoured to re-establish the ancient Egyptian government. They tried to link themselves with the Old Empire by using the same royal titles, the same language, and even the same orthography in the inscriptions. Art revived again, but though the works of art of this time possess great elegance and prettiness, yet the spirit is dead within them, and we feel that the men who created them were leading an artificial life.

The 26th dynasty is in fact therefore a renaissance period; people attempted consciously to revive a civilisation belonging to the past. This dream of a new kingdom of the Pharaohs lasted barely a century; Cambyses attacked it in the year 525 B.C., and it collapsed at the first blow.

PRINCE MR'EB, SON OF KING CHUFU (L. D., ii. 20 f.)

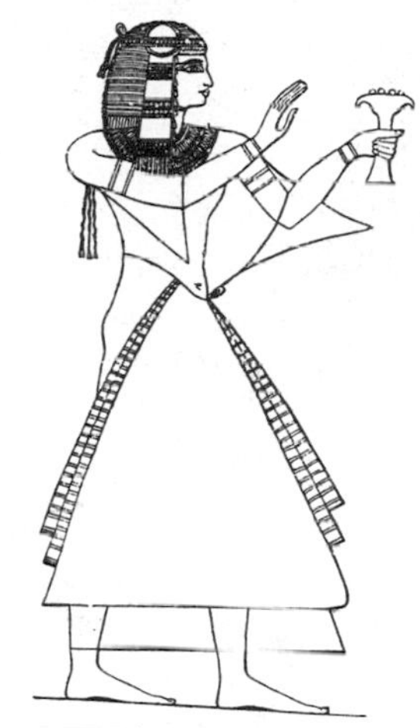

PRINCE MENT'UHERCHOPSHEF, SON OF RAMSES III. (L. D., ii. 217 a.)

Egypt next became a Persian province; several rebellions were cruelly suppressed, and the country was entirely ruined. Egypt was afterwards subdued by Alexander, and at the division of his empire fell to the share of Ptolemy and his family; finally, in the year 30 B.C., the country became a Roman province.

During this long period of foreign rule the priesthood kept up the fiction of the existence of an independent Egyptian kingdom. Darius and Alexander, Ptolemy and Hadrian, are all regarded in the temples as true Pharaohs. Even in the year 250 A.D., Decius is spoken of as Pharaoh in a hieroglyphic inscription, written at a time when the greater part of the Egyptian nation had embraced Christianity.

We intend in this work to consider only the three periods of ancient Egyptian history, the Old, the Middle, and the New Empire; the constitution of the Egypt of later centuries, of Egypt under the Libyans, the

Ethiopians, the Assyrians, the Persians, the Greeks and Romans, is too complicated for us to treat of together with the Egypt of older days. Yet in limiting ourselves to the time between the 4th and the 21st dynasty, we have at least eighteen centuries to review, that is, a period equal to that which divides the modern Romans from those of the time of the emperors.

We can well understand that it was impossible that these ages should pass over the Egyptian people without leaving some traces; and indeed if a courtier of the palace of Chufu could by a miracle have visited the court of Ramses III., he would have believed himself to be in a foreign country. No one would have understood his speech, the learned alone could have deciphered his writing, and his attire would only have been recognised from the representations of the gods or from the statues of the kings. I must now beg my readers to keep in mind the following fact: in point of time the Old Empire is as far removed from the New Empire as are the times of King Arthur, the hero of romance, from the more prosaic days of Queen Victoria.

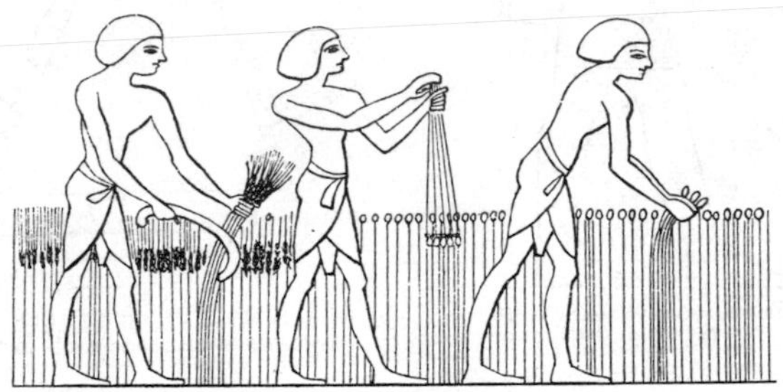

NECHEBT, THE PATRON GODDESS OF THE KING.

CHAPTER IV

THE KING AND HIS COURT

THE idea of a state, as bequeathed to the world by the Greeks and Romans, was as strange to the mind of Eastern nations of old as it still is to that of the modern Oriental.

In the East the idea prevailed, and still exists, that the whole machinery of the state is set in motion by the will of the ruler alone; the taxes are paid to fill his treasury, wars are undertaken for his renown, and great buildings are erected for his honour. All the property of the country is his by right, and if he allows any of his people to share it, it is only as a loan, which he can reclaim at any moment. His subjects also belong to him, and he can dispose of their lives at his will.

This is merely the theoretical view, which is impossible to carry out in practice, for the king, though supposed to dispose of everything as a god, is rarely able to act independently. It is true that the great body of the nation, now such an important element in the modern state, was unrecognised in old times; yet other factors existed which could render a ruler powerless, however absolute he might appear to be.

Around the king were the old counsellors who had served his father, and whom the clerks and officials were accustomed blindly to obey, as well as the generals with the troops in their pay, and the priesthood with their unlimited power over the lower classes. In the small towns the old rich families of the nobility, residing in their country seats, were nearer to the homes of the people than the monarch dwelling in his distant capital. The king was afraid to offend any of these powerful people; he had to spare the sensitive feelings of the minister; discover a way of gratifying the ambition of the general without endangering the country; watch carefully that his officers did not encroach on the rights of the nobility; and above all keep in favour with the priests. It was only when the king could satisfy all these claims, and understand at the same time how to play off one party against another, that he could expect a long and prosperous reign. If he failed, his chances were small, for there lurked close to him his most dangerous enemies, his nearest relatives. There always existed a brother or an uncle, who imagined he had a better claim to the throne than the reigning king, or there were the wives of the late ruler, who thought it a fatal wrong that the child of their rival rather than their own son should have inherited the crown. During the lifetime of the king they pretended to submit, but they waited anxiously for the moment to throw off the mask. They understood well how to intrigue, and to aggravate any misunderstanding between the king and his counsellors or his generals, until at last one of them, who thought himself slighted or injured, proceeded to open rebellion, and began the war by proclaiming one of the pretenders as the only true king, who had wrongfully been kept from the throne. The result was always the same; the others admired the boldness of their rival and hastened to imitate it, until there were as many pretenders as there were parties in the kingdom. It made little difference who won in the fight, he made his way to the throne through the blood of his opponents, and then began a struggle with those who had helped him. If he possessed good luck and energy he was able to clear them out of his way; otherwise he became a tool in the hands of those around him, who, at the first sign of independence, would cause him to be murdered and place a more docile ruler on the throne in his place.

In the meantime, in those parts of the country where there was no civil war, events followed their peaceful course—the labourer worked in his field, and the clerk in his office, with oriental indifference as if nothing were happening. The people however felt it bitterly when the government was weak. The taxes were raised, and were gathered in irregularly to satisfy the greed of the soldiers, the officials became more shameless in their extortions and caprices, and the public buildings, the canals and the dykes, fell into decay. Under these circumstances the nobility and priesthood alone flourished; when no central power existed they became more and more independent, and were able to obtain fresh concessions and gifts from each new claimant. The next powerful ruler had to spend long in reducing the country into order, and even then he could not flatter himself that his work would endure, for in the East the same fate awaited each ruling family.

The troublous conditions which we have sketched from the Oriental history of the Middle Ages were in force at all periods in ancient Egypt. The inscriptions may lead us to believe that an ideal kingdom existed in that country—a kingdom where, surrounded by his *dear friends* and *wise princes*, a *good god* cared like a father for his country; was adored by his subjects; feared by his enemies; and revered by the priests as the "true son of the Sun-god"; when we look closer however we see the same fatal conditions which ever had such evil results in Eastern history.

In the preceding chapter the reader will have seen how frequently there occurred periods of political disorder, yet our knowledge is confined to those of long duration, we know scarcely anything of the short disputes about the succession to the crown. The kings who made war on each other, were generally mere puppets in the hands of ambitious men, as we see by an inscription of a certain Bay, chief treasurer to the King Septaḥ of the 19th dynasty, in which Bay boasts quite openly that he "had established the king on the throne of his fathers."[1]

Even powerful rulers lived in constant danger from their own relatives, as is shown by the protocol of a trial for high treason of the time of Ramses III. The reign of this king was certainly a most brilliant one, the country was at last at peace, and the priesthood had been won by the building of great temples and by immense presents. All appeared propitious, yet even in this reign those fatal under-currents were at work which caused the speedy downfall of each dynasty, and it was perhaps due only to a happy chance that this king escaped. A conspiracy broke out in his own harem headed by a distinguished lady of the name of Tey, who was certainly of royal blood, and indeed may have been either his mother or stepmother.[2] We know not which prince had been chosen as aspirant for the crown (in the papyrus he is only mentioned by a pseudonym), but we see how far the matter had progressed before discovery, by the letters of the ladies of the harem to their mothers and brothers: "Excite the people, and stir up those who bear enmity to begin hostilities against the king." One of the ladies wrote to her brother, who was commanding the army in Ethiopia, and ordered him explicitly to come and fight against the king.[3] When we see how many high officials had taken part or were cognisant of this conspiracy we realise the seriousness of this danger to all eastern kingdoms. I have intentionally represented the adverse side of this form of government; and I would ask the reader always to remember that, behind all the pomp and splendour which surrounded the Egyptian king and his court, conditions probably lay hidden no better than those described above.

The dignity of *king* in Egypt goes back to prehistoric ages. The insignia of the Pharaohs evidently belong to a time when the Egyptians wore nothing but the girdle of the negro, and when it was considered a special distinction that the king should complete this girdle with a piece of skin or matting in front, and should adorn it behind with a lion's tail. We know not how long elapsed before this chief of a half-savage race became the divine Pharaoh, nor can we now determine what wars preceded the gradual union of the separate Egyptian provinces into one state. We know only that before the time of the Old Empire there must have been a long period in which Egypt was divided into two states, the south and the north, or as they are called in the Egyptian formal style, "the two countries." Both must have been powerful states equal in importance, so that there was no question of the incorporation of the one into the other; and after the union both remained independent, only

[1] L. D., iii. 202 a, c.

[2] The consort of his father at any rate bears this same name, Mar. Cat. d'Ab., 1170.

[3] Pj. T., 4, 2; 5, 3.

connected by that doubtful bond called personal union. The king of Egypt might call himself *lord of both countries*, or the *uniter of the two countries*, or as in later times the *Ruler of Egypt*, yet his official title was always the "King of Upper Egypt and the King of Lower Egypt." It was the same with the titles of his servants; originally they were the superintendents of the two houses of silver, or of the two storehouses, for each kingdom had its own granary and its own treasury. Such a personal union could not last; even in Egypt it soon became a fiction, though it was kept up at all times in the titles of the king.

The royal names and titles always appeared to the Egyptians as a matter of the highest importance. The first title consisted of the name borne by the king as a prince. This was the only one used by the people or in history; it was too sacred to be written as an ordinary word, and was therefore enclosed in an oval ring in order to separate it from other secular words. Before it stood the title "King of Upper Egypt and King of Lower Egypt." Thus *e.g.* King of Upper Egypt and King of Lower Egypt, Chufu. Under the Old Empire the idea arose that it was not suitable that the king, who on ascending the throne became a demigod, should retain the same common name he had borne as a prince. As many ordinary people were called Pepy, it did not befit the *good god* to bear this vulgar name; therefore at his accession a new name was given him for official use, which naturally had some pious signification. Pepy became "the beloved of Rê‘"; ’Ess’e, when king, was called, "the image of Rê‘ stands firm"; and Ment’uḥôtep is called "Rê‘, the lord of the two countries." We see that all these official names contain the name of Rê‘ the Sun-god, the symbol of royalty. Nevertheless, the king did not give up the family name he had borne as prince, for though not used for official purposes, it yet played an important part in the king's titles. It was the name which attested the high birth and the royal descent of the ruler, and as according to loyal belief the royal race was supposed to be descended from the sun-god Rê‘, the title *Son of Rê‘* was placed with special significance before this name, *e.g.* the prince Amenemḥê‘t was therefore called as king: "the King of Upper Egypt and the King of Lower Egypt: Rê‘, the speaker of truth, the son of Rê‘: Amenemḥê‘t." The style was not even then complete, for on his accession the king took three other titles: "Horus"; , "lord of the diadem of the vulture and of the snake"; and , "the golden Horus"; these testify to his divine nature, for Horus is the youthful, victorious sun-god, and the two diadems are crowns belonging to the gods. To these three titles are again added three surnames, *e.g.* a king of the 13th dynasty is called: "Horus, who united the two countries, the lord of the diadem of the vulture and of the snake, of abiding splendour, the golden Horus, souls of the gods, the King of Upper Egypt and the King of Lower Egypt: 'Rê' of splendid life,' the son of Rê': 'Sebekḥôtep.'"

Such are the phrases necessary to designate the Egyptian king in full style, and even these long titles were often insufficient to content the loyalty of the scribes of the new Empire; their reverence for their ruler sometimes even found expression in a short psalm appended to his name; *e.g.* the dating of a stele, erected under Ramses II., on the way to the gold mines of Nubia, runs thus:

"In the 3rd year of His Majesty Horus: the strong bull, beloved by the goddess of truth, the lord of the diadem of the vulture and of the snake: who protects Egypt, and subdues the barbarians, the golden Horus: full of years, great in victories, the King of Upper Egypt and the King of Lower Egypt: Rê', strong in truth, chosen of Rê', the son of Rê', Ramses, the beloved of Amon, giver of everlasting life, the beloved of the Theban Amon Rê', the lord of the temple, the throne of the two countries, shining daily on his throne amongst men as his father Rê'.

"The good lord, the lord of the south,—the Horus with the bright plumes of the temple of Edfu, the beautiful silver hawk, who protects Egypt with his wings, preparing shade for mankind; the castle of strength and of victory,—who came out terribly from his mother's womb, in order to take to himself fame, extending his borders,—the colour of his body is as the strength of the war-god Mont—the god Horus, the god Set—Heaven rejoiced at his birth; the gods said: we have brought him up; the goddesses said: he was born of us, to be the leader of the kingdom of Rê'; Amon said: I am he who made him, I seated truth in her place; for his sake the earth is established, the heavens satisfied, the gods contented—the strong bull against the miserable Ethiopians, his roaring rages against the negroland: whilst his hoofs trample the Troglodytes, his horn pushes them—his spirit is mighty in Nubia, and the fear of him reaches to the land of Kary, his name is famous in all countries because of the victories which his arms have won—at the mention of his name gold comes out of the mountains, as at the name of his father; the god Horus of the land of Baka—he is greatly beloved in the land of the south, as Horus at M'e'ama, the god of the land of Buhen.

"The king of Upper Egypt and the king of Lower Egypt, Rê', strong in truth, the chosen of Rê'—from the loins of Rê', the lord of crowns, Ramses, the beloved of Amon, the daily giver of eternal life like his father Rê'."[1]

When the reader has made his way through the stupefying clatter of these empty phrases (which were used even of the weakest monarch), he is still ignorant of the contents of the inscription, for we should express all that he has read by the words "In the 3rd year of Ramses II." These exaggerated titles show us that the Egyptians believed their king to be a kind of deity, and in fact always so designated him.

[1] Prisse, Mon. 21.

One difference existed between king and god: while Amon, Rê', Osiris, and Horus are called *the great gods*, the king as a rule had to be content with the appellation, *the good god*. Each king was of divine birth, for as long as he was acknowledged sovereign, he was considered as the direct descendant of Rê'. This belief was not affected by the fact that in course of time the throne passed frequently from one family to another; it was not more difficult for the genealogists of the New Empire to trace the relationship of the usurper Setnacht or of the Libyan Sheshonk to the old race of kings, than for the Arab genealogists to trace the descent of the royal families of Northern Africa, in spite of their Berberic blood, from the Arab comrades of the Prophet. In modern times the historians of the seventeenth and eighteenth centuries have done the same for other royal families. Thus the Egyptian kings did not hesitate to call their predecessors their ancestors, for it was always easy to construct some relationship with them. The people were also early accustomed to view their rulers as gods, for in the beautiful song of the 11th dynasty, concerning the passing away of all things earthly, we read: "the gods who were of old, rest in their pyramids."[1]

The Egyptians avoided using the name of the reigning monarch, in the same way as we feel a certain awe at needlessly pronouncing the name of God. They therefore spoke of the king as: "Horus the lord of the palace, the good god, his Majesty, thy Lord," or (usually under the New Empire) instead of all these designations, they used the indefinite pronoun *one* to signify sacred power—"One has commanded thee," "One is now residing at Thebes," would be, in the older style, "The king has commanded thee," or "The king resides at Thebes." When royal deeds are mentioned, the name of the ruler is used in a way common to many nations; *e.g.* as the Turks call their government "the sublime Porte," so the Egyptians of all ages preferred to speak of the government buildings rather than of the ruler. "The Palace, the king's house, the great double hall"[2] and above all the "great house (*per'o*) are the usual appellations for the king; the last was used so commonly that the Hebrews and Assyrians employed it (Pharaoh) almost as the actual name of the Egyptian monarch.

In the early period this idea of the divinity of the king was not carried to its final consequences; temples were not erected, nor were sacrifices offered, to the *good god* whilst he dwelt amongst men. This custom appears to have been a new departure in the time of the New Empire, and it is noteworthy that the temple, in which Amenḥôtep III. adores himself (the mystical official expression is adores his *living earthly image*—*i.e.* that of the sun-god), was not on Egyptian soil. This new venture was only made when the Egyptian religion was introduced into Nubia.[3]

[1] Harr., 500, 14, 4.

[2] An., 4, 4, 10.

[3] Ed. Meyer, Gesch. des Alterthums, § 225.

The king was of course distinguished from his subjects by his costume; the tokens of royal dignity have been so exactly described, and so much importance has been attached to them, that we must dwell a little on their gradual development. Under the Old Empire the royal ornaments were very simple.[1] It is easy to see that the usual form of the royal dress originated in very primitive times. In prehistoric ages, when the only garment was a girdle round the loins, with two or three ties hanging down in front, it was considered a luxury that the ruler should replace these ties by a piece of matting or fur, and, as further decoration, should add the tail of a lion behind. In the rock steles of the quarries of Sinai the King Sa'ḥurê' is seen standing clothed in this way, killing his enemies the Beduins. This is only an ancient symbolical representation, and we must not imagine that the king really wore this costume of a savage chief. In the time of the 5th dynasty the loin girdle had long become the dress of the lower orders, all the upper classes in Egypt wearing a short skirt. The king wore this skirt sometimes over, but more usually under his old official costume. Both corners of the piece of stuff were then rounded off, so that the front piece belonging to the girdle could be seen below. Sometimes the whole was made of pleated golden material, and must have formed quite a fine costume.

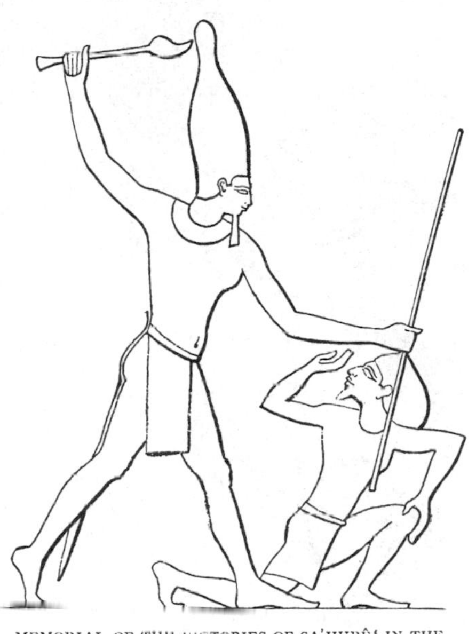
MEMORIAL OF THE VICTORIES OF SA'ḤURÊ' IN THE WADI MAGHARA (L. D., ii. 39 f.)

THE USUAL ROYAL COSTUME IN THE OLD PERIOD.

His Majesty shaved off both hair and beard as carefully as his subjects, and like them he replaced them by artificial ones. Even in these respects he was distinguished from the people, for the artificial beard which he fastened under his chin was longer than that usually worn under the Old Empire. The king also covered his head with a head-dress of peculiar form (see pp. 43, 45) the sides of which fell over his shoulders in two pleated lappets; it was twisted together behind, and

[1] Pictures of kings of the Old Empire, L. D., ii. 2 a, c. 39 f, 116; Statues of Cha'frê' at Gizeh.

hung down like a short pigtail. The *uraeus*, the symbol of royalty, is always found on his head-dress; this brightly-coloured poisonous snake seems to rear itself up on the brow of the king, threatening all his enemies, as formerly it had threatened all the enemies of the god Rê'.

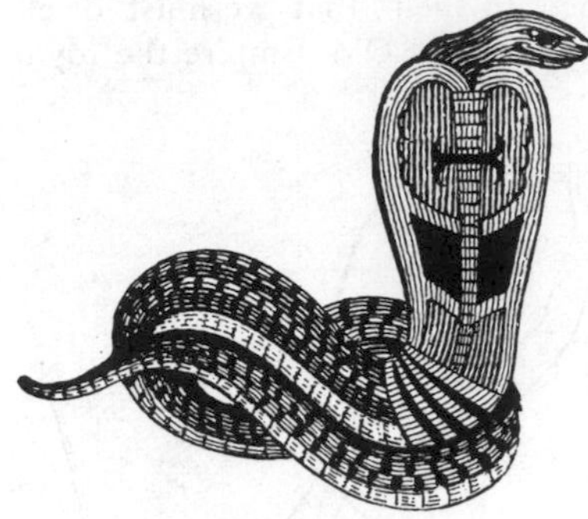

THE SACRED URAEUS SNAKE.

On festive occasions the king would wear his crown, either the white crown of Upper Egypt, a curious high conical cap, or the scarcely less quaint red crown of Lower Egypt with its high narrow back, and the wire ornament bent obliquely forward in front. Sometimes he wore both crowns, the *double crown*, the white one inside the red, and the wire stretching forward from the former.

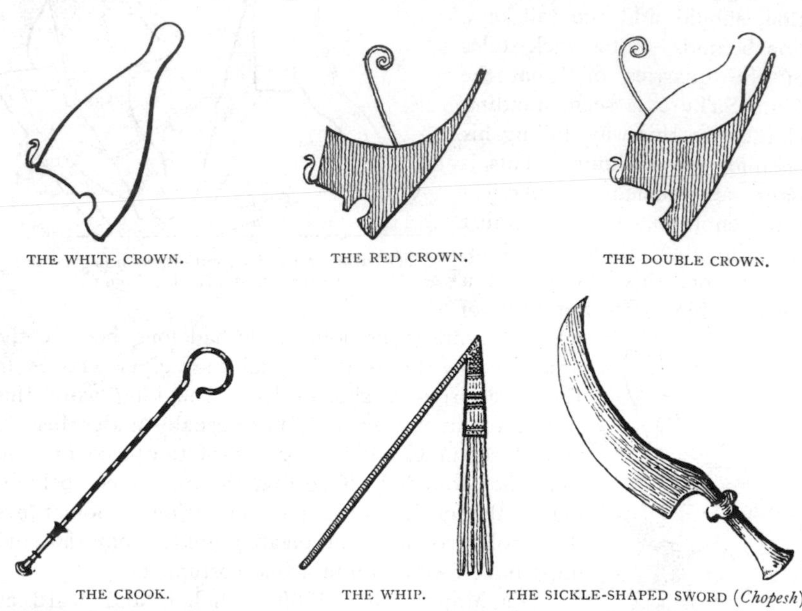

THE WHITE CROWN. THE RED CROWN. THE DOUBLE CROWN.

THE CROOK. THE WHIP. THE SICKLE-SHAPED SWORD (*Chopesh*).

The crook and the flail also served as royal insignia, and the sickle-shaped sword, called from its shape, the thigh (*Chopesh*), seems also to have been a symbol of royalty.

The king appeared at times in the costume of a god; he then either bound his royal girdle round the narrow womanish garment in which the people imagined their divinities to be dressed, or he wore one of the strange divine diadems constructed of horns and feathers, and carried the divine sceptre.[1]

[1] L. D., ii. 2 a.

The royal insignia were very complex even in the time of the Old Empire; in later times they were essentially the same, though more splendid in appearance. In the later period special importance was attached to the front piece of the royal skirt, which was covered with rich embroidery, uraeus snakes were represented wreathing themselves at the sides, and white ribbons appeared to fasten it to the belt. If, according to ancient custom, the Pharaoh wore nothing but this skirt, it was worn standing out in front in a peak, which was adorned with gold ornamentation. Usually, however, the kings of the New Empire preferred to dress like their subjects, and on festive occasions, they put on the long transparent under dress as well as the full over dress, the short skirt being then worn either over or under these robes. The crowns also remained unchanged, while the diadems of the gods with their horns and feathers[1] came more into fashion than in the earlier periods. It was also the custom that Pharaoh, even in times of peace, should wear his war-helmet, the *Cheperesh*; this was quite in character with the warlike spirit of this age.

THE KING IN THE COSTUME OF THE GODS (L. D., ii. 39 f.)

a

b

c

USUAL ROYAL COSTUME UNDER THE NEW EMPIRE.

a, Short skirt over the under dress; double crown. (Offering of an ointment box.) *b*, Short skirt under the same; war helmet. (Drink offering and incense.) *c*, Short skirt; under and over dress; diadem of the gods. (Offering of wine.)

We have written thus much about the costume and ornaments of the

[1] Stele of Kuban, l. 8: the fillet and the double feather are part of the king's costume when in council.

king, but a whole volume would be required to describe them completely; so minutely were they represented by the Egyptians. The lords of the royal toilette had the charge of their proper employment; there were many of these officials under the Old Empire, and they seem to have held a high position at court. These officials were called the "superintendent of the clothes of the king,"[1] the "chief bleacher,"[2] the "washer of Pharaoh,"[3] and the "chief washer of the palace."[4] Even the sandals had their special custodian,[5] and for the wigs there were the "wig-maker of Pharaoh,"[6] the "upper and under wig-makers of the king,"[7] and the "superintendent of the wig-makers."[8] It was the duty of those officials, who had the care of the monarch's hair, to take charge of the other numerous head-dresses of the king; they were called "keepers of the diadem,"[9] and boasted that they "adorned the brow of their god," or of "the Horus."[10] There was a special superintendent and clerk, the "chief metal-worker and chief artist for the care of the royal jewels"[11]—which at the same time formed part of the charge of the treasury; the superintendence of the clothes of the king was also vested in the same department.[12]

KING IN THE LATER FORM OF THE ROYAL APRON, AND IN THE HEAD CLOTH. He offers incense before the god.

There were not so many of these officials in later times, yet under the Middle Empire, "the keeper of the diadem who adorns the king" had a high position at court. He had the title of "privy councillor of the two crowns," or "privy councillor of the royal jewels, and maker of the two magic kingdoms."[13] Divine power was ascribed to the crowns of Upper and Lower Egypt, which are referred to as the *magic kingdoms*, and under the Middle Empire a regular priesthood, instituted by the keepers of the diadem, was appointed to these two crowns. The office of keeper of the diadem seems to have been suppressed under the New Empire, or it may have been replaced by

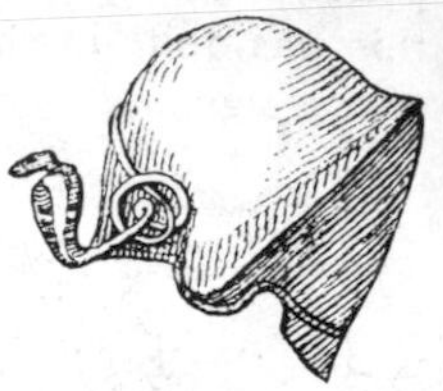

ROYAL HELMET (*Cheperesh*).

[1] R. J. H., 83; Mar. Mast., 185.
[2] Mar. Mast., 185, 198 f.; Stele of 'Euf'e in the Brit. Mus. (L. A.)
[3] Stele of 'Euf'e; Mar. Mast., 198. [4] Mar. Mast., 70. [5] Ä. Z., 1882, p. 20.
[6] L. D., ii. 91 b.
[7] L. D., ii. 95 f.; R. J. H., 60; L. D., ii. 65 ff.; Mar. Mast., 250. [8] R. J. H., 60.
[9] L. D., ii. 35 ff. 65 ff.; R. J. H., 60; Mar. Mast., 250; Br. Dic. Supplm., 670.
[10] L. D., ii. 35 ff. 65 ff.
[11] R. J. H., 60, 78 (97); Mar. Mast., 101, 116, 135, 233 ff., 250.
[12] Mar. Mast., 251 ff.; R. J. H., 90; L. D., ii. 100 c.
[13] The titles of these and other officials are found on the Steles of Chent-em-sete and Chent-em-sete-ur (L. A.), both of the Anastasi collection; the latter is now in the Brit. Mus.

the "overseer of the ointments of the king's treasury, superintendent of the royal fillet of the good god."[1]

The *throne of the living one*, the *great throne* on which the king *shone* when giving audience, belongs also to the royal insignia. In later

KING TUET-'ANCH-AMUN (DYN. 18) ON HIS THRONE GIVES AUDIENCE TO THE GOVERNOR OF ETHIOPIA ḤUY.

The king wears the war helmet, and holds the whip and sceptre; the governor bears the sceptre, and (as a sign of his rank) the fan. The canopy is adorned at the top with uraeus snakes, below with griffins, the symbol of wisdom, over whom the king rules. By the king are written his names: "the King of Upper Egypt and the King of Lower Egypt," "the god Rê' for all beings," "the son of Rê'," "Tuet-'anch-Amun, the lord of Hermonthis," who lives for ever like Rê' (L. D., iii. 115).

times this throne certainly could not be recognised by its shape or in any other way as a special symbol of royal dignity. A canopy raised on

[1] Mar. Cat. d'Ab., 1122.

pretty wooden pillars, a thick carpet on the floor, a seat and footstool of the usual shape; the whole brilliantly coloured and decorated,—such was the *great seat of Horus*, according to the numerous representations of the time of the New Empire. When we examine the decoration, we see that it befits a royal throne; negroes and Asiatics appear to carry the seat, and a royal sphinx, the destroyer of all enemies, is represented on either arm at the side. On the floor, and therefore under the feet of the monarch, are the names of the enemies he has conquered, and above, on the roof, are two rows of uraeus snakes,[1] the symbol of royal rank.

It was the custom of the court that the Pharaoh, or rather, according to the poetical language of Egypt, that the *sun-god* should shine when he rose from the horizon, and showed himself to the people; therefore whenever we see the Pharaoh outside his palace, he is surrounded by the greatest splendour. When according to ancient usage he is carried out in a sedan-chair, he is seated within it in full dress, two lions striding support the chair, the poles of which rest on the shoulders of eight distinguished courtiers.[2] The fan-bearers accompany the king, fanning him with fresh air and waving bouquets of flowers near his head, that the air round the *good god* may be filled with sweet perfumes. The ordinary fan-bearers walk in front and behind the monarch, but the high official, who accompanies the king "as his fan-bearer on the right" carries a beautiful fan and a small bouquet merely as the insignia of his rank, and leaves the work to the servants.

A representation at Tell el Amarna of King Chuen-'eten visiting his god the Sun-disk,[3] shows us how the royal family set out:—

The procession moves out of the courts of the royal palace surrounded by the greatest pomp and splendour. Two runners with staves hasten first to clear the way through the inquisitive crowd for the king's chariot. Following close behind them comes His Majesty drawn by fiery richly-caparisoned horses, with which the servants can scarcely keep pace. On either side is the bodyguard on foot, running; Egyptian soldiers and Asiatic mercenaries armed with all kinds of weapons; their badges are borne before them, and behind them the officers follow driving. After the king's chariot come those of his consort and of his daughters, two of the young princesses drive together, the elder holds the reins, while the younger leans tenderly on her sister. Behind them come six carriages with the court ladies, and on either side six more with the lords of the bed-chamber. Runners and servants hasten along on both sides swinging their staves.

A more splendid spectacle can scarcely be imagined than this procession as it passed quickly by the spectators; the gilded chariot, the many-coloured plumes of the horses, the splendid harness, the coloured fans, the white flowing garments, all lighted up by the glowing sun of Egypt.

When the Pharaoh died and was buried, or rather as the Egyptians

[1] L. D., iii. 76, 77, and other similar passages.

[2] L. D., iii. 2 b, c. 121a. This account refers to the time of the New Empire.

[3] See the interesting representations in the tomb of Mry-Rê' at Tell el Amarna (L. D., iii. 92-94).

would have said, "when he like the sun-god has set below the horizon, and all the customs of Osiris have been fulfilled for him; when he has passed over the river in the royal bark and gone to rest in his eternal home to the west of Thebes," then the solemn accession of his son takes place. "His father Amon, the lord of the gods, Rê', Atum, and Ptaḥ beautiful of face, the lords of the two countries, crown him in the place of his forefathers; joyfully he succeeds to the dignity of his father; the country rejoices and is at peace and rest; the people are glad because they acknowledge him ruler of the two countries, like Horus, who governs the two countries in the room of Osiris. He is crowned with the Atef-

KING ḤAREMḤÊB IS CARRIED BY SOLDIERS; BEFORE AND BEHIND ARE THE REAL FAN-BEARERS, NEAR HIM A DISTINGUISHED "FAN-BEARER ON THE RIGHT OF THE KING."
The ornamentation of the throne is the binding together of the flowers of Upper and Lower Egypt, signifying the union of the two halves of the kingdom (L. D., iii. 121 a).

crown with the uraeus; to which is added the crown with the double feathers of the god Tatenen; he sits on the throne of Harmachis, and is adorned like the god Atum."[1]

We know little of the details of the ceremonies of the day of accession; it was kept as a yearly festival,[2] and celebrated with special splendour on the thirtieth anniversary.[3] One representation only is known of a festival which apparently belongs to the coronation festivities,[4] *i.e.* the great processional and sacrificial festival, which the king solemnises to his father Min, the god who causes the soil to be fertile. It was natural

[1] Harris, i. 76, 1-4. [2] Coronation festival, L. D., iii. 31 b. 13. [3] L. D., iii. 174 d., 175 f.
[4] L. D., iii. 162-164, ib. 212-213 (more fully W. iii. lx.), in both places amongst pictures of the life of the king.

that the king should begin his reign over this agricultural country with a sacrifice to the god of the fields.

We first see how the king, "shining as the sun," leaves the "palace of life, steadfastness, and purity, and is borne towards the house of his father Min, to behold his beauty." The Pharaoh is seated under a canopy in a richly decorated sedan-chair, he is carried by some of his sons, while others fan him with their large fans. Two priests walk in front burning incense; a third, the reciter-priest, reads "all that is customary before the king as he goes forth." A company of royal relatives, royal children and great princes, precede the king, others follow; at the head of the procession are drummers and trumpeters, while in the rear march the soldiers.

In the meantime the god Min has left his sanctuary and advances to meet the king. Twenty priests bear the covered stand, on which is the image of the god; others fan the god with bouquets and fans. The "white bull," sacred to the god, walks pensively before him, and a long procession of priests follow, carrying the insignia of kingship, and divine symbols; also images of the royal ancestors, the statues of the kings of Upper and Lower Egypt. In the meantime the reciter-priest reads from the strange book the "words of the negroes," and the procession advancing meets that of the king, which is waiting on a terrace, where two flag-staves bearing the head-dress of the god have been erected. Here the priest lets fly four geese, to carry the news to the gods of the four quarters of heaven, that "Horus the son of Isis and Osiris has received the white and the red crown, that King Ramses has received the white and the red crown."[1]

When the monarch has thus been proclaimed king to the gods, he offers his royal sacrifice in the presence of the statues of his ancestors. A priest presents him with the golden sickle, with which he cuts a sheaf of corn, he then strews it before the white bull, symbolising the offering of the first fruits of his reign. He then offers incense before the statue of the god, while the priest recites from the mysterious books of the "dances of Min." When the Pharaoh, with these and similar ceremonies, has taken upon him the dignity of his father he next receives the congratulations of his court. If any of the high officials are unavoidably absent, they send congratulatory letters: *e.g.* the treasurer Qagabu sends the following poem to Sety II. on his coronation,[2] that it may be read in the palace of Meryma'‘t in the horizon of Rê‘:—

"Incline thine ear towards me, thou rising Sun,
Thou who dost enlighten the two lands with beauty;
Thou sunshine of mankind, chasing darkness from Egypt!
Thy form is as that of thy father Rê‘ rising in the heavens,

---

[1] According to a legend Horus employed the same messengers to announce his accession to the other gods. Cp. the representation of his accession, L. D., iv. 57-58.

[2] An. 4, 5, 6 ff. The writing belongs to the first year.

Thy rays penetrate to the farthest lands.
When thou art resting in thy palace,
Thou hearest the words of all countries;
For indeed thou hast millions of ears;
Thine eye is clearer than the stars of heaven;
Thou seest farther than the Sun.
If I speak afar off, thine ear hears;
If I do a hidden deed, thine eye sees it.
O Rê‘, richest of beings, chosen of Rê‘,
Thou king of beauty, giving breath to all."

If we may believe what Diodorus[1] tells us of the daily life of the king, we shall find the order of each day most strictly regulated for the Pharaoh. At daybreak the king despatches and answers his letters, he then bathes and robes himself in his state garments and assists at the sacrifice in the temple. There the high priest and the people pray for the god's blessing on the king, and the priest gives him to understand, in a figurative way, what is worthy of praise or blame in his manner of ruling. After this homily the king offers sacrifice, but does not leave the temple till he has listened to the reading from the sacred books on the deeds and the maxims of famous men. His manner of life during the remainder of the day is exactly laid out for him, even as to the times for his walks, or for his frugal meals of goose-flesh, beef, and wine. Everything, Diodorus tells us, is arranged as strictly and reasonably as if "prescribed by a physician."

It is not possible that the rulers of a kingdom, which flourished for 3000 years, should really have been such puppets as Diodorus represents. This historian gives us the ideal of a pious king, according to the priestly ideas of later times, and in fact the later kings of the 20th dynasty may have led such lives under the governance of the Theban ecclesiastics, until the high priests judged it more expedient to ascend the throne themselves. Yet there is some truth in many features of this description even as regards the more ancient periods, for the Egyptian king had always to play a religious part. In the same way as each Egyptian of high standing exercised a kind of priestly office in the temple of his god, so the king was considered the priest of all the gods. Whenever we enter an Egyptian temple, we see the king represented offering his sacrifice to the gods. In most cases this is symbolic of the presents and revenues with which the king endowed the temple, but it is not probable that they would have had these representations if the king had not sometimes officiated there in person. At many festivals (*e.g.* the above-mentioned festival of the god Min) it is expressly declared in the official style of the inscription, that the chief business of the king is to "give praise to his fathers, the gods of Upper and Lower Egypt, because they give him strength and victory, and a long life of millions of years."[2]

It was part of the king's work to guide the government and carry on the wars, but in theory his duty towards the gods was still more important. Being, in very deed, "the son of Rê‘, who is enthroned in his heart, whom

[1] Diodorus, i. 70.

[2] Stele of Kuban, line 7, and many other examples.

he loves above all, and who is with him, he is a shining embodiment of the lord of all, created by the gods of Heliopolis. His divine father created him to exalt his glory. Amon himself crowned him on his throne in the Heliopolis of the south, he chose him for the Shepherd of Egypt, and the defender of mankind."[1] When the gods blessed the country, it was for the sake of *their son;* when after many failures they allowed some undertaking to succeed, it was in answer to the prayers of *their son.* With these ideas what is more natural than that the people should consider the king to be the mediator for his country? He alone with the high priest might enter the Holy of Holies in the temples, he alone might open the doors of the inner sanctuary and "see his father the god."

RAMSES II. MAKES AN OFFERING BEFORE THE GODDESS NEBTHẠT.

He "gives two jugs of milk to his mother." The goddess promises him, in consequence, "that he shall endure eternally like the heavens."

The monarch could scarcely fulfil all these religious duties, as well as those of the administration which were expected of him. His *cabinet*[2] formed the centre of the government, to which all the chief officials had to "render their account,"[3] and to which "truth must ascend." When reports were concluded, they were laid before the ruler, and special questions were also brought to him for his decision; this was the case, at any rate, in the strained conditions of the time of the New Empire.

When thieves were caught, tried, and found guilty, the court was not allowed to pronounce sentence; the report was made to the Pharaoh, who decreed what punishment was to be awarded;[4] when houses were allotted to labourers, the king was importuned about it.[5] In short, there was nothing which might not, under certain circumstances, be brought before the Pharaoh, and if he were not able personally to sift the matter, he was obliged to appoint a delegate[6] to take his place. We who know the pleasure the Egyptian scribe took in lawsuits, realise how many reports the king had daily to read, and how many royal orders he had to give. The monarch had also to journey through the country and examine in person the condition of the buildings, etc. We learn how more than

[1] See L. D., iii. 24.

[2] , old spelling , e.g. R. J. H., 95. Cp. Br. Dic. Suppl., p. v. 'aḥ'a.

[3] d'd sm'e, e.g. An., 4, 4, 9.

[4] Pap. Amherst, 3, 9 and 4, 3.

[5] Insc. Hier. Char., 12.

[6] Abb., 6, 14.

once the king travelled through the desert in order to understand the position of the quarries and of the oases.[1]

The king had of course trustworthy officials to assist him in this work; the chief of these was the T'ate, the "governor," whom we may consider as the leader of the government, and who communicated with the king on state affairs through the "speaker."[2] In difficult cases the king summoned his councillors, or (as they were called under the New Empire) "his princes, who stand before him,"[3] and requested their opinion. The king often appointed his son and heir as co-regent,—this was the case under most of the kings of the 12th dynasty. We read that he "appoints him his heir on the throne of the god Qeb; he becomes the great captain of the country of Egypt, and gives orders to the whole country."[4]

The "great house," therefore, in which the king resided was not only the dwelling-place of a god (his *horizon* as the Egyptians were accustomed to call it), but also the seat of government, the heart of the country. This double definition was carried out in the disposition of the royal house, which was always divided into two parts, an outer part serving for audiences; an inner one, the dwelling of the "*good god.*" The outer division is the large battlemented enclosure, which bore the name of *Usechet* the wide; the inner part is the narrow richly decorated building *'Aḥ'a*, lying in the background of the enclosure.[5]

These two parts of the palace were sharply defined, especially under the Old Empire, when the titles of the court officials showed to which division their owners belonged. Audiences were held in the "*usechet*"; the highest government officials, the "great men of the south" and the Judges, were therefore called the "overseers" "the governors of the vestibule,"[6] or "the governors of the writing business of the vestibule."[7] The palace *'Aḥ'a* on the other hand was the home of the king, and whoever was called *governor of the palace* was either a prince or a personal servant of the king, a lord-chamberlain.[8]

In the palace itself, under the Old Empire, there were various divisions: there was the, the great hall of pillars, which was used

[1] L. D., ii. 149 f., iii. 140 b.

[2] , and : the former belongs to the old period, the latter often occurs after the time of the 18th dynasty.

[3] Stele of Kuban, l. 11; L. D., iii. 187.

[4] Harris, i. 75, 10.

[5] The form here given of the palace belongs to the Old Empire (e.g. L. D., ii. 48. Mar. Mast., 248, 424); it is the traditional form in later representations (e.g. W., iii. pl. lx.). The palace of the New Empire appears in several different ways (see ch. ix.), but it always contains this division, bearing indeed the same names: 'aḥ'a, An., 4, 5, 9; usechet, An., 5, 19, 6.

[6] L. D., ii. 48 ff., 103 c.; R. J. H., 86, 87; Mar. Mast., 124 ff., 214 ff., 228 ff. etc.

[7] Mar. Mast., 214 ff.

[8] cherp, 'aḥ'a with princes, L. D., ii. 34 g.; R. J. H., 65, with other court officials, e.g. R. J. H., 82 f.; L. D., ii. 35 ff., 89 a.; Mar. Mast., 160 f., 236 ff.; mer 'aḥ'a, R. J. H., 78.

for council meetings, and, still more important, there was the *house of adoration*, the king's room. Only the king's sons, his nearest friends, and the governor of the palace, were allowed to bear the title of "Privy councillor of the house of adoration," a *gentilhomme de la chambre du roi*, as they would say at the French court. The Egyptian king had several palaces[1] in the different towns of his kingdom, and Ramses II. and Ramses III. made for themselves noble palaces even in the two temples, which they built to Amon on the west side at Thebes.[2] We should expect in this ceremonious country, that the palaces should receive particular names, and we find, *e.g.*, that of Sety II. called "Beloved of the goddess of truth."[3]

Even in modern times it is considered a special honour to have personal intercourse and to associate with the ruler of the state. If this be the case now, when we consider him only as the chief officer and the first nobleman of the land, how much greater would the honour be in Egypt where the Pharaoh was looked upon as a god. He who was chosen to enjoy this great happiness never forgot to inscribe it in his tomb for the benefit of posterity; and many are the phrases and the titles which he used to express his sense of the dignity conferred upon him: "He knew the place of the royal foot, and followed his benefactor in the way,[4] he followed Horus in his house,[5] he lived under the feet of his master,[6] he was beloved by the king more than all the people of Egypt, he was loved by him as one of his friends, he was his faithful servant, dear to his heart, he was in truth beloved by his lord."[7] Over and over again we meet with these phrases in the tombs of the great men, and all that they signify is that the deceased belonged to the court circle, or in the Egyptian language to the the "*Chosen of the Guard.*" These courtiers watched jealously lest one should approach the monarch nearer than another; there were certain laws, the "customs of the palace and the maxims of the court," which were strictly observed by the officials who "allowed the courtiers to ascend to the king."[8] This presentation of the courtiers in order of precedence was openly considered as a most important business, and those whose duty it was to "range the princes in their places,[9] to appoint to the friends of the king their approach when standing or sitting,"[10] boast how excellently they performed their duty.

We know little more of the ceremonial of the Egyptian court; the fact that King Shepseskaf allowed Ptaḥshepses, one of his grandees, to kiss his foot instead of kissing the ground before him, shows us how strict etiquette was even under the Old Empire. It is noteworthy that the man

[1] Even under the Old Empire, "Governor of the noble dwellings of the King," L.D., ii. 35 ff. "Privy councillor of the king in all his dwellings," Mar. Mast., 195.

[2] L. D., iii. 159; Harris, i. 4, 11. That these funerary temples were at least nominally dedicated to Amon we see from L. D., iii. 167; Harris, i. 3, 11.

[3] An., 4, 5, 6.

[4] Louvre, C. 170.

[5] Louvre, C. 55.

[6] Passim.

[7] R. J. H., 11.

[8] Ä. Z., 1882, 204.

[9] Cp. e.g. Ä. Z., 1882, 10.

[10] Mar. Cat. d'Ab., 764.

chosen out for this high honour was not only the high priest of Memphis, but also the son-in-law of His Majesty.[1] Under the Old Empire these conventionalities were carried farther than in any later time; and the long list of the titles of those officials shows us that the court under the pyramid-builders had many features in common with that of the Byzantines.

Under the New Empire it seems to have been rather out of fashion, at any rate for the highest officials, to *kiss the earth:* the words may occur occasionally in the inscriptions, but in the pictures the princes only bow, either with their arms by their sides or with them raised in prayer before His Majesty. The priests also, when receiving the king ceremoniously at the gates of the temples, only bow respectfully, and even their wives and children do the same as they present the Pharaoh with flowers and food in token of welcome; it is only the servants who throw themselves down before him and *kiss the earth* at the sight of the monarch.[2]

It seems to have been the custom under the New Empire to greet the king with a short psalm when they "spoke in his presence" (it was not etiquette to speak "to him")—*e.g.* when the king had called his councillors together, and had set forth to them how he had resolved to bore a well on one of the desert roads, and had asked them for their opinion on the subject, we might expect them straightway to give him an answer, especially as already on their entrance into the hall they had "raised their arms praising him." The princes considered it necessary however to make a preamble as follows: "Thou art like Rê' in all that thou doest, everything happens according to the wish of thy heart. We have seen many of thy wondrous deeds, since thou hast been crowned king of the two countries, and have neither seen nor heard anything equal to thee. The words of thy mouth are like the words of Harmachis, thy tongue is a balance, and thy lips are more exact than the little tongue on the balance of Thoth. What way is there that thou dost not know? Who accomplishes all things like thee? Where is the place which thou hast not seen? There is no country through which thou hast not journeyed, and what thou hast not seen thou hast heard. For from thy mother's womb thou hast governed and ruled this country with all the dignity of a child of royal blood. All the affairs of the two countries were brought before thee, even when thou wast a child with the plaited lock of hair. No monument was erected, no business was transacted, without thee. When thou wast at the breast, thou wast the general of the army, in thy tenth year thou didst suggest the plan of all the works, and all affairs passed through thy hands. When thou didst command the water to cover the mountain, the ocean obeyed immediately. In thy limbs is Rê', and Chepr'e thy creator dwells within thee. Thou art the living image on earth of thy father Atum of Heliopolis. The god of taste is in thy mouth, the god of knowledge in thy heart; thy tongue is enthroned in the temple of truth;

[1] R. J. H., 80. [2] From the picture, L. D., iii. 92 ff.

God is seated upon thy lips. Thy words are fulfilled daily, and the thoughts of thy heart are carried out like those of Ptaḥ the creator. Thou art immortal, and thy thoughts shall be accomplished and thy words obeyed for ever."

When the princes had expressed their admiration of the young king in this pretty but in our opinion exaggerated, senseless style, they might then address him directly: "O King, our master," and answer his question.[1]

Special titles served to signify the degree of rank the great men held with respect to the king. In old times the most important were the *friend*, and the *well-beloved friend* of the king. These degrees of rank were awarded at the same time as some promotion in office. A high official of the 6th dynasty received the office of "Under-superintendent of the prophets of the royal city of the dead," and at the same time the rank of "friend"; when later he was promoted to be "Chief of the district of the Nubian boundary," he became the *well-beloved friend*.[2] Promotion to a certain rank was not exactly connected with certain offices, it was given rather as a special mark of favour by the king.

Amongst the "*nearest friends*" of king Pepy, was one belonging to the lower rank of "Overseer of Scribes"; in this case he was invested with a title of honour usually reserved for higher officials.[3] The princes of the royal household were as a matter of course raised to this rank sooner than others, for whilst as a rule no high priest, no "treasurer of the god," bears the title of "*friend*," the sons of the king holding these positions are often called the "*nearest friends*" of their father.[4] Though these titles were generally given only to the highest officials, yet some of the "great men of the South" are counted as "*friends*," while many chief judges[5] are without this rank. It seems that officers in the palace received it when called to be "Privy-Councillors of the honourable house,"[6] while the high priests appear, as we have said, to be entirely excluded.

The rank of *friend* was kept up in later times, though it did not play so important a part as before. Under the New Empire the title of "fan-bearer on the right hand of the king" was given to princes, judges, high-treasurers, generals, and others of the highest rank. They had the

[1] Stele of Kuban. It is possible that the redactor of this inscription may have embellished it in a poetical manner.

[2] Ä. Z., 1882, p. 8.

[3] Stele of Pepy-sed in the Brit. Mus. (L. A.).

[4] High priests without rank: R. J. H., 79 ff., 93 ff.; Mar. Mast., 74 ff., 123.157; Mar. mon. div., 18. With rank: L. D., ii. 22 c. Treasurers of the god, without rank: L. D., ii. 97 a. 100 b.; Mar. Mast., 88, 162, 198 ff. With rank: R. J. H., 89; Mar. Mast., 189, 191.

[5] Chief judges without rank: L. D., ii. 45 ff.; Mar. Mast., 228 ff. With rank (e.g. princes): L. D., ii. 15.34 g., 41.75; R. J. H., 65, 96.153; Mar. Mast., 124 etc.

[6] Palace officials, without rank: Mar. Mast., 116, 135, 136, 250; L. D., ii. 65, 95 f.; R. J. H., 78, 88. As *friends*, R. J. H., 82; Mar. Mast., 236. As *nearest friends*, L. D., ii. 35 ff., 86, 89 a; R. J. H., 6.60; Mar. Mast., 160.175 ff., 185.

privilege of carrying as insignia, a fan and a small battle-axe[1] of the shape represented below. The axe, symbolic of the warlike character of the New Empire, shows that this title was originally given to those of high military rank, and in fact we find some of the standard-bearers and fan-bearers in the army[2] carrying this fan. The fan was also given to ladies, and the maids of honour of the queen and the princesses often bear it.[3] That it was certainly considered a great honour, we judge from the fact that the happy possessor was never depicted without it,—even when the hands are raised in prayer, the fan or the axe is represented on the band on the shoulder.[4]

I have observed above that those who were raised to the rank of "*fan-bearer*" received also the title of "*nearest friend*," which under the New Empire signified essentially the same dignity. Similar conservative customs in maintaining names and titles may often be observed under the New Empire, *e.g.* notwithstanding that all the conditions of the state had altered, yet we see that under Thothmes III. the royal bark bears the same name, "Star of the two countries," as the bark of King Chufu fifteen hundred years previously.[5]

INSIGNIA OF HIGH RANK UNDER THE NEW EMPIRE.

We have as yet considered the king only from his official side, as a demigod high above all other human beings. This descendant of the Sun-god was also however, in spite of his divine nature, a private individual; so that although nominally the whole country belonged to him, yet, at any rate under the Old Empire, he had his own private property, the "house of the palace," which had its own administration[6] and perhaps its own storehouse[7] and its own court of justice.[8] As the Pharaoh had his own property although in theory all the country belonged to him, so also he had his own consorts although, according to ancient ideas, all the wives of his subjects were his.[9]

There was only one legal wife, the queen; she was of royal or of high noble birth, and indeed she may have been the "daughter of the god"[10] *i.e.* of the late king, and therefore the sister of her husband. Her titles testify to her rank at court; the queen of the Old Empire is called:

[1] We find this axe certainly in the time of the 18th dynasty, L. D., iii. 98, 104, 105; later it is often wanting.

[2] L. D., iii. 92. There is no difference between standards and fans, they serve for both, L. D., iii. 100 b.

[3] L. D., iii. 101.

[4] L. D., iii. 98.

[5] L. D., iii. 17 a, cp. L. D., ii. 18 ff.

[6] For the various grades in this department of , the inscriptions onwards from L. D., ii. 49 ff., 55 ff. will be found specially instructive.

[7] Mar. Mast., 100.

[8] Mar. Mast., 70.

[9] Pyramid of Un'es, l. 629.

[10] R. J. H., 153.

"She who sees the gods Horus and Set" (*i.e.* the possessor of both halves of the kingdom)
"the most pleasant,
the highly praised,
the friend of Horus,
the beloved of him who wears the two diadems."[1]

The queen under the New Empire is called—
"The Consort of the god,
the mother of the god,
the great consort of the King;"[2]
and her name is enclosed like that of her husband in a cartouche.

The queen appears as a rule to have been of equal birth with her husband; she took her share in all honours. Unfortunately the monuments always treat her as an official personage, and therefore we know scarcely anything of what took place in the "rooms of the royal wife."[3] The artists of the heretic king Chuen'eten alone emancipate themselves from conventionalities, and give us a scene out of the family life of the Pharaoh. We see him in an arbour decked with wreaths of flowers sitting in an easy chair, he has a flower in his hand, the queen stands before him pouring out wine for him, and his little daughter brings flowers and cakes to her father.[4]

After the death of her husband the queen still played her part at court, and as *royal mother* had her own property, which was under special management.[5] Many of the queens had divine honours paid to them even long after their deaths,—two especially at the beginning of the New Empire, 'Aḥ-ḥôtep and 'Aḥmose Nefert'ere, were thus honoured; they were probably considered as the ancestresses of the 18th dynasty.

Besides the chief royal consort, and other consorts, the Pharaoh possessed a harem,[6] whose inmates, the *secluded*, under the supervision of an ancient matron,[7] attended to the pleasures of the monarch. High officials, *e.g.* the "governor of the royal harem,"[8] the scribe of the same,[9] the "delegate for the harem"[10] looked after its administration, and a number of doorkeepers prevented the ladies from holding useless intercourse with the outer world.[11] These *secluded* were some of them maidens of good Egyptian family, but many were foreign slaves. King Amenḥôtep III.

[1] Mar. Mast., 183, 208, 225, R. J. H., 153. [2] L. D., iii. 132 o.

[3] These "nest suten (hieroglyphs) en ta ḥemt suten" have a special administration: L. D., iii. 242 d.; see also ib. 100 d. [4] L. D., iii. 98. [5] L. D., iii. 100 d.

[6] The harem is called (hieroglyphs) (Mar. Cat. d'Ab., 686) (hieroglyphs) (ib. 719) under the New Empire (hieroglyphs). The name which occurs frequently (hieroglyphs), seems to signify the family dwelling-house in a wider sense, as the children (ib. 702) and the mother (L. D., iii. 100 d.) of the king reside in it.

[7] Mar. Mast., 138 ff. [8] P. J. T., 4, 4; L. D., iii. 242 d (a higher officer).

[9] P. J. T., 4, 5.5, 10 (N. E.); Mar. Cat. d'Ab., 686.719 (M. E.) [10] P. J. T., 5, 9.

[11] Stele of Kefnen under Amenemḥê't III. (L. A., "Mus. Eg., 70"), P. J. T., 5, 1. All these harem officials are themselves married, and therefore are not eunuchs.

RAMSES II., ACCOMPANIED BY HIS SONS, STORMS A SYRIAN FORTRESS.

The Princes Ment'uherchopshet and Cha'emuêse are engaged in the hand-to-hand mêlée; the Princes Meryamun, Amenemu'ea, Sety and Setpenrê' are in command near the penthouses under which the troops advance to the attack; two princes (unnamed) have climbed up the scaling ladders. (After L. D., iii. 166.)

received as a gift from a certain prince of Naharina, his eldest daughter and 317 maidens, the choicest of the *secluded*.[1] We see from this statement what a crowd of women must have lodged in the house of the women belonging to the court of Pharaoh.

We know scarcely anything of the harem life, except that the inmates had to provide musical entertainments for the monarch. On one occasion only a king allows us a glimpse into his harem; in the building in front of the great temple of Medinet Habu we see representations of Ramses III. with his ladies.[2] They, as well as their master, are dressed solely in sandals and necklets, they wear the coiffure of royal children, and therefore some scholars have thought them to be the daughters of the king. But why should the daughters of Ramses III. be depicted here and not his sons? It is also quite contrary to Egyptian custom to represent the members of the royal family with no names appended. We can therefore conscientiously consider these slender pretty ladies to be those

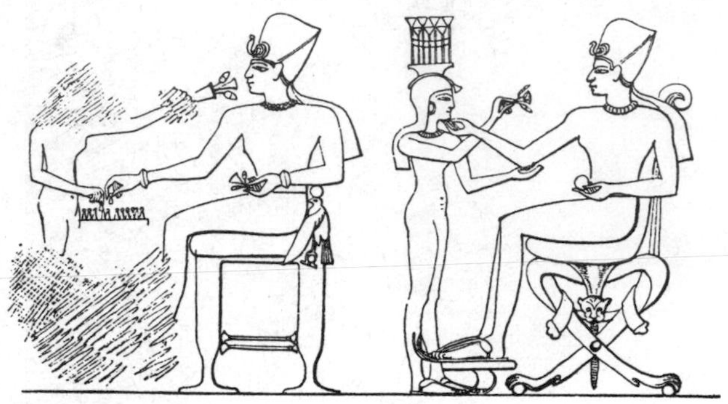

KING RAMSES III. WITH THE LADIES OF HIS HAREM.

who plotted the great conspiracy against the throne of Ramses III. of which we have spoken above. In these pictures no indication is given of this plot; the ladies play the favourite game of draughts peacefully with their master, they bring him flowers, and eat fruit with him.

Under these circumstances it was natural that posterity should not fail the Egyptian kings, though all did not have so many children as Ramses II., of whom we read that he had 200 children; of these 111 sons and 59 daughters are known to us.[3] In the older periods at any rate special revenues[4] were put aside for the maintenance of these princes. Under the Old Empire they also received government appointments, *e.g.* one called the "treasurer of the god"[5] had to fetch the granite blocks out of the quarries of the desert; others officiated as high priests in the temple of Heliopolis,[6] and others again (bearing the title of "prince of the blood," *erpa'te*) became the "chief judges" or the "scribes of the divine

[1] Ä. Z., 1880, p. 82.

[2] L. D., iii. 208 a. b. d. The uraeus snake in d. ought certainly to be a flower.

[3] L. D., iii. 179; Mar. Abyd., i. 4.

[4] L. D., 26, 53.

[5] R. J. H., 89. L. D., ii. 18. Mar. Mast., 188 f.

[6] L. D., ii. 22 c. Mar. mon. div., 18.

book,"[1] and nearly all of them were, in addition, "Chief reciter-priests of their father," and belonged, as "governors of the palace," to his inner circle of courtiers.

Under the New Empire, when the army came more to the fore, they preferred to be invested with military titles, and were called the generals of their father. They assisted zealously at the battles, and were the first to venture up the ladders when a castle was stormed; at least so the official representations of battles inform us.[2] Those even who devoted themselves to the priestly profession, and who in their old age were high priests, as Cha'emuêse the pious son of Ramses II., were not excluded in their youth from taking part in the battles.[3]

The princes, or, as they are called under the New Empire, the "divine offspring,"[4] can be recognised by their robes. In later times they also retained during their lifetime the side-lock, the old badge of childhood, though not in its original form, for instead of a plaited lock of hair, they wore a fringed band.

The princes were brought up in the home of their father, and in a special part of the palace, the *shep* ; their tutor , who was one of the highest court officials, was called, strange to say, their *nurse*. Paḥri, the prince of El Kab under Amenḥôtep I., was *nurse* to the prince Uad'mes;[5] Semnut, the favourite of Queen Chnemt-amun, was *nurse* to the princess Ra'nofru;[6] and Ḥeqerneḥeḥ, a grandee at the court of Amenḥôtep II., had the care of the education of the heir-apparent, Thothmes II., and of seven other princes.[7] In addition to these male nurses, the real female nurse played an important part at court, *e.g.* at the court of the heretic king Chuen'eten, the "great nurse who nourished the god and decked the king" was an influential personage.[8] "Decking the king" signifies some duty the nurse performed at the coronation; in the time of the Middle Empire a "keeper of the diadem" boasts that he had "nourished the god and beautified the Horus, the lord of the palace."[9]

A SON OF RAMSES III., THE FAN, SYMBOLIC OF RANK, IN HIS HAND. (L. D., iii. 214.) (Cp. also the representations of two princes in the vignette on page 51, preceding chapter.)

There was a pretty custom in the time of the Old and Middle Empire: the king allowed other boys to be educated at court with his own sons.

[1] L. D., ii. 15, 34 g., 41 f.; R. J. H., 65, and L. D., ii. 12 f.; Mar. Mast., 178 f.

[2] L. D., iii. 166; cp. also ib., 154, 156.

[3] L. D., iii. 166.

[4] L. D., iii. 176 b. Pap. Mallet, 4, 1.

[5] L. D., iii. 10 b. The above date is not quite certain.

[6] L. D., iii. 25.

[7] L. D., iii. 69. Other tutors, Mar. Cat. d'Ab., 702, 703 (M.E.), 1103 (N.E.).

[8] L. D., iii. 105 f.

[9] Stele of a Chent-em-sete from Abydos (L. A.).

Ptaḥshepses, who later became high priest of Memphis, was brought up by king Menkarē' "amongst the royal children in the great house of the king, in the room and dwelling-place of the king, and was preferred by the king before all the other boys." When Menkarē' died, Shepseskaf, who succeeded him, kept him amongst the princes and honoured him before all the other youths. When Ptaḥshepses became a man, his Majesty gave him "the great royal daughter Ma'tcha' to wife, and his Majesty wished her to live with him rather than with any other man."[1] It was the same under the Middle Empire, for a nomarch of Siut relates with pride how he had received swimming lessons[2] with the royal children, and a high officer of the palace boasts that as a child "he had sat at the feet of the king, as a pupil of Horus, the lord of the palace."[3] Another man relates:[4] "His Majesty seated me at his feet in my youth, and preferred me to all my companions. His Majesty was pleased to grant me daily food, and when I walked with him, he praised me each day more than he had the day before, and," he continues, "I became a real relative of the king." These last words are easy of explanation: the same honour was bestowed upon him as upon Ptaḥshepses—he received one of the daughters of the king for his wife.

In the time of the Old Empire we continually meet with these , "royal relatives," holding different dignities and offices. We can rarely discover what their relationship was to the king, and we suspect that those who were only distantly connected with the royal family made use of this title which had formerly been given to their ancestors. Under the 12th dynasty, it is expressly stated when any one was a "*real* royal relative," and the words "royal relative," when used alone, began to have an ambiguous meaning.

[1] R. J. H., 79. [2] R. J. H. 289 = Mar. mon. div., 68 d.
[3] Stele of a Nebpu-Usertesen from Abydos (L. A.).
[4] Stele of a Chent-em-sete from same place (L. A.).

A KING OFFERS WINE BEFORE THE SPHINX, THE EMBLEM OF ROYAL DIGNITY.

EGYPTIAN ORNAMENTATION FOR A CEILING.
Consisting of Conventional Lotus Flowers.

CHAPTER V

POLITICAL CONDITIONS IN EGYPT UNDER THE OLD EMPIRE

IN the following pages I shall endeavour to give a sketch of the constitution of the Egyptian state, as it existed at the different historical periods; at the same time I must beg my learned reader to consider how many are the difficulties connected with this first attempt, especially with the treatment of the most ancient period. The tombs of the Old Empire may indeed faithfully give us the names of all the offices held by the deceased, but even if we work our way patiently through these wearisome lists of empty titles, we are scarcely any the wiser for our trouble. Out of thirty or more titles borne by one of these great men, we may perhaps understand the meaning of twenty, but there will be barely ten of which we can say what duties belonged to the office designated by a certain title. Still less do we know which was the principal office held by the deceased, or what connection there was between all his various dignities. These great men nearly always contented themselves with enumerating with evident delight a bare list of titles, given them by the gracious favour of the king. They call themselves "Governor of the town," "Director of the land," and "Chief prophet," but they do not tell us where the town, the land, or the temple was situated over which they ruled; nor do they say what were the duties they had to perform. If we read the long list of titles in the tomb of "Un'e the prince, the administrator of the south, the chief reciter-priest, the nearest friend of the king, the leader of great men, the sub-director of the prophets of the pyramids of King Pepy and King Merenrêʿ, the director of the treasure-houses, the scribe of the drinks, the superintendent of the two fields of sacrifice,"[1] etc., we should never realise that this was the man of whom we read in another inscription, that his

[1] R. J. H., 2.

duties were to order stone to be cut for the pyramid of the king and to examine all the state property. Still less should we guess that in his youth Un'e officiated as a judge, and that later he commanded the Egyptian army in a dangerous war. His titles in no way indicate what were the most famous achievements of his life, and meanwhile others who bear the title of "Commander of the soldiers" may never have been in action.

The materials we possess for the period of the Middle Empire are rather more satisfactory, and much that is good exists for that of the New Empire, but unfortunately only a small part is as yet accessible. Great research has been necessary to put together even this short account of the history of the Egyptian government; the essential features are probably fairly accurate, the details will naturally in the future require rectifying and supplementing. The classical writers and the inscriptions of the later temples agree in informing us of the traditional division of Egypt into about forty provinces, and the monuments of the earlier periods show us that this was in fact an old national division: many of the names of these provinces occurring in the inscriptions of the Old Empire. The basis alone of this division remained unchanged; in certain particulars there were many alterations and fluctuations, *e.g.* in the number and in the boundaries of the provinces, especially in the Delta, which appears later to have been entirely divided into twenty provinces, in imitation of the twenty provinces of Upper Egypt. In the Delta, where under the Old Empire there was but one province,[1] , we find later an eastern and a western province, and in another case, the province , of which part was called the "west country," was later divided into a northern and a southern province. In later times we hear nothing of other ancient provinces, such as the "east province," or the east and west crocodile provinces, at any rate not under those names. In the same way our knowledge of the divisions of the Delta under the Middle Empire[2] agrees in general features but not in details with the later division.

Under the Middle and also under the Old Empire, each province was the seat of an ancient noble family, who for generations inherited the government and the high-priesthood of its temple.[3] It is true that these provincial princes could only actually bequeath to their children the family estate and the membership in the priestly college of their native temple; but if there were no special circumstances against it, the Pharaoh would always bestow the government on the great landowner of the province, and in choosing their high priest, the priests could scarcely

[1] Provinces of the Old Empire: L. D., ii. 3-7; R. J. H., 95; Mar. Mast., 437.

[2] The inscriptions of Beni Hasan, Siut, and Bersheh are especially instructive for the provinces of the Middle Empire.

[3] Cp. with the inscriptions of Beni Hasan, what I have ascertained from the texts of Siut, Ä. Z., 1882, p. 161 f. The nomarchs of the Old Empire are easily recognisable by their titles, yet they do not usually state their place of residence; we cannot therefore determine whether the governorship of the provinces was hereditary.

pass over the richest and most important personage amongst them. At any rate in his own town they would leave him in the enjoyment of the titles of his ancestors, even if he himself did not perform all the duties. It has been conjectured, with great probability, that these provinces with their nobility, their coats-of-arms and their own militia, were the remains of independent little princedoms, and that therefore they represent the most ancient political state of the country. Such a period must be of great antiquity, for other conditions seem to lie at the root of the political constitution of the Old Empire, which, as we have seen in the preceding chapter, appears to have consisted of two kingdoms, connected by the bond of personal union. The government of the two states remained separate, and only once under the Old Empire do we meet with a high official who united in his person the governorship of the whole country, viz. Kagemn'e, the "director of the whole country, of the south and of the north."[1]

As a rule the twofold division was always maintained; the whole government was split up into "two houses," and the temple property, or the public lands, belonged to the "two houses, the southern and the northern."[2] In theory all state property was divided into two parts, and the high officials, whose province it was to superintend the treasury or the granaries, were always called the superintendents of the "two houses of silver," or of the "two storehouses."[3] Even if the treasury or granary contained the revenues of but one province or of one town, they yet formed part of the two "houses of silver," or of the two storehouses which received the revenues of the two countries. The royal jewels were also prepared in "two workshops," and kept in "two houses of gold;"[4] the two abodes of food" were for the maintenance of the living, the "two fields of sacrifice"[5] for that of the dead. Originally the war department was double, but in early times they seem here to have felt the need of concentration, for the single form[6] is more often used than the double for this department as well as for the king's court, and for the courts of law.

The system of government as far as we can judge does not seem to have been quite the same for the two halves of the kingdom; *e.g.* while the "great men of the south" ruled over Upper Egypt, there do not seem to have been any corresponding "great men of the north." Each state may have maintained its former organisation even after the union. At the same time we know so little of the Delta under the Old Empire, that it is impossible to form a decisive opinion; we shall therefore confine ourselves

[1] L. D., ii. 97 b, perhaps identical with the old wise man of the same name, mentioned in the papyrus Prisse.

[2] Temple estate : L. D., ii. 88. Fields : Mar. Mast., 115.

[3] Houses of Silver : L. D., ii. 45 ff., 73 ff., 77 ff. ; Mar. Mast., 124 ff., 228 ff. Granaries : L. D., ii. 45 ff., 73 ff., 77 ff.

[4] Workshops : L. D., ii. 45 ff. ; Mar. Mast., 124 ff., 228 ff. ; Houses of gold : L. D., ii. 75, 103.

[5] Abodes of food : L. D., ii. 27 ff. ; Mar. Mast., 228 ff. Fields of sacrifice : R. J. H., 2.

[6] Double : L. D., ii. 73 ff. Single : Mar. Mast., 214 ff., 228 ff.

in the following pages to the conditions in Upper Egypt, which certainly played the chief part politically.

Upper Egypt, officially styled "the South," was divided into a great number of districts, each possessing local government. We do not know how far these were identical with the provinces of the country. There were altogether thirty "great men of the south,"[1] many of these, however, had a merely nominal share in the government, their district consisting of the "desert," the "Nile," or the "fisheries."

These governors, who always bore the proud title of "First under the king," [hieroglyphs], had a double function, judicial and administrative. The governor was the [hieroglyph] judge, and the [hieroglyph] chief of the district (as perhaps the latter title may be translated)[2] in his department, and if a large town were situated in the latter, he was also ruler [hieroglyphs] of this town. A number of lesser offices were apparently connected with this principal one; we say *apparently*, because for the most part these lesser offices were only empty titles. The members of this ancient bureaucracy were fond of creating a special title for each function of their judicial or administrative work; for instance, they had to pass on the royal orders to their district or their town, they therefore entitled themselves "Privy councillor of the royal orders," and as their duty consisted in directing the public works, they called themselves "Superintendent of the works of the king" and "Superintendent of the royal commissions." If they collected the taxes of corn and cattle, or commanded the local militia, they bore the title of "Superintendent of the sacrificial and provision houses," or "Superintendent of the war department"; if they had an office for the different secretaries, connected with their government or judicial work, they then assumed the title of "Superintendent of the royal scribes," or "Superintendent of the legal writers." In addition, they had various priestly duties. As judges, they were priests of Ma't the goddess of truth; their loyalty constrained them to be priests of the king and of his ancestors; finally, they were almost always invested (I know not why) with the office of prophet of the frog-headed goddess Ḥeqt.[3]

We do not know how large a district was governed by one of the "great men of the south"; it was certainly not a whole province. The great chiefs [hieroglyphs] of many provinces belong, however, to this collegiate

[1] [hieroglyphs] Cp. the interesting passages quoted by Brugsch, Dic. Suppl., 927 ff. According to the later quotations, they were exactly the same as judges, though originally they were so only incidentally; what Diodorus (i. 75) says about the choice of these thirty judges by the three towns of Thebes, Memphis, and Heliopolis, can at most apply only to the latest epoch.

[2] L. D., ii. 3, shows that this title does not signify (as Brugsch maintains) "Inspector of the canals and dykes," but has a more general sense. (Cp. also ib. 100 b, where this title follows that of "Superintendent of the desert.")

[3] Titles of Chiefs of the Districts, e.g. L. D., ii. 3 ff., 27 ff., 60 ff., 72, 84, 88; Mar. Mast., 118 ff., 164 ff., 211-214 ff., 243 ff.; R. J. H., 52, 77-86.

number;[1] the "great one of the south," 'Amt'en a contemporary of King Snofru, was prince of the 17th province, prince of the eastern Feyum, and possessed in addition the dignity of district chief in several of the provinces of the Delta.[2] On the other hand, there were "great men of the south," who had no administrative duties in the south, and who yet, by special favour of the king, were considered members of the collegiate assembly, *e.g.* Ra'ḥôtep, the high priest of Heliopolis, a town scarcely belonging to the *south;* the departments over which he ruled as "district chief" were certainly peculiar: they were the fisheries and the Nile.[3] The government of these departments was given to him, in order that a personage so important should have a seat in the great council; a seat was also generally given to the superintendent of the agricultural department.

The thirty were not all of equal rank, for some were deputy superintendents,[4] and at the head of all stood the distinguished "governor of the south." This was a very high office; after Un'e, the favourite of King Pepy, had served the king faithfully many years, and had risen to high honour, Merenrê', the successor of Pepy, appointed the worthy old man to be "Governor of the south" and "Chief of the great men," and gave him at the same time the rank of *prince.* Un'e relates that this was a token of special favour, and that he strove by his good government of the south to show himself worthy of the confidence of his master. He apportioned the duties justly, and twice he ordered the registration of all the properties and revenues which the king possessed in the south. This had never been done before, and on account of his energy Un'e was then named "real governor of the south"; *i.e.* his office was not merely nominal, as had perhaps been the case with many of his predecessors. As we have seen, this honour was given by special royal favour; not long before the time of Un'e it had been bestowed upon a nomarch of the 15th province of Upper Egypt.[5]

We know little of the government of the "north country," the Delta. Under the Middle Empire we meet with a "governor of the north country." This dignity may have existed in an older period, although it is strange that the title never occurs amongst the numberless titles in the older tombs. The Delta was also governed by district chiefs, as is shown by the inscriptions in the tomb of the above-mentioned 'Amt'en, the "great man of the south,"[6] the same tomb, which now forms one of the chief treasures of the Berlin Museum. 'Amt'en governed the 17th province and the eastern half of the Feyum in the *south,* but in his

[1] E.g. the nomarch of the 15th province: L. D., ii. 113. [2] L. D., ii. 3-7.

[3] Mar. mon. div. 18. In the same way a somewhat later colleague of the same. L. D., ii. 22 c.

[4] L. D., ii. 61 a; Mar. Mast., 164 ff.

[5] Inscriptions of Un'e: Ä. Z., 1882, p. 20 f. R. J. H., 2. Others holding this office: L. D., ii. 60 ff., 113.

[6] L. D., ii. 3-7; in every way an important but very difficult inscription. Amongst other things it treats of the landed property of the deceased, and the part taken from it for the funerary worship.

tomb these appointments are not to be compared to those which he possessed in the Delta, where he was "Prince of the great house" in perhaps a dozen large towns. It is not certain whether he had actually to govern the towns or only the crown property, the property of the "great house" contained in them. His position was at all events very important, for it constituted him "district chief in the province of each town." In this way he ruled the sacred city of Dep[1] (the later Buto), the "city of the two dogs" in the province of Mendes, several towns in the province of Saïs, the town Sent in the east of the Delta and others. In each of these provinces he was also a "district chief," and in the country to the west of

STATUE OF RA'ḤÔTEP IN THE MUSEUM OF GIZEH.

Saïs, where he governed the town of Ḥes-uar, he was "Prince of agriculture." The most remarkable of his towns however was the "Cowhouse," probably situated in one of the oases (perhaps the modern Farafrah). As prince of this town he was district chief of the "foreign country," *i.e.* the desert, and again in the same capacity he was "chief of the Beduins," and "Master of the hunt" of the king. The latter was his favourite distinction, for in his tomb he allowed nothing to be represented except the game brought in by his servants. Besides his administrative duties, 'Amt'en as usual had judicial and priestly functions to perform; he was prophet and leader of the priests of various divinities, and "agricultural judge" in the "province of the Ox."

'Amt'en also relates to us the history of his career, how that although

[1] Another district chief of this town. R. J. H., 63, 65.

of high birth (he was a "royal relative") he was obliged to work his way up from below. He was at first "scribe of the house of food" (perhaps a superintendent of a provision depôt); he then rose gradually to be "district chief" and "deputy agricultural judge" in the "province of the Ox" in the west of the Delta. After he had filled various positions, amongst others that of "governor of all the royal harvest," those high dignities were bestowed upon him which he retained till his death.

This inscription contains almost all that we know about the government of the north country, and suffices to show that the organisation there was less traditional than in the south. 'Amt'en received such and such towns, he became chief in certain provinces, but he acquired none of those titles and additional posts which were always connected with such appointments in the south. He ruled the province of Saïs, but he was neither the "superintendent of buildings" nor of "commissions" nor of "writing affairs,"—titles such as these he owed to his districts in Upper Egypt; an organised bureaucracy seems to have been unknown in the Delta. From these facts we conclude that a great difference existed between the civilisation of the two halves of the kingdom. Upper Egypt possessed a thoroughly organised ancient administration, while simpler conditions held sway in Lower Egypt.

As we see from the above description, the constitution of the Old Empire was one of decentralisation. The numerous small districts into which the country was split had their own courts of justice, their own storehouses for corn, and their own militia. The central power which held these somewhat loose organisms together was the "Chunu,"—the *inner*, *i.e.* the public treasury; it had property in all the provinces of the country, over which its representative, the "governor of the south," had the control,[1] and besides the treasure houses of the different provinces, there was also a central finance department, which at the same time had the care of the clothes and ornaments of the monarch. This "house of silver of the treasury" employed numerous men, the "superintendent," the "deputy-superintendent," and the "scribes of the house of silver," with their chief.[2] The house of silver [hieroglyph] belongs however to the great department of the treasury [hieroglyph] or [hieroglyph], and the rank of lord high treasurer was one of the highest in the kingdom [hieroglyph]. It was his duty to collect and value all precious things "that are given by heaven, or brought forth by the earth, or brought down by the Nile"; perfumes from the incense countries, minerals from the mountains, and costly blocks from the quarries.[3] The practical work of the department,

[1] R. J. H., 2; Ä. Z., 1882, p. 21.

[2] L. D., ii. 100 c; R. J. H., 90; Mar. Mast., 251 ff. Cp. also ib. 233 ff.

[3] L. D., ii. 149 c; Mar. Cat. d'Ab., 654; Louvre, C. 2. Borchardt has shown (Ä. Z., 1890, 87-92) that [hieroglyph] does not signify "lord high treasurer," but rather denotes a degree of rank, which was usually borne by various high officials, especially by the "Superintendent of the treasury,"

the labour of obtaining and transporting these precious things, was generally in the hands of the second officer,[1] the "treasurer of the god," [hieroglyphs], a half military rank much desired by the sons of the king. This officer must have been a man of many gifts[2] in order to fulfil the various duties which were expected of him. His expeditions would take him into the deserts and into hostile countries, he was therefore "Superintendent of the infantry," and of the "house of war," and "Chief superintendent of the young men." He was "Superintendent of the shipping" in order to command the transport ships, and therefore the care of the other ships of the kingdom was placed in his hands, and he was considered the admiral of the state.[3] He had to see that the blocks were dragged through the desert, therefore he was the "Superintendent of the gangs of workmen of the god"; and as his journeys and voyages were generally undertaken for the royal buildings, he was also the "Superintendent of all the works of the king," or "of his commissions."

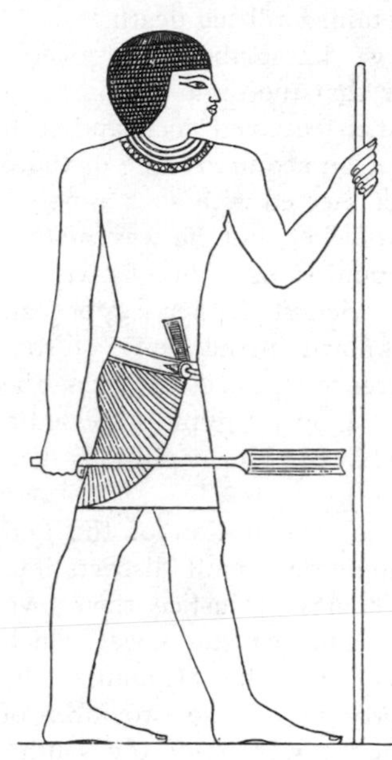

PRINCE MER-'EB.
Treasurer of the god, under King Chufu (after L. D., ii. 21).

Other departments of the state seem also to have had similar central superintendence, *e.g.* the "chief of the granaries," who collected the corn tax, the most important part of the customs.[4] There was also a central department for the superintendence of agriculture, which on account of the inundation required uniform government. The "superintendent of agriculture, and of the scribes of agriculture," therefore held office in "both houses, that of the south and that of the north," *i.e.* in both divisions of Egypt.[5] In the same way for the forests of the anterior

the real lord high treasurer. The [hieroglyphs] ranks between the [hieroglyphs] "Prince" and the [hieroglyphs] "nearest friend."

[1] This is the case at any rate under the Middle Empire. See L. D., ii. 137 a. He may have been called "treasurer of the god" because he worked specially for the temples and tombs.

[2] Cp. on the subject of these officials, Ä. Z., 1882, p. 6; L. D., ii. 18 ff., 97 a, 100 b; Mar. Mast., 162, 188 ff., 198 ff.; R. J. H., 78, 89 (=Mar. Mast., 191).

[3] At Beni Hasan (L. D., ii. 127) he commands the ship which conveys the body of the nomarch to Abydos.

[4] [hieroglyphs] Mar. Mast., 108. A superintendent of the south: L. D., ii. 60 ff. Stele of a Sebekḥôtep (Dyn. VI., L. A.). A chief judge: L. D., ii. 73 ff., 77 ff., 103 c.

[5] L. D., ii. 94 d, 110 c; Mar. Mast., 104, 115, 135, 150; R. J. H., 85/101. An exception is made in the case of the "superintendent of the agricultural scribes of the Nome of the Ox." Mar. Mast., 437.

country (*i.e.* the boundary district between Nubia and Egypt), the possession of which was of importance for shipbuilding, there was a special department, at the head of which stood the "high superintendent of the anterior country of the Pharaoh."[1]

The administration of justice was also centralised. We meet with the office of judge [hieroglyph] in many forms. One of the least important of the judicial posts, one often held by sons of the higher judges, was that of "judge and superintendent of the scribes"[2] [hieroglyphs]. Another was that of "judge belonging to the city of Nechent" [hieroglyphs]; the latter is sometimes said to assist the high-judge "on all secret occasions,"[3] a third was the [hieroglyphs] which may signify the judge of agriculture.[4] These lower judicial appointments were held as a rule by the "great men of the south" or by their sons, and their jurisdiction extended over the town or the province of their respective great lords. All the judges belonged to one of the "six great houses," that is, to one of the great law-courts, in which "the secret words" were discussed,[5] and the chief of these great men, the superintendent of the south, was a member of all the six.[6] At the head of this court of justice[7] stood the "Chief judge," [hieroglyphs], who was at the head of the whole jurisdiction of the country. The chief judge was always of very high birth; if not one of the sons of the king,[8] he would be one of the "high priests of the great gods,"[9] or a "hereditary prince,"[10] or at least a "real prince."[11]

There was good reason for this, for the chief judge held the highest appointment that could be bestowed under the Old Empire. He was the [hieroglyphs] T'ate, the chief of the whole administration—the governor, or as we may translate this title, the "leader of the great men of the south and of the north,"[12] the "second after the king in the court of the palace."[13]

At all ages of Egyptian history this was the most popular position in the kingdom. When the poet describes the palace of the king, he adds,

[1] For the [hieroglyphs] see Ä. Z., 1882, pp. 4, 8, 25, 26 (in which much correction is needed). Br. Dic. Suppl., 944, 949; L. D., ii. 72, 88 c, 111 k.

[2] For the sons of higher judges, see Mar. Mast., 164 ff., 214 ff., 228 ff. Other examples, R. J. H., 52, 78, 99; Mar. Mast., 158, 224; L. D., ii. 43 ff., 110 l—n.

[3] The inscription of Un'e is specially instructive on this subject (Ä. Z., 1882, p. 2 ff.). Also R. J. H., 64; L. D., ii. 16.

[4] E.g. R. J. H., 5; Mar. Mast., 105. Also amongst the titles of 'Amt'en, L. D., ii. 3 ff.

[5] [hieroglyphs] Mar. Mast., 70.118 ff., 164 ff., 214 ff.; L. D., ii. 84.

[6] L. D., ii. 60 ff.

[7] L. D., ii. 103 c, 77 ff.; Mar. Mast., 124 ff., 228 ff.

[8] L. D., ii. 15, 34 g, 41 ff.; R. J. H., 65.

[9] R. J. H., 96 f., 153 f.; Mar. Mast., 149.

[10] L. D., ii. 77 f.

[11] L. D., ii. 73 ff.

[12] R. J. H., 153 f., 304.

[13] R. J. H., 303 f.

that in it there "rules a governor with a merciful heart for Egypt,"[1] and of the god Amon he can say nothing better than that he is "as gracious towards the poor as a good governor."[2] Even the sun-god could not carry on his rule without the help of a good governor, and for this office he chose Thoth, the god of wisdom.[3]

The popular idea was that earthly governors and chief judges ought to vie in wisdom with their heavenly prototype; therefore wise sayings were ascribed to wise governors of old time. It was comprehensible to the naïve understanding of the people that Kagemn'e or Ptaḥ-ḥôtep should have owed their high position as judges to their great wisdom; they even believed that the excellent sayings of the former on the "being of man" had induced King Snofru to name him governor and superintendent of the town.[4] The governors also cherished high ideas about their own position—Ment'uḥôtep, chief judge under Usertsen I., boasts that he had "charmed the heart of the king more than all the dwellers in the two countries, he was beloved amongst the friends of the king and mighty against his enemies, full of power in the two countries, and the first in the valleys of the desert, and in the two countries. He had been the only one loved by the king, without any equal, great men came to him bowing down to him, and all the people rejoiced in his light."

This was not strange, for it was the duty of Ment'uḥôtep "to give the laws, to promote men in their appointments, to adjust the places for the boundary stones, and to settle the quarrels of the officials. He made peace throughout the country, as a man of truth in the two countries, a faithful witness like the god Thoth. He, the chief of the judges, through the words of his mouth, caused brothers to return home in peace; the writings of Thoth were on his tongue; and he surpassed in righteousness the little tongue of the balance. He knew the secrets of every one; he listened well and spoke wisely; he made those to tremble who were disposed to be hostile to the king, he kept the barbarians in check, and made the Beduins to live in peace."[5]

This agrees with what we hear of the governors from other sources. A certain Amony-seneb, priest at Abydos under the 13th dynasty, relates to us with pride that the governor sent his clerk to him as a messenger to summon him, he went with the clerk, and found the governor in his own hall, and there he received his commission.[6] Apparently it was a great honour for a priest of lower rank to be summoned into the direct presence of the great man. Even the "great men of the south" had to be introduced into his presence and to throw themselves on their faces before him.[7] Respect towards the governor was even carried so far that we sometimes find added to his name the words "Life, health, happiness," which are usually appended only to the names of kings and princes.[8] It was also an unparalleled

[1] An., 4, 6, 6. [2] Bol., 1094, 2, 4. [3] Destruction des Hommes, l. 74.
[4] Prisse, 2, 9 and 4, 1. [5] With omissions from R. J. H., 303-304. [6] Louvre, C. 12.
[7] Stele of 'Entef, the chief of the cabinet, of the 39th year of Usertsen I. (L. A.).
[8] Under Usertsen I., L. D., ii. 122.

sign of his dignity that the same ceremonial expressions were used with him as with the kings: *e.g.* people might not speak *to* the chief jndge but *before* him, they did not write *to* the governor, but they *laid a letter before him.*[1]

It was natural that men in such a powerful position should gradually widen their sphere of influence. Under the Old Empire the chief judges often usurped the superintendence of the treasury also; they were superintendents of the "houses of silver" and of the granaries,[2] and even bore the proud title of "Lord high treasurer."[3] They also officiated as high priests,[4] or in later times they were usually governors of the chief town.[5] These chief judges often retained the rank of "first under the king,"[6] which they had held before attaining the above high position; in the same way many of them retained in after-life all the dignities of their former appointments. Thus the number of offices they then held grew to be enormous, *e.g.* a certain Ka'e is said to have held more than forty,[7] yet this multiplicity of appointments did not hinder them from exercising the high office of judge, *e.g.* we know that they personally conducted the inquiry in the secret state process against the members of the royal household.[8]

This hasty sketch of the constitution of the Old Empire shows but the leading features. The hierarchy of the bureaucracy was carried into the smallest details. Above the scribes and the superintendent of the scribes, stood a chief, and between the prophets and their superintendent were the sub-superintendents and the deputy superintendents.[9] Then there were "first men," "chiefs," "great men," "associates," as well as other dignitaries. There was wide scope for the ambition of the Egyptian official, who, if he longed for them, could always obtain high-sounding titles; there was *e.g.* the splendid title "Chief of the secrets," or, as we should say, of the privy council. There were privy councillors connected with all branches of the government. The officers of the palace became "privy councillors of the honourable house,"[10] the judges became "privy councillors of the secret words of the court of justice,"[11] and the chiefs of the provinces became "privy councillors of the royal commands."[12] He who directed the royal buildings was called "privy councillor of all royal works."[13] A general was the "privy councillor of all barbarian countries,[14] and the high priest of Heliopolis, who also officiated as astrologer, was even called the "privy councillor of the heavens."[15] These titles were so meaningless

[1] Abb., 5, 6, 16.
[2] L. D., ii. 73 ff., 77 ff.; Mar. Mast., 124 ff., 228 ff.
[3] R. J. H., 65; L. D., ii. 34 g, 41 ff.
[4] Mar. Mast., 149.
[5] R. J. H., 153 ff. (6th dynasty).
[6] L. D., ii. 104 b; cp. with ib. 103 c. Cp. also L. D., ii. 73 with ib. 78 a.
[7] Mar. Mast., 228 ff.; cf. L. D., ii. 45 ff.
[8] Inscription of Un'e, A. Z., 1882, p. 5, 11.
[9] The order of these degrees of rank is uncertain.
[10] L. D., ii. 41; R. J. H., 97 ff., and many other examples.
[11] L. D., ii. 60 ff., 84; Mar. Mast., 164 ff., 214 ff., and frequently.
[12] Mar. Mast., 150, 164 ff., 214 ff.
[13] L. D., ii. 23.
[14] L. D., ii. 100 b.; Mar. Mast., 162.
[15] Mar. Mast., 149. In the time of the New Empire he wears a dress bespangled with stars.

that the Egyptians generally contented themselves with the first half of them, *e.g.* they would say "Chief of the secrets" in the same way as we should abbreviate our titles of privy councillor of the kingdom or of the admiralty, into privy councillor alone.

All these titles were not invented in the time of the 5th and 6th dynasties, they are of older origin, for we find in them indications of political conditions which have no significance in historical times; *e.g.* the town of El Kab (the old Nechebt or Nechent) plays a peculiar part in the list of titles; under the Old Empire, as I remarked before, many judges bore the title: "Belonging to the town of Nechent,"[1] and "Chief of the town of Nechebt" is the usual designation of the king's "chief reciter-priest"[2] who assisted him at his worship. Possibly in a still more ancient period this court appointment was the privilege of the nomarchs of El Kab, and afterwards the title was retained by those princes and courtiers who recited the holy writings before the monarch.

From what we have said, it will be seen that the structure of the old Egyptian kingdom was somewhat lax. As long as the royal power was strong, the princes of the provinces, the so-called nomarchs, were merely officials governing under the guidance of the court, the centre of government. As soon as this central power became weaker the nomarchs began to feel themselves independent rulers, and to consider their province as a small state belonging to their house. An external circumstance, viz. the places they chose for their tombs, indicates whether a race of nomarchs considered themselves as officials or princes.

Under the 4th and 5th dynasties the "great men of the south," without exception, were buried in the burial-place of the capital, near their king, like the other officers of his household. Under the 6th dynasty, however, the dynastic families of Middle Egypt preferred to rest in their native soil, and at Sheikh Said, at Zawiet el Meitin, and at Kasr Saiyad, the governors of those nomes hollowed out splendid grotto tombs in the rocks of their homes, as if the burial-ground of Memphis were no longer their rightful place. In the succeeding period of anarchy this custom took root amongst the nomarchs, and under the mighty kings of the 12th dynasty each provincial prince in Middle Egypt was laid to rest in his own territory.

Amenemḥê't I., founder of the 12th dynasty, tried to reorganise the divided kingdom; but to accomplish this difficult task it was necessary not only to reduce the independent princes to be obedient vassals of the crown, but also to take away from many of them a part of their property. The old boundaries of the districts had long been disregarded, powerful governors of towns or provinces had seized the territory of their weaker neighbours, and in this way had constituted small kingdoms for their own families. In such cases the king took energetic measures: he "passed through the country shining like the sun-god Atum, in order to punish

[1] Ä. Z., 1882, 5.

[2] [hieroglyphs] interchanges always with [hieroglyphs].

wrong and to reinstate what was devastated. He divided the towns the one from the other, and appointed the boundary of each town. He replaced the boundary stones, and made them firm as the heavens." He also determined for each province its share in the Nile and in the various canals; and "because he so loved the truth" he took as the foundation of this division "what was written in the books, and what he found in the old writings."[1]

Yet though this king may have succeeded by force of arms in punishing wrong-doing and re-establishing order, he was never able completely to subject the nomarchs who had risen to such great power. The tombs and inscriptions of Beni Hasan show us plainly that the nomarchs who were buried there considered themselves firstly princes of their provinces, and secondly servants of the king. Whatever they boast of having done, they did, as they expressly state, for their province; they warded off famine from it, and at the head of its troops they fought for the king.[2] Their ancestors boasted that they were beloved by the king more than all his other servants; on the other hand they, in their tomb inscriptions, boast of being "beloved by their town."[3] In fact, they stand in closer relationship to their people than to their king, and two-thirds of the inhabitants of their province are named after the ruling family.[4] Even in the reckoning of time we find that whereas in the state the computation was by the years of the king's reign, in the nome of the Middle Empire it was by the years of the nomarch.[5]

The nomarchs of the Middle Empire, like the vassals of the Middle Ages, though faithful to Pharaoh as their liege lord, were no longer his servants. Though the bureaucratic state of the Old Empire had become a feudal state, yet this brought about no great change in the country, and everything depended upon the king's bestowing the provinces on faithful devoted men. He could do this the more easily as the sons[6] were not the sole heirs, but also the sons of the daughters;[7] the Pharaoh therefore had a sufficient choice of candidates.

We see how the nomes passed from one family to another by the inscriptions (often referred to in this work) in the tomb of the nomarch Chnemḥôtep at Beni Hasan. The two provinces of the Gazelle and of the Jackal lay on the left bank, some way below Siut, where, owing to a bend, the Nile flowed close to the western mountains, thus leaving a plain of about 14 miles broad and 90 miles long. The small piece of arable land on the right bank, with the high-sounding name of the *Horizon of Horus*,[8] was too insignificant to form a province, and was therefore joined to the eastern desert. Its chief town bore the curious name of Men'at Chufu, the Nurse of Chufu; this town cannot have been far from the

[1] L. D., ii. 124. [2] L. D., ii. 122. [3] L. D., ii. 122; Louvre, C. 1, and frequently.

[4] Cp. the remarks on this subject in chap. viii. [5] L. D., ii. 122.

[6] The son of the nomarch follows his father in office; L. D., ii. 122, 134 c.

[7] It is probable from the following inscription that the sons of the daughters were sometimes considered heirs-presumptive; other passages coincide with this. I shall return to this obscure point in chapter viii. [8] L. D., ii. 124, l. 35.

capital of the Nome of the Gazelle, for the tombs belonging to both were in the same place, near the modern Beni Hasan, at a spot devoted to the lioness-headed goddess Pasht. When Amenemḥê't I. subdued this district, he gave orders by a "decree of his mouth" concerning the town Men'at Chufu. He named the ruler "hereditary prince, prince and ruler of the eastern lands in Men'at Chufu, he fixed the southern boundary, and established the northern as firm as the heavens." The desert formed the eastern boundary, the middle of the Nile the western. The new prince must have shown himself worthy of the confidence of his lord, for when long afterwards the governorship of the neighbouring Nome of the Gazelle fell vacant, Amenemḥê't bestowed that also on him. He again appointed the limits of his territory southwards to the Nome of the Hare, northwards to that of the Jackal, as was denoted by the newly-erected boundary stones. All within these limits, and on the other side between the middle of the stream and the desert, "water, fields, groves, and sand,"—all was to belong to him. At the same time the new nomarch retained his own inheritance, the town of Men'at Chufu and the government of the eastern lands. At his death in the eighteenth year of Usertsen I., it appears that the king preferred again to separâte these two princedoms: a son of the name of Nacht received the family property of Men'at Chufu; and Amony, who was certainly a son of the late prince, inherited the Nome of the Gazelle.[1]

Men'at Chufu afterwards fell into the hands of another family. A daughter of the old prince called Baket, the *olive tree*, had married a prince of the town, Neḥer'e, governor of the town of Ḥat-Ra'-sḥetp-eb, who may also have belonged to the family of the nomarch of the neighbouring Nome of the Hare. The son of this marriage was called Chnemḥôtep. In the nineteenth year of Amenemḥê't II., the governorship of Men'at Chufu, which had become vacant, perhaps owing to the death of Nacht, was given by the Pharaoh to Chnemḥôtep, whom he considered the heir of the family. Chnemḥôtep, seeing how advantageous it had been to have an heiress-presumptive for his mother, married Cheti, the daughter of the prince of the Nome of the Jackal. His speculation was successful, for under Usertsen II. his eldest son Nacht inherited that nome. The limits of the Nome of the Jackal being uncertain, Nacht besought the king to revise them, or, as he expressed it in pretty but obscure fashion, he besought the monarch to allow his "great rewards to reach his water." The king granted his request; he "erected a memorial for himself in the Nome of the Jackal, in that he restored there what he found in ruins. He divided the towns from each other, and appointed to each its province, revising all after the ancient books." He placed a boundary stone on the south, but on the north where his land touched the Nome of the Sceptre which had been hostile, he placed fifteen boundary stones. On the east the nome was to extend to the middle of the stream, and on the west as far as the mountains.

[1] L. D., ii. 122. Amony remarks positively that he inherited the Nome of the Gazelle from his "old father"; the date is given directly after.

Nacht was appointed at the same time to be superintendent of the south. We see his career was a promising one, and as one of his brothers, the younger Chnemḥôtep, was greatly in favour at court, the prospects of the family were brilliant.

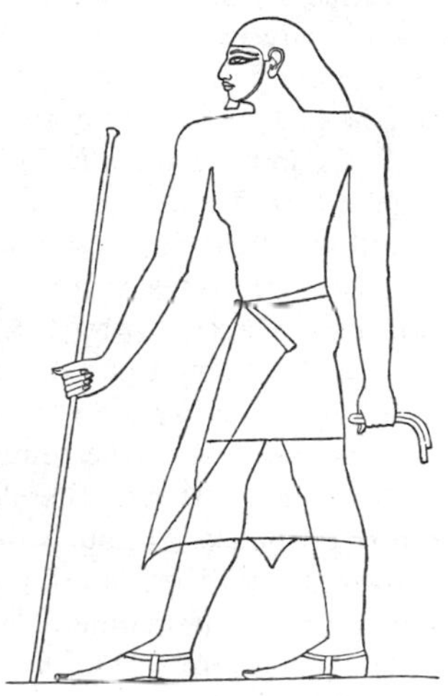

THE NOMARCH CHNEMḤÔTEP (after L.D., ii. 131).

Whilst the inscriptions of Beni Hasan thus teach us the history during one century of the inheritance of the nomes of Middle Egypt, another inscription at Siut, of the same period, allows us a glimpse into the circumstances relating to the property of one of these nomarchs.[1] They are, as may be imagined, of a most intricate nature, for the properties and revenues which he inherited from his ancestors, *i.e.* "the house of his fathers," were always separate from the "house of the prince"—that is, from the estates and rents with which the office of nomarch was endowed. The former was in reality his own property; he could give it up or dispose of it at will; the other was only held as a fief from the king, and even if he disposed of small portions from the "house of the prince," these gifts were not binding by law, and could be claimed at any time afterwards by a niggardly successor. The whole of the two estates, with the "servants, the cattle, the gardens, and other things" belonging to them, naturally formed a rich possession, and in addition there were all kinds of emoluments and taxes. The nomarch received, for instance, a leg of all the bulls sacrificed in the necropolis, also his share of the bulls sacrificed in the temple, and the brotherhood of the "hour-priests" of the sanctuary of 'Epuat sent whole cows and goats for the "provision of the prince." It was important for the personal property of the nomarch that his family should have their share in the management of the temple, and that therefore he should be a member by birth of the priestly college; as such he would draw a certain income from the temple property, and have his share in "all the bread, beer, and meat that came into the temple." This would belong to him by inheritance, and he could do as he pleased with it. There was also a third source of income. The nomarch generally took the first place in the priestly college, and as chief prophet he received certain emoluments, *e.g.* a piece of roast beef from each ox slain in the temple, and a jug of beer on the days of processions. We must add that though these properties belonged as a rule to the same person, yet this was purely incidental, and it was only his hereditary family property, the "house of his fathers," that the nomarch might dispose of quite freely.

Amony ruled for many years in the Nome of the Gazelle, which

[1] Cp. Ä. Z., 1882, p. 159 ff.

Usertsen I. had bestowed upon him; he relates to us how a good nomarch should govern in his office.[1] He says: No young son have I injured, no widow have I molested, no labourer have I arrested, no shepherd have I banished, no superintendent of workmen was there whose labourers have I taken away from their work. In my time there were no poor, and none were hungry in my day. When the years of famine came I ploughed all the fields of the nome from the southern to the northern boundary; I kept the inhabitants alive and gave them food, so that not one was hungry. I gave to the widow even as to her who had a husband, and I never preferred the great to the small." Amony was therefore "greatly beloved, and his popularity ever increased; he was a ruler beloved by his town." He was also in favour with the king. All that the "royal house" ordered to be done in his nome went through his hands, and he showed himself specially useful in collecting the revenues. In the twenty-fifth year of his rule he was able to save out of the temple properties of his nome 3000 draught oxen for the king. It was therefore no wonder that he was "yearly praised in the royal house," so much the more because he acted with perfect honesty, delivered up all revenues, and put by nothing for himself. As nomarch, Amony also commanded the troops of the nome, and three times he had to lead them out. The first time he took part in the Nubian campaign before he himself was nomarch, "according to the wish of the palace he took the place of his old father," and in Ethiopia he won to himself "praise which reached to heaven." His second expedition was the escort of a prince with 500 of his soldiers to the gold mines in Nubia; and in the third he conducted the governor of the chief town and 600 warriors to the quarries of Hamamat.

In the same way as the nome was a state in miniature, its government was a diminutive copy of the government of the state.[2] The nome also had its treasury, and the treasurer, who was an important personage, had the oversight of all the artisans, the cabinetmakers, carpenters, potters, and smiths, who worked for the nomarch. He even built the tomb for his master, and he was so highly esteemed by the nomarch that he was allowed to travel in the boats with the princes. There were also the superintendent of the soldiers, who commanded the troops of the nome, the superintendent of the granaries, the superintendent of the oxen, the superintendent of the desert, a number of superintendents of the house, and a host of other scribes and officials.

The accompanying illustration shows us part of the government offices of Chnemḥôtep; they are in a court which appears to be surrounded by a wall. The building on the left is the treasury, in which we see the weighing of the money that has just been received. The treasurer Bak'te squats on his divan inspecting the work, whilst, outside, his scribe, Neternacht, makes a record of the proceeding. Close by is the building for the

[1] L. D., ii. 122.

[2] All that follows on this subject is according to the pictures in the tomb of Chnemḥôtep, L. D., ii. 126 ff. We see here that the treasurer built the tomb of Chnemḥôtep, L. D., ii. 125, l. 222.

"superintendence of the property of the revenues," and here the scribes are especially busy. The harvest is just over and the corn is being brought into the granaries; each sack is filled in the sight of the overseer and noted down, and when the sacks are carried up the steps to the roof of the granary, the scribe Nuteruḥôtep receives them there, and writes down the number emptied through the opening above. In this way any peculation on the part of the workmen is avoided, and the officials check each other. The nomarch is thus surrounded by a court *en miniature*, and like the king he has his "speaker," [hieroglyphs] who brings him reports on all subjects.

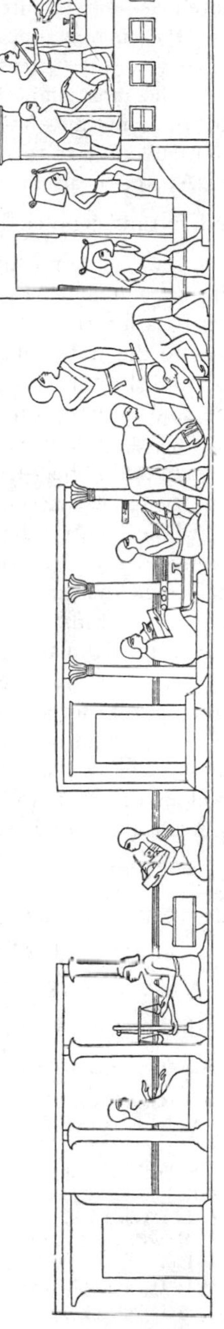
GOVERNMENT BUILDING OF THE NOME OF THE GAZELLE (after L.D., ii. 127).

During the time of the Middle Empire, owing to the independent position of the nomarch, the constitution of the state had become looser, but on the other hand one department of the government, a department centralised even under the Old Empire, viz. the superintendence of the royal treasury and property, remained unchanged. In fact most of the high officials interred in the burial-ground of Abydos belong to this department, which at this time was held in even greater honour than ever. It formed apparently the central point of the state. We find a whole list of "houses" with their superintendents [hieroglyphs]; they are the bureaus, the writing and account rooms, of the different government departments, and it was the duty of their overseers "to reckon up the works, to write them down by the thousand, and to add them together by the million."[1] The old office of "superintendent of granaries" is now called "the house of the counting of the corn," and the director takes a high position.[2] The superintendence of the oxen, or the "house of the reckoning of the oxen," is placed under the "superintendent of the oxen of the whole country," who also bears the title of "superin-

[1] Mar. Cat. d'Ab, 661.

[2] [hieroglyphs] stele of 'Enḥer-nacht, from the Anastasi collection (L. A.); Mar. Cat. d'Ab., 388.

tendent of the horns, claws, and feathers."[1] The "superintendence of the storehouses"[2] is often combined with the latter, and finally there is also the finance department, the house of silver of the Old Empire,[3] called also the "great house."[4] This last department appears to have been the most important of all, and to have even included the others, *e.g.* we sometimes find the superintendence of the storehouse and of the oxen subordinate to the treasury department.[5]

At the head of the treasury department was the high official whose rank is thus denoted and who called himself with bold exaggeration, the "governor of all that exists, or that does not exist."[6] At the king's command he gave out of his treasury, sacrifices for the gods and sacrifices for the deceased,[7] and it was he who "fed the people,"[8] *i.e.* he gave to the state officials their salaries in bread and meat. Even under the Old Empire the position of the lord high treasurer was a very high one, and in later times his influence was, if possible, still greater; he is entitled *e.g.* "the greatest of the great, the chief of the courtiers, the prince of mankind;[9] he gives counsel to the king, all fear him, and the whole country renders account to him."[10] One is mentioned as the "captain of the whole country, the chief of the north country,"[11] and another the "chief commander of the army."[12] Yet, notwithstanding their high rank, they performed the duties of their office in person; we meet with one in the quarries of Sinai,[13] another journeying to Arabia,[14] and another on his way to the Nubian gold mines.[15] It was incumbent on them personally to endow one of the great temples at home with the precious things they brought from foreign countries.[16]

The second official of the treasury, the "treasurer of the god," whose chief business consisted in the superintendence of the transport of precious things, is to be met with in the mines,[17] in Nubia,[18] or on the way to Arabia.[19] He is still the "conductor of the ships," and the "director

[1] Mar. Cat. d'Ab., 590, 601, 679. Stele of Kems'e in the Kestner Collection, and of Ra'-sḥetp-'eb-'anch at Leyden (L. A.); L. D., ii. 150 a.

[2] stele of Ra'-sḫetp-'eb-'anch at Leyden (L. A.); Mar. Cat. d'Ab., 691, 384, 582.

[3] Mar. Cat. d'Ab., 594.

[4] Mar. Cat. d'Ab., 654, 762; Louvre, C. 2. Stele of Ra'-cheper-ka at Leyden (L. A.) There were six great houses, L. D., ii. 150 a, as there were six courts of law ; this denotes some division of the kingdom, or of Upper Egypt, into six parts.

[5] L. D., ii. 150 a; Mar. Cat. d'Ab., 647; Ä. Z., 1882, 203.

[6] L. D., ii. 150 a.

[7] Stele of Ra'-sḥetp-'eb-'anch at Leyden (L. A.), Louvre, C. 2.

[8] R. J. H., 303-304.

[9] Mar. Cat. d'Ab., 647.

[10] L. D., ii. 150 a.

[11] Stele of Ra'-cheper-ka at Leyden (L. A.).

[12] Mar. Cat. d'Ab., 647.

[13] L. D., ii. 137 a, 140 n.

[14] L. D., ii. 150 a; Ä. Z., 1882, 203.

[15] L. D., ii. 144 d.

[16] L. D., ii. 135 h, after comparison with the original.

[17] L. D., ii. 137 a, c, g, 144 q.

[18] L. D., ii. 144 c.

[19] Ä. Z., 1882, 204.

of the works," but his title has been changed to correspond with the spirit of these times, in which the hierarchy of the bureaucracy was more emphasised than under the Old Empire; he is therefore called in the first place the "cabinet minister of the hall of the treasurer,"[1] or the "cabinet minister (or "chief cabinet minister") of the house of silver,"[2] at the same time he retains his old title, but only as a title, not as designating his office. The "cabinet minister" also held a high place at court; one boasts that "he had caused truth to ascend to his master, and had shown him the needs of the two countries,"[3] and another relates that he had "caused the courtiers to ascend to the king."[4]

The titles of the lower treasury officials were also changed, and instead of using their old designation of *treasurer*, they preferred the more fashionable one of "assistant to the superintendent of the treasurer."[5]

We have already seen that many of the chief treasurers claim by their titles to be the highest official in the state. As such however we must generally regard the "governor and chief judge"; he may of course at the same time be the "chief treasurer."[6] Frequently under the Middle Empire this "chief of chiefs, director of governors, and governor of counsellors, the governor of Horus at his appearing," receives the government of the capital town;[7] in later times this becomes the rule.

The above may suffice as a brief sketch of official life under the Middle Empire. A characteristic feature of this time is that, in addition to the high officials of the Old Empire, the subordinate ones come into greater prominence than before. Their number is legion, *e.g.* the treasury department possesses, in addition to the above-mentioned personages, the "deputy governor of the treasurers;"[8] the "clerk to this governor,"[9] the "clerk of the house of silver,"[10] the "chief clerk of the treasury,"[11] the "custodian of the house of silver,"[12] the "superintendent of the officials of the house of silver,"[13] etc. Evidently these lower officials have become personages of distinction and importance, and even if unable to make a show of long titles, or call themselves the "privy councillors" or "friends" of the king, yet, like the members of the old aristocracy, they kept servants and slaves,[14] and erected for themselves splendid tombs at Abydos. They have formed a middle class in the nation.

1 Mar. Cat. d'Ab., 764. 588. Stele of Sa-setet under Amenemḥê't III. (L.A.).
2 L. D., ii. 137 a, c, g, etc.
3 Mar. Cat. d'Ab., 764.
4 Ä. Z., 1882, 204.
5 L. D., ii. 137 f. g.; L. D., ii. 135 h., after comparison with the original.
6 R. J. H., 303/4.
7 L. D., ii. 149 c. Cover of the sarcophagus of a Usertsen (L. A.).
8 L. D., ii. 137 a.
9 Mar. Cat. d'Ab., 635, 627.
10 Mar. Cat. d'Ab., 635.
11 Mar. Cat. d'Ab., 627.
12 Mar. Cat. d'Ab., 677. Stele of Sa-setet (L. A.).
13 Mar. Cat. d'Ab., 677.
14 E.g. a stonemason. Mar. Cat. d'Ab., 724.

How this came to pass is quite evident; it was the result of a process which always plays a part in the life-history of all states. The passions of mankind which influence the government of a kingdom are the same in all places and at all times, and as a rule therefore the development of a state follows the same course. The high official is always of opinion that in the interest of the state he ought to undertake the duties of his colleague as well as his own, so as to render the system of government more uniform and simple. If one man succeeds in holding two offices, each of his successors will endeavour to do the same, and thus the union of the two dignities becomes the rule. In the course of centuries, through the ambition of the officials, the government becomes more and more centralised, the high dignitaries of the state continually add other offices to those they already hold, until we find at last an abnormal condition, like that existing under the ancient Empire, when a great number of offices were vested in one person.

The result of this unwholesome concentration of all the authority in few hands follows as a matter of course. The most energetic man who is in charge of thirty departments cannot really perform the smallest part of the duties of each. No one at the same time can judge, govern the treasury, command the troops, direct the buildings, wait on the king in the palace, sacrifice to Horus or to the late Pharaoh, superintend the temple, and I know not what else besides. The happy possessor of all these honours soon contents himself with the direction of the departments, leaving the work of each to his subordinates, and as some duties are of more importance than others, he confines his energies to the former, leaving the latter entirely to the inferior officials; but though he gives up the work, he still nominally holds the office for the sake of the much-coveted title. This state of things rights itself in time, for instead of the power, which the great men thought to have gained, they find themselves merely in the possession of a number of high-sounding titles.

Egypt underwent the above process in very early times. Under the Old Empire many titles lay under the suspicion of being only empty titles, and conscious of this fact their owners added to them the word *real*. Thus a certain Tepem'anch of the time of the 5th dynasty[1] calls himself

"the *real* nearest friend of the king,
the *real* director of commissions,
the *real* judge and chief of the district,
the *real* judge and chief scribe,
the *real* judge and scribe."

Doubtless under the Middle Empire many of the terms of distinction borne by the nomarchs in Middle Egypt were mere titles; indeed the fact that those who bear them protest that they are *really* chief prophets,[2] or *really* royal relatives, indicates that all their pretended dignities are not equally trustworthy. The nomarchs of Siut, Beni Hasan, and Bersheh bear the title of "lord high treasurer," although we never

[1] Mar. Mast., 195. [2] Mar. mon. div., 168 c. = R. J. H., 287.

meet one of them in Sinai or in Hamamat. In this case it was evidently a title that they retained from old times; perhaps one or other of their ancestors really fulfilled the duties of that office, and Pharaoh conferred the honour of the title on his posterity.

Before we further pursue the subject of the development of the state, we must take a glance at those social conditions on which the constitution of the state rested in old times.

At the beginning of this chapter I showed that there existed an aristocracy, the *nobility* [hieroglyph], in whose hands lay the government of the towns and of the nomes to which they belonged. They sat in the seats of their

PEASANT WOMEN BRINGING TRIBUTE FROM THE VILLAGES OF "LAKE, CAKES, WINE MOUNTAINS, FUNERAL SACRIFICES," etc.
From the grave of T'y (after Bädeker, Lower Egypt, p. 411).

"fathers, the nobility of ancient days,"[1] and they present the best example of a hereditary nobility. Their riches consisted chiefly in landed property, and in their tombs we see long processions of peasant men and women representing the various villages belonging to the deceased. The names of the places are inscribed by the side and give us many interesting particulars. Most[2] are names derived from their chief products:—"fish, cake, sycamore, wine, lotus, provision of bread, provision of beer, fish-catching," etc., and as these designations might repeat themselves, the name of the master is added:—"the fish-catching of Peḥen," "the lotus of Peḥen," "the lake of Enchefttka," "the lake of Ra'kapu," etc. Some proprietors prefer religious names, thus S'abu, high priest of Ptaḥ, named his villages:—"Ptaḥ gives life," "Ptaḥ gives everlasting life," "Ptaḥ acts rightly," "Ptaḥ causes to grow,"[3] etc. Others again loyally choose names of kings: *e.g.* a Ptahḥotep called his villages: "S'aḥurê' gives beautiful orders," "'Ess'e, who loves the truth," "Horus wills that Userkaf should live," "Mut wills that Kaka'e should live," "Ḥar'ekau has splendid diadems," "Ḥar'ekau gives splendid rewards."[4] We conjecture that these royal names, which are often those of past ages, may have belonged to those Pharaohs who bestowed the

[1] Leyden, v. 4 (twice).
[2] E.g. Mar. Mast., 185, 186, 276, 305, etc.
[3] R. J. H., 95.
[4] R. J. H., 84. 89.

property on the family. The above-mentioned S'abu, who lived under Tet'e, would in this case have received several villages from Un'es and 'Ess'e the preceding kings; but one of his estates, the *honourable*, had probably been given to his ancestors by the ancient king Cha'frê'. S'abu's villages were not all situated close to Memphis, where he held his office, but were scattered throughout the Delta.

Numerous functionaries were of course necessary to direct large properties; these are frequently represented; there are "scribes," "directors of scribes," "stewards," "directors of affairs," "scribes of the granaries," etc. Very often the highest appointments in the superintendence of property are given to the sons of the great lord.[1] There was also always a special court of justice belonging to the estate, to supervise the lists of cattle,[2] and before this court the mayor of the village would be brought[3] when behindhand with the rents of his peasants. Besides the labourers there were numerous workmen and shepherds belonging to the property; these went out

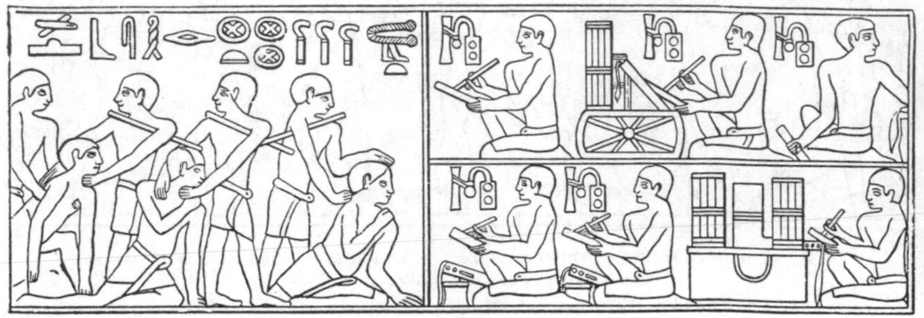

THE MAYOR OF THE VILLAGE BROUGHT TO RENDER ACCOUNT.
(Representation in the grave of T'y. After Bädeker, Lower Egypt, p. 409.)

to war with their lord, and formed various bodies of troops, each bearing their own standard.[4] Under the Middle Empire the conditions of large landed proprietors appear to have exactly resembled those above described.

The study of the representations in the tombs of the Old Empire might lead us to the conclusion that the population of Egypt during that period consisted only of the people represented there, viz. the great men of the kingdom with their large domains, their high appointments, and priestly offices; their subordinates, the lower officials of all kinds; and lastly, the crowd of serfs, labourers, and peasants. No others are represented in the tombs, we never have the least glimpse of free peasants, artisans, or shopmen. Such peculiar social conditions might be the result of special political events, but it is difficult to understand how so high a civilisation could be developed in such an unnatural and one-sided community. Serfs could scarcely have brought Egyptian art and handicrafts to that perfection which we see represented in the tombs of the Old Empire.

We have in fact no convincing proofs that the Egypt of the earliest ages consisted of such a nation of slaves. We must not forget that we owe all our knowledge to tombs erected by members of the highest class

[1] L. D., ii. 9.11. [2] L. D., ii. 61 b. [3] Bädeker, Lower Egypt, p. 409. [4] L. D., ii. 9.

of society. It was natural that these princes and royal relatives should wish to hand down to posterity the names of their faithful servants, and that they should cause to be represented the peasants, shepherds, and artisans who worked on their property. On the other hand, they had no interest in immortalising in their tombs those citizens of inferior rank who had no connection with them, either as servants or otherwise; and if we wonder why the latter did not build tombs for themselves, we must not overlook the fact that probably the custom of building indestructible tombs began only in the time of the Old Empire. The highest of the land alone allowed themselves this luxury, and (as far as we can judge from the excavations of Lepsius and Mariette) there were scarcely a thousand tombs built in the burial-ground of Memphis during the three hundred years of the 4th and 5th dynasties. It was only under the Middle Empire that tomb-building began to be common in a wider circle, and in the necropolis of Abydos we find countless cenotaphs, commemorating those who belonged certainly to the lower rank of officials. At the same time with these "scribes of the harem" or "of the nomes,"[1] we meet with many other persons on the field of Abydos, bearing no title or rank; these may be wealthy free citizens, possessors of smaller properties, rich merchants, or tradesmen. These tombs are not of less importance than those of the royal officials; the deceased had their "master of the household," and their male and female servants,[2] and often some member of the family had entered the official career.[3] They are therefore of the same social rank as the servants of the state.

A poem of very ancient date tells us in fact of tradesmen who were neither the serfs of high lords, nor officials of the state, but who worked for their own living. One is said to travel through the Delta "in order to earn wages," another, a barber, goes from street to street to pick up news, a third, a maker of weapons, buys a donkey and sets forth for foreign parts to sell his wares.[4] In the same poem we read that the weaver must always sit at home at his work, and if he wishes to get a little fresh air, he must bribe the porter; we see therefore that the poet considers him to be a bondservant.[5]

[1] Mar. Cat. d'Ab., 686, 561.
[2] Mar. Cat. d'Ab., 611, 704, 705.
[3] Mar. Cat. d'Ab., 709, 715, 729.
[4] Sall., 2, 5, 5 ff.; Sall., 2, 5, 3 ff.; Sall., 2, 7, 4 ff. = An., 7, 2, 6 ff.
[5] Sall., 2, 7, 2 ff. = An., 7, 2, 3 ff.

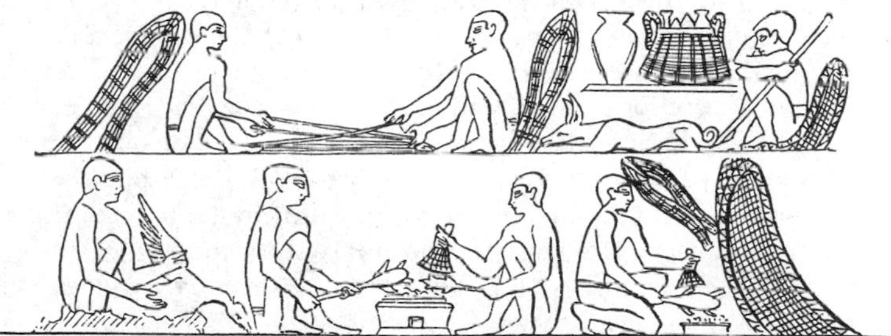

SHEPHERDS COOKING, OF THE TIME OF THE OLD EMPIRE (after Perrot, p. 36).

EGYPTIAN DECORATION FOR A CEILING.

CHAPTER VI

POLITICAL CONDITIONS IN EGYPT UNDER THE NEW EMPIRE

IN spite of all changes and innovations, the Middle Empire rested on the same political basis as the Old Empire; on the other hand, under the New Empire, the constitution of the state must be regarded as a new creation, differing as much from that of the old period as the military government of the first Napoleon differed from the feudal kingdom of St. Louis. Many of the old courts of jurisdiction and many titles still existed in this later period, but the fundamental principles of the government were so much changed that these resemblances could only be external.

In the first place, under the New Empire the provincial governments on which the old state rested have entirely disappeared; there are no longer any nomarchs; the old aristocracy has made way for royal officials, and the landed property has passed out of the hands of the old families into the possession of the crown and of the great temples. This is doubtless the effect of the rule of the Hyksos and of their wars.

The Theban dynasties maintained the struggle against these foreign rulers for generations; they did not fight for the freedom of the small princedoms, but for their own interest. They conquered the country and drove out the barbarians, scarcely from those patriotic impulses to which we of the modern world pretend. They looked upon their conquest as their own hardly-won possession, and simply took the place of the foreign rulers. We can well understand that King Ta'a would not only receive no support from the petty princes, but that they would resist him, preferring to remain vassals of the foreign ruler in Ḥatu'ar rather than submit to one of their equals. In fact we find that after the war of liberation rebellions still arose, which A'ḥmose had to crush; we read especially of a certain Tet'e-'an, who "collected the evildoers" and marched against him, and whom A'ḥmose conquered in a pitched battle.[1] On the other hand, A'ḥmose was obliged to reward with high titles those princes who had supported him, and therefore in the beginning of the 18th dynasty we meet with distinguished private men bearing the title of the "first son of the king";[2] the renunciation of their claims being evidently bought from them by the bestowal of high rank. The family of the "first royal son" of El Kab certainly kept this title during four generations, and Amenḥôtep, the son of Ḥapu, the celebrated wise man of the court of Amenḥôtep III., belonged to it.[3] Whatever the details may have been, we may accept as a general fact that Ta'a and A'ḥmose exterminated the old nobility very much as the Mamluks were exterminated by Mehemed Ali, and as the latter obtained the greater part of all the property in the kingdom by the confiscation of the estates of the Mamluks, so the former absorbed in like manner the property of the small princedoms.[4] Thus arose those abnormal agrarian conditions found in later Egypt by which all property, with the exception of the priest's fields, belonged to Pharaoh, and was rented from the crown by a payment of 20 per cent. In Gen. xlvii. these conditions are declared to be due to the clever policy of Joseph.

The New Empire was founded by the power of arms, and established by wars in the north and south; no wonder therefore that it became a military state, and that the soldiery rose to greater power than ever before. The army had as yet played but an insignificant part; even under the Middle Empire the Nubian wars were carried on by the militia of the individual nomes; one element of a standing army alone was present, viz. the "followers of the king", a body-guard, which we meet with so often and so exclusively in Nubia that we conjecture that it was employed as the garrison of the subjected country.[5] Everything seems changed under the New Empire: we continually meet with the infantry, the chariot-force with their officers, and the "royal scribes"; on the borders and in the conquered country we find mercenaries with their chiefs, while in the interior the foreign troops of the Mad'oi act as military and police. For the most part these warlike services are rendered to Pharaoh by barbarians, and under Ramses II. we meet with Libyans and Shardana in Egyptian pay.

SOLDIER OF THE MIDDLE EMPIRE
(Picture at Siut. After Wilk., I. 202.)

[1] L. D., iii. 12 d., 22. [2] L. D., iii. 9, 43 a. b. [3] L. D., iii. 42 a. b.

[4] We see that after a civil war A'ḥmose himself bestowed lands on his favourites (L. D., iii. 12 d., 21). This fact supports the above theory, for he probably granted them a share in the booty.

[5] L. D., ii. 136 e. g., 144 b. h. i. k., 138 a. g.

It follows that an army of mercenaries, such as we have described, would soon become a powerful factor in the state, and would interfere in many ways in the government. That this was the case we can often gather from the correspondence of the scribes which is still extant. The "chief of the soldiers" orders exactly how and where a certain canal is to be dug,[1] and his deputy not only orders blocks of stone to be transported, but also undertakes the transport of a statue.[2] The king's charioteer, holding a high position in the army, watches over the transport of monuments,[3] and the chief of the militia does the same.[4] Thus we see that officers of the army have stepped into the places of the former "high treasurer," and of the "treasurer of the god." A few centuries later the mercenaries thrust the Pharaoh from his throne, and set up their great chief in his place.

SOLDIER OF THE NEW EMPIRE (after L. D., iii. 121 b.).

The Egyptian kingdom however was fated first to succumb to another power; threatening signs of this danger are seen under the New Empire. I speak of the priesthood, whose place in the kingdom became more and more abnormal after the 18th dynasty. Signs of the rise of their power are plainly to be traced on the burial-field of Abydos, where in like manner we saw the rise of the lower official class under the Middle Empire: from the time of the 18th dynasty the tombs of priests and temple officials are to be found on all sides.

There was no lack of priests in the older time, but, with the exception of the high priests of the great gods, most of the priesthood held inferior positions bestowed upon them by the nomarchs and by the high officials. We hear but little also of the estates or of the riches of the temples; at most we only meet with the "treasurer" of a sanctuary.[5] Under the Middle Empire the conditions are somewhat different: we find a "scribe of the sacrifices,"[6] and a "superintendent of the temple property,"[7] a "lord treasurer of the temple,"[8] and even a "scribe of the corn accounts and superintendent of the granaries of the gods of Thinis."[9] The above however were of little importance compared to the numberless "superintendents of the cabinet," and the "keepers of the house," belonging to the treasury. Under the New Empire all is changed; the fourth part of all the tombs at Abydos belong to priests or to temple officials. The individual divinities have special superintendents for their property,[10] for their fields,[11] for their cattle,[12] for their granaries,[13] and for their storehouses,[14] they have directors for their buildings,[15] as well as their own

[1] An., 5, 21, 8 ff. [2] Leyden, 348, 7. [3] Leyden, 349. [4] Leyden, 348, 6, 7.
[5] Mar. Mast., 96, 97. [6] Mar. Cat. d'Ab., 552. [7] Mar. Cat. d'Ab., 566.
[8] Mar. Cat. d'Ab., 551. [9] Mar. Cat. d'Ab., 694.
[10] Mar. Cat. d'Ab., 1202, 1153 (=1219), 1049. Cp. especially as to the working of this department, Leyden, 348. [11] Ib., 1085. [12] Ib., 1144, 1080.
[13] Inscription in the hier. char., 29. [14] Mar. Cat. d'Ab., 430. [15] Ib., 424, 1163.

painters and goldsmiths,[1] their servants and slaves, and even the chief barber[2] has his place in all the great sanctuaries. These temple officials are for the most part men of distinction and note. Thus we see that the priesthood under the New Empire forms one of the most important elements of the kingdom. This is not surprising, for just at that period religion undermined and stifled the energies of the nation; kings exhausted their resources in building gigantic temples, or in giving the booty of towns to the god Amon, and barren religious representations take the place of the old bright pictures of daily life. It was natural that the priesthood should thrive on the religious fanaticism of a decaying nation. When we read in the Harris papyrus of the immense treasures that one king alone bestowed on his "fathers the gods," we are not surprised that the servants of these gods should soon rival the kings in power, and indeed at last entirely thrust them aside.

The captains of the mercenaries on one hand, powerful priests on the other, take the place under the New Empire of the old aristocracy. It is not purely accidental that we find joining forces with the above a third determining factor, one that only arises when a kingdom is in an unhealthy state, viz. the *slaves* belonging to the ruling class.

The pictures representing the court life of the nomarch Chnemḥôtep (alrẹady frequently mentioned) show us the chiefs of the kitchen and of the garden, and besides them several household servants, bearing the title ; they belong apparently to the princely kitchen, for they assist at the slaying of animals and bring roast meat, jars of wine, and food, to their master.[3] We learn, however, from a Berlin stele, that a distinguished family of that period had four such servants, who presided over the "bakery" and the "fruit-house."[4] We meet with them also forming the lowest rank of service in other households of this time, as for instance in the house of one master who possessed no office at all under government.[5] We therefore do no wrong to the if we translate this word by the term *slave*.

Under the 19th dynasty these slaves rise to importance in the state and attain high honours. One is a clerk of the treasury,[6] another gives orders to the officers as to how the monuments should be erected,[7] and under Ramses IX. we even meet with two *prince slaves*, who rank immediately after the high priests. They are the "royal slave Nesamun, scribe to Pharaoh, and director of the property of the high priestess of Amon Rê‘," and the "royal slave Nefer-ke-Rê‘-em-per-Amun, speaker to Pharaoh."[8] We shall meet with both in the next chapter in the discharge of their official duties, and shall have occasion to consider their abnormal position in the kingdom.

[1] Mar. Cat. d'Ab., 1084 and 1204. [2] Ib., 1079. [3] L. D., ii. 128, 129.
[4] No. 7311, as a trusted servant. [5] Mar. Cat. d'Ab., 563; Louvre 7 (L. A.).
[6] P.j.T., 4, 14. [7] An., 5, 24, 4. [8] Abb. pass.

These slaves were mostly of barbarian birth; of the eleven mentioned as belonging to the court of Ramses III. five bear foreign names: one is, *e.g.* the Libyan Ynene, whilst another rejoices in the good Phœnician name of Mahar-ba'al.[1] Many also who bore Egyptian names were probably of foreign origin. Their foreign birth makes us suspect that *slaves* are here intended, and a passage in a poem, describing in long-winded measures the triumph of the king, leaves us in no doubt that such is the case. It is there stated that the older of the Cilician captives who are led in triumph before the King's balcony are to work in the brewery; the younger are either to be boatmen, or when they have been bathed, anointed, and clothed, to be slaves to his Majesty.[2] These became the favourites of the kings of the New Empire, who seem to have tried, in the same way as the Sultans of the Middle Ages, by the purchase of slaves, to create for themselves a trustworthy surrounding. The slaves here take the place of the Mamluks, and I need hardly say that the same motive, viz. distrust of his own subjects, led the monarch in both cases to have recourse to this strange expedient, by which slaves rose to high positions in both states. As a matter of fact the slaves (like the Mamluks) were not always faithful to their masters,—some of them, *e.g.*, took part in the great conspiracy against Ramses III.[3]

Amongst the court officials also we often meet with foreigners who may have been slaves. For instance, the office of "first speaker of his Majesty," whose duty was to take charge of the intercourse between the king and his attendants, was, under King Merenptaḥ, invested in the Canaanite Ben-Mat'ana, the son of Jupa'a, from D'arbarsana.[4] At court he of course assumed an Egyptian name; he was called "Ramses in the temple of Rê'"; and as this distinguished name might also belong to some of his colleagues, he bore the additional name of the "beloved of Heliopolis." All barbarians were probably not so conscientious as Ben-Mat'ana in confessing their foreign origin, consequently we may suppose that many of the officials named after the reigning king may have been Phœnicians or Cilicians.

We have already remarked that the feudal system of the country had probably come to a violent end; something however remained of the old provincial governments, though in a much changed form.[5] The College of the Thirty is mentioned now and then, at any rate in poetry.[6] The old nomarch title of "prince" is also still borne by the governors of great towns such as Thebes or Thinis,[7] but they have lost the influence and power which these princes possessed under the Middle Empire. They have become purely government officials without any

1 P.j.T., 2, 2; 4, 12, 14, 15. 2 An., 3, 8, 3; An., 4, 16, 2. 3 P.j.T., 4, 12, 14, 15.
4 Mar. Cat. d'Ab., 1136 = Mar. Ab., ii.; T., 50.
5 We might consider the "the scribe Paḥri, prince of Nechebt, the superintendent of the Prophets," as a nomarch in the old sense; he lived in the beginning of the 18th dynasty, L. D., iii. 10 to 11. 6 E.g. An., 5, 9, 5. 7 Mar. Cat. d'Ab., 403; 1080.

political significance; Thebes possessed two of these princes, one for the town proper, the other for the quarter of the dead.[1] If we may trust a representation of the time of Sety I., the "south and the north" were formerly governed by 19 princes.[2]

Between the Pharaoh and the government officials a deputy of the monarch now appears on the scene; he is the "chief mouth," *i.e.* "chief of chiefs, and director of directors of the works"; under Queen Chnem-tamun he was her favourite servant, but as a rule the heir-presumptive of the throne occupied this position.[3] At the head of the government itself however we still find the "chief judge" and "governor," of whom there are now often two contemporaneously.[4] In the old time these men nearly always held at the same time another high office, viz. that of "lord treasurer." Under the New Empire and probably earlier[5] they govern the *town, i.e.* the seat of government, whether it were Thebes,[6] Memphis,[7] or Ramses in the Delta, the newly-founded city of the 19th dynasty.[8] In the capital the last appeal, even in temple cases,[9] was to the *governor,* who ranked even above the high priests.[10] When the labourers were unable to get their corn delivered to them at the right time, after exhausting all other resources, they appealed to him. Each criminal case was brought before him, and he had to conduct the inquiry and the prosecution. In short, he was the first police magistrate of the capital, and probably also of the whole kingdom. Under the New Empire a priestly personage was often chosen as governor and "superintendent of the town"; either the high priest of the great Theban god Amon,[11] or the high priest of Ptaḥ, the great god of Memphis.[12] He then united in his person the highest temporal and spiritual power, and was not only "Chief of the great men of the south and of the north," but also "Superintendent of the prophets of the south and of the north," or, as we should say, both minister of the interior and minister of public worship.

The ancient departments of the royal property were also maintained, that of the *house*[13] (*i.e.* of the landed property), that of the granaries,[14]

[1] Abbott pass.

[2] L. D., iii. 128 b. We must not overlook that, ib. 76, the "first men of the south and north" together with the "superintendent of the house" consist only of 34 persons.

[3] Senmut: L. D., iii. 25 1.; Ḥaremḥêb (first "chief mouth" and then "deputy"). Transactions of Bib. Archæ., iii. 486 ff.; Ramses II. ("deputy" at his birth, and at the age of ten years "chief mouth" to his father); Stele of Kuban, l., 16, 17; Ramses III. (was *erpa'te* and then at the same time great "chief mouth for the countries of Egypt, and giver of orders for the whole country;" Harr., 75. 10. Under Ramses IX. an *erpa'te* accompanies the governor; Insc. in the hieratic character, Pl. I.

[4] Under Ḥaremḥêb the "two superintendents of the town, of the south and of the north"; Düm. Hist. Insch., ii. 40 e. Under Ramses III., Düm. Hist. Insch., i. 26, 27; Harr., 10. 10, for the two halves of the kingdom. Under Ramses IX., on the contrary, the south and the north are ruled by the same governor, as we see from Abbott, 6. 22.

[5] First probably under the 6th dynasty R. J. H., 153-4; M. E.—L. D., ii. 122; Mar. Cat. d'Ab., 755; Louvre, C. 4. C. L. A.

[6] Abb. pass.

[7] Berlin Museum, 2290.

[8] Mar. Cat. d'Ab., 1138.

[9] Insc. in the hierat. char. 29.

[10] Abb. 7, 3.

[11] Mar. Cat. d'Ab., 408.

[12] Berlin Museum, 2290.

[13] "Superintendent of the house" and "great superintendent of the house": Mar. Cat. d'Ab., 441-449.

[14] Abb., 3, 3; L. D., iii. 76, 77.

and that of the oxen,[1] and the various superintendents were men of note, able to erect splendid tombs for themselves. The office of "superintendent of the granaries" was especially important, for in spite of all conquests and tributes, the real wealth of Egypt lay in the produce of corn. The "superintendent of the granaries" had to take care that this was plenteous, that it should suffice for the maintenance of all the officials, soldiers, and serfs; he had to control and to demand rich supplies from the "superintendents of the estates (?) of Pharaoh and the chief officials of the south and of the north, from the miserable land of Ethiopia to the confines of the country of Naharina."[2] It was a great day each year for the country when the superintendent of the granaries in solemn audience presented to the monarch the "account of the harvests of the south and of the north";[3] and if he, like Cha'-emḥê't, the superintendent of granaries to Amenḥôtep III., could announce to his master that the inundation was good, and that there had been "a better harvest than for thirty years," then his Majesty would show special honour to his faithful servant, and in the presence of the monarch he would be anointed and decked with necklets of great value.[4]

CHA'EMHÊ'T, SUPERINTENDENT OF THE GRANARIES OF AMENḤÔTEP III. (after L. D., iii. 77 e).

The department of the treasury, however, though in quite an altered form, still held the highest place in the government. We hear little more of the "treasurer"[5] except the empty title of "lord treasurer" which is still borne by the governors;[6] the "treasurers" have disappeared as well as the "superintendents of the cabinet." Their work is done for the most part by soldiers, and the rest, that belonging to what we should call the finance department, has been taken over by the "house of silver," which formerly formed a subdivision only of the treasury. At the head of the latter are various "superintendents of the house of silver,"[7] distinguished men, who rank directly after the governor.[8] Under them are the "deputies"[9] and the "scribes of the house of silver," whose correspondence will occupy much of our attention; we shall see how they deliver up the wood to the shipbuilders,[10] how they cause the palace of the king to be decorated,[11] and how they take charge of the commissariat for the court when travelling.[12]

1 Lee, I. 2. 2 L. D., iii. 77. 3 L. D., iii. 77. 4 L. D., iii. 76.

5 A "lord treasurer" is mentioned L. D., iii. 3 a. b. Mar. Cat. d'Ab., 1061, and Stele of Kuban, l. 11. Here he is still at work. The "superintendent of the house of silver" bears the title of lord treasurer, L. D., iii. 242.

6 Mar. Cat. d'Ab., 408.

7 That there were several at the same time we see from P.j.T., 2, 1, 5, 2.

8 Insc. in the hier. char. 29. 9 L. D., iii. 242. 10 An., 4, 7, 9 ff.

11 An., 4, 16, reverse side. 12 An., 4, 13, 8 ff., 15, 1 ff.

The care of the crown jewels was also, as in old times, vested in the treasury department, forming part of the duties of the "superintendent of the ointments of the treasure-house of the lord of the two countries, of the superintendent of the royal diadem of the good god."[1] The superintendent of the house of silver had therefore a number of artists under him: the "deputy of the artist of the house of silver," the "chief painter," and the "scribe of the painters," as well as the "chief architect of the house of silver."[2] We must also mention a few other officials who belong here, for instance the "keeper of the scales of the house of silver," who boasts that he has not diminished the revenues of the gods, nor falsified the tongue of the balance."[3] Also the distinguished librarian of the house of silver, the "chief keeper of the books,"[4] and the "scribe of the tribute granary."[5]

TREASURY OFFICIAL, WEIGHING RINGS OF GOLD (after L. D. iii., 39 a).

The letters between the "scribe 'Ennana" and his predecessor and tutor Qagabu, the scribe of the house of silver, give us a good illustration of the working of this department. Both belonged probably to the treasury department in the Town of Ramses, though 'Ennana was stationed in the east of the Delta.

Qagabu receives a commission from his chief, "Parê'-em-ḥeb, the superintendent of the house of silver," to have the palace of the king repainted during his absence;[6] and leaves to 'Ennana the more prosaic part of the work. The latter with the workman Ser-Amen-nacht, is also to repair a bark of acacia wood, which has been out of the water for many years, and which is falling to pieces. Qagabu writes to him, "When you receive my letter, go together and look at the acacia planks which remain with the divine bark in the storehouse at Resnu, and choose out four boards which are very long, very broad, and very beautiful, and use them as side planks for the acacia bark which is with them in the storehouse, putting two boards on each side. See then what else is left of good wood for facing, and repair it from bow to stern."[7]

[1] Mar. Cat. d'Ab., 1122. [2] L. D., iii. 242, as funeral procession of those placed before.
[3] Mar. Cat. d'Ab., 1102. [4] An., 6, 3, 13. [5] Mallet, 3, 2.
[6] An., 4, 16, reverse side.
[7] An., 4, 7, 9 ff. The word used may be "beams" instead of "planks," the words "*side planks*" and "repair" are entirely hypothetical.

Another time he commissions him to inspect the vineyard of the temple of Amon in the town of Ramses and to deliver up the wine that was pressed. 'Ennana faithfully carried out these instructions, and sent to his predecessor the following account of his journey, which gives us a good example of the formal style used in such official reports; he says:[1] "When I came to Nay-Ramessu-Mry-Amun on the bank of the Poter, with the transport boat of my Master and with the two span of oxen of the house of Sety II. in the temple of Amon enduring for millions of years, I then appointed the number of gardeners for the gardens of the house of Sety II. in the temple of Amon enduring for millions of years. I found:

Gardeners:	Men	7
	Youths	4
	Lads	4
	Boys	6
	Total	21 souls.

"List of the wine which I found sealed by the head gardener T'at'ery:

Wine	Jars	1500
Shedeḥ-Drink	"	50
Pauer-Drink	"	50
'Enharmaa Fruits	Baskets	50
Bunches of Grapes	"	50
	Packages	60

"I laded the two ox waggons of the house of Sety II. in the temple of Amon enduring for millions of years, and drove up stream to the town of the house of Ramses II. of the great image of Rê' Harmachis. I there delivered them into the hands of the official in charge of the house of Sety II. in the temple of Amon enduring for millions of years, and I now write this report to my master."

A much more important commission was also placed in the hands of 'Ennana; viz. the commissariat of the court. The king when he travelled required that everything should be prepared at the various places where he proposed to stop, and the "scribe of the house of silver" had almost more than he could do to provide everything needed for the stay of the court. His chief sent him a letter telling him of the proposed arrival of "Pharaoh his good lord," and exhorting him to follow the instructions exactly as to the order of the stages, and on no account to allow himself to be guilty of any indolence.[2] The task was not a light one, as the quantities concerned were very large. Six kinds of *good bread*, in all 16,000 pieces, were required, of other bread 13,200 pieces, of various kinds of cake 4000 pieces, and 200 baskets. In addition 100 baskets of

[1] An., 4, 6, 10 ff.

[2] An., 4, 13, 8 ff. Whether *ḥtp* means exactly a basket I cannot tell, it may signify a reed box. A similar letter, An., 4, 15, 1 ff., is in more general terms.

dried meat, 90 jars of butter, and corresponding quantities of milk, geese, etc. The number of baskets of figs, grapes, and other fruits was also considerable; 100 wreaths of flowers were necessary to deck the jars of wine, 100 loads of hay for the horses, 2000 pieces of wood for kitchen fuel as well as 200 loads of coal. The usual baskets of the treasury did not suffice for the packing and transporting of these quantities, and therefore the clerk had also to order 500 new reed baskets from the basket-makers.

Let us hope that 'Ennana got through his difficult task well, and thus escaped the threatened censure. It would have been considered a *great crime*, had he allowed Pharaoh to "travel to Heliopolis, without all his requirements in his rear."[1]

On another occasion 'Ennana really fell into serious embarrassment. Amongst other duties, he had to superintend a number of peasants, who worked as serfs on the fields, while their wives were busy weaving for the state. Some months previously he had handed over to his chief, the "superintendent of the house of silver," certain large quantities of material woven by these women, and he was now prepared to hand over the 178 pieces of stuff which had been woven since that time. Meanwhile another high official, the "master of the house" (*i.e.* the superintendent of the estate), to whom the harvest of these peasants was due, discovered that the work also of the wives ought to be given in to *him*, and there was probably some truth in his view of the matter. He accordingly went boldly to 'Ennana, and, as the latter said, "did to him all manner of evil." He then caused him to be brought by three of his servants before Ḥuy, the superintendent of the soldiers, and Ptaḥemḥeb, the scribe, who in that city had the care of the registration of the serfs. A list of his peasants—containing, as he maintained, many errors—was placed before 'Ennana, and on the strength of this list the superintendent of the property proceeded against him. "When the register of the peasantry had been made out to me," wrote 'Ennana to Qagabu, "he excited people against me to say 'Give up the work of the peasants.' Thus he said. And yet I had already given in the work of the peasants to the superintendent of the house of silver, and the work had been accepted more than five months before, in the second summer month! He then took from me the woven work that I was about to give in to the superintendent of the house of silver. I subjoin a list of the work that was taken from me, that the superintendent of the house of silver may see it:

Royal linen	No. of pieces	87
Linen	"	64
Good linen of Upper Egypt .	"	27
	Total	178"

'Ennana at length summoned his opponent before *the princes*, and

[1] From An., 4, 10, 8 ff.

through their intervention the affair seems, outwardly at any rate, to have been adjusted; yet he still had many vexations to bear from the superintendent of the house. "When the latter sent out the two scribes of the soldiers to fetch in the harvest, they took away for the second time two peasant women from the village of Pa'eshemu, and ordered 'Ennana to give them a youth, though he had only the one who kept the cattle of the proprietor Thothmes." This and many other things the superintendent of the estate did to 'Ennana merely out of revenge; he said openly to him: "This happens to you because you gave up the woven work of the peasant women to the superintendent of the house of silver." 'Ennana was able to do nothing against his powerful enemy: he could only beseech his chief Qagabu to speak a word for him to the "great one of the house," who was over the wicked "superintendent of the house," so that at least he might get back the four peasant women

SCRIBES OF THE OLD EMPIRE (after L. D., ii. 9).

who had been taken from him with no pretext of justice.[1] Whether this step was successful, or how the matter further developed, we know not.

Numerous documents have come down to us, showing how the accounts were kept in the department of the "house of silver," and in similar departments; the translation of these is however extremely difficult, owing to the number of unknown words and the abbreviations they contain. These documents show exactly how much was received, from whom and when it came in, and the details of how it was used. This minute care is not only taken in the case of large amounts, but even the smallest quantities of corn or dates are conscientiously entered. Nothing was done under the Egyptian government without documents: lists and protocols were indispensable even in the simplest matters of business. This mania for writing (we can designate it by no other term) is not a characteristic of the later period only; doubtless under the Old and the Middle Empire the scribes wrote as diligently as under the New Empire. The pictures in the old tombs testify to this fact, for whether the corn is measured out, or the cattle are led past, everywhere the scribes are present. They squat on the ground, with the deed box or the case

[1] An., 6, the first letter.

for the papyrus rolls by them, a pen in reserve behind the ear, and the strip of papyrus on which they are writing, in their hands. Each estate has its own special bureau, where the sons of the proprietor often preside.[1] We find the same state of things in the public offices: each judge is also entitled "chief scribe," and each chief judge is the "superintendent of the writing of the king"; one of the great men of the south is called

Superintendent of the writing on agriculture,
Director of the writing in the agricultural department,
Director of the writing on agriculture, (?)
Head scribe, scribe of the king,
Director of the writing of petitions[2]; (?)

in short, we see that all the government business was done in writing. To *superintend* and to *write deeds* was much the same thing, according to Egyptian ideas, and a "scribe" was an official. In later times there were a host of scribes in each department—in the house of silver, to which 'Ennana and Qagabu belonged, there were at least nine,[3] and even the army was under bureaucratic government, the "scribe of the troops" being one of the chief officers.

There were also scribes who personally assisted the heads of the various departments, as *e.g.* the governor,[4] the "prince" of a town,[5] or the "superintendent of the house of silver";[6] these officials doubtless often exercised great influence as the representatives for their masters. The monarch also always had his private secretary; under the Old Empire we find the "scribe in the presence of the king,"[7] under the Middle Empire the "scribe witness in the presence of the king,"[8] and under the New Empire the "royal vassal and scribe of Pharaoh."[9]

The well-known proposition that what cannot be put into documental form does not exist was in force in Egyptian affairs, and the following phrase was therefore often added to business letters: "I write this to you, that it may serve as a witness between us, and you must keep this letter, that in future it may serve as a witness."[10] Copies also were made of certain deeds, so that original and copy might vouch for each other.[11] Nothing was given out by the treasury department without a written order, and even an official who wanted to take his *annual quantum* of fuel and coal from the treasury was not able to get it before the superintendent of the house of silver had given him a written order.[12] Full written details were also necessary; in vain a "chief of the militia" tried to obtain a number of serfs from the commander of the mercenaries; not one could be given up to him until he brought a list of names.[13] The chief entirely approved of these formalities. This punctiliousness extended to the smallest details; if oxen were borrowed for threshing, the driver had a list of the

[1] L. D., ii. 9. [2] Mar. Mast., 150, and many similar passages. [3] An., 4, 9, reverse side.
[4] Abb., 1, 11. [5] Abb., 6, 11.
[6] Abb., 1, 12, at the same time chief of a storehouse.
[7] E.g., Mar. Mast., 229. [8] Mar. Cat. d'Ab., 567, 627, 628, 630. [9] Abb., 2, 5.
[10] Mallet, 4, 6; An., 5, 14, 6. [11] Mallet, 6, 1, 11. Berlin Pap., 47 (Ä. Z., 1879).
[12] Mallet, 5, 6. [13] An., 5, 25, 6 ff.

cattle given to him [1] and if a workman received his ration of corn, a formal receipt was given to him with it.[2]

The scribe engrossed deeds in this wise: "to be copied" [3] or "to be kept in the archives of the governor." [4] The documents were then given into the care of the chief librarian [5] of the department they concerned, and he placed them in large vases and catalogued them carefully. Thus a librarian of the 20th dynasty records that he had examined two of his vases of books in the sixth year of the king.[6] The first of them contained (if I understand rightly) two accounts belonging to private people, which were kept in the archives; the protocol of a revision of the "wreaths" for the temple of Amon, and two large rolls and four small ones, containing deeds belonging to the temple of Ramses III.:

"Total number of rolls found in the vase of books . . . 9."

In the other vases were kept the deeds relating to the lawsuit against the tomb-robbers, of whom we shall have to speak in the following chapter. It contained the following documents:

"Receipt for the gold, silver, and copper which was found stolen by the workers in the necropolis . . .	1
The re-examination of the Pyramids	1
The trial of certain people found desecrating a tomb on the waste ground of the town	1
The examination of the pyramid of the king Rê'-sechem-mery-taue	1
The examination of the tomb of the governor Ser, carried out by the metal-worker U'ares	1
List of the copper goods stolen by the thieves in the Necropolis called 'Place of beauties'	1
The names of the thieves	1
The trial of Paiqaḥay, formerly controller, now out of office	1"

Two papyrus rolls now in the Berlin Museum were actually found in a vase.[7]

The above history of the development of the Egyptian empire could be much amplified by further research, especially with regard to the New Empire; the essential features would however remain unchanged. Instead therefore of giving further details, I propose to describe a number of incidents illustrative of the constitution of the Egyptian bureaucracy. They all refer to the officials of the New Empire, with whom however the servants of the old state had probably much in common with those of whom we shall now speak. I am chiefly indebted for these particulars

[1] An., 9, 3. [2] Ä. Z., 1880, 97. [3] Berlin Pap., 47. [4] Abbot, 7, 16.

[5] Keeper of archives to the treasury department, An., 6, 3, 12. Others Sall., 1, 3, 5, and frequently.

[6] Vienna papyrus edited by Brugsch, Ä. Z., 1876, pl. 1. My translation is untrustworthy in places, the text needing much revision. [7] Passalacqua, Catalogue raisonné, p. 207.

to the so-called didactic letters, *i.e.* the correspondence partly real, partly fictitious, between a tutor and his pupil, or, what comes to the same thing, between a higher official and his subordinate. It was the custom in the later period that whoever wished for an official career should first be placed under the supervision of a superintendent or a scribe of the treasury, not only to learn his practical work, but also for his education and intellectual training. It is evident that such a professional training would induce narrow views of life. The doctrine taught by these teachers was that the position of "scribe," *i.e.* the official position, stood above all others ; the latter resembled the donkey, while the scribe was as the driver who drove the heavily laden beast before him.[1] "His position is princely and his writing materials and books are sweet and rich ;"[2] for the industrious student attains to position, power, and riches.

Position, power, and riches could not indeed be won even by the most diligent, unless his superior, "his lord," as the Egyptians said, was pleased to bestow them upon him. The scribe was therefore obliged before all things to try and stand well with his chief, and for this purpose he followed the recipe, which has been in use during all ages : "Bend thy back before thy chief,"[3] taught the wise Ptaḥḥôtep of old, and the Egyptian officials conscientiously followed this maxim. Submission and humility towards their superior officers became second nature to them, and was expressed in all the formulas of official letter-writing. Whilst the chief writes to his subordinates in the most abrupt manner : "Do this or that, when you receive my letter," and rarely omits to add admonitions and threats, the subordinate bows down before him in humility. He does not dare to speak directly to him, and only ventures to write "in order to rejoice the heart of his master, that his master may know that he has fulfilled all the commissions with which he was intrusted, so that his master may have no cause to blame him." No one was excepted from writing in this style ; the scribe 'Ennana writes thus to "his master Qagabu, the scribe of the house of silver," and in the same way he assures "Parê'emḥeb the superintendent of the house of silver" of his respect.[4] Besides this official correspondence, personal submission and affection are also often expressed towards a superior, and a grateful young subordinate sends the following lines to his chief :[5]

> "I am as a horse pawing the ground,
> My heart awakes by day,
> And my eyes by night,
> For I desire to serve my master,
> As a slave who serves his master."

The manner in which he "serves his master" could surely have been carried out without these night watches ; he builds him a villa in his imagination, and describes it to him in twenty-four lines of poetry. In return, the duty of the chief towards his subordinate was to protect his rights from

1 Ä. Z., 1880, 96. 2 An., 5, 10, 8 = Sall., 1, 3, 10 ; cp. An., 5, 9, 5. 3 Prisse, 13, 9.
4 An., 4 pass. and An., 4, 16 reverse side, as well as An., 6. 5 An., 4, 8, 8.

the encroachments of others, *e.g.* a scribe, wronged by one of his colleagues, complains to his master that he was as if he had no chief, that he was without protection even as a widow.[1]

Manifold were the small troubles which had to be endured by the official in his career. A certain official trusting in the fact that his superior was a "servant of Pharaoh, standing below his feet," *i.e.* living at the court, ventured to depart a little from the instructions he had received touching a distant field in the provinces. But *his master*, hearing of it, sent a letter of admonition to the guilty official: "One of my servants (he wisely does not name the accuser) came and told me that you are acting dishonestly with regard to that part of my field which lies in the district of Ta- . . et-Rê'. What does it mean that you in this way violate my instructions?"[2] Well for the servant who got off so lightly, for it often happened that a "royal order was brought to him," *i.e.* that his reprimand came from the central authority. Thus it happened that a high official of the treasury did not sufficiently examine certain people (I cannot quite make out who are meant by the T'ektana) who came into Egypt out of the oasis; he allowed them to depart, and he then had to send one of his scribes to the oasis. This negligence was considered a great crime; it appeared incredible to the officials of the royal treasury that such was the state of the affair; they still hoped that the gods Rê' and Ptaḥ would hear a more satisfactory account. Yet "shouldst thou," as the prince wrote, "have allowed the T'ektana spies to have escaped, where wilt thou then turn? Into what house wilt thou flee? Like a sandstorm it would fall on thy head."[3] He was advised with threats to bring the matter into order, and immediately on receipt of "this writing of the Pharaoh" to his scribe, to send the swiftest courier to the oasis and to order him on pain of death to bring back one of the T'ektana.

A scribe had not only to fear severity from those above him, but also annoyances from his colleagues and his comrades. Each high official watched jealously that no one should meddle with his business, and that the lower officials should give up their accounts and the work of the serfs to him and not to one of his colleagues. He was always ready to regard small encroachments on his rights as criminal deviations from the good old customs, and to denounce them as such to the higher powers, and when not able to do this, he vexed his rival in every way that he could.[4]

Another misfortune which could always befall an official was to be sent to a bad locality. There were such in Egypt, and those who had to live in the oases or in the swamps of the Delta had good right to complain. A letter has come down to us[5] written by one of these unfortunate scribes to his superior; he was stationed in a place otherwise unknown to us—Qenqen-taue, which he said was bad in every respect. If he wished to

[1] An. 6, 3, 8-9.

[2] An. 5, 27, 3-7. The kind of dishonesty spoken of in the text I do not understand.

[3] An., 4, 10, 8 ff.

[4] Abbott and An., 6.

[5] An., 4, 12, 5 ff.

build, "there was no one to mould bricks, and there was no straw in the neighbourhood." What was he to do under these circumstances? "I spend my time," he complains, "in looking at what there is in the sky (*i.e.* the birds), I fish, my eye watches the road . . . I lie down under the palms, whose fruit is uneatable. Where are their dates? They bear none!" Otherwise also the food was bad; the best drink to be got was beer from Qede. Two things there were indeed in plenty in Qenqen-taue: flies and dogs. According to the scribe there were 500 dogs there, 300 wolf-hounds and 200 others; every day they came to the door of his house to accompany him on his walks. These were rather too many for him, though he was fond of two, so much so that, for want of other material to write about, he describes them fully in his letter. One was the little wolf-hound belonging to one of his colleagues; he ran in front of him barking when he went out. The other was a red dog of the same breed with an exceptionally long tail; he prowled round the stables at night. The scribe had not much other news to give from Qenqen-taue, except the account of the illness of one of his colleagues. Each muscle of his face twitches. "He has the Uashat'ete illness in his eyes. The worm bites his tooth." This might be in consequence of the bad climate.

Another scribe, a native of Memphis, writes how much he suffers from *ennui* and home-sickness in his present station; his heart leaves his body, it travels up-stream to his home. "I sit still," he writes, "while my heart hastens away, in order to find out how things are in Memphis. I can do no work. My heart throbs. Come to me Ptaḥ, and lead me to Memphis, let me but see it from afar."[1] He was indeed considered fortunate who escaped these unpleasant experiences, and remained at home, or was sent to the same station with his father; his friends all congratulated him. Thus Seramun, the chief of the mercenaries and of the foreigners, writes to Paḥripedt, the chief of the mercenaries, who has been sent to the same place in the Syrian desert where his father was already stationed: "I have received the news you wrote to me: the Pharaoh, my good lord, has shown me his good pleasure; 'the Pharaoh has appointed me to command the mercenaries of this oasis.' Thus didst thou write to me. Owing to the good providence of Rê', thou art now in the same place with thy father. Ah! bravo! bravo! I rejoiced exceedingly when I read thy letter. May it please Rê' Harmachis that thou shouldst long dwell in the place with thy father. May the Pharaoh do to thee according to thy desire. Mayest thou become ever more powerful; write to me I pray thee by the letter-carrier, who comes here from thee, and say how it goes with thee and with thy father."[2] That official was indeed happy, to whom the Pharaoh was thus well disposed, who "received rewards from the king, and was in favour with the king in his time."[3] The poet truly says of him:

"Thou dost live, thou art happy, thou hast good health,
Thou art neither in poverty nor in misery.

[1] An., 4, 4, 11 ff. [2] An., 5, 11, 7 ff. [3] An., 4, 4, 3.

Thou art as enduring as the hours—
Thy purposes endure, thy life is long—
Thy words are excellent.
Thine eye sees what is good,
Thou dost hear what is pleasant,
Thou seest good things, thou hearest pleasant things,
Thou standest firm, and thine enemy doth fall,
He who spake against thee is no more."[1]

Such good fortune does not befall men by chance, it is the gift of the great god Amon Rê'.[2] Qagabu, the scribe of the house of silver, trusted in him when, longing for promotion, he said: "Thou wilt find that Amon fulfils thy desire in his hour of graciousness. Thou art praised in the midst of the princes and dost stand firm in the place of truth. Amon Rê'! thy great Nile overflows even the mountains, he is the lord of the fish, rich in birds, all orphans are satisfied by him—therefore do thou promote princes to the place of princes, place the scribe Qagabu before Thoth, thy (scribe) of truth."[3]

"Visible tokens of recognition" (the modern synonym for orders of merit) were not wanting in this well-ordered state. As early as under the Middle Empire a high officer boasts that "the gold had been given to him as a reward,"[4] and this decoration became quite usual under the military government of the 18th dynasty.[5] The biographers of the generals of these warrior kings never forget to relate how many times the deceased received from his lord "the reward of the gold." A'ḥmose, son of 'Ebana the Admiral, was seven times "decorated with the gold"; the first time he received the "gold of valour" was as a youth in the fight against the Hyksos, the last time as an old man in the Syrian campaigns of Thothmes I. His contemporary, namesake, and fellow-countryman, the general A'ḥmose, was decorated with the gold by each of the kings under whom he fought, while Amenemḥeb, the general under Thothmes III., won it six times under this monarch. Each time it was "for valour"; he brought his captives from beyond the Euphrates, he captured Syrian chiefs, or at the head of the most daring he stormed a breach in the wall of a town.

What was this decoration, the possession of which was so coveted by the distinguished men of all times? It was not one simple decoration like our modern orders, or the "chains of honour" of the 16th century, but it consisted of valuable pieces of jewelry of different kinds. Thus the *gold*, which was "bestowed in the sight of all men," upon Amenemḥeb before Kadesh, consisted of a lion, three necklets, two bees, and four bracelets—all worked in the finest gold; the rewards, which he won some time later in the country of T'echse, consisted of the very

[1] An., 5, 14, 7-15, 5, with omissions. The closing lines also literally, An., 4, 3, 11.
[2] An., 4, 4, 2.
[3] An., 4, 10, 5 ff.
[4] L. D., ii. 138 a.
[5] For the bestowal of the "gold" compare the inscriptions of A'ḥmose (L. D., iii. 12 d.), of Amenemḥeb (Ä. Z., 1873, 1), of Paser (Ä. Z., 1883, 135), and especially of A'ḥmose Pennechebt (Prisse, Mon. 4 and Ä. Z., 1883, 78).

same objects again. Amenḥôtep I. bestowed the "gold" upon the general A'ḥmose in the form of four bracelets, one vessel for ointment, six bees, a lion, and two hatchets; Thothmes I. was still more generous, he gave him four golden bracelets, six golden necklets, three ointment vases of lapis-lazuli, and two silver clasps for the arms. We see that the value of the metal alone in such a present was very great, and yet the "reward of the gold" was valued more for its symbolic signification than for its intrinsic worth. The richest and the highest in the land vied with each other in order to be rewarded in solemn fashion by the king "before all the people, in the sight of the whole country." We do not know how the investiture was carried out in the camp, or on the battlefields of those warlike kings, but the remarkable tomb-pictures describing the court life of the heretic king Chu-en-'eten show us how the ceremony was conducted at home in time of peace.

The "divine father 'Ey" played a prominent part at court in the new town, the *Horizon of the Sun.*[1] He had not held high rank under the old hierarchy, but he had risen to be the confidant of the above king, perhaps owing to the active part he had taken in the royal efforts at reformation. He does not seem to have held high religious rank; at court he bore the title of "fan-bearer on the right side of the king," and of "royal truly loved scribe;" he had the care of all the king's horses, but in the hierarchy he never rose higher than the rank of "divine father," which he had held at the beginning of the reformation. His consort Tey helped him much in his advancement at court; she had been the nurse and instructress of the king.

It was natural that being such a favourite with the monarch he should receive public honours, and that the gold should be bestowed upon him. In fact he received this distinction at least twice; the first time was before his marriage with Tey.[2] In the representation he resorts to the palace of the king in a chariot escorted by numerous fan-bearers and servants. In the background of the picture we see his majesty with the queen on the balcony of the palace; they are respectfully greeted by the multitude. The king, turning to his treasurer, commands him to decorate 'Ey; "Put gold on his neck, and on his back, and gold on his feet, because he has heard the doctrine." The treasurer orders his servants to bring jewels of all descriptions, golden chains, necklets, and beautiful vases for ointment; and whilst he notifies on his writing-tablet how much the royal treasures are diminished on that day, his servants entwine the throat and neck of

[1] The representations of the gold-bestowal in the pictures in the two tombs of 'Ey; L.D., iii. 108-109 and L. D., iii. 103-105, referring to L. D., iii. 97. In the second representation the golden hands amongst the jewels should be noticed. See also Wilk., iii. pl. 64 of the 19th Dyn.

[2] It seems to me that there is no doubt that Tombs 1 and 3 of the southern tombs at Tell-el-Amarna belong to one and the same man; this is proved by the identity of name, title and time. First he had tomb No. 3 prepared for himself, but after his marriage he ordered the construction of tomb No. 1 with its more splendid pictures, for himself and his noble wife. In addition to these, later as king of Thebes, he built for himself a third tomb, in which also his body was destined to find no repose!

'Ey with chains of gold. 'Ey raises his arms rejoicing, and the king nods to him pleasantly from the balcony. On this day also the provision house of the king was spoiled for the sake of 'Ey; for the king ordered vases of wine and great quantities of food to be taken to the house of his favourite.

When 'Ey received the *gold* for the second time, he was the husband of Tey, and we see, by the manner in which it was awarded him this time, that he was nearly connected with the royal house by his marriage. It was now with royal pomp that the carriages of the distinguished bride and bridegroom were conducted to the palace; companies of runners and fan-bearers escorted them, Syrian and Nubian soldiers formed their bodyguard, and 'Ey even brought ten scribes with him, to write down the gracious words with which his lord would honour him.

(After L. D., iii. 108.)

Now when 'Ey and Tey came below the royal balcony, they received an honour far beyond their expectation: the king did not call upon his treasurer to adorn them, but he himself, his wife, and his children, wished as a personal favour to bestow the gold decoration upon these faithful servants of his house. Leaning on the coloured cushions of the balustrade of the balcony, the monarch threw necklets down to them; the queen, with the youngest princess 'Anchesenpa'eten in her arms, threw down chains of gold, and the two older princesses, Meryt-'eten and M'aket-'eten, shared in the game and scattered bracelets. Showers of jewels were poured out over 'Ey and Tey; they were not able to carry them, still less to wear them all. 'Ey wore seven thick necklets and nine heavy bracelets; the servants had to carry the rest to his home. The crowd broke out into shouts of praise when they saw the graciousness of the monarch, and the boys who had followed 'Ey danced and jumped for joy. Proudly the happy pair returned home, and the rejoicing which arose there when they came in sight was indeed great. Their servants came joyfully to meet them; they kissed 'Ey's feet with rapture, and threw themselves in the dust before the gifts of the king. So loud were the shouts of joy that they were heard even by the old porters, who were squatting before the back buildings far away from the door. They asked each other in surprise: "What mean these shouts of joy?"

And one of them said to his boy: "Runner, go and see what this great rejoicing means." "I go, I go," said the boy, and he soon returned with the news, "They are rejoicing over 'Ey, the divine father, and over Tey; they have become creatures of gold!" Thus every one rejoiced on this "beautiful occasion."

This custom of giving presents as a mark of esteem and honour was in vogue for a long time: towards the close of the 20th dynasty we hear of a certain Pennut, who ruled over a district of Nubia, and who through the instrumentality of the governor of Nubia received two silver bowls of precious ointment as a mark of high distinction.[1]

Owing to the power and to the gifts bestowed by the favour of the king, riches now began to make their appearance amongst the officials; and whoever could afford it, indulged in a beautiful villa, a fine carriage, a splendid boat, numerous negroes,—as lackeys, servants, and house officials,—gardens and cattle, costly food, good wine, and rich clothing.[2] The following example will give an idea of the riches which many Egyptian grandees gained in this way. It was an old custom in Egypt, which has lasted down to modern days, that on New Year's Day "the house should give gifts to its lord."[3] Representations in the tomb of a high official of the time of Amenḥôtep II. (his name is unfortunately lost) show us the gifts he made to the king as a "New Year's present."[4] "There are carriages of silver and gold, statues of ivory and ebony, collarettes of all kinds, jewels, weapons, and works of art." The statues represent the king and his ancestors, in various positions and robes, or in the form of sphinxes with the portrait head of the monarch. Amongst the weapons are axes, daggers, and all manner of shields, there are also coats of mail, several hundred leather quivers of various shapes, 680 shields of the skin of some rare animal, 30 clubs of ebony overlaid with gold and silver, 140 bronze daggers and 360 bronze sickle-shaped swords, 220 ivory whip-handles inlaid with ebony, etc. In addition, numerous vases of precious metal in curious Asiatic forms, two large carved pieces of ivory representing gazelles with flowers in their mouths, and finally there is the *chef-d'œuvre* in the form of a building overgrown with fantastic plants bearing gigantic flowers, amongst which tiny monkeys chase each other. This was probably part of a kind of service for the table in precious metal.

The splendid Theban tombs in which the chiefs of the bureaucracy of the New Empire rest, give us also the same idea of great riches. There were of course comparatively few of the officials who rose to such distinction; the greater number had to live on their salaries, which consisted as a rule of payment in kind—corn, bread, beer, geese, and various other necessaries of life, which are "registered in the name" of the respective official.[5] We hear, however, of payments in copper also; a letter from Amenem'epet to his student Paibasa assigns to the former 50

[1] L. D., iii. 229, 230.
[2] An., 4, 3, 2 ff.
[3] Inscription of Siut: Ä. Z., 1882, 164, 177.
[4] L. D., iii. 63, 64.
[5] An., 1, 11, 8-12, 5.

Uten (*i.e.* about $4\frac{1}{2}$ Kilo) of copper "for the needs of the serfs of the temple of Heliopolis."[1]

It seems, however, that the storehouses of ancient Egypt were scarcely better supplied than the coffers of the modern country; we have at any rate in the letters of that time many complaints of default of payment. A servant named Amenemu'e complains to the *princes* that "in spite of all promises no provisions are supplied in the temple in which I am, no bread is given to me, no geese are given to me."[2] A poor chief workman only receives his corn after he has "said daily for ten days 'Give it I pray.'"[3] The supplies might indeed often await the courtesy or the convenience of a colleague. "What shall I say to thee?" complains a scribe: "give ten geese to my people, yet thou dost not go to that white bird nor to that cool tank. Though thou hast not many scribes, yet thou hast very many servants. Why then is my request not granted?"[4]

To supplement his salary the official had often the use of certain property belonging to the crown. In this matter proceedings were very lax, and the widow of an official generally continued to use the property after her husband's death. In fact, in one case, when the mother of an official died, who had had the use of one of the royal carriages, the son tried to obtain permission from his chief, for his sister who had been left a widow a year before, to use the aforesaid carriage. Although his superior did not at once agree to the request, yet he did not directly refuse him; he told him that if he would visit him when on his journey, he would then see what he could do.[5]

There is the reverse side to this apparent generosity of the Egyptian government; it is evident that he who uses state property is bound to pay a certain percentage of what it enables him to earn; he only holds it in pledge.

The greater part of the harvests which the peasant-serfs reaped from the treasury lands, as well as the material woven or spun by their wives, belonged of course to the state, and was collected mercilessly. However bad the harvest might have been, the scribe came to the peasants' houses accompanied by negroes with sticks; he demanded the corn, it was no use for them to say that they had none; they were beaten nearly to death by the negroes.[6] Even from those who did not belong to the class of serfs, a tax was as stringently *demanded*,[7] and the scribe of the governor even broke into the house of the woman Takaret, who would not give up the firstling of her cow.[8] These taxes were paid as unwillingly then as they are now, and many of the people thought that they paid far more than was right. The appeal, which the servant Amenemu'e made to the *princes* has come down to us. The servant Thothmes of the temple of Thoth had, during the four years from the 31st to the 34th year, required of him as follows:[9]

[1] An., 3, 6, 11 ff. [2] Mallet, 2, 5 ff. [3] Ä. Z., 1880, 97.
[4] An., 5, 11, 2-6. [5] Tur., 16. Cp. also An., 5, 14, 5, "the ass of Pharaoh."
[6] An., 5, 15, 6 ff. = Sall., 1, 5, 11 ff. [7] The word here is *shed*. [8] An., 5, 14, 1 ff.
[9] Mallet, 1, 1 ff. Certain details of this translation are hypothetical.

Skins, raw, 4 pieces, worth in copper 8 Uten.
Skins, made up into coats of mail, 1 piece, worth in copper 5 Uten.
Stick, prop-stick, inlaid work, 1 piece, worth in copper 4 Uten.
Stick, scrape stick, 1 piece, worth in copper 1 Uten.
Paper, 1 strip.
Paper, 1 roll.
Hoe 1, worth in copper 2 Uten.
Corn, $2\frac{3}{4}$ bushels.
Meal, do.
Paper, 1 roll.

In the 4th year he had again to supply three strips of paper and four Uten of copper; on an average therefore, he had to pay five Uten (about $\frac{1}{2}$ Kilo) of copper in the year—a considerable sum for a servant. This was the harder for him because, as he bitterly complains, the provisions with which the state ought to supply him did not come in. This does not seem to have been at all unusual. The supplies provided by the state might be detained on the way, and might never come into the hands of the rightful owner, but if the gift were entered to his name, the duty charged upon it was nevertheless required from him. Thus, *e.g.*, a shepherd of the name of Thothmes lost a donkey, and a certain Pa'ere, who ought to have given it up, had chosen on some pretext to keep the useful animal. Thothmes therefore wrote him the following letter of admonition:

"Channa, the officer of the company *Shining as the Sun* stationed in the country of D'aper, gave thee a donkey and told thee to give it to Thothmes. But thou hast not given it to me. Then I seized thee when thou wast at Memphis with Amenmose the chief of the stable, and said to thee: 'Give it to me.' Thou didst then say to me: 'Take me not before the judgment; I have the donkey, but if thou dost send to fetch it, I will not give it up.' Thus thou didst say, and thou didst swear by the life of thy lord that thou wouldst cause it to be brought to me. Behold, however, thou hast not sent it to me, and now they demand from me the work of the donkey, year by year, while it has been with thee."[1]

The *work* of the donkey here spoken of is the tax which Thothmes had to pay for the use of the animal.

To each of the great departments in Egypt belonged artisans and labourers, who were divided into "companies." We meet with one of these companies [hieroglyphs] on the domains of the rich proprietors of the Old Empire, and, headed by their banner-bearer, we see them reviewed by the great lord. The rowers of each great ship formed a *company*, and even the genii who conducted the bark of the sun through the night bore this name. The workmen of the temple and of the necropolis were organised in the same way; the Egyptian official always thought of the lower orders merely as a crowd—one single workman did not exist for him

[1] Ä. Z., 1881, 118.

any more than one single soldier exists in the mind of our chief officers. They were only considered *en masse;* the criminal courts alone had to do with them as individuals. In speaking of an individual workman, we must always add the name of the chief under whom he worked and that of the department to which he belonged: "the workman Userchopesh, under the chief workman Nachtemḥê't of the Necropolis."[1] I scarcely know whether serfs were included in these companies of workmen; as a rule there seems to be a distinction between the workmen and the bond-servants of the temple or necropolis. Artisans were also sometimes bond-slaves, *e.g.* the "metal-worker Paicharu of the western town, bondservant of the house of Ramses III. in the temple of Amon, subject to the first prophet of Amon Rê‘,"[2] or the "artist Setnacht" of the same temple, "subject to the second prophet of Amon Rê‘."[3] The artisans, however, were not generally reckoned in the department of the *companies* of workmen; the serfs had to carry water, catch fish, cut wood, fetch fodder, and do similar work.[4]

At the head of each company of workmen stood the chief workman, who bore the title of "Chief of the Company"; he was not very much above his people, for we have an instance of a man, who in one place is designated simply as a "workman," and in another more precisely as "chief workman."[5] He was nevertheless proud of his position and endeavoured, like the higher officials, to bequeath his office to one of his sons.[6] However unimportant his position might be, he was at any rate a great personage to his workmen. He carefully kept notes in a book about their diligence. On a rough tablet of chalk in the British Museum[7] a chief workman has written down the names of his forty-three workmen and, by each name, the days of the month on which the man failed to appear. Many were of exemplary industry, and rarely missed a day throughout the year; less confidence could be placed in others, who failed more than a fortnight. Numberless are the excuses for the missing days, which the chief workman has written down in red ink; the commonest is of course *ill,* in a few instances we find *lazy* noted down. A few workmen are *pious* and "are sacrificing to the god"; sometimes a slight indisposition of wife or daughter is considered a valid reason for neglect of work.

We have some exact details about the conduct of a *company* of workmen, who were employed in the City of the Dead at Thebes, in the time of Ramses IX. We do not know precisely what their employment was, but they seem to have been metal-workers, carpenters, and similar craftsmen. Their chief kept a book[8] with great care, and entered everything remarkable that happened to his *company* during the half-year.

[1] Abb., 6, 5. [2] Abb., 4, 13. [3] Amh., 4, 4.

[4] Cp. the interesting list of the serfs of the Necropolis: Tur. 35-38.

[5] Abb., 5, 13 and 6, 5.

[6] In the Pap. Salt we read of a son of a chief workman who succeeded his father.

[7] Inscriptions in the hieratic character, T. 20, 21.

[8] Turin papyrus edited by Lieblein. Two hieratic papyri in the museum of Turin, ib. the translation of Chabas.

He also noted each day whether the men had "worked" or had been "idle." For two full months (from the 5th of Phamenoth to the 11th of Pachons) no work was required, though by permission the time was registered as working days; during the next two months also half the time was kept as a festival. Nevertheless the workmen did not suffer owing to lack of work, they received their rations each day whether they worked or not. Four times in the month they seem to have received from different officials a larger allowance (perhaps 200-300 kgrm.) of fish, which appears to have formed their chief food. Each month they also received a portion of some pulse vegetable, and a number of *jugs*, which may have contained oil and beer, also some fuel and some corn. With regard however to the latter there is a story to tell. It is one of the acknowledged characteristics of modern Egypt that payments can never be made without delays, so also in old Egypt the same routine seems to have been followed with respect to the payments in kind. The letters and the documents of the officials of the New Empire are full of complaints, and if geese and bread were only given out to the scribes after many complaints and appeals, we may be sure that still less consideration was shown to the workmen. The supply of corn was due to our *company* on the 28th of each month; in the month of Phamenoth it was delivered one day late, in Pharmuthi it was not delivered at all, and the workmen therefore went on strike, or, as the Egyptians expressed it, "stayed in their homes." On the 28th of Pachons the corn was paid in full, but on the 28th of Payni no corn was forthcoming and only 100 pieces of wood were supplied. The workmen then lost patience, they "set to work," and went in a body to Thebes. On the following day they appeared before "the great princes" and "the chief prophets of Amon," and made their complaint. The result was that on the 30th the great princes ordered the scribe Chaemuêse to appear before them, and said to him: "Here is the corn belonging to the government, give out of it the corn-rations to the people of the necropolis." Thus the evil was remedied, and at the end of the month the journal of the workman's *company* contains this notice: "We received to-day our corn-rations; we gave two boxes and a writing-tablet to the fan bearer." It is easy to understand the meaning of the last sentence; the boxes and the writing-tablet were given as a present to an attendant of the governor, who persuaded his master to attend to the claims of the workmen.

The condition of the workmen of the necropolis was just as deplorable in the 29th year of Ramses III.; they were almost always obliged to enforce the payment of every supply of the food owing to them by a strike of work. On these occasions they left the City of the Dead with their wives and children, and threatened never to return unless their demands were granted. Documents have come down to us showing that at this time the sad state of things went on for half a year. The month Tybi passed without the people receiving their supplies; they seem to have been accustomed to such treatment, for they waited full nine days before again pushing affairs to extremities. They then lost patience, and on the 10th of Mechir "they crossed the five walls of the necropolis and said: 'We have been starving for 18 days:' they placed themselves behind the temple of Thothmes III." In vain the scribes of the necropolis and the two chiefs of the workmen tried to entice them back by "great oaths," the workmen were wise and remained outside. The next day they proceeded further, even as far as the gate at the southern corner of the temple of Ramses II.; on the third day they even penetrated into the building. The affair assumed a threatening aspect, and on that day two officers of the police were sent to the place. The priests also tried to pacify the workmen, but their answer was: "We have been driven here by hunger and thirst; we have no clothes, we have no oil, we have no food. Write to our lord the Pharaoh on the subject, and write to the governor who is over us, that they may give us something for our sustenance." Their efforts were successful: "on that day they received the provision for the month Tybi." On the 13th of Mechir they went back into the necropolis with their wives and children. Peace was re-established,[1] but did not last long; in fact only a month. Again in Phamenoth the workmen crossed the wall of the City of the Dead, and driven *by hunger* they approached the gate of the town. Here the governor treated with them in person; he asked them (if I understand rightly) what he could give them when the storehouses were empty; at the same time he ordered half at least of the rations that were overdue to be paid down to them.[2]

In the month of Pharmuthi the supplies seem to have been duly given out, for our documents mention no revolt; but in Pachon the workmen suffered again from want. On the second day of the latter month two bags of spelt were remitted as the supply for the whole month; we cannot be surprised at their resenting this reduction in their payment, and at their resolution to go down themselves to the corn warehouse in the harbour. They only got as far as the first wall of the City of the Dead; there the scribe Amennachtu assured them he would give them the rest of the spelt if they remained quiet; they were credulous enough to return. Naturally they did not receive their corn now any more than before, and they were obliged again to "cross the walls," after which the "princes of the town" interfered, and on the 13th of the month ordered fifty sacks of spelt to be given to them.[3]

We see that in Egypt, to a certain extent, these workmen played the part of our proletariat. We must not, however, imagine that their life was a very wretched one. On the contrary, the workman had his wife, or more frequently a friend who lived with him as his wife; he had his own house, sometimes indeed situated in the barren necropolis, and often he even had his own tomb. He was educated to a certain degree, as a rule he could read and write, and when speaking to his superiors, he frequently expressed himself in high-flown poetic language.[4] At the same

[1] Tur., 42, 43, 2-5, 48, 17-23.

[2] Tur., 43, 6 ff., 44, 45, 1-5.

[3] Tur., 45, 6 ff. 46.

[4] Abb., 6, 5 ff.

time we cannot deny that his written attempts are badly expressed and present an inextricable confusion of sentences.

The morality of the workmen has little to rest upon, if we may believe the long accusations which they prefer against each other. The chief workman Paneb'e, under King Sety II., must have been exceptionally bad.[1] He stole everything that came in his way: the wine for the libations, a strap from a carriage, and a valuable block of stone; the latter was found in his house, although he had sworn that he had not got it. Once he stole a tool for breaking stones, and when, after searching for it vainly for two months, "they said to him: 'It is not there,' he brought it back and hid it behind a great stone. . . . When he stationed men to cut stones on the roof of the building of King Sety II., they stole some stone every day for his tomb, and he placed four pillars of this stone in his tomb." In other ways also he provided cheaply for the equipment of his tomb, and for this object he stole "two great books" from a certain Paḥerbeku, doubtless containing chapters from the Book of the Dead. He was not ashamed even to clear out the tomb of one of his subordinates. "He went down into the tomb of the workman Nachtmin, and stole the couch on which he lay. He also took the various objects, which are usually provided for the deceased, and stole them." Even the tools which he used for the work of his tomb were royal property.

He continually turned his workmen to account in various ways for private purposes: once he lent them to an official of the temple of Amon, who was in need of field labourers; he commissioned a certain Nebnofr to feed his oxen morning and evening, and he made the wives of the workmen weave for him. He was also charged with extortions of all kinds, especially from the wives and daughters of his workmen. He was guilty also of cruelty: once he had some men soundly bastinadoed in the night; he then took refuge on the top of a wall, and threw bricks at them.

The worst of all was his conduct to the family of the chief workman Nebnofr. While the latter was alive, he seems to have lived in enmity with him, and after his death, he transferred his hatred to the two sons, especially to Neferḥôtep, who succeeded his father in his office. He even made an attempt on his life. "It came to pass that he ran after the chief workman Neferḥôtep . . . the doors were shut against him, but he took up a stone and broke open the door, and they caused people to guard Neferḥôtep, for Paneb'e had said that he would in truth kill him in the night; in that night he had nine people flogged, and the chief workman Neferḥôtep reported it to the governor Amenmose and he punished him." Paneb'e, however, extricated himself from this affair, and finally he seems to have made away with Neferḥôtep; notwithstanding this he appears to have lived on in peace, because, if we may believe the accusations against him, he killed those who could have borne witness against him.

[1] See the complaint against him in the Salt Pap. Another similar complaint of one workman against another, Turin Pap. 47/48. I have tried in my translation to imitate the awkward style which is so characteristic of this text.

We find, as we have said above, that as a rule these free or semi-free workmen always formed *companies*, while the bondservants belonging respectively to the temple or to the necropolis[1] and the peasant-serfs on the estates were really organised in a military manner, and were reckoned as part of the army.[2] They had their officers of different grades, some of whom were chosen from their own ranks; they were led by standard-bearers, who were certainly chosen out of the soldiers.[3] We cannot doubt that these men were *slaves* in our sense of the word, and that they formed part of the property of the crown or of the temple as much as the land or the cattle. Their names were entered in a register by the officials of the house of silver, who travelled about for this purpose accompanied by an officer and his soldiers,[4] who branded them with the seal of the department.[5] These slaves were despised by the scribes, who said they were without *heart*, *i.e.* without understanding, and that therefore they had to be driven with a stick like cattle. The following verses refer to the slaves:

"The poor child is only brought up
That he may be torn from his mother's arms;
As soon as he comes to man's estate
His bones are beaten like those of a donkey;
He is driven, he has indeed no heart in his body."

The scribe has to provide for these slaves:

"He takes the lists of them in his hand,
He makes the oldest amongst them the officer,
The youngest of them he makes the bugler."[6]

Many of these slaves were prisoners of war; they were handed over from the booty, and sent wherever they were wanted. They were passed on from one department to another, just as if they had been oxen or donkeys, and occasionally the same fate befell them as sometimes befalls oxen or donkeys as they pass through the hands of different officials; they disappeared and left no trace. There lived, for instance, a prophet of the temple of Thoth named Ramses, to whom the crown had given a Syrian slave to use as a labourer, yet the latter never came into his possession; he was lost on the way. Ramses then besought his son to take up the matter, and to find out where the slave was. Bekenamun, his son, the libation scribe, exerted himself so energetically that he was

1 *Smdt* of the temple: An., 4, 4, 9 and many other examples; of the Necropolis: Abb., 5, 11; Tur., 37, 2.

2 Brugsch shows, Wb. Suppl. p.v., that *'eu'ait* means the peasantry. A *u'au* of the latter: P.j.T., 6, 4. A "standard-bearer" of the latter P.j.T., 2, 4. "Superintendent of the peasantry": An., 3, 5, 5 Rs. and often as officers in the wars.

3 Similar officers of the serfs: Brugsch, Wb. Suppl., p. 579. An., 5, 10, 5 f. also standard-bearers: Abb. 7, 5.

4 An., 4, 4, 8 ff. An., 5, 10, 5 f. An., 5, 7, 6. An., 6, 2, 11, 3, 5.

5 An., 5, 7, 6; Harr., I. 77, 5, as to the custom of branding, cp. An., 5, 10, 1; and what Brugsch alleges Ä. Z., 1876, p. 35 ff.

6 Both of these passages are from An., 5, 10, 3 ff. = Sall. 1, 3, 5 ff.

able at any rate to send his father the following rather unsatisfactory answer:

"I have made inquiries about the Syrian, who belonged to the temple of Thoth, and about whom thou didst write to me. I have ascertained that he was appointed field-labourer to the temple of Thoth, and placed under thee in the third year on the 10th of Payni. He belonged to the galley slaves brought over by the commandant of the fortress. His Syrian name is Naqatey, he is the son of Sarurat'a, and his mother's name is Qede; he comes from the country of Artu and was galley slave on the ship of Kenra, the captain of the galley. His guard told me that Cha'em'epet, officer of the royal peasantry, took charge of him, in order to send him on. I hastened to Cha'em'epet, the officer of the royal serfs, but he pretended to be deaf, and said to me: The governor Meryti-Sechemt took charge of him to send him on. I therefore hastened to the governor Meryti-Sechemt, and he with his scribes pretended to be deaf, and said: We have not seen him! I then went to the officer at Chmunu and said to him: I pray thee to order that the Syrian field-labourer, whom thou didst receive for the temple of Thoth, should be sent to the prophet. I shall sue him before the high court of law."[1]

Let us in conclusion briefly state what we know or surmise about the social conditions under the New Empire. The landed property was partly in the hands of the state, partly in those of the priesthood; it was tilled by peasant-serfs; there seem to have been no private estates belonging to the nobility, at any rate not under the 19th dynasty. The lower orders consisted mostly of serfs and foreign slaves, the higher of officials in the service of the state or of the temples. Between these two extremes there was certainly a middle class of artisans and shopmen, but they came little to the fore. It is only owing to the fact that many stelae exist, on which the names of the deceased are inscribed without any titles, that we know there must have been well-to-do people, who were not state officials. These may have been the "people of the country,"[2] whose wives are entitled the "dwellers in the town."[3]

We cannot now determine whether they, as well as the priests, officials, and soldiers, played an important part in the development of their country. One fact however is clear to our eyes: the bad administration, which still distinguishes modern Egypt, the extravagance of the upper classes, the extreme poverty of the lower, all this is of ancient date. The same king Ramses III. who gave 185,000 sacks of corn yearly to the temples,[4] was often unable to hand over fifty sacks a month to his starving workmen in the necropolis. The stereotyped appeals: "We hunger, no provision is given to us,"[5] form a sad commentary to the vainglorious phraseology of the inscriptions, which speak of the might and of the riches of the king.

[1] Bologna 1086, l. 9 ff.; many details uncertain.

[2] Abb., 4, 1.

[3] Ib. and many examples.

[4] This calculation is taken from Harr., I.

[5] Tur., 76, 6.

TOMBS IN THE NECROPOLIS, FROM A STELE AT GIZEH.

CHAPTER VII

THE POLICE AND THE COURTS OF JUSTICE

THE documents of the great lawsuit under King Ramses IX. (about 1100 B.C.), against the bands of thieves in the Theban city of the dead, give us a distinct picture of the work of the government police under the 20th dynasty, of how crime was tracked, and how trials of suspected persons were conducted.[1] This *cause célèbre* (for such it certainly was) has a special attraction for us, from the fact that it throws a sidelight upon the many disagreements and intrigues that went on in the heart of the government of the capital; the acts of this lawsuit form therefore a good sequel to the description of the Egyptian bureaucracy, which I have drawn up in the preceding chapter.

The *Governor* was, as I remarked above, at the head of the government in the capital; at the same time it was of course impossible that he should concern himself about the various details. For each half of the town, he had therefore as his subordinate a *prince*, who carried on the duties of the old Theban nomarch. The eastern part, the city proper, was under the "prince of the town," the western part, the city of the dead, under the "prince of the west," or the "chief of the police of the necropolis."

At the time of our lawsuit the higher office was held by a certain *Paser*, the lower by a certain *Paser'a*, and as is not unusual even now with colleagues at the head of two adjacent departments, they lived in open enmity with each other. Their enmity was no secret; and if a discontented subordinate of Paser'a thought he observed anything wrong in the city of the dead, he went to Paser and related the tittle-tattle to him, as a contribution to the materials which he was collecting against his colleague.[2] When therefore in the 16th year important thefts were perpetrated in the necropolis, it was not only Paser'a, the ruler of the city of the dead, who, as in duty bound, gave information to the governor,

[1] For the following, cp. Pap. Abbott, Pap. Amherst, also my work upon these documents: Ä. Z. 1879, 81 ff. 148 ff.

[2] Abb. 5, 16. 6, 21.

but Paser also, the prince of the town, did not let slip this opportunity of denouncing his colleague to the chiefs in council. It is characteristic of the sort of evidence presented by Paser that precisely that royal tomb which he declared to have been robbed was found at the trial to be uninjured: evidently his accusation rested on mere hearsay.

The court of justice, before which both princes had to give their evidence, consisted of "Cha'emuêse, the superintendent of the town and governor," assisted by two other high officials, the *scribe* and the *speaker* of Pharaoh, or according to their full titles: "the royal vassal Nesamun, scribe of Pharaoh and chief of the property of the high-priestess of Amon Rê', king of the gods;" and "the royal vassal Neferkerê'-em-per-Amun, the speaker of Pharaoh."

When these three *great princes* heard of the attempt on the *great noble necropolis*, they sent out a commission of inquiry on the 18th Athyr to investigate the matter on the spot; for this commission they appointed not only the prince of the necropolis himself and two of his police officers, but also a scribe of the governors, a scribe belonging to the treasury department, two high priests, and other confidential persons, who were assisted in their difficult task by the police. As inspectors[1] these officials went through the desert valleys of the city of the dead carefully examining each tomb which was suspected. The result is related in the following document which enumerates the "pyramids and mummy-pits examined on this day by the inspectors."

"(1) The *eternal horizon* of King Amenḥôtep I., having a depth of 130 yards, lying to the north of the garden-temple of Amenḥôtep, which was supposed to have been broken into by thieves, according to the evidence given by Paser to the governor Cha'emuêse, the town-superintendent; to the royal vassal Nesamun, the scribe of Pharaoh, the chief of the property of the high-priestess of Amon Rê', king of the gods; and to the royal vassal Neferke Rê'-em-per-Amun, the speaker to Pharaoh; the great princes—

"Examined this day:

"It was found uninjured by the inspectors.

"(2) The pyramid of the king: the son of Rê' 'Entef the great, lying to the north of the court of the temple of Amenḥôtep, the pyramid itself being in ruins, and a stele having been placed in front of it, on which is represented the king with his dog Beḥka at his feet—

"Examined this day:

"It was found uninjured.

"(3) The pyramid of King 'Entef. It was found that a boring had been made by the thieves, they had made a hole of 2½ yards at the *base* (?) and had thus made their way out of the outer hall of the ruined tomb of 'Euray, superintendent of the sacrifices to Amon:

[1] The [hieroglyphs] may be officers of control; An. 4, 7, 7, they receive the wine supplied by the vineyards of the temple of Amon. This is also the opinion of Chabas.

"It was uninjured, the thieves had not been able to penetrate into the interior.

"(4) The pyramid of the king 'Entef the great. It was found that a boring had been made by the thieves at the place where the stele stands—

"Examined this day:

"It was found uninjured, the thieves had not been able to effect an entrance.

"(5) The pyramid of the king Sebekemsaf. It was found that the thieves had bored a mine and penetrated into the mummy chamber; they had made their way out of the outer hall of the tomb of Nebamun, the superintendent of food under Thothmes III. It was found that the king's burial-place had been robbed of the monarch; in the place also where the royal consort Nubch'as was buried, the thieves had laid hands on her.

"The governor and the prince-vassals ordered a thorough examination to be made, and it was proved exactly by what means the thieves had laid hands on this king and on his royal consort."

This was, however, the only pyramid that had really been broken into; all the other royal tombs were uninjured, and the scribe was able with pride to draw up this sum total at the bottom of the deed:

"Pyramids of the royal ancestors, examined this day by the inspectors:

Found uninjured, Pyramids	9
Found broken into, Pyramids	1
Total	10"

Matters had gone worse with the tombs of private individuals: of the four tombs of the distinguished "singers of the high-priestess of Amon Rê' king of the gods," two had been broken into, and of the other private tombs we read—"It was found that they had all been broken into by the thieves, they had torn the lords (*i.e.* the bodies) out of their coffins and out of their bandages, they had thrown them on the ground, they had stolen the household stuff which had been buried with them, together with the gold, silver, and jewels found in their bandages." These were however only private tombs; it was a great comfort that the royal tombs were uninjured. The commission sent in their report at once to the *great princes.* At the same time the prince of the necropolis gave in to the prince-vassals the names of the supposed thieves, who were immediately taken into custody. The lawsuit against them did not give much trouble.

There were eight thieves who had violated the tomb of King Sebekemsaf, most of them were servants in the temple of Amon. Amongst them were masons, and apparently these had forced the subterranean way into the interior of the tomb. They "were examined," that is "they were beaten with sticks both on their hands and feet;" under the influence of this cruel bastinado they confessed that they had made their way into the pyramid and had found the bodies of the king and queen there. They said: "We then opened the coffins and bandages in which they lay. We found the noble mummy of the king . . . with a long chain of golden amulets and ornaments round the neck ; the head was covered with gold. The noble mummy of this king was entirely overlaid with gold, and his (coffin) was covered both inside and out with gold, and adorned with precious jewels. We tore off the gold, which we found on the noble mummy of this *god*, as well as the amulets and ornaments from round the neck, and the bandages in which the mummy was wrapped. We found the royal consort equipped in like manner, and we tore off all that we found upon her. We burnt her bandages, and we also stole the household goods which we found with them, and the gold and silver vessels. We then divided all between us ; we divided into eight parts the gold which we found with this *god*, the mummies, the amulets, the ornaments, and the bandages."

This public confession was not enough ; the thieves were also obliged to identify the scene of their crime—there seems to have been a law to this effect. The governor and the royal vassal Nesamun commanded the criminals to be taken in their presence, on the 19th of Athyr, to the necropolis where they identified the pyramid of Sebekemsaf as that to which their confession referred. Their guilt being finally established, the *great princes* had now done all they could in the case, for the sentence of punishment had to be pronounced by the Pharaoh himself, to whom they, together with the princes of the town, at once sent the official report of the examination. Meanwhile the thieves were given over to the high priest of Amon, to be confined in the prison of the temple "with their fellow thieves."

The examination of the city of tombs was however not yet concluded ; fresh suspicions arose which had to be followed up. A man of bad repute, who three years before had been *examined* by a predecessor of the present governor, had lately confessed at an *examination* that he had been into the tomb of Ese, the wife of Ramses II. and had stolen something out of it. This was the "metal-worker Peicharu, son of Charuy and of Mytshere, of the west side of the town, bondservant of the temple of Ramses III. under Amenḥôtep, the first prophet of Amon Rê‘ king of the gods." He belonged to the dregs of the populace, as is shown by the name of his mother, which signifies *little cat*. Suspicion was thus aroused that the part of the necropolis in which the nearest relatives of the king were buried (called *the place of beauties*) had been visited by the thieves, and the great princes resolved to sift the matter thoroughly. They therefore caused the metal-worker to be blindfolded and carried in their presence to the necropolis. "When they arrived there, they unbandaged his eyes, and the princes said to him : 'Go before us to the grave out of which, as thou dost say, thou hast stolen something.' The metal-worker went to one of the graves of the children of the great god King Ramses II., which stood open, and in which no one had ever been buried, and to the house of the workman Amenem'ent, son of Ḥuy of the necropolis, and he said : 'Behold, these are the places in which I have been.' Then the princes ordered him to be thoroughly examined (*i.e.* bastinaded) in the great valley, and they found nevertheless that he knew of no other place besides these two places which he had pointed out. He swore that they might cut off his nose and his ears, or flay him alive, but that he knew of no other place than this open tomb and this house, which he had shown to them.

"The princes examined the tombs and the large chambers in the *place of the beauties* in which the beautiful royal children, the royal consorts, the royal mothers and fathers of the mothers of the Pharaoh rest. They were found uninjured." The joy of the princes was great, for the matter was not nearly as bad as had been represented. In order to put an end to all the reports which were current in the town on the subject, they at once sent a "great embassy to the town consisting of the inspectors, the chiefs of the workmen of the necropolis, the officers of the police, the police, and all the bondservants of the necropolis of western Thebes."

We can well imagine that this *embassy* was of a rather tumultuous character, and that those who believed in the maladministration of the necropolis were little pleased at this demonstration. One high official was especially vexed with it, Paser, the chief of the government of the town proper—"the prince of the town" whose enmity towards Paser'a, the prince of the necropolis, has been mentioned above. Part of the information which had led to the examination of the necropolis had been sent directly by him; he had maintained officially that the tomb of Amenḥôtep I. had been robbed. The contrary was now established, and with the exception of the one pyramid of Sebekemsaf, all the royal tombs were found to be in good order. He believed nevertheless that he had not lightly launched his accusations against the government of the city of the dead, but had followed trustworthy information, and even now he had two discontented scribes of the necropolis who were furnishing him with more material concerning the abuses in the administration there.

It is not surprising that under these circumstances Paser felt a suspicion which we ourselves can scarcely suppress even now when we read through these old deeds. Had the examination been really as thorough as was represented; or rather were not the great princes trying to hush up the abuses of the necropolis? At the close of second day of trial, when the royal vassal Nesamun was holding a sitting in the Temple of Ptaḥ, Paser met some who had taken part in the investigation, and could not restrain his vexation. He declared openly that he had no faith in the embassy which had been sent with so much fuss, that he was now quite aware of how matters were passing in the necropolis, and that he would inform the Pharaoh directly upon the subject.

This declaration on the part of Paser was immediately reported to Paser'a, and the threat seems to have awakened fear in the heart of the latter. The next day he sent a long letter to the governor informing him of the declarations and threats of his colleague, evidently with the view of inducing the governor if possible to take judicial measures against Paser before he should carry out his threats. This letter was written in a very excited mood; a copy in somewhat shortened form, with the omission of the usual opening and closing sentences, is to be found amongst the documents still extant relating to this *cause célèbre*. The most remarkable passage runs thus:

"The royal vassal Nesamun, the scribe of Pharaoh, held a sitting. The prince of the town was with him. The latter stationed himself near the temple of Ptaḥ and quarrelled with the people of the necropolis. The prince of the town said to the people of the necropolis: 'You have rejoiced before the door of my house. Was I indeed the prince who gave information to the monarch? You rejoice on this account only. You have been there; an examination has been made; and you have found all in order. Only the tombs of Sebekemsaf and of Nubch'as his royal consort were found broken into—the tomb of one great ruler only, while reports were given in with regard to ten. The anger of the great god Amon Rê' king of the gods against his monuments abides surely in that tomb.'[1] Thereupon thus answered the workman Userchopesh, who was under the chief workman Nachtemḥê't of the necropolis: 'All the kings, together with their royal consorts, the royal mothers and royal children, who lie in the great noble necropolis, and who rest in the *place of beauties*, are uninjured. They guide and protect the plans of the Pharaoh their son, who watches over them, and who has caused them to be thoroughly examined.' The prince of the town answered him: 'Thou dost maintain proudly what thou dost say; that was indeed no small speech. Pooh!' thus said the prince of the town.

"The prince of the town again began to speak for the second time, and said: 'The scribe Ḥor'e, son of Amennacht of the necropolis Chenuchen'e, came into my house to the great . . . of the town, and brought me information of three important matters, which were taken down in writing by my scribe and by the scribe of the two districts of the town. The scribe Peibasa of the necropolis also told me of two other matters (five therefore altogether) which were also taken down in writing. It is impossible to be silent concerning them. Pooh! they are such great crimes that they deserve execution, death, and every kind of punishment. Now I shall write to the Pharaoh on the subject, so that a man may be sent by the Pharaoh to ruin you.'

"Thus spake this prince of the town to them, and he swore ten oaths that he would do this. I heard these words, which were spoken by the prince of the town to the people of the Pharaoh's noble great necropolis enduring for millions of years in western Thebes, and (herewith) I report

[1] The meaning of this disconnected and very difficult speech seems to be: "I care nothing about the business, for the accusation to the king did not proceed from *me*" (this was only half the truth). Then ironically: "It is very fine that you have only found *one* royal tomb violated, and of course this injury must not be attributed to bad administration, but was caused by the special anger of the gods against that king."

them to my lords, for it would be a crime for any one in my position to hear such words and to keep them secret. Though I could not be present myself at the great speech made by the prince of the town, yet it was told to me by the scribes of the necropolis Chene, who stood amongst the people close by. Alas! my feet could not carry me so far. I now report them to my lord, and may my lord cause some one to be fetched who was present when the words of the prince of the town were spoken. The scribes of the necropolis reported them to me. I said, 'I will write on the subject to the Pharaoh.' It is, however, a crime of those two scribes of the necropolis that they should have gone to this prince of the town with their reports; their ancestors certainly never made reports to him, but to the governor when he was in the south. If he happened to be in the north, then the royal police of the necropolis would go with their documents to the place where the governor was staying.

"On the 20th Athyr in the 16th year, witnesses were brought before me to testify as to these words of the prince of the town, and I now lay them before my lord in writing, so that my lord may send to-morrow to fetch an ear-witness."

In fact this challenge was received by the governor on the next day, at the time when he was presiding at a session. The document was entered amongst the acts in this wise:

"Behold the superintendent of the town, the governor Cha'emuêse, has ordered to be brought before him:

Of the temple of Ramses III., servants of the first Prophet of Amon,	The metal-worker Peicharu, son of Charuy, the metal-worker T'aroy, son of Cha'emopet, the metal-worker Peikamen, son of T'aroy.

"The governor said to the great princes of the great court of justice of the town. 'On the 19th of Athyr, in the 16th year, in the presence of the royal vassal, the scribe of the Pharaoh, this prince of the town said some words to the inspectors and workmen of the necropolis, at the same time speaking abusively of the great chambers, which are found in the *place of beauties*. I, the governor of the country, went thither with the royal vassal Nesamun, the scribe of Pharaoh. We have examined the places where the prince of the town said that the metal-workers of the temple of Ramses III. in the temple of Amon had been, and we found that they were uninjured. He was (therefore) found guilty in everything that he had said. Now behold the metal-workers stand before you, let them tell everything that took place.'

"Audience was given to them, and it was found that the people knew none of those chambers in the *places of the Pharaoh* (*i.e.* the necropolis), against which this prince of the town had spoken. He was declared guilty in the matter.

"The great princes spared the lives of the metal-workers of the temple of Ramses III. They were sent back the same day to Amenḥôtep, the first prophet of Amon Rê'. A document was written on the subject, and was placed in the archives of the governor."

Our documents do not inform us how this unpleasant business proceeded further; perhaps both parties found it advisable to put it aside and not to bring it before the Pharaoh. Neither had anything to gain by this step; the prince of the town had said things which were certainly foolish, and which could easily be construed as treasonable; and the prince of the necropolis also, and his patron the governor, could scarcely boast of a clean conscience. The condition of affairs in the necropolis was certainly very bad, for though possibly one only of the royal tombs had been violated, yet the private tombs had "all been broken into by the thieves."

After this great investigation everything seems to have gone on in the old way; three years later, in the first year of Ramses X., about sixty arrests were made of persons supposed to be thieves.[1] Those who fell under suspicion this time were not poor serfs, but, for the most part, officials of a low rank amongst whom we even find a scribe of the treasury of Amon, a priest of Amon, and a priest of Chons. Many of the others were "out of office," *e.g.* a "former prophet of the god Sobk," from Per'onch, a town in the Feyum, probably a fictitious personage. Most of the thieves were of course Thebans, others had come from the neighbouring places for the sake of this lucrative business. They did not rob the same part of the necropolis as their predecessors of the 16th year, but turned their attention to the barren valley now called the Biban el Moluk. Here they robbed the outer chambers of the tombs of Ramses II. and Sety I., and sold the stolen property; their wives, who were also arrested, may have been their accomplices in this matter. The Berlin museum actually possesses an object which in all probability belonged to their plunder—a bronze funerary statuette of King Ramses II. The thieves broke off the gold with which it was overlaid, and flattened and mutilated the graceful figure; they then threw away the bronze as worthless into some corner, where by a happy chance it was preserved to us. The robbery might not have been discovered had not the thieves finally quarrelled over the division of the spoil, and one of them, who thought himself ill used, went to an officer of the necropolis and denounced his comrades.

This great capture by the Egyptian police could not save the royal tombs from their impending fate. Owing to their isolated position in the bare desert valley, the violation of the tombs and the thefts continued as formerly, and a few years later the state officials confessed openly that they were powerless against the thieves. They were obliged to abandon the tombs which were exposed to danger, and to try only to save the royal bodies; even these were somewhat injured and had to be restored as well as possible. Distracted by fear, they dragged the bodies from tomb to tomb; *e.g.* the mummy of Ramses II. was first placed in the tomb of Sety I., and when that tomb was threatened, in that of Amen-

[1] Abbott, 8, and Pap. Mayer, which I unfortunately only know from Goodwin's short annotations. Ä. Z., 1873, 39 f. 1874, 61 ff.

hôtep I. Finally there was nothing further to be done but in the darkness of the night to bring the bodies that remained, and hide them in an unknown deep rocky pit in the mountains of Dêr-el-baḥri. So greatly did they fear the thieves that the priests no longer dared to inter in state the mummies of the royal house, but hid them also in this hiding-place. They were well concealed there. All the great monarchs of the New Empire—Ra'sqenen, who expelled the Hyksos, the sacred queen A'ḥmose-nefert-'ere, the ancestress of the 18th dynasty, Amenḥôtep I., Thothmes II., Thothmes III. the great conqueror, Sety I., the great Ramses II. and many others rested here unmolested till quite modern times. It was only about the year 1875 that the fellahs of the village of Qurna, the modern robbers of the Theban necropolis, found this pit; they guarded their secret with care until the summer of 1881 when it was discovered by the energetic measures of the Egyptian authorities. It was a great day for science when on 5th July 1881 the officers of the Bulak Museum entered this most wonderful of all tombs. When the marvellous tidings were telegraphed to Europe many shook their heads incredulously; the news was too much like a fairy tale. In no other branch of archaeology has such a remarkable find been recorded; and we owe our good fortune to those bands of thieves with whose lawsuits we have been so busy above.

UERCHUU, THE ROYAL RELATIVE, THE ROYAL SCRIBE OF PHARAOH, JUDGE AND SUPERINTENDENT OF SCRIBES, JUDGE AND SUPERINTENDENT OF THE TWO COURTS OF JUSTICE, ETC., RIDES OUT IN A SEDAN CHAIR.

Before him is his runner, behind him his fan-bearer. (After L. D., ii. 43*a*.)

We have already had occasion to speak of the courts of justice of the older period (see p. 87 ff.). Under the Old Empire Upper Egypt possessed six courts of justice or *great houses*, at the head of which was an all-powerful chief judge. Each of the "thirty great men of the south" was a judge and a district chief, and as such was also a "privy councillor of the pondering of the secret words of the great house,"[1] that is, he was member of one of the six courts of justice;[2] the chief of these great men, the "governor of the south," as "privy councillor of secret words of the six great houses," alone had a seat in all. Before these great men rose

[1] Instead of this title we find as an exception a great man of the south, who is called "Superintendent of the royal audience of the pondering of all words." (Mar. Mast., 109).

[2] Brugsch first rightly distinguished these *great houses*, as well as the words for *judge* and *chief judge* (Dict. Suppl., 390 ff.).

to the rank of full judge, they usually superintended the office work of the court; they were entitled "judge and scribe,"[1] "judge and deputy superintendent of the scribes,"[2] or later in their career "judge and chief of the scribes,"[3] finally they were promoted by the favour of Pharaoh to be one of the thirty great men of the south. Besides these collegiate judges, there were individual judges, as the [hieroglyphs] and the [hieroglyphs] who seem to have belonged to no court of justice. The latter, the "judges belonging to the town of Nechent," officiated as assistants of the chief judge; they gave audience with him "on all secret occasions," and like him they represented "the king, the royal household, and the six great houses."[4]

HORUS WEIGHS THE HEART OF THE DECEASED IN THE UNDERWORLD: IN THE OTHER SCALE IS THE HIEROGLYPH [hieroglyph], THE SIGN FOR TRUTH.

The goddess Ma'at is watching that the weighing is right; Thoth, the god of wisdom, is waiting to write down the result. (After L. D., iii. 78.)

The administration of justice was evidently well organised, and played an important part in the state. The judges had a special patron saint, Ma'at the goddess of truth; all judges of high rank served her as priests, and the chief judge wore a little figure of this goddess round his neck as a badge of office.[5]

The most ancient constitution of the courts of justice seems to have perished early under the Middle Empire; as far as I know, we only meet with one of the lower orders of judges, that "belonging to the town Nechent"; and this is probably a mere title of the nomarchs of Beni Hasan and Siut. The office of chief judge, on the other hand, in connection with the dignity of governor, survived even under the New Empire. Probably this office, like others which also outlived the Old Empire, had long become a sinecure, and survived only as the addition of a traditional title. Under the New Empire we still find the "governor of the six great houses,"[6] though these ancient courts of justice had long since ceased to exist except in name. The court of justice of the New Empire had not only an entirely different constitution, but differed also in name from that of the Old Empire. The *great house* was formerly a permanent assembly of high government officials, the [hieroglyphs] was a court of justice, in which the members varied. It consisted of "wise men and

[1] R. J. H., 84. 91. 97. [2] Ib. 52. 78. 99. [3] Ib. 52.

[4] Ä. Z., 1882, pp. 2-3, 10-12. Cp. also L. D., ii. 16 = R. J. H., 64.

[5] We see from passages quoted by Brugsch, Dict. Suppl., 390, that this ornament spoken of by Diodorus was really the traditional badge of the chief judge. [6] Br., Dict. Suppl., 392.

princes,"[1] that is of priests and officials, who "formed the great court of justice;" on a certain day they assembled at the gate of a temple, *e.g.* "near the two stelae in the court of Amon, at the gate 'adoration,'[2] or near the great gate, 'contented with truth,' of King Ramses II., opposite that of Amon."[3] On the latter spot there stood in fact a "justice hall of the Pharaoh,"[4] which became so famous as a place of justice that a deceased poet amongst the justified of the nether world entitles it the "excellent gate, 'contented about the doing of truth.'"[5] We see by the fact that the court of justice was called the "court of this day,"[6] that those who were qualified by their official or priestly office to serve did not all sit at the same time, and in fact the composition of the court varied very much. On the 21st of Athyr in the 16th year of Ramses IX. the court of justice sitting in judgment on the princes of the town consisted of:

"The governor Cha'emuêse, the superintendent of the town.
Amenḥôtep, the first prophet of Amon Rê', king of the gods.
Nesamun, of the temple of Ramses IX. enduring for millions of years, the prophet of Amon Rê', king of the gods.
The royal vassal Nesamun, the scribe of the Pharaoh, and chief of the house of the high priestess of Amon Rê', king of the gods.
The royal vassal Neferkerê'-em-per-Amun, the speaker of the Pharaoh.
Ḥor'e, the deputy of . . .
The fan-bearer of the household of Ḥor'e.
Paser, the prince of the town."[7]

In this case the lay element preponderated, but on the 14th of Phaophi in the 46th year of Ramses II. we find the members of the court consisted of:

"Bekenchons, the first prophet of Amon.
Ueser-mont, the prophet of Amon.
Ram, the prophet of Amon.
The prophet Uennofre of the temple of Mut.
The prophet Amen-em-'en of the temple of Chons.
The (holy father?) Amen-em-opet of the temple of Amon.
Amenḥôtep, the priest and reader of Amon.
Any, the priest and reader of Amon.
The priest Ḥuy of the temple of Amon.
The accountant Ḥuy of the court of justice of the town."[8]

In this case therefore we find nine priests and but one layman, *i.e.* the permanent scribe of the court who reported the lawsuit.[9] It was right that there should be a permanent official in these affairs of law, for the protocol was the determining document of the process, the whole transaction being

[1] Abb., 7, 2. [2] Abb., 7, 1. [3] Ä. Z., 1879, 72.
[4] Ä. Z., 1879, 72. [5] An., 4, 4, 7. [6] Ä. Z., 1879, 72. Abb., 7, 2.
[7] Abb., 7, 3 ff. The closing sentence might be construed thus: "the fan-bearer of the household of the prince," yet this rendering presents a grammatical difficulty.
[8] Ä. Z., 1879, 72.
[9] These scribes of the court are also called "the royal scribes of truth." Mar. Cat. d'Ab., 433, 1216.

conducted by word of mouth. In the civil court, the plaintiff first preferred his complaint, the court being seated [1] and the contending parties standing;[2] the court then declared that the case was *heard*, and summoned the defendant to answer. After the defence, the court gave sentence. The victor, then turning to the other party, stated the award adjudicated to him, and the one who had lost declared with the words "I do it, indeed I do it, I do it," that he submitted to the sentence of the court.[3] It was the same in criminal cases, except that the accusations [4] were addressed to the governor, who took the place of the plaintiff. In these cases also the sentence was not always pronounced by the court. It sufficed for the court to declare the guilt of the prisoner, to "find him guilty"; [5] the deed was then sent to the Pharaoh,[6] and it was left for him to decide what punishment should be inflicted.

The laws which guided the king and courts in their decisions are unfortunately unknown to us. Some of them were said to have been of divine origin; a deed informs us that the criminal should be condemned to the "great punishment of death, of which the gods say 'do it to him,'" and it expressly states further that this decree of the gods is written in the "writings of the divine words." [7] Diodorus probably says truly that he was informed that the sacred books of law had been composed by Thoth the god of wisdom.[8] He may also be right on the whole with regard to what he states as to the contents of the old laws. It is quite probable that murder either of a free man or of a slave, as well as perjury, was punishable with death; treachery with the cutting out the tongue; the forgery of acts or seals with the cutting off the hand.[9] It sounds more doubtful when Diodorus tells us that the infanticide had to hold the corpse of her infant three whole days in her arms; [10] the refinement of such a punishment savours rather of the invention of the Greek philosophers. Punishment was regarded as the necessary consequence of crime, which pursued the delinquent to his destruction; he who is punished,[11] "his crime seizes him,[12] it overtakes him and undoes him."

Besides these old sacred laws, there were others originating in historical times. Diodorus informs us expressly of laws made by certain wise kings,[13] and in fact the old chief judge Mentuḥôtep boasts that he had "given laws." [14] Under the 12th dynasty the canon of the old laws was not considered finally closed, and the same is probably true of later times.

There were of course particular cases, which formed exceptions to the usual procedure of justice described above. Acts were committed by those immediately surrounding the king which could not be passed over, but which it was not prudent to expose to the eyes of the people. In such cases, as in all autocratic states, the Pharaoh broke through the usual

[1] Abb., 7, 2. [2] An., 6, 6, 12. Tur., 16, 8.
[3] Cp. the Berlin Pap., 47, pub. Ä. Z., 1879, 72 ff. A fragment of a similar text is now at Munich.
[4] Ä. Z., 1879, 153. [5] Abb., 7, 14. [6] Amherst, 3, 9. [7] Lee, 1, 7, 2, 5. [8] Diod., 1, 94, 75.
[9] Diod., 1, 77, 78. [10] Diod., 1, 77. [11] Pj. T., 4, 1. 6, 1. [12] Pj. T., 4, 2.
[13] Diod., 1, 94. [14] "*Dada hpu*," R. J. H., 303.

course of justice, and, passing by the highest of his law officials, he intrusted the trial to one of his confidants. We know of a case of this kind as early as the 6th dynasty. We quote from the autobiography of Un'e the favourite of King Pepy, whom we have already frequently mentioned. He relates: "When the lawsuit was conducted secretly in the royal household against the great royal consort 'Emtese, his majesty ordered me to appear in order to direct the proceedings—I alone, no chief judge, nor governor, nor prince was present; I alone, because I was agreeable and pleasant to the heart of his majesty, and because his majesty loved me—I myself, I compiled the written report; I alone and one single judge belonging to the town Nechent. Yet formerly my office was only that of a superintendent of the royal anterior country, and no one in my position had ever in earlier times heard the secret affairs of the royal household. I alone was excepted, his majesty allowed me to hear them because I was more agreeable to the heart of his majesty than all his princes, than all his nobles, and than all his servants."[1] Un'e was not inexperienced in such affairs, for before he was made superintendent of the anterior country, he himself had officiated as assistant to the chief judge ("as judge, belonging to the town Nechent").

We have a more detailed account of a similar lawsuit of later time, concerning the great harem conspiracy under Ramses III. In dealing with this wretched business the Pharaoh again avoided the regular law-courts, and appointed a number of trusted personages to form a special court of justice, and gave them discretionary powers over the life and death of the criminals. The following short report of the proceedings of this lawsuit may in fact have been arranged for the royal archives. The official origin of the report is probable from the exceeding precaution displayed by the compiler, who wisely avoids going into detail.[2] At the same time, even from his short account, we see that the affairs with which this trial was concerned were such as were better not proclaimed from the housetops. Certain persons belonging to the royal household (fictitious names alone are given) had conspired against his majesty and planned an open rebellion. The harem formed the centre of the conspiracy. One of the oldest inmates, Tey, had a son Pentuêre, "who also bore another name" (therefore probably a prince); Tey conspired with another lady of the harem, to "excite enmity against their lord," probably with the object of placing Pentuêre on the throne. Most of the officials of the women's apartments were inculpated in the conspiracy; the higher ones took an active part—they had "taken counsel with the women;" the lower ones had probably known of the conspiracy, they had been present at some of the consultations of the conspirators, and had thought it best at any rate to be silent about the matter, even if they did not agree to it. We see how promising the affair must have appeared to those interested.

[1] Ä. Z., 1882, 10-12.

[2] The description here given of the great trial for high treason under Ramses III. is taken from: the judiciary Papyrus of Turin, Papyrus Lee, and Papyrus Rollin, 1888. Cp. Ä. Z. 1879, 76 ff.

It was most important for Tey and her companions that the highest official of the harem, the "great man of the house Pai-bek'e-kamen," should join actively in the conspiracy, for through him they were able to correspond with the outside world. "He took their words out to their mothers and brothers outside," and this communication ran thus: "Excite the people, goad on the enemies to begin hostilities against their lord." For the moment indeed they remained quiet; the troops that were stationed in Ethiopia were to be the first to rise against the Pharaoh and attack Egypt. The commander of these troops had been won over to the conspiracy; his sister belonged to the harem, and she had by her letters initiated him into the secret. Other high officers and officials, including even the high priest of the goddess Sechemt, joined zealously in the preparations for the rebellion. They thought it right to use every means; even the help of the magic art was called in to do harm to the king. The royal "superintendent of the cows," a man of high rank, procured a magical book from the Pharaoh's own library, and according to its directions he made certain wax figures which were smuggled into the palace, where they were supposed to cause lameness and illness.

These designs against the king's health may not have been so dangerous perhaps as the others by which there is no doubt that his throne was seriously threatened. We do not know how it came about that the conspiracy was discovered in time; one day the conspirators (they are officially styled the "abomination of the land") were arrested, and brought before a kind of court-martial, consisting of officials of high and low rank, whom the king believed worthy of his special confidence. The instructions given to this court of inquiry have come down to us, and in them we read the following characteristic passage: "What the people have spoken, I do not know. Hasten to investigate it. You will go and question them, and those who must die, you will cause to die by their own hand, without my knowing anything of it. You will also cause the punishment awarded to the others to be carried out without my knowing anything of it." We see that the Pharaoh would have nothing to do with the affair; the criminals were too closely connected with him, the conspiracy was too dangerous for him to institute official law proceedings against them, which would drag into publicity affairs of which it was better for the people to know nothing, and which would oblige the monarch himself to award the punishments to the guilty. He therefore preferred to give discretionary powers to certain persons whom he trusted, and they were to despatch the wretched business as quietly and quickly as possible. They were also to avoid making a sensation by the punishments; whoever deserved death was to die by suicide.

The judges proceeded with their sad business; the work was so heavy that they had to divide themselves into two commissions. One, consisting of six members, the "great princes of the court of inquiry," undertook principally the trial of the harem officials; the other of five members, all "vassals" of the king, had fewer but more weighty crimes to judge;

they pronounced death sentences only. These sentences are short and monotonous:

"The great criminal Mesd-su-Rê' formerly vassal. He was brought to trial because he had conspired with Pai-bek'e-kamen, who had been chief of the house, and with the women, to stir up malcontents to act with hostility against their master.

"He was brought before the great princes of the court of inquiry. They investigated his crime, they found him guilty, they caused his punishment to be carried out."

With people of lower rank the proceedings were more summary:

"The wives of the doorkeepers of the harem, who had joined with their husbands in the conspiracy, were placed before the princes of the court of inquiry, were found guilty, and their punishment was ordered to be carried out: six persons."

The following is an example of the sentence passed on a distinguished delinquent: "Pentuêre, who formerly bore another name. He was brought before the court, because he had joined with his mother Tey, when she conspired with the women of the harem, and because he acted with hostility against his lord. He was brought before the vassals, that they might question him. They found him guilty; they dismissed him to his house; he took his own life."

The concise nature of these deeds shows that it was considered desirable that as little as possible of the history of the conspiracy should be passed down to posterity. We cannot tell with certainty what were the names of any of the culprits, for many of the names that are entered are evidently perverted. One vassal is called Mesd-su-Rê', = "the sun-god hates him," another high officer Be'n-em-Uêse, = "bad in Thebes;" it stands to reason that these could not be the real names of these persons of high rank. Probably in truth their names were Nefr-em-Uêse = "good in Thebes," and Mer-su-Rê' = "the sun-god loves him," but the zealous loyalty of the scribes of our report distorted these names into others of bad significance. Before the investigation had been brought to a close, an incident occurred which shows us plainly how disturbed were the conditions in the Egyptian court of old. Three of the king's six confidants who formed the first commission had to be suddenly arrested. The accused women of the harem had formed close friendship with them, they had sought them out and, with them and with Pai'es the chief culprit, they had "made a beer-house" that is they had held a revel. This was an unheard-of breach of confidence, they "lost the good tokens of favour which had been shown to them by the king," when he had appointed them to be judges. But "their guilt seized upon them," and "their punishment was fulfilled by the cutting off of their noses and ears."

The two great lawsuits which we have already described in this chapter give us a complete, though scarcely happy, picture of criminal justice in Egypt; as to civil law unfortunately there is scarcely any material to help us. The two non-criminal law documents which we possess are so much injured that it is impossible to quote from them; the disputes about *mine* and *thine*, which occasionally fill private letters, are very obscure, and neither wills nor bills are to be found. Fortunately for our subject we have a number of contracts (the *sealed*, as the Egyptians called them), such as were frequently concluded by people of rank in order to ensure certain revenues for religious services after death. Such are the ten contracts concluded with the priesthood of his town by Ḥapd'efa'e, a nomarch of Siut in the time of the Middle Empire; they are in perfect preservation and deserve more study.[1] It does not seem that Ḥapd'efa'e had much to gain by them; he wished to secure that his five statues, which he had placed in his tomb and in the temples of Siut, should receive from the priesthood a yearly offering of bread, beer, and meat. He wished also to provide for the "kindling of the lights," *i.e.* the illumination of the statues, which took place on many festivals; he therefore bound the priest, who had the care of the lamps in the temple, regularly to provide the wicks for this illumination. The objects which Ḥapd'efa'e secured by his ten contracts appear to us very insignificant—besides these he had bequeathed for his tomb worship an endowment of "fields, servants, cattle, gardens, and other things"—and we scarcely understand why he did such honour to these ten deeds, as to write them down for us *in extenso* in sixty gigantic lines in his tomb.

The priesthood, with whom he concluded his contracts, would naturally do nothing without a corresponding return; he had to pay them for all the offerings they were to offer. He did this partly by gift of lands in his own possession, partly by surrendering certain rights. As he himself belonged by birth to the priestly college of the god 'Epuat, he had a right to a share of the temple rations, supplied out of the temple property to the individual priests; in order to pay his colleagues it was therefore the simplest way for him to renounce part of these rations on behalf of himself and his heirs.

These deeds of purchase of Ḥapd'efa'e are all couched in the same strictly regular form:

"Contract concluded between A and B,
that B should give x to A,
whilst A should give y to B.
Behold, B was therewith content."

All sorts of clauses are interpolated, which for the most part contain more detailed business provisions. This plan ought fully to content lawyers. It is in no wise a deed on the conclusion of the completed contract (this would run: a contract *was* concluded, etc.), but it is in fact rather the superscription, or the table of contents of the contract. We

[1] Cp. with all that follows my work Ä. Z., 1882, p. 159 ff. Similar "sealed rolls for payment" (*chetemt dbau*) were concluded for the same object by the priests of Abydos with people of rank: Mar. Abyd., ii. 25.

might almost imagine that the scribe had ventured to change the formula somewhat when these deeds were inscribed in the tomb.

The seventh contract gives us an example of one of the shortest:

"Contract, concluded between the late chief prophet Ḥapd'efa'e and the great priest of Anubis for three wicks to be delivered to him (to the priest); the same to be burnt in the lamps of the temple of Anubis:
one on the fifth intercalary day, on the New Year's Eve,
another on New Year's Day,
another on the 17th of Thoth, the eve of the festival of Uag.

For this he shall give him: 1000 field measures from the estate of his fathers, as the price for these three wicks, which he shall deliver to my funerary priest, in order to burn in the lamps.

Behold, he was therewith content."

Others, however, are more detailed and are provided with many clauses and reasons, as *e.g.* the third:

"Contract, concluded by Ḥapd'efa'e the prince and chief prophet, with the official staff of the temple, that they should give him bread and beer on 18th Thoth, the day of the festival of Uag, whilst he should give them: 24 temple days, out of his property from the estate of his fathers, and not in any way out of the property of the estate of the nomarch; in fact, four days for the chief prophets, two days for each of them.

"Behold, he said to them:

"1. A temple-day is $\frac{1}{360}$ of the year. If all the bread, beer, and meat that is received daily in this temple be divided, the $\frac{1}{360}$ of the bread and beer and of everything that is received in this temple, is a temple-day which I give to you.

"2. It is my property from the estate of my fathers, and not in any way from the property of the estate of the nomarch, because I am indeed a son of a priest as each of you are.

"3. These days shall form the remuneration for each future staff of priests, that they may deliver to me this bread and beer, which they shall give to me.

"Behold, they were therewith content."

A list is appended, which shows how the requisition of bread and beer was to be divided between the ten members of the "official staff" of the temple; each should give 2 jugs of beer and 200 rolls of bread, but the chief priest, who was to be paid by four temple-days, was to supply 4 jugs of beer and 400 rolls of bread.

These three clauses of the document are very interesting. The first declares what Ḥapd'efa'e means us to understand by the day's ration of the temple. It was never to be taken as the receipts of any given day, but the receipts of the whole year were to be added together and $\frac{1}{360}$ of the same was to be regarded as the average ration. The other clauses were to protect him from the suspicion, which might be suggested, that he was disposing of revenues which were not his own by inheritance; he declares that he belongs by birth to the priesthood, and has, therefore, full rights to the revenues of that position. Finally, the third clause again points out what were the good offices for which he renounces to his colleagues the fifteenth part of his yearly income as priest.

We see from these instances that there existed a complete system of drawing up contracts, and this is confirmed by the facts contained in these curious records. It is most remarkable how limited were the testamentary powers of the nomarch; again and again emphasis is laid on the fact that he can only dispose of that part of his property and revenue which was really hereditary in his family. As high priest of his temple, for instance, he was entitled to a roast piece of the bulls sacrificed in the temples; he might wish that subsequently this piece should be offered to his statue on great processional days, but he could not himself arrange this. Membership of the priestly college might be hereditary in his family but not the dignity of high priest, and therefore he could not dispose of those particular revenues due to the latter. In order to arrange any small affair according to his wish it was necessary to set in motion a complicated system of judicial machinery. In his capacity as a private individual he concludes a contract with himself as chief prophet for the time being, and purchases from himself the roast piece in question, in return for two of the above-mentioned rations. In order that this contract should be incontestable, he expressly obtains the consent of the priestly body to the transaction.

A people who could so clearly grasp the double nature of an individuality as to allow him to conclude contracts with himself, was certainly long past the time of judicial infancy, and had attained to a highly developed legal status. Unfortunately, as has already been said, there is barely any material from which we can learn much of the subject.

The tomb of Ḥapd'efa'e contains extracts at any rate of one other document of legal nature, viz. the provision which he exacted from his funerary priest,[1] when he endowed him "with fields, with servants, with herds, with tanks, and with all kinds of other things." The office of funerary priest was usually hereditary in one family, there was therefore danger that the properties belonging to that office should at some time be split up by inheritance. Ḥapd'efa'e forbids this expressly: "these things shall only belong to one of thy sons, the one whom, above thine other children, thou dost desire to be my funerary priest . . . and he again shall not divide it amongst his children." Similar statutes concerning the funerary tomb-priests, exist of the time of the Old Empire,[2] they also contain detailed provisions about the inheritance of endowed property, and directions are given how disputes are to be settled between individuals entitled to it. Unfortunately these sadly injured inscriptions do not explain to us the particulars of the stipulations, yet they show us that there existed in that old time such an organised system of jurisprudence, that

[1] Mar. Mon. div., 64, 9-12.

[2] R. J. H. I. Mar. Mast., 318—both much injured.

the decree of this statute alone ensured sufficient protection against the encroachments even of posterity. The favourite prayer to the gods, commonly used in other parts of the world, on occasions of similar endowments, finds no place here; it is enough that the founder of the endowment should express his will in a formal manner.

It was quite otherwise in later times; *e.g.* when the chief officer Amenḥôtep, son of Ḥapu, who lived under Amenḥôtep III., founded the little temple of Dêr-el-Medineh dedicated to Amon Rê' in Thebes, he did not consider his foundation sufficiently safe without calling down the anger of the gods on any one who should injure it. On the 8th of Choiakh in the 21st year, when the king visited the new sanctuary, the following decree was published by certain high officials of the state, viz. Amenḥôtep the governor, Meryptaḥ the superintendent of the house of silver, and the scribes of the army:[1] "Hear the decree, issued at the establishment of the temple of Kak, belonging to the hereditary prince, the royal scribe, Amenḥôtep called Ḥuy, the son of Ḥapu . . ., that his temple of Kak, with the slaves belonging thereto both male and female, should endure eternally from son to son, from heir to heir, and that no one should ever transgress this decree, for as long as this temple stands upon earth, it is sacred to Amon Rê', king of the gods, who is king eternally and the protector of the dead.

"If the general and scribe of the soldiers, who shall be my successor, shall find that the temple of Kak has fallen into decay, and that certain belonging thereto have been taken away from the slaves who raise the corn for my endowment,—if he then uphold all the laws and ordinances of Pharaoh, then shall his bodily life be satisfied.

"But those who transgress them and render no account thereof, upon them shall fall the destruction of Amon, the lord of Thebes, who will not allow them to be satisfied in their office of royal scribe of the army, which they have received for me! He will deliver them up to the wrath of the king on the day of his anger, his snake diadem shall spit fire on the crown of their head destroying their sons. It shall eat their body, and they shall become like the snake Apophis (the enemy of the sun-god), on the New Year's Day. They shall be drowned in the ocean, which shall conceal their bodies; they shall not receive the funeral services of the just, they shall not eat the food of the god Qerte, they shall not cool themselves on the water, on the course of the river. Their sons shall not succeed them, their wives shall be used shamefully even in their sight. Honourable men shall not enter their houses as long as they are upon earth, and they shall not enter, nor be led into the palace (?). They shall not hear the voice of the king when he rejoices. They shall be slain on the day of destruction, and men shall call them miserable. Their bodies shall be sick, they shall hunger without food; their bodies shall die! Above all, this curse shall fall upon the governor, the treasurer, the superintendent of the

[1] This decree has only come down to us in an abstract of later time: Inscript. in the Hier. Charact., T. 29. Edited by Birch (Chabas, Mélanges, I. p. 324 ff.) and Brugsch (Ä. Z. 1875, p. 123 ff.).

storehouse, the first prophet, the holy fathers, the priests of Amon to whom this edict has been read, which has been issued for the temple of Kak, belonging to the hereditary prince, the royal scribe Amenḥôtep the son of Ḥapu, if they do not take care of his temple of Kak.

"If, however, you shall take care to protect the temple of Kak, with the slaves both male and female, who raise corn for my property, then shall all good befall you. Amon Rê', king of the gods, shall reward you with a happy life. . . . Honours shall be heaped upon you ; you shall see the sons of your sons, and the heirs of your heirs. You shall be sent on embassies which the king shall reward. Your bodies shall rest in the netherworld after a life of 110 years. Your food-offerings shall be increased as well as what otherwise is due to you.

"What I have said shall fall also upon those officers of the militia which belong to the district of the prince of the western town, called Cheftḥer-nebs, who shall not maintain my endowment for each day, and all my festivals at the beginning of the months ; their bodies shall not thrive. But if they attend to all these words, which are issued as a command, and are obedient, and do not turn aside from them, good shall befall them, even as to the just. They shall rest in the city of the dead after a good old age."

The man who issued this decree, so rich in curses, was considered by later generations as the model of a wise man.[1] This document will scarcely appear to us of the modern world as a special proof of his wisdom, and those ancient founders, who drew up their documents without invoking the help of the gods will probably stand higher in our esteem than the celebrated Amenḥôtep, the son of Ḥapu, who, on account of his wisdom, as Manetho tells us, "appeared to partake of the divine being."

[1] Ä. Z., 1875, 123. 1876, 26. 1877, 147. His father and his family, L. D., iii. 43 b.

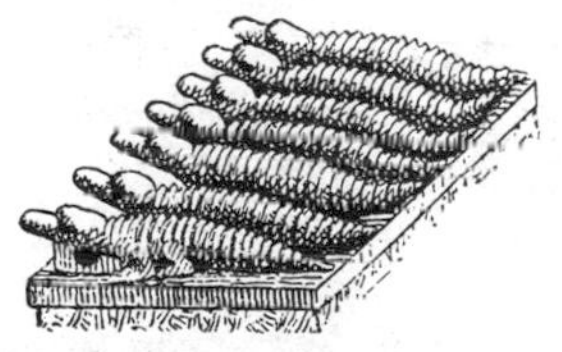

AMULET IN THE BERLIN MUSEUM.

GROUP OF M'AYPTAḤ, THE PRIEST OF PTAḤ, WITH HIS FAMILY.

On the left is his wife, Ḥa'tshepest, "the lady full of charms, of grace, and of love"; on the right is his daughter, 'En'euhay, the "favourite of the Pharaoh." The small figures represent a second daughter and her son, who dedicated the statues (Berlin, 2297).

CHAPTER VIII

FAMILY LIFE

IT has often been said that the essential difference between the civilisation of the West and of the East consists in the different status of woman. In the West she is the companion of man, in the East his servant and his toy. In the West, at one time, the esteem in which woman was held rose to a cult, while in the East the question has been earnestly discussed whether woman really belonged to the human race.

This view of the matter, however, is just neither to the East nor to the West; for the teaching of Mohammed with regard to woman represents as great an extreme on one side, as the sentimental cult of woman in the Middle Ages on the other. The position of woman is very much the same amongst all nations who have attained a certain degree of culture, unless that position is affected by particular religious views such as those of Mohammedanism or Christianity. As a rule, one woman is the legitimate wife and the mistress of the house; at the same time the man may, if his fortune allow it, keep other women, and it is generally considered that the slaves of the household belong to him. This state of things, which appears to us most immoral, does not seem so in the eyes of a primitive people; on the contrary, the slave feels it as a disgrace if she does not "find favour" in the sight of her lord. Such were the views of marriage which were held in ancient Egypt. One woman alone was the legitimate wife of the husband, "his dear wife," "the lady of the house"; yet when we obtain a glimpse into the interior of a well-to-do household, we find also "beautiful singers" and other attendants in the "house of the women." The relationship between husband and wife appears to us at all times to have been faithful and affectionate. When they are represented together, we frequently see the wife with her arm tenderly round her husband's neck, the children standing by the side of their parents, or the youngest daughter crouching under her mother's chair.[1] The wife helps her husband to superintend the household;[2] she and the children look on while he is netting birds,[3] or she accompanies him in his boating expeditions for sport through the swamps.[4] The inscriptions of the Old Empire praise the wife who is "honoured by her husband,"[5] and the old book of wisdom of the governor Ptaḥḥôtep, declares him to be wise who "founds for himself a house, and loves his wife."[6] How deeply affectionate a marriage might be is shown by the touching confessions of a widower, which have been preserved to us in a Leyden papyrus of late date. After the death of his wife 'Anch'ere, he fell ill and a magician seems to have told him that it was his wife who sent him this misfortune; he then wrote a sorrowful letter to the "wise spirit" of 'Anch'ere and laid it upon her tomb in the hope of propitiating her. He complains: "What evil have I done to thee, that I should find myself in this wretched state. What then have I done to thee, that thou shouldest lay thy hand upon me, when no evil has been done to thee? From the time when I became thy husband till now—have I done anything which I had to hide from thee? . . . Thou didst become my wife when I was young, and I was with thee. I was appointed to all manner of offices, and I was with thee; I did not forsake thee nor cause thine heart any sorrow. . . . Behold, when I commanded the foot soldiers of Pharaoh together with his chariot force, I did cause thee to come that they might fall down before thee, and they brought all manner of good things to present to thee . . . When thou wast ill with the sickness which afflicted thee, I went to the chief physician, and he made thee thy medicine, he did everything that thou didst say he should do. When I had to accompany Pharaoh on his journey to the south, my thoughts were with thee, and I spent those eight months without caring to eat or to drink. When I returned to Memphis, I besought Pharaoh and betook myself to thee, and I greatly mourned for thee with my people before my house.[7]

Polygamy was quite the exception, we rarely find two wives ruling in a house at the same time; there are, however, a few instances at different

[1] E.g. L. D., ii. 10 b.
[2] L. D., ii. 13.
[3] Mar. Mon. div., 17.
[4] L. D., ii. 130. Wilk., ii. 107.
[5] R. J. H., 82; Mar. Mast., 308, and other examples.
[6] Prisse, 10, 8
[7] Leyden, 371; a better edition by Maspero, Etud. égypt., p. 145 ff. The above follows the latter in as far as this difficult text can be translated with tolerable certainty.

periods. Amony, the "great man of the south," who probably died at the beginning of the reign of Amenemḥê't II., had two wives. One Nebet-sochet-ent-Rê' (or as she was generally called, Nebet), may have been his niece; she bore him two sons and five daughters; by the other, Ḥnut, he had certainly three daughters and one son. A curious circumstance shows us that the two wives were friends, for the lady Nebet-sochet-ent-Rê' called her second daughter Ḥnut, and the lady Ḥnut carried her courtesy so far as to name all her three daughters Nebet-sochet-ent-Rê'.[1] We meet with the same custom a century later, and indeed, as it appears, in a lower class. One of the thieves of the royal tombs possessed two wives at the same time, the "lady Taruru and the lady Tasuey, his other second wife."[2]

Royal double marriages frequently occur; *e.g.* Ramses II. had two great "royal consorts," Nefret-'ere-mer-en-mut and 'Eset-nofret, and when he concluded his treaty with the Cheta king, he brought the daughter of that monarch also home to Egypt as his wife. Political reasons doubtless led to this third marriage; the union with the Princess Ra'-ma'-uer-nofru was the seal of the bond of friendship with her father, and the Pharaoh could give no lower place to the daughter of his mighty neighbour than that of his legal wife. Similar motives also probably led to double marriages amongst private individuals; as we have seen above, many daughters of rich men in Egypt possessed valuable rights of inheritance in their father's property. The history of one of the nomarch families of Beni Hasan gives us a case in point. Chnemḥôtep, son of Neḥer'e, with whom we had so much to do in the previous chapter, owed the possession of the Nome of the Gazelle to the fortunate marriage of his father with the heiress of the prince of that house. In order to secure the same good fortune for his children, he married Chety, the heiress of the Nome of the Jackal, and, in fact, through this marriage, his son, Nacht, succeeded later to this province. But though Chety was treated with all the respect due to her high rank as his "beloved wife," and as "lady of the house," and though her three sons alone were called the "great legitimate sons of the prince," yet the love of Chnemḥôtep seems previously to have been bestowed upon a lady of his household, the "mistress of the treasury, T'atet." Contrary to former custom, Chnemḥôtep caused this lady and her two sons, Neḥer'e and Chnemḥôtep, the "sons of the prince," to be represented in his tomb, immediately behind his official family.[3] She also accompanies him in his sporting expeditions, though she sits behind Chety, and does not wear as beautiful a necklet as the legitimate wife.[4] At the funeral festival of the same Chnemḥôtep, we meet with Chety and T'atet in a covered boat with the "children of the prince and the women," guarded by two old servants of the princely court.[5] There is no doubt that these *women* belong to the harem of the prince, to the "house of the secluded," as they

[1] Mar. Cat. d'Ab., 627. A similar case of this period, ib. 586. But of the three women, ib. 1161, two are stated to be "*former*," and therefore descend from former marriages.

[2] Ä. Z., 1873, 40. [3] L. D., ii. 128. 132. [4] L. D., ii. 130. [5] L. D., ii. 126.

were wont to say. The harem is rarely mentioned in the tombs, yet doubtless at all times it existed as one of the luxuries of the rich. We have already (p. 74), spoken of the royal house of women, which was strictly guarded. It was the duty of the inmates to cheer Pharaoh by songs,[1] and the ladies of private harems had also to be skilled in similar accomplishments; in the tomb of the courtier T'y, of the fifth dynasty, we see the ladies of the harem dancing and singing before their master.[2] We have also a picture of the harem under the New Empire. In a tomb at Tell el Amarna, belonging to the close of the eighteenth dynasty, a distinguished priest called 'Ey has caused his house to be represented.[3] After passing through the servants' offices, the store rooms, the great dining hall, the sleeping room, and the kitchen, at the further end of a piece of ground, the visitor came to two buildings turned back to back and separated by a small garden. These were the women's apartments, 'Ey's harem, inhabited by the women and children. A glance shows us how the inmates were supposed to occupy themselves; they are represented eating, dancing, playing music, or dressing each other's hair; the store rooms behind were evidently full of harps, lutes, mirrors, and boxes for clothes. The possession of such a harem would, of course, be restricted to men of the upper class, for the same reason as it is in the East at the present day—on account of the expense.

ONE OF THE TWO HOUSES FOR WOMEN BELONGING TO 'EY (after L. D., iii. 106 a).

We do not know what formalities were necessary for the conclusion of a legal marriage in Egypt, or to "found for oneself a house,"[4] as the Egyptians said; there were probably, as in Greek and Christian times, formal marriage contracts. It may be also that it was customary, as in later times, to have the "year of eating," the first year of probation, after which, by the payment of a certain sum of money, the marriage might be annulled. There existed also another custom foreign to our ideas, the marriage with a sister; this became common in Egypt during the Ptolemaic and Roman periods. Most of the Ptolemies married their sisters, and under the Emperor Commodus two-thirds of all the citizens of Arsi

[1] Mar. Mast., 138 f.
[2] Brugsch, Gräberwelt, 81, 83.
[3] L. D., iii. 106 a.
[4] Prisse, 10, 8; L. D., iii. 12 d.

had done the same.[1] Marriage with a sister shocks our moral sense, but seemed most natural to the Egyptians, just as in modern Egypt marriage with a cousin is considered to be most sensible and right. The gods set an example in point; the brothers Osiris and Set having married their sisters, Isis and Nephthys.

In the royal family of the eighteenth dynasty, we find that A'ḥmose-Nefert-'ere married her brother, A'ḥmose; a lady named A'ḥmose was consort to her brother Thothmes I., and 'Ar'at to her brother, Thothmes IV., and so on.[2] In the inscriptions of all ages we often meet with the words "his beloved sister," where we should expect the words "his beloved wife." It is impossible that all these passages should refer to unmarried ladies keeping house for their bachelor brothers; "thy sister, who is in thine heart, who sits near thee"[3] at the feast, or "thy beloved sister with whom thou dost love to speak,"[4] these ladies must stand in a closer relationship to the man. No other explanation also is possible of the fact that two stone masons, who directed the work in the quarries of Hamamat, each had "his sister" with him.[5] Surely two old maids could not have had the touching affection to follow their brothers into this terrible hot desert.

At the same time it is probable that these *sisters* were not all really married to their brothers, as Lessing's Just very rightly remarks, "there are many kinds of sisters." In the Egyptian lyrics the lover always speaks of "my brother" or "my sister," and in many cases there can be no doubt that the *sister* signifies his "beloved," his *mistress*. A stele in the Berlin museum[6] tells us for instance that a certain Amenemḥeb worshipped in the temple of Osiris, accompanied by his mother and his seven sisters; the latter were probably the seven ladies of his harem. We know that in late Roman time laxer forms of union were substituted for the strict indissoluble tie of marriage, but probably many Egyptians of earlier ages preferred to enter into a loose bond with a "sister" rather than conclude a formal marriage with a wife.[7] This state of affairs appears to have been very common amongst the lower classes. We happen to have two complaints presented by five labouring women; of four it is said that they "live with" such and such a workman, of one only that she is the *wife* of her husband.[8]

The moral condition of the "company of workmen," the Egyptian proletariat, appears to have been very low; it seems to have been a

[1] Cp. Wilcken, Arsinoit. Steuerprofess. (Reports of the Royal Prussian Ak. d. Wiss., 1883, p. 903.)

[2] It has been conjectured from the titles of the daughters of Ramses II. that this king married his own daughters. This is however an error, for every princess at her birth received the title of "royal consort." See Maspero, Guide, p. 342.

[3] Ä. Z., 1873, 60. [4] After Wilk., iii. pl. lxvii. [5] L. D., ii. 138 b. [6] Nr., 2091.

[7] Wiedemann (Hierat., Texts, p. 16) also conjectures that the term *sister* indicates a form of marriage. He thinks that the expression refers to the probationary marriage. With this I cannot agree.

[8] Tur., 47, 8; Salt, 2, 2-3. The word *ḥbsuy* (literally, she who clothes her husband) may mean *mistress*. Ä. Z., 1873, 39. The men are called their "*husbands*."

common crime amongst the workmen to "assault strange women."[1] We cannot shut our eyes to the fact that the social principles of the Egyptians on this point were almost as lax as those of classic antiquity. No reasonable being would take offence at the *naïveté* with which things are spoken of, or drawn as common signs in writing, which, according to our modern feelings, ought to be carefully hidden. On the other hand, when we see the series of obscene pictures, drawn and annotated by a caricaturist of the twentieth dynasty,[2] and when we think that this book was found in a tomb, we are shocked at the morality of a nation which could supply the deceased with such literature for the eternal journey. Finally, what can we say when an ancient sacred book[3] describing the life of the deceased Pharaoh in bliss, assures him, with the addition of some words we cannot quite understand, that in heaven he will "at his pleasure take the wives away from their husbands."

There were of course plenty of women who did not belong to "good women"[4] (that is to the respectable class); as in other countries of antiquity, these women were often those whose husbands had left them, and who travelled about the country. The strange woman was therefore always a suspicious character; "beware," says the wise man,[5] "of a woman from strange parts, whose city is not known. When she comes do not look at her nor know her. She is as the eddy in deep water, the depth of which is unknown. The woman whose husband is far off writes to thee every day. If no witness is near her she stands up and spreads out her net: O! fearful crime to listen to her!" Therefore he who is wise avoids her and takes to himself a wife in his youth;[6] first, because a man's own house is "the best thing";[7] secondly, because "she will present thee with a son like unto thyself."[8] It was considered the greatest happiness to possess children, and the relationship between parents and children offers us a delightful picture of Egyptian family life.

"Thou shalt never forget what thy mother has done for thee," teaches the wise 'Eney, "she bare thee and nourished thee in all manner of ways. If thou forgettest her, she might blame thee, she might 'lift up her arms to God, and He would hear her complaint.' After the appointed months she bare thee, she nursed thee for three years. She brought thee up, and when thou didst enter the school, and wast instructed in the writings, she came daily to thy master with bread and beer from her house."[9]

The esteem which the son felt for his mother was so great that in the tombs of the Old Empire, the mother of the deceased is as a rule represented there with the wife, while the father rarely appears. On the funerary stelae of later times also, it is the usual custom to trace the descent of the deceased on the mother's side, and not, as we usually do, on that of the father. We read of "Ned'emu-sneb, born of Sat-Hathôr; of Anḥôr,

[1] Salt, 2, 2 ff. Tur., 47, 8, ib. 57, 5 f.
[2] An example may be found, Tur., 145.
[3] Unas, 629.
[4] Tur., 47, 8.
[5] Pap. de Boul., i., 16, 13 ff.
[6] Pap. de Boul., i. 16, 1 ff.
[7] Golenischeff, Conte égypt., in the Transactions of the Berlin Oriental Congress, ii. 104.
[8] Pap. de Boul., ib.
[9] Pap. de Boul., i. 20, 17 ff.

born of Neb-onet, or of Sebekreda, born of Sent," but who were the respective fathers we are not told, or they are only mentioned incidentally. It is possible that this strange custom and the similar custom in East Africa, may have arisen from the belief that a child's birth can be proved from the mother's side only, the father must be always supposititious. The necessary consequence of this belief follows; and to this day amongst the nobility of the tribes of the Tuarek, the dignity of chief is inherited not by his son but by the son of his sister;[1] it is considered as more certain that the sister of the deceased belongs to the race of the chieftain than that the son of the chieftain is his own. It appears that a similar custom as to the inheritance in noble families prevailed in ancient Egypt, but instead of the son of the sister, the son of the eldest daughter was the heir. We have already mentioned (p. 92), that under the Middle Empire the nomes passed from one family to another through heiresses; thus he who married an heiress (as she was called), would gain for his son the inheritance of his father-in-law. In the older period we meet these hereditary princes, *rp'ate*, at every turn; they evidently formed the highest aristocracy. Even in these families, however, the inheritance did not always pass to the son of the daughter, we have contemporary instances of its passing, as is more natural to our minds, directly to the son himself. Thus Nacht inherited the town of Men'at Chufu from his father; Amony inherited the Nome of the Gazelle in the same way, and Dḥut-ḥôtep inherited the Nome of Bersheh from his father, Gay. Yet in spite of all exceptions the institution mentioned above must be considered as an old-established custom. So much was it part of the flesh and blood of the nation, that the "father of his mother" was considered the natural protector of a rising youth.

If an official succeeded in a brilliant career, it was the maternal grandfather who took the most interest: "When he is placed at the head of the court of justice, then the father of his mother thanks God."[2] Under the new Empire we hear of a young officer who is received into the royal stables, "for the sake of the father of his mother," and when obliged to go to the wars, he "gave his property into the charge of the father of his mother."[3]

Nevertheless these beliefs and customs were not able to disturb the natural relationship of father and son. On the contrary, at all periods it was the heartfelt wish on every father's part that he should leave his office to his son," that "his child should sit in his chair after he was gone;[4] it was also the son's sacred duty "to cause his father's name to live." In both particulars, the gods had left an example for men of all times; Horus had avenged his deceased father Osiris, and justified his name against the

[1] Hanoteau, Grammaire de la langue Tamachek, p. 15. [2] Sall. 2, 11, 3.

[3] An., 3, 6, 4, 7. Cp. also L. D., iii. 12 d., where the "son of the daughter" endows the tomb to the "father of his mother."

[4] Stele of Nebpu-Usertsen in the Brit. Mus. (L. A.), and other similar instances.

accusations of Set, for he himself had ascended the "throne of his father," and had put the Atef crown of his father on his own head.

A father could not do very much to insure that his son should succeed him, Pharaoh had to decide that matter with his counsellors, but they (if they were piously inclined), considered it their duty as far as possible to follow the dictates of this pious claim, and to "place every man on the throne of his father."[1] The duty of the son was the easier to fulfil, on account of the manner in which he had to cause his father's name to live: viz. to maintain his tomb and to offer the necessary sacrifices there on festival days. More than *one* pious son assures us in his autobiography that he had fulfilled these sacred duties; *e.g.* the nomarch Chnemḥôtep relates: "I have caused the name of my father to increase, and have established the place for his funeral worship and the estate belonging thereto. I have accompanied my statues (*i.e.* those of the family on days of procession) into the temple. I have brought to them their offerings of pure bread, beer, oil, and incense. I have appointed a funerary priest, and endowed him with land and labourers. I have established offerings for the deceased on every festival of the Necropolis."[2] These duties towards the deceased descended in direct line to the head of the family, but at the same time the obligation rested on the other members, even of later generations; they also had to keep up the established worship, and to honour their ancestors (their nobles[3] as they were called) on festival days. The Pharaohs especially had to honour their ancestors, "the forefathers of the king." In spite of this reverence for their ancestors, we doubt whether, with the exception of the royal family, there existed much family pride amongst the ancient Egyptians. It is well known from the inscriptions in the Egyptian tombs, that nothing that was adapted to increase the fame of the deceased would be lightly passed over in silence. Yet amongst the numerous inscriptions of the Old and Middle Empire, we rarely find any praise of the famous ancestors of the deceased; as a remarkable exception a high priest of Abydos boasts that he had built his tomb "in the midst of those of his fathers to whom he owed his being, the nobles of ancient days."[4] The family of the deceased is scarcely spoken of, even the grandfather being rarely mentioned.[5] When the deceased was descended from a king, he tells posterity of his genealogy; but this is an exceptional case, *e.g.* in one of the tombs of the Old Empire, in the place where the name of the deceased is usually given, we find this genealogy.[6]

"The king Snefru.

His great legitimate daughter Nefretkau.

Her son, Neferma'at, the high treasurer.

His son, Snefru-ch'af, the high treasurer, priest of Apis, nearest friend

[1] Louvre, C. 26. [2] L. D., ii. 124, 81 ff. [3] Ä. Z., 1882, 168.

[4] Leyden, v. 4 (L. A.)

[5] Louvre, C. 170. Stele of an Amenemḥê't, son of 'Entef, son of Kemse, of the 12th year of Amenemḥê't II. (L. A.); Leyden, v. 3 (L. A.), the grandfather is mentioned, but his name is not given.

[6] L. D., ii. 16=R. J. H., 64.

of the king, prince, belonging to the town Nechent, belonging to the town Pe.

Snefru-ch'af was therefore a descendant of King Snefru, the genealogy being

Snefru — Wife?

Husband? — The lady Nefretkau.

Neferma'at — Wife?

Snefru-ch'af.

We see from the defectiveness of this genealogy, in which even the name of the grandfather is not given, how little Snefru-ch'af thought of his family history; the only fact that interested him was that he was related to a Pharaoh. The same holds good in later times; it is always the individual who is spoken of, very seldom the race or family.[1] It is only during the latest epoch of Egyptian history, in the times of the Ethiopian kings, of the Psammetichi and of the Persians, when people gloried in the remembrance of the former greatness of the nation, that we meet with complete genealogical trees; it was natural that at this period men should be glad if possible to boast of direct descent from an official of king Ramses.

Another circumstance confirms the above statement. In the course of generations, a nation possessing genealogical sense unconsciously forms surnames, even when they only consist of vague appellations, such as are used by the old Beduin families. There is no trace of such names amongst the Egyptians, not even amongst the noble families of the Middle Empire. We reach the decadence of the Egyptian kingdom before we meet with even a tendency to use family names; in the time of the foreign Libyan rulers the descendants of the old family of the Pharaohs called themselves "sons of King Ramses," thus forming a race of the "sons of Ramses," the "Ramessides."

Names therefore with the Egyptians were entirely individual, and if we may say so, lack historical significance. Notwithstanding they offer much that is interesting, and a closer study of them will reward an attentive student. Names were of course subservient to fashion, and very few were in common use at all periods, though the ideas they expressed have much similarity.

The more simple names indicate briefly the bodily or intellectual qualities of the bearer. Thus the names of some distinguished men of the Old Empire are *Little*, *Young*, or *Content*, while one lady is called simply the *Beautiful*. Under the Middle Empire we meet with men named *Healthy* and *Strong*, with women called *Beauty*, *Resembling*, *Sweet*, *Verdant*,

[1] A genealogy of seven generations of painters of the temple of Amon, at the beginning of the 18th dynasty; Lieblein, 553. A genealogy up to the great grandfather (Dyn. 19); ib. 888.

or *She is healthy;* and under the New Empire some of the men are named *Tall*, *Beautiful of Face*, and the ladies, *Strong* and *Large-headed*.[1] Names of animals are not infrequently used: *Ichneumon*, *Silurus*, *Lion*, *Wild lion*, *Tadpole*, *Daughter of the crocodile*, *Horse;* and under the New Empire we find *Tomcat* and *Kitten*.[2] From the vegetable world we have the female name *Beautiful sycamore*.[3] Names referring to the good reputation of the bearer are found, *e.g.* *Praised*, *Beloved*, *Loved one*, *Worthy of thanks*, *Beautiful is what he does;*[4] these are naturally very numerous amongst the ladies. We not only find, *First favourite*, *Beautiful mistress*, *Loving one*, *My mistress is as gold*, and *This is my queen;* but also, with bold exaggeration, *Beloved by the two countries*, and *Ruler of the two countries*.[5]

Numerous names at all times are evolved from family affection, and express, often in touching fashion, the joy of the parents over their child. *Beautiful day* and *Beautiful morning*,[6] are in remembrance of the joyful day of a boy's birth; the child is *My own*, or the *Only one*, the parents love him as *Their eyes*, and he is *Their most beautiful* or *Their riches*. The father says of him, *I have wished it*, he is *Acceptable* and *Welcome*.[7] The daughter is called *Beautiful as her father*, and the *Ruler of her father;* at her birth it is said *Beauty comes*, and at the birth of the son *Riches come*.[8] Those who are gone live again in the children, *The Brothers live*, *His father lives;* and mournfully the widower says to the baby, *Replace her*. The family now survives, the *Mothers* are born again in the daughters, and *His name lives* through them;[9] all hopes are centred on the son, and the father in his mind's eye already sees him as his *Protector*, the *Prince*, the *Chief*, or he thinks of him as succeeding him, and therefore names him, even in his infancy, *Chief of the mercenaries*.[10]

Religion, as a matter of course, played a great part in this affair of name-giving,—men liked to be named after that god whom their family chiefly served; women desired above all to be called after Ḥatḥôr, the goddess of love. Some of these religious names are in praise of the gods; *e.g.* the following, which were favourite names under the Old Empire: *Sokar shines with spirit*, *Ptaḥ acts rightly*, *Rê' is beautiful*, *Beautiful is the countenance of Ptaḥ*, *Rê' is content*, *God is rich*.[11] They may

[1] I give a transcription of the names, and indicate the periods by the letters, O: M: and N; O: Sher'e, ned'es, ned'em-'eb, nefert. M: Sneb, nechty, nefru, sent, benr'et, uad'et, senebtesc. N: Qa, neferḥer, t'enra, ta-'at-d'ad'a.

[2] O: ḥet'es, ḥu'a, ma. M: Ma-ḥesa, ḥefner, gef, sat-'epa, ḥt'or. N: M'eu, Myt-šer'eu.

[3] M: Neḥt-nefret.

[4] O: Ḥesy. M: Mery, meryt. N: Nefer-sechru. O: Nefer-'ert-nef.

[5] M: Ḥ'at-shepest. N: Ḥnut-nefret. M: merert, nebt'e-m-nub, ḥnut'e-pu, meryt-taui. N: nebt-taui.

[6] N: Hau-nefer. M: Duat-nefret.

[7] N: Pay'e, u'at'e. M: Merte-sen. N: Tasen-nefer. O: D'efat-sen. N: 'ab-en'e, nefert-'eu. N: 'Ey-m-ḥôtep.

[8] O: Nefret-en-ets. M: Nebt-'et. O: 'Ey-nefer, 'Ey-d'efa.

[9] O: Snu-'anch. M: 'Etf-'anch, deba-set, mut, renf-'anch.

[10] O: Sat. N: Pa-sei, pa ḥri, pa-ḥri-pedt. The latter, An., 5, 11, 7 ff., as chief of the mercenaries and his son.

[11] O: Seker-ch'a-bau, Ptaḥ-ch'a-merut, Ptaḥ-nefer-'ert, Ra'nofer, Nefer-ḥer-en-Ptaḥ, Ra'ḥôtep, Neter-user.

also express thankfulness or trust in the gods, *e.g.* the old names of *Ptaḥ causes me to live*, *Amun is her riches*, *Belonging to Ptaḥ*, *Servant of Rê‘*, and the curious one of *Brother of Amon.*[1] Names of the latter kind are especially numerous in the time of the Middle Empire, *e.g. Son of Mont*, *daughter of Ḥatḥôr*, *Comrade of Sobk*, *Of Amon*, *The gift of Amon*; other favourite names give glory to the gods, *e.g. Amon first*, *Sobk first*, or *Ḥatḥôr first.*[2] During the religious revival, under the New Empire, there was, of course, a superabundance of religious names; many follow the older forms, *e.g. Given by the bark of Osiris*, or *Amon is content*, *Of Set*, *Of Ḥôr*; others are disposed in new forms as, *Born of the Moon*, *Rê‘ gave him birth*, *Amon in the desert*, *Amon at the feast*, *Hôr in the bark*, *Mut in the bark.*[3] These new names have rather a peculiar, we might almost say a theological character; they express religious learning rather than simple piety, for instance, the knowledge as to which gods accompany the sun-god in his bark in the heavens. From the time of the Middle Empire every one bears the name or the title of a god, the men are called *Hôr*, *Chons*, *Uennofre*, or *Lord of the gods*, women, *Sechemt*, or *Lady of Denderah.*[4]

We cannot be surprised that the Egyptian officials, who always tried to show their loyalty, should often name their children after the kings. Under the Old Empire we find combinations such as *Cha‘frê‘ lives*, *Snefru is beautiful*, *Pepy endures*, *Pepy is strong*;[5] under the New Empire those are preferred which signify the piety of the Pharaoh, *e.g. Sety in the house of Thoth*, or *Nefer-ke-rê‘ in the house of Amon.*[6] After the 11th dynasty, however, it was customary to give sons the name of the monarch without further addition, as well as the prenomens and titles of the king, as *Shining in Thebes*, the *Bull with the understanding heart*, and even titles such as, *Lord of the two Countries*, and *Your lord*, are used under the New Empire.[7]

This custom of naming the children after the Pharaoh without the addition of any epithet, of calling the children Amony when an Amony was on the throne, or ’Entef during the reign of an ’Entef, is the cause of great confusion. The kings of the 11th dynasty were either ’Entef, Amony, or Mentuḥôtep, and these names survived in many families; some of the kings of the 12th dynasty were called Amenemḥê‘t, others Usertsen, and the great courtiers named their children after them. Under the 12th dynasty, therefore, these five names meet us at every turn; for instance, out of

[1] O: Ptaḥ-s‘anchu’e, Amend’efas, Nsu-Ptaḥ, Ḥent-Rê‘, Sen-Amun. Such names as Sen-Amun, Ḥatḥôr-sat, etc., may perhaps be elliptical, and be understood to mean: "the brother (given) by Amon," "the daughter (given) by Ḥatḥôr, etc.

[2] M: Sa-Ment’u, Sat-Ḥatḥôr, Sebek-’ere, Amony, Amendadat, Amenemḥê‘t, Sebekemḥê‘t, Ḥatḥôremḥe‘t.

[3] N: Neshemt-dadat, Amenḥôtep, Sety, Ḥor’e, ’E‘aḥmose, Ra‘messu, Amen-em-’ent, Amenemḥêb, Ḥar-em-u’e, Mut-em-u’e.

[4] M: Ḥôr, Chensu. N: Uennofre, Neb-nuteru, Sechemt. M: Nebt-’ent.

[5] O: Cha‘frê-‘anch, Snefru-Nofer, Pepy-ded’e, Pepy-necht.

[6] N: Sety-m-per-Dḥoute, Nefer-ke-rê‘-em-per-Amun.

[7] N: Ch‘amuêset, Ka-men-’eb; Nebtauey, Neb-seny—both the latter are elliptical forms: "he who *belongs* to the lord of the two countries."

twenty-seven male members of a family, thirteen are called Usertsen.[1] In the same way later the names Aḥmose and Amenḥôtep continually occur under the 18th dynasty, and that of Ramses under the 20th. Those especially well disposed (and what Egyptian official did not wish himself to be thought well disposed) seem not to have been content with naming their children after the monarch, but to have re-named them when a new Pharaoh ascended the throne. Thus under Usertsen I., the "chief judge and governor" was called after that monarch, though we can scarcely believe that the first official of the kingdom was born during his reign. It is far more likely that he was born under Amenemḥê‘t, and bore some other name, which was changed to the royal name at the accession of the new Pharaoh.[2] We meet with many similar cases.

The adoption of the royal name must doubtless have caused much confusion in the kingdom; but this confusion must have been still greater at the courts of the nomarchs of the Middle Empire; for in the time of the 12th dynasty, the custom arose for the officers of the household of the great men to call themselves and their children after their lord, in the same way as the state officials after the Pharaoh. The following instance may give an idea of the incredible confusion which was the result. The province, whose governors were buried at Beni Hasan, was governed at the beginning of the time of the Middle Empire (I know not in what order), by princes bearing the names of Amony, Chnemḥôtep, Netruḥôtep, Chety, Baqt'e, Nacht and Neternacht.[3] The consequence was that at the court of the Chnemḥôtep, son of Neher'e, whom we have so frequently mentioned, two-thirds of all the officials of the nome bore the name of this prince. Amongst his servants there were at least eleven of the name of Chnemḥôtep, nine of Neternacht, four of Chety, four of Baqt'e, two of Netruḥôtep, two of Amony, and one of Neḥer'e. One-third only bore names after their own pleasure.

The worst element in this confusion remains to be told; the Egyptians often went as far as to give brothers or sisters the same name. Thus S‘abu, high priest of Memphis under the Old Empire, named his second son S‘abu, but contented himself with giving to the four others the name of Ptaḥshepses. His eldest son and successor followed his example, for he called at least two of his sons Ptaḥshepses, and a third S‘abu.[4] Under the Middle Empire also we meet with a family in which three daughters were called Nebet-sochet-ent-Rê‘, and there are many similar cases.[5]

In order to distinguish those of the same name from each other, nick-names or pet names were doubtless provided for daily life; the inscriptions with their stiff official style rarely inform us what these were. Under the Old Empire the son was often distinguished from his father of the same name by the addition of *the Little*.[6] In time double names were formed from these nicknames, and the great lords and ladies of the pyramid age

[1] Louvre, C. 170. [2] L. D., ii. 122. [3] Cp. their tombs, L. D., ii. 142-143.
[4] R. J. H., 94; Mar. Mast., 378. It is doubtful which of the two generations is the older.
[5] Mar. Cat. d'Ab., 627. [6] E.g. Mar. Mast., 316, 325, and other examples.

often bear a "little name" as well as a "great" or "beautiful name.[1] The first is the child's name commonly used, as Ḥet'es ; the second is a high-sounding name with some good signification, as *Sokar shines with spirit.* A certain lady Tepes has, for instance, the additional great name of *Beautiful is the peace of Ḥatḥôr*, the lady Beb'e *Golden peace*, and a certain Ḥeba *Beautiful leader.* A lady of the harem is called *Servant of Rē'*, as well as *Amiable.* In later times also we often meet with double names, *e.g.* Kay Usertsen, Usertsen Senebsenebneb, and a nurse Senebtese, who bears the additional name of *My heaven endures.*[2]

Sometimes in order to give an individuality to a name in common use, it was somewhat changed. Thus with the children of the abovementioned high priest S'abu and Ptaḥshepses, the youngest son was called by the pet name Ptaḥshep [3] instead of Ptaḥshepses. With adults also we find similar familiar abbreviations of long names. Pepy-ded'e, *Pepy endures* is abbreviated to Ded'e, *endures.*[4] Amendadat and Sebekdadau'e, *The gift of Amon* and *Sobk bestows me* often become Dadat and Dadau'e, *Gift* and *Bestows me ;* Nebet-sochet-ent-Rê', the *Mistress of the fields of Rê'*, is curtailed to Nebet, *Mistress*, etc.[5] Numerous senseless pet names, which have come down to us from the time of the Old Empire, are probably abbreviations of much older names ; such are: 'Es'e, Ses'e, 'Ess'e, 'Et'e, Tet'e, 'Ett'e, 'Ep'e, Pep'e, 'Epp'e, 'Eff'e, Kek'e, Beb'e, T'et''e (they were probably pronounced Atôti, Apôpi,[6] etc.) With other nations a name as lisped by a child is often used as a term of endearment ; *e.g.* the English pet names of Dick or Dicky for Richard, Watt and Watty for Walter, Bob or Bobby for Robert. Evidently Bob and Bobby answer to Egyptian forms of the same kind ; for instance, in later times, under the New Empire, we meet with names such as T'ut'y, T'ut'eu, Tey, Naney, Tepa, Pepyu, Papepe, and others.

It may be concluded, from what we have said, that the Egyptians attached less importance to names than other nations of the same degree of civilisation. This is strange, for on the other side they thought much of a name enduring to posterity. According to the Egyptian faith, one could do nothing better for any one than by inscriptions and representations to "cause his name to live," and nothing worse than to allow it to perish. The Egyptians zealously endeavoured to root out and destroy the names and figures of people they hated ; this act of revenge was common at all periods, and was practised by kings as well as by private individuals. Thus we find in a tomb of the Old Empire, preserved intact, that the names and representations of two of the sons of the deceased have been carefully chiselled out, evidently according to the father's orders, who, after the building of his tomb, had occasion to be displeased with these sons.[7]

A stele from Abydos, which is now in the museum at Leyden,

[1] Ren nod'es, ren'a and ren nofer. E.g. Mar. Mast., 74 ff., 357, 360, 375, 400, 436, and frequently.
[2] For the latter, Louvre, C. 13.
[3] R. J. H., 94 ; Mar. Mast., 378.
[4] Mar. Mast., 401 f.
[5] Mar. Cat. d'Ab., 627.
[6] Cp. Tt'e, "Αθωθις, 'Epepy "Απωφις.
[7] Mar. Mast., 376.

belonged to a very distinguished man, the "hereditary prince, and the prince, the nearest friend of the king, the high priest with the right to wear the royal apron, the judge and prophet of Ma'at, the great priest of Osiris," etc., in short, to a high priest of Abydos. In his youth he had held a government appointment; "bearing the order of the king, he had done what the king pleased," his office was "famous in all the country" and King Usertsen I. "set him amongst his friends, because he was excellent in the eyes of his majesty." Finally, he succeeded his father as high priest of Abydos, and died after holding this office for twenty-four years. There is nothing in the long inscription to show us that any cloud had come between him and the court, and yet after his death something wrong must have been discovered about him, or some enemy of his must have come into power, for his name has been so carefully erased in the two places where it formerly stood that no sign of it can be read.[1]

It follows as a matter of course that the Pharaohs did the same towards rival kings or towards those predecessors whom they disliked. Many examples could be given: for instance, Thothmes III. caused to be chipped out all the names and figures of Chnemtamun his sister, who probably had kept him in tutelage much longer than was right. If we examine closely the mutilated monuments of Queen Chnemtamun we find other injuries, which were not due to the anger of her brother and guardian. The name and figure of the god Amon is carefully erased everywhere, evidently by the heretic king Chuen'eten, who instituted the worship of the sun's disk, and throughout his reign tried consistently to strike out the name of Amon in all the temples and tombs in the Nile valley. This fanatic attempted to establish the worship of one god, in order that his "name should endure for ever in the mouth of the living."

The mother had the charge of the child during its infancy, she nursed it for three years and carried it on her neck,[2]—this corresponds exactly to the custom of the modern Egyptians. During the first years of their childhood the boys,[3] and very often the girls also,[4] went nude. A grandson of King Chufu was content with nature's own costume even when he was old enough to be a "writer in the house of books," *i.e.* went to school.[5] Many children wore the short plaited lock on the right side of the head, following the example of the youthful god Horus, who was supposed to have worn this side-lock. I cannot say whether all children of a certain age wore this lock, or whether originally it was worn as a mark of distinction by the heir, as the pictures of the Old Empire would lead us to believe.[6] It is also uncertain how long it was worn, in one poem the "royal child

[1] Leyden, v. 4 (L.A.)

[2] Pap. de Boul., i. 20, 17 f.

[3] O. E.: L. D., ii. 8, 11, 19, 20, 22, 23, 27, etc. N. E.: L. D., iii. 10 b.

[4] Nude: O. E.: L. D., ii. 10, 23, 54. N. E.: L. D., iii. 8 b. Clothed: L. D., ii. 27, 36.

[5] L. D., ii. 23.

[6] Most of the children of the O. E. are without this lock; it appears, L. D., ii. 11, 23, 73; Düm. Res., 8; Perrot, p. 142. A little princess of the N. E.: L. D., iii. 8 b. A full grown girl in the harem: ib. 106 a. A little prince: L. D., iii. 10 b. Under the twentieth dynasty the royal children usually wear a broad band instead of the lock.

with the lock" is a "boy of ten years old;"[1] on the other hand, the young king, Merenrê' (Dyn. VI.), wore the lock all his life,[2] and the royal sons of the New Empire certainly wore it even in their old age.[3]

The years of childhood, the four years in which each was a "wise little one,"[4] *i.e.* a good child, were spent as they are everywhere all over the world. The toys, such as the naughty crocodile, the good little man who would jump, and the beautiful dolls which moved their arms,[5] show us that the little Egyptian girls were just like other children.

1. DOLL IN FORM OF OUR "PIN-CUSHION DOLLS," WITH LONG HAIR (Brit. Mus. After Wilk., ii. 64. A similar one in Berlin).

2. DOLL. THE HAIR IS GONE (Brit. Mus. After Wilk., ii. 64).

There were flowers also and pet birds in the nursery; and we find that Sechentchak, the above-mentioned little "writer in the house of books," was not ashamed to take a poor hoopoo about with him.[6] Boyhood, the time of education, followed the period of childhood, which under the New Empire closed with the fourth year.[7] The school boy had also his proper costume, which in old times seems to have consisted of a girdle only.[8] The Egyptians realised that it was a father's duty to superintend the education of their children, as we learn from the favourite dialogues between

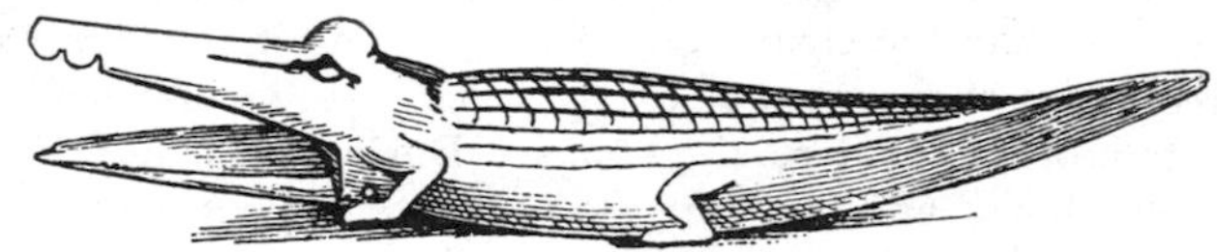

CROCODILE WITH MOVABLE JAW
(Leyden. After Wilk., ii. 64. A similar one in Berlin).

a father and a son contained in the didactic literature. As a matter of fact, even at this tender age, the children of the upper class were frequently sent away from home; they were either brought up in the palace with the royal children,[9] or they had to enter the school belonging to one of the government departments to prepare for their official career.[10] Besides the purely scientific instruction of which we shall have to treat in the

[1] Inscrip. of Kuban, l. 16. [2] Maspero, Guide, p. 347. [3] L. D., iii. 166, and frequently.

[4] Inscription of the high priest Bekenchôns at Munich.

[5] Dolls of the eleventh dynasty, of wood and ivory, with movable arms: Maspero, Guide, p. 250.

[6] L. D., ii. 23. [7] Inscription of the high priest Bekenchôns.

[8] Cp. Ä. Z., 1882, 2, and the passages referred to there.

[9] Cp. the passages referred to above, p. 78.

[10] The high priest Bekenchôns, for instance, was from his fifth to his fifteenth year assigned to one of the royal stables.

14th chapter, and the gymnastic exercises such as swimming;[1] the school-course consisted above all in the teaching of ethics, practical philosophy, and good manners. From a book edited probably in the time of the Middle Empire, but written under king 'Ess'e (Dyn. V.),[2] we learn how a father ought to instruct his son: "Be not proud of thine own learning, but do thou take counsel with all, for it is possible to learn from all. Treat a venerable wise man with respect, but correct thine equal when he maintains a wrong opinion. Be not proud of earthly goods or riches, for they come to thee from God without thy help. Calumnies should never be repeated: messages should be faithfully delivered. In a strange house, look not at the women; marry; give food to thy household; let there be no quarrelling about the distribution. For the rest, keep a contented countenance, and behave to thy superiors with proper respect, then shalt thou receive that which is the highest reward to a wise man; the "princes who hear thee shall say: 'How beautiful are the words which proceed out of his mouth.'"[3]

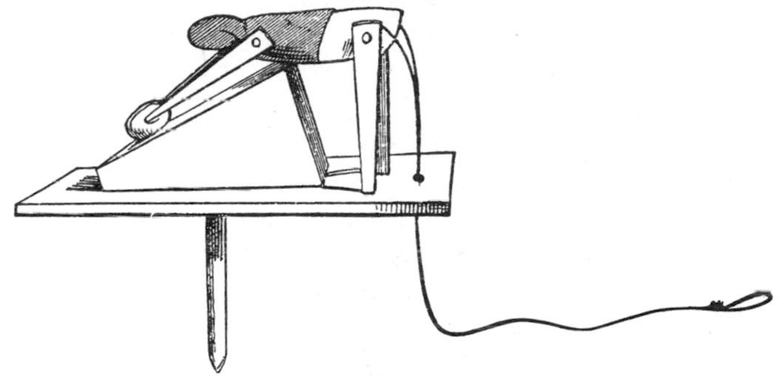

JOINTED DOLL, REPRESENTING A SLAVE CRUSHING CORN
(Leyden Museum. After Wilk., ii. 64).

A similar *instruction* of the time of the New Empire gives still more detailed advice. Be industrious, "let thine eyes be open, lest thou become a beggar; for the man that is idle cometh not to honour."[4] Be not importunate nor indiscreet; "enter not uninvited into the house of another; if he bids thee enter thou art honoured. Look not around, look not around in the house of another. If thine eye see anything, be silent about it, and relate it not outside to others, lest if it be heard, it become to thee as a crime worthy of death.[5] Speak not too much, for men are deaf to the man of many words; be silent rather, then shalt thou please, therefore speak not.[6] Before all things guard thy speech, for "a man's ruin lies in his tongue.[7] Man's body is a storehouse, full of all manner of answers. Choose therefore the right one and speak well, and let the wrong answer remain imprisoned in thy body."[8] Behave with

[1] Inscription at Siut: R. J. H., 289, 6 = Mar. mon. div., 68 d.
[2] The second half of the Pap. Prisse. [3] Prisse, 19, 2-3. [4] Pap. de Boul., i. 18, 13 ff.
[5] Ib. 16, 9 ff. with hypotheses. [6] Ib. 16, 17 f. [7] Ib. 20, 9. [8] Ib. 20, 9 ff.

propriety at meals, and "be not greedy to fill thy body.[1] Eat not bread whilst another standeth by, unless thou shalt lay his hand on the bread also. . . . One is poor, another is rich, but bread remains to him that is generous. He that was rich in the year that is past, may even in this year become a vagrant."[2] Never forget to be respectful, and "do not sit down whilst another stands, who is older than thou, or who holds a higher office than thou dost."[3]

These rules for good conduct are enough to show how much the higher classes thought of good manners, and the strict formulae of letter writing (which we shall discuss in the 15th chapter), though they varied according to the rank and position of the correspondents, show us that the Egyptians of the New Empire were lovers of strict etiquette. The formalities of society were certainly not less ceremonious then, than those of the Mahommedan inhabitants of Egypt are now.

[1] Ib. 21, 7. [2] Ib. 21, 3 ff. From the context the word is supposed to be *vagrant*. [3] Ib. 19, 10 ff.

ISIS WITH THE CHILD HORUS.
(Porcelain statue in the Berlin Museum).

RESTORATION OF A COUNTRY HOUSE (after the picture p. 176).

CHAPTER IX

THE HOUSE

IN speaking of the architecture of ancient Egypt, our minds turn involuntarily to those wonderful temples and tombs, the ruins of which are the glory of the valley of the Nile. These gigantic buildings, however, form in reality an exception to the usual style of building in Egypt, where the houses were as slight and perishable as the temples were strong and eternal. Instead of thick walls, the houses had walls of Nile mud; instead of gigantic pillars, pretty wooden supports; instead of stone roofs, rafters of palm trunks. One feature alone they had in common, the rich colouring which adorned every part of the house as well as of the temple. It may seem surprising that, in spite of the great skill of the Egyptians in building, they should never have used the "eternal stones" for their dwelling houses. The Nile mud offers however such an easy workable material, that for buildings which were not to endure for ever it would have seemed absurd to substitute it by quarried stone. The climate also had to be considered; a building was required which kept off the violent heat of the sun, but allowed plenty of air to enter everywhere; a solid stone building would scarcely have been pleasant during the great summer heat of Upper Egypt. A light erection with small airy rooms, hangings of matting over the windows, standing amongst shady trees, and if possible near the cool water—such was the house best fitted for the Egyptian climate, and such was the house built by the ancient Egyptians at all periods.

There was of course a great difference between one house and another. If we leave on one side the *houses* of the peasants (they lived probably in mud-huts like the modern fellahin) the house of a citizen living with a small household in the narrow streets of the town would perhaps consist merely of a small court with a few rooms at the back, and a flight of steps leading up to the flat roof. This is the plan of the better sort of village houses in Egypt now, and corresponds with some small models of houses in our museums, though the latter probably represent store-houses rather than dwelling-houses.[1] The illustration below somewhat resembling a box gives the usual character of these small dwelling-houses. It seems to represent a house with thick slanting walls of mud replaced by thin walls of laths below the windows; above is a small upper story open to the flat roof in front. A thick pillar, probably of mud, like the similar supports in modern Egyptian houses, forms the only decoration of the little house.

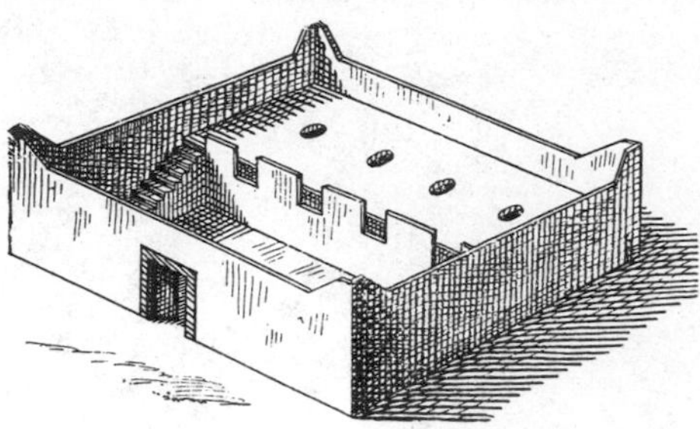

MODEL IN THE LOUVRE (after Perrot-Chipiez).

On the other hand, the great lord who lived in his park outside the town was not content with a building of this sort; he wanted a house for himself, another for his wife, another for the kitchen, a reception hall for distinguished guests, a provision house, dwellings for the servants, etc. As is the case now in the East, a palace of this kind must really have constituted a town-quarter.

MODEL OF A HOUSE. UNKNOWN PERIOD (Louvre. After Perrot-Chipiez).

[1] The model in the Louvre certainly represents a granary; the holes in the top are to pour in the corn. In the court of the one in the Brit. Mus. (Wilk., i. 351), is a woman pounding corn in a mortar; it was formerly full of corn. A stove is in the court of the one in the Gizeh Museum (Maspero Guide, p. 293 f.) They all probably represent places in which bread might be prepared, and this renders it intelligible why they put these models in the tombs.

Unfortunately it is now almost impossible to form an exact picture of the appearance of an ancient Egyptian town, for nothing remains of the famous great cities of ancient Egypt except mounds of rubbish; not even in Memphis nor in Thebes is there even the ruin of a house to be found, for later generations have ploughed up every foot of arable land for corn. The only ruins that remain are those of the town "Horizon of the Sun,"[1] built for himself by the reformer Chu-en-'eten, and destroyed by violence after his death; this city lay outside the arable country, and therefore it was not worth while to till the ground on which it had stood. We can still trace the broad street that ran the whole length of the town which was about three miles long and half a mile broad, and see that on either side of the street were large public buildings with courts and enclosures. It is impossible to trace how that part of the town occupied by the numerous small private buildings was laid out.

It is probable that the great towns in ancient Egypt often changed their position, like the eastern towns of the Middle Ages. It was customary in the East that a mighty monarch should begin at his accession to "build a city;" he generally chose an outlying quarter of the town or a village near the capital as the site of his palace, and transferred to it the seat of his government. Occasionally this new place was permanent, but as a rule it was never finished, and disappeared a few generations later, after a successor had established a new residence for himself. Thus the capital in the course of centuries moved hither and thither, and officially at least changed its name; this was the case with almost every great city of the East. A king might also choose a new plot of ground far from the capital without its becoming on that account more permanent.

We know for certain that this was customary with the Pharaohs of the New Empire; Thebes was indeed maintained as the capital of the kingdom, on account of her great sanctuaries, but the king resided in some newly-founded city bearing the name of the founder. The new city was built "after the plan of Thebes"[2] with granaries and storehouses, with gardens and tanks that it might be "sweet to live in,"[3] and the court poet sung of her glory in his "account of the victory of the lord of Egypt:"[4]

"His Majesty has built for himself a fortress,
'Great in victory' is her name.
She lies between Palestine and Egypt,
And is full of food and nourishment.
Her appearance is as On of the South,
And she shall endure like Memphis.
The sun rises in her horizon
And sets within her boundaries,[5]
All men forsake their towns
And settle in her western territory.
Amon dwells in the southern part, in the temple of Sutech,
But Astarte dwells towards the setting of the sun,

[1] Plan of Tell el Amarna, L. D., i. 63, 64.
[2] An. 3, 2, 1.
[3] Ib.
[4] An., 4, 6, 1 ff.
[5] That is: the king lives in her.

And Ud'oit on the northern side.[1]
The fortress which is within her
Is like the horizon of heaven,
'Ramses beloved of Amon' is god there,
And 'Mentu in the countries' is speaker,
The 'Sun of the ruler' is governor, he is gracious to Egypt,
And 'Favourite of Atum' is prince, to whose dwelling all people go."

In the same way we know that Amenemḥê't, a king of the Middle Empire, built a town for his residence in the Feyum, and erected his pyramids close by. The last circumstance explains what otherwise would appear most strange.

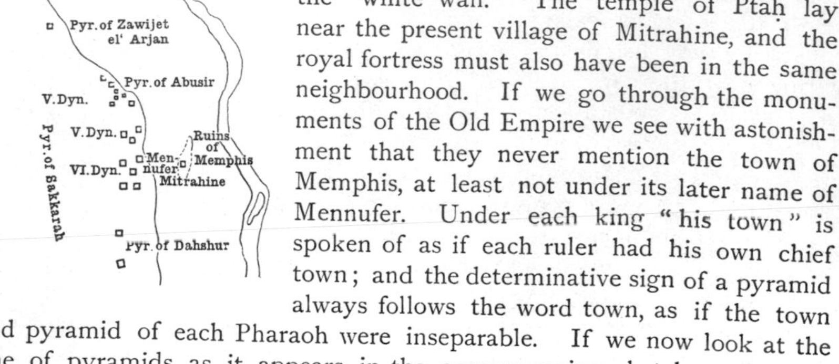

We are accustomed to accept the Greek tradition that the kings of the pyramid age resided at Memphis, the city of the ancient temple of Ptaḥ and of the famous citadel of the "white wall." The temple of Ptaḥ lay near the present village of Mitrahine, and the royal fortress must also have been in the same neighbourhood. If we go through the monuments of the Old Empire we see with astonishment that they never mention the town of Memphis, at least not under its later name of Mennufer. Under each king "his town" is spoken of as if each ruler had his own chief town; and the determinative sign of a pyramid always follows the word town, as if the town and pyramid of each Pharaoh were inseparable. If we now look at the line of pyramids as it appears in the accompanying sketch, we become aware of the striking fact that the pyramid which we know to be the most ancient is very far removed from the old site of Memphis.

If we accept the general opinion that Chufu and Cha'frê' resided at Memphis then we must also admit the strange fact that they built their tombs three miles from their capital, whilst the desert ground in the immediate neighbourhood was wholly bare of buildings. It is difficult to believe this; it is far more likely that the town of Chufu was in reality near his pyramid. The residence of Cha'frê' and of Menkerê' was also probably at Gizeh, that of the kings of the 5th dynasty at Abusir and to the north of Sakkarah, whilst that of the Pharaohs of the 6th dynasty was close to the site of the later town of Memphis. In corroboration of this opinion we find that the oldest pyramid erected close to Memphis, the tomb of Pepy, was called Mennufer, the same name that Memphis bore later. The *town* of King Pepy probably bore the same name as his pyramid, and from that town the later town Mennufer—Memphis—was developed, which in the course of time grew to be a gigantic city with the

[1] The position of the temple of each divinity indicated the part of the sky where that divinity was supposed to dwell.

famous temple, the "house of the image of Ptaḥ," and the fortress of the "white wall." Whilst the residences of the older kings have completely disappeared, leaving no trace except their pyramids, the residence of Pepy prospered on account of its vicinity to an important town.

The ruins of the towns having disappeared, it is very difficult to form any idea of an ancient Egyptian dwelling-house, and we should be quite powerless to do so, were it not for some coffins in the form of houses belonging to the time of the Old Empire. If we look at the picture of the coffin of King Menkerê' (Dyn. IV.) which once stood in his pyramid at Gizeh and now lies at the bottom of the Adriatic, we see at the first

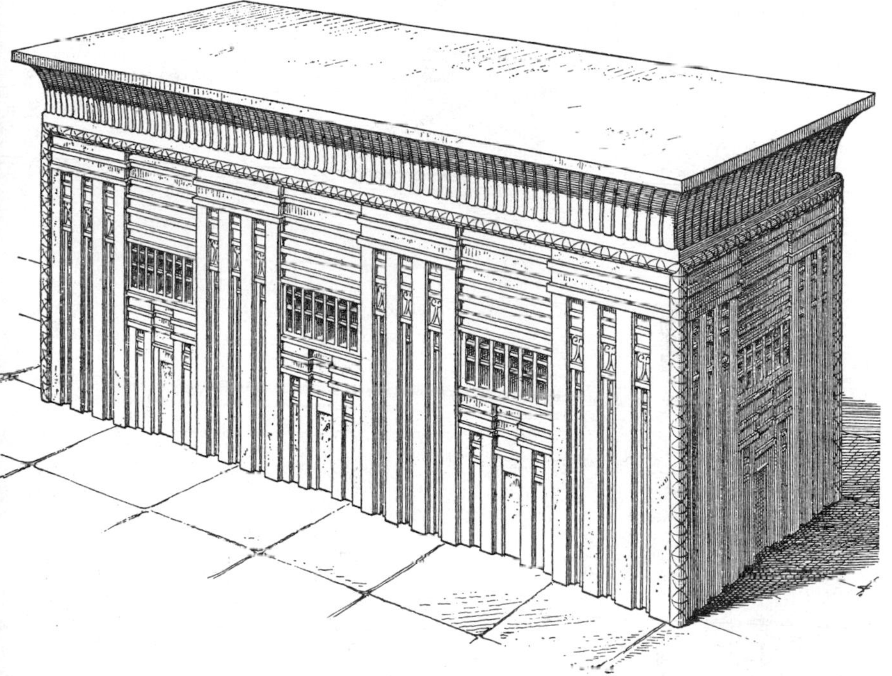

SARCOPHAGUS OF MENKERÊ' (after Perrot-Chipiez).

glance that it represents a house.[1] This house had three doors on the long side and one on the short side; above each was a latticed window. Graceful little pillars, projecting slightly from the wall, support the beams, on which rests the concave portion of the flat roof. A mere glance convinces us that this house was built by a carpenter and not by a mason; we can see clearly how the horizontal beams fit into those that are vertical. There are no large wall-spaces as there are

[1] Coffins in the form of houses: King Menkerê', Perrot, p. 109. Chufu'anch, Perrot, p. 188, 189. Coffin at Gizeh, L. D., i. 30. The splendid house-shaped coffin of Mentuḥôtep (Berlin) of the Middle Empire, which as we see was fully painted.

in brickwork; the whole house is put together of thin laths and planks. Trunks of palms are used only at the corners and for the beams of the roof. The ordinary character of these buildings is seen by the accompanying sketch from Chipiez; the details are rather arbitrary.

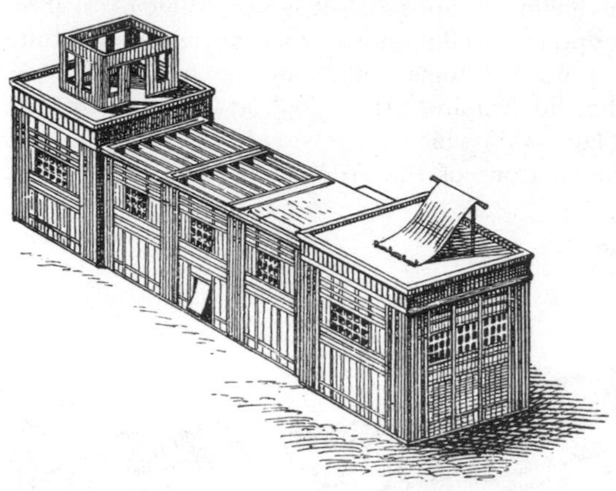

RESTORATION OF A HOUSE OF THE OLD EMPIRE (after Perrot-Chipiez).

This style of building was no exception to the rule, as we see by the numerous representations of doors in the Memphite tombs. A door, similar to the door of an ancient house, was chiselled within the tomb on the west wall,[1] and this is always very much like those seen on the above coffin. Its form is sometimes simple, sometimes rather ornamental, but it is always painted in bright colours.

Doubtless the houses were also adorned in this brilliant manner; each lath, each board, was either painted or gaily figured. The broader piers

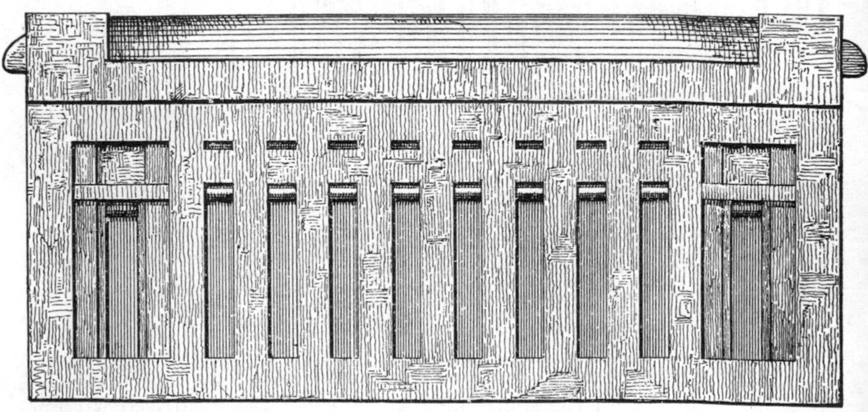

COFFIN OF THE OLD EMPIRE IN THE FORM OF A HOUSE (after L. D., i. 30. Tomb 98 at Gizeh).

were, however, hung with carpets, each with its own pattern and its own colour.[2] Such a building would appear most strange under our grey sky, but in the Egyptian sunlight the pretty systematic arrangement of the woodwork and the richness of the colour must have been most effective.

[1] False doors in tombs, Perrot, p. 181 (=Pl. 13, 14), 512, 513; L. D., i. 25, 26, 29, 41; L. D., ii. 10, 11, 16, 17, 33, 48, etc.

[2] Perrot, Pl. 13, 14; L. D., ii. 98.

All the houses of the rich however were not so highly decorated. The accompanying illustration represents a coffin of an unknown man, and gives us an example of a model of a house of much simpler construction. The smooth undivided walls are evidently of brick, the recess containing the door alone shows distinct wooden construction. The disposition of the rooms in this house must also have been very different from the above-mentioned luxurious wooden building; this one has only two doors altogether, the walls of the back of the house and of the two short sides being pierced alone by windows.

The dimensions of some of these old palaces were very considerable, thus 'Amt'en, the great man of the south, with whom we have had so much to do (pp. 83-85), built a house for himself "two hundred ells long and two hundred broad," a square building therefore, with each side measuring over a hundred yards.[1] Unfortunately we know very little of the arrangement of the furniture of these buildings. Once only, in the tomb of Ymery, a superintendent of the royal property,[2] part of the inside of a house is given. Ymery has caused himself to be represented there seated in a pillared hall receiving the funerary offerings. Four rows of light wooden pillars nearly 20 feet high, with capitals in the form of flowers, support the flat roof. A gaily coloured carpet is hung between the pillars at the back; screened in this way from the sight of the servants, Ymery sits here on a high backed seat under which crouches his greyhound 'Eken'e. The room is filled with tables of food and jugs of liquid, and from a bar, which runs the whole length of the room below the ceiling, hang pieces of roast meat. This is evidently the great dining-hall, which then, as well as a century later, constituted the chief room of an Egyptian palace.

Rugs, like those which adorn Ymery's chair, evidently play a great part in the decoration of the room, and we shall scarcely make a mistake in thinking that the inner sides of the walls were hung with carpets like the outer. The lower part of the wall remained uncovered: with real artistic sense they preferred a dado of a heavier style, and therefore allowed the timber-work to be seen. This was the more decorative as they understood how to make the woodwork in alternate pieces cut cross and lengthwise.[3] The round trunks of the palms which formed the roof were also often left uncovered that they might be seen. In some cases they were splendidly decorated like those beautiful roofs in the tombs, which we admire so much. The Egyptians preferred to have the doors and windows small and high; there was a wooden roller at the top of each which served to roll up the mat which hung over the opening.

Let us now pass over the long series of centuries dividing the Old from the New Empire, and we shall find that though for this later period

[1] L. D., ii. 7. The courts and storehouses were of course included in this reckoning.

[2] L. D., ii. 52.

[3] L. D., ii. 20. In this tomb a piece of stone wall is seen below the painted woodwork, and in the houses also a few feet of the brickwork may sometimes have been visible below.

we have at our disposal more material than before, yet we are still unable to give a wholly satisfactory picture. The representations of houses and palaces which we get from the tombs of Thebes and Tell el Amarna are unfortunately drawn in the same unfortunate style as the Egyptians used for landscape. When an Egyptian artist represented a man or an animal he gave the contours clearly and reasonably in profile, but when he had to draw a great building, a temple, or a garden, his good genius forsook him. In treating such an important and complex object he wished if possible to show every part of it; he therefore did not draw the house from the front nor from the side, but made a picture of both sides together, and when the house had an upper story with three chambers, he put these three rooms close by also. He considered his duty accomplished when he had placed all the details before the spectator, but he did not care whether the spectator understood how these details fitted together.

We have to face another difficulty in order to comprehend these pictures; the Egyptian artist has no sense of proportion between the different parts of the representation. If, for instance, the king is standing in one of the rooms of the building in question, our artist would, regardless of truth, draw that room ten times as large as all the others together, and even in one picture he frequently changes his standard of measurement. The reader must beware of these peculiarities in considering the following restorations of Egyptian buildings.

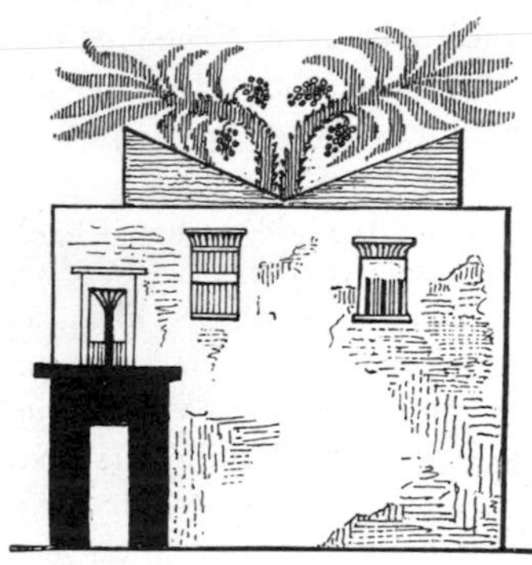
After Wilk., i. 361.

The pictures in the Theban tombs, representing the small country houses of Egyptians of rank, instruct us as to the outside of private houses of the time of the New Empire.

One of these is a low two-storied building, and like all the houses of this time very bare on the outside. It has smooth white-washed brick walls, and the plain white surface is only varied by the projecting frames of the door and windows. The ground floor seems to have no windows, but the first story has, in addition to its two windows, a kind of balcony. The roof, above which we can see the trees of the garden behind, is very strange,—it is flat, but has a curious top, which perhaps answers to the *Mulkuf* of the modern Egyptian house; an oblique construction of boards which catches the cool north wind and conducts it into the upper story of the house.

We see in the Theban wall-picture on p. 176[1] a country house of the

[1] After Ros. M. C., 68 (=Perrot, p. 453, after Champ. mon. 174). My opinion differs considerably from that of Perrot, who thinks this picture represents all four sides of the building together, which is I think quite erroneous. The picture (which apparently is unfinished) is only a part of a larger one, as we see by the fact that the lower part of the wall and half of the door on the right side are wanting. It would be quite worth while to search for the rest.

time of the 18th dynasty; it was not represented on account of its special grandeur, but as being the scene of a home-festival. In the open porch before the house are the vessels of wine, while the food is on tables adorned with garlands; numerous jars, loaves, and bowls stand close by, hidden by a curtain from the guests who are entering. Whilst the latter greet their host a jar of wine with its embroidered cover is carried past, and two servants in the background, who seem to be of a very thirsty nature, have already seized some drinking bowls.

The house itself lies in a corner of the garden, which is planted with dark green foliage trees, figs, and pomegranates, and in which there is also an arbour covered with vines. The garden is surrounded by a wall of brownish brick pierced by two granite doors. Though the house has two stories it strikes us as very small; it has only one door which, as was customary at that time, is placed at one side of the principal wall and not in the middle. The ground floor seems to be built of brick and to be whitewashed; it is lighted by three small windows with wooden lattice-work; the door has a framework of red granite. The first story is in quite a different style, the walls are made of thin boards, the two windows are large, their frames project a little from the wall and are closed by brightly coloured mats. This story contains probably the principal room of the house, the room for family life. A curious fact confirms this supposition: the window-hangings have a small square piece cut out at the bottom allowing the women to see out of the windows without themselves being seen. A similar arrangement exists now in modern Egyptian houses.

The roof of the second story rests on little pillars and is open on all sides to the air. Ventilation is much thought of also in the other parts of the house, for the whole of the narrow front is left open and can only be closed by a large curtain of matting. In our picture this is only half drawn up, so as to conceal the interior of the ground floor from the guests. In order to protect this part of the house from the great heat of the Theban sun, a wonderful canopy, borne by six thin blue wooden pillars, is carried over the whole building, and brought forward like a porch in the front of the house. Our picture shows us how this porch was used; it was the place in which the Egyptians enjoyed the pleasures of life; here they could breathe the sweet breath of the north wind and enjoy the flowers and trees of the garden. An excellent restoration of this house forms the frontispiece to this chapter.

The above details show plainly that the gentlefolk of Egypt preferred to live far from the bustle of the world; this is still more apparent in the case of another house of the same epoch. The gentleman to whom the garden described on p. 195 belonged had his house hidden in the farthest corner of his garden, behind high leafy trees screening it from inquisitive eyes. People passing on the canal would only see the tops of the trees over the white wall: the simplicity of the house corresponds with its hidden situation. It is a one-storied building with a higher wing

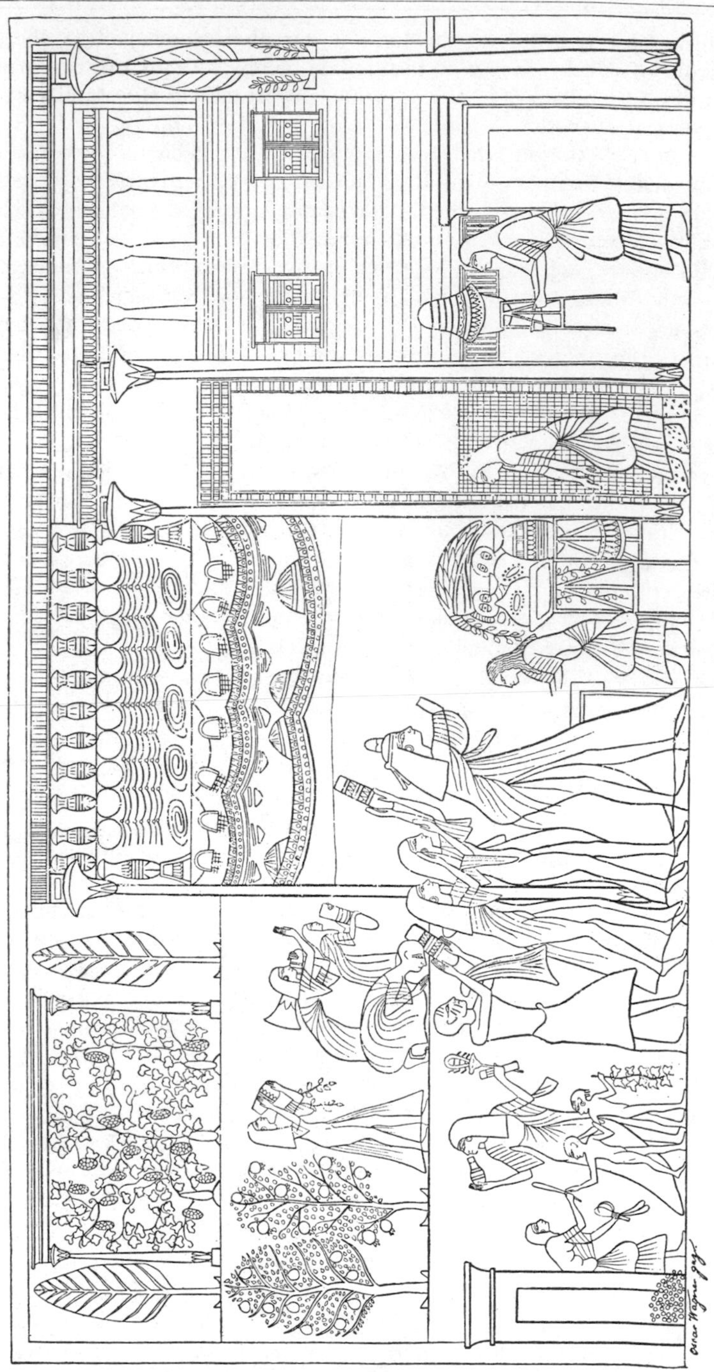

VISIT TO A COUNTRY HOUSE (after Ros. M. C., 68).

something like a tower on the left; it has plain wooden walls, the only decoration of which consists in the hollow below the roof and the projecting frames and pillars of the windows. Unfortunately the details of the plan are very obscure.

A country house, such as we have described above, cannot be considered as a complete example of the house of an Egyptian gentleman. It is so small that it would be impossible to find room for a large household. There are no servants' rooms, no storerooms, no kitchens. All these offices, which might be dispensed with in the country, are absolutely necessary in a town house: the number of servants employed in the household of a rich man will alone give us an idea of the size required for his residence.

The plans of the houses which are given in the tombs of Tell el

HOUSE OF MERYRÊ'—SIDE VIEW (after L. D., iii. 93).

Amarna are in fact quite different from the above. Instead of a single building with several stories we here find a number of one-storied rooms and halls grouped round small courts. This characteristic is common to all, though the details of the plans may vary a good deal according to the taste or the wealth of the proprietor. The two houses represented in the tomb of the high priest Meryrê' are perhaps the most simple in their arrangement; one is drawn from the front, the other from the side. They seem both to have belonged to that wealthy priest.[1] The new city extended a long way, and it is quite conceivable that he may have thought it necessary to have one house near the temple and another near the palace

[1] After L. D., iii. 93 and 96 b. I have a suspicion that both pictures represent the same building, in spite of all the variations in detail.

of his master. The two buildings resemble each other very much, and in our description we will treat them as the same.

The ground plan was rectangular, and the whole was surrounded by a wall which could only be entered on the short side in front of the house where there was the principal door with a small door on either hand. Inside the wall was a court where we see the servants busy sweeping and sprinkling with water. The farther wall of this court forms the front of three small

HOUSE OF MERYRÊ'—FRONT VIEW (after L. D., iii. 96).

buildings. The arrangement of the two side rooms is obscure—we can only see a row of pillars in the interior of them; the central building however certainly served as a vestibule to the great hall which lay behind. This vestibule is a coquettish kiosk borne by four pretty pillars, the wall in front only reaching half way up. The top of this wall and the posts of the doors are adorned with rows of uraeus snakes in bronze. There is a porch in front of the vestibule, like that in the country house mentioned above.

Passing through the kiosk we enter the most important room in the Egyptian house, the great dining-hall supported by pillars. The large dining table stands in the middle covered with dishes, bowls of fruit, and loaves of bread; roast meat and other articles of food are placed upon smaller tables; there are also flowers and gay necklets, the requisites for an Egyptian dinner-party. In the back part of the hall a row of immense wine jars are built into the wall. On either side of the table stand one or two arm-chairs, and close to one of them is a basin with a jug of water; evidently the present Oriental custom of pouring water over the hands after eating is no modern innovation.

Behind the dining-hall, but separated from it by a small court, are the store-rooms and a sleeping apartment. The room on the right side of the latter is not entered directly from the court but through a small ante-chamber; a large bed piled high with pillows and bolsters stands in the middle.

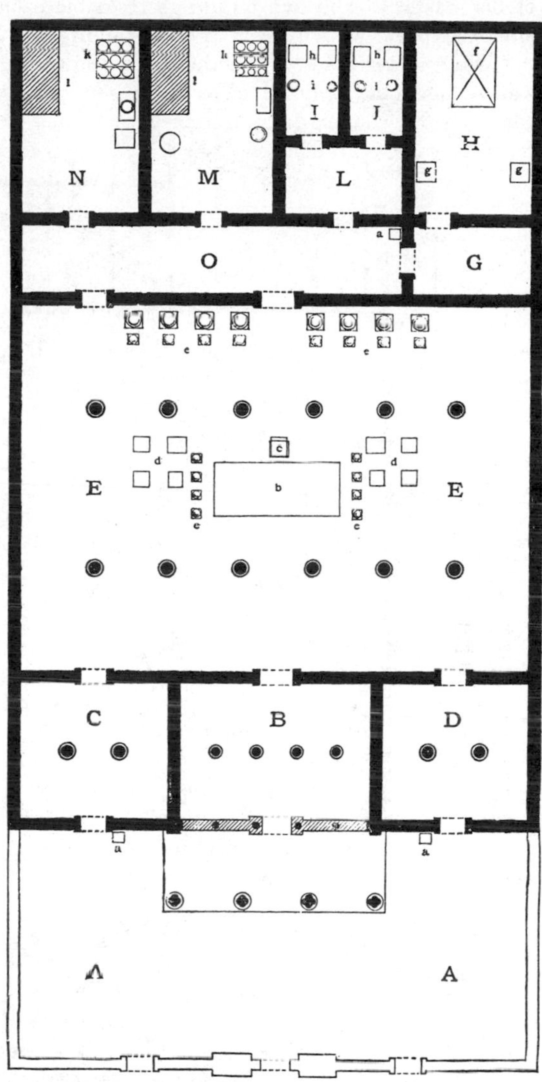

PLAN OF THE HOUSE OF MERYRÊ' (after L. D., iii. 93).

A. Court.
B. Vestibule with porch.
C, D. Porters' rooms.
E. Dining hall.
G. Vestibule.
H. Bedroom.
I, L. Bakery.
M, N. Kitchens.
O. Court.

a. Seats for the porters.
b. Large table.
c. Seat for the master.
d. Small tables.
e. Jugs.
f. Bed.
g. Toilet-table.
h. Table with bread.
i. Bowls on stands.
k. Jugs.
l. Hearth.

To the left is the bakery, consisting of an ante-room and two other rooms; here a workman is busy pounding corn in a great mortar. Two large rooms filled with jars serve as kitchens; in each room there is a low hearth.

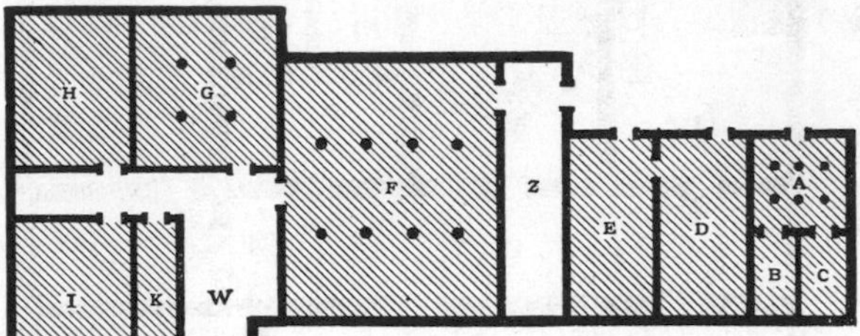

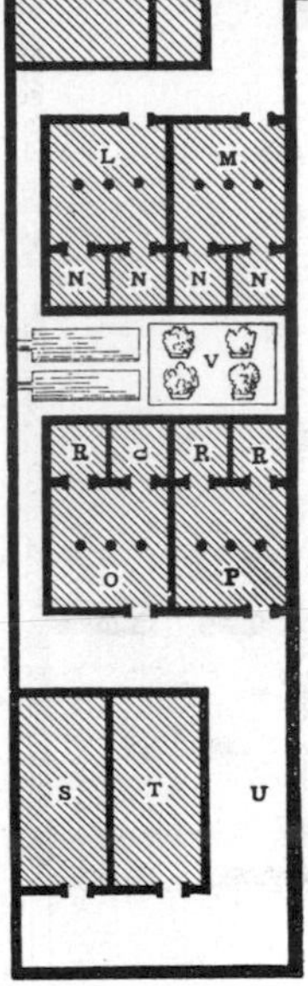

Two doors [1] lead to these rooms behind; the larger door is in the middle of the dining-hall, and is evidently destined for the company and for the servants when waiting at meals. The servants usually however passed through the vestibule to the left into the left side of the hall, which was left unfurnished, and thence through a little door into the court at the back. There was no direct way from the storerooms into the street, the servants had always to pass through the great hall; a fault in the plan which seems strange enough. Another curious fact about Meryrê''s house is that there were no women's apartments. This puzzle is easily explained by the inscriptions in his tomb: in no place is his wife mentioned. Meryrê' therefore was an old bachelor. This is also the reason that in one of his dining-halls we see but one chair; the great lord ate his dinner alone. The accompanying plate gives a restoration of this interesting building. The artist has succeeded very well in giving to the surroundings the general character of an ancient Egyptian town.

PLAN OF THE HOUSE OF 'EY (after L. D., iii. 106).

A. Servants' room.
B, C. Bedchambers.
D, E. Pantries.
F. Dining hall.
G. Bedroom.
H. Dining-room.
I. Kitchen.
K. Bakery.
M, L, O, P. Women's apartments.
N, R. Bedchambers for the women.
S, T. Kitchens for the servants.
Y. Garden.
U, W, Z. Courts.

A house of very different plan was that in which the above-mentioned (p. 119) "holy father" 'Ey lived with his family at Tell el Amarna.[2] The shape of the plan was again rectangular, with the short side parallel to the street; it was therefore impossible to have the usual arrangement of courts and buildings.

The stately enclosed court with its three doors and the three vestibules

[1] This refers to the one building, the other possesses but one entrance door: therefore in the latter the left side of the dining-hall is not left free.

[2] After L. D., iii. 106 a. The smaller corner-room is completed from Prisse's publication of this plan. It is doubtful whether the ground-plan was really rectangular, or whether it is so represented from want of room.

RESIDENCE OF A WEALTHY EGYPTIAN OF THE TIME OF THE 18TH DYNASTY.

AFTER THE PLANS L. D., III. 93, 96. RESTORATION BY P. LAUSER.

The walls are broken away to show the interior of the vestibule on the left, and of the great dining-hall.

beyond are not to be found here; if we enter from the street we find ourselves in front of three small buildings, and of these the one on the left alone (the room of the servant on duty) has rather a dignified appearance, the other two being merely additional storerooms for wine and oil. Were it not for the fan-bearers standing in front of the door, no one would guess that this insignificant house was the residence of the mighty favourite of Pharaoh. To the right of these buildings we pass through a small door into a narrow court, where the servants are busy with their brooms and water-pots. The stately building beyond is the dining-hall, which is arranged in the usual manner.

PART OF THE HOUSE OF 'EY. Rooms G-N (after L. D., iii. 106).

A door leads from the back of the dining-hall into a court, through which we reach the kitchen and the master's bedroom. In the middle of the latter is an immense four-post bedstead, near which stand three small beds, which may be intended for 'Ey's children. A second smaller dining-room adjoins the bedroom; it contains as usual two arm-chairs with footstools, a large dining table, and jars of wine; the jug and wash-basin have also not been forgotten. Apparently 'Ey and his wife Tey only used their great dining-hall on festive occasions.

This court and the long wing which stretches to the

left of it is the scene of the daily life of the household. Servants are grouped together in the corners, gossiping busily over the news of the day; sitting on low stones before the entrance to the master's rooms are the porters, who join, though from a distance, in the interesting conversation.

If we leave the court on the left and go round the kitchen we find ourselves in front of a handsome building which is nothing less than the harem belonging to 'Ey—the dwelling of his wife, of her attendants, and of his children. He possessed two similar houses turned back to back, and separated by a small garden containing trees and tanks of water. Each house is divided into two rooms supported by pillars, behind each of which are two other rooms for the musical instruments and the toilet requisites. No work was ever done here. Behind the two houses for the women, at the further end of the piece of ground, are two other kitchens, apparently intended for the servants, several of whom are squatting round this building, busily intent on eating their dinner from small tables.

The houses which we have now considered suffice to give us an idea of the private dwellings of the New Empire. If we put aside the question of the above-mentioned country houses, we find that the following parts belong to the complete town house of the 18th dynasty: a great vestibule with an ante-room for the porter; behind that the large dining-hall, the principal room in the whole house; beyond, a small court, to the right of which was the sleeping apartment of the master; to the left, the kitchen and store-room. Then beyond still further follows the house for the women and the garden.

Doubtless this plan holds good for all the large private houses, and even the king's palace differed only in size and grandeur.[1] The palace has a vestibule with a principal door and two side doors; three small buildings with a row of pillars extending along the front forms the further side of this vestibule. The central building (answering to the kiosk-like ante-chamber in the house of Meryrê') is often represented in the tombs of Tell el Amarna; the king and queen appear on the balcony above, to show themselves to their faithful servants and to throw down presents to them. This balcony, the *smshd*, which is frequently mentioned, forms a characteristic part of the royal palace; the king *appears*[2] on it to inspect the heaps of tribute below and the slaves who are led before him. This "great balcony" was therefore richly decorated; it consisted of "good gold" or of "lapislazuli and malachite."[3] Behind the three ante-chambers are the state rooms, two immense dining halls, and adjoining one of these is the kitchen and the sleeping apartment of the monarch. In the latter his bedstead stands surrounded by flowers in bloom.

Not far from the temple of Medinet Habu there is a ruin, which is

[1] The palace of the king: L. D., iii. 108-109; the details are very obscure owing to the change in the scale of measure. The kiosk of the palace: L. D., iii. 103, 108; the remarkable building L. D., iii. 99, with its ramp seems to belong here.

[2] Harr., i. 4, 12.

[3] Ib. and An., 3, 7, 5.

probably the remains of a royal castle. Ramses II. and Ramses III. had, as I have already remarked (p. 70), laid out certain palaces near the temples which they had founded on the western bank. The pleasing building with narrow rooms, like a tower, so well known by the name of the

SEAT OF THE TIME OF THE 4TH DYNASTY (after L. D., ii. 44).

ARM-CHAIR OF THE TIME OF THE 5TH DYNASTY (after L. D., ii. 74 c).

"Pavilion of Medinet Habu," belongs to the noble royal palace, which Ramses III. built here for himself "like the hall of Atum, which is in the heavens, with pillars, beams, and doors of silver, and a great balcony of good gold upon which to appear.[1]" Contrary to custom Ramses III. built the front of his palace of quarried stone, and therefore the ruins of this part remain whilst no trace is left of the palace proper.

CHAIR IN THE LEYDEN MUSEUM (after Wilk., i. 410).

We have fortunately very definite knowledge about the furniture of the ancient Egyptian house; it was distinguished at all periods by elegance and good sense. The chairs and couches were specially handsome;

[1] Harr., i. 4, 11.

they were often made of ebony inlaid with ivory,[1] and from the earliest period it was customary to shape the feet like the paws of a lion, and if possible to bring in the head of a lion also, as if the king of beasts were offering his back as a seat to the great lord. The most ancient form of seat is a wooden stool covered by a cushion, and carved into the form of a lotus-flower behind, while the legs are shaped like those of

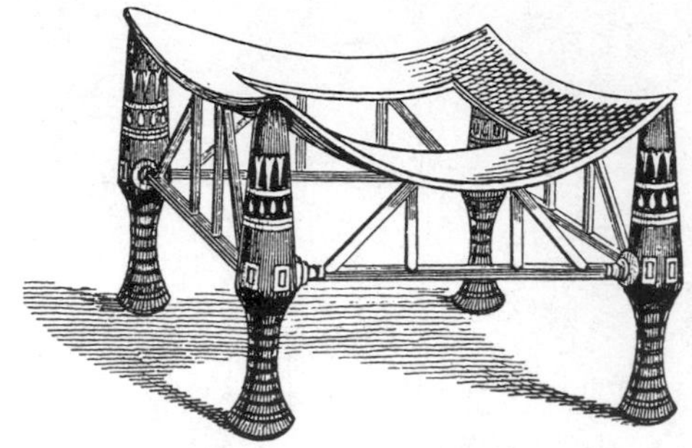

STOOL MADE OF EBONY INLAID WITH IVORY (British Museum. After Wilk., i. 413).

FROM A THEBAN WALL PICTURE IN THE BRITISH MUSEUM.

a lion.[2] It is intended for one or for two persons, and appears to have been used even down to the time of the New Empire. Under the 5th dynasty this seat usually had high sides and a back.[3] These seats are too high and stiff to appear at all comfortable, and in fact under the Middle Empire the back was sloped and the sides were lowered.[4] Under the New Empire seats like that seen in the accompanying illustration were in general use. The reader will recognise that they resemble those given in the above representations of houses from Tell el Amarna.[5] They are as a rule covered with thick downy cushions, and rarely, as in old times, with a simple stuffed leather seat.[6] Most of them are higher than the corresponding seats of the Old Empire, and a footstool is therefore necessary.[7] There are many other forms of

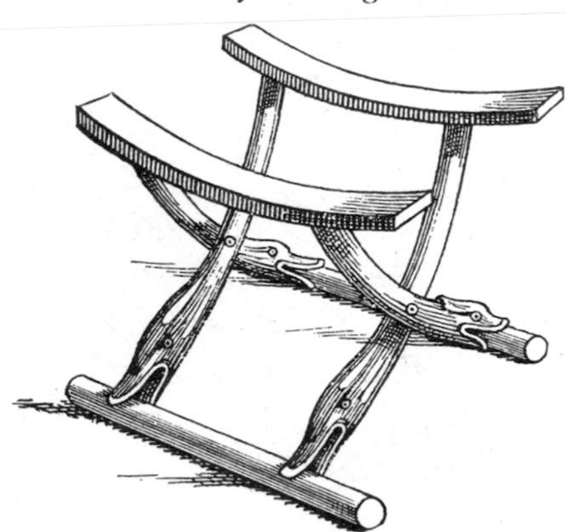

CAMP STOOL IN THE BRITISH MUSEUM (after Wilk., i. 411).

[1] L. D., ii. 19. Cp. Wilk., i. 413, 414.

[2] Dyn. IV.: L. D., ii. 10, 11, 13, 17 d, 19. Dyn. V.: L. D., ii. 44, 51. Dyn. XII.: L. D., ii. 134 b. Dyn. XVIII.: L. D., iii. 9.

[3] L. D., ii. 42, 47, 52, 56, 57, 61, 74 c.

[4] L. D., ii. 127.

[5] L. D., iii. 39, 64, 99, 100, 208 d, 230, there are exceptions without the lions' paws.

[6] See the illustration (chap. xi.) of the wall-picture now in the British Museum. A similar leather seat is preserved (Wilk., i. 414).

[7] After L. D., iii. 100, 208 d, 230.

seats besides these splendid examples, such as stools without backs or lions' paws, made out of palm branches lightly put together; stools made of ebony of careful workmanship; seats which could be folded together like our camp-stools,[1] and low seats for old people, thickly cushioned like our sofas, etc.[2]

The couch also belongs here. It is really only a broader seat, decorated

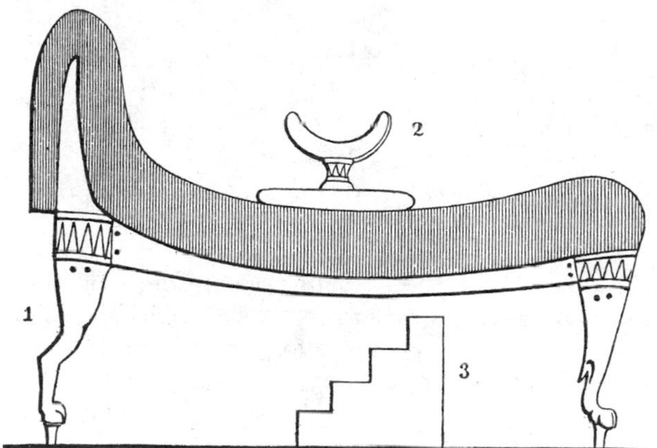

COUCH (1), WITH HEAD-REST (2); THE LITTLE STEPS (3) BELOW SERVE TO GET UP ON THE COUCH (Tomb of Ramses III. After Wilk., i. 416).

usually with lions' paws and frequently with a great lion's head.[3] Cushions might be piled up on these couches, as the reader can see in the sleeping apartments in our plan of a house; as a remarkable contrast to the enjoyment of comfort which this suggests we find that a wooden head-rest was used as a pillow at all periods. This was pushed under the neck so that the head hung free over the cushions; the artificial wig of the sleeper thus remained uninjured, this being the sole *raison d'être* of this uncomfortable object.

The Egyptians originally had no tables, at least not of the shape

which has come down to us from classical times. Under the Old Empire high or low stands of the above shapes were used. These were often made of

[1] L. D., iii. 64, 105. Camp-stool with a high back and cushions. L. D., iii. 208 a.
[2] L. D., ii. 126 (M.E.) This is evidently the throne [hieroglyph] of the hieroglyphics.
[3] E.g. L. D., ii. 126.

coloured stone.[1] On each was placed a jug or cup, or *e.g.*, as a preparation for meals, a flat basket which then served as a dinner-plate ; a low framework of thin laths was also in use, especially as a stand for jars. These

lath-stands in later times constituted the only form of table that was used ; in the houses of Tell el Amarna we see them of all sizes in the dining-hall of the master as well as in the bedrooms and kitchens. It is but rarely that we find the old stands for jars and baskets, and then as a rule only in representations of offerings.[2]

Instead of cupboards they used large wooden boxes to keep their

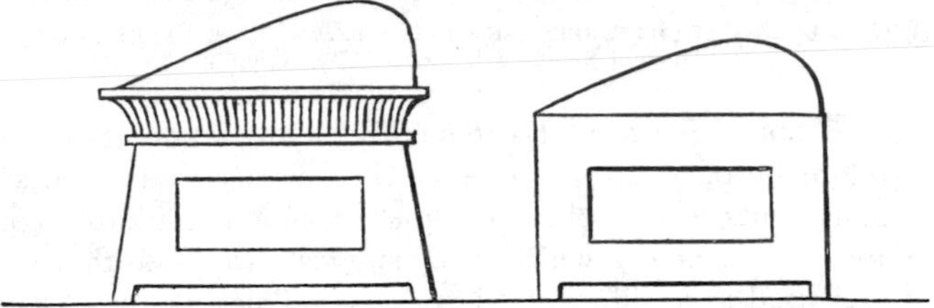

clothes and such like property. Under the New Empire these were generally in the shape of the accompanying illustration with a round cover rising high at the back.[3]

In order to obtain a right idea of an Egyptian interior, to the list of furniture which we have already considered, we must finally add carpets and curtains. A tomb of the 5th dynasty[4] shows us how the walls were covered with coloured matting ; in other tombs of the same period we see screens about the height of a man, formed of perhaps sixty pieces of different patterns ; they stand near where the master sat.[5] Thick rugs for covering the floor are found at all periods. The chair of the master is placed on one ; and when the ladies sit on the floor at the feasts, beautiful rugs are spread for them.

1 The colour certainly of the stone : L.D., ii. 19, 20. What the little notch means above and below on these stands I cannot tell. It sometimes happens (e.g. L. D., ii. 57 b) that the foot and the basket are firmly joined together.

2 The stands of the tables of offerings are higher than those of the Old Empire.

3 The boxes of the Old Empire which I know have flat covers : L. D., ii. 96. Bädeker, p. 409.

4 Perrot-Chipiez, Pl. 14.

5 L. D., ii. 57, 63, 64.

From the above-mentioned pictures from Tell el Amarna we can see in what grand style an Egyptian lord lived, and we may be sure that he required a vast number of servants. Our knowledge of these dependants is gleaned chiefly from the details that we have of the courts of the nomarchs of the 12th dynasty. The chief of the household consisted of an old "superintendent of the provision house," who had the charge of the store-rooms.[1] He had the supervision of the bakery as well as of the slaughter-house, and grew so stout in the exercise of his duties that at the funeral festival of his master he was not able to carry his own offering.[2]

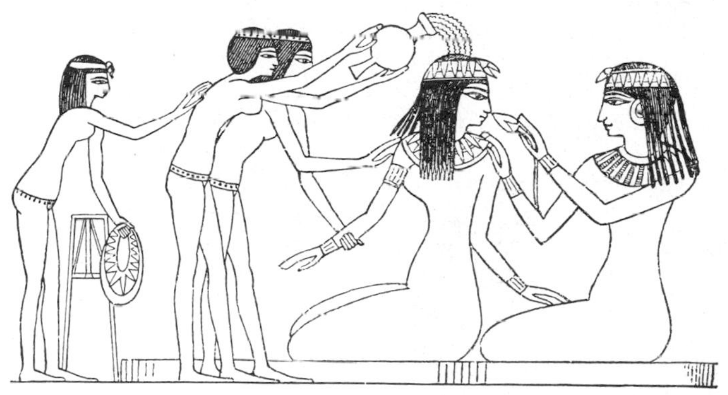

A LADIES' PARTY UNDER THE NEW EMPIRE (after Wilk., ii. 353. Thebes).

At the head of the kitchen stood the "superintendent of the dwelling;"[3] the serfs[4] were subject to him; the "superintendent of the bakehouse"[5] governed the bakery and the "scribe of the sideboard"[6] was originally appointed to take charge of his master's drinks. To these we must add the porter, the baker, the gardener, and other under-servants, as well as handicraftsmen and women who worked for the master. Smaller households under the Middle Empire were arranged of course in a more modest manner, yet they often had their serfs,[7] bakers,[8] and other servants,

[1] A storeroom is seen in a picture of Tell el Amarna (Wilk., i. 349, 348) it contains twenty-four small rooms, in which are kept various assorted breads, drinks, fish, fruit, boxes of clothes, and vessels of precious metal. Close by are the granaries. Unfortunately we cannot discover from Wilk. whether these buildings belong to a private house; I therefore pass over them here.

[2] L. D., ii. 126, 128.

[3] as chief of the kitchen: Ros. M. C., 83, 2. Mar. Cat. d'Ab., 740.

[4] L. D., ii. 128, 129. Cp. the remarks p. 105.

[5] L. D., ii. 131. Ib. 126.

[6] L. D., ii. 131. He is generally spoken of as scribe of the libations, and is therefore a priestly official.

[7] Mar. Cat. d'Ab., 650. Everything in the following remarks applies to the Middle Empire.

[8] Mar. Cat. d'Ab., 606, 634. What the (ib. and frequently) are, I do not know.

who were certainly some of them bond-servants; there were also female slaves:[1] pretty Syrians were often chosen to wait on the master.[2] In the royal court at any rate there were bond-servants, who were under their "great superintendent"; and amongst the upper servants of the household there were certainly many foreign imported slaves.[3] But these royal "provision superintendents,"[4] "superintendents of the dwelling,"[5] serfs,[6] "bearers of cool drinks,"[7] "scribes of the sideboard,"[8] "preparers of sweets,"[9] as they are called, were people of importance and respectability, and the more so because the Egyptians at all times were very fond of good cooking.

It sounds indeed very modest when, in the prayers for the deceased, the Egyptian prayed that he might have for his nourishment in heaven bread and beer, goose and beef; but a glance at the lists of offerings in the tombs shows us that they knew very well that all bread and all meat was not the same thing. These curious lists claim for the deceased not less than ten sorts of different meat, five kinds of birds, sixteen kinds of bread and cake, six kinds of wine, and four of beer, and eleven varieties of fruit, as well as "all manner of sweet things,"[10] etc. These dishes were not passed down from one generation to another, as is the case with a primitive people; rather they were like our dishes, subject to fashion. We have the *menu* of the meal which was to be prepared for a king of the 19th dynasty in the various towns he passed through on his journey with the court; and in the list of ten varieties of bread and five sorts of cake there is scarcely one which was in common use under the Old Empire.[11] They had foreign dishes as well as those of home manufacture. In a very ancient sacred book we read that the gods eat the fine bread of Qamḥ, *i.e.* the קמח of the Semites.[12] The names also of a good many of the dishes of the New Empire show them to be importations. It was from the neighbouring northern countries, particularly Syria, Asia Minor, and Mesopotamia, that the Egyptians procured culinary delicacies. For the "princes" there were the "great well-baked loaves" made from the corn of T'uret (פלת), and for the soldiers various kinds of Syrian bread from Qamḥ,[13] as the Keleshet bread, and especially the Arupusa (ἀλφός). They obtained good wine from Charu; beer from Qede; fine oil from 'Ersa, Cheta, Sangar, 'Emur, T'echesa, and Naharena; the best figs came from Charu.[14] These articles of food were however not always really imported;

[1] Ib. 615, 705.
[2] Ib. 690, 697. Louvre C., 170.
[3] An., 4, 16, 2=An., 3, 8, 3.
[4] Mar. Cat. d'Ab., 384, 582, 691.
[5] Ib. 751. Cp. also p. 190, note 3.
[6] M. E.: ib. 642, 659, 671, 684.
[7] Ib. 644.
[8] O. E.: R. J. H., 2. M. E.: Mar. Cat. d'Ab., 707.
[9] O. E.: L. D., ii. 95 a. M. E.: Mar. Cat. d'Ab., 723. N. E.: ib. 406.
[10] Cp. the group of lists of offerings of the O. E. in Dümichen, tomb-palace of Petamenap T., 18-26.
[11] An., 3, 14, 12 ff.
[12] In the pyramid texts: Teti, 57. In the old lists of offerings (Dümichen, ib. 66) next to the words, "the bread which is in the country" (63) that is the native bread. The writing also seems to indicate a foreign product.
[13] An., 4, 17, 6. Cp. An., 4, 13, 12 ff.
[14] An., 4, 15, 2 ff.

besides the real "Qede beer from the port,"[1] there was the Qede beer which was brewed in Egypt by foreign slaves.[2]

We know very little unfortunately of how the dishes were prepared. The favourite national dish, the goose, was generally roasted over live embers; the spit is very primitive—a stick stuck through the beak and neck of the bird.[3] They roasted fish in the same way, sticking the spit through the tail.[4] The roast did not, of course, look very appetising after this manner of cooking, and it had to be well brushed by a wisp of straw before being eaten. A low slab of limestone served as a hearth; even the shepherds, living in the swamps with their cattle, took this apparatus about with them. In the kitchen[5] of Ymery, superintendent of the domain of King Shepseskaf, the hearth is replaced by a metal brasier with pretty open-work sides. In the same kitchen we see how the meat is cut up on low tables and cooked; the smaller pots have been placed on a brasier, the large ones stand on two

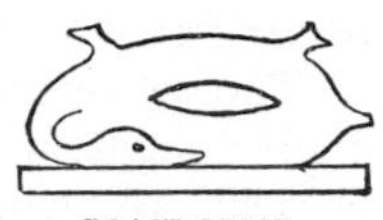

ROAST GOOSE.

SHEPHERDS IN THE FIELDS. (From an Old Empire tomb at Sakkarah, now at Gizeh. After Perrot-Chipiez.)

supports over the open fire. It is only when we come to the time of the New Empire that we find, in representations of the kitchen of Ramses III., a great metal kettle with feet standing on the fire; the kitchen boy is stirring the contents with an immense two-pronged fork. The floor of the whole of the back part of the kitchen is composed of mud and little stones, and is raised about a foot in order to form the fireplace, above which, under the ceiling, extends a bar on which is hung the stock of meat.

Bread-making held a high place in the housekeeping at all periods, bread in different forms being the staple article of food with the people.[6] We know therefore a good deal about it. We may take it for granted that the Egyptians, at any rate in the older periods, had no mills; we never find one represented in their tombs. On the contrary, in the time of the Middle as well as of the New Empire we find representations of great mortars in which one or two men are "pounding the corn" with heavy pestles, just in the same way as is done now in many parts of

1 An., 3, 3, 6.

2 An., 4, 16, 3=An., 3, 8, 5.

3 Roast goose—O. E.: L. D., ii. 66, 77; Bädeker, 404. Cp. L. D., ii. 52.

4 L. D., ii. 10.

5 Kitchens—O. E.: L. D., ii. 52 (=Ros. M. C., 84, 3=W., ii. 35). M. E.: Ros. M. C., 83, 87. N. E.: Ros. M. C., 86=W., ii. 32; L. D., iii. 93, 106 a.

6 The Pap. Harr., i. speaks of thirty sorts of bread used in the temples. (Piehl, Dict. du pap. H., p. 101). The word bread is also often used in Egyptian to signify food.

Africa.[1] They obtained finer flour however by rubbing the corn between two stones. The lower larger stone was fixed and sloped towards the front, so that the prepared flour ran into a little hollow in the front of the stone. Under the Old Empire the stone was placed on the ground and the woman who was working it had to kneel before it; under the Middle Empire a table hollowed out in front took the place of the lower stone, the woman could then stand, and her work was thus rendered much lighter.[2]

The second thing to be done in the making of bread was the kneading of the dough, which could be done in different ways. Shepherds,[3] in the fields at night, baking their cakes in the ashes, contented themselves with "beating the dough" in an earthen bowl and lightly baking their round flat cakes over the coals of the hearth or in the hot ashes only. Little sticks served as forks for these hungry people to take them out of the

SERVANT CRUSHING CORN.
Limestone statuette at Gizeh (after Perrot-Chipiez).

SERVANT KNEADING DOUGH.
Limestone statuette at Gizeh (after Perrot-Chipiez).

glowing embers, but before they could eat them they had first to brush off the ashes with a wisp. It was otherwise of course in a gentleman's house.[4] Here the dough was placed in a basket and kneaded carefully

[1] The pounding of the corn—M. E.: Ros. M. C., 67. N. E.: L. D., iii. 93; W., ii. 204; Ros. M. C., 85 (=W., ii. 32). Cp. also the Coptic **EYNE** "Mill" and the names of towns such as . In one of these towns one of the legends of the gods expressly mentions a miller. (Destr. des hommes, l. 18).

[2] Grinding between stones—O. E.: Perrot, 74, 663, 664. Statuette in Berlin, No. 7706. M. E.: L. D., ii. 126 (=Ros. M. C., 67, 7); Ros. M. C., 5, 6; W., ii. 190. The model of the house also belongs to this time, W., i. 351.

[3] Shepherds baking bread—O. E.: L. D., ii. 66 (=Ros. M. C., 84, 4); ib. 77; ib. 96, 105.

[4] Kneading bread in a basket—O. E.: Perrot, 33, 661, 662; Br. Dic. Suppl., p. 167. M. E.: L. D., ii. 126; Ros. M. C., 67, 1. N. E.: Ros. M. C., 84 (=W., ii. 34).

with the hands; the water was pressed out into a pot placed underneath the basket. The dough was then fashioned by the hand into various shapes similar to those we now use for pastry, and these were baked on the

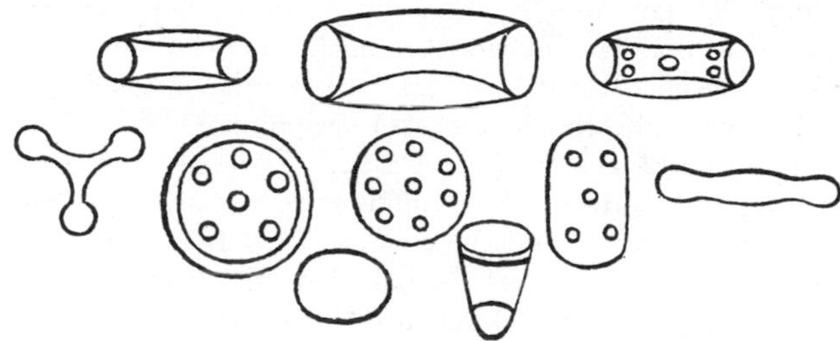

SHAPES OF CAKES OF BREAD UNDER THE MIDDLE EMPIRE (after L. D., ii. 126, 128, 129).

conical stove.[1] I purposely say *on* the stove, for the Egyptians seem to have been satisfied with sticking the cakes on the outside of the stove. A picture of the time of the New Empire gives us a tolerable idea of one of these stoves; it is a blunted cone of Nile mud, open at the top and

THE ROYAL BAKERY. (From the tomb of Ramses III. After Wilk., ii. 34, where by mistake only one of the cakes is represented below on the left as stuck on the stove.)

perhaps three feet high. The fire is burning in the inside, the flames burst out at the top, and the cakes are stuck on the outside.

The same picture shows us also the court-bakery of Ramses III.[2] The dough here is not kneaded by hand—this would be too wearisome a method when dealing with the great quantities required for the royal

[1] Stoves—M. E.: Ros. M. C., 67, 2, cp. those of the Old Empire, Brugsch, Gr. W., 159. N. E.: Ros. M. C., 85 (=W., II, 34).

[2] The bakery of Ramses III.—Ros. M. C., 84=W., ii. 34.

household—it is trodden with the feet. Two servants are engaged in this hard work; they tread the dough in a great tub holding on by long sticks to enable them to jump with more strength. Others bring the prepared dough in jars to the table where the baker is working. As court baker he is not content with the usual shapes used for bread, but makes his cakes in all manner of forms. Some are of a spiral shape like the "snails" of our confectioners; others are coloured dark brown or red, perhaps in imitation of pieces of roast meat. There is also a cake in the shape of a cow lying down. The different cakes are then prepared in various ways—the "snails" and the cow are fried by the royal cook in a great frying pan; the little cakes are baked on the stove.

A special part of the royal kitchen is "the pure," that is the brewery

TABLE FOR FOOD. OLD EMPIRE (after L. D., ii. 57 b).

ALABASTER BOWL. Alnwick Castle Museum (after Wilk., ii. 42).

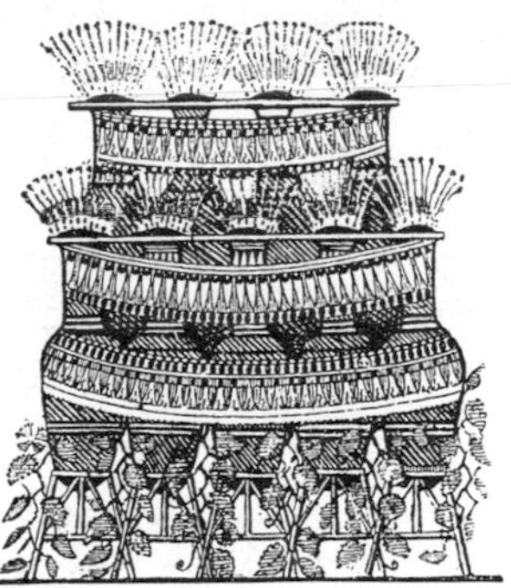

WINE-JARS ADORNED WITH WREATHS AND EMBROIDERY (wall picture in the British Museum).

WASHING-STAND.

in which beer is prepared.[1] Beer was the favourite drink of the Egyptian people, and even the deceased in their state of bliss could not get on without beer any more than without bread. This drink was in favour at all times; under the Old Empire men made four sorts of beer, amongst these was "black beer," *i.e.* beer of a dark colour;[2] under the New Empire foreign beer from the neighbourhood of Qede in the east of Asia Minor was preferred; in Greek times the Egyptians drank Zythos beer, of which

[1] [hieroglyphs] An., 4, 16, 3 = An., 3, 8, 5. "Superintendent of the provision of the brewery:" Mar. Cat. d'Ab., 1073. The *mer-'est-u'ab* of the Middle Empire may belong here (ib. 751).

[2] List of offerings in Dümichen, Grabpal. of Petamenap.

Diodorus says that its smell was as the smell of wine. We know little about the preparation of beer; all accounts however agree that it was made from ground barley, or as it was called, the "corn of Upper Egypt."[1]

Under the Old Empire the Egyptians squatted for their meals,[2] two people generally at one little table, which was but half a foot high, and on which was heaped up fruit, bread, and roast meat, while the drinking bowls stood underneath. They ate with their hands, and had no compunction in tearing off pieces of goose. In later times common people ate in the same way,[3] whilst the upper classes of the New Empire preferred to sit on high cushioned chairs and to be waited upon by men servants and female slaves.[4] After eating, water was poured over the hands, corresponding to the modern Oriental custom; in the dining-rooms, therefore, we often find a jug and basin exactly like those of a modern wash-stand.[5] In ancient Egypt table decoration was a fine art. Large lotus flowers were used for the dining tables; and under the New Empire the jars of wine and beer were always adorned with covers of embroidered work;[6] "wreaths of flowers for the wine-jars" were indispensable, and when the court travelled through a town it was just as necessary that the servants should procure the 100 wreaths as the 29,200 loaves or the 200 bushels of coal.[7] In the same way as the tables were decked with flowers, the guests at the banquet were adorned with sweet-smelling flowers and buds; they wore lotus buds in their hair, and held them out to each other to smell, just as the guests amongst other nations pass glasses of wine to each other at the present day.

This custom is not so unimportant as some might think; it is founded on the love of flowers and green plants which is so characteristic of the Egyptian people. Everywhere on the monuments we meet with flowers; bouquets of flowers are presented to the gods; the coffins are covered with wreaths of flowers; flowers form the decoration of the houses, and all the capitals of the pillars are painted in imitation of their coloured petals. The Egyptian also loved shady trees. He not only prayed that the "Nile should bestow every flowering plant in their season" upon his departed soul, but also that his soul might sit "on the boughs of the trees that he had planted, and enjoy the cool air in the shade of his sycamore."[8] The arable fields, the shadeless woods of palms, the bare mud soil, scarcely provided the scenery which he most admired, he therefore tried to supply the want by landscape gardening. In the oldest periods there were parks and gardens;[9] and the gentleman of ancient Egypt talked with pride of his

[1] Beer from barley: Leps. Totenb., 124, 5. Destruction des hommes, l. 18, and all the Greek accounts. From the "corn of Upper Egypt": Dümichen, List of offerings of Medinet Habu, p. v. That the corn of Upper Egypt was barley, cp. Br. Dic. Suppl., 460.

[2] L. D., ii. 52.

[3] L. D., iii. 106 a.

[4] Cp. the illustrations of a feast in the 11th chapter, as well as the arrangement of the dining-halls in our plans of houses.

[5] L. D., iii. 93, 106 a.

[6] O. E.: L. D., ii. 98. M. E.: L. D., ii. 129. N. E.: passim.

[7] An., 4, 14, 6.

[8] Louvre, C. 55, and many similar examples.

[9] L. D., ii. 7.

shady trees, his sweet-smelling plants, and his cool tanks. All the sentiment with which we regard the woods and meadows of nature, the Egyptian felt towards his well-kept garden; to him it was the dwelling-place of love, and his trees were the confidantes of lovers.

On the "festival day of the garden," that is, on the day when the garden was in full bloom, the wild fig-tree calls to the maiden to come into the shade of the fig leaves as a trysting-place:

"The little Sycamore
Which she planted with her hand,
She begins to speak,
And her (words are as) drops of honey.
She is charming, her bower is green,
Greener than (the papyrus).
She is laden with fruit,
Redder than the ruby.
The colour of her leaves is as glass,
Her stem is as the colour of the opal . . .
It is cool in her shadow.
She sends her letter by a little maiden,
The daughter of her chief gardener
She makes her haste to her beloved:
Come and linger in the (garden) . . .
The servants who belong to thee
Come with the dinner things;
They are bringing beer of every (kind),
With all manner of bread,
Flowers of yesterday and of to-day,
And all kinds of refreshing fruit.
Come, spend this festival day
And to-morrow and the day after to-morrow . .
Sitting in my shadow.
Thy companion sits at thy right hand,
Thou dost make him drink,
And then thou dost follow what he says . . .
I am of a silent nature
And I do not tell what I see
I do not chatter."[1]

The Pharaoh shared this love for trees and flowers, and tried to turn his city into a garden. Ramses III. *e.g.*, planted trees and papyrus plants in Thebes,[2] and in the new town which he founded in the Delta he made "great vineyards; walks shaded by all kinds of sweet fruit trees laden with their fruit; a sacred way, splendid with flowers from all countries, with lotus and papyrus, countless as the sand."[3] It is not a mere saying that flowers from all countries were planted there; for the enjoyment of gardening and of raising flowers had really led to the importation of exotic plants. Three hundred years previously it had been the pride of Queen Chnemtamun that she had caused "thirty-one growing incense trees" to

[1] From the love-songs of a Turin papyrus (Tur., 79-83, edited by Maspero, Étud. égypt., i. p. 217 ff).

[2] Harr., i. 7, 11.

[3] Harr., i. 8, 3-4. "Lotus" is hypothetical.

be brought from the incense countries of the Red Sea:[1] Ramses III. repeated this difficult experiment and had the court of Amon planted with these rare shrubs.[2]

Two remarkable pictures from Theban tombs of the time of the New Empire[3] give us further details as to the arrangement of the gardens and country houses of the upper classes; in each we see that the proprietor loved the quiet of the country. A high wall shut out the outside world;

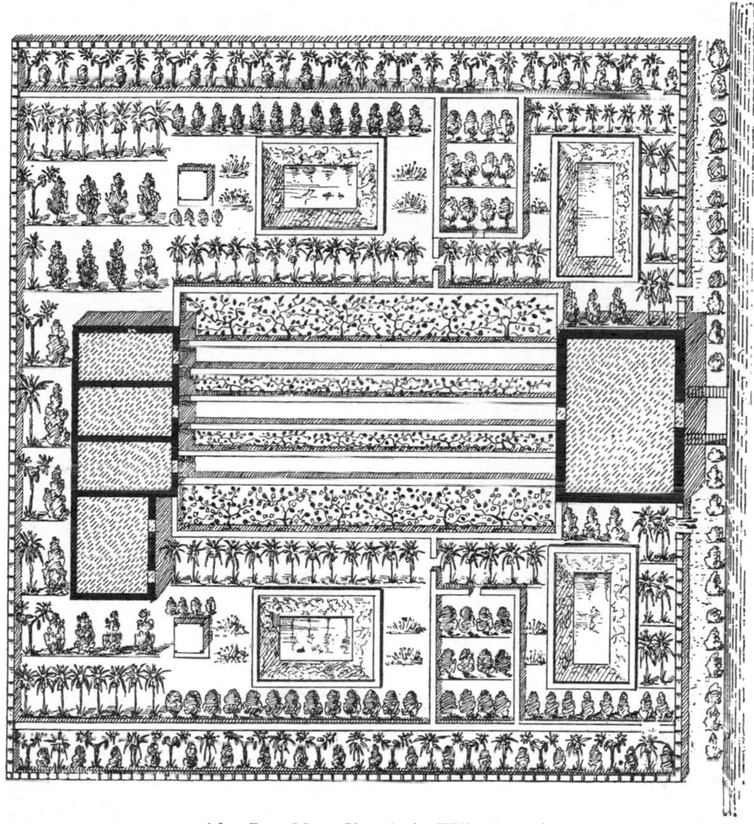

After Ros. Mon. Civ., 69 (=Wilk., i. 377).

the house was invisible at the further end of the garden under the shade of old trees, and only approached by narrow garden paths. The gentleman who owned the large piece of ground seen in the above plan,[4] concealed

[1] Düm., Hist. Inscrip., ii. 18.

[2] Harr., i. 7, 7.

[3] Besides the illustration here spoken of, see the above illustration of a country house.

[4] The plan mentioned is published, Ros. M. C., 69 (=Wilk., i. 377). The restoration of the garden offers no difficulties, the Egyptian painter has evidently forgotten to put in the two gates in the upper part of the picture but they can be restored from the lower part. The restoration of the

his house in the furthest corner of the garden; no sound from the stirring life on the canal could penetrate his seclusion, no profane eye could see his house over the walls or over the tops of the trees.

A high castellated wall surrounds the piece of ground, which is almost square; there is no entrance except in front, where a broad flight of steps leads down from the large porter's lodge to two small doors which open upon the canal. Through the chief entrance, adorned with the name of the reigning king, we pass out of a small door directly into the vineyard, which is seen in the centre of the plan. The luxuriant vines with their large purple grapes are trained on trellis-work built up with stone; through these vine-walks the path leads straight up to the house.

If we pass, however, through either of the side doors we come to a part of the garden resembling a small park; here there is a fish-pond surrounded with palms and shrubs. Part of this garden is separated off by a wall, inside which are trees of a light green colour; this may be a nursery plantation, or it may contain rare trees.

Two doors lead out of this garden; one into the palm-garden which occupies a narrow strip on either side of the piece of ground, the other door leads into the hinder portion of the garden. Whether we enter the right or left side we now come again to a "cool tank," and to rest here was the delight of the Egyptian. A pretty little arbour stands at the head of the pond; here the master would sit in the evening and watch the water-birds at their play in the water amongst the lotus and papyrus plants.

Finally at the back, surrounded by a double row of palms and high trees, lies the house itself, apparently an irregular one-storied building. The principal part is built against the back wall of the vineyard and has three rooms opening into the garden. On the left side a wing is built out which seems to be higher than the central portion; it has two doors in front and two windows at the side. The whole house is strikingly bare, and the monotony of the timber walls is only somewhat relieved by the pillars and frames of the windows and by the gaily coloured hollow below the roof. There is no reason why this building should be more richly decorated. It is quite hidden amongst the trees, and passers-by would be sufficiently impressed by seeing the stately lodge in front.

The form of the garden here given seems to have been that usual in the older periods. In the beautiful park laid out by the oft-named 'Amt'en, chief hunter to King Snefru, he had "dug a great tank and planted fig-trees and vines." "In the middle of the garden" (exactly as in our plan) "he made a vineyard, which yielded him much wine."[1]

It was very natural that the Egyptians should think so much of the vineyard, for though beer was the great national drink, yet at all times wine was a favourite beverage. Under the Old Empire they distinguished six sorts of wine, *e.g.* white, red, black, and northern wine.

house is, notwithstanding, very difficult; I have chosen the easiest solution, yet it seems very exceptional that, with a garden laid out so carefully and symmetrically, the house should have been so unsymmetrical.

[1] After L. D., ii. 7.

The latter corresponded to the various Delta wines, the Mareotic, the Sebennytic, and the Teniotic wines, which enjoyed such a high reputation in Græco-Roman times. Vines were much grown throughout the country; for instance, Ramses III. planted "vineyards without number" in the southern and northern oases, as well as many others in Upper and Lower Egypt. He appointed foreign slaves to till them, and dug "tanks with lotus flowers" growing in them.[1] Above all he undertook the care of the celebrated mountain vineyard called *Ka-en-Qêmet*, the genius of Egypt, which yielded "sweet wine."[2] This great vineyard, which was "inundated like the two countries, whose large olive-trees were full of fruit, which was surrounded by a long wall and planted with great trees by all the paths, which yielded oil as the sand of the sea-shore,"[3]—was the great garden-plot of the temple of the Theban Amon,[4] to which temple at any rate it belonged from the beginning of the reign of Ramses III., who confirmed this gift of his ancestors and founded a treasure-house and a sanctuary in it.[5]

The pictures of the Old Empire show us how vines were grown and cultivated.[6] They were trained over trellis-work supported by wooden forks, or, in the time of luxury of the 6th dynasty, borne by wooden pillars. Much care was taken in their cultivation; the individual plants were watered from earthen pots, and the swarms of birds were frightened away with cries and slings. After the grapes, which seem to have been of a curious long shape, had been picked and collected in baskets, they were carried to the wine-press, which was of the most primitive kind, like those still to be seen in the south of Europe. It consisted of a long low box over which was erected a wooden framework higher than a man. The box being filled with grapes, five or six men then stepped into it, raised their arms and grasped the upper boards of the framework, and trod the grapes with their feet; we see by the quick movement of their feet that they had to hold on to the boards to keep themselves from falling. Under the New Empire the shape of these wine-presses was more convenient and more artistic; the workmen held on by cords, this gave them scope for freer movement, and as the wine was pressed out it ran through the openings below into great vats.[7]

However carefully the men might tread out the grapes there would always remain a certain amount of the sweet juice, which could only be extracted by more energetic measures. The careful Egyptian did not despise this residuum, but obtained it by squeezing the pressed grapes in a sack. A great sack of light yellow matting was filled with grapes and then wrung

[1] Harr., i. 7, 10-11. [2] An., 3, 2, 6. [3] Harr., i. 8, 5 ff.

[4] Cp. the wine-jars which came from that temple, Ä. Z., 1883, 34.

[5] Harr., i. 8, 8 ff.

[6] Grape-harvest: L. D., ii. 53, 61, 111. Watering of the vines: Düm. Res., 8. Scarecrows: L. D., ii. 53, 61. Treading of the grapes: L. D., ii. 53, 61, 96, 111. Düm. Res., 8. Wine-press with the sack: L. D., ii. 13, 49, 53, 96, 111. Düm. Res., 8 (exceptional). Filling jars: L. D., ii. 13, 49, 53, 111. Fastening up: L. D., ii. 13, 61. Sealing: L. D., ii. 96. An instructive picture of the New Empire: L. D., iii. 11 d.

[7] Grape-harvest and wine-press of the New Empire: Wilk., i. 385. L. D., iii. 11 d. In the latter picture the workmen seem to be holding on to a cloth.

like a piece of linen from the wash-tub. Sticks were put through the two loops which were formed of the ends, and it was then wrung by four powerful men. Each turn of the sack made the work harder, at last it became impossible to turn the sticks again, the sack was twisted as far as it would go, and if the workmen gave way in the least, it would untwist

THE WINE-PRESS OF THE NEW EMPIRE.

Above on the right is a little temple to the goddess of the harvest, before whom has been placed an offering of grapes and wine on this harvest day. Below is seen the filling of the great wine-jars with jugs (after Wilk., i. 385. Theban tomb picture).

itself. At this critical moment we see how the men show their greatest skill. Two hold the sticks firmly at the lower ends, two others jump on their backs, seize the sticks at the upper ends and pull them back, a fifth swings himself up between the two sticks and presses them apart with his hands and feet. This feat does not go unrewarded, the wine flows out in a dark stream into the earthenware jar standing below. This is the usual method of procedure under the Old Empire.

After L. D., ii. 53.

We have no account of the further process in the treatment of the grape juice, we only see how the wine jars were filled from the great vats, how they were fastened up, and how, finally, they were sealed by the treasurer. As a matter of course we see the scribes sitting close by and noting down the number of jars of wine that are filled.

Under the New Empire, as in Greek and Roman times, it was a favourite custom to mix several sorts of wine together. The following picture shows us how they filled a large vessel by siphons with three sorts of wine; the festive decoration of the vessels indicates that this mixing is taking place at the time of a feast.

We must not forget to mention the fig-tree, which together with the vine was grown at all periods in ancient Egypt. We meet with the fruit everywhere, and we also find representations of the trees in the old tombs.[1] The fig-trees have thick gnarled trunks, and seem scarcely to reach 16 feet in height; their boughs however, are strong enough to allow the gardeners to climb up and gather the fruit into flat baskets. When the gardeners are unable to climb up into the trees themselves, they send tame monkeys into the branches to gather the fruit for them, as we see in the illustration below.

THEBAN TOMB PICTURE (after Wilk., ii. 314).

[1] Fig harvest: L. D., ii. 53, 61, 127.

MONKEYS HELPING WITH THE FIG HARVEST (after L. D., ii. 127).

HEAD OF NEFERHOR, KEEPER OF THE GRANARY ARCHIVES (Berlin Museum, 2303; his wife sits by him).

CHAPTER X

DRESS

As long as we regarded the antiquities of ancient Egypt as unknown quantities, and contented ourselves with marvelling at them as wonderful curiosities, the strange impression of the whole made us overlook the various differences between the individual monuments. Even when we had gradually learnt to divide Egyptian history into its long epochs, it was still a good while before our sight became sharp enough to recognise in all their significance the great differences between the productions of these several epochs. For a long time men spoke of Egyptian art, Egyptian religion, and Egyptian language as if they had not experienced any very great changes during three thousand years, and made up their minds that the Egyptian character was one peculiarly conservative. Now we know that there is no justification for this conclusion. During the three thousand years of their history, the language, the faith, and the art of the ancient Egyptians changed neither more nor less than that of any other nation under the same conditions; it was solely owing to our want of knowledge that we underestimated these differences for so long.

This holds good also about dress, a point which amongst civilised people is perhaps subject to most changes. It is altogether false to speak of "the Egyptian costume" as expressing one style of dress, for it was just as much ruled by fashion as the dress of other nations. Under the Old Empire a short skirt was worn round the hips; under the Middle Empire a second was added; and under the New Empire the breast also was covered. If we look closer we find many other changes within these great epochs. If during one century the skirt was worn short and narrow, during the next it would be worn wide and shapeless, whilst during a third it was fashionable only when peculiarly folded. The various classes are also distinguished by their costume,—the royal costume differs from that of the courtiers, and the household officials of the great lords are not dressed like the servants, the shepherds, or the boatmen. Evidently here also fashion ruled: the costume of the higher classes was soon imitated by those next

SIMPLEST FORM OF SKIRT (after L. D., ii. 4).

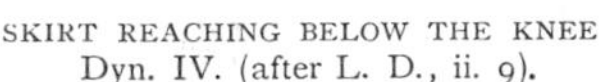

SKIRT REACHING BELOW THE KNEE Dyn. IV. (after L. D., ii. 9).

beneath them; it then lost its fashionable character,—the great lords relinquished it to the people, and assumed a new one. Thus after the close of the 5th dynasty the old royal costume was imitated by the great lords of the kingdom, and later it passed down to be the official dress of the higher artisans; thus the same costume in which the courtiers of King Snefru appeared at court was worn not long afterwards by household officials.

We must also add other distinctions; the old men wore longer warmer clothing than the young men, and for the king's presence men dressed better and more fashionably than for the home or for the hunt. The material on this subject is inexhaustible, and deserves more detailed consideration than is possible within the narrow limits of this book. I must content myself with bringing forward the principal types of the various dresses.[1] The reader however will I hope receive the impression

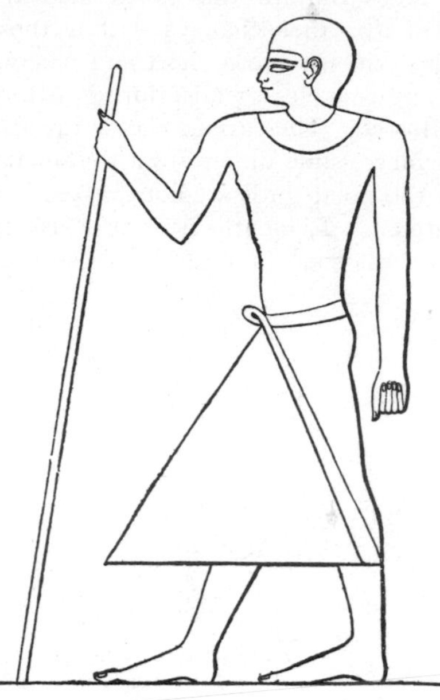

that, in spite of the simplicity of its component parts, dress was subject to comparatively frequent changes.

The most ancient dress worn by persons of high rank seems to have been the simple short skirt which was the foundation of all later styles of dress. It consisted of a straight piece of white stuff, which was wrapped rather loosely round the hips, leaving the knees uncovered. As a rule it was put round the body from right to left, so that the edge came in the middle of the front. The upper end of this edge was stuck in behind the bow of the girdle which held the skirt together.[2] In the beginning

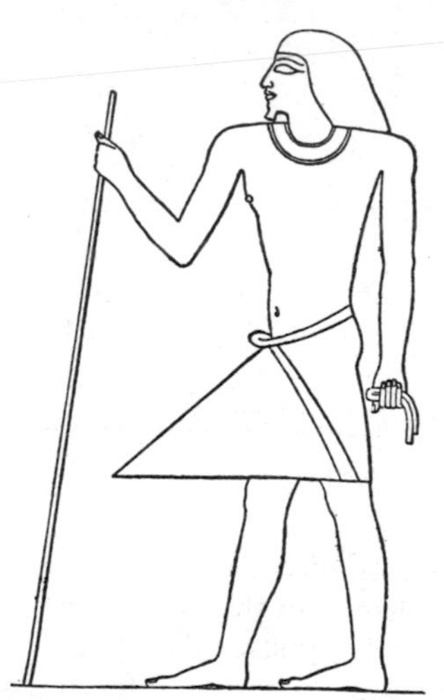

THREE PICTURES OF SENED'M-'EB, CALLED MEHY (Dyn. V.), with the skirt unusually broad (L. D., ii. 74, 78).

[1] The material at hand for these researches is very abundant, but the difficulties in turning it to account are so great, that I must beg for special indulgence. Those who have studied more statues than I have will doubtless differ from my opinion in many particulars. The clothing on the reliefs is treated very superficially, and becomes quite unintelligible in the publications where the original colours are left out. Besides, for artistic reasons the dress is often drawn inaccurately on the reliefs and frescoes, nearly always in fact when the person is represented looking to the left.

[2] The skirt is white: L. D., ii. 19. That the girdle was separate from the skirt is probable from the picture, L. D., ii. 112.

of the 4th dynasty we find that even the great lords were content with this dress in its simplest form;[1] more usually however, even under the Old Empire, it was the dress of scribes, servants, and peasants.[2]

After the time of Cha'frê', the builder of the second pyramid, it became the fashion to wear the skirt longer and wider; at first this innovation came in with moderation,[3] but towards the close of the 5th dynasty it exceeded good taste, and we can scarcely understand how a beau at the court of King Un'e managed to wear this erection in front of him—perhaps he had a support to hold it out. Under the 6th dynasty we

SKIRT WITH ERECTION IN FRONT.
(Representation of Nebemchut. After L. D., ii. 13.)

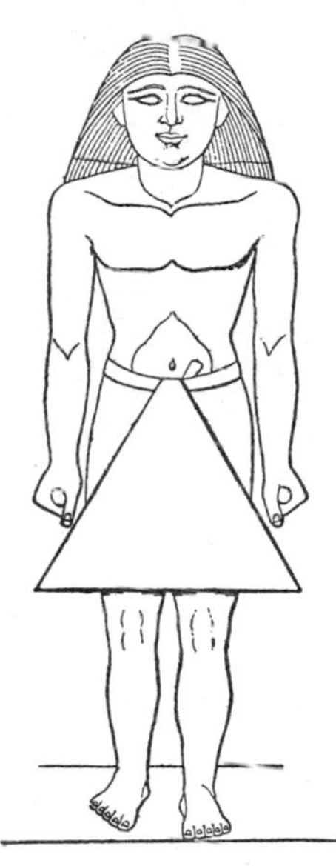

SKIRT WITH ERECTION IN FRONT.
(Statue of Uerchuu. After L. D., ii. 44.)

meet with the same costume though not so much exaggerated. The servants and peasants of this time began to wear their skirts wider,[4] the household officials of the great lords having already set them an example in this direction.[5]

There is a strange variation in this skirt, which appears to have been in much favour amongst the great lords of the 5th and 6th dynasties; by some artificial means they managed to make the front of the skirt stand out in a triangular erection. There were several slight differences in this fashion. If the edge of the skirt formed a loose fold it was regarded merely as a variation of the ordinary dress; if on the other hand the

[1] L. D., ii. 3, 4.
[2] L. D., ii. 4, 8, 22, 25, 32, 44, 45, 63, etc.
[3] L. D., ii. 8, 9.
[4] L. D., ii. 105.
[5] L. D., ii. 69.

erection was quite symmetrical and reached above the girdle,[1] then it was considered to be quite a novel and quaint costume.

In addition to these various forms of the short skirt, we meet with exceptional cases of men wearing long dresses, reaching from the waist to the feet.[2] The deceased are represented in this dress when seated before the tables of offerings, receiving the homage of their friends still

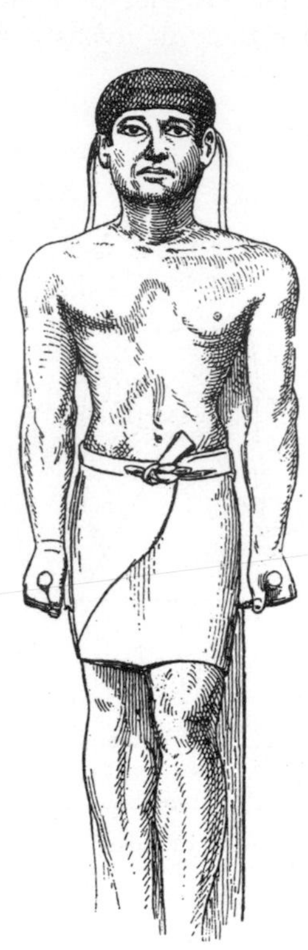

GALA SKIRT WITHOUT BORDER.
(Statue of Nofer at Gizeh. After Perrot-Chipiez, 628.)

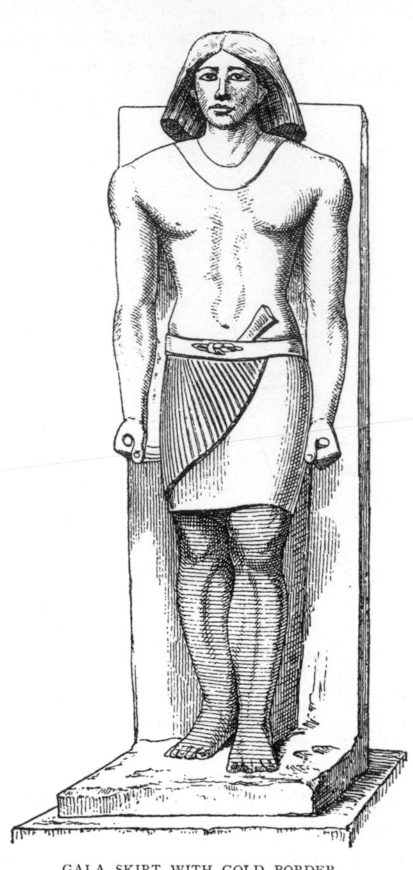

GALA SKIRT WITH GOLD BORDER.
(Statue of Ra'nofer at Gizeh. After Perrot-Chipiez, 655.)

living; it is doubtless the dress of an old man, the same as was worn probably just before death.

In addition to these every-day costumes, the great lords of the Old Empire possessed one intended only for festivals. As is usual in such cases, this festive costume does not resemble the fashionable dress of the

[1] We suspect that this erection (like a similar one in the dress of the New Empire) may have been a separate piece of stuff from the skirt, fastened on in front to the girdle.

[2] L. D., ii. 3, 6 (plainly characterised as an old man), 23, 30, 31 b.

time, but follows the more ancient style. It is in fact merely a more elegant form of the old, narrow, short skirt; the front is rounded off so that it falls in little folds, and the belt is fastened by a pretty metal clasp. In spite of numerous representations, it is difficult to see how this clasp was made; the narrow ornamented piece, which is nearly always raised above it, is perhaps the end of the girdle; it is certainly not the handle of a dagger, as has been generally supposed. Finally, the fore-part from the middle of the back was often further adorned by a pleated piece of gold material, thus forming a very smart costume.[1] To complete this festive garb a panther skin was necessary, which was thrown over the shoulders by the great lords when they appeared in "full dress." The right way of wearing this skin was with the small head and fore paws of the animal hanging down, and the hind paws tied together with long ribbons over the shoulder. It was the fashion, when sitting idle, to play with these ribbons with the left hand.[2]

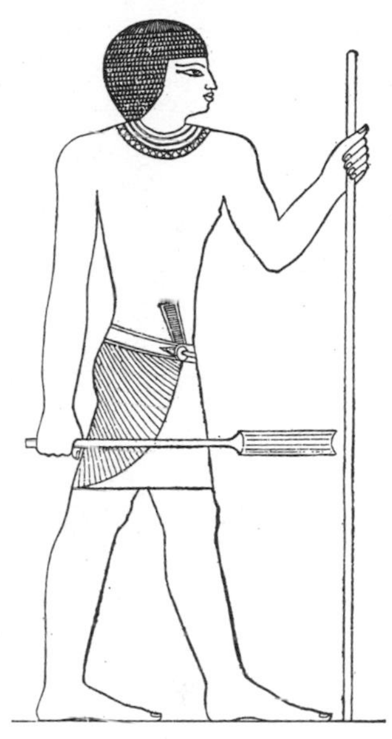

GALA SKIRT WITH GOLD BORDER.
(Prince Nor'eb. After L. D., ii. 20.)

SIMPLE SKIRT OF THE MIDDLE EMPIRE.
(Official of Chnemhôtep. L. D., ii. 131.)

During the dark ages which elapsed between the 6th and 12th dynasties, dress underwent no great change; the skirt meanwhile became a little longer, so that it reached to the middle of the leg.[3] Under the Middle Empire it again became narrower and less stiff; for this purpose it was slightly sloped in front, and hung rather lower than behind. Between the legs, if possible, it was the right thing to show one or two points, which belonged to the inner part of the skirt.[4] Men also liked to decorate the outer edge with an embroidered border,[5] or to pleat the front prettily.[6] Ordinary people wore this skirt of thick material, but men of high rank, on the contrary, chose fine white material so transparent

[1] E.g. the statue 94 in the Berlin Museum, as well as one in the Louvre A, 46, 102, 105. That this pleated material is golden we see by the pictures, L. D., ii. 19, 20, 21. Louvre A, 102; A, 105. It is white, ib. A, 46.

[2] Cp. L. D., ii. 18, 19, 21, 22, 23, 30, 31 b, 32, etc. Perhaps it was the prerogative of a certain high rank.

[3] L. D., ii. 126, 127, 130, 131.

[4] L. D., ii. 127, 130, 131. Plainly seen in the statue at Berlin of Sebekemsaf (brother of queen Nubch'as). Berlin 1188 in the *sons* of the deceased, but not in his *servants*.

[5] L. D., ii. 126, 127.

[6] L. D., ii. 126, 127.

that it revealed rather than concealed the form of the body. It was then necessary to wear a second skirt under the transparent outer one. Those who had the right to wear the *Shend'ot*, the short royal dress, liked to wear it as the inner skirt.[1] Contemporary with this double skirt, which marks a new epoch in the history of Egyptian dress, appears the first clothing for the upper part of the body. One of the princes of the Nome of the Hare, who were buried at Bersheh, wears, as is seen in the illustration below, a kind of mantilla fastened together over the chest.[2] In a second representation the same lord appears in a most unusual costume; he is wrapped from head to foot in a narrow dress apparently striped; such a dress seems to have been worn by old men under the Middle Empire.[3]

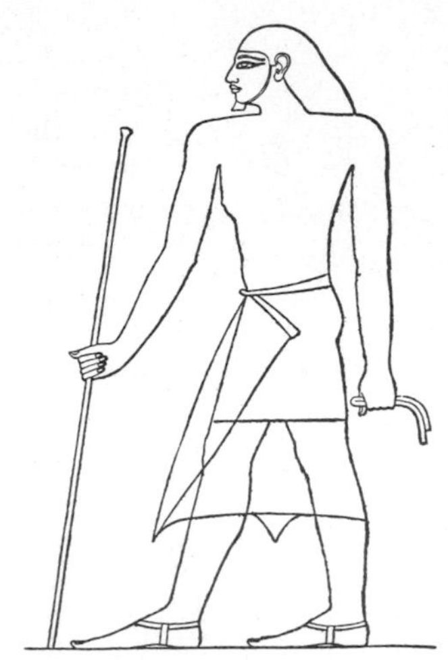

DOUBLE SKIRT OF THE MIDDLE EMPIRE. (The nomarch Chnemḥôtep. L. D., ii. 131.)

During the interval between the Middle and the New Empire there was little innovation in dress, but the more stylish forms of men's clothing entirely superseded the simpler fashions. The priests alone kept to the simple skirt; all other persons wore an outer transparent skirt and a short inner one, both of which still retained the old shape.[4]

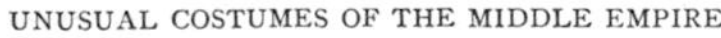

UNUSUAL COSTUMES OF THE MIDDLE EMPIRE. (The Nomarch Dḥuthôtep. L. D., ii. 134 d, e.)

[1] Inner skirts of the usual kind: L. D., ii. 128, 130, 131, 134 d. Royal skirt: L. D., ii. 130.

[2] L. D., ii. 134 b, d.

[3] L. D., ii. 134 e. Also ib. 126 (Chnemḥôtep), 127 (the old servants of the latter).

[4] L. D., iii. 9 f, 10 a, 12 a, and others, 62 b, 69 a. Very great lords wore also the royal skirt underneath: L. D., iii. 9 e.

The rapid development of the Egyptian Empire, and the complete revolution in all former conditions, soon brought in also a quick change of fashion. About the time of Queen Chnemtamun dress assumed a new character. It became customary to clothe the upper part of the body also, a short shirt firmly fastened under the girdle was adopted now as an indispensable article of dress by all members of the upper class; the priests alone never followed this fashion. To promote free movement of the right arm this shirt appears to have been open on the right side, while the left arm passed through a short sleeve.[1] During this period each generation adopted its own particular form of skirt. At first the inner

OF THE TIME OF AMENHÔTEP III.
The outer skirt is longer than the inner (after L.D., iii. 77 e).

COSTUME OF THE FIRST HALF OF THE 18TH DYNASTY (L. D., iii. 12 a).

OF THE TIME OF CHUEN-'ETEN.
The outer skirt is raised, the inner one has become longer (after L. D., iii. 101).

skirt remained unchanged whilst the outer one was shortened in front and lengthened behind.[2]

Towards the close of the 18th dynasty, under the heretic king Chuen-'eten, the inner skirt was worn wider and longer, whilst the upper one was looped up in puffs, so as to show the under one below it. The front of the outer one was formed of thick pleats, the inner one also was often pleated, and the long ends of the girdle were allowed to hang down.[3]

In the gala costume of this period the outer skirt grew to be of less significance than the inner. The latter developed into a wide pleated dress, whilst the former retrograded into a piece of linen folded round the

[1] In several pictures the shirt appears to be open on both sides, and to be sleeveless, whilst at the same time, in other postures of the arm, the sleeve is plainly visible. Again in figures standing facing the right, the disposition of the dress in the pictures is changed, and the sleeve appears on the right arm. Shirts with two distinct sleeves are rare, though the governor of Ethiopia certainly wears one; L. D., iii. 230.

[2] Part of a picture (representation of an offering) in the British Museum, L. D., iii. 69 a, 77 e.

[3] E.g. L. D., iii. 91 a, 93, 101, 104; Wilk., i. 442. The inner skirt pleated in front: L. D., iii. 97 e, 103. Berlin, 7316.

hips. At the same time we find very various costumes in the representations,—sometimes the piece of linen is wrapped round the body in such a way as to cover the back of the legs behind and yet to be quite short in front;[1] sometimes it assumes the form of the ancient skirt;[2] sometimes it is wound twice or thrice round the body.[3]

FESTIVE COSTUMES OF THE END OF THE 18TH DYNASTY.
1. The oft-mentioned 'Ey with the gold ornaments bestowed on him by the king, L. D., iii. 105.
2. Amenḥôtep, the governor of Ethiopia, ib., 115. 3. His colleague Ḥuy, ib. 116.

COSTUME OF THE 19TH DYNASTY (L. D., iii. 176 f).

COSTUME OF THE 20TH DYNASTY WITH A PIECE OF MATERIAL PUT ON IN FRONT (L. D., iii. 217 a, 231).

The dress of the great lords of the 19th dynasty corresponds very nearly to that of the great men of the time of Chuen'eten described above, except that the puffs of the outer skirt were smoothed out, and that it was worn somewhat longer during the later period.[4]

[1] L. D., iii. 105. [2] L. D., iii. 115. [3] L. D., iii. 115, 116. Berlin, 7278, 7316
[4] L. D., iii. 128 b, 153, 162, 176 f, 183 b.

In the time of Ramses III. a fashion was adopted which had already been employed for festive garments;[1] the outer skirt, which was only used for ornamental purposes, was entirely given up, and a broad piece of material, cut in various shapes, was fastened on in front like an apron.[2]

RAMSES II. IN A CLOAK.

Meanwhile the clothing of the upper part of the body remained essentially the same, though after the time of the 19th dynasty it was worn fuller than before.[3] We sometimes find also a kind of mantle, which fits the back closely and is fastened together in front of the chest. The kings usually appear in it;[4] other people only wear it on festive occasions.[5]

In addition to the usual forms of dress, the development of which we have just considered, there were at all periods certain garments which were only worn by individuals of rank, and which we must conclude to be robes of office. We must of course give the first place to the royal costume of the king, the skirt with the lion's tail and with the ends rounded off, between which hung down the narrow strip of stuff which was the most ancient symbol of royalty. We have already shown (p. 59) how this costume became more splendid in course of time, and we may well surmise that those changes were due in great part to the spirit of imitation; the great lords tried as far as possible to dress like the Pharaoh. The festive costume of the Old Empire was the first result of imitation; the edge in the front of the skirt was rounded off and adorned with golden embroidery, so that the wearer should in his dress, when seen at any rate from the right side, resemble His Majesty. It is only towards the close of the 5th dynasty that we first occasionally meet with a costume exactly resembling the royal skirt, except that it was not made of gold material nor furnished with a lion's tail. It was worn as a hunting costume under the Middle Empire as well as in the beginning of the New Empire, when men of high rank wore it when hunting birds or spearing fish.[6]

OLDER FORM OF THE ROYAL SKIRT.

[1] E.g. under King Ḥaremḥeb in a funeral procession. Wilk., iii., plates 67, 68. Cp. also L. D., iii. 117.

[2] L. D., iii. 217 a, 229, 230, 231. In order rightly to understand this costume, see, e.g., statues 2303, 2287, in the Berlin collection.

[3] E.g. L. D., iii. 153, 183 b, 214. In the latter instances the skirt seems to pass through the girdle, so that it covers the back.

[4] L. D., iii. 1, 91 a, 92, 98 b, 101, 115, etc. Cp. also the above plate iv. representing the Turin statue of Ramses II.

[5] Wilk., iii., plates 67, 68.

[6] O. E.: L. D., ii. 60. Berlin, 1118, 1119. M. E.: L. D., ii. 130 (alike also in the length of the royal beard). N. E.: L. D., iii. 9 e; Wilk., ii. 107.

Under the Middle Empire however it appears that a law was passed limiting such imitations, and the wearing of the *Shend'ot* (the royal skirt)

CHNEMḤÔTEP HUNTING BIRDS (after L. D., ii. 130)

was only granted to certain dignitaries. Many great lords of the 12th dynasty expressly claim this privilege, and in later times the high priests of the great sanctuaries bear as one of their proudest titles *wearer of the Shend'ot.*[1] These limitations were not of much use, and in the time of confusion between the Middle and the New Empire the royal skirt was adopted by an even wider circle. Under the 18th dynasty the chiefs of all the departments wore it on official occasions, and even when they gave way to the fashion of the time and wore an outer long skirt, they fastened the latter up high enough for the symbol of their office to be visible underneath.[2] Officials whose duties were very circumscribed, such as the "chief of the peasants," or the "chief of the waggoners," chief masons, sailors, and drivers of the time of the New Empire, often wore skirts very much resembling the *Shend'ot.*[3]

AFTER A WALL PICTURE IN A THEBAN TOMB (now in the British Museum).

We may regard as another token of high rank

[1] passim. The high priest of Memphis wears a very similar skirt as early even as the 4th dynasty. Mar. Mast., 74 75.

[2] L. D., iii. 76 a, b, 77 c.

[3] L. D., iii. 10, 41, 76 a, 77 b. The middle piece in the case of these subordinate officials is often longer and more pointed.

the strips of white material which great lords of the Old Empire so often wound round the breast or body,[1] when they put on their gala dress; or allowed to hang down from the shoulders,[2] when in their usual dress they went for a walk in the country; or when they went hunting. A broad band of this kind was no protection against the cold or the wind, it was rather a token by which the lord might be recognised. In the same way the overseer of the fishermen or labourers was known by a narrow band round the neck.[3] The narrow ribbons, which we so often see great men of all periods holding between their fingers, may have the same signification.[4]

Another dress, seen at the first glance to be a robe of office, is that of the chief judge and governor, who was the highest official of the Egyptian government; he wore a narrow dress reaching from the breast to the ankle, held up by two bands fastened with a metal clasp behind at the neck. This great lord wore his head shaven like the priests—probably because he was also *ex officio* the high priest of the goddess of truth.[5] We shall speak later of the many changes in the dress of the priests and of the soldiers.

A GOVERNOR UNDER RAMSES IX. After a rough sketch on a limestone slab (Insc. in the hier. char. i.)

Let us now cast a glance on the clothing of the lower classes, which was essentially different from that of the upper classes considered above. Subordinate officials are generally rather behind the fashion; under the Middle Empire they wore for instance the short skirt of the Old Empire, and under the New Empire the longer one of the Middle Empire. The people proper however,—the peasants, shepherds, workmen, servants,—always contented themselves with a very simple costume. When dressed for the presence of their master they generally wore a short skirt of the kind that was fashionable at the beginning of the 4th dynasty.[6] When at work it was put on more loosely, and with any violent movement it flapped widely apart in front.[7]

This skirt was generally of linen; yet certain shepherds and boatmen of the Old Empire appear to have contented themselves with a clothing of matting; these men are remarkable also for the curious way of wearing their hair and beard, corresponding to that of the oft-mentioned *marsh*

[1] L. D., ii. 19, 22, 23, 72, 86, 89, etc.

[2] L. D., ii. 9, 12, 19.

[3] L. D., ii. 12, 107.

[4] Under the O. E., e.g. L. D., ii. 74 b. M. E.: L. D., ii. 131. N. E.; passim.

[5] L. D., iii. 121 a. Inscr. in the hier. char., i. Berlin Museum, 2290. Louvre A, 72.

[6] O. E.: L. D., ii. 4, 8, 19, 21, 22, 25, etc. M. E.: L. D., ii. 127, 131, etc. N. E.: L. D., iii. 3 a, 26, 41, 94, 105 a, etc. Wilk., ii. 34.

[7] O. E.: L. D., ii. 13, 24, 25, 32, 33 b, etc. M. E.: L. D., ii. 126, 127. N. E.: L. D., iii. 10 a.

folk.[1] The labourers of the New Empire also wore rough skirts of matting, which they were wont to seat with a piece of leather.[2] Finally, people who had to move about much, or to work on the water,[3] wore nothing but a fringed girdle of the most simple form like that still worn by many of the African tribes, a narrow strip of stuff with a few ribbons[4] or the end of the strip itself hanging down in front.[5] A girdle of this kind could not, of course, cover the body much, the ribbons were displaced with every movement, and the boatmen, fishermen, shepherds, and butchers often gave it up and worked in Nature's costume alone.[6] The feeling of shame so strongly developed with us did not exist in ancient Egypt; the most common signs in hieroglyphics sometimes represented things, now not usually drawn.

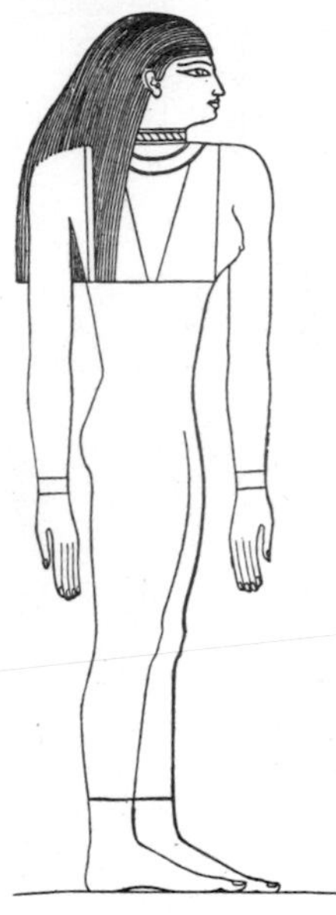

ORDINARY DRESS UNDER THE OLD EMPIRE (Princess Sed'et, Dyn. IV. After L. D., ii. 21).

According to our ideas it becomes a woman rather than a man to love dress and finery; the Egyptians of the Old Empire however held a contrary opinion. Compared with the manifold costumes for men, the women's dress appears to us very monotonous, for during the centuries from the 4th to the 18th dynasty, the whole nation, from the princess to the peasant, wore the same dress. This consisted of a simple garment without folds, so narrow that the forms of the body were plainly visible. It reached from below the breasts to the ankles; two braces passed over the shoulders and held it up firmly. In rare instances the latter are absent,[7] so that the dress is only prevented from slipping down by its narrowness. The dress and braces are always of the same colour,[8] white, red, or yellow; in this respect also there existed no difference between that of mother and daughter, or between that of mistress and maid. In the same way all wore it quite plain, unless perhaps the hem at the top might be somewhat embroidered.[9]

E'T'E, WIFE OF SECHEMKA (Louvre A. 102, after Perrot-Chipiez).

It is very rarely, as we have said, that we find dresses of a different

[1] L. D., ii. 69, and frequently.

[2] L. D., iii. 40. Wilk., ii. 100.

[3] O. E.: Butchers; L. D., ii. 4, 24, 25. Shepherds; ib. 23, 24, 35. Boatmen; ib. 28, 45. Fishermen; ib. 9, 46. Birdcatchers; ib. 46. N. E.: Corn workers; L. D., iii. 10. Temple cooks; ib. 96. Sailors; Düm. Flotte, i.

[4] Under the O. E. at most two or three; seldom four (L. D., ii. 56) or more (ib. 24).

[5] L. D., ii. 9, 12 b, 106.

[6] L. D., ii. 9, 12 b, 20, 43.

[7] Mistress; L. D., ii. 15.

[8] White; L. D., ii. 83, 90. Red; ib. 19, 20, 21. Yellow; ib., 57 58.

[9] L. D., ii. 5, 8 c, 11, 15.

fashion. 'Et'e, wife of Sechemka, the superintendent of agriculture, wears a white dress richly embroidered with coloured beads, covering the breasts and cut down in a V between them. It is worn with a belt and has therefore no braces. Another dress, which we find rather more frequently, covers the shoulders though it has no sleeves ; the neck also is generally cut down in a V.[1] In the following illustration, representing the beautiful

LADY OF THE OLD EMPIRE IN A CLOAK (Statue of Nofret, Gizeh, after Perrot-Chipiez).

statue of Nofret, the wife of the high priest Ra'ḥôtep, is seen a cloak which is worn over the usual dress.

Under the Middle Empire women's dress seems to have changed but little, and in the beginning also of the 18th dynasty the modifications were but trifling;[2] contemporary however with the changes in men's dress which followed, it assumed a new character, due partly to the great political change in the position of Egypt in the world. Following the

[1] Perrot, 637, 659. L. D., ii. 57 (under a dress with braces ?) ib. 58 (the neck is cut out in a round).

[2] It is characteristic of these later periods that one or both of the braces should be left off; M. E. : with two or with one, L. D., ii. 128 ; without any, ib. 130. N. E. : with both embroidered, L. D., iii. 9 f. ; with one, ib. 9 d, 42 ; without any, ib. 9 e.

new fashions of the day, women wore two articles of clothing—a narrow dress leaving the right shoulder free, but covering the left, and a wide cloak fastened in front over the breast; as a rule both were made of such fine linen that the forms of the body were plainly visible.[1] The hem of the cloak was embroidered, and, when the wearer was standing still, hung straight down. In course of time, under the New Empire, this

DRESS AND CLOAK OF THE TIME OF THE NEW EMPIRE (after Perrot-Chipiez).

costume evidently underwent many changes, all the details of which are very difficult to follow, because of the superficial way in which the Egyptian artist represented dress. On every side we are liable to make mistakes. If we, for instance, take the picture here given of the princess Bekten'eten by itself we should conclude that the lady was wearing a single white garment, it is only when we compare it with the

[1] E.g. L. D., iii. 62 c. Wall pictures in the Brit. Mus. (see the plates in the following chapter): Berlin, 2297, 7278, 8041. Incidentally we may mention that the Greek figures of Isis wear this cloak fastened together between the breasts.

more detailed contemporary picture of a queen that it is possible rightly to understand it. In both cases the same dress and cloak are worn; but while in the one case the artist has given the contours of both articles of dress, in the other he has lightly sketched in the outer edges only, and thus as it were given the dress in profile. Even then he is not consistent; he shows where it is cut out at the neck and where the cloak falls over the left arm, but he quite ignores that it must cover part of the right arm also.[1]

FEMALE COSTUME OF THE END OF THE 18TH DYNASTY (after L. D., iii. 100. See also illustration, p. 46).

Under these circumstances I shall content myself with bringing forward the most important types which can be distinguished with some certainty in women's dress of the time of the 19th and 20th dynasties. The next development was to let the cloak fall freely over the arms as shown in the accompanying illustration;[2] soon afterwards a short sleeve was added for the left arm, whilst the right still remained free.[3] Finally, towards the close of the 20th dynasty, a thick underdress was added to the semi-transparent dress and the open cloak.[4] We have one costume which deviates much from the usual type, and which belongs certainly to the second half of the New Empire; it is seen on one of the most beautiful statues in the Berlin museum;[5] it consists of a long dress which seems to have two sleeves, a short mantilla trimmed with fringe on the shoulders, and in front a sort of apron which falls loosely from the neck to the feet. We noticed above the dress of a man in which in similar wise a kind of apron hung down from the belt: the representation of the husband of this lady shows us that both these fashions were in vogue at the same time. Contemporary with the complicated forms of female costume we sometimes meet with a very simple one, a plain shirt with short sleeves, reaching up to the neck; this, however, seems only to have been worn by servants.[6]

The dress of the women of the lower classes never differed much from that of the ladies; peasant women and servants for the most part wore clothes of almost the same style as those of their mistresses. Their dress allowed of very little movement, and could not therefore be worn for hard work,—at such times women like men were contented to wear a short skirt which left the upper part of the body and the legs free.[7] The dancing

[1] I need scarcely observe that those same difficulties arise more or less in all Egyptian representations of dress.

[2] L. D., iii. 93, 94, 97 a, e, 117, 172 e.

[3] L. D., iii. 184 a, 186, 196, 201 a, 202 f.

[4] L. D., iii. 229, 230, 231 a. These pictures show also the sleeve of the cloak particularly clearly.

[5] Berlin, 2303.

[6] L. D., iii. 42, 91 a. Wilk., i. 392.

[7] O. E.: Perrot, 662, 664. M. E.: L. D., ii. 126, 127.

girls of ancient times, doubtless from coquettish reasons, were wont to prefer the latter dress decked out with all sorts of ornaments rather than a more womanly costume.[1] For similar reasons the young slaves under the New Empire, who served the lords and ladies at feasts, wore as their only article of clothing a strip of leather which passed between the legs, and was held up by an embroidered belt (see the two plates in the following chapter); the guests liked to see the pretty forms of the maidens.[2]

Considered as a whole, the development of female dress followed very much the same course as that of the men. In both cases under the Old Empire the forms were very simple; there was little change till the beginning of the New Empire, at which time, with the great rise of political power, there was a complete revolution in dress. In both cases

CLOAK WITH THE ARMS FREE (after L. D., iii. 217 e).

CLOAK WITH SLEEVE (Dyn. XX. After L. D., iii. 2).

CLOAK WITH SLEEVE AND A DOUBLE DRESS (after L. D., iii. 231 a).

the change consisted in the introduction of a second article of clothing, and the two new dresses correspond with each other in possessing a sleeve for the left arm only, while the right arm is left free for work. Another remarkable coincidence is that at the same time in the clothing of both sexes appearance seems so much to have been studied. It is quite possible that these changes were effected in some degree by foreign intercourse,—how far this was the case we cannot now determine. This influence, however, could only have affected details, for the general character of Egyptian dress is in direct contrast to that which we meet with at the same time in North Syria. The Syrians wore narrow, close-fitting, plain clothes in which dark blue threads alternated with dark

[1] L. D., ii. 36, 61 a, 101 b, 126.

[2] Theban wall-pictures now in the Brit. Mus. Wilk., ii. 353.

red, and these were generally adorned with rich embroidery. In Egypt wide robes with many folds of white transparent linen were worn, without any adornment, the merit of this clothing consisting in the absolute purity and the finest texture. It was really not thus originally in ancient Egypt. The dress of the Old Empire appears sometimes to have been made of thick material;[1] in the oldest period the dress of women is more often coloured than white,[2] and under the Middle Empire it is sometimes green and sometimes of various colours.[3] Colour disappeared disproportionately early from the dress of the men,[4] and though, according to the inscriptions, red, green, or blue material is still said to be required by the divinities or by the deceased,[5] this had long been replaced amongst the living by fine white linen.

SYRIAN AMBASSADOR IN THE TIME OF TUET-'ANCH-AMUN. In the original the threads of the dress are alternately blue and red (after L. D., iii. 116).

This proscription of colour was doubtless due to the desire for more absolute cleanliness of body; the same wish which led the Egyptians to shave both hair and beard. It was natural that with such ideas those workmen whose duties were to wash the clothes, played a special part, and

"The washer, he who washes on the dyke,
Neighbour to the crocodile as he swims up stream,"

After L. D., ii. 102 (Beni-Hasan).

is a favourite figure in poetry.[6] We have already remarked (p. 62) that the "royal chief washer" and the "royal chief bleacher" were amongst

[1] E.g. the statue, Perrot, 637.

[2] White; L. D., ii. 96. Red; ib., 19, 21. Yellow; ib., 57, 58. Many coloured; Louvre A, 102.

[3] Green; Mar. Cat. d'Ab., 620. Many coloured; Berlin, 13. As a rule however white under the Middle Empire; Berlin, 1183, 1188.

[4] Again yellow; L. D., ii. 55, 57, and Berlin, 1109 (Dyn. VI.). Otherwise as far as I can judge always white or white with gold. Under the 6th dynasty in several instances (Berlin, 7764, 7765), striped materials, whether coloured cannot be determined.

[5] Cp. on the names of these colours, Br. Dic. Suppl., 172.

[6] Sall., 2, 8, 2 ff=An., 7, 3, 5 ff. Similar instances, e.g. An., 4, 10, 5. D'Orbiney, 10, 8 ff.

the higher court officials. In the domestic life of private houses the great washing day was an important event, important enough to be introduced into the series of pictures in the tombs.[1] Three pictures of the time of the Middle Empire represent workmen watched by the *chief washer* busy at small tanks with the *washing* and *wringing*. We see them beating the wet clothes with wooden staves; they sprinkle them holding their arms up high; they hang one end of the folded piece of linen over a post, put a stick through the other end, and wring it with a good deal of force. They then stretch and fold up the linen, and finally the *chief washer* packs it up in a great bundle. Washing and bleaching however were not considered all that was necessary for good laundry work; ingenious methods were also devised to mark the folds required by fashion, and which the fine linen would scarcely assume by itself. By what means exactly the Egyptians contrived to do this we can scarcely decide, though it is an interesting conjecture of Wilkinson's that these regular folds in the dresses

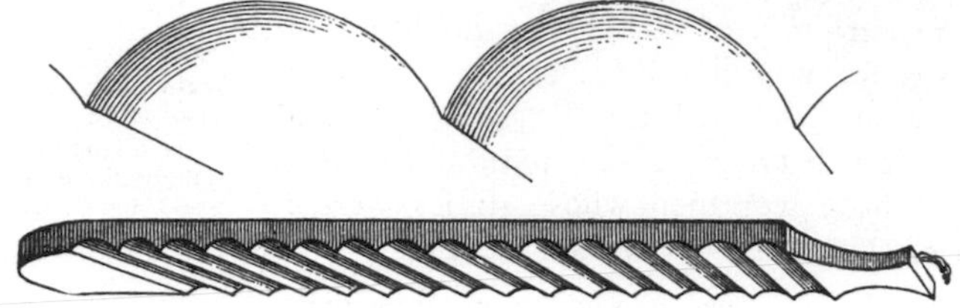

WOODEN INSTRUMENT IN THE MUSEUM AT FLORENCE.
The hollows are represented below in their original size (after Wilk., i. 185).

were pressed in by means of a board such as is shown in the accompanying illustration.

The character of the dress of a nation however does not depend merely upon clothes; the ornaments, the shoes, and the manner of dressing the hair are all important elements. In Egypt the latter was of great importance, and we must treat it in more detail. It has often been maintained that the ancient Egyptians, like their modern descendants, shaved their heads most carefully, and wore artificial hair only. The following facts moreover are incontrovertible: we meet with representations of many smoothly shaved heads on the monuments, there are wigs in several museums,[2] and the same person had his portrait taken sometimes with short, at other times with long hair. Herodotos also expressly states of the Egyptians of his time that they shaved themselves from their youth up, and only let their hair grow as a sign of mourning. An unprejudiced observer will nevertheless confess, when he studies the subject, that the question is not so simple as it seems at first sight. The same Herodotos remarks, for instance, that in no other country are so few bald heads to

[1] Representations of washing at Beni Hasan: L. D., ii. 126 (with inscriptions above). W., ii. 173 (only 4-13). Ros. M. C., 42, 1-2.

[2] London (Wilk., ii. 329), Berlin (ib. 330), Gizeh several (Maspero Guide, p. 332), one in Paris.

be found, and amongst the medical prescriptions of ancient Egypt are a number of remedies for both men and women to use for their hair. Still more important is it to observe that in several of the statues belonging to different periods little locks of natural hair peep out from under the edge of the heavy wigs.[1] We must therefore conclude that when a man is

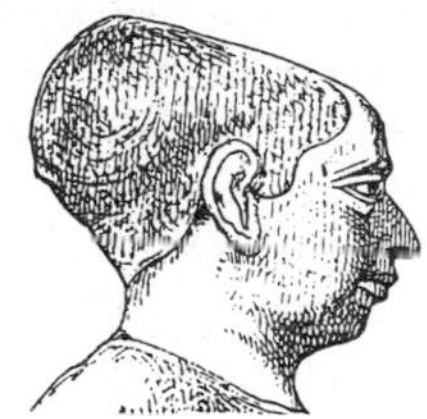

THE HEAD OF THE DWARF AT GIZEH.

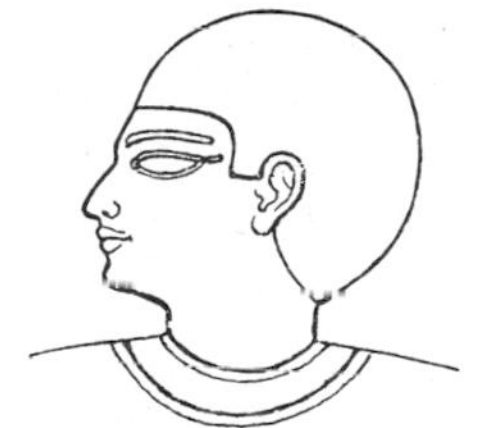

CONVENTIONAL REPRESENTATION OF THE SAME WIG.

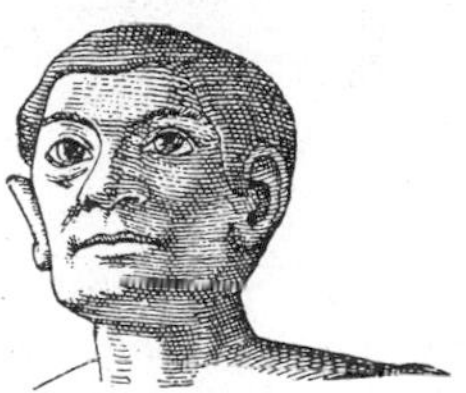

HEAD OF THE SCRIBE AT THE LOUVRE.

said to be *shaven* we are as a rule to understand that the hair is only cut very short, and that those persons alone were really shaven who are represented so on the monuments, viz. the priests of the New Empire.

As a fact the monuments of the Old Empire show that short hair (as seen in the accompanying illustrations) was originally the fashion for all classes;[2] for the shepherd and the boatman as well as for the prince, and was even worn by those in court dress.[3] At the same time the great

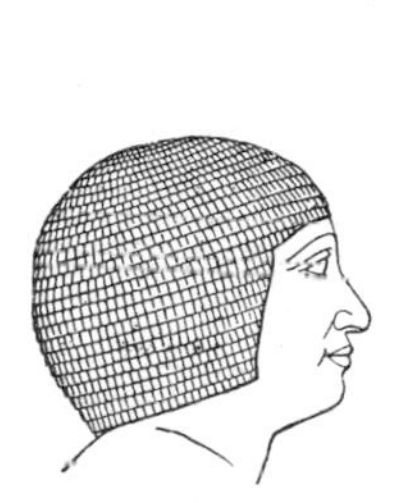

LITTLE CURLS OVER THE CROWN OF THE HEAD (after L. D., iii. 290).

CONVENTIONAL REPRESENTATION OF THE SAME WIG.

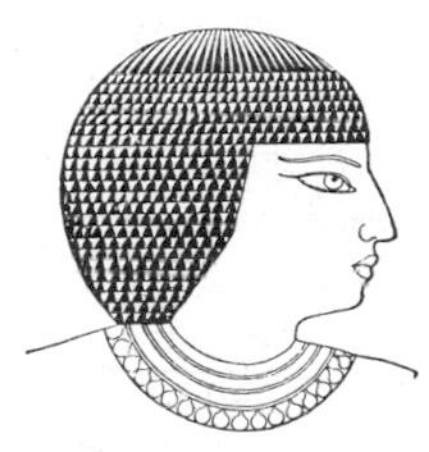

THE LITTLE CURLS OVER THE FOREHEAD ONLY (after L. D., ii. 21).

lords possessed also a more festive adornment for their heads in the shape of great artificial coiffures. Amongst them we must distinguish two kinds of wigs, the one made in imitation of short woolly hair, the other of long hair. The former consisted of a construction of little curls arranged in horizontal rows lapping over each other like the tiles of a

[1] In the head-dresses of ladies of the O. E.: Perrot, 141, 142, 658, plate viii. In the case of a lady of the N. E.: Berlin, 7278; in the case of a man: Berlin, 2296.

[2] Sometimes (Louvre A, 102; ib. Salle civile 6) the short-cut hair is only indicated by a grey colour, whilst a lock of hair (on the 1st statue) is coloured black. The other colours of these coiffures are striking—white, L. D., ii. 19, 57, 58; yellow, ib. 90; red, ib. 19.

[3] L. D., ii. 8 b, 11.

roof;[1] as a rule very little of the forehead was visible, and the ears were quite covered as well as the back of the neck. The details vary in many particulars, though this description is correct as a whole. The little curls are sometimes triangular, sometimes square; the hair is sometimes cut straight across the forehead, sometimes rounded; in many instances the little curls begin up on the crown of the head, in others high on the forehead; other differences also exist which can be ascribed only to the vagaries of fashion. It strikes us as humorous that the people should ape this attire of their masters; in the earliest times the master alone and one or two of his household officials wore this wig, but in the time of the 5th dynasty we have many representations of workmen,

LONG CURLY WIG (after Perrot, 655).

LONG CURLY WIG (after the picture of Uerchuu from L. D., ii. 44 a).

CONVENTIONAL REPRESENTATIONS OF THIS HEAD-DRESS (after the picture of Cha'frê'a'nch from L. D., ii. 9; and the picture of Meḥy from L. D., ii. 74 c).

shepherds, or servants adorned with this once noble head-dress. On the other hand the second wig, that of long hair,[2] seems never to have been displaced from its exclusive position, although it was certainly a more splendid head-dress than the stiff construction of little curls. In the long-haired wig the hair fell thickly from the crown of the head to the shoulders, at the same time forming a frame for the face; while round the forehead, and also at the ends, the hair was lightly waved. The individual tresses were sometimes twisted into spiral plaits.

Nevertheless, this marvel of the Egyptian wig-maker's art, with all the variations which it admitted, did not content the dandy of the Old Empire;

[1] Good examples of the usual forms of wigs—to the crown of the head: L. D., iii. 289, 10; 290, 13, 14, 16; L. D., ii. 23, 36, c. To the forehead: L. D., iii. 288, 2, 4, L. D., ii. 5, 10 b, 19, Perrot, 644. Cut round on the forehead: Perrot, 637, 141. Cut square on the forehead: Perrot, 659, 142. Conventional drawing of the same: L. D., ii. 9, 10 a (only discernable by the ear being hidden). Black: L. D., ii. 19, 57 c. Dark grey: L. D., ii. 19. Light yellow: L. D., ii. 57 a. Carried by people: L. D., ii. 45 c, d, 66, 67-70. Düm Res., 8, 9. A very unusual shape, L. D., ii. 50 b.

[2] Good examples of long wigs—Front view: L. D., ii. 11, 44; Perrot, p. 10, 655. Side view: L. D., iii. 288, 3, 5, 289, 7-9; L. D., ii. 3, 9, 25, 27. Waved: L. D., ii. 89, iii. 288, 3. Twisted tresses: Düm. Res., 8, 9, 12 (Dyn. V.) The ear visible: L. D., ii. 43 b.

and he exerted himself to make his head-dress still more imposing. A certain Shepsesrê‘, who held the office of superintendent of the south at the court of King 'Ess'e, must have been specially anxious to excel in this respect. He caused four statues to be prepared for his tomb each representing him in a special coiffure. In two he wears the usual wigs, in the third his hair is long and flowing like that of a woman, and in the fourth he wears a wig of little curls, which reaches down to the middle of his back.[1] The latter must have been an invention on the part of the wig-maker, for it would be impossible ever to dress a man's natural hair in such a wonderful manner. The same might be said of the wig which became the ruling fashion under the 6th dynasty. This consisted of a senseless combination of the two earlier forms; the long-haired coiffure, the whole style of which is only possible with long tresses, being divided, after the fashion of the other, into rows of little curls, though its waving lines were retained.[2]

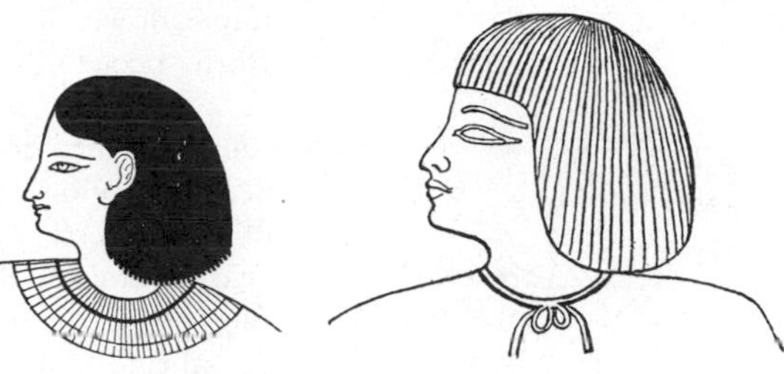

SHORT-HAIRED WIGS (after L. D., iii. 77 e, 115. Cp. also the head of the scribe, p. 210).

Under the Middle Empire there was little change in the fashion of wearing the hair. The men of the upper classes still seem to have kept to the two ancient forms of wig,[3] while the lower classes let the hair grow freely;[4] neither did the fashion change immediately on the expulsion of the Hyksos, but only with the rise of the Egyptian political power.[5] From this time, viz. from the second half of the 18th dynasty, fashions evidently rapidly succeeded each other, and we are not always able, from the

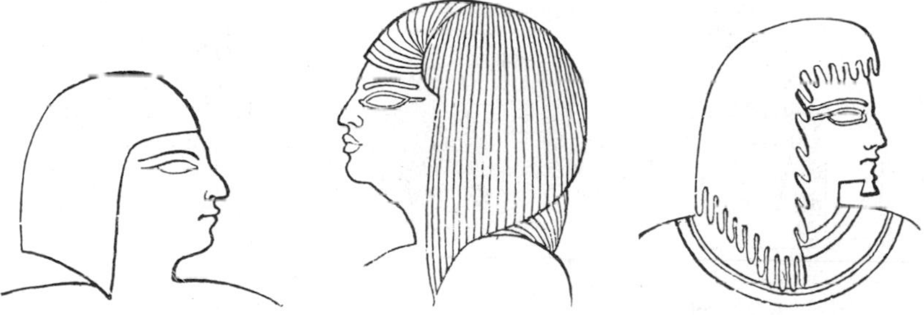

HEAD-DRESSES WHICH COVER THE SHOULDERS (after L. D., iii. 121 b, 100, 173 c).

[1] L. D., ii. 64 bis.

[2] L. D., ii. 110 f, g, 111 d; Berlin, 7764, 7765.

[3] The shorter, L. D., ii. 121, 128, 130; the longer, ib. 126, 129, 131. In both the ear is often left uncovered.

[4] L. D., ii. 126, 132.

[5] Short wigs: L. D., iii. 1. Long ones: ib. 9 e. With little curls: ib. 39 c. Very long ones hanging down the back: ib. 9 f, 10 a.

material at our command to say exactly how long one single fashion lasted. We may distinguish two principal coiffures, a shorter one often covering the neck, and a longer one in which the thick masses of hair hung down in front over the shoulders. Both occur in numerous more or less anomalous varieties. A simple form of the shorter coiffure is shown in the accompanying representation of the head of Cha'emḥê't, the superintendent of granaries; straight hair hangs down all round the head, being cut even at the back.[1] As a rule however men were not content with anything so simple; fashion demanded curly hair,[2] or at least a fringe of little curls framing the face, and a single tress hanging down loosely at the back.[3] The second coiffure, which covers the shoulders, does not differ much in its simplest form from the shorter one; generally however it is a far more stately erection.[4] The ends of the hair as well as the hair round the face are also sometimes curled[5] in a charming though rather unnatural manner, as we see in representations of several great men of the 18th and

After L. D., iii. 77 a. Cp. also the frontispiece to this chapter.

WIG OF LONG HAIR (after L.D., ii. 21).

WIG OF SHORT HAIR (after Perrot, plate ix.).

WIG OF LONG HAIR (Perrot, 659).

19th dynasties. The hair which falls over the shoulders is twisted into little separate curls forming a pretty contrast to the rest of the hair, which is generally straight.[6]

Both forms of coiffure which we have described were worn by all men of rank of the 18th and 19th dynasties; we see that they were really wigs,

[1] L. D., iii. 76 b, 77 e. Similar ones: ib. 98 a, 153; Berlin, 2289, 2296 (above the ears the natural hair is visible).

[2] L. D., iii. 76 b.

[3] Cp. also the wall pictures in the British Museum shown in the following chapter.

[4] L. D., iii. 93, 116, 121 a, 128 b, 176, 187 d.

[5] L. D., iii. 173 c; Berlin, 7316.

[6] Many variations in detail: L. D., iii. 77 a; Berlin, 2277, 2287, 2293, 2298 2303 7278 7316, and others. Firstly, under Thothmes III., with still shorter ends: Louvre A, 53.

and not natural hair, by the change of coiffure worn by one and the same person.[1] They lasted on into the 20th dynasty, at which time we also find long freely-waving hair.[2]

Under the Old Empire the women of all classes wore a large coiffure of straight hair, hanging down to the breast in two tresses.[3] Many pictures

After Wilk., ii. 339.

After a Picture in the Brit. Mus.

prove to us that these wonderful coiffures also were not always natural, for occasionally we find not only the servants without them, but also the grown-up daughters and the mistresses themselves,[4] while the head appears to be covered with short hair.[5] In a few instances we find a shorter form of coiffure worn occasionally by ladies of high birth. The hair does not hang longer than to the shoulders, and under the wig in front the natural hair can generally be seen covering the forehead almost to the eyes.[6]

After Perrot, 795.

During the long period of the Middle Empire, fashion, as regards ladies' hair, remained wonderfully stationary, the only innovation we can remark is, that the ends of the two tresses were formed into a pretty fringe.[7] With the great changes which Egyptian dress underwent towards the middle of the 18th dynasty[8] several new fashions in ladies' as well as men's coiffures arose contemporarily, and apparently followed the same course. These seem to have been due to the desire for a freer and less stiff arrangement of the hair. The heavy tresses which formerly hung down

1 E.g. L. D., iii. 103 and 105; ib. 76 b, and 77 a, e.

2 L. D., iii. 2 b.

3 E.g. L. D., iii. 289, 11-12; L. D., ii. 20, 32, 33 a, 40 b; Perrot, 659.

4 Ladies: L. D., ii. 25, 27, 74 c, 90. Daughters: L. D., ii. 8 b, 19, 22 a, 25, 27. Servants: L. D., ii. 9, 17 c, 35, 36 c, and Perrot, 663.

5 It is white or yellow, and is exactly like the corresponding coiffure of the men.

6 Perrot, 141, 142, 658; plate viii.

7 With fringe: L. D., ii. 128. Without fringe: ib. 130.

8 The old coiffure: L. D., iii. 42; in curled hair: Berlin, 2289, 2298.

in front are now abandoned; and the hair is made to cover either the whole of the upper part of the body[1] or it is all combed back and hangs behind.[2] The details vary very much. Sometimes the hair falls straight down,[3] sometimes it is twisted together in plaits,[4] at other times it is curled.[5] Some women wear it long, others short and standing out; some frame the face with wonderful plaits,[6] and others with short tresses.[7] Nearly all, however, twist the ends of several plaits or curls together, and thus make a sort of fringe to the heavy mass of hair, as is shown in the frontispiece to the eighth chapter.

A more graceful head-dress is that worn by the girl playing a musical instrument, in the London picture so often mentioned (see the following chapter); curly hair lightly surrounds without concealing the shape of the head, whilst a few curls hang down behind like a pig-tail. In very similar fashion a young servant has arranged her plaits; three thick ones form the pig-tail, and eight smaller ones hang down over each cheek.[8]

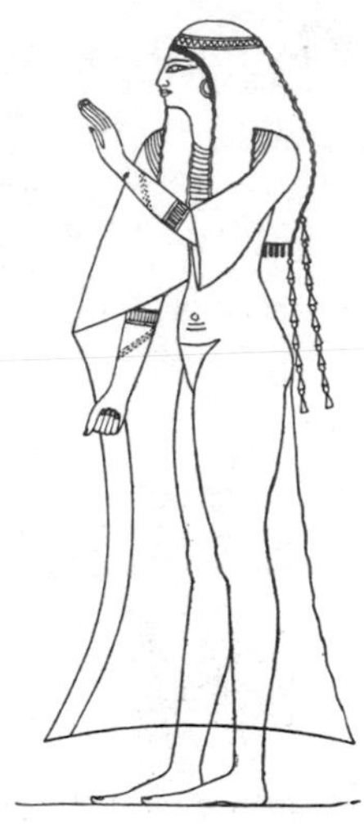

COIFFURE OF THE 20TH DYNASTY (after L. D., iii. 2).

All these coiffures were worn by the ladies of the 18th dynasty; later, especially under the 20th dynasty, ladies came back to the old manner of dressing their hair, and again allowed a heavy tress to fall over each shoulder. They turned aside indeed very much from the old simplicity, they crimped their hair, and those who could afford it allowed their wigs to reach to below the waist.[9] I say *wigs*, for most of these coiffures must have been artificial, as we see by the fact that short coiffures were also worn on various occasions by the same ladies.[10] To one of these ladies belonged the wig in the Berlin Museum (shown in the illustration above), the long curls of which appear now very threadbare.

WIG IN THE BERLIN MUSEUM.

[1] L. D., iii. 62 c. 94, 97 a, and frequently.
[2] L. D., iii. 100, in the statue.
[3] E.g. L. D., iii. 94.
[4] E.g. Perrot, p. 795.
[5] Theban wall pictures in the Brit. Mus. Berlin, 2297, 7278 (the natural hair is visible below).
[6] L. D., iii. 2, 240 a. Wilk., ii. 339. Very complicated: Berlin, 2297, 2303.
[7] E.g. L. D., iii. 240 c.
[8] L. D., iii. 42.
[9] L. D., iii. 240 c. Shorter: ib. 2 and ib. 230. A beautiful example framing the face: Berlin, 2303.
[10] Under the M. E.: L. D., ii. 127. Under the N. E., in ladies of rank: L. D., iii. 91.

It is not composed of human hair, but of sheep's wool; and these cheap preparations were doubtless usually worn.[1]

This custom of wearing artificial hair strikes us as very foolish, though perhaps not so much so as another custom with which it is closely allied. The same exaggerated idea of cleanliness which led the Egyptian to regard long hair as something unclean and to be removed, caused him to feel a grudge against his beard. He shaved it off, in contrast to his Mahommedan descendants, who, though they shave their heads, regard the beard as too sacred to be touched. In all epochs of Egyptian history it is very rarely we find that a gentleman wears even a small moustache,[2] shepherds alone and foreign slaves let their beards grow—evidently to the disgust of all cleanly men.[3] Yet in Egypt the notion, familiar to all oriental nations, that the beard was the symbol of manly dignity, had survived from the most primitive ages. If therefore on solemn occasions the great lords of the country wished to command respect, they had to

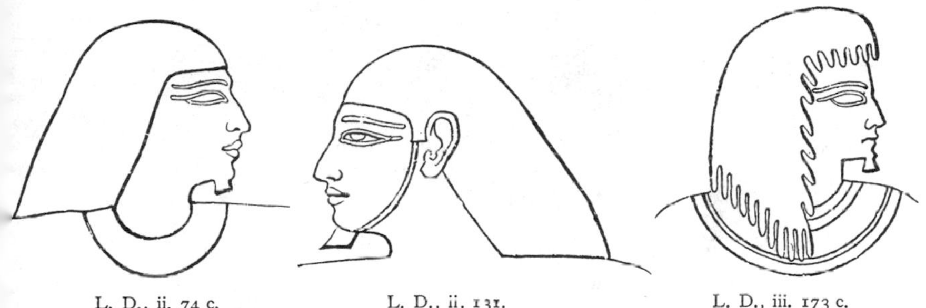

L. D., ii. 74 c. L. D., ii. 131. L. D., iii. 173 c.

BEARDS OF THE OLD, MIDDLE, AND NEW EMPIRE.

appear with beards, and as the natural beard was forbidden, there was no other course but to fasten on an artificial one underneath the chin. This artificial beard is really the mere suggestion of a beard, it is only a short piece of hair tightly plaited,[4] and fastened on by two straps behind the ears.[5] Every one would willingly have done without this ugly appendage; men of rank under the Old Empire put it on sometimes when they appeared in their great wigs on gala days, but they often left it off even on these occasions, and scarcely ever did one of them allow it to be represented on his portrait statue; he felt that it was disfiguring to the beauty of the face.[6]

[1] Even the wig of a queen is found to consist of a mixture of black sheep's wool and human hair. Maspero Guide, p. 332.

[2] A small natural moustache, Perrot, 639; Louvre A, 41, 104. The same with a trace of beard on the chin, L. D., ii. 83 b—all under the Old Empire.

[3] E.g. under the O. E.: L. D., ii. 69; under the M. E.: L. D., ii. 132; under the N. E.: L. D., iii. 10 a.

[4] The shape is well given: Düm. Res., 9, 12; L. D., ii. 22 a.

[5] These straps do not always appear on the sculptures; in spite of their absence, we must always regard these beards as artificial, as the same person is represented sometimes with, sometimes without, a beard.

[6] An exception is found in one of the four statues represented in the tomb; L. D., ii. 64.

It was more common under the Middle Empire and was worn even by the officials of the nomes and of the estates,[1] though very seldom by those of more ancient times.[2] Under the New Empire again it was seldom worn, *e.g.* none of the courtiers of Chuen'eten wear it; it was considered as a fashion of past days, and only appropriate for certain ceremonies.[3] A longer form of the artificial beard belongs strictly to the royal dress, and though we find it occasionally worn by the nomarchs under the Middle Empire, it was as much an encroachment on the royal prerogative as the wearing of the Shend'ot.[4] Finally, the gods were supposed to wear beards of a peculiar shape; they were longer by two

KING OF THE OLD EMPIRE (L. D., ii. 39 f). NOMARCH OF THE MIDDLE EMPIRE (L. D., ii. 130). KING OF THE NEW EMPIRE. THE GOD OSIRIS.

finger-breadths than those worn by men, they were also plaited like pig-tails and bent up at the end.[5]

Egyptian costume, as far as we have already considered it, shows a comparatively rich development; on the other hand the history of the foot gear is very simple. In no point of apparel, in fact, did the nation remain so faithful to old traditions. At a time when people paid great attention to the various gradations of style in clothes and wigs, and when they were also strenuously striving after greater cleanliness, men and women, young and old almost always went barefoot, even when wearing the richest costumes. Under the Old and the Middle Empire women seem never to have worn sandals, while great men probably only used them when they needed them out of doors,[6] and even then they generally gave them to be

[1] L. D., ii. 128, 131, on a solemn occasion.

[2] E.g. L. D., ii. 9.

[3] E.g. L. D., iii. 9 e, 29 a, 77 a, 116, 173 c; Berlin, 2277, 2287, 7316, etc., when in ceremonial dress.

[4] L. D., ii. 129, 130.

[5] Once also under the New Empire upon a man who is bringing offerings for the deceased ancestors, and therefore is officiating as Horus (L. D., iii. 9 f); the deceased often wear it when they are in the form of Osiris, especially in the representations on the mummy cases.

[6] O. E.: L. D., ii. 13, 54, 79, 80; Perrot, 91. Single ones; L. D., ii. 98 b. M. E.: L. D., ii. 126, 131.

carried by the *sandal-bearer* who followed them.[1] Sandals were more frequently used under the New Empire; still they were not quite naturalised, and custom forbade that they should be worn in the presence of a superior.[2] Consequently sandals were all essentially of the same form. Those here represented have soles of leather, of papyrus reed or palm bast, the two straps are of the same material; one strap passes over the instep, the other between the toes.[3] Sometimes a third strap is put behind round the heel[4] in order to hold the sandal on better; somtimes the front of the sandal is turned over as a protection to the toes.[5] The sandal with sides belongs perhaps to a later period, it approaches very nearly to a shoe.

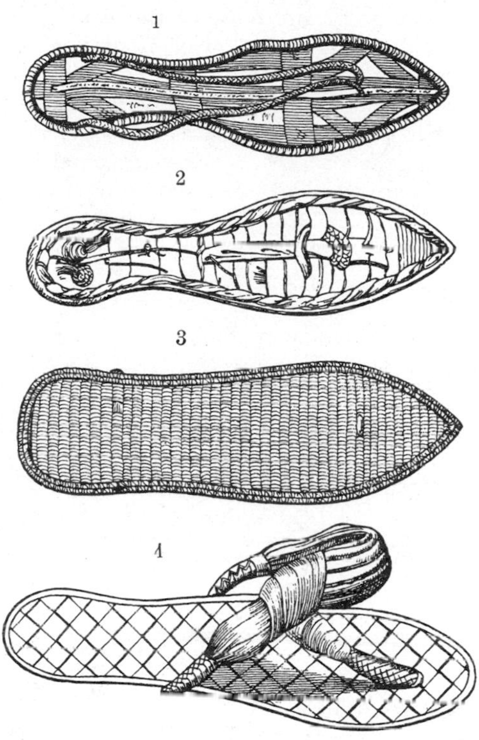

1, 2, UPPER AND UNDER SIDE OF A SANDAL (Alnwick Castle). 3, Ditto. 4, Berlin (after Wilk., ii. 336, 337).

We have laid great stress, as the reader will see by the various illustrations to this chapter, on the accessories of dress, and on ornament. At all periods both men and women wore coloured embroidered necklets,[6] as well as bracelets for the wrist and the upper arm;[7] anklets were also worn as ornaments by the ladies.[8]

[1] Sandal-bearers—O. E.: specified as *of the king*, Ä. Z., 1882, 20. M. E.: L. D., ii. 131. N. E.: servant carrying those of her mistress, Wilk., i. 392.

[2] Princes in the king's presence without sandals whilst he wears them himself, e.g. L. D., iii. 76 b, 77 c.

[3] Leather sandals in pictures such as, L. D., ii. 49 b, or Ros. Mon. civ., 64, 1.

[4] E.g. L. D., ii. 131. L. D., iii. 77 e, 98 b.

[5] E.g. L. D., iii. 1, 115, 224.

[6] Necklets for men—O. E.: narrow, blue, L. D., ii. 18, 19, 20, 21, 22, 32, 36 c, 46, etc.; blue and green on white, Louvre A, 102, 104, 105. M. E.: L. D., ii. 130, 134 b, d, etc. (narrow). N. E.: broad, with leaf-shaped ornaments reaching to the breast, passim. Necklets for women—e.g. O. E. and M. E. (mostly blue, narrow, and often a second narrow row round the neck): L. D., ii. 19, 20, 21, 32, 33, etc.; Perrot, plate ix.; Louvre A, 102. N. E.: broader than those for men, otherwise alike, passim. Simple strings of beads as necklets are rare, and indeed only customary under the New Empire; on a man, Berlin, 2297; on a woman, Perrot, 795.

[7] Frequent at all periods, under the O. E., blue (L. D., ii. 19, 21); under the M. E., green with blue necklets (Berlin, 1188).

[8] Under the O. E. (blue): L.D., ii. 20, 27, 46.

Earrings were probably first introduced into Egypt by foreigners, in the time of the New Empire. Under the 18th dynasty they consisted of broad ornamented disks; under the 20th of large rings.[1] Rings for the fingers, of which many are preserved, were generally seal rings; they bear for the most part the name of the reigning king.

After L. D., iii. 77 e. An example also of a peculiar covering for the leg, this being the only known representation of the same.

The members of the royal family wore a special covering for the head. The Pharaoh wore his crowns, his helmet, or his folded kerchief (see p. 60 f.). His sons wore (at any rate under the New Empire) a kerchief with a broad band, which took the place of the youthful sidelock, the ancient princely badge; they also wore a diadem round the head. The queen wore the so-called vulture head-dress, in which that sacred bird, the protector of the king

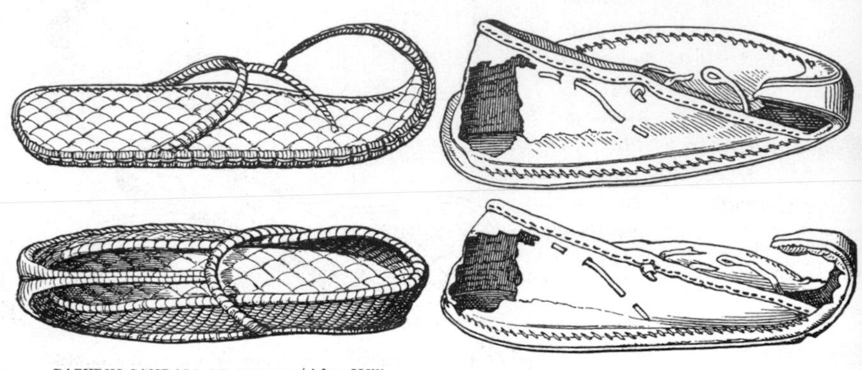

PAPYRUS SANDALS AT BERLIN (After Wilk., ii. 336).

SANDALS OF GREEN LEATHER IN THE SALT COLLECTION (after Wilk., ii. 336).

in battle, appeared to spread his wings over the head of the queen. Ordinary people contented themselves, when in gala costume, with wearing a wreath or a coloured ribbon round the hair. Women as a rule also wore the same; under the Old Empire only we occasionally find a man wearing a diadem.[2]

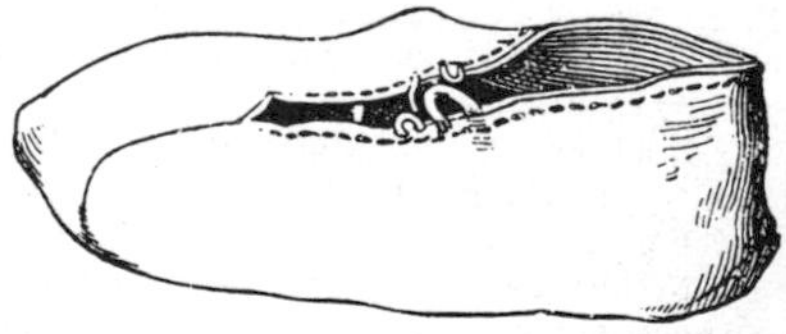

SHOE OF GREEN LEATHER IN THE SALT COLLECTION (after Wilk, ii. 336).

Men possessed one badge of honour however above women—a very important one, according to Egyptian ideas. We refer to the various sticks which men of rank of all epochs carry in such a dignified manner. To our profane eyes the differ-

[1] Disk-shaped: Wall pictures in London; Berlin, 7278; Perrot, 795. Rings: L. D., iii. 2, 217 e (both 20th dynasty).

[2] Man with diadem: L. D., ii. 73, 97 b; Düm. Res., 14; Berlin, 1118.

ences between the various sticks appear to be trifling and one stick seems as good as another; but to the Egyptian each had its own significance and its particular name. The stick in common use was of man's height, as a rule smooth or with a knob at the top.[1] It was used as a walking stick and as a support when standing still. Next there was the staff of this form, which was carried as a symbol of command, as is signified by its name, *cherp* = first. A similar staff, bearing the name of *sechem* = mighty, evidently served the same object. A fourth with the head of a fabulous animal at the top, was originally the sceptre of the gods, but was used later even by private individuals as a walking

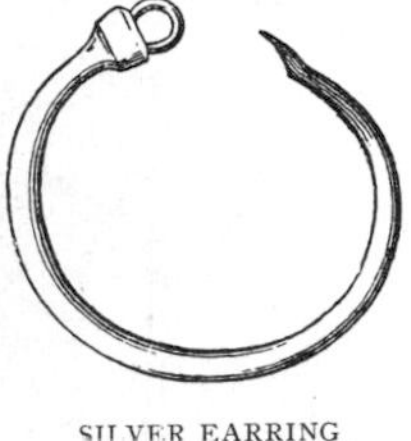

SILVER EARRING (after Wilk., ii. 349).

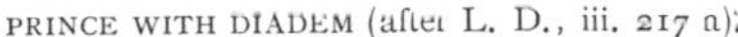

PRINCE WITH DIADEM (after L. D., iii. 217 a).

QUEEN WITH VULTURE HEAD-DRESS (after L. D., iii. 217 e).

stick.[2] We have perhaps given examples enough. Many forms of sticks were also imported from foreign parts, *e.g.* the *shebet* staff of the Canaanites called the *shabd*.[3]

The following distinction has been drawn between the apparel of primitive and civilised nations, viz. that the former love the effect of splendid clothes, the latter on the other hand beautify the body itself; according to this dictum we shall find that the Egyptians of the Old Empire were not far removed from the primitive standpoint. The painting and rouging of the face, the oiling of the limbs and of the hair, was as important to them as their clothes; and even the deceased were not happy without seven sorts of salve and two sorts of rouge.[4] In their

[1] E.g. quite smooth: L. D., ii. 20 f, 21, 78 a. With knob: ib. 13, 104 c. With hook: Wilk., iii. lxvii.

[2] Wall picture in the Brit. Mus. (gentleman in the country).

[3] E.g. Mallet, 1, 7.

[4] Thus always in the lists of offerings of the Old Empire.

sculpture also, in which slight deviations from nature were allowed, the Egyptians liked to represent the marks of paint adorning the eyes.

Two colours were chiefly used—green, with which under the Old Empire they put a line under the eyes ; and black, with which they painted

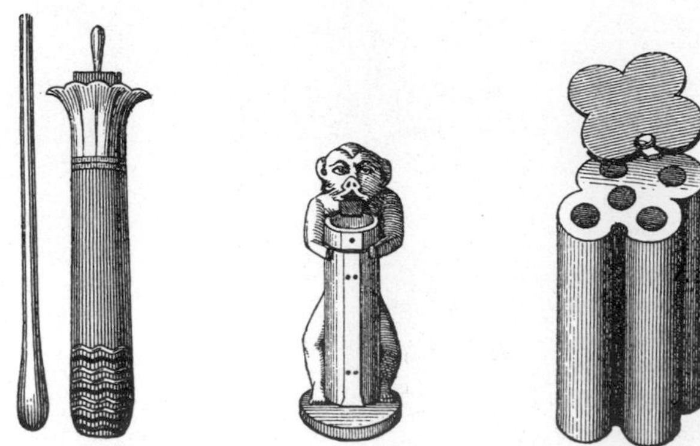

POTS FOR PAINT FOR THE EYES : 1, In the shape of a pillar, next to it the little stick for putting it on. (Brit. Mus.) 2, Held by a monkey, cover and pin are missing (Alnwick Castle). 3, For four different kinds (ditto). (After Wilk., ii. 348.)

the eyebrows and eyelids, in order to make the eyes appear larger and more brilliant. As a cosmetic stibium was chiefly used. It was imported from the East ; the best kind, called *mesd'emt*, was evidently very costly. This custom still exists in Egypt, and in this land of ophthalmia the same healing properties are ascribed to *koḥl* as were formerly to *mesd'emt*. It was customary also to paint other parts of the body as well, and from the picture of the singer to Amon (p. 216), we surmise that that lady has had her arm tatooed.[1] The caricature here depicted evidently represents a lady who is rouging her lips,[2] and surveying herself complacently at the same time in the metal mirror which she holds with the rouge pot in her left hand.

LADY ROUGING HERSELF : IN HER LEFT HAND SHE HOLDS THE MIRROR AND THE ROUGE POT (from the obscene papyrus, Tur., 145).

We can scarcely realise the importance of oil in ancient Egypt. Oil was a necessary of daily life, and the hungry unpaid workmen complain in the same breath that no food is given them to eat, and that no oil is

[1] L. D., iii. 2.

[2] Tur., 145.

given to them.[1] These workmen had probably to be contented with native fat, but the soldiers demanded imported oil—*oil from the harbour.*[2] People of rank always obtained their oils and perfumes from foreign countries,[3] in preference from the south coasts of the Red Sea, which supplied the precious *Qemi,* the ointment so often mentioned and so often represented, which was used under the New Empire for oiling the head.[4] The oil was not used as we should naturally imagine. A ball about the size of a fist was placed in the bowl of oil; the consistency of the ball is unknown, but at any rate it absorbed the oil. The *chief anointer*, who was always to be found in a rich household,[5] then placed the ball on the head of his master, where it remained during the whole time of the feast, so that the oil trickled down gradually into the hair.

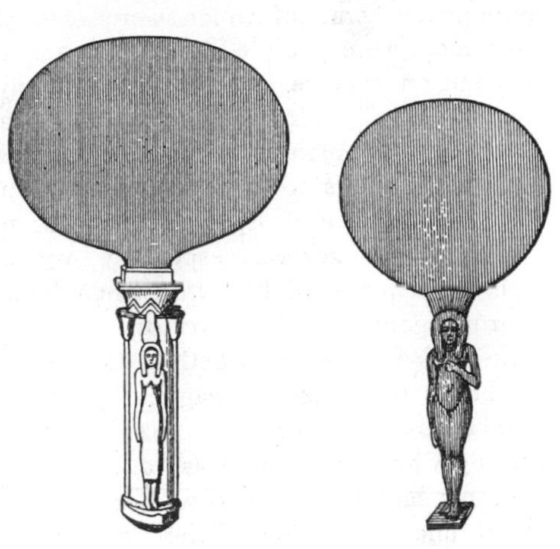

METAL MIRRORS (after Wilk., ii. 351).

Oil in Egypt was also symbolic; it was an emblem of joy. On festival days, when the king's procession passed, all the people poured "sweet oil on their heads, on their new coiffures."[6] At all the feasts cakes of ointment were quite as necessary as wreaths, and if the king wished specially to honour one of his courtiers he ordered his servants to anoint him with *Qemi*, and to put beautiful apparel and ornaments upon him.[7] It was considered a suitable amusement at a feast for persons to perform their toilettes together, and while eating they would anoint themselves, or put on new necklets and exchange flowers.

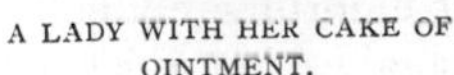

A LADY WITH HER CAKE OF OINTMENT.

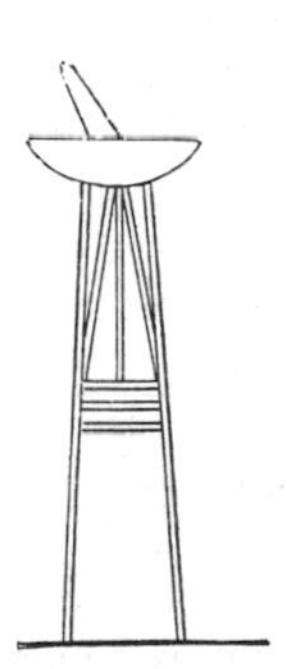

BOWL FOR OINTMENT. Others in the picture p. 120.

[1] Tur., 43, 3. [2] An., 4, 15, 4. [3] See the details in chap. xix.

[4] Scenes of anointing: L. D., iii. 76 b, 230; Wilk., i. 426. Ointment on the heads in all pictures of funerary feasts, on stelae, etc.

[5] An., 4, 3, 8. [6] An., 3, 3, 2.

[7] L. D., iii. 76 b; Düm. Hist. Inscrip., ii. 40.

To give an agreeable odour to the body the Egyptians used many kinds of perfume, above all one well known to the Greeks, the *Kyphi*, consisting of myrrh, broom, frankincense, buckshorn, and several other ingredients, some of which were obtained from foreign plants. These substances were pounded and then mixed together, and a certain quantity was put on the fire, and then "the smell in the house and of the clothes was pleasant." Honey also was added and pills concocted, which when chewed "by women made the breath of their mouths sweet."[1] The latter receipt brings us to the cosmetics, which occupy so large a space in the medical literature of Egypt. It is curious that, amongst this wig-wearing people, the doctor was especially worried about hair; men as well as women[2] required of him that when their hair came out he should make it grow again, as well as restore the black colour of youth to their white locks. We know not whether these Egyptian physicians understood this art better than their colleagues of modern times; at any rate they gave numberless prescriptions. For instance, as a remedy against the hair turning white the head was to be "anointed with the blood of a black calf that had been boiled with oil." As a preservative against the same misfortune the "blood of the horn of a black bull," also boiled with oil, was to be used as an ointment. According to other physicians "the blood of a black bull that had been boiled with oil" was a *real* active expedient against white hair. In these prescriptions the black colour of the bull's hair was evidently supposed to pass into the hair of the human being. We read also of the "fat of a black snake" being prescribed for the same object.[3] When the hair fell out, it could be renewed by six kinds of fat worked up together into a pomade—the fat of the lion, of the hippopotamus, of the crocodile, of the cat, of the snake, and of the ibex. It was also considered as *really* strengthening to the hair to anoint it with the "tooth of a donkey crushed in honey." On the other hand queen Shesh, the mother of the ancient King Tet'e, found it advisable to take the hoof of a donkey instead of the tooth, and to boil it in oil together with dog's foot and date kernels, thus making a pomade. Those with whom this did not take effect might use a mixture of the excreta of gazelles, sawdust, the fat of the hippopotamus, and oil;[4] or they might have recourse to the plant *Degem*, especially if they belonged to the community which believed in this plant as a universal remedy.[5]

The physician however had not only to comply with the wishes of the lady who desired to possess beautiful hair herself, but unfortunately he had also to minister to the satisfaction of her jealousy against her rival with the beautiful locks. "To cause the hair of the hated one to fall out," take the worm *'an'art* or the flower *sepet*, boil the worm or the flower in oil, and put it on the head of the rival. A tortoise-shell boiled, pounded, and

[1] Eb. 98, 12; cp. also Ä. Z., 1874, 106 ff.
[2] In the prescriptions, Eb., 65 ff, both are often expressly mentioned.
[3] The prescriptions are quoted, Eb., 65, 8, 16, 19; 66, 1.
[4] Quoted, Eb., 66, 9, 20, 15, 21.
[5] Eb., 47, 19.

mixed in the fat of a hippopotamus was an antidote against this cruel artifice, but it was necessary to anoint oneself with the latter "very very often" that it might be efficient.[1]

With this little glimpse of the life of the harem we will take our leave of the subject of Egyptian dress, which has kept us longer than may seem right to many a reader.

[1] Eb., 67, 3 ff. Perhaps it would be more exact to say "of the hated one."

CARICATURE OF A BADLY SHAVEN, BALD-HEADED MAN.
(From the Turin obscene papyrus.)

WINE PARTY UNDER THE NEW EMPIRE.

The host and hostess are the scribe of the King Ḥaremḥeb, and his wife Ese; the guests are the chiefs of the mercenaries of his majesty (after Wilk., i. Pl. xi. = Perrot, 796).

CHAPTER XI

RECREATION

As a nation advances towards the higher stages of civilisation, there are many pursuits which, though no longer necessary as in past times for the maintenance of life, do not nevertheless fall into oblivion. Though exercised more rarely, they appear to give purer pleasure than before, and with the absence of constraint the hard work of former ages becomes a delight and a sport. When we first obtain a glimpse of the Egyptians, centuries had probably elapsed since they had been obliged to spear fish or to kill birds with a throw-stick in order to obtain food. Yet in later times these two arts were pursued with far greater pleasure than net-fishing or bird-snaring. Similar instances are to be found in the history of all people and all ages.

It stands to reason however that these old crafts could only be exercised later by those who cared little what they gained by them. In the Egypt of historical times nets and snares were used when fish and geese were really needed, and the spear and the throw-stick were employed only by wealthy men or men of rank for amusement rather than for use. This kind of recreation seems to have been confined to the aristocracy, and it was even thought to be the particular privilege of these great men,—the master alone might be a sportsman, the servant's duty was to occupy himself in more useful ways. This view of the matter, which is familiar to us from the feudal customs of the Middle Ages, seems to have been general in Egypt, for as a rule the great men, when spearing fish or killing birds with the throw-stick, are always represented in their most honourable costume, in the royal skirt,[1] and even with the royal beard.[2] This sport in the marshes was not in their opinion an indifferent matter, it was a precious privilege, a princely right.

[1] O. E.: L. D., ii. 60; Berlin, 1118, 1119. M. E.: L. D., ii. 130. N. E.: L. D., iii. 9 e; Wilk., ii. 107.
[2] L. D., ii. 130.

At the beginning of this book I showed that, at the commencement of the historical period in Egypt, the cultivation of the land was already far advanced. Much of the country formerly covered by marshes and tropical forests was already arable land. At the same time old river beds remained; stretches of marsh and half-stagnant water, overgrown as of old with papyrus reeds, offered shelter to the hippopotamus, the crocodile, and to numberless water birds. This was the happy hunting-ground of the great lords of ancient Egypt, the oft-mentioned "backwaters," the "bird tanks of pleasure." They played the same part in Egyptian life as the forest in German folk lore; the greatest delight perhaps that the Egyptian

After L. D., ii. 130.

knew was to row in a light boat between the beautiful waving tufts of the papyrus reeds, to pick the lotus flowers, to start the wild birds and then knock them over with the throw-stick, to spear the great fish of the Nile and even the hippopotamus, with the harpoon. Pictures of all periods exist representing these expeditions, and we have but to glance at them in order to realise how much the Egyptians loved these wild districts, and how much poetry they found in them.

We see how the great papyrus shrubs lift up their beautiful heads high above the height of man, while "their roots are bathed" as a botanist says, "in the lukewarm water, and their feathery tufts wave on their slender stalks." With the help of other reeds and water plants they form an impenetrable thicket—a floating forest. Above, there swarm, as now in the Delta, a cloud of many thousand marsh-birds. We see in our picture that it is the close of the breeding season; a few birds are still sitting on their nests, which are built on the papyrus reeds and swayed by the wind, while most of the others are flying about seeking food for their young. One bird is chasing the great butterflies which are fluttering round the tops of the papyrus reeds; another with a long pointed beak darts down upon a flower in which he has discovered a cockchafer. In the meantime danger threatens the young ones; small animals of prey, such as the weasel and the ichneumon, have penetrated into the thicket, and are dexterously climbing up the stems of the reeds. The startled parents hasten back, and seek to scare away the thieves with their cries and the flapping of their wings.

Meanwhile in a light boat formed of papyrus reeds bound together the Egyptian sportsman makes his way over the expanse of water in this marsh;[1] he is often accompanied by his wife and children, who gather the lotus flowers and hold the birds he has killed. Noiselessly the bark glides along by the thicket, so close to it that the children can put their hands into it in their play. The sportsman stands upright in the boat and swings his throw-stick in his right hand; with a powerful throw it whizzes through the air, and one of the birds falls into the water, hit on its neck. This throw-stick is a simple but powerful weapon—a small thin piece of hard wood, bent in a peculiar way; when thrown it hits its mark with great strength, then returns in a graceful curve and falls at the feet of the marksman. The natives of Australia still use the same weapon in a somewhat different form under the name of a boomerang.[2] It is most remarkable that in many of the pictures of the New Empire a tame cat accompanies the sportsman and brings him the fallen birds out of the thicket into the boat.[3]

The bag after such a hunting expedition was necessarily very light; we have already said this was purely sport. The great numbers of water-birds required for Egyptian housekeeping were caught in a less delightful but much more effective manner; a large bird-net was used, which we often see represented in the tombs. The net was spread on a small expanse of water surrounded by a low growth of reeds. Judging from the representations, it was often 10 to 12 feet long and about five feet wide. It was made of netted string and had eight corners.[4] When

[1] Bird-hunting with the throw-stick—O. E.: L. D., ii. 12, 60, 106 (large boat with many oars); Berlin, 1118 (without any companions). M. E.: L. D., ii. 130 (coloured). N. E.: W., ii. 104 (we see the throw-sticks fly through the air), 107, 108; L. D., iii. 9 e, 113 c.

[2] Many exist in the Museums, e.g. Berlin, 4734 (L. D., ii. 130, yellow).

[3] Cats at the bird hunt: W., ii. 107, 108. The bird sitting in the bow of the boat, W., ii. 104, 107, 108, may serve as a decoy bird. This does not appear under the Old Empire.

[4] The construction of the net is not easy to understand. Wilk., ii. 110, shows the meshes. The net is open, L. D., ii. 130, close by we see it amongst the hieroglyphics in its closed form. Bird-catching with a net—O. E.: Mar. mon. div., 17. Perrot, 35 (important); L. D., ii. 9, 12 a; 42, 43, 46. Düm. Res., 8; L. D., ii. 105, and the same in the tomb of T'y. M. E.: L. D., ii. 130 (coloured) the fowler sits hidden behind a mat). N. E.: Wilk., i. 290; ii. 102.

spread, the sides were drawn well back and hidden under water plants; in order to draw it up, a rope which ran along the net and was fastened behind to a clod of earth, had to be pulled hard.

How they enticed the birds into the net, whether by bait or by a decoy bird, I can scarcely tell, for the favourite time for representa-

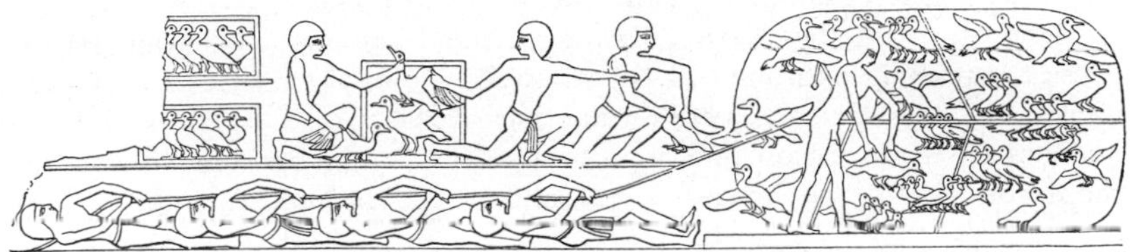

BIRD-CATCHING UNDER THE OLD EMPIRE (after L. D., ii. 46).

tion on our monuments is always the moment when the net is being drawn together. Three or four fellows who have thrown off every useless bit of clothing, hold the long rope, and wait in breathless attention for the command to draw the net together. In the meantime the master has

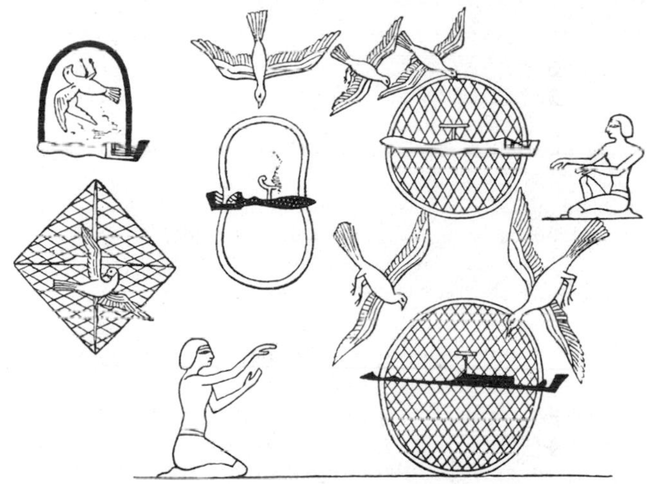

BIRD-TRAPS, SOME OPEN, SOME CLOSED. From a tomb of the Middle Empire at Beni Hasan (after Wilk., ii. 103).

slipped through the bushes close to the net, and has seen and heard that the birds are caught in the snare. He dares not call out to his men for fear of scaring the birds, so he gives them the signal by waving a strip of linen over his head. The workmen then pull the rope with might and main, they pull till they literally lie on the ground. Their efforts are rewarded, for the net is full of birds, thirty or forty great water-birds being caught in it; most as we see are geese, but an unfortunate pelican has also wandered in. The latter has little chance of mercy from the bird-catcher, who now gets into the net and seizes the birds one by one by their wings, and hands them to his men; of these the first appears to be breaking the wings, while the others place them in large four-cornered cages, first sorting them, for the Egyptians loved order; "those in the box?" asks one of another meanwhile.[1]

The cages are then carried home on hand-barrows, where the fattest geese are proudly exhibited to the master; one of the species *ser*, though unusually fat, is far surpassed by another of the species *terp*. From the marshes on this occasion they also bring lotus flowers for wreaths and for the decoration of the house—a present is also brought in from the net

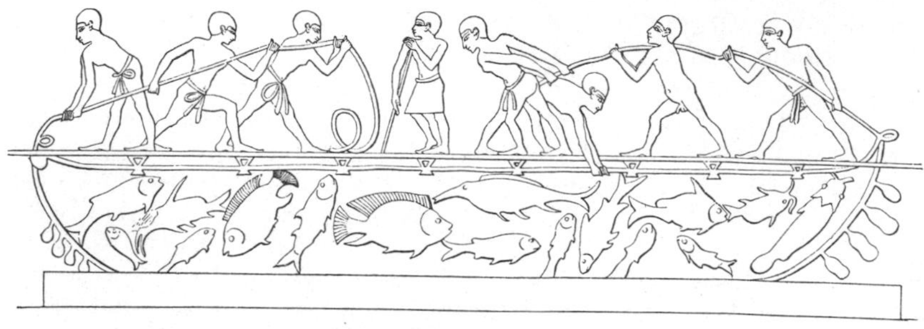

CATCH OF FISH UNDER THE OLD EMPIRE (after L. D., ii. 9).

for the young master; a gay hoopoe, which he almost squeezes to death with the cruel love of a child.[2]

As we have already remarked, this manner of bird-catching was not mere sport in the early ages of the 5th and 6th dynasties; at that time there was a special official on many estates, the "chief bird-catcher,"[3] and the people also thus obtained their favourite national dish, viz. roast goose. They evidently pursued this sport regularly, and indeed a picture of the time of the New Empire shows us how they salted down the remaining birds in large jars.[4]

When however, instead of prosaic geese, they wanted to catch the pretty birds of passage, the "birds of Arabia who flutter over Egypt smelling of myrrh,"[5] they used traps baited with worms.[6] It was a favourite pastime even for ladies[7] to sit in the fields all day long, waiting for the moment when at last they should hear the "wailing cry of the beautiful bird smelling of myrrh."[8]

Fishing was also very popular in ancient Egypt; the peaceful well-stocked waters of the Nile invited the inhabitants of the country to this

1 Düm. Res., 8.
2 Düm. Res., 8, 9, L.D., ii. 105.
3 L. D., ii. 105, also Br. Gr. W., 68 a.
4 Wilk., i. 290.
5 Harr., 500, 12, 3.
6 Ib. 12, 4, 7.
7 Cp. the song, Harr., 500, 12, 2 ff.
8 Ib. 12, 6.

easy sport. The most primitive manner of fishing, viz. with the spear,[1] was only pursued later as a sport by the wealthy. For this purpose the Egyptians used a thin spear nearly three yards long, in front of which two long barbed points were fastened. The most skilful speared two fish at once, one with each point. Angling was also considered a delightful recreation for gentlemen; we see them seated on chairs and rugs fishing in the artificial lakes in their gardens.[2] The common fishermen also did not despise line fishing.[3] As a rule however the latter fished in a more effective manner, with the bow-net[4] or with the drag-net.[5] We see how the latter is set upright in the water, quite in the modern style, with corks fastened on the upper edge and weights on the lower. Seven or eight fishermen then drag it through the water to the land. The catch is a good one, about thirty great fish are caught at one haul, and lie struggling on the bank. Many are so heavy that a man can only carry one at a time; a string is put through the gills of the others, and they are carried in a row on a stick to the fish dealers.

These dealers are seated on low stones before a sort of table, cleaning out the inside of the fish and cutting them open so as to dry them better. The fish were then hung upon strings in the sun to dry thoroughly; when the fishermen were far from home, they began this work on board their boats.[6] These dried fish were a great feature in Egyptian housekeeping; no larder was without them,[7] and they formed the chief food of the lower orders.[8] They were the cheapest food of the land; much cheaper than corn, of which the country was also very productive. The heartfelt wish of the poorer folk was that the price of corn might be as low as that of fish.[9] Fish was also a favourite dish with the upper classes; and the epicure knew each variety, and in which water the most dainty were to be caught.[10] It was therefore a most foolish invention of later Egyptian theology to declare that fish were unclean to the orthodox and so much to be avoided, that a true believer might have no fellowship with those who ate fish.[11]

Besides the birds and fish, there dwelt in the marshes two giants of the animal world, the hunting of which was attended with considerable danger, viz. the hippopotamus and the crocodile. Both were regarded with timid respect, which was carried in some districts to religious reverence. The hippopotamus especially, with his senseless furious roar, and his "extremely pugnacious, restless nature"[12] was accounted the embodiment

[1] O. E.: Berlin, 1119. M. E.: L. D., ii. 130, Ros. M. C., 25. N. E.: Wilk., ii. 107 (the end of the spear is feathered like an arrow).

[2] Wilk., ii. 115 (N. E.).

[3] O. E.: Perrot, p. 14=Bädeker, p. 413. M. E.: L. D., ii. 127=Wilk., ii. 116, with and without a rod. Fish hooks perhaps, L.D., ii. 96.

[4] Bow-nets, Bädeker only, p. 411 (O. E.).

[5] Large net—O. E.: L. D., ii. 9, 42 a; 43 a, 46, 106; Ros. M. C., 24. Cp. also Br. Gr. W., 69-71. M. E.: L. D., ii. 130. N. E.: Wilk., ii. 102. Transport of fish—L. D., ii. 9, 12. Killing the fish—L. D., ii. 9, 12, 46; Düm. Res., 8; Ros. M. C., 25.

[6] Wilk., ii. 102.

[7] Wilk., i. 340.

[8] Cp. p. 125.

[9] Br. Dic. Suppl., 1015.

[10] An., 4, 15, 5 ff.

[11] Mar. mon. div., 6, 151, 152.

[12] Barth, Travels in Africa, v. 229.

of all that was rough and wild. The crocodile, on the other hand, was regarded as the terrible ruler of the water, and it was believed that the water-god Sobk assumed his shape. Both have now deserted Egypt, but formerly they were as numerous in that country as in tropical Africa. The pictures of the time of the Old Empire represent them frequently—the crocodile lying in wait for the cows when they should come into the water, the hippopotamus in blind rage attacking the rudder of a boat, or even seizing a crocodile with his powerful teeth. The crocodile was hunted, in spite of its sanctity as being sacred to the water god; and that there are no representations of this sport is owing probably to the fact that they had scruples of conscience about it. There were no religious scruples however about the hippopotamus, and men of rank of all times liked to have representations of hippopotamus-hunting in their tombs,[1] the more so because the spice of danger made them proud of their success. They seem to have pursued the hippopotamus only

'ACHECH, THE GRIFFIN (after Wilk., iii. 312). THE SAG (after Wilk., iii. 312).

on the water from their boats; a harpoon served as weapon, the shaft of which freed itself from the point as soon as the animal was hit. If the wounded animal dashed down into deep water, the hunter allowed him to do so, by letting out the line attached to the harpoon, though there was danger of the boat being carried under. The hippopotamus was soon obliged to rise to the surface to breathe, and then the sportsman could wound him again. Gradually, as in our whale fisheries, the powerful animal was exhausted by frequent attacks, and finally a rope was thrown over his great head and the creature was dragged to land.

The Libyan deserts and the Arabian mountains still offer great opportunities for sport, and in old times this was yet more the case, for many animals which formerly inhabited these regions are only met with now in the Sudan. Flocks of ibex climbed about the mountains, herds

[1] Hippopotamus-hunting—O. E.: L. D., ii. 77; Perrot, p. 14 (=Bädeker, p. 413). M. E.: Wilk., ii. 128. N. E.: Wilk., ii. 129, after W., ii. 127; this sport is often represented in the Theban tombs, the pictures are unfortunately generally injured. Fully described, W., ii. 127, the harpoon of the O. E. does not seem to have been so complicated as the one there described of the N. E. It is doubtful, according to Wilkinson's figure, whether it was a lasso which was thrown over the animal's head. It might be a net like that still used in Africa to throw over the heads of wild boar.

of gazelles sported about the sand dunes; there were also antelopes and animals of the cow kind. The hyaena howled and the jackal and fox prowled about the mountains on the edge of the desert; there were also numerous hares and hedgehogs, ichneumons, civet cats, and other small

THEBAN TOMB-PICTURE OF THE TIME OF THE NEW EMPIRE (after Wilk., ii. 92).

animals. There was big game too for the lovers of an exciting hunt; they could follow the "furious" leopard or the "savage-looking" lion.[1] Possibly the imaginative huntsman hoped also to obtain as a prize one of

[1] Beautiful representations of wild animals—O. E.: L. D., ii. 6, 11, 46, 96; Düm. Res., 8, 9. M. E.: L. D., ii. 131, 132. N. E.: Wilk., ii. 92.

those marvellous animals spoken of by everybody, but which no living man had ever seen,[1] the *'achech*, the swiftest of all animals, which was half-bird, half-lion; or the sphinx, that royal beast with the head of a man or of a ram, and the body of a lion; or the winged gazelle, or even the *sag*, the creature uniting the body of a lioness with the head of a hawk, and whose tail ended in a lotus flower. All these animals and many others of similar character were supposed to exist in the great desert, and Chnemḥôtep, the oft-mentioned governor of Middle Egypt under the 12th dynasty, caused a panther with a winged face growing out of his back to be represented amongst the animals in his great hunting scene. He was probably of the opinion that such a creature would cause the neighbourhood of Beni Hasan to be unsafe.

The Egyptians of all ages loved desert hunting. We know that the kings of the Old Empire had their own "master of the hunt," who was also district chief of the desert;[2] and as regards the Pharaohs of the New Empire, we often read of their hunting in person. Thothmes IV., accompanied only by two lions, used to hunt in the neighbourhood of Memphis,[3] and we read of his son Amenḥôtep III., that during the first ten years of his reign he killed with his own hand "110 savage lions."[4] Packs of dogs were usually employed in desert hunting; they were allowed to worry and to kill the game.[5] The hunting dog was the great greyhound with pointed upright ears and curly tail; this dog (under the name of *Slughi*) is still in use for the same purpose on the steppes of the Sudan. It is a favourite subject in Egyptian pictures to show how cleverly they would bury their pointed teeth in the neck or in the back paws of the antelopes. These graceful dogs also ventured to attack the larger beasts of prey. A picture of the time of the Old Empire represents a huntsman who, having led an ox to a hilly point in the desert, lies in wait himself in the background with two greyhounds. The ox, finding himself abandoned, bellows in terror; this entices a great lion to the spot, and the huntsman watches in breathless suspense, ready in a moment to slip the leash from the dogs and let them fall on the lion,[6] while the king of animals springs on the head of the terrified ox.

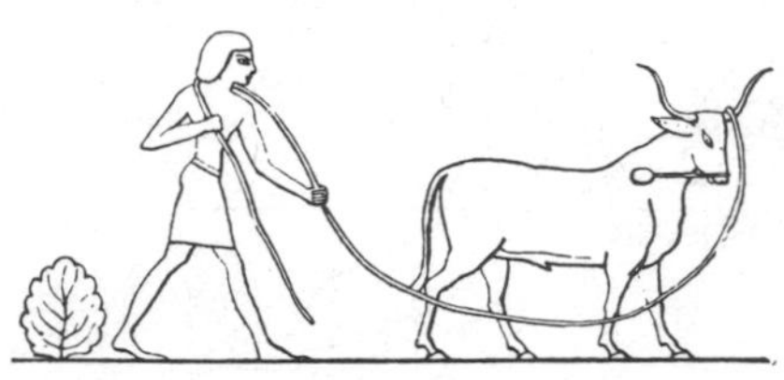

PICTURE OF THE TIME OF THE MIDDLE EMPIRE (after Wilk., ii. 87).

The Egyptians were also fond of taking antelopes alive, not in order to stock their parks with them, but to fatten them with their cattle. They

[1] Fabulous animals: L. D., ii. 131; Wilk., ii. 93, iii. 309-312; Ros. M. C., 23; Maspero, Guide, p. 169, rightly recognises that sphinxes belong here.

[2] L. D., ii. 3. He carries the throw-stick—did they also use it in desert hunting?

[3] L. D., iii. 68.

[4] Frequent inscriptions on the scarabs of his reign.

[5] O. E.: Düm. Res., 8; L. D., ii. 6, 46. N. E.: Wilk., ii. 92 = Ros. M. C., 15. Perrot, 291, is interesting; the hunting ground seems to be surrounded with a net.

[6] Düm. Res., 8.

seem to have caught the ibex of the hills by hand;[1] in the desert however they employed the lasso, a long rope with a ball at the end, which when thrown at an object wound itself round it.[2] A skilled sportsman would throw the lasso so that the rope wound round the legs and body of the animal, while the end twisted itself in the horns. A powerful jerk from the huntsman then sufficed to throw the animal helplessly on the ground.

We might almost surmise that the Egyptians felt that scorn for shooting weapons common to so many nations; at any rate representations of sport with bow and arrow are much rarer than those of hunting.[3] Even when shooting they employed dogs to start the game, and possibly beaters armed with sticks to drive the animals towards the sportsmen. With the powerful bow and the arrows a yard long it was quite possible to kill even lions.

A passionate sportsman is also as a rule a great lover of animals, and it delights him at home to be able to have under his immediate observation the game which flies past him when out hunting. The wealthy Egyptians therefore at all times kept menageries, in which they brought up the animals taken by the lasso or by the dogs in the desert, as well as those brought into Egypt by way of commerce or as tribute. From the neighbouring deserts they obtained the lion and the leopard (which were brought to their masters in great cages), the hyaena, gazelle, ibex, hare, and porcupine, were also found there;[4] from the incense countries and from the upper Nile came the pard, the baboon, and the giraffe;[5] and from Syria the bear and the elephant.[6] They felt still greater delight when these animals were tamed, when the Ethiopian animal the *ka'eri* was taught to dance,[7] and to understand words;[8] or when the lion was trained to conquer his savage nature and to follow his master like a dog.[9] Ramses II. possessed a tame lion which accompanied him to battle,[10] and which lay down in the camp at night before the tent of the royal master.[11] Pet apes are found at all periods; these were imported from foreign parts.[12] Nebemchut, an Egyptian courtier in the reign of King Cha'frê', possessed two uncouth long-maned baboons, and, accompanied by them, he with his wife inspected the work of his artisans, and certainly the great lord mightily enjoyed the inspection of his people which the apes undertook for their part.[13] Most people however contented themselves with one small monkey, which we sometimes see sitting under a chair busy pulling an onion to pieces, or turning out the contents of a basket; and though as a rule the monkey was

[1] L. D., ii. 46.

[2] O. E.: Düm. Res., 8; L. D., ii. 96. M. E.: Wilk., ii. 87. The rope in which the huntsman seems entangled is certainly the lasso. Düm., ib.

[3] L. D., ii. 131-132, Wilk., ii. 88, 89. Both, M. E.

[4] L. D., ii. 11, 50 b, 107; Düm. Res., 9, etc.

[5] Düm. Flotte, 2. Wilk. i. Pl. ii. a. b.

[6] Wilk., i., Pl. ii. b.

[7] An., 5, 8, 7=An., 3, 4, 1.

[8] Bol., 3, 9.

[9] Bol., 3, 9.

[10] L. D., iii. 184 a.

[11] L. D., iii. 155.

[12] Mentioned as early as in the pyramid of Unas, 423. Under the New Empire baboons and monkeys were brought from Arabia (Düm. Fl., 2).

[13] Baboons under the Old Empire: L. D., ii. 13, 107.

the lady's pet, yet several gentlemen have their pet monkeys represented with themselves in their tombs.[1]

We can well understand that the Egyptians with their love for animals should at all times have shown special affection towards man's most faithful companion, the dog. Probably no wealthy household was complete without the splendid great greyhounds,[2] still employed in the Sudan under the name of Slughi. They were most precious to the huntsman, for they were swifter than the gazelle and had no fear even of a lion. The Egyptian who was no sportsman however also loved to have these beautiful creatures about him; they accompanied him when he went out in his sedan chair, and lay under his chair when he was in the house. If we may believe the representations of a Memphite tomb, Ptaḥḥôtep, a high official under the 5th dynasty, insisted upon keeping his three greyhounds with him, even while he was listening to the harps and flutes of his musicians, in spite of the howls with which these dogs of the Old Empire seem to have accompanied the music. These greyhounds, the T'esem, do not appear to have been natives of Egypt; under the New Empire at any rate they seem to have been brought from the incense countries of the Red Sea. Nevertheless this breed of dog was always popular in Egypt, and a tale of the time of the 20th dynasty relates how a prince preferred to die rather than part from his faithful greyhound.

Under the Old Empire, besides the T'esem, we meet with a small earless dog, which was also used for coursing; it may be that in former times they also tamed the prairie dogs.[3] Under the 11th dynasty there were certainly three different breeds of dog known in Egypt, and later there appear to have been even more. It is interesting that the names given by Egyptian huntsmen to their dogs were often foreign ones. Of the four dogs represented on the stela of the ancient King 'Entef, the first two are called Beḥka'e and Peḥtes, which, as the accompanying inscription informs us, mean "gazelle" and "black"; it is not quite clear what the fourth name Teqeru signifies, the third is 'Abaqero, in which Maspero has recognised with great probability the word Abaikour, the term by which the Berberic nomads of the Sahara still call their greyhounds.[4]

In Egypt, the land of cattle-breeding, the bull held the same place of old as the lion does now in our poetry; in Egypt "the strong bull" was the incorporation of strength and resistless power, and the poets describe in detail how, with his horns lowered, he rushes on the enemy and

[1] Monkeys: L. D., ii. 36 c. Düm. Res., 10. L. D., iii. 9 f, 12 a; Berlin, 7278, and frequently. With a man, Berlin, 7276.

[2] Greyhounds (Cp. R. Hartmann, Ä. Z., 1864, p. 20) under the New Empire come from Punt (Düm. Fl., 2). Representations under the Old Empire: L. D., ii. 17 c, 47, 50 a, 52, 107; Düm. Res., 10. Cp. also the hunting pictures of the O. E.

[3] Cp. Düm. Res., 8, 9, and the remarks of R. Hartmann on the subject—the latter thinks the dog in the lion-hunt is a calf. On the other hand, that the animals considered by Hartmann to be prairie dogs were used for hunting, appears improbable, from the absence of the collar, which is always worn by the true hunting dog.

[4] R. J. H., 161 = Mar. mon. div., 49. Other names of dogs: L. D. ii. 17 c, 47, 52. Ros. M. C., 16, 5; Berlin, 1192.

tramples him underfoot. It was therefore quite natural that the Egyptians should take great pleasure in bull-fights, and should keep bulls for this purpose.[1] In the arena the fighting bulls had their special names; one represented below is called "the favourite," the name of the other may signify the "broad striker."[2] Shepherds with short sticks assisted as umpires, and "loosed" the bull that was worsted from the horn of his opponent, which had pierced through his dewlap. When the fight between the two short-horned bulls was at an end, a powerful animal of the long-horned race, adorned for the festival with a gay cloth, was brought in to fight the victor.

The pleasure and excitement felt at a bull-fight were intensified at the gymnastic games, of which the representations belong to all epochs. One

PICTURE OF THE TIME OF THE MIDDLE EMPIRE. From Beni Hasan (after Wilk., ii. 77).

favourite game was sailor-stabbing, in which, for the amusement of their masters, boatmen stood up in their bulrush skiffs, and thrust at each other with their long poles.[3] The men also had wrestling matches for the same purpose. These were fought in such earnest that many of the combatants had to be carried off the field.[4] There were prize fighters too, who fought with short sticks, and wore a small piece of wood tied to the left arm to protect themselves from the blows of their opponent.[5]

Women also appeared before their masters to perform gymnastic feats,[6] or to dance, more frequently in the latter capacity, for no feast was considered complete without dancing. To the Egyptian mind it was the natural expression of joy—to rejoice and to dance were synonymous expressions in their poetry. When the harvest was gathered in, and the peasant sacrificed the first fruits to Min the god of Koptos, he danced to testify his joyful thankfulness to the god, and when the festivals of the great goddesses of pleasure Ḥatḥôr and Bastet were solemnised, dancing was considered as necessary as the shouting for joy or the carrying of wreaths.

We know little of these peculiar national dances. In one of them the dancers held two short sticks in their hands, like our *bones;* and in fact in one of the harvest representations of the Old Empire we see the workmen

[1] M. E.: Wilk., ii. 75, 77. N. E.: Wilk., ii. 75, 76.

[2] Wilk., ii. 75, 76.

[3] O. E.: Perrot, 41; Wilk., ii. 74; Ros. M. C., 104, 105; M. E.: L. D., ii. 130.

[4] Ros. M. C., 111-115.

[5] Wilk., ii. 72.

[6] Wilk., ii. 54, 68.

taking part in this dance; they have laid aside their clothes, and run with quick movements clapping their sticks together.[1]

Dancers were almost always present at the "feast of Eternity,"—that is the feast held in honour of the deceased; in fact the procession accompanying the statue of the deceased was generally headed by dancers.[2]

WRESTLING SCENES OF THE TIME OF THE MIDDLE EMPIRE. From Beni Hasan (after Wilk., ii. 71, and ib. i. 394).

Under the Old Empire their movements appear to have been very measured. They first step slowly forwards one after another, the foot scarcely raised above the ground; they raise their arms over the head, turning the inner part of the hand upwards; next they stretch the right arm obliquely upwards and put the left behind the body. As a rule four persons only took part in this "beautiful dance," though sometimes there might be more than a dozen. The music consisted always of three or four female singers behind the dancers.

Though these dances appear very monotonous on the reliefs, yet

[1] L. D., ii. 56 a; Cp. ib. 52, the writing of *'eba* "to dance."

[2] Dancing men—O. E.: L. D., ii. 14 a, 41, 52, 53 a, 109. Dancing women—O. E.: L. D., ii. 35, 36, 61 a, 101 b.

with close attention we can distinguish different figures. At the funerary festival, for instance, the singers and the dancers stand opposite each other with a table of food between them.[1] On another occasion [2] behind the singers there stands a little pillar adorned with the head of a cat, representing Bastet the goddess of pleasure, close by is a little nude dwarf; doubtless both were to play their part in the further development of the dance.

When dancing, men wore as a rule the ordinary short skirt, they sometimes also put on a girdle tied in a bow behind.[3] Women dancers also rarely wore long dresses;[4] like the men, they generally wore nothing but the short skirt round the hips. In addition they put on all manner of coquettish ornaments—bracelets, necklets, anklets; they wound ribbons round the upper part of the body, and put on a wreath of flowers. According to the inscriptions these dancers and singers belonged

FEMALE DANCERS UNDER THE OLD EMPIRE (after L. D., ii. 101 b).

to the harem of the great man concerned.[5] In addition to these simple dances, in which a large number of people could join, there were others,[6] in which two dancers formed a difficult group together. These dances are also distinguished by their name [hieroglyphs] *t'eref* from the ordinary dances [hieroglyphs] *'eb.* Three of these figures are represented in a tomb of the end of the 4th dynasty. The two dancers, wearing a fringed girdle as their only clothing, stand opposite each other with outstretched arms grasping each other by the hand. Both perform exactly the same movements. In one figure they raise one arm and one foot towards their partner, in another they draw up their foot like a crane, in the third they turn away from each other and appear to be about to run away to either side. Each of these groups has its own name (*e.g.* the second appears to be called *the pillar*); to the Egyptian, each group represented a certain scene.

[1] L. D., ii. 35. [2] L. D., ii. 36. [3] L. D., ii. 14 a. [4] Ib. 35.
[5] Ib. 35, 52, 101 b; Br. Gr. W., 81.
[6] Figure dancing—O. E.: L. D., ii. 52. M. E.: ib. 126. Wilk., i. 505.

The figures which were danced at the funerary feast of the nomarch Chnemḥôtep in the time of the 12th dynasty, are comparatively easy to

After L. D., ii. 126. Cp. with the group on the left, the relief represented above, p. 59.

understand; they are seen in the accompanying illustration from Beni Hasan. The dress of the dancers consists apparently of short bathing

PICTURE OF THE TIME OF THE MIDDLE EMPIRE. From Beni Hasan (after Wilk., ii. 65).

drawers only; for the further amusement of the spectators they have tied up their hair in the shape of the royal crown of Upper Egypt. One figure, in fact, parodies a royal group, one of the frequent victory reliefs, in which the monarch seizes the kneeling barbarian by the hair, and swings his sickle-shaped sword above his head. This group is called "Under the feet," the superscription over the relief being always, "all nations lie under thy feet." Another group in the same picture is called *the wind*: one woman bends backwards, till her hands rest on the ground, a second performs the same movement above her, a third stretches out her arms over them. Possibly the former represent the reeds and grasses bent by the wind.

In the tombs of Beni Hasan we have also representations of women playing with balls, which was considered, as we see by the costume of the

FEMALE DANCERS UNDER THE NEW EMPIRE, THE TALL ONES WITH KETTLEDRUMS, THE SHORT ONES WITH CASTANETS (Relief at Gizeh, after Perrot-Chipiez).

performers, as a variety of dancing.[1] These dancers excelled in all kinds of skilful tricks. We see them playing with several balls at once, or catching two balls with their arms crossed. They get into all sorts of curious positions at their play; they stand on one leg, jump high into the air, or ride on the back of one of their companions.

Whilst the character of the dances of the older period was quiet and measured, the dances of the New Empire were more like those of the East of the present time.[2] The girls are dressed in long transparent clothes, and with tambourine or castanets in their hands they turn round and round in quick time, bending their bodies in a coquettish manner.

[1] Wilk., ii. 65, 66. Balls ib. 67, similar ones in Berlin and Paris.

[2] Wilk., i. 439, 443, pl. xi.; Perrot, 701; Ros. M. C., 96, 98, 99.

The old Egyptians took no more offence at these questionable movements of the dancers than do the modern Egyptians of to-day; it was a favourite amusement to look on at this dancing, and at social parties dancers were invited for the entertainment of the guests. The accompanying plate[1] shows us a feast of this kind. The girls, wearing nothing but girdles, stand close to the wreathed wine jars; they go through their twists and turns, clapping their hands to keep in time. Meanwhile one woman plays the flute, and three others sing a song, evidently in praise of the pleasures of the cool happy time of inundation, during which season, as is the custom at the present day, the feast was given:

> The earth-god causes his beauty to grow in the heart of every creature,
> This is the work of Ptaḥ's hands, this is balm to his breast,
> When the tanks are full of fresh water,
> And the earth overflows with his love.

Every large household had its harem and the inmates were careful

BLIND SINGERS. Picture from Tell el Amarna (after Wilk., i. 442).

that music and song should never fail at any feast, secular or sacred. In the royal household moreover, where the musicians were very numerous, they were under a superintendent, who may be regarded as a professional. A number of names of these ancient choir-masters have come down to us. Under the Old Empire we meet with a certain Ra'ḥenem, the "superintendent of the singing,"[2] who was also the superintendent of the harem. There were also three "superintendents of the royal singing" who were at the same time "superintendents of all the beautiful pleasures of the king"—their names were Snefrunofr, 'Et'e, and Rê'mery-Ptaḥ; the two last were singers themselves and boast that they "daily rejoice the heart of the king with beautiful songs, and fulfil every wish of the king by their beautiful singing." At court they held a high position, they were

[1] Feast with music and female dancers. Amongst the guests in the upper row two married couples sit in front on arm chairs, behind them on stools sit alternately secular and priestly gentlemen. (After a Theban tomb picture of the 18th dynasty in the Brit. Mus.)

[2] Mar. Mast., 139 f. The reading of the name is uncertain.

FEAST, WITH MUSICIANS AND DANCING GIRLS.

Wall picture from a Theban tomb in the British Museum. (After a photograph by Wilke.)

"royal relatives," and priests of the monarch and of his ancestors.[1] Under the New Empire we find Ḥ'at-'euy and Ta[2] singers to Pharaoh, and Neferronpet the "superintendent of the singers to Pharaoh,"[3] who was at the same time "superintendent of the singers of all the gods," and therefore at the head of the musical profession in Egypt.

HARP UNDER THE OLD EMPIRE (after L. D., ii. 61 a).

It is certainly not accidental that in the pictures of the Old Empire[4] the women appear always to sing without, and the men with, instrumental accompaniment; the women's voices were considered pleasant to listen to alone, but the men's, on the other hand, were preferred with harps and flutes. Nevertheless the men alone seem to have been regarded as artists, the women probably sang only as an accompaniment to the dances. It was the usual custom for

PRIESTS PLAYING HARPS. From the tomb of Ramses III. (Ros. M. C., 97).

singers to mark the time by clapping their hands; men waved their arms quickly when singing, while etiquette forbade the women to do more than move their hands. We see that, according to Egyptian ideas, these barbaric customs and correct singing were inseparable, for the word *to sing* is written at all times by the sign of a hand.

Even under the New Empire this custom of beating time was in use,

[1] Mar. Mast., 153; R. J. H., 3-4, 88; L. D., ii. 59.

[2] Mar. Cat. d'Ab., 1115, 425.

[3] Mar. Cat. d'Ab., 1159. His brother is superintendent of the harem, and priest of the crowns.

[4] Female singers at the dance. O. E.: L. D., ii. 36 c, 52, 53 a, 61 a, 101 b. Singers with music—O. E.: L. D., ii. 36 c, 52, 53, 61, 74.

more scope however was allowed in their manner of singing, and male and female voices were employed individually, or together with instruments.[1] The blind, of whom there have always been many in Egypt, were much liked as singers;[2] the best school for female singers was at Memphis.[3]

The harp[4] was always the favourite instrument; harps of two sizes were in use, that of medium size had six or seven strings, while the larger

GIRL PLAYING THE LUTE. THE PLECTRUM WITH WHICH SHE STRIKES HER THREE-STRINGED INSTRUMENT HANGS BY A STRING. Theban tomb-picture of the time of the New Empire (after Perrot-Chipiez).

one had often twenty strings; for the former the performer was seated, for the latter he was obliged to stand. A very small harp, played resting on the shoulder, appears only in the time of the New Empire.[5] The

[1] Male singers: Wilk., i. 442, 462. Female singers: ib. 440, 441. Both together: ib. 441.

[2] Wilk., i. 438, 442.

[3] An., 3, 3, 7.

[4] Harps of the O. E.: L. D., ii. 36 c; 52, 53, 61, 74. Of the M. E.: Wilk., i. 442. Of the N. E.: Wilk., i. 436, 438, 441, 442, 462, 464, pl. xi.

[5] Wilk., i. 465. Here belong also the small instruments in Berlin and London, ib. 473, 474.

construction of the harp does not always seem to have been the same, for instance, the resonance chamber at the lower end of the instrument is found only during a later period.[1]

The lute was also in common use, its name 𓄤 *nefer* is one of the commonest signs in hieroglyphics. Its Egyptian name was derived from the Semitic *n. b. l.*; it was played by striking it with the plectrum, and seems to have been a very primitive instrument, possessing originally only one string.[2] The trigonon, the small three-stringed harp, first appears under the New Empire; in still later times it became very common. This instrument may possibly have been of foreign origin,[3] as was doubtless the lyre. We meet with the latter but once before the time of the 18th dynasty, and then indeed in the hands of a Beduin bringing tribute. It is frequently represented after the Egyptians had continuous intercourse with the Semites, and was evidently the fashionable instrument of the New Empire.[4] It is found of all sizes and shapes, from the little instruments with five strings, which ladies could easily hold, to those with eighteen strings, some of which were six feet high, the performer having to stand by them. The reader can see lyres of different sizes together with lutes and harps in the picture of the house, p. 181.

BEDUIN OF THE TIME OF THE MIDDLE EMPIRE PLAYING THE LYRE (after L. D., ii. 133).

The flute was the only wind instrument in use. There were two forms of flute under the Old Empire; the long flute, [hieroglyphs], which the player held obliquely behind him, and the short flute [hieroglyphs], which was held horizontally when played.[5] Under the New Empire these were

[1] Under the O. E. at any rate, L. D., ii. 53. Under the M. E. an open sounding-box may have been fastened under the end of the harp, cp. Wilk., i. 442. Under the N. E. small instruments constructed with a belly, e.g. Wilk., i. 473, 442; large ones with an ornamented box. The tone was also strengthened by placing the harp on a pillar instead of on the ground; cp. Wilk., i. 438, 462, 464.

[2] Wilk., i. 481, 482, 483, pl. xi.—all of the N. E. That the lute existed previously we only judge from the hieroglyphs.

[3] L. D., iii. 106, Wilk., i. 469, ib. 470, an example in the Louvre with twenty-one strings, others ib. 474.

[4] Wilk., i. 439, 441, 470, 476, ib. 477, 478. Examples are preserved in Berlin and Leyden.

[5] Flutes of the O. E.: L. D., ii. 36 c, 52, 61, 74.

almost suppressed in favour of double flutes, as *e.g.* that played by the musician in the accompanying plate.[1]

Finally we must mention the round and square kettledrums,[2] and the castanets,[3] which were the instruments usually played by the dancers, also the barrel-shaped drum and the trumpets of the soldiers; we shall then have enumerated almost all the instruments on which the ancient Egyptians of the various periods depended for their musical pleasure.[4]

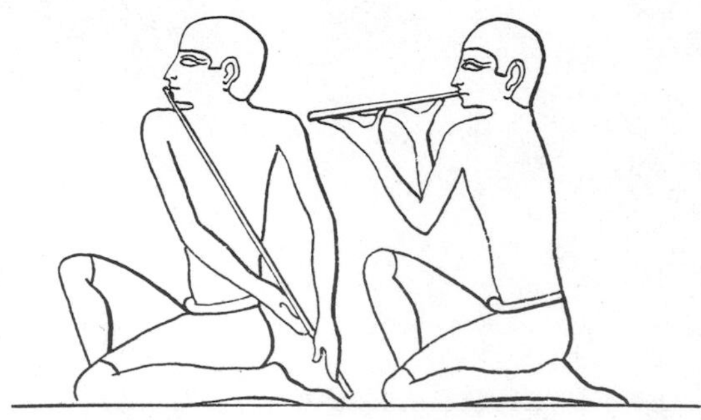

FLUTE-PLAYERS UNDER THE OLD EMPIRE (after L. D., ii. 74).

Under the Old Empire instrumental music seems to have been performed solely by men, and to have served merely as an accompaniment to the voices. The instruments commonly used at a concert of that time consisted of two harps, a large and a small flute; while close to each musician stood a singer, who also beat time by clapping his hands.[5] On rare occasions the harp was employed alone to accompany singing,[6] but at this earlier period flutes were never used alone.[7] Under the New Empire on the other hand women performers were more frequent, and female as well as male voices were combined with all manner of instruments. A large harp, two lutes (or a lute and a lyre) and a double flute were used at this later period as the usual accompaniment to the voices.[8]

During the performance of music and dancing at feasts, the guests in no way appear so engrossed in these pleasures as is required by etiquette at our musical soirées. On the contrary, they drink and talk, and busy themselves with their toilette. As I remarked above, the Egyptian idea of a social feast was that the guests should be anointed and wreathed by the attendants, that they should receive new necklets, and that lotus

[1] Double flutes of the N. E.: Wilk., i. 436, 438, 439, 440, 441. A single one, ib. 440, 486. Flutes in the Brit. Mus., ib. 486.

[2] Kettledrums: Perrot, 701; Wilk., i. 439, 443.

[3] Perrot, 701, 838. In many museums, often in the shape of a hand.

[4] A curious instrument of the M. E.: Wilk., i. 442. In An., 4, 12, 2, the flutes are called *uad'ʿa'e* and *uar*, and the stringed instruments *ken'en'euru*, and *nat'ache*. Of these foreign barbaric names we can only identify the last but one, the *kinnôr* or lyre.

[5] L. D., ii. 52, 61, 74.

[6] L. D., ii. 53.

[7] They were thus employed under the N. E.; cp. the above illus. from the Brit. Mus.

[8] E.g. Wilk., i. 438, 440, 441. At sacrifices, L. D., iii. 236.

EGYPTIAN LADIES AT A FEAST.

flowers and buds should be placed on the black tresses of their wigs. If we look at the feast represented in the accompanying plate,[1] or at any one of the many similar pictures[2] of the New Empire, we see how absorbed the women of the party are in their own adornment; they give each other their flowers to smell, or in their curiosity they take hold of their neighbour's new earrings.[3] The serving boys and girls go round offering ointment, wreaths, perfumes, and bowls of wine. They challenge the guests at the same time to "celebrate the joyful day"[4] by the enjoyment of the pleasure of the present moment; the singers also continually repeat the same as the refrain to their song. They sing to the guests as they quaff the wine:

> "Celebrate the joyful day!
> Let sweet odours and oils be placed for thy nostrils,
> Wreaths of lotus flowers for the limbs
> And for the bosom of thy sister, dwelling in thy heart
> Sitting beside thee.
> Let song and music be made before thee.
> Cast behind thee all cares and mind thee of pleasure,
> Till cometh the day when we draw towards the land
> That loveth silence."[5]

or:

> "Celebrate the joyful day, with contented heart
> And a spirit full of gladness."[6]

or:

> "Put myrrh on thy head, array thyself in fine linen
> Anointing thyself with the true wonders of God.
> Adorn thyself with all the beauty thou canst.
> With a beaming face celebrate the joyful day and rest not therein.
> For no one can take away his goods with him,
> Yea, no one returns again, who has gone hence."[7]

The guests, hearing these admonitions to enjoy life while they may, before death comes to make an end of all pleasure, console themselves with wine, and finally, as was considered suitable at every feast, "the banquet is disordered by drunkenness."[8] Even the ladies do not refrain from excess, for when they at last refuse the ever-offered bowl, they have already, as our picture shows, presumed too much on their powers. One lady squats miserably on the ground, her robe slips down from her shoulder, the old attendant is summoned hastily, but alas! she comes too late.[9] This conclusion to the banquet is no exaggerated caricature. In

[1] Feast. In the upper row three married couples, in the lower eight ladies, the gentlemen sit behind on simple stools. (Theban tomb picture of the 18th dynasty now in the Brit. Mus.)

[2] See particularly Ros. M. C., 79, also Wilk., i. 424, 426, 427, 430, pl. xi.

[3] Wilk., ii. 21.

[4] That this was a cry to the guests we see by Wilk., pl. xi., where the servant thus apostrophises one of the guests, the chief of the mercenaries. Cp. also Ros. M. C., 96.

[5] Düm. Hist. Inscrip., ii. 40. Cp. Ä. Z., 1873, 60 ff. Also Records of the Past, vol. vi. p. 129.

[6] Wilk., i. pl. xi.

[7] Harr., 500, 14, 10 ff.; Cp. also Records of the Past, vol. iv. p. 118.

[8] Turin love songs, Maspero, Etud. Egypt. i. 228.

[9] A similar picture, Wilk., i. 393.

other countries and in other ages it may also happen that a lady may drink more than she need, but in the Egypt of the New Empire, where this pitiful scene is perpetuated on the wall of a tomb, it was evidently regarded merely as a trifling incident, occurring at each banquet, and at which no one could take offence.

The Egyptians were not content with the feasts instituted at great festivals, but when the opportunity arose, they were quite willing without

FROM A THEBAN TOMB OF THE TIME OF THE NEW EMPIRE (after Wilk., i. 392).

any particular reason to arrange a "house of beer," *i.e.* a small banquet.[1] We have already seen an instance of this (p. 144) in which the judges had arranged one of these pleasure parties with the accused, and had heavily to atone for their indiscretion.[2] Well might the wise 'Eney teach: "Drink not beer to excess! . . . The words that come out of thy mouth, thou canst not recall. Thou dost fall and break thy limbs, and no one reaches out a hand to thee. Thy comrades go on drinking, they stand up and say: 'Away with this fellow who is drunk.' If any one should then seek thee to ask counsel of thee, thou wouldst be found lying in the dust like a little child."[3] These words of wisdom, however, were as useless as those of Dauuf, who entreated his son to content himself with two jugs of beer and three loaves of bread.[4] The Egyptian youth seems to have followed his own sweet will, and one teacher wrote sorrowfully to his pupil as follows:[5]—

"I am told: thou dost forsake books,
Thou dost abandon thyself to pleasure,
Thou dost wander from street to street;
Every evening the smell of beer,
The smell of beer scares away men (from thee),
It destroys thy soul.

[1] P j. T., 6, 1; Mar. mon. div., 6, 134, and in the passage lately quoted from the Turin love songs.
[2] P j. T., 6, 1. [3] Pap. de Boul., i. 17, 6 ff. [4] Sall., 2, 10, 6.
[5] An., 4, 11, 8 ff. Also the beginning of Sall., i. 9, 9 ff.

Thou art as a broken oar,
That can guide to neither side,
Thou art as a temple without its god,
A house without bread.

Thou art caught as thou dost climb upon the walls,
And dost break the plank,
The people flee from thee,
And thou dost strike and wound them.

Oh that thou didst understand that wine is an abomination,
And that thou wouldest abjure the *shedeh* drink,
That thou didst not set thy heart on cool drinks,
And that thou wouldest forget the T'enreku.

Now thou art instructed how to sing to the flute,
To recite (?) to the pipe (?),
To intone to the lyre,
To sing to the harp."

Girls are also represented in the company of an inebriated man; they embrace him and he sits by them "imbrued with oil, and with a wreath of cotton weed round his neck."[1] He may then pat himself in a contented way, but when he tries to get up, he tumbles and falls down and "bespatters himself with mud like a crocodile."

It was not however at all necessary for the young men to fill up their idle hours with pleasures such as these; even in old times there were games and many other kinds of recreation with which they could refresh themselves after their studies. They had bows and arrows with which they might shoot at targets made of the skin of some animal,[2] or they had a game they played similar to one of our own, in which by a powerful throw a point was driven obliquely into a block of wood, whilst the opponent had to drive it out again with his own point.[3] There was also a game with two hooks and a ring,[4] and many others, about which we can ascertain nothing from the monuments. For those who did not care for these trials of strength, there were games of chance or of skill. It is doubtful whether dice go back to the older period of Egyptian history,[5]

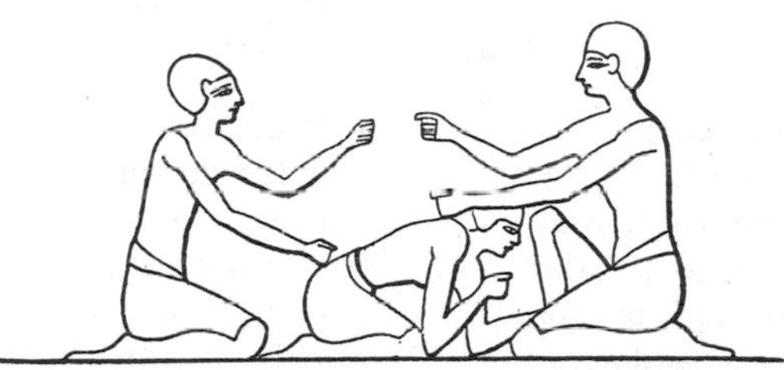

UNKNOWN GAME OF THE TIME OF THE MIDDLE EMPIRE; POSSIBLY THE MAN KNEELING HAD TO GUESS WHO STRUCK HIM (after Wilk., ii. 61 = Ros. M. C., 102).

[1] Both expressions used in this passage, [hieroglyphs] and [hieroglyphs], must refer to the Egyptian *demimonde*. The former appears to signify "nurse," the orthography of the latter is connected with *meses* to give birth.

[2] Wilk., i. 406, ib. 27.

[3] O. E.: in the tomb of Ptaḥḥôtep; M. E.: Wilk., ii. 69.

[4] M. E.: Wilk., ii. 62.

[5] Cp. Wilk., ii. 62.

but the game now known in Italy by the name of *mora* was possibly played by the Egyptians round a pot even under the Old Empire.[1] In the same way we also find another old game for which concentric circles were drawn on the ground.[2] Each of the players put a stone inside the circles, but what was exactly the object of the game or how it was played we cannot determine, as we only possess one single picture in which it is represented. The game of draughts, of which we have many repre-

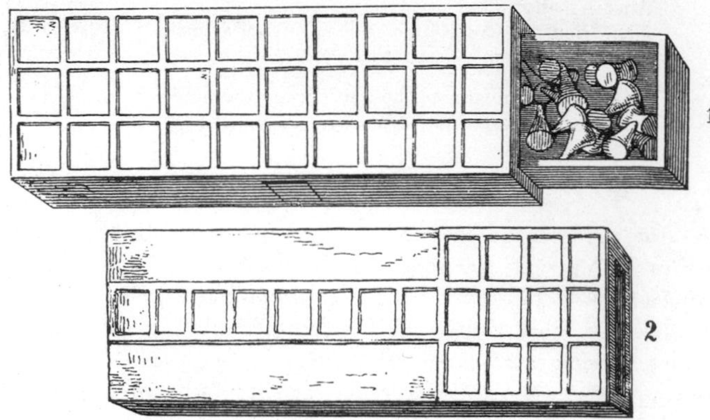

BOARD FOR A GAME, FROM THE ABBOTT COLLECTION. Front and back view (after Wilk., ii. 58).

sentations,[3] as well as many boards in existence,[4] is almost as obscure as the other games. This was the favourite game of the ancient Egyptians, the game which they were allowed to play even in the nether world.[5] We know that there were many ways of playing this game; this is proved by the various boards which we possess, but it is impossible now to determine the particular construction of each game.

[1] O. E.: perhaps Br. Gr. W. 137; N. E: Wilk., ii. 55, round a pot.

[2] O. E.: Wilk., ii. 61. Another puzzling game, Wilk., ii. 70.

[3] O. E.: L. D., ii. 61; M. E.: Wilk., ii. 57 = Perrot, 258; N. E.: Wilk., ii. 59, 60; L. D. iii. 208.

[4] Wilk., ii. 58 (= Prisse monum., 49, p. 9); Mar. mon. div., 51 j (= Maspero, Guide, 3182); Maspero, Guide, 3183, ib. 4673.

[5] Book of the Dead, chap. 17 superscription.

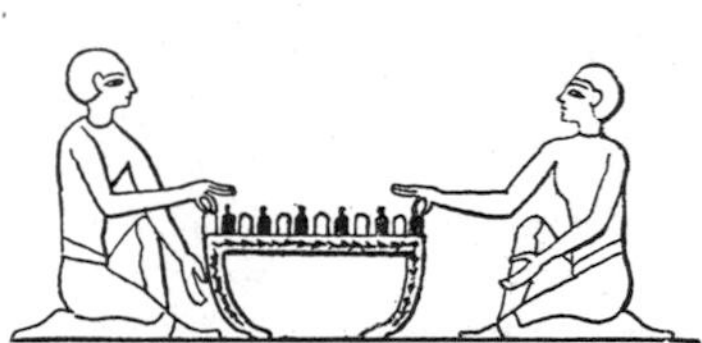

GAME PLAYED ON A BOARD. Picture of the time of the Middle Empire at Beni Hasan (after Wilk., ii. 57).

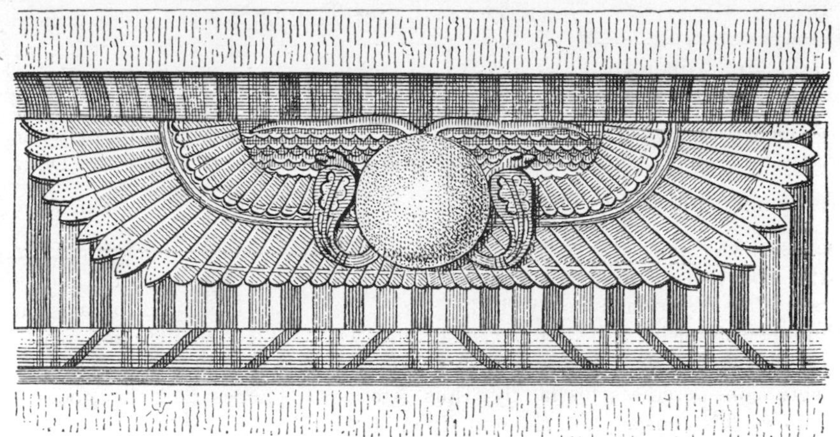

CHAPTER XII

RELIGION

WERE it possible to describe the life of the ancient Egyptians without touching upon a subject of such moment to them as their religion, I would gladly do so, for it is not possible as yet to give a satisfactory scientific account of the faith of this ancient nation. In spite of the enormous amount of material that we possess in the shape of religious texts and pictures, our knowledge of the subject is still very elementary, and in the following sketch much must still be considered as hypothetical.[1] It is most probable that originally the whole country did not profess a common religion. It is true that there are certain representations which continually recur, and which seem common to all parts of Egypt, as for instance, that of Rê‘, the sun-god, passing through the heavens in his bark, or of heaven as a goddess bending over the earth, but these representations have little to do with religion itself. He who needed superhuman help turned rather to a god more akin to himself, the *god of his town*. Each town, and indeed each village, possessed its own particular divinity, adored by the respective inhabitants, and by them alone. Thus the later town of Memphis was faithful to Ptaḥ, of whom they said, that as a potter on his wheel he had turned the egg from which the world was hatched. The god Atum was the "town god" of Heliopolis; in Chnum we find Thoth, in Abydos Osiris, in Thebes Amon, in Hermonthis Mont, and so on. The goddess Ḥatḥôr was revered in Denderah, Bastet in the town later called Bubastis, while in Sais the people adored the warlike Neit, who was probably of Libyan origin. The names of many of these deities show them to be purely local gods, many being

[1] I have, as a rule, followed the views of Piltschmann and Ed. Meyer.

originally called after the towns, as, "him of Ombos," "him of Edfu," "her of Bast"; they are really merely the genii of the towns. Many were supposed to show themselves to their worshippers in the form of some object in which they dwelt, *e.g.* the god of the town Dedu in the Delta (the later Busiris) in the shape of the wooden pillar 𓊽. The form chosen was generally that of some animal: Ptaḥ manifested himself in the Apis bull, Amon in the ram, Sobk of the Feyum in a crocodile, and so on. The Egyptians believed that each place was inhabited by a great number of spirits, and that the lesser ones were subject to the chief spirit; in some instances they formed his suite, his divine cycle; sometimes they were considered as his family, thus Amon of Thebes had the goddess Mut for his consort, and the god Chons for his son.

The religious conditions described above exist *mutatis mutandis* everywhere amongst nations in a low state of development; with the progress of Egyptian civilisation they changed in many essential points. As the Egyptian peasants of the different nomes began to feel that they belonged to one nation, and as the intercourse increased between the individual parts of this long country, the old religion gradually lost its disconnected character. It was natural that families travelling from one nome to another should take the gods they had hitherto served to their new homes, and that, like every novelty, these divinities should win prestige with the inhabitants. It is conceivable that the god of a particularly great and mighty town should be believed to exercise a sort of patronage, either politically or agriculturally, over that part of the country dependent upon that centre. When any god had attained this prominent position, and had become a *great god*, his worship would spread still farther. He had more opportunities than the other gods of giving help and working miracles, he therefore won more renown than they did. If the fame of a god spread through the whole country, and if pilgrims came from afar to his sanctuary, still greater results ensued. The worshippers of other less celebrated deities then discovered that their divinity was really the same as the more famous god. It was no obstacle that the names were utterly different, *e.g.* in far distant ages the worship of Osiris, belonging originally to Abydos, spread over the whole of Egypt, and gods as distinct from him as Sokar of Memphis and the pillar of Dedu were identified with him.

The consequence was that with the progress of civilisation the religion underwent a process of simplification. The small local gods shrank into the background by the side of their more fortunate colleagues, who tended more and more to merge into each other. Thus the cruel Sechmet and the gracious Bastet were almost considered as special forms and names of the more famous goddess Ḥatḥôr; and in later times we may also add of Mut of Thebes. At length Ḥatḥôr herself had to suffer identification with Isis. In the same way, as the reputation of the sun-god increased, other gods grew more like him. Few Egyptian gods escaped identification with Rê', not even the water god Sobk, in spite of his crocodile form.

The development of a common mythology advanced hand in hand with the process described above. At the period when each individual place revered its special divinity, the respective inhabitants had woven for their god a history of special actions and destinies which had little or no connection with the stories of the divinities worshipped in other localities. When however the local cults were fused into a national religion, the legends of the gods were united to form a mythology which, in its most important particulars, became the common property of the nation.

The evolution of Egyptian religion described above took place in prehistoric times. In the oldest records we possess, the so-called pyramid texts, the development was complete, and the religion had essentially the same character as in all after ages. We find a very considerable number of divinities of each rank, the greater with their sanctuaries in various towns, one being always acknowledged as pre-eminent; individual gods are sometimes expressly distinguished the one from the other, sometimes considered as identical; we find a mythology with myths which are absolutely irreconcilable existing peacefully side by side; in short, an unparalleled confusion. This chaos was never afterwards reduced to order; on the contrary, we might almost say that the confusion became even more hopeless during the 3000 years that, according to the pyramid texts, the Egyptian religion "flourished."

From century to century progress was made, at any rate in one direction, viz. in the amalgamation of the divinities to one type. More especially the sun-god Rê' formed a central point for this kind of union; Amon of Thebes, Horus of the East, Horus of Edfu, Chnum of Elephantine, Atum of Heliopolis, and it may be many others, were considered under the New Empire as *one* god. This course would gradually lead to the abolition of polytheism, and in fact this tendency is very apparent. Thus, *e.g.* in the phraseology of the hymn to the sun-god, the divine amalgam, composed of Amon, Rê', Harmachis, Atum, is called the "only god, in truth, the living one." At the same time, the existence of the various sanctuaries proves that these were but empty phrases; as long as Atum, Chnum, and Horus still possessed their individual sanctuaries and priesthood, the fusion of these gods could not be complete, notwithstanding these beautiful words. Above all, the priests of those gods naturally withstood these anti-polytheistic theories of the New Empire, especially those who, being the richest, had most to lose by them,—the priests of Amon. It is no accident that the only practical attempt that we know of in this direction turned, in the time of momentary triumph, with rage against Amon, as if it had experienced most resistance from that god. This attempt was undertaken by the son of Amenḥôtep III., the last king of any importance of the eighteenth dynasty,[1] and consisted in no less a change than the substitution of all the gods of past times by one single deity, the "great living sun-disk," or, according to his official title, "the sun ruling the two horizons, he who rejoices in the horizon in his name: splendour abiding

[1] Cp. p. 45 ff., though there may be much to change in this conception of the ancient religion.

in the sun-disk."[1] In fact, it was not a sun-god who was adored, but the material sun itself, which, by the hands of his beams, bestowed upon living beings that "eternal life which was in him."[2] This new deity, therefore, did not bear the name of any of the old sun-gods, nor is he called simply the *sun*, but he is called [hieroglyphs], *'etn*, the *sun-disk*, a word not contaminated by having been used in the old religion.

It is probable that this religious revolution was borne along by an undercurrent of support in the nation, or at least in the educated classes; finally however it was carried out by the zeal of a monarch. King Amenḥôtep IV. (or as he was called after the reformation, Chuen'eten, splendour of the sun-disk) established thc *doctrine*, this is evidently the official term for the new religion,[3] for a number of years as the state religion. The above title, referring to the sun-disk, shows that from the first the new faith was formulated dogmatically; nevertheless, we can only judge of this teaching by the hymns,[4] in which adoration is paid to "the living sun-disk, besides whom there is no other." He created all things, "the far-off heavens, mankind, the animals, the birds; our eyes are strengthened by his beams, and when he shows himself all flowers grow and live; at his rising the pastures bring forth, they are intoxicated before his face, all the cattle skip on their feet, and the birds in the marshes flutter with joy." It is he "who brings in the years, creates the months, makes the days, reckons the hours, he is the lord of time, according to whom men reckon." These ideas and expressions are similar to those found in the hymns to the sun-god in the older religion; the innovation brought in by Chuen'eten therefore was essentially only the idea that the one God, "the God living in truth," was to be an article of real faith, and no longer merely a phrase.

Yet, in spite of the fact that the new faith was founded on the old teaching, it stood really in absolute opposition to the latter. The fury with which the reformer persecuted the old gods, especially the Theban god, finds its parallel only in the history of fanaticism. The name and figure of Amon were erased everywhere, and to accomplish this act of vengeance against the god whom they detested, Chuen'eten's people even penetrated into the interior of the private tombs. The goddess Mut, the consort of Amon, fared no better. The king would no longer live in the town, which had been the residence of his ancestors, but built a new town in Middle Egypt to be the seat of government in place of the impure Thebes. He thought it necessary, also, to change his name of Amenḥôtep, because the name Amon belonged to the old faith; he also decreed a change of orthography in order to remove a sign, to which there was the same objection. The word *maut* (mother) had hitherto been written [hieroglyphs], it

[1] In two variations which may correspond perhaps to changes in dogma.

[2] L. D., iii. 106 b.

[3] L. D., iii. 97 e, 107 a, d.

[4] The following is from the hymns: L. D., iii. 97 a and 106 b. Similarly, 98 a and 107 b.

was now changed to , because, in the old fashion of spelling, the word signified also the name of the goddess Mut.

It is evident that a reformer who went so rashly to work as to try to set aside the whole history of a people with one stroke, could create nothing permanent. The results of the work of Chuen'eten were ruined after a few years, and in the reaction his buildings were razed to the ground. The old faith was re-established unchanged, and there was never any more question of the *doctrine* of the heretic. The result of this episode was the same as that produced by all reformations that fail; the victorious old faith grew still more rigid against every innovation than it had ever been before. After the eighteenth dynasty the Egyptian religion became, if possible, more confused and more lifeless than ever; this was certainly partly due to the victory obtained by the priests of Amon over the king, who perpetrated the crime of thinking that their religion was not the height of perfection.

The reader must not expect that in a sketch of Egyptian religion I should give special details about the individual gods and their actions. In the first place, a discourse on this subject has little concern with Egyptian life, theological details would lead us far from our subject, and moreover, an exact description of the Egyptian pantheon consists of little more than an empty list of the names of gods and temples. Most of the Egyptian gods appear to us as lifeless, characterless figures. They have their appointed names, they also bear some fixed epithet, such as "father of the gods," "king of the gods," "of beautiful countenance"; in their pictures they are distinguished from mankind by a special dress[1] and a special beard;[2] and they are distinguished from each other by certain animal heads, crowns, and attributes. This is all however, and those who expect to find living beings like the Greek gods will be much disappointed with these meaningless puppets of gods.

But, on the other hand, we should be very unjust to the Egyptians if we thought that their deities were, to *their* minds, the mere shadows that they appear to us in the inscriptions. Like the Greeks, the Egyptians allowed their imagination to weave all manner of legends round the gods, and to remodel their shapeless great genii into beings, acting and feeling as human beings of decided character. There was also a system of mythology connected with the Egyptian gods, and if we now know little of the stories of these divinities, and are obliged to content ourselves with their names and representations, it is owing merely to the fact that the texts omit to inform us about these myths. The religious writings refer continually to mythological events, they call Isis the "lady of the marshes," and Horus the "avenger of his father," or they make mention of a "certain day when the words are to be offered up at Heliopolis," but very few texts tell us anything further about these matters.

[1] The dress resembles the short ancient underdress of women. The representations of the gods were all determined under the Old Empire: cp. L. D., ii. 2 c, 115 e.

[2] See p. 226.

Originally, the compilers of these religious texts were evidently content to give these allusions only, because the myths were so well known that a mere reference to them was sufficient. In later times there were other reasons for this reticence; the old books containing these myths were considered too sacred to be placed where profane eyes might see them, in the tomb chapels or in the temple halls; even the gods themselves were supposed to wash seven times before reading the words of these sacred books.[1] At this later period also, even the representations of these myths at the temple festivals were considered[2] as a great secret, and the reader will remember how conscientiously and carefully Herodotos avoids

THE GOD ATUM OF HELIOPOLIS (with human head and double crown).

THE GOD MONT OF HERMONTHIS (with hawk's head, sun-disk, and feathers).

THE GOD SOBK OF THE FEYUM (with crocodile head, horns, sun-disk, and feathers).

relating what he had learnt concerning the mythological reasons for the strange festival customs on these occasions.

The mythological tales which, in spite of the hazards of fortune, have come down to us, are very few in comparison with the multitude which must formerly have existed, and, unfortunately, the fragments which remain[3] are of different periods, and belong to writings of very various character. Nevertheless, the following brief account is given here, in order that the reader may obtain some idea of ancient Egyptian myths, in default of better sources of information.

In the primaeval ages of the world, the sun-god Rê‘ appeared on the

[1] Destruction des hommes, l. 78.

[2] Under the eighteenth dynasty this was evidently not the case, for, as we shall see below, we find the representation of one of these festivals in a Theban tomb.

[3] A collection from Egyptian and Greek sources of these fragments of myths, many of which are contained in the Sall. iv., and in magical formulae, is one of the first requisites needed for the study of Egyptian religion. Before this is compiled, all speculations respecting the Egyptian gods are of little use.

dark ocean of the god Nun, and undertook the government of the world. This did not happen without a struggle; finally however the victory remained with Rêʿ, and the "children of the rebels" were delivered up to him on the terrace of the town Chmunu.[1] He now reigned in peace as "king of men and gods,"[2] and as long as he was in full possession of his powers, no one attacked his government. But his youth was not eternal; his limbs became stiff with old age, his bones changed to silver, his flesh to gold, his hair to real lapis-lazuli.[3] Then happened what happens also to earthly kings when they grow old: his subjects became rebellious, more especially the wise goddess Isis,[4] who was wiser than all men, than all gods and spirits. She knew all things in heaven and earth as well as Rêʿ himself, but there was one thing which she did not know—and this want of knowledge impaired her power—the secret name of Rêʿ. For this god "of the many names" kept his special name secret, the name on which his power was founded, the name which bestowed magical might on those who knew it. As Isis could in no way learn this secret name, she had recourse to the stratagem related in the following lines:

"The age of the god stirred in his mouth,
And caused him to spit on the earth,
And what he spat fell on the ground.
Isis then kneaded it with her hand
Together with the earth which was there;
She formed a noble worm with it
And made it like a spear.
She did not put it living about her face,[5]
But threw it down rolled together (?) on the path,
On which the great god was wont to walk
At his pleasure through his two countries.

The noble god stepped forth in his splendour,
The gods, those who serve the Pharaoh, accompanied him,
And he walked as he did each day.
Then the noble worm stung him . . .
The divine god opened his mouth
And the voice of his majesty reached unto heaven.
His cycle of gods cried, 'What is it? what is it?'
And the gods cried, 'Behold! behold!'
He could not answer them,
His jaw bones chattered,
All his limbs trembled
And the poison invaded his flesh,
As the Nile invades her territory (?).

When the great god had calmed his heart,
He cried out to his followers:
'Come to me, you, the offspring of my body,
You gods, who were formed from me,

---

[1] Book of the Dead, 17, 5 ed., Nav.

[2] Destruction des hommes, l. 1; Turin, 131, 13.

[3] Destruction des hommes, l. 2.

[4] For all that follows see Turin, 131 ff., 77, 31. Cp. concerning this text the work of Lefébure, A. Z., 1883, 27 ff., who first acknowledged its importance and made a good translation of it.

[5] A play on the uraeus snake, which rears itself above the face of the sun-god.

That Chepr'e may tell it to you:
Something malignant has attacked me,
My heart knows it, mine eyes see it not,
My hand did it not,
I know not who (?) has done this.
I have never felt pain approaching unto it,
There is no illness worse than this.'

'I am a prince and the son of a prince,
The divine progeny of a god.
I am great and the son of a great one.
My father devised my name.
I am he of many names and of many forms,
And my form is in every god. . . .
My father and my mother told me my name,
And it has remained hidden in my heart since my birth,
So that magical power should not be given to a magician against me.
I had gone out to look at that which I had created
I was walking through the two countries which I had created;
Then something stung me, what I know not.
It is not fire,
It is not water,
My heart is full of heat,
My body trembles
And all my limbs quake.'

'Now, then, bring me the divine children,
Those who speak wisely
With an understanding tongue,
Whose power (?) reacheth to the heavens.'
Then the divine children came to him,
Each of them full of grief;
There came also Isis with her wisdom,
Whose mouth is full of the breath of life,
Whose decree banishes pain,
And whose word gives life to those who no longer breathe.
She said, 'What is it? what is it, divine father?
Behold! a worm has done thee this wrong,
One of thy children has raised his head against thee.
Therefore, he shall fall by means of an excellent magic,
I will cause him to yield at the sight of thy rays.'

The splendid God opened his mouth:
'I was walking upon my way
And traversing the two countries and the foreign lands,
For my heart would look upon that which I had created.
Then was I bitten by a worm which I did not see.
It is not fire,
It is not water,
And I am colder than water,
And I am hotter than fire.
All my limbs perspire greatly,
I tremble, mine eye is not steady,
And I do not see the sky.
Water streams down my face as in the time of summer.'
Then spoke Isis to Rê':
'Tell me thy name, divine father,

For that man lives who is called by his name.'
'I am he who created heaven and earth, and piled up the mountains,
Who made all living creatures.
I am he who made the water and created the great river,
Who made the *Bull of his mother*,
Who begets all.
I am he who created the heavens and the secret of the horizon,
And I have placed there the souls of the gods.
I am he, who when he opens his eyes, it becomes light,
When he closes his eyes, it becomes dark;
The water of the Nile flows when he commands,
But the gods know not his name.
I am he who makes the hours and creates the days.
I am he who begins the year and creates the inundation.
I am he who made the living fire . . .
I am Chepr'e of the morning and Rê' at mid-day
And Atum at evening time.'
The poison did not yield, it went farther,
The health of the great god began to decline.

Then spoke Isis to Rê':
'That is not thy name that thou tellest me.
Tell it to me that the poison may go out,
For the man who is called by his name lives.'
The poison, however, burnt like a furnace,
It was stronger than flame or fire."

Then Rê' could no longer withstand the torment; he told Isis his name and regained his health through her magic power. Nevertheless, even after he was healed, the strong rule of the old sun-god had lost its vigour, and even mankind became hostile against him; they became angry and began a rebellion. The measures which Rê' took against this danger are related in another very ancient book.[1]

"His majesty spake to those who were his followers: 'Call to me my Eye (*i.e.* the goddess Ḥatḥôr), Shu and Tefnut, Qeb and Mut, together with the divine fathers and mothers, who were with me when I was still in the ocean, and call to me also Nun (*i.e.* the god of this primaeval ocean). Let him bring his courtiers with him, let him bring them softly (?), so that mankind shall not see and escape (?), he shall come with them to my great palace, in order that they may give me their excellent counsel.' . . . Then these gods were conducted thither, and these gods threw themselves down on both sides of his majesty and touched the ground with their faces, that he might tell his desire before the father of the most ancient gods, who made man, and who created wisdom.

"Then they spake before his majesty: 'Speak to us that we may hear.' Then spake Rê' to Nun: 'Oh, thou most ancient god! from whom I was begotten, and you, the ancestors of the gods! behold the men who were begotten from mine eye, they plot (evil) against me. Tell me what you would do against them, for I will not slay them till I have heard what you shall say about it.'

[1] Destruction des hommes.

"Then spake the majesty of Nun: 'Oh, my son Rê', thou god who art greater than he who made him, and than those who created him! remain seated on thy throne, for the fear of thee will be great, if thou dost (but) turn thine eye upon those who have conspired against thee.' Then answered the majesty of Rê': 'Behold, they have fled to the mountains, for their heart is full of fear, because of what I have said to them.' Then they spake before his majesty: 'Shoot forth thine Eye, that it may slay the evil conspirators. . . . Let the goddess Ḥatḥôr descend, and when that goddess shall arrive, then shall she slay the men on the mountains.' Then spake the majesty of this god: 'Go in peace, Ḥatḥôr.' . . . Then spake this goddess: 'By thy life! it shall be good for me when I subject mankind'; but the majesty of Rê' said: 'I will subject them (and) slay them.'"

THE GODDESS SECHMET: BEFORE HER STANDS RAMSES II., WHO IS OFFERING HER FLOWERS.

This last speech of the god was especially important in Egyptian theology, for, as the sacred book informs us, because Rê' spoke to the goddess of "subjecting" (*sochm*) them, therefore the latter bore from that time the additional name of *Sechmet.* This goddess, Sechmet, is well known to us as the lion-headed goddess of war, who is so often represented as angry and as wading in blood.

In the night therefore Ḥatḥôr descended to the earth and began to make a terrible massacre of those sinful men, those even who were flying up stream into the mountains being included in it. She was so terrible in her fury that the whole town of Chenensuten ran with blood. Then Rê' determined to stop the massacre, and save at any rate a part of mankind. The means he employed however to stop his terrible messenger in the continuance of the slaughter were rather strange. "Call now to me swift messengers," he said, "that I may send them forth (as) the shadow of a body." They brought him these messengers immediately, and his majesty the god spake: "Hasten to the island of Elephantine, and bring me much *dada* fruit." They brought him this *dada* fruit and he gave it to the god Sektet, who is in Heliopolis, to grind. When the slaves had crushed some barley to make beer, they put this *dada* fruit in the mixing jar together with the blood of men, and they thus made ready 7000 jugs of beer.

When now his majesty, the King of Upper Egypt and King of Lower Egypt Rê', came together with those gods, in order to inspect this beer, as day dawned behold this goddess had slaughtered the men as they passed up stream. Then spake His Majesty Rê': "How good that is; I will protect mankind from her." Then spake Rê', "Bring hither the beer to the place where she is slaying mankind." Thus it happened, in the twilight, the jugs of beer were poured out so that they overflowed the fields. The result of this was curious. "When this goddess came thither in the morning, she found these fields inundated, and her face (was mirrored) beautifully therein. She then drank thereof and was satisfied; she went about drunk and recognised mankind no longer."[1]

Thus Rê' saved a remnant of mankind from the bloodthirsty, terrible

FIGURE OF THE COW OF HEAVEN, BORNE BY THE GOD SHU, AND SUPPORTED BY OTHER GENII.

On her body, which is adorned with stars, the bark of the sun voyages twice. It is exactly described in this illustration how the latter amplifies the sacred book spoken of above; explanatory marginal writings are also given, and indeed with the express statement as to whether they were to be turned towards the right or towards the left (*m shat*).

Hathôr, but he himself had no pleasure in his victory; "his heart was weary of being with them," and he withdrew to rest on the back of the cow of heaven, after he had named Thoth, the god of wisdom, as his deputy upon earth. Before however he left this world, he called the earth-god Qeb, and enjoined upon him to be extremely careful as to snakes and worms, for he could not forget how much harm had come to him through a worm.

Still more popular than even these stories of the sun-god, was the myth of Osiris and of his wicked brother Set, the Greek Typhon.[2] Qeb the earth-god and Nut the goddess of heaven had four children, the gods

[1] Another version of this legend causes wine instead of beer to be made out of "the blood of those who formerly fought against the gods." Cp. Plutarch, De Iside (ed. Parthey), 6.

[2] All that follows, when not otherwise stated, is according to Plutarch, De Iside, 13 ff.

Osiris and Set, and the goddesses Isis and Nephthys. Osiris was the husband of Isis, and Set of Nephthys; to the former was given the government of the earth. His rule was full of blessing for mankind, for he taught the inhabitants of Egypt to till the ground, and gave them laws. But the evil Set laid wait for him and devised a conspiracy: "he secretly took the measure of Osiris' body, and accordingly prepared a beautiful, richly-adorned chest, which he brought in at the feast. When all had rejoiced at the sight of its beauty, Typhon promised jestingly to give the chest as a present to the one who would exactly fill it when lying in it. All tried it, but it would fit no one, till at last Osiris got into it and lay down. The conspirators then hastened to throw the cover over it, closed the chest on the outside with nails, poured hot lead over it, carried it out to the river and sent it by the Tanitic mouth to the sea." Thus Osiris died: his consort Isis however followed the advice of the god of wisdom and fled into the swamps of the Delta. Seven scorpions escorted her flight. Wearied out, she came one evening to a house of women, but the mistress was frightened by the escort of the goddess and closed her door to the homeless one. The scorpion Tefen then crept under the door and stung the child of the mistress. But when Isis heard the grief of the mother her anger melted away; she laid her hand on the child and gave it new life. Afterwards, when in the swamps, Isis herself gave birth to a son, Horus, whom Buto (*Ud'ot*), the goddess of the North, successfully hid from the vengeance of Set. Buto could not however guard him from every mischance, and once when Isis came to his hiding-place she found him lying lifeless on the ground,—a scorpion had stung him. Then Isis prayed for help to the sun-god Rê', and he caused the sun-bark to stop and sent down Thoth the god of wisdom, who gave the child new life.[1]

Whilst Horus thus grew up in the marshes, Isis wandered through the world seeking the chest with the body of Osiris; she was accompanied and protected by the jackal-headed god Anubis, the bastard son of Osiris and Nephthys. At last she found what she sought. The waves of the sea had washed up the chest on the Phoenician coast at Byblos, and a tree, near which the chest was stranded, grew up so quickly that it quite enclosed it. The king of the country however, admiring the great tree, caused it to be felled, and placed it under his house as a pillar with the hidden coffin inside it. There Isis, who had entered the service of that king as nurse, found it; she revealed herself as goddess, and drew out the coffin from the pillar. She brought it by ship to Egypt, where she wept in solitude over the body of her husband; then she hid the coffin, and went to the sacred town of Buto to see after her son. But when hunting by moonlight Set found the hidden coffin, and wreaked his anger on the corpse of his adversary; he tore it to pieces, and these he scattered to the winds. Then Isis went through the marshes in a bark seeking the different limbs of her husband. Wherever she found one she buried it,

[1] The two last incidents are not from Plutarch, but from an Egyptian source, edited by Brugsch, Ä. Z., 1879, 1 ff.

and men revered each of those spots as the grave of their benefactor Osiris, *e.g.* the town of Busiris in the Delta, the burial-place of his backbone, and Abydos where his head rested in a small chest. When Horus had grown up to be a young man, he left his hiding-place in Buto in order to avenge the death of his father. He had to encounter a terrible fight with Set, in which one of Horus' eyes was torn out and Set suffered a

KING SETY I. OFFERS WINE BEFORE OSIRIS, "TO THE CHIEF GOD OF THE WEST (I.E. OF THE KINGDOM OF THE DEAD), THE GREAT GOD, THE LORD OF ABYDOS, UENNOFRE, THE LORD OF ETERNITY, THE RULER OF ETERNITY."

Behind Osiris are "the Great Isis, the divine mother," and "Horus the son of Isis and of Osiris."

yet worse mutilation; finally Thoth separated the combatants and healed their wounds.[1] Set however was vanquished, and he acknowledged as the new monarch Horus, who now assumed the sacred Atef crown and ascended the throne of his forefather the god Qeb. Horus thus became king of men; his father however from this time ruled over the deceased in the kingdom of the dead, as "King of eternity." Osiris died in truth, and the other members of his divine family have also died since; their souls alone still live as the stars in the sky; that of Isis as the dog-star, that of Horus as Orion.[2] The soul of Osiris however dwells in the bird Benu, the phoenix of the Greeks, which we see in our illustration, perched on the branches of the sacred tree above the coffin of Osiris.

1 E.g. this is mentioned in the Book of the Dead, 17, 30 ff.

2 Plutarch, De Iside, 21. This is also contained in the pyramid texts, in which the soul of mankind is represented as a third star, travelling through the sky with the dog-star and Orion.

Other legends also treat of the fight between Horus and Set; legends which originally can have had nothing in common with that related above. In one we read that Set and Horus were two brothers, who formerly divided Egypt between them; another relates that Horus took the form of a great sun-disk with coloured wings, and after a long conflict with his adversary Set and his followers, he gained the victory near the town of Edfu. Therefore the winged sun-disk was placed over all the doors into the temples, that the image of Horus might drive away all unclean spirits from the sacred building; this decoration so constantly carved over the temple entrances may be seen at the head of this chapter.

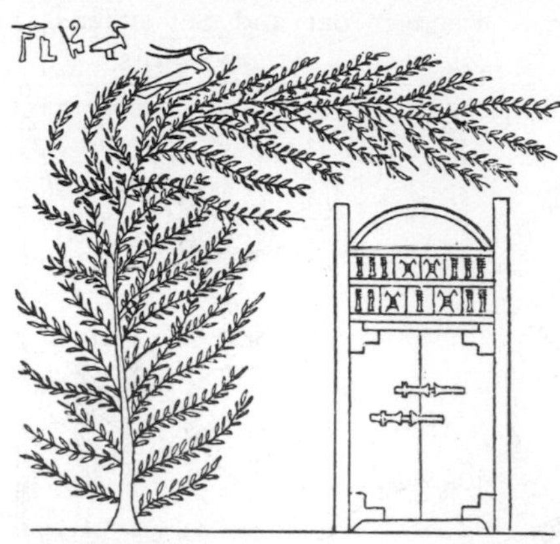

AFTER WILK., III. 349, FROM A TOMB TO HAU.
The tree is perhaps the Abaton of the tomb of Osiris, of which Plutarch speaks, de Iside, 20. Over the bird is written "Soul of Osiris."

The above contains essentially all that we know of Egyptian mythology. The gods mentioned in these legends, Rê', Osiris, Isis, Horus, Set, have become nearly as real to us as the inhabitants of the Greek Olympus; but the immense number of the Egyptian gods, known to us only in their theological literature or temple pictures, remain, as I said before, entirely shadowy personages. If, for instance, we were to put together everything that is related in the texts of Ptaḥ and Amon, the great gods of Thebes and Memphis, we should still know but very little of either; for though, like the other gods, they must once have also possessed myths, yet the texts contain scarcely a word concerning them. Finally, it is entirely erroneous to maintain that the Egyptian divinities were merely abstract phantoms, such as they seem to us; we only know too little of them. For centuries the great sun-god Rê' appeared just as colourless as all the other divinities, until by happy chance, two long fragments of his myth were brought to light, and he became the characteristic figure which we now recognise.

The worshippers of these gods were always faithful to them, and each individual strove to stand well, if not with all the gods, at any rate with the god of his home. He brought the first fruits of his harvest to the servants of the god;[1] he avoided what the god hated, and took care of the animal beloved by the divinity; and in order that "the god should not be angry with him, he solemnised the feast of his god and repeated his festivals";[2] he made the furthermost room of his house into a little chapel,[3]

[1] Thus at Siut under the M. E. Cp. Ä. Z., 1882, 169, 180.
[2] Mar. Cat. d'Ab., p. 1.
[3] Pap. de Boul., i. 16, 3.

and placed there a little image of the god; he put his offering on the stone table of offerings, and he recited daily his "adoration" before him. In the court of his granary,[1] or near his winepress,[2] he erected a little sanctuary to Renenutet, the goddess of the harvest, and placed there a table of offerings with wine and flowers. This was not a mere show of piety, at any rate not with those who were serious-minded, for one of their wise men taught: "the sanctuary of the god—clamour is an abomination to him. Pray for thyself, with a loving heart, in which the words remain hidden; that he may supply thy need, hear thy words and accept thy offering."[3] These and other evidences of private piety are however quite eclipsed by the pious offerings of the state.

The activity of the state, or to express ourselves in an Egyptian manner, that of the king for the gods, was so excessive, particularly under the New Empire, that the state must be regarded as really maintaining the religion of the country. The state and the priesthood are alone responsible for its prosperity, and in this matter the people are but the fifth wheel to the coach. The king builds the temple; the king bestows treasure, the long lists of offerings are said to be royal gifts; scarcely anything worth mentioning comes from private individuals. In the same way, it is the king who is always represented in the temple, and it is the king for whom prayers are offered in the temple. No mention is made of the pious worshippers. The temple services appear to have been of a strictly official character; it is quite conceivable indeed that they never rose to a higher standard.

The daily acts of worship performed by the priest *du jour*[4] are known from several contemporary sources[5] to have been essentially the same in the case of the various gods. Whether it were Amon or Isis, Ptaḥ or the deceased to whom divine honours were to be paid,[6] we always find that fresh rouge and fresh robes were placed upon the divine statue, and that the sacred chapel in which it was kept was cleansed and filled with perfume. The god was regarded as a human being, whose dwelling had to be cleansed, and who was assisted at his toilet by his servants.

These ceremonies doubtless differed both in detail and extent at the various sanctuaries; *e.g.* the priest at Thebes had about sixty ceremonies to perform, whilst at Abydos thirty-six were found to be sufficient. The form and object of the worship however were always the same, though the details might vary. As a general rule also, the priest had to recite an appointed formula at each separate ceremony.

At Abydos,[7] the priest first offered incense in the hypostyle hall, saying: "I come into thy presence, O great one, after I have purified

[1] Wilk., i. 348. [2] See the illustration, p. 198. [3] Pap. de Boul., i. 17, 1 ff.

[4] Cp. for this definition of the title of the ritual of Amon, Pap. Berlin, 55.

[5] Lemm's Ritual of the Theban gods; Ritual book of the service of Amon, that of Abydos, Mar. Ab., i. pp. 34-76 of the text.

[6] Cp. the ritual of Schiaparelli: Il libro dei funerali. Many examples also in the pyramid texts.

[7] I follow here Mar. Ab., i. pp. 34-56. The texts are so much injured, that many points in the above are hypothetical.

myself. As I passed by the goddess Tefnut, she purified me . . . I am a prophet, and the son of a prophet of this temple. I am a prophet, and I come to do what ought to be done, but I do not come to do what ought not to be done." . . . He then stepped in front of the shrine of the god and opened the seal of clay with these words: "The clay is broken and the seal loosed that this door may be opened, and all that is evil in me I throw (thus) on the ground." When the door was open, he first incensed the sacred uraeus snake, the guardian of the god, greeting it by all its names; he then entered the Holy of Holies, saying: "Let thy seat be adorned and thy robes exalted; the princes of the goddess of heaven come to thee, they descend from heaven and from the horizon that they may hear praise before thee. . . . He next approached the "great seat," *i.e.* that part of the shrine where the statue of the god stood, and said: "Peace to the god, peace to the god, the living soul, conquering his enemies. Thy soul is with me, thine image is near me; the king brought to thee thy statue, which lives upon the presentation of the royal offerings. I am pure." The toilet of the god then commenced—"he laid his hands on him," he took off the old rouge and his former clothes, all of course with the necessary formulae. He then dressed the god in the robe called the Nems, saying: "Come white dress! come white dress! come white eye of Horus, which proceeds from the town of Nechebt. The gods dress themselves with thee in thy name *Dress*, and the gods adorn themselves with thee in thy name *Adornment*." The priest then dressed the god in the *great dress*, rouged him, and presented him with his insignia: the sceptre, the staff of ruler, and the whip, the bracelets and anklets, as well as the two feathers which he wore on his head, because "he has triumphed over his enemies, and is more splendid than gods or spirits." The god required further a collarette and an amulet, two red, two green, and two white bands; when these had been presented to him the priest might then leave the chapel. Whilst he closed the door, he said four times these words: "Come Thoth, thou who hast freed the eye of Horus from his enemies—let no evil man or evil woman enter this temple. Ptaḥ closes the door and

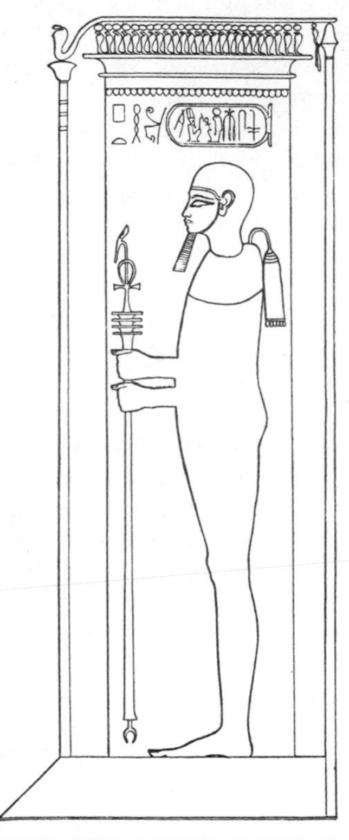

CHAPEL WITH A FIGURE OF PTAḤ OF MEMPHIS, AS HE WAS ADORED AT KARNAK UNDER RAMSES II.

The chapel, as well as the baldachin which encloses it, are adorned with uraei (After L.D., iii. 147 b.)

Thoth makes it fast, closed and fastened with the bolt." So much for the ceremonies regarding the dress of the god; the directions were just as precise concerning the purification and incensing of the room, and the conduct of the priest when he opened the shrine and "saw the god." According to the Theban rite,[1] for instance, as soon as he saw the image of the god he had to "kiss the ground, throw himself on his face, throw himself entirely on his face, kiss the ground with his face turned downwards, offer incense," and then greet the god with a short psalm.

The image of the god spoken of above must have always been very small. In the Holy of Holies was a shrine, the so-called *naos*, inside which was a richly-adorned little bark (see the accompanying illustration), containing the figure of the god.[2] The statue could therefore have been only about two feet high; it probably resembled the little bronze figures of which we possess such a number. We know no more, for this sacred image of the god was so strictly guarded from profane eyes that as far as is known it is never once represented in the temple reliefs.[3] Even the pictures of the Holy of Holies show only the divine bark, adorned fore and aft with the head of the animal sacred to the god, and manned with a crew of small bronze figures of kings and gods; in the centre is the little deck cabin like a little temple, which for further protection is covered with a canopy of some stuff material.[4] This bark was carried round in procession on great festivals, and to the outside world it was itself the image of the god. There is really nothing very remarkable in this circumstance, for in the worship of other nations also, the shrine or the processional carriage of the god, which alone is seen by the people, stands at last to them for the figure of the god itself. It is however characteristic of Egypt that a boat should play this part in that country. The Egyptian idea of travelling was always by Nile boat; the god also would therefore, according to their views, require a Nile boat to go from place to place.

Not only had the priest to dress and serve his god, but he had also to feed him; food and drink had to be placed daily on the table of offerings, and on festival days extra gifts were due. In other countries these offerings have been generally maintained by the gifts of pious individuals, and in Egypt also this was probably originally the case; but, as we have said before, under the New Empire especially the state stepped into the place of the people, and if private individuals brought offerings, these were quite insignificant in comparison with the great endowments made by the kings.

We have much information as to the extent and the kind of offerings; on the outer wall of the great temple of Medinet Habu there still exist parts of a list of the offerings instituted by Ramses II. and Ramses III. for this sanctuary, which was erected by them. These may have been

[1] Lemm, Ritual Book, p. 29 ff. 47.

[2] Cp. e.g. Mar. Ab., i. 32 of the plates.

[3] Except perhaps the pictures of quite late date in the secret passages at Denderah.

[4] We see plainly in many pictures that the canopy is of some material, for we can see the strings with which it is tied together below.

SACRED BARK OF AMON RÊ‘, OF THE TIME OF THOTHMES II., AT KARNAK.

richer than those of earlier temples, though they would certainly not equal those of Karnak and Luxor. If we leave on one side the less important items, such as honey, flowers, incense, etc., and consider simply the various meats, drinks, and loaves of bread placed on the tables of offerings, we shall find as follows: every day of the year the temple received about 3220 loaves of bread, 24 cakes, 144 jugs of beer, 32 geese, and several jars of wine.[1] In addition to this revenue, which was doubtless chiefly used for the maintenance of the priests and the temple servants, special endowments were established for special days. There were extra offerings for the eight festivals which recurred every month. On the second, fourth, tenth, fifteenth, twenty-ninth, and thirtieth days of each month, 83 loaves, 15 jugs of beer, 6 birds, and 1 jar of wine were brought into the temple; while on the new moon and on the sixth day of the month the offerings amounted to 356 loaves, 14 cakes, 34 jugs of beer, 1 ox, 16 birds, 23 jars of wine.[2] Still more important were the offerings on great festival days, of which there was no lack in the ecclesiastical year of ancient Egypt. Thus, for instance, a feast of ten days was solemnised in the last decade of the month Choiakh to the Memphite god Ptaḥ-Sokaris-Osiris; the temple of Medinet Habu took part in this festival. If we again pass over the unessential items, the following list of offerings shows us the royal endowment for these festival days:[3]

Choiakh.	Loaves of Bread of various kinds.	Cakes.	Jugs of Beer.	Oxen and other Cattle.	Geese and other Birds.	Jars of Wine.
21	145	30	15	—	4	2
22	310	10+x	24	—	6	—
23	298	50	110	?	?	?
24	258	40	168	3	—	2
25	1237	50	30	1 (?)	5	2
26	3694	600	905	5	206	33
27	305	30	51	—	12	3
28	50	—	14	—	5	2
29	385	40	20	—	6	1
30	177	2	?	1	6 (?)	15 (?)

Yet Ptaḥ-Sokaris-Osiris was only a god of the second rank at Medinet Habu; at the great festivals of Amon, the offerings were doubtless far more numerous.

One question forces itself involuntarily upon the reader, what became of all this extra food after it had fulfilled its purpose of lying on the altar before the god? We might think that it would be brought into the provision-house and used gradually for the maintenance of the temple servants and priests; the various amounts of the offerings would then merely prove

[1] Dümichen, Calendar inscriptions, 1-2.

[2] Dümichen, Calendar inscriptions, 3-7; restored and translated by Dümichen. The calendar lists of offerings of Medinet Habu.

[3] Dümichen, Calendar inscriptions, 22-31.

the greater or less importance of the feast. If however we consider lists such as the above, we perceive that the matter is not so simple; for if on the different festival days the number of loaves of bread varies from 50 to 3694, and the jugs of beer from 15 to 905, the birds from 4 to 206, the different degree of sanctity between the individual days could not account for so much variation. The 26th of Choiakh, the feast of Sokaris, was evidently the principal day of the whole festival, but it could not be twenty times more holy than the 30th of Choiakh, the sacred day, when the pillar of Ded was erected. It is much more likely that there was a more practical reason for the choice of these numbers: the food probably supplied different numbers of persons, and these persons were not divine images, but the priests and the laity who took part in the festival. The number of the latter probably varied much on the different festival days; according as the festival was a closed or an open one, the crowd at the feast to consume the offerings would vary in proportion. This would also explain the difference in the quality of the food; at one time the people assisting would belong to the upper classes, and would require roast meat and cake; at another time the lower classes preponderated, and for them loaves of bread would suffice.

The great festivals, of which I have here spoken, were, as far as we know, of very much the same character, the chief feature being a representation of some important event in the history of the god whose day was celebrated. Under the Middle Empire, for instance, on the festival of Osiris of Abydos, the former battles of this god were represented; the "enemies of Osiris were beaten," and this god was then carried in procession to his tomb in Peqer, the cemetery of Abydos, and buried. Afterwards there was a representation of "that day of the great fight," on which "all his enemies" were beaten at the place "Nedyt."[1] The festival of 'Epuat, the god of the dead, celebrated at Siut, must have been very similar; he was also "conducted by a procession to his tomb," which was situate in the necropolis there.[2] Indications of this kind are frequent, especially in the later texts; nevertheless, with our ignorance of the mythology on which these festivals are founded, we are seldom able to understand them. We are aware that such a god *appears* on such a day (*i.e.* is carried round in procession), and resorts to the temple of a god his friend, but we know nothing of the legend which would explain the motive of his visit.

I have already given an illustration (p. 65) depicting the public proceedings on a similar great festival; I will add here the description of another festival, which I found in a Theban tomb.[3] It is the feast of the "erection of the pillar Ded," at the close of the above-mentioned feast of Ptaḥ-Sokaris-Osiris, in the month of Choiakh: this special festival was of the greater importance because it was solemnised on the morning of the royal jubilee. The festivities begin with a sacrifice offered by the king to Osiris, the "lord of eternity," a mummied figure, wearing on his head

[1] Stele 1204, at Berlin, imperfectly published, L. D., ii. 135. [2] Ä. Z., 1882, 164.

[3] Tomb of Cheruf in Assasif, under Amenḥôtep III.

the pillar *Ded*, 𓊽. The Pharaoh then repairs with his suite to the place where, lying on the ground, is the "noble pillar," the erection of which forms the object of the festival. Ropes were placed round it, and the monarch, with the help of the royal relatives and of a priest, draws it up. The queen, "who fills the palace with love," looks on at the sacred proceedings, and her sixteen daughters make music with rattles and with the jingling sistrum, the usual instrument played by women on sacred occasions. Six singers join in a song to celebrate the god, and four priests bring in the usual tables of offerings to place them before the pillar which is now erect.

So far, we can understand the festival; it represents the joyful moment when the dead Osiris awakes to life again, when his backbone, represented in later Egyptian theology by the Ded, stands again erect. The farther ceremonies of this festival however refer to mythological events unknown to us. Four priests, with their fists raised, rush upon four others, who appear to give way, two others strike each other, one standing by says of them, "I seize Horus shining in truth."[1] Then follows a great flogging scene, in which fifteen persons beat each other mercilessly with their sticks and fists; they are divided into several groups, two of which, according to the inscription, represent the people of the town Pe and of the town Dep. This is evidently the representation of a great mythological fight, in which were engaged the inhabitants of Pe and Dep, *i.e.* of the ancient city of Buto, in the north of the Delta. The ceremonies which close the sacred rite are also quite problematic: four herds of oxen and asses are seen driven by their herdsmen; in the accompanying text we are told, "four times they go round the walls on that day when the noble pillar of Ded is erected."

We cannot conceive an Egyptian god without his *house*, the 𓉟, in which he lives, in which his festivals are solemnised, and which he never leaves except on processional days. The site on which it is built is generally *holy ground*,[2] *i.e.* a spot on which, since the memory of man, an older sanctuary of the god had stood. Even those Egyptian temples which seem most modern have usually a long history; the edifice may originally have been very insignificant, but as the prestige of the god increased, larger buildings were erected, which again, in the course of centuries, were enlarged and rebuilt in such a way that the original plan could no longer be traced. This is the history of nearly all Egyptian temples, and explains the fact that we know so little of the temples of the Old and of the Middle Empire; they have all been metamorphosed into the vast buildings of the New Empire.

The oldest form of Egyptian temple is known to us through the

[1] Horus "shining in truth" is one of the names of Amenḥôtep III.

[2] Inscription in the temple of Ramses III. at Karnak.

inscriptions of the ancient Empire; *a* is a temple of the god Set;[1] *b* of a god whose name is not given.[2] Both seem to be hovels of wood and lattice work; over the doors we see a barbaric ornamentation of bent pieces of wood; one temple, like those of later date, is adorned with flag-staves; the entrance appears to be closed by a paling. Such buildings as these are common amongst nations of low civilisation, and the plan of them may go back to those prehistoric ages of which I have spoken above (ch. ii. pp. 34, 35).

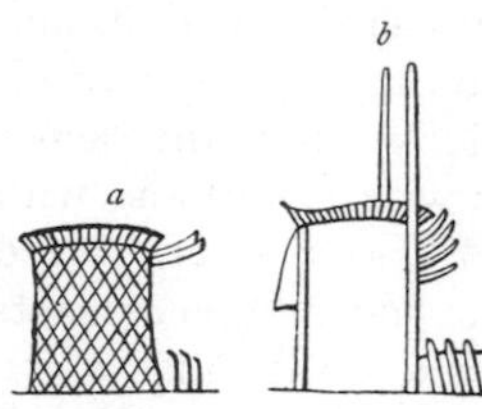

Certain ruins of temples of the time of the Old Empire still exist, viz. the pyramid temples and the splendid though enigmatical building not far from the great Sphinx; these possess the grand features of later architecture. The parts that remain appear to have been merely the substructures; they consist of immense square buildings, constructed partly of costly material, but without ornament or sculpture; the division of the space unfortunately is not certain. On the other hand, the few remains that we have of temples of the Middle Empire are essentially in harmony with the plans of those of the New Empire, and if we may trust the statement of a very late inscription,[3] the same disposition of the various halls which we meet with after the time of the New Empire was customary even in the time of the 6th dynasty. We cannot here enter into a discussion concerning the variations of the plans of the various sanctuaries, which were often due to accidental circumstances; it will suffice to give a description of a typical Egyptian temple.

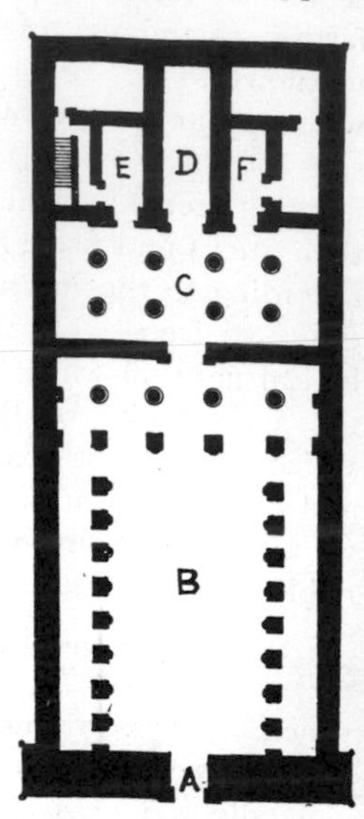

TEMPLE OF AMON RÊ' AT KARNAK, BUILT BY RAMSES III. (A specimen of the usual type of temple.)

A. Pylon, B. Court, C. Hypostyle Hall, D. Chapel of Amon, E. Chapel of Mut, F. Chapel of Chons. Both the latter have side-rooms, one of which contains the staircase leading to the roof.

The approach to the sanctuary was by a paved road, with sphinxes on either side. One or more of the so-called *pylons* stood in front of the temple. These great gates were flanked with two towers, which may originally have actually served as a protection for the entrance; under the New Empire, however, they stood inside the surrounding wall of the sanctuary, and were then purely decorative; their coloured walls and the high flag-staves and obelisks were intended to impress the visitor with the sanctity of the place he was about to enter.

[1] Mar. Mast., 74.

[2] Mar. Mon. div., 18 b.

[3] One inscription tells us that the temple of Denderah, according to its first plan, was built under the 6th dynasty.

THE TEMPLE OF LUXOR. RESTORATION BY GNAUTH, CHIEF COMMISSIONER FOR PUBLIC BUILDINGS.

The smaller building to the side of the temple is supplied hypothetically. On the other side of the river is the "west end of the town," with tombs and funerary temples.

Immediately beyond the pylon was the great court, surrounded by a colonnade of massive pillars. In the further wall of the court was the entrance into the so-called hypostyle hall, a gigantic hall supported by pillars, and lighted by small windows under the roof. The festivals were celebrated in the columned court and the hypostyle hall, but these were not the abode of the god. He dwelt in the central one of the three dark chapels situate behind the hypostyle hall; here was kept the divine bark with the image of the god; the two adjoining rooms belonged as a rule to his consort and to his son. These three chapels were the most holy parts of the temple; "he who enters must purify himself four times," was written close to the doors of these chapels.[1] Often, as at Karnak and Luxor, the Holy of Holies had a second entrance at the back, and behind it were all kinds of rooms serving as storerooms for temple provisions, etc.

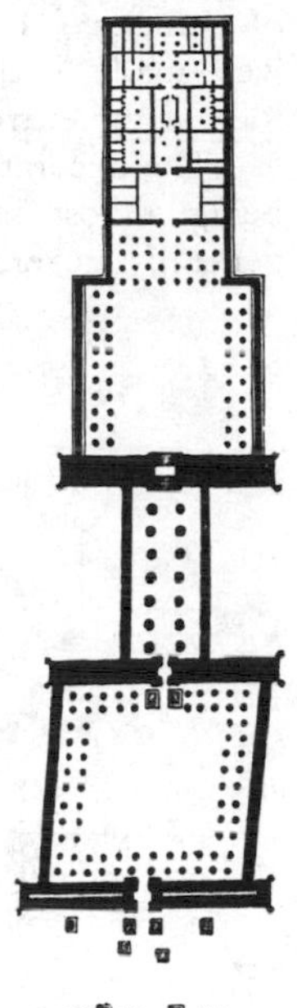

GROUND-PLAN OF THE TEMPLE OF LUXOR. (After Perrot-Chipiez.)

The above description may be considered as the general plan of all the larger temples; smaller temples were content with fewer rooms,—thus the pretty little temple erected by Thothmes III. at Medinet Habu consisted of but one hall, supported by pillars and columns, shut in on the outer side by a screen of intercolumnar slabs. In the centre was the sanctuary of Amon; at the further end were three chambers dedicated to Amon, Mut, and Chons. These few rooms might well suffice for the temple of a suburb of the capital.

The fact that the plans of the temples seem to us most complicated arises from the circumstance that they were not built from one design. Temples such as Luxor, or more particularly Karnak, owe the development of their plan to the many hands which have worked at them. Each king, fired with ambition to build, designed some new addition to the temple of the Theban Amon; he wished his plan to surpass if possible any previous project, but it was granted to few to complete the work they had designed. Thothmes I. erected his pylon at Karnak, and thought thus to have completed the façade for ever; he also began but never finished those splendid buildings intended to meet this façade, and to unite that great temple with the temple of Mut. Amenḥôtep III. spoilt this plan by adding another pylon in front, and the kings of the 19th dynasty went so far as to place their gigantic hypostyle hall before this latter pylon, so that the façade of the 18th dynasty was left in the very centre of the temple; a new pylon (the fourth), greater than any other, formed the entrance. Incredible as it may appear, the temple was not yet complete; when

[1] E.g. in the temple of Ramses III. at Karnak, the regular simple plan of which answers exactly to the description here given.

Ramses III. built his little temple to the Theban gods, he placed it in part closely in front of the façade of the great temple. Afterwards, the Libyan princes felt it their duty to build an immense hall of pillars in front again, which curiously enough happened exactly to cross the temple of Ramses III. If we consider that at the same time similar additions were made to the back of the temple and to the interior, we gain a little idea of the extreme confusion of the whole.

The decoration of the temple corresponded with its sacred character, being almost throughout purely religious. The walls and pillars were generally covered from top to bottom with representations of the gods;

THE GOD SET TEACHES THE KING THOTHMES III. TO SHOOT WITH THE BOW (Karnak, L. D., iii. 36 b).

the brilliant colouring brightening the broad spaces in the building. These pictures were little more than pure decoration, and their monotony is almost incredible. We see the king standing in a stiff posture, dressed in a costume of ancient date, with the great divinities of the temple. The principal god holds the sign of life ☥ to his nose; the goddess blesses him, laying her hand on his shoulder; the third and youthful god looks on, and Thoth the scribe of the gods marks down the "millions of years," which these divinities bestow upon the Pharaoh.[1] The following scenes also constantly occur: two gods embrace the monarch, or a goddess gives him her breast;[2] Horus and Set, the gods of war, teach him to shoot with bow and arrow;[3] or the monarch stands in supplication before several gods seated on their thrones in two columns one

[1] L. D., iii. 15, and frequently. [2] L. D., iii. 35 b, and frequently.
[3] L. D., iii. 36 b, and frequently.

over the other, all being exactly alike;[1] or these divine puppets themselves approach the Pharaoh in two long rows, in order to express their thanks to him for this "beautiful monument."[2] That these reliefs were purely decorative and served no other purpose than to enliven with their colour the large blank spaces of walls and pillars, we see by the fact that they are repeated on the corresponding parts of the architecture, where they are all turned in the opposite direction for the sake of symmetry.

KING RAMSES II. RECEIVES FROM AMON RÊ', "THE LORD OF KARNAK," WHO IS SEATED IN A CHAPEL, THE SIGN OF THE NUMBERLESS FESTIVALS WHICH HE SHOULD YET LIVE TO SEE;

The god says: "My beloved son of my body, lord of the two countries, *User-ma' Rê'*, chosen of Rê', I give thee the two countries in peace, I give thee millions of festivals in life, duration, and purity." Mut, the consort of Amon, "the lady of heaven and the ruler of the gods," says: "I place the diadem of Rê' on thy head, and give thee years of festivals, whilst all the barbarians lie beneath thy feet." The moon-god Chons, the child of the two gods, says: "I give thee thy strength."

The same may be said of numberless inscriptions of the temples; their contents are quite secondary to their decorative purpose. The god assures the king over and over again in these words,[3] "I give thee years of eternity and the joyful government over the two countries. So long as I exist, so long shalt thou exist on earth, shining as King of Upper Egypt and King of Lower Egypt on the throne of the living. As long as heaven endures thy name shall endure, and shall grow eternally, as a reward for this beautiful, great, pure, strong, excellent memorial that thou hast erected to me. Thou hast accomplished it, thou ever-living one."

[1] L. D., iii. 36 c, d, and frequently.

[2] L. D., iii. 37 b, and frequently.

[3] L. D., 45 a, and many other instances.

In other places the god says, "I bestow upon thee life, duration, purity," or, "I bestow upon thee the everlasting life of Rê' and his years, as monarch of the two countries; the black and the red land lie beneath thy throne, as they lie daily beneath that of Rê'.[1] Or, again, "My son, whom I love, my heart rejoices when I see thy beauty; thou hast renewed for me once more my divine house, as the horizon of the sky. For this reason I give to thee the eternal life of Rê' and the years of Atum."[2]

When we have read these interesting assurances, *mutatis mutandis*, some dozen times in one temple, we may perhaps be encouraged by finding the god speaking to the king as follows: "Welcome, thou good god; I place thy victory over every nation, and the fear of thee in the hearts of the nine nations of the bow. Their great ones come as *one* man to thee with their backs laden. I place the fear of thee in the two countries, and the nine nations of the bow shall bow when thou dost call."[3] But if we think to have found a new thought, we shall be disappointed when we read on the next wall, "Son of my body, whom I love, thou lord of power over all the countries! The people of the Nubian Troglodytes lie slain beneath thy feet. I allow the princes of the southern countries to come to thee, bringing their tribute and their children on their backs and all the beautiful gifts of the south. Their lives are in thy hand, they live or die as thou pleasest."[4] Or, again, "Welcome! Thou hast captured what thou didst desire, and hast slain those who crossed thy border. My sword is with me, it falls upon the countries; thou dost cut off the heads of the Asiatics. I allow thy power to be great, and subject each country to thee, that they may see how strong is thy majesty, like to my son when he is angry."[5]

It must strike every one that all these representations and inscriptions are compiled more to the honour of the kings than to that of the gods. The exaggerated loyalty that leads to this abuse of the inscriptions is found also, in a curious way, in the appellations of the various temples, which were dictated by the same spirit. The ancient names of the great temples, as Opet, for the Theban temple of Amon, 'Esher, for the temple of Mut, etc., were after a time replaced by names which identify the temple with the name of the reigning king. The most ancient example of this custom is found under the Middle Empire; the temple of Sobk, in Shedt, the capital of the Feyum, under Amenemḥê't III., is designated as, "that Amenemḥê't may live for ever in the house of Sobk of Shedt."[6] Under the New Empire the formula would run somewhat otherwise, "the temple of the millions of years of Amenemḥê't, in the house of Sobk."[7] The sense is the same in each case; the temple is a building which is indissolubly connected with the memory of that monarch who had rendered it the greatest services.[8] Thus also, for instance, under

[1] L. D., iii. 119 g. [2] L. D., iii. 125 a. [3] L. D., iii. 127 b.
[4] L. D., iii. 210 a. [5] L. D., iii. 211. [6] L. D., ii. 138 e.
[7] In Egyptian there are two different words for *house*, the *ḥt* of the king and the *pr* of the god.
[8] This is the most simple explanation; otherwise we might think that the king was worshipped in each temple, and that they wished to emphasise this fact.

Ramses III., the temple of Amon is called "the temple of Ramses III. in the house of Amon"; that of Rê', "the temple of Ramses III. in the house of Rê'"; that of Ptaḥ, "the temple of Ramses III. in the house of Ptaḥ," and so on. These names were only appropriate of course in those cases, where a king had actually built or richly endowed the temple; nevertheless they were applied indiscriminately to all temples and all monarchs; and when we find that under Sety II. the temple of Amon in the town of Ramses is called "the temple of the millions of years of King Sety II. in the house of Amon,[1] it does not follow from this alone that that king had rendered it any special services.

The property of the god, his *house*, ▭ (*i.e.* his estates), and his herds bear similar names; the latter are also called the "house (or the herd) of Ramses III. in the house of Amon," as if the reigning king had bestowed them all upon the god.

The great gods however possessed several temples, houses, and herds, and it was necessary to distinguish them from each other by slight variations in the common name. For this purpose the monarch was designated in one case by his throne name, in another by his family name, "the temple of Userma'rê' Mi-Amun in the house of Amon," is different from the "temple of Ramses ḥeq On in the house of Amon," though both are names of the same king. They also distinguished the temples by adding some epithet; thus the temple of the sun at Heliopolis was called the "temple of Ramses ḥeq On in the house of Rê'," and the later temple, at Tell el Yehudeh, north of Heliopolis, the "temple of Ramses ḥeq On in the house of Rê' built for millions of years."[2] The choice of these names was not accidental, they were of course officially conferred by the king.

We cannot take leave of this subject without casting a glance upon the buildings belonging to the temple, the storehouses, the dwellings for the priests, etc. They were situate in the so-called temple circuit, *i.e.* inside those great walls which enclosed a wide circle round the temple, and which can still be traced in many of the ruins. The dimensions of these temple enclosures may be judged from the fact that that of southern Karnak comprised about twelve acres, and that of middle Karnak, probably, fifty-seven. Even if these were of unusual size, they show us that each of the great temples, with its additional buildings, courts, and gardens, occupied quite a town quarter. The buildings comprising this sacred quarter were constructed, for the most part, of brick, and therefore have mainly disappeared;[3] and we should not therefore be in a position to form a picture of the temple surroundings did not the representations in the tombs come to our assistance. It is again the tombs of Tell el Amarna which have preserved this record for us.

When King Chuen'eten left the residence of his fathers and founded the town of the "Horizon of the Sun," in Middle Egypt, for himself and

[1] An., 4, 7, 1.

[2] The Harris I. papyrus is full of similar examples, which can be easily studied in Piehl's Index.

[3] Close to the Ramesseum the vaulted storerooms are still in existence.

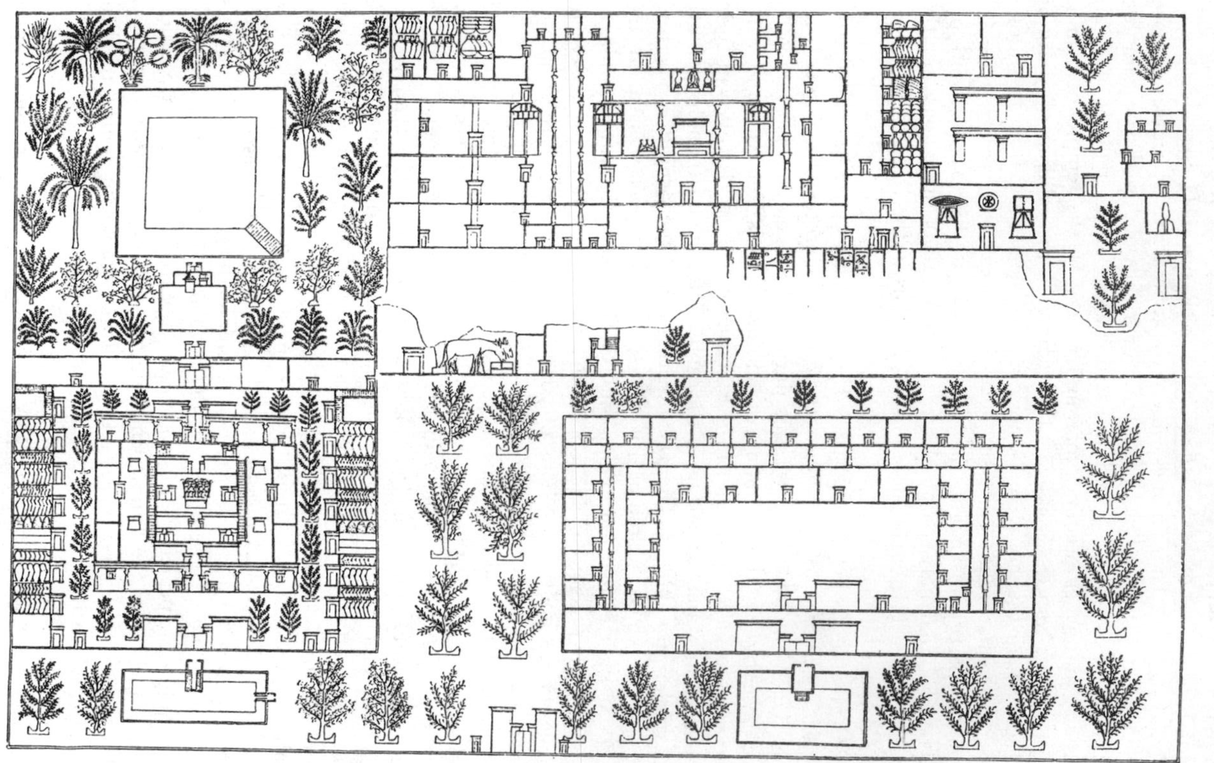

THE ADJOINING BUILDINGS OF THE TEMPLE OF THE SUN-DISK
(From the tomb of Meryrê', at Tell el Amarna. L. D., iii. 95.)

his god, he took care that there should be splendid temple-buildings in his new city, and one of his faithful courtiers, the high priest Meryrê', has, in the pictures of his tomb, transmitted to posterity the story of their grandeur. They are interesting enough to reward particular attention, the more so as they elucidate much that has already been described.

The temple is in general built after the usual plan of the great temples, though there are certain curious details in the architecture.[1] Passing through the immense pylon adorned with flag-staves, we enter a large court in the middle of which stands the great altar of the god, which is reached only by a flight of steps; the altar is richly laden with slaughtered oxen and geese and decked with flowers. In order to show that this court is open to all worshippers, it is not closed by thick walls, but by a chain of structures with portals. The doors of the latter stand open, except at the back part of the court, where there is a wall to separate it from the fore part.

Three smaller chambers lie behind the central one; the hypostyle hall is noteworthy, it is supported by sixteen large pillars. Six small buildings standing in this central part of the temple may perhaps have served as storerooms. The termination of the whole building is formed by two grand halls or courts against which sixteen rooms are built, which evidently constitute the special places for worship. In the middle of each hall stands a great altar.

Close behind this great temple stands a second smaller one, consisting of a great hall surrounded by smaller rooms, in front of which there is a hypostyle hall with rows of pillars and statues of the king, as well as a small court.

Passing from the "House of the Sun" proper, we come to the adjoining buildings. The large temple is surrounded on all sides by a small court, which has one entrance only. No one could reach the temple without passing through this gate, and this entrance was guarded in a military manner, for two houses close by in the court were evidently inhabited by watchmen. To the left of the great gate a wall divides off a corner of the court,—here the animals for the sacrifices were killed. Possibly the more refined contemporaries of Chuen'eten found less enjoyment in the slaughtering of animals than their ancestors of the time of Chufu, who seem to have represented that subject with particular pleasure.

The little temple behind is also surrounded by a court; here also there is the walled-off slaughter-yard to the left of the entrance. In the rear is a small building which served as a kitchen, and a larger one, probably the bakery, for in it people seem to be kneading dough. Thus we see that the space in the court to the left of the temple was devoted to household offices; I cannot tell for what purposes that on the right-hand

[1] The anterior temple, L. D., iii. 96 c, the posterior, ib. 96 a; both are shown in the picture, L. D., iii. 94. It is instructive to compare the two representations; we see the freedom with which the Egyptian painter treated detail. The remarkable picture, L. D., iii. 102, possibly represents also the smaller posterior temple, though the variations are indeed very great.

side was used; perhaps for worship, for we see there a seated group of singers, who are devoutly singing their hymns accompanied by the harp.

It appears that the large piece of ground at the back of the smaller temple was taken up with the dwellings of the priests and servants, as well as by the granary and the treasury belonging to the temple; our illustration gives a tolerably clear idea of these buildings.[1]

The piece of ground which appears to have been connected with the temple by a side-door is surrounded by a wall into which admission can only be gained by one gateway. The space between the buildings is laid out as a garden and planted with trees, each trunk is surrounded by a little heap of earth; there are also two tanks to facilitate the watering of the young plants.

The great building to the right of the entrance consists of thirty-seven rooms, which are arranged in two rows round a rectangular court; a colonnade between these rows forms a corridor for the rooms behind; there is another small court in front of the house. This building may have contained the offices for the management of the temple property, or the dwellings for the servants.

Beyond, there lies another building, far larger and grander than the one described above. A large hall supported by two rows of columns, and a parallel smaller hall with one row, appear to serve as courts; between them and round them is a complicated series of halls, rooms, and storerooms. We are probably right in regarding the principal building, surrounded by courts and stabling, as the dwelling-house of the priest.

To the left, on the smaller part of the piece of ground, is the provision-house. On each side of a court, well guarded by gates and walls, lie eight chambers filled with all manner of gigantic jars; from the hindermost chamber a staircase leads to a story above, the low rooms of which are seen in our illustration. These rooms are the temple storerooms; the curious building in the middle of the provision-house may be the treasury. In the court of the provision-house is a second similar building with stately doors and adorned with rows of pillars; in the court of the latter building, separated from the outer world by threefold walls, we find the central point of the whole plan, a square building with four closed doors. The roof of this edifice is arranged as a kind of temple and provided with an altar on which thank-offerings may be offered to the god out of the fulness of his gifts. Steps outside lead up to this altar on the roof.

Finally, behind the storehouses, protected from idle visitors by walls and closed gates, is a garden or grove with a large tank in the centre. We do not know whether this artificial lake with its flight of steps leading down to the water was merely for the refreshment of the priests, or served, as at Karnak for instance, for certain ceremonies at the festivals. It is

[1] After the remarkable picture, L. D., iii. 95, which has been explained in several ways; e.g. Perrot and Maspero consider the storehouse to have been a palace. The above explanation appears to me to be tolerably certain, but its position with regard to the temple is uncertain.

also uncertain whether the small building on the bank was for pleasure or for more serious purposes.

As centuries elapsed the ruling idea in Egyptian life became more and more religious, and at the same time also the servants of religion gradually attained that high position which to us appears unnatural. The history of the growth of priestly influence is one of the most interesting studies in Egyptology, but it is beset with very many difficulties, and the following sketch of this history must therefore be accepted with all caution. Before however we approach this dangerous topic, it will be as well to explain the meaning of those priestly titles which most frequently occur.

We will first consider the dignity of *Ue'b.* The writing of the name [hieroglyphs] shows that the duty of this priest was to pour out the drink-offering. The signification of the word points to another of his functions. Ue'b signifies *pure*, and in fact under the Old Empire this priest, the Ue'b or the "prophet and Ue'b," or the "superintendent of the Ue'bs of the Pharaoh," had to examine into the purity of the sacrificial animals; it was only when *he* had smelt the blood and declared it *pure*, that the pieces of flesh might be laid on the table of offerings.[1] The word Ue'b serves also as a general term for priest.

More important perhaps than the Ue'b was the *Cherḥeb*, [hieroglyphs], the *reciter-priest*.[2] His duty was to recite from the holy books, and as, according to Egyptian faith, magical power lay hidden in these old religious texts, the people believed, at any rate under the New Empire, that the Cherḥeb was a magician. This power was especially ascribed to the "first reciter-priest" of the king.[3]

The largest class of the priesthood however were the [hieroglyphs], *servants of the god*, the ecclesiastics whom, after Greek custom, we usually call prophets.[4] The latter appellation has become so customary that I have retained it in this book, and when I use this most inappropriate term, I must ask my readers, once for all, not to think of the Hebrew prophets, those religious leaders who stood in conscious opposition to the priesthood. Still less did these Egyptian prophets *prophesy*; the term *prophet* is here only another word for priest.

The above three titles and several other similar but less frequent ones, were in use from the oldest to the latest period, but it would be a mistake always to attribute the same significance to them. On the contrary, the status of the clergy, and in consequence the ideas connected with these appellations, varied; a prophet of the time of Ramses II. would

[1] L. D., ii. 68; Düm. Res., xi., and another representation from the same tomb.

[2] Literally, "he with the book." Cp. Br. Wb. Suppl., 804.

[3] Pap. Westcar, passim, as to the "first reciter-priest" under the O. E.: cp. above, p. 90.

[4] Why the Greeks called them thus we know not.

occupy a very different position from that occupied by a prophet of the time of Chufu.

It cannot be accidental that under the Old Empire, when religion was not so important a factor in the life of the people as during the later epochs, the religious administration was far more the common property of the people than it ever afterwards became. Almost every man of rank under the Old Empire held, in addition to his secular calling, one or more priestly appointments, and the women devoted themselves to the service of the temple as much as the men. The dignity of the priesthood was in part the privilege of those who held state appointments; thus, the judges were generally priests of the goddess of truth,[1] whilst the "great men of the south" served as a rule the goddess Ḥeqt.[2] Usually also priestly offices were hereditary in individual families of rank, the members of which served the god of their home even when living at court, far from the town of their fathers.[3] High officials undertook also the duties of other priestly offices in order to show their loyalty. Thus, the pious kings of the fifth dynasty founded a number of places of worship to the sun-god; and their courtiers, therefore, gave special preference to the service of the god of these new sanctuaries.[4] It was also a matter of course that men of high rank should adore the reigning Pharaoh or one of his ancestors.[5] Women also, as I said before, took their part in these various cults;[6] as a rule however they served the two goddesses, Neit and Ḥatḥôr.[7]

Whilst most of the priestly offices were vested in private individuals holding additional appointments, there were others requiring continual service in the temple, which had of course to be served by ecclesiastics proper; these were, on the one hand, the lowest,[8] and, on the other hand, the highest offices. The high priests of the great sanctuaries held a peculiar position which is still recognisable by their titles. They are not called "superintendents of the prophets," or "first prophets," or "great priests," as are the chiefs of the temple officials of lower rank, but they bear titles which characterise them as quite peculiar personages, I might almost say as personages quite outside the ordinary priesthood. The high priest of Heliopolis[9] is called "he who is great in regarding," he bears also the additional titles, "He who sees the secret of heaven," and "Chief of the secrets of heaven," as if he were the chief astronomer; his colleague

[1] R. J. H., 81, 87; Mar. Mast., 165, 218, 229, etc.

[2] Cp. above, p. 82.

[3] Cp. e.g. the priestly titles of the father, Mar. Mast., 198, 199, with those of the son, ib. 200.

[4] Mar. Mast., 112, 199, 200, 233, 243, 248, 250, 259, etc.

[5] I do not here refer to the funerary worship of the kings ("priest of the pyramids") which I shall speak of in the following chapter, but to the worship of the king himself, which appears to have been a separate matter ("prophet of the king"), as Mar. Mast., 89, 92, 198, 200, 217, 243, 248, 259, etc. Here belongs also the "prophet of the Horus, who is in the palace," ib. 228.

[6] Prophetess of Thoth, Mar. Mast., 183; of 'Epuat, ib. 162; of the king, ib. 90.

[7] Prophetess of Neit, ib. 90, 162, 201, 262, etc., of Ḥatḥôr, ib. 90, 107, 162, 201, etc.

[8] An official therefore is rarely ue'b of a god (Mar. Mast., 295), but always prophet.

[9] Mar. Mon. div., 18; Mar. Mast., 149. Perhaps also Mar. Mast., 140.

of Memphis however,[1] who served the Egyptian Hephaistos, the "Ptaḥ who creates works of art,"[2] is styled the "Chief leader of artists," as if the temple were the workshop of the god, and he his chief assistant.[3] Similar titles were doubtless borne by the high priests of all the greater temples, though we cannot always identify them under the Old Empire.[4]

Under the Old Empire, as well as to a certain degree under the Middle Empire, the laity took an active share in public worship. In the temples of the jackal-headed gods 'Epuat and Anubis at Siut, we find at this time, besides the official priesthood, an "hour priesthood,"[5] *i.e.* a brotherhood of pious laymen, who seem to have delegated one of their number every month to the service of their god,[6] whilst they, as a body, took part in the processions on great festival days.[7] They had no share in the temple property or revenues,[8] and if the citizens of Siut gave them a present from the first fruits of their fields, the gift was dictated purely by private piety.[9]

The same arrangement was in existence at the great temple of Osiris at Abydos, where, besides the five appointed priests, there were many prophets;[10] these formed the "hour priesthood."[11] Though, as under the Old Empire, these laymen might take part in the temple worship, yet, apparently, they had already forfeited much of the original dignity of their position in the temple. There is not one of the higher officials of the Middle Empire whose tomb remains to us (and their number is legion), who has thought it worth while to tell posterity that he had been a prophet in this or that temple. Indeed, had we not expressly learned of the existence of the hour priesthood from the above-mentioned inscription, we should have concluded, from the study of the other material we possess, that the lay element had already been as jealously excluded from the temple worship as it was afterwards under the New Empire.

The great nobles, the nome princes, form an exception to this rule; they state expressly in the long list of their antique titles that they served as priests the god of their nome.[12] It was also customary in these families that the women should dedicate themselves as priestesses to the goddess Ḥathôr.[13]

The priesthood proper of a god, in contradistinction to the hour priesthood, his "officials,"[14] *qnbt*, formed a small col-

[1] Mar. Mast., 74 ff., 112 ff., 123, 157; R. J. H., 93-95. [2] Stele of Kuban, l. 19.

[3] He works, in fact, with his artists for the king; cp. Mar. Mast., 204, 205.

[4] The possession and use of a high priestly title, such as the above, was a proof of the ancient dignity of a temple; the fact that the Theban Amon had originally only a "first prophet" shows the late date at which this god rose to importance.

[5] Cp. Ä. Z., 1882, 163; Brugsch, Dic. Suppl., 318, has recognised the meaning of the word.

[6] Ä. Z., 1882, 180.

[7] In the contracts at Siut their presence in the temple at certain festivals seems to have been an understood thing, e.g. ib., 167. [8] Ib., 163. [9] Ib., 169, 180.

[10] Mar. Cat. d'Ab., 711. [11] A similar priesthood is mentioned, Louvre, C. 12 (L. A.).

[12] Thus at Beni Hasan: L. D., ii. 121, 143 g; at Bersheh: ib. 134 c, 135 a-d.; at Siut: R. J. H., 285, 286, 290; Mar. Mon. div., 68 a.

[13] L. D., ii. 143 g; R. J. H., 293. [14] Ä. Z., 1882, 163.

legiate assembly at each temple, membership being hereditary from father to son.[1] The prince of each respective nome officiated as chief, and always bore the title of "superintendent of the prophets." At the same time the superintendence exercised by the prince was often only nominal, for many princes state expressly that they have *really* exercised this office.[2] It was also not sufficient in itself to be the son of a nomarch and high priest in order to succeed to the priestly office of the father; for though the priestly rank may have been hereditary, yet the distinct degree of rank was certainly not so,[3] at the same time we may be sure that neither the Pharaoh nor the priests themselves would lightly pass over the richest and most distinguished member of the college in the choice of their chief.

It sometimes happened that a prince, in whose town several temples were situate, belonged at the same time to the priesthood of these various temples.[4] He also frequently held several appointments in the same temple; for instance, he might be at the same time "Superintendent of the prophets," "Superintendent of the temple," and "Superintendent of the oxen of the god."[5]

The *official staff* of a temple consisted, as we have said before, of comparatively few persons, at Siut for instance of ten;[6] at Abydos, as it appears, of only five priests.[7] Each of these had his own special title; thus the collegiate assembly of the Osiris of Abydos was composed of

"The great Ue'b," *i.e.* the high priest,[8]
The treasurer of the god,
The scribe of the god's house,
The reciter-priest,
The *Mete-en-sa.*"

At the temple of 'Epuat at Siut however, as well as in other places, we find a "Superintendent of the storehouse"; a "Superintendent of the house of worship"; a "Scribe of the house of the god"; a "Scribe of the altar," and others. We see that these titles are generally derived from the business duties which the priests exercised in the administration of the temple property, but it would be a mistake to suppose that they were merely administrative officials of the sanctuary. On the contrary, they are priests *par excellence*: "I am the son of a priest like each of you," said Ḥapd'efan'e, the nomarch of Siut, to the priests, in order to demonstrate unquestionably his priestly rank.[9]

This close connection of the *official staff* to the temple is also borne out by the fact that the members enjoyed certain claims on the revenues of the god. The worth of the natural products that *comes out* to them

[1] Ä. Z., 1882, 171, where in the translation of l. 28, ~~we~~ ought to read "son of a priest." Also 171, 176, 178, where the priesthood is expressly stated to be inherited from the father.

[2] Mar. Mon. div., 68 c; R. J. H., 284.

[3] Ä. Z., 1882, 162 note.

[4] Mar. Mon. div., 68 a. L. D., ii. 142 c.

[5] Thus Mar. Cat. d'Ab., 637. Similarly L. D., ii. 121, and frequently.

[6] Ä. Z., 1882, 173.

[7] Mar. Cat. d'Ab., 711.

[8] That this title was given to the "Superintendent of the prophets" of Abydos is attested by Mar. Cat. d'Ab., 742, and Leyden, v. 4.

[9] Ä. Z., 1882, 171.

(to retain an Egyptian expression), is certainly not much, if we may judge by what they received in the temple of Siut. In the latter temple, the yearly salary[1] of each member of the staff was valued at about 360 jugs of beer, 900 loaves of white bread, and 36,000 ash-baked cakes of little worth; this came to such an insignificant sum that the recipient might sell it for one daily lamp-wick, such as were used in funerary worship. In fact, a high priest of Siut thought nothing of renouncing the rations due to himself and his heirs for twenty-seven days in each year, *i.e.* sacrificing a twelfth part of his priestly income in exchange for some very trifling benefits for his funerary festivals.[2]

We may conclude, judging from the small stipends allowed to the priests of so considerable a town as the ancient Siut, that, even under the Middle Empire, the part played by the priests was of little importance. The great rise of the priesthood to be the most important factor in the kingdom dates from the complete revolution of ancient conditions which took place under the 18th dynasty. I have already (p. 105) shown that the evidence of this rise of the priesthood is especially found in one place in Egypt. In the cemetery at Abydos, where, under the Middle Empire, very few priests or temple officials were interred, we find that, without exaggeration, 25 per cent of those buried there under the New Empire belonged to the priestly class; moreover if the latter held a state appointment in addition, it was evidently considered as secondary to their position in the temple.[3]

The ruling part played by the priesthood under the New Empire necessarily brought about a great modification in the constitution of that body. The position of the priesthood, in fact, changed essentially, though not equally so in all the temples. The old conditions were retained longer in the smaller country sanctuaries, and in the large ancient temples, than in those temples of the new capital which rapidly rose to importance and did not possess old traditions.[4]

It is not the place here to investigate the various differences between the priests of the individual temples under the New Empire. It is sufficient for our purpose to consider the circumstances of those ecclesiastics who took precedence in the country, and of whom we have most knowledge.

We know very little of the priests of Amon of old times,[5] but under the New Empire there were five degrees of rank amongst the officials of that god;[6] the first, second, and third prophets, the divine father, and the

[1] Ä. Z., 1882, 172.

[2] Ä. Z., 1882, 171, 176, 178.

[3] Examples of these double appointments are found: firstly, in the case of high priests (L. D., iii. 237, a. b., Mar. Cat. d'Ab., 408); secondly, in the case of a few others who superintend the temple estates (Lieblein, 187, 666, 904; L. D., iii. 26, 1 d).

[4] We may specify here that the hour priesthood mentioned at Abydos under the 18th dynasty (R. J. H., 21, 14), we only meet with in other places at a later period. It is a matter of course that a title such as that of the high priest of Memphis remained unchanged.

[5] Under the Middle Empire, a *second prophet* is mentioned (Mar. Cat. d'Ab., 389), also a Ue'b (ib. 745), and a *ḥri sgr* (ib. 393) of Amon.

[6] Expressly mentioned on the statue of Bekenchôns. Cp. also the account in the Pap. Berl., 47 (Ä. Z., 1879, 72).

Ue'b; the latter also officiated in his temple as reciter-priest.[1] The age at which a priest, if he were fortunate, might attain to these various degrees of rank, is shown by the biography of the high priest Bekenchôns, who served and died under Ramses II.[2] From his fifth to his fifteenth year he received a military education in one of the royal stables; at the age of sixteen he entered the service of Amon as Ue'b. He held this inferior rank till the age of twenty, after which he officiated as *divine father* for twelve years. When he was thirty-two he entered the order of prophets; for fifteen years he served as third, and for twelve years as second prophet. Finally, in his fifty-ninth year, the monarch raised him to be "first prophet of Amon and chief of the prophets of all the gods." Every one was not so fortunate, for many a rich and distinguished Egyptian died as Ue'b, or as "divine father," without attaining any higher rank.[3] It does not seem to have been possible to dispense with serving in the lower ranks, for even the highest ecclesiastics note them down in their list of titles,[4] and the sons of the high priests begin their career as Ue'b.[5]

It follows that individual priestly dignities were not hereditary, and it is to be regarded merely as nepotism when we frequently find the son succeeding his father in his office of first prophet.[6] The priesthood itself was also no longer as a rule hereditary, for we find sons of priests as superintendent officials, and sons of officials as priests.[7] The members of one and the same family also often served different gods,[8] showing that the priesthood was regarded as any other profession, in which it was of the first importance to gain a good livelihood, irrespective of any particular temple.

We do not know what were the respective functions of the various priests of Amon, we only know that amongst other duties the second prophet had the superintendence of the artists of the temple.[9] The high priest however, the "first prophet, was a good father to his subordinates, he educated their youth, he stretched out his hand to those on the road to ruin, he maintained the life of those in need,"[10] but the first duty of the high priest, who lived under these great royal builders, was to direct the buildings for the enlargement of the temple. He had to

[1] Both titles expressly connected in the tomb of Paser (Sheikh Abd-elqurna, Dyn. 19; from my own copy), in the case of his second son. Cp. also Lieblein, 606 (ue'b and χ rḥb), where similar lists of titles (L. D., iii. 200 a, 237 e) only mention the ue'b.

[2] On his statue in the Glyptothek at Munich.

[3] E.g. the divine father Nefrḥotp, whose beautiful tomb is at Sheikh Abd-elqurna; the tomb of 'Ey, who became king when holding and retaining that rank, and others.

[4] Thus the high priest, L. D., iii. 237 c (Liebl., 559), and the second prophet (Liebl., 606).

[5] Thus the high priest just mentioned, Rome, son of Roy (L. D., iii. 237 c).

[6] In addition to those mentioned in the above note, Amenḥôtep, ib. l. l. e. Also the two, L. D., iii. 62 b.

[7] The governor, Paser, mentioned in a preceding note, was for instance the son of a first prophet, and a son of Paser again became Ue'b.

[8] Cp. e.g. the four high priests of the various gods, Liebl., 905, or the instance, ib. 585, in which the father served Amon, the son Osiris.

[9] Tomb of the second prophet, Pu'em-rê', at Assasif, of the 18th dynasty (in part, L. D., iii. 39 c). Also Amh., 4, 4, of the 20th dynasty.

[10] Biography of Bekenchôns.

"do splendidly in his temple as great superintendent of the works,"[1] even if he delegated the direction of the building itself to other special officials. In addition, he was general of the troops of the god, and governed his "house of silver."[2] The position the high priests of Amon attained, owing to the fact that the temple they governed was by far the largest and the richest in Egypt, must have been very abnormal; it was therefore the more dangerous for the state when the kings of the New Empire, contrary to true political principles, made the other temples also subordinate to them. The first prophet of Amon became, not only "superintendent of the prophets of the gods of Thebes," but also "superintendent of the prophets of all the gods of the South and of the North,"[3] in other words, the whole priesthood of the Egyptian temples was subject to him.[4] The state seems even to have taken care to humble the other temples and make them dependencies of the temple of Amon, for we repeatedly find that the dignity of high priest in other temples was given to some member of the collegiate body at Thebes; *e.g.* a first prophet of Amon was, at the same time, high priest of Memphis;[5] a second prophet of Amon, high priest of Heliopolis,[6] and a chief superintendent of the oxen of the Theban god was high priest of Anḥôr.[7]

We have seen that, under the New Empire, the lay element almost disappeared from the priesthood; at that period however it came forward so much the more in another branch of public worship. In all temples, but above all in that of Amon, we find , female singers (or rather *musicians*, as we might perhaps translate the word), and indeed in great numbers. We scarcely meet with one lady, under the New Empire, whether she were married or unmarried,[8] the wife of an ecclesiastic or layman, whether she belonged to the family of a high priest[9] or to that of an artisan,[10] who was not thus connected with a temple. This institution of *singers* was remarkable however for the singular idea associated with it. The god was, in fact, regarded as an earthly prince, and the singers, who made music in his presence, were the beautiful singers, the inmates of the house of women. The singers formed the harem of the god,[11] and

[1] Biography of Bekenchôns.

[2] L. D., iii. 200 a.

[3] Thus in the tomb of the father of the above-mentioned Paser, Mar. Cat. d'Ab., 408, Liebl., 559; L. D., iii. 200 a. Statue of Bekenchôns.

[4] The servants "of all the gods" (without the words "of the South and North"), only known to us from Abydos, viz. a divine father (at the same time first prophet of Osiris, Mar. Cat. d'Ab., 1086), a superintendent of the fields (at the same time second prophet of Anḥôr, ib. 372), a superintendent of the singers (ib. 1159), and a scribe of the sacrifices (ib. 1128), serve "all the gods" of this town; see also Maspero, Guide, p. 286.

[5] Sem of Ptaḥ, title of Neb-notru in the tomb of Paser.

[6] Statue of Amen'anen at Turin, incompletely given, Liebl., 606.

[7] Mar. Cat. d'Ab., 1144.

[8] The latter, e.g. Mar. Cat. d'Ab., 1179.

[9] Liebl., 905.

[10] Four daughters of an artist, Liebl., 944; the wife of a shoemaker, Mar. Cat. d'Ab., 1174; wives of weavers, ib. 1175, 1187.

[11] It follows that the higher rank (the chief concubine) requires the existence of lower concubines; the latter are represented by the singers, who evidently belong to the lower rank; Abb., 3, 17, says expressly that the singers belonged to the house of the earthly consort of the god.

they held various degrees of rank as in an earthly harem; certain women of high rank had the honour of bearing the splendid title of "chief concubine" of the god.[1] At the head of the mystical harem at Thebes there stood the legitimate consort,[2] called the "wife of the god," the "hand of the god," or the "adorer of the god," and to her house belonged the singers.[3] This lady, usually the queen herself, represented the heavenly consort of Amon, the goddess Mut, and to her therefore belonged special high honours which seem sometimes to have even given her a political importance. Later, under the Saites, we find these women nominally rulers of Thebes, and there are many indications that at the beginning of the 18th dynasty they held a similar position. At public worship their duty was to play the sistrum before the god; probably there was not much more for them to do in their official capacity, for we find that a child could be invested with this high rank. The wife of the god possessed also a large property, administered by a "great man of the house."

THE *SINGER* TACH'A, SISTER OF PENNUT, OFFICIAL IN THE NUBIAN DEPARTMENT; She is carrying the sistrum, the instrument of temple music (Dyn. XX., L.D., 231 a).

Before I pass on to describe the worldly possessions of the ecclesiastical profession, their property, and its administration, I will make a few remarks on the vestments of the priests, the history of which corroborates well what I have said above of the development of a special rank of priesthood under the New Empire.

The priesthood of the Old Empire do not seem to have been distinguished by a characteristic dress; all the priests, even the high priests of Memphis and Heliopolis, wore, as a rule, exactly the same costume as other people. A few, as the high priest of Ptaḥ,[4] wore badges while exercising their office; others, as the priests of the dead, or the Ue'b,[5] wore their usual dress and coiffure even whilst they officiated. Under the Middle Empire however we see that the officiating priest, at the funeral sacrifice of the nomarch Chnemḥôtep, wears a skirt of more ancient fashion than the others who are present, and this tendency is more observable when we come to the priestly costume under the New Empire. During the latter period the servants of the gods seem to have felt that they belonged to a special caste, that the chief property of the nation was in their care, and that therefore it was no longer suitable that they should follow the secular vagaries of fashion. The priests never wore the mantle or double dress; they wore the simple plain skirt of former times, doubtless because it appeared to them that true piety flourished best

[1] The members of the family of a high priest, L. D., iii. 132 q; Liebl., 991; of other distinguished families, Mar. Cat. d'Ab., 1137, 1139.

[2] Cp. my remarks in Sweinfurth's pamphlet, "Alte Baureste im Uadi Gasus," in the Transactions of the Berlin Academy, 1885.

[3] Abb., 3, 17.

[4] Mar. Mast., 74, 75.

[5] L. D., ii. 10 and often; ib. 68.

during those old periods. Men of all ages have woven a halo round the past, and even our ecclesiastics are wont to regard the early centuries of Church history as a period when purer faith reigned; they also still wear the same costume as their forefathers of the sixteenth century.

STATUE OF AMEN'ANEN, HIGH PRIEST OF HELIOPOLIS, AND SECOND PROPHET OF AMON UNDER AMENḤÔTEP III.
(Turin Museum.)

The priests of the New Empire showed that they were the disciples of past pious ages by their dress, which they wore in private life even at feasts;[1] the high priests alone may have been allowed to wear ordinary dress.[2] The details of the costume vary a good deal, probably according to the rank or the special duties of the wearer. Many are represented wearing the narrow short skirt, common at the beginning of the 4th dynasty;[3] others the long wide skirt, such as was usually worn under the Middle Empire.[4] Some wound a scarf round the upper part of the body;[5] others put on over the skirt a curious wide cape which reached to below the arms;[6] others (like the singer represented, p. 252), wrapped the whole body in a great cloak.[7] We see that the *Sem* at the funeral sacrifice wears a panther skin,[8] as does also the high priest of Heliopolis, who as "Chief of the secrets of heaven," has the skin adorned with stars.[9] Finally, the chief priest of Memphis, under the 18th and 19th dynasties, wore round his neck as his badge of office the same curious ornament that was worn by the same official under the 4th dynasty.[10]

[1] Wall picture in Brit. Mus., see pl. opposite p. 248.
[2] L. D., iii. 174, 175, and the Turin statue here represented.
[3] See the above-mentioned wall picture.
[4] L. D., iii. 128 b, 162.
[5] Thus the high priests, L. D., iii. 128 b. Cp. also p. 150.
[6] L. D., iii. 14. Cp. also p. 276.
[7] In the same way the temple servants, L. D., iii. 94.
[8] Passim. Also under the M. E.: L. D., ii. 127.
[9] See the accompanying illustration.
[10] O. E.: Mar. Mast., 74, 75. Statue of Ra'nofer at Gizeh (975). N. E.: Statue of Ptaḥmose at Florence (Catal. gener., i. 197). Relief of Cha-'em-uêse at the Louvre (Revillout, Setna, frontispiece).

Whilst the dress of the priests varied in so many particulars, the custom of shaving the head seems to have been common amongst all the ecclesiastics of the New Empire. They shaved doubtless from reasons of cleanliness, as Herodotos clearly states. Men of other professions, as we have related in the tenth chapter, cut their hair very short, and wore artificial coiffures. The priests, on the other hand, did not, even when out of doors, protect their bare heads from the heat of the sun;[1] at feasts also they wore no wigs, though they anointed the skin of their heads with oil, like the other guests who wore hair.[2] This was the custom in later times, but under the Old Empire, even in the manner of dressing the hair, there existed no difference between the clergy and the laity, they all wore the same style of coiffure.

SEKER-CHA'BAU, THE HIGH PRIEST OF MEMPHIS.
(After Catal. gener. del Museo di Firenze, vol. i. p. 198.)

The priesthood of the New Empire owed their great power, and even their final triumph over the king himself, chiefly to their riches. Their riches were due for the most part, as far as we know, to royal gifts, for we rarely find it stated that a private citizen endowed a building to the gods.[3] All the kings, from the very oldest period, followed the same fatal course; some were more generous than others, as for instance the pious kings of the 5th dynasty;[4] thus even under the Old Empire many temples were rich enough to keep their own military force.[5] The Nubian conquests of the kings of the 12th dynasty opened out those gold districts to Egypt, and the temples received their share of the booty; for instance, the chief treasurer Ychernofret was sent by Usertsen III. on a special mission to Abydos,[6] "to erect monuments to his father Osiris, the god of the west, and to adorn the most secret place (*i.e.* the Holy of Holies) with the gold which His Majesty had brought in victory and triumph from Nubia." Ychernofret obeyed the order of the king and endowed the barks and the vessels of the god with lapis-lazuli and malachite, with electron and all manner of noble stones.

[1] E.g. L. D., iii. 128 b.

[2] See the above-mentioned London wall-picture.

[3] The foundation of Dêr el Medîneh (see p. 148) is an exception in point; cp. also L. D., iii. 236, where the private individual H'eyna is mentioned in connection with the temple of Amon. Under the New Empire there is no mention of the great number of small gifts, which we find amongst the offerings of later times.

[4] According to later tradition at any rate, Pap. Westcar, 9, 25 ff.

[5] Cp. the titles of the high priests of Heliopolis, Mar. Mon. div., 18. Also in the inscription of Un'e (Ä. Z., 1882, 14).

[6] Stele 1204, Berlin.

The golden age for the temples however began with the Asiatic expeditions of the 18th dynasty. The remains of an inscription at Karnak[1] give us an idea of the gifts of Thothmes III. to Amon: fields and gardens "of the most excellent of the south and of the north"; plots of ground in a higher situation, "overgrown with sweet trees," milch cows and other cattle, quantities of gold and silver and lapis-lazuli. In addition, Asiatic and negro prisoners, at least 878 souls, men and women, who were to fill the granaries of the god, spin, weave, and till the ground for him. Finally, Thothmes III. settled upon Amon three of the conquered towns, 'En'eugsa, Yenu'amu, and Ḥurenkaru, which had to pay a yearly tribute to the god. He also established special additional sacrifices for the festival days, besides richly increasing those already established. In the same way we hear that Sety I. "bestowed upon his father Amon Rê' all the silver, gold, lapis-lazuli, malachite, and precious stones, which he carried off from the miserable country of Syria"; and as the picture accompanying this inscription shows, lordly vases also of precious metal and of curious shapes; these were the much-admired productions of the ancient Syrian goldsmiths.[2] In addition to this generous present, the king gave "the great men of the countries, which he had brought in his hand," as slaves for the storehouse of Amon.[3] Each king of the New Empire boasts in almost identical words of these practical proofs of his piety; we might therefore be tempted to consider this constant self-praise of the Pharaohs, like so much in the Egyptian texts, to be merely empty conventional phrases. Our incredulity would however, in this case, exceed the limits of truth, for some at least of these kings gave gifts to the temples, exceeding all that we could consider probable. The happy chance which has preserved to us the so-called "great Harris Papyrus," allows us to bring numerical proofs on this matter. King Ramses III., at his death, left a comprehensive manifesto, in which he gave full details of all that he had done for the temples of his country during the thirty-one years of his reign. The figures in these lists are evidently taken from the account books of the state and of the various temples, and ought therefore to be worthy of credence.

This great papyrus is 133 feet long, and contains 79 pages of very large size; it is divided into five sections, according to the recipients of the gifts. The first section contains the gifts to the Theban temples; then follow the presents to Heliopolis, to Memphis and to the smaller sanctuaries of the country; finally, the fifth section gives the sum total of all the donations.[4] The individual sections are in strict order; this much facilitates our finding our way through the long lists of payments. In the first few pages of each section the king recounts the large buildings, the lakes and gardens he has laid out for each respective god; special gifts are particularly mentioned here beforehand, without specification of payments.

[1] L. D., iii. 30 b. [2] L. D., iii. 127 b. [3] L. D., iii. 127 b, 129.
[4] Harr. i. 1-23, Thebes; 24-42, Heliopolis; 43-56, Memphis; 57-66, smaller temples; 67-74, total.

The second rubric[1] gives in exact figures the precise presents of the king; his gifts of golden vessels, of fields and vineyards, of slaves and cattle. The third rubric[2] contains the account of the *duties*, or (as may be translated), the "work of the subjects of the temple, which the king gives to them as their yearly income," the account therefore of what the sanctuary ought to receive from those who had to pay rent to the temple independently of the monarch. Finally, the fourth rubric[3] shows the quantity of gold, fabrics, cattle, corn, incense, etc., that the Pharaoh gave towards the sacrifices of the god.

I shall now give a few examples from the fifth section, which, as I have said, gives the total sums of all the gifts which Ramses III. bestowed upon the various places of worship during the thirty-one years of his reign.

The following may be mentioned as special gifts from the king:

169 towns (nine in Syria and Ethiopia),
113,433 slaves,
493,386 head of cattle,
1,071,780 plots of ground,
514 vineyards and tree gardens,
88 barks and galleys,
2,756 images of the god (containing 7,205 uten and 1 qed of gold, and 11,047 uten and $\frac{1}{4}$ qed of silver),[4]
10,001 uten and 8 qed of precious black bronze,
97,148 uten and 3 qed of embossed bronze vessels,
47 uten and 6 qed of lapis-lazuli,
18,168 pieces (*sic*) and 1 qed of various precious stones;
etc.

The *duties*, *i.e.* the charges imposed upon the temple subjects, were as follows:

2,289 uten $4\frac{1}{2}$ qed of golden vessels and ornaments,
14,050 uten 2 qed of silver vessels and ornaments,
27,580 uten of bronze,
4,575 robes, finely woven,
3,795 uten of yarn,
1,529 jars of incense, honey, and oil,
28,080 jars of wine and similar drinks,
4,204 uten $7\frac{3}{5}$ qed of silver, the worth of various things paid in as a tax,

[1] Thebes, 10-11; Heliopolis, 31, 32 a 6; Memphis, 51 a—51 b 2; minor gods, 61-62 a 10; total, 67-68 b 3.

[2] Thebes, 12 a-b; Heliopolis, 32 a, 7-32 b; Memphis, 51 b, 3-52 a 3; minor gods, 62 a, 11-13, without special rubric; total, 68 b, 4-70 a 1. The word signifies here, as always in later times, the charges imposed.

[3] Thebes, 13 a ff.; Heliopolis, 33 a ff.; Memphis, 52 a 4 ff.; smaller gods, 62 b ff; total, 70 a 2 ff.

[4] One uten contains 91 g.; 1 qed, 9.1 g.

460,700 sacks of corn, the duty imposed upon the labourers,
326,995 geese,[1] the duty imposed upon the bird-catchers,
961 oxen from Egyptian herds,
19 oxen, the duty imposed on the countries of the Syrians,
12 ships of precious wood,
78 ships of ordinary wood ;
etc.

For the sacrificial funds the following payments were made from the royal treasury :

1,663 uten of golden vases and ornaments,
3,598 uten 8 qed of silver vases and ornaments,
30 uten $9\frac{1}{8}$ qed of real lapis-lazuli, malachite, and ruby (?),
327 uten 9 qed of black bronze,
18,786 uten 7 qed of embossed bronze vases,
50,877 robes, finely woven,
331,702 jars of incense, honey, and oil,
35,130 jars of *qadarut'e* incense,
228,380 jars of wine and similar drinks,
1,075,635 amulets, scarabaei, and seals of precious stone,
2,382,605 various fruits,
20,602 oxen
367 gazelles } of various kinds,
353,719 geese
1,843 bags } of salt and natron,
355,084 bricks
161,287 loaves
25,335 loaves } of various kinds of bread,
6,272,421 loaves
285,385 cakes,
466,303 jugs of beer,
3,100 uten of wax,
494,000 fish,
19,130,032 bouquets of flowers,
3,260 pieces of wood for fuel,
3,367 lumps of coal,
1,933,766 jars of incense, honey, oil, fat, etc.,
5,279,652 sacks of corn ;
etc.

If we take the similar items of the presents, duties, and sacrificial gifts, and reckon them together, we find that, for the thirty-first year, the sum total of the principal items for the Egyptian temple will be somewhat as follows :

1,015 kg. 336 g. of gold,
2,993 kg. 964 g. of silver and silver goods,

[1] The writing 426,995 here is erroneous ; there seem also to be other small errors in the figures of the other accounts.

940 kg. 3 g. of black bronze,
13,059 kg. 865 g. of bronze,
7 kg. 124 g. of precious stones,
1,093,803 valuable stones,
169 towns,
1,071,780 plots of arable ground,
514 vineyards and gardens of trees,
178 ships,
113,433 slaves,
514,968 head of cattle (particularly oxen),
680,714 geese,
494,800 fish,
2,382,605 fruits,
5,740,352 sacks of corn,
6,744,428 loaves of bread,
256,460 jars of wine,
466,303 jugs of beer,
368,461 jars } of incense, honey, and oil;
1,933,766 jars }
etc.

In order to give the reader an idea of the very large sums concerned, I may remark that, though the value of metal has gone down so much at the present time, yet the quantity of precious metal mentioned here would amount to about £200,000, and we must not forget that the same six or seven million Egyptians who, in addition to taxes paid to the state, devoted this treasure *ad majorem dei gloriam,* had also to maintain the temples of Medinet Habu, Karnak, Tell el Yehudeh, etc. The capacities of this small country were indeed much overtaxed for the unproductive purpose of temple worship.

These conditions were rendered most unsound by the unequal distribution of the treasure. Had all the temples in the country shared alike, no single one would have risen to excessive power and riches. From political reasons however, Ramses III. also endowed *one* temple especially, the same in fact that had received the richest gifts from his predecessors. This was the sanctuary of the Theban god Amon, who bore off the lion's share of all that was given by these generous monarchs. For instance, out of the 113,433 slaves that Ramses presented to the gods, no fewer than 86,486 fell to Amon; also 421,362 head of cattle out of 493,386; 898,168 plots of land out of 1,071,780; 433 vineyards out of 514, and so forth; the 2756 gold and silver figures of the gods were exclusively for that god, as well as the 9 foreign towns; and it must be regarded as exceptional that he only received 56 out of the 160 Egyptian towns. We shall probably be quite on the safe side if we reckon that three-quarters of all the royal gifts went into the treasury of Amon. Even the Theban deities who were co-divinities with the "king of the gods" had to content themselves with a very modest share; the god Chons and the goddess Mut together only receiving 3908 slaves out of the 86,486.

The earlier kings of the New Empire had also delighted to fill the coffers of their favourite god Amon, who thus finally possessed property entirely eclipsing that of all other gods. The papyrus of Ramses III. again enables us to prove this fact by figures. I remarked above that, reckoned together with the royal gifts, are the duties which each temple received yearly from its own subjects. These were the duties paid by the bondservants of the temple, the artisans, the peasants living on the temple property, and the shepherds who kept the temple flocks; duties therefore, which represented, for the most part, the sum for which the temple property was leased, and which may be regarded as the rental of the temple property, thus giving us an idea of its size. In the following list the revenues of the later Theban sanctuary are placed side by side with those of the ancient celebrated temples of Heliopolis and Memphis, as well as with those of the lesser gods of Egypt.

List of temple revenues of	Thebes	Heliopolis	Memphis	The lesser gods
Gold articles in uten	569.6	—	—	—
Silver " "	10964.9	$586.3\frac{11}{12}$	$98.3\frac{11}{12}$	—
Bronze " "	26329	1260	—	—
Fine linen, clothes	3722	1019	$133\frac{1}{2}$	—
Yarn, in uten	3795	—	—	—
Incense, honey, oil in jars . . .	1049	482	—	—
Wine, etc., in jars	25405	2385	390	—
Duties imposed on the people, various objects, worth in silver uten . .	3606.1	$456.3\frac{1}{2}$	141.3	—
Taxes on the labourers, sacks of corn .	309950	77100	37400	73250
Vegetables, bundles	24650	4800	600	3300
Flax, bundles	64000	4000	—	3300
Tax from the bird-catchers, geese .	289530	37465	—	—
Oxen from the Egyptian herds . .	849	98	$15\frac{1}{2}$	—
" from Syrian herds . . .	17	—	—	—
Live geese.	544	548	135	—
Barks of rare wood	12	1	—	—
" of ordinary wood . . .	31	7	—	—

If we compare these figures, it is impossible to have any doubt that under the 20th dynasty Amon of Thebes possessed at least five times as much property as the sun-god of Heliopolis, and ten times as much (and probably much more) as Ptaḥ of Memphis. Yet both the last-mentioned gods were formerly the chief and the richest gods in the whole country.

The enormous properties belonging to the temples required of course a far more complicated machinery for their administration than had been necessary for the more modest possessions of the old sanctuaries. Under the Middle Empire certain members of the priestly college were deputed to manage the affairs of the treasury, the commissariat and the correspondence;[1] the work of these departments not being heavy was easily despatched,

[1] See the remarks above on the *qnbt* of Abydos and Siut.

and there were hardly any officials in these temples except the servants.[1] Under the New Empire it was quite otherwise; the priests were no longer able to do the work of administration alone, but required a host of officials to help them. This was the case in all temples,[2] but of course especially so in that of the Theban Amon. This god possessed a central bureau for the administration of the *house*,[3] *i.e.* of the temple property, and also special departments for the treasury,[4] for *agriculture*,[5] for the *barns*,[6] for the *cattle*,[7] and for the *peasants*;[8] and each of these departments had its *superintendent*, who was of princely rank,[9] as well as its *scribes*. In the temple of Amon there was also a *chief scribe* of high rank, who had the care of the title-deeds of the sanctuary,[10] and as in a large temple under the New Empire new buildings and restorations were always going on, the god was obliged to have his own building department, which was over *all works*.[11] It follows as a matter of course that the needful number of artisans and artists of all kinds had to be forthcoming, from the painter to the stone-mason.[12] In order to maintain order in the temple and on the property, the god possessed his own militia with chief and subordinate officers;[13] and as many secular transactions occurred under his administration, he had also his own prison.[14] We know little of the great staff of lower officials, which must have existed under these conditions, for this class do not come within our ken. We have however many monuments of people like the "superintendents of the sacrificial storehouse,"[15] "door-keepers" of all kinds,[16] "barbers,"[17] all of whom must to a certain extent have lived in easy circumstances.

These remarks on the temple administration would have still more interest for us did we know what connection existed between these various offices, and how it comes to pass that we find some at one time, others at another time, united in one person. It is easy to understand

1 The few exceptions that I know however may in part be only so apparently; see above, p. 104.

2 Superintendent of the property of Chons: Mar. Cat. d'Ab., 1153; Superintendent of the provision-house of Horus, ib. 430; Superintendent of the workmen of Min, ib. 424; temple scribe of Ptaḥ, ib. 1131; Superintendent of the oxen of Anḥôr, ib. 1080, etc.

3 Superintendent, L. D., iii. 25, 26; Harr., 10, 8; Abb., 8 a, 25, 27; Liebl., 610, 611, 666, 838, 1044; Mar. Cat. d'Ab., 1202; Scribe Liebl., 641.

4 Tomb of 'Enn'e at Sheikh Abd-elqurna; L. D., iii. 200 a.

5 Liebl., 624; Mar. Cat. d'Ab., 1085.

6 Superintendent: Tomb of 'Enn'e, L. D., iii. 25 k., 26. "Scribe of the corn accounts": L. D., iii. 38 g.

7 Chief superintendent: Liebl., 904-997; Mar. Cat. d'Ab., 1144. Superintendent: Liebl., 187, 620, 845, 995. Scribe of the accounts: Liebl., 663.

8 L. D., iii. 25, 38 g.

9 Harr., i. 10, 3.

10 : tomb of Ramses at Dra-abulnega; Liebl., 927.

11 "Director of the works": Tomb of 'Enn'e at Sheikh Abd-elqurna; "Superintendent" of the same: Liebl., 946; L. D., iii. 200 a. Tomb of Ramses at Dra-abulnega.

12 See also for more detail, chap. 16.

13 Mar. Cat. d'Ab., 1158. Liebl., 970; ib. 967; ib. 1186; ib. 835; Mar. Cat. d'Ab., 1063.

14 Amh., 4, 3.

15 Leibl., 674.

16 Liebl., 682, 686, 762, 802, etc.

17 Mar. Cat. d'Ab., 1079. Cp. also Liebl., 1245.

that the high priest himself should nominally, in addition to the high priesthood, hold one or other important office; but it is not clear, for instance, why the superintendence of the buildings was at one time held as an additional appointment by the chief scribe,[1] and at another time by the superintendent of the granaries;[2] this is the more obscure because the former had also the superintendence of the cattle of the god, and the latter had the care of the treasure-houses, and "sealed all the contracts of the temple of Amon." It is a characteristic fact that these high temple officials were also frequently officials of the state as well;[3] the gradual change of government from the old monarchy into the hierarchy of the 21st dynasty, when the power was vested in the high priests of Amon, is clearly foreshadowed in this plurality of appointments. The royal authority did not however submit to that of the priests without a struggle, and it may be that the Reformation of Chuen'eten, as well as the disturbances at the close of the 19th dynasty, when "no sacrifices were brought into the temple,"[4] were owing in great part to the efforts made by the Pharaohs to stem the overwhelming torrent of the rising power of the priesthood of Amon. As a matter of fact, both episodes served only to defeat their own object.

[1] Tomb of Ramses at Dra-abulnega.

[2] Tomb of 'Enn'e at Sheikh Abd-elqurna.

[3] Thus the Ramses mentioned above; the superintendent of oxen: Liebl., 187, 904, and other examples.

[4] Harr., i. 75, 6.

VASES FOR THE RECEPTION OF THE VISCERA OF THE MUMMIES.
The covers bear the heads of the four genii under whose protection the viscera were placed.

CHAPTER XIII

THE DEAD

IN the preceding chapter we discussed the practical effect of religion on the life of the nation rather than the religious ideas of the people themselves; in like manner we will now consider what the Egyptians really did for their dead rather than endeavour to comprehend the confused notions which they held as to the life after death. In order to understand the subject we must however first make a few general remarks on the future state of the deceased.

From the earliest ages it was an article of faith amongst the Egyptians that man existed after death, but where and how he existed was not so clear to their minds. Some thought that he was to be found amongst the stars in the sky, others that he sat on the branches of the trees with the birds, and others that he remained on earth where his bones were laid to rest. At some periods of their history they believed that it was his special privilege to appear sometimes in one form, sometimes in another—one day as a heron, another as a cockchafer, and yet another as a lotus-flower on the water. At other times he was supposed to live in a kingdom of light—the *duat*, the dwelling-place of the gods, who travelled with the happy dead, "on those beautiful ways where the glorified travel." The peasants believed, on the other hand, that he went to the fields of *Earu*, where the barley and the spelt grew to the height of seven cubits; that here he would plough the land and reap the harvests, and when tired in the evening, he would sit under his sycamore, and play draughts with his companions.

Yet the Egyptians never clearly explained how the various parts of the human personality were connected together after death. They did not consider man as a simple individuality; he consisted of at least three parts, the body [hieroglyph], the soul [hieroglyph], and the ghost, the image, the double, or the genius, according as we translate the Egyptian word [hieroglyph] *ka*. The latter is evidently the most important; it is an independent spiritual being, living within the man, and through its presence bestowing upon the man "protection, intelligence, purity, health, and joy."[1] No man nor god was conceivable without his *ka*, which grew up with him and never left him. The *ka* of a child assumed a childlike appearance, and like the child wore the youthful side-lock. He is his faithful companion, and when the gods are represented bearing the new-born prince in their arms, they also carry his double with him.[2]

In sculptural art the *ka* is distinguished by certain characteristics, common to it whether it is represented as two arms[3] without a body, or as a complete human figure.[4] These characteristics are a staff and the sign [hieroglyph], the former bearing the head[5] the latter the name of the respective man. In the case of a private individual both face and name are the same as those belonging to his human body. The *ka* of a king, on the other hand, possesses a special sacred appellation, the so-called Horus name; thus for instance the "living *ka* of the lord of the two countries" of Thothmes III. is called "the victorious bull, which shines in Thebes."

After the death of a man, just as during his lifetime, the *ka* was still considered to be the representative of his human personality: it is not clear to us, nor perhaps was it even to the Egyptians, what part the "living soul" played in the matter. The *ka* was supposed to exist after death under very different conditions from those he had enjoyed upon earth; it was therefore necessary to take many precautionary measures to avoid every mischance. The body had to be preserved that the *ka* might take possession of it when he pleased. A statue of the deceased had to be kept in some safe place that the *ka* might find in that image those individual features which the corpse had lost. His favourite household goods had to be provided for him, that he might live in the tomb as he had lived on earth. Finally and chiefly, food and drink had to be placed for the *ka* on the table of offerings in the tomb, for otherwise he might suffer hunger and thirst, or even, so the Egyptians thought, be obliged to feed on his own excreta. Though these conceptions were of a very vague and in many ways of a very contradictory nature, yet they exercised an immense influence on the life of the Egyptians. In consequence of this belief they

[1] L. D., iii. 35 b, and frequently.

[2] L. D., iii. 75 a, b.

[3] The sign [hieroglyph] doubtless sprang originally from the representation of the *ka* by two arms.

[4] E.g. L. D., iii. 34 b.

[5] In the instances before us, the *ka* represented is always that of a king, it therefore always bears the little head of a king.

mummified their bodies, they built their indestructible tombs, they established endowments for the sacrifices for the dead, they preserved statues and household goods in the tombs,—in short it is to their faith in the *ka* that we owe all our knowledge of the home life of the people.

In addition to the above-mentioned provisions for the benefit of the deceased, we must mention one of peculiar nature resting on the Egyptian belief in magic, which was very characteristic of that nation. Magical formulae not only affected the living, but also the dead, *e.g.* if any one repeated the following words in a tomb: "An offering which the King gives, an offering which Anubis gives, thousands of bread, beer, oxen geese, for the *ka* of N. N.," he would, through the repetition of this formula, ensure to the deceased the enjoyment of these funerary meats. It was, therefore, most necessary that at the funerary feast a reciter-priest should repeat these formulae, and the inscriptions also conjure each later visitor to the tomb, by what he holds most sacred, by his children, his office, his king, and by the god of his home, to say "thousands of bread, beer, oxen, and geese," on behalf of the deceased.

There was a special development of these magical formulae in early times. As the reader will remember from the foregoing chapter, the people believed that Osiris was murdered by Set, avenged by his son Horus, and that afterwards he rose to new life. A similar fate was to be desired for each mortal man; those who were left behind hoped that, like Osiris, the deceased would rise to new life; and that in his son, who took care of his tomb and honoured his memory, as worthy a successor would arise as Horus had been to Osiris. With this object the magical formulae recited in the tomb were composed like those used by Horus to his father Osiris, in the belief that thus it would go as well with the deceased as formerly with the god who had been slain. This faith, which we meet with everywhere in the beginning of the Old Empire, gave the characteristic form to all the customs of funerary worship. From the time of the Middle Empire the deceased is addressed directly as the *Osiris N. N.*, as if he were that god himself; and the epithet is always added, *of true words*, because formerly the *words* of Osiris had been found true in the dispute with his enemies. Anubis is represented holding his body as he had held that of Osiris, and Isis and Nephthys weep for him as if he himself had been the husband of Isis. These conceptions were so widespread that they finally reacted on the god himself, and raised him to an importance which he scarcely possessed originally. Before all other gods Osiris became the god of the dead; even Anubis, the protector of the dead, played but a secondary part, —Osiris was the king of the realm of the blessed.

This latter favourite idea was thus further developed by the Egyptian imagination. The blessed dead were supposed to form the nation who worked for Osiris and were governed by him; his officers were composed of terrible demons, who guarded his gates, or who sat as assessors in his great hall of judgment. In this *hall of the two truths*, by the side of the king of the dead, there squatted forty-two strange daemonic forms, with heads of snakes or hawks, vultures or rams, each holding a knife in his hand. Before these creatures, *eater of blood*, *eater of shadows*, *wry head*, *eye of flame*, *breaker of bones*, *breath of flame*, *leg of fire*, *white-tooth*, and others of like names, the deceased had to appear and confess his sins. If he could declare that he had neither stolen, nor committed adultery, nor reviled the king, nor committed any other of the forty-two sins, and if the great balance on which his heart was weighed (see p. 139) showed that he was innocent, then Thoth, the scribe of the gods, wrote down his acquittal. Horus then took the deceased by the hand and led the new subject to his father Osiris, just as in this world an earthly prince would present a deserving man to the Pharaoh.

From a material point of view also Osiris gained much advantage when he became the great god of the dead; the places where he was honoured rose to the highest importance, especially Abydos, whence seems to have originated the Osiris legend. In the earliest ages this town was an obscure village, but after the close of the Old Empire it became the most sacred place in Egypt, and the wish of every pious man was to rest there near Osiris. The place maintained its supremacy down to Greek times. Under the Ptolemies a tomb of Osiris was connected with each new sanctuary, the great god Set was converted into a Satan because he had murdered Osiris, and to the Roman world Serapis and Isis became the Egyptian gods *par excellence*. All this indicates that the doctrine of Osiris influenced not only the funerary worship, but also all the religion of the country.

The above remarks will suffice for the needful understanding of the funeral customs and festivals for the dead. I must repeat however, that besides these conceptions, there were others both of older and of more recent growth, which were often directly contradictory, and, as far as we know, have never satisfactorily been explained. It is impossible from the texts to answer even elementary questions as to the constitution and the position of the kingdom of the

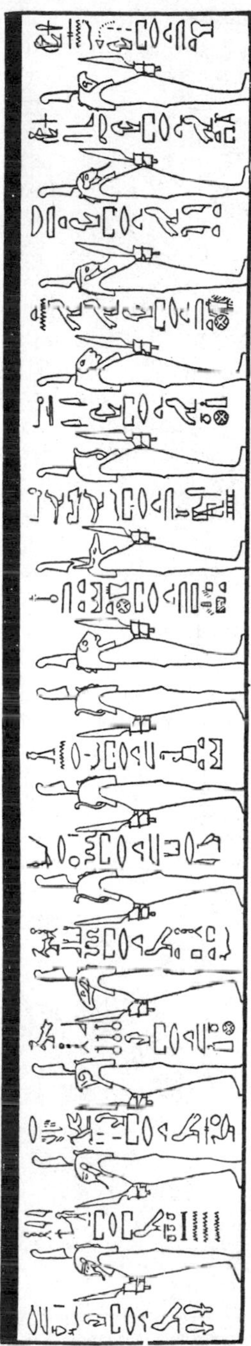

THE JUDGES OF THE DEAD.

blessed; for centuries one obscure idea was grafted on another scarcely less obscure, until the one became less clear than the other, and there is now no hope of arriving at a right understanding of the whole.

When the Egyptians saw the sun disappear behind the western mountains it was natural that they should imagine that in the west lay the entrance into the hidden land ; therefore, when no special circumstances prevented, they always built their tombs on the edge of the western desert. For at least 3000 years they thus buried their dead; and as they preferred not to go far into the desert, the strip of ground which bounded the fertile country must have been filled with bodies in a way which defies description. According to the lowest reckoning, from the time of the Old Empire to the Christian epoch, 150,000,000 to 200,000,000 human beings must have died in Upper Egypt alone, and these must have nearly all found their last resting-place in a strip of desert about 450 miles long.

We must not imagine that there was the same immense number of *tombs*, for in the older period at any rate, the higher classes alone possessed tombs, the lower orders were simply buried in the sand of the desert. Mariette chanced to find the burial field for the poor of Memphis;[1] the bodies lay about three feet below the surface with no coffins nor bandages; at most a little brick building had sometimes been constructed to separate one of rather higher standing from his neighbour. Small alabaster bowls and bones of animals showed that food and drink had been given to them.

Thus originally the building of a real tomb was apparently the privilege of the highest class, and if we reckon that through the great excavations of Lepsius and Mariette five hundred tombs of the Old Empire were brought to light, and even if we conclude that one-tenth of the tombs have been discovered (a conclusion far beyond probability), we shall find that during the 4th and 5th dynasties 5000 persons alone could have been thus buried. In other words, out of a population of 5,000,000, 700 persons at most could have annually afforded themselves this luxury.[2]

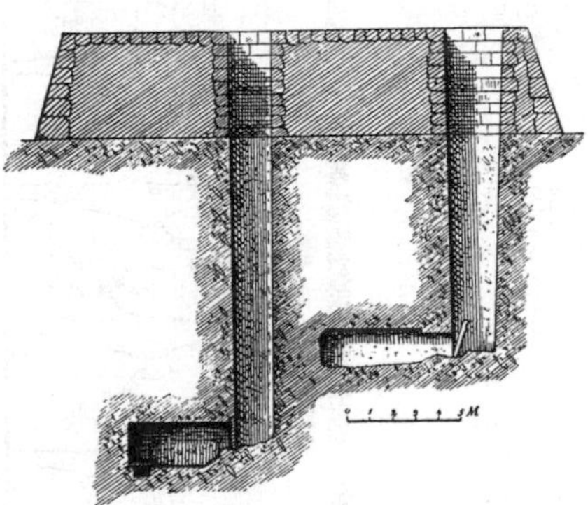

SECTION OF A MASTABAH AT GIZEH WITH TWO SHAFTS, EACH OF WHICH LEADS TO A MUMMY CHAMBER.

(After L. D., i. 22, restored by Chipiez.)

The tombs of the Old Empire, the so-called mastabahs, all bear the same character. This form of tomb seems to have originated in the oblong heaps of stones which were raised in prehistoric times over the grave of a deceased prince in order to protect his body. The

[1] Mar. Mast., 17.

[2] These are, of course, very vague reckonings; they certainly show however, with certainty, the approximate proportion.

mastabahs of the time of Chufu are really similar heaps of stone covered with a casing of sloping flat blocks. The real grave that contains the body lies deep under this stone construction ; it is a narrow chamber hewn out in the rock, to which a shaft leads down from the roof of the mastabah. When the body has been hidden in this chamber, the door is walled up, and the shaft filled with great blocks of stone. The tomb was not built merely to protect the body, it was also the place to which the friends could bring offerings for the *ka* of the deceased, and could recite the necessary formulae before him. A portion therefore of each tomb was so arranged that the worshippers might look towards the west, the entrance into the hidden land ; and in fact the decoration of this part of the tomb

MASTABAH TOMBS IN THE NECROPOLIS OF GIZEH, RESTORED BY PERROT-CHIPIEZ.
In front of the tombs are the entrances to the funerary chapels, on the roofs the openings to the shafts.

always represented that entrance in the form of a narrow door. In the most simple mastabahs this false door, on which the name of the deceased and prayers for the dead were written, was usually outside on the east wall, so that the worship went on in front of the tomb in the road. As a rule, however, a small chamber was cleared out at the south-east corner, and on the further wall, looking towards the west, is found the false door with the inscriptions. These chambers represent the great scientific value of the mastabahs, for their walls are covered with inscriptions and pictures, from which we have obtained all our knowledge of the Old Empire. Whatever was dear to the deceased or valued by him is represented or related here,—his titles, his estates, his workmen and officials, but all with reference specially to the tomb and to the funerary worship. We must not imagine this chamber in the mastabah to be of large size ; it occupies often but a fiftieth part of the great massive stone construction.[1] The mastabahs are also of very various sizes,—some are quite small, covering perhaps an area of 24 square yards; others close by may cover an area of more than a quarter of an acre.

In addition to the above chamber, the mastabah contained a second smaller room, the so-called *serdâb*, in which the statue of the deceased was hidden. This *serdâb* (the word is Arabic and signifies cellar) was only separated by a wall from the chapel, so that the *ka*, who inhabited the statue, should be near at hand during the sacrifices and during the recitation of the funerary formulae; frequently, in fact, there was also a narrow hole through the partition, so that the incense might better pass into the *serdâb* to the statue.

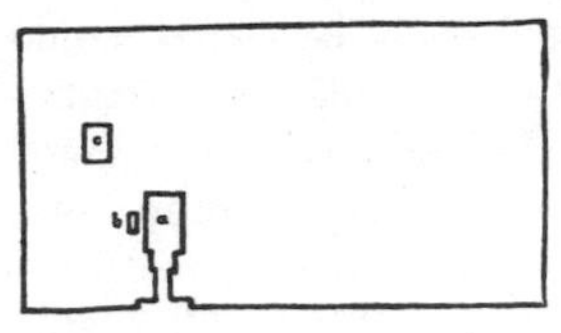

GROUND-PLAN OF A MASTABAH. (After Mar. Mast. 341.) A. Chapel, B. Serdab, C. Shaft leading to the mummy chamber.

The furniture of the funerary chamber seems to us rather scanty: before the false door is placed a stone table of offerings; and close by, the high wooden stands with bowls for offerings of drink and oil. Other objects which the chamber originally contained have doubtless been stolen in old times, for this chamber was always easy of access. The mummy chambers also have almost invariably been robbed by these ancient thieves, in spite of the careful way in which they were walled and filled up, so that we know very little of the oldest manner of burial. A large simple oblong sarcophagus, which sometimes contained a wooden coffin, enclosed the body, which was always mummied and bandaged. Over the face the deceased sometimes wore a mask of cartonage. In the coffin was usually placed the wooden or stone head-rest used in life as a pillow, with which the deceased could not dispense for his eternal sleep.

The mastabah tombs described above are all found in the burial-places in the neighbourhood of the later town of Memphis; they were built entirely by the aristocracy, who wished to rest near their monarch. Towards the end of the Old Empire, when the power of the king declined, the nobility of the nomes began to prepare their tombs near their own homes, and at the same time we find a change in the form of tomb. Instead of the mastabah, the rock-tomb was now preferred everywhere. This tomb had only been used before in a few cases on the low plateaus of Gizeh and Sakkarah; it presented however the form most suitable for the higher and steeper rocky sides of the valleys of Upper Egypt. The details of the plan of these rock-tombs vary a good deal according to the riches of the family, and according to the ruling fashion; the chief characteristics are however common to all, even to tombs of different periods. Through a stately portico we reach the place of worship, which consisted of one or more spacious chambers, the walls of which were covered with reliefs or paintings of the customary kind. In a corner of one of these chambers

[1] E.g. Mar. Mast., 232, 236, 341.

there was a shaft (the so-called well), the opening of which was hidden, for it led to the mummy chamber. Sometimes several persons were buried in one tomb, which would then contain several wells. As it was not possible to have a *serdâb* in a grotto-tomb, the statues of the deceased were placed, in accordance with later custom also, in a niche of the furthermost chamber. One of the old princes of Elephantine, whose tomb was discovered in 1886, resorted to a curious expedient as decoration,—he had the stone pillars of the funerary chapel carved to represent the mummies who were buried below. These grotto-tombs of the Middle Empire, with their columned halls and often tasteful entrances (cp. p. 24), stand higher in an artistic sense than the shapeless stone masses of the mastabahs with their narrow chambers. In dimensions also many of the former equal the latter, and tombs like those at Siut, with their large halls, still compel our admiration, even in this country of gigantic buildings.

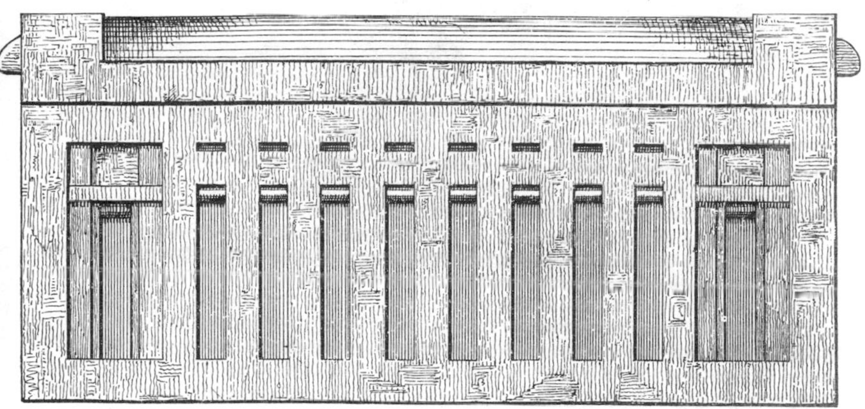

COFFIN OF THE OLD EMPIRE IN THE FORM OF A HOUSE. (After L. D., i. 30.)

As with the mastabahs so with the grotto-tombs, it was of course men of rank only who could afford them; they were far beyond the means of the middle class, who, after the close of the Old Empire, began to build small tombs for themselves. The latter prefered to build at Abydos, the city of Osiris; and they were as a rule content with a shallow well to contain the coffin. Over this was built a little brick pyramid on a low pedestal, the whole being then plastered with Nile mud and whitened. In front of this pyramid there was sometimes, as in our illustration, a small porch, which served as a funerary chapel; in other cases the offerings and prayers were offered in the open air in front of the tomb, where was placed a stone slab, the funerary stela. These stelae, which are so numerous in our museums, were originally identical with the false doors of the mastabahs, and represented the entrance into the netherworld: they indicated the place to which the friends were to turn when they brought their offerings. The stelae in these little tombs of the poorer people were of course of very small dimensions—most were less than three feet high—and consequently their original signification was soon forgotten. Even at the beginning of the Middle Empire the door form disappeared completely, and the whole space of the stone was taken up with the representation of the deceased seated before a table of offerings receiving gifts from his relations and servants. Soon afterwards it became the custom to round off the stone at the top, and when, under the New Empire, pictures of a purely religious character took the place of the former representations, no one looking at the tomb stela could have guessed that it originated from the false door.

The latter tombs remained in vogue till far into the time of the New Empire; and the burial-grounds of Abydos and Thebes must have been covered with many hundreds of these little white pyramids. From their

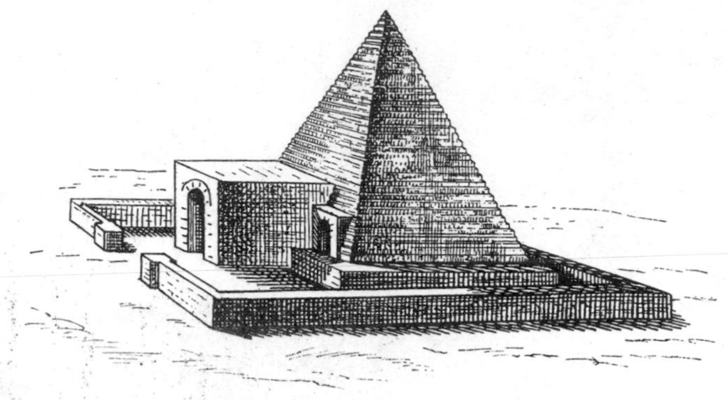

TOMB OF THE MIDDLE EMPIRE AT ABYDOS. (After Perrot-Chipiez.)

slight style of building they have now almost entirely disappeared, and the short shaft in which formerly the coffin was hidden is left bare, and looks like a hole filled with rubbish.

There are a great number of grotto-tombs at Thebes of the time of the New Empire, which, comparatively speaking, are little injured. Those indeed which possessed a brick porch have lost that part, but the funerary chapels are often in excellent preservation. They usually consist of a wide chamber of little depth, on the two narrow sides of which are placed the stelae; whilst in the middle of the back wall is generally the entrance to a narrow long room. In the latter as a rule was the well with the coffin, and seated in a niche in the further wall were usually the life-size statues of the deceased and his wife carved in the rock. Though these tombs often contain other chambers in addition to the above, yet their dimensions do not as a rule nearly equal the similar tombs of the Middle Empire. The pictures also, however interesting they may be, are not executed with the same finish; we rarely meet with careful reliefs; the walls are generally plastered with Nile mud and hastily though brightly painted. We see that under the New Empire the upper classes were not so particular as to the plan of their tombs, while the desire for a burial, in accordance with all the requirements of religion, had reached what we may comparatively call the lower orders of the nation,—under the 20th dynasty we even hear of a chief workman who constructed a tomb for himself.[1] This man may indeed have been an exception to the rule, yet his example probably induced others to take the opportunity of sharing a rock tomb together. Many of the latter tombs have been found; they were evidently laid out by contractors and the places let out in them. The people who are buried in them belong, as far as we can ascertain, mostly to the middle class.[2]

Though the architectural plan of the tombs of the New Empire was simpler than that of those of the old period, yet gradually many other things had come to be necessary for the full salvation of the soul of the deceased. The sarcophagus under the Old Empire was a four-cornered stone chest with few inscriptions and very little adornment; under the Middle Empire however it had quite a gay appearance. False doors were painted on the outside, as well as invocations to the protector of the dead, while the inside was closely inscribed with religious texts. The inner coffins also were generally similarly inscribed all over. Evidently they believed that these formulae, the *glorifications* as they called them, the repetition of which was so useful for the deceased, would exercise the same effect if they wrote them out for him instead of repeating them. In later times, when these formulae increased more and more in number, they had not room enough for them on the sides of the coffin; under the New Empire therefore they were written out on a roll of papyrus, and this so-called Book of the Dead was bound up inside the bandages of the mummy. Thus as it was not now necessary that the coffin should have smooth sides fit for inscriptions, the Egyptians began to think more of its artistic form. The inner coffins, which were of wood or cartonage, were as a rule shaped like the mummy, and on the cover of the outer stone sarcophagus used by people of rank was represented the deceased lying at full length. The embalmment and the complicated system of bandaging the body seem to have become more perfect under the New Empire as compared with the older period; as yet however we can give no details on this point. One innovation only is apparent, viz. the treatment of the viscera. The heart, upon the weight of which depended the decision as to the innocence of the deceased in the judgment before Osiris, was now taken out of the body and replaced by a stone scarabaeus. The so-called scarabaeus, the great cockchafer of southern countries, was considered an especially mysterious and sacred animal, and the figure of this insect was almost as symbolic to the followers of the Egyptian religion as the cross is to the Christian. If this sacred emblem therefore were substituted for the sinful heart, and further if the invocation were added that it "might not rise up as a witness"

[1] Salt, 2, 6 ff. Cp. ib., Rev. 1, 2.

[2] Cp. the detailed account of a tomb of this kind by Passalacqua, Catalogue raisonné, p. 197 ff.

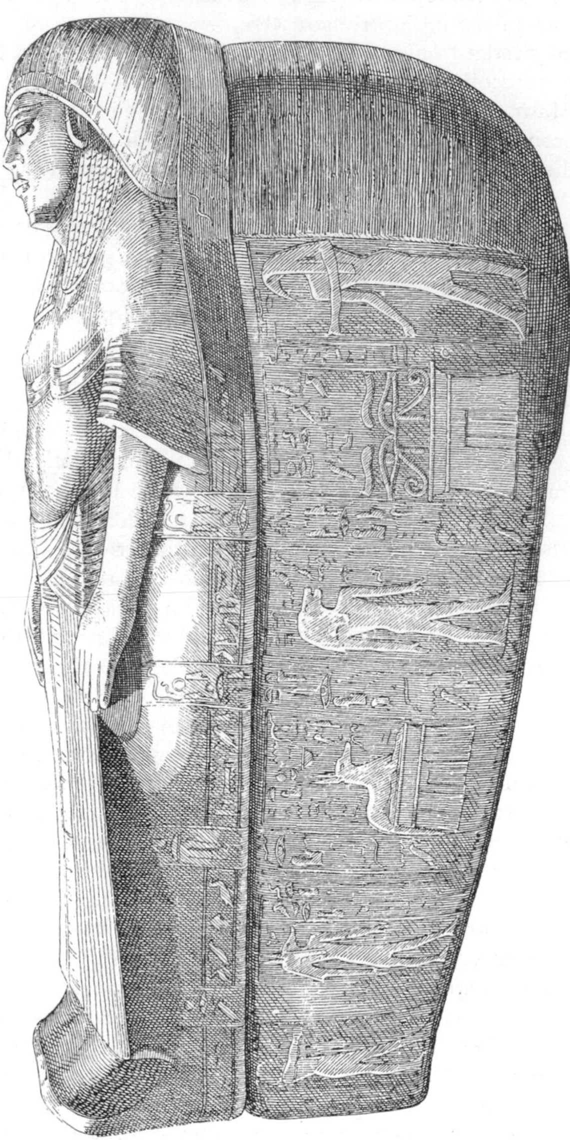

COFFIN OF THE SCRIBE 'EN'EUA, DYN. 19, MEMPHIS. (Now in the Louvre: after Perrot-Chipiez.)

against his master, it would be of essential use to the deceased. The old anxiety however, lest the deceased might suffer from hunger and thirst, led to further special precautions concerning those organs of the body which might suffer from these disagreeable sensations. They were taken out of the body and placed in four jars, each under the protection of a particular genius. These genii are 'Emset, Ḥape, Duamutf, and Ḳebḥsneuf; as sons of Osiris they could protect the deceased from hunger;[1] each of the jars with the viscera (from an ancient misconception we term them canopic vases) has a cover, as is seen in the illustration at the head of this chapter, in the shape of the animal head of its protecting genius.

Before the invention of these jars many precautionary measures were taken to ward off the much-dreaded danger of hunger, in case the sacrifices and magical formulae should fail of effect. Under the Old and the Middle Empire food was given to him in imperishable form; alabaster figures of roast geese, and wooden jars of wine were supposed, by the indwelling of certain magical power, to satisfy his hunger and thirst. In the same mysterious way his food was also supposed to be cooked for him in the little wooden models of kitchens, which resembled those in which his servants had formerly roasted his beef and prepared his food; whilst statuettes of servants pounding corn or kneading dough were believed to provide bread for the deceased. The same faith in the magical power of wooden figures was shown when they placed a little boat with oars near the coffin; this was to ensure to him the possibility of travelling. Besides these models of servants and of sailors which replaced the earthly domestics of the departed, there were many other figures of a different kind which served him as bondservants. These are the so-called funerary statuettes, or as they are termed in Egyptian the Ushebte, *i.e.* the *answerers*, a curious name which admits of a simple explanation.[2] As we remarked above, the Egyptian conception of the Fields of the Blessed was that of an arable country of peculiar fertility; there ploughing and reaping, watering and carrying away the earth went on just as in the fields on earth. As this land was most productive, the idea of being obliged to cultivate it was always attractive to the Egyptian peasantry, who formed the bulk of the Egyptian nation. But the case was otherwise with the great lords. On earth they had never followed the plough nor used a scythe, it was not therefore a cheerful prospect to them that Osiris might call upon them to work in the fields for him. In order to escape this unpleasant contingency the members of the upper classes had whole boxes of these little wooden and faïence figures, the *answerers*, buried with them, so that whenever the name of the deceased should be called upon to work, they should *answer* for him and do the work for him. On earth a man of wealth or a distinguished scribe left his work to his bondservants; so, thanks to this invention, he could do the same in the Blessed Land.

[1] Pyramid of Tet'e, l. 60.

[2] There is no doubt as to the truth of this explanation, which is given by Maspero.

If, even after all these precautions, something should yet be wanting for the happiness and repose of the deceased, there were still the amulets, which could protect him from all harm. Little models of wands or of papyrus rolls, amulets for the fingers, sacred eyes of Horus, and other curious things, were laid by the side of the mummy or were hung in a chain round its neck; gradually the demand for these amulets increased so much that the manufacture of them became a symbol of Egyptian industry. In the same way as the beautiful vases of the Greeks are found in all those countries with which the Greeks traded, so these little talismans abound in every place where the Egyptians carried on their commerce, as a sign of their activity and of their joyless imagination.

From what we have said above, we see that an Egyptian would deem it a terrible misfortune, if at death he were not laid to rest in a tomb which answered to all these magical requirements; every one therefore who was not thoughtless or irreligious began to build a tomb as soon as possible, that is as soon as his means allowed. For instance, Un'e, the oft-mentioned contemporary of king Pepy, began his tomb when he had scarcely completed half his official career.[1] Owing to his beginning the building so early in life one drawback was unavoidable; the names of his sons were handed down to posterity as children with no titles, for every father was not so lucky as D'ad'aem'onch, the ancient "treasurer of the god" who prepared a special place in his tomb for his son "when he was still a child," and was able even then to designate him as his successor in his office.[2] To our minds this might be a small misfortune, but to the Egyptian, who was so proud of his titles, it was such an important matter that he resorted to the curious expedient of leaving an empty space before the name of his infant son, which the latter might fill in later to say how far he had been prospered by the favour of the Pharaoh. We should scarcely have been aware of this custom had not a stele been preserved to us in which the son had forgotten later to fill up the space.[3] A similar case exists with regard to a wife—Cha'emḥê't, the superintendent of the granaries of king Amenḥôtep III., mentioned above (see p. 108), built himself a splendid tomb in Thebes before he had settled his marriage arrangements. He was either still unmarried, or he had not decided which lady of his harem he should raise to be his legitimate wife. The statue of his wife is seated by him in his tomb, but in the inscription a space is left after the words "his dear wife, the lady of his house."[4] Evidently Cha'emḥê't died before he had made up his mind what name to insert.

The most pious and the most careful might however sometimes die without having built a tomb, for as the wise 'Eney taught his son, "the messenger comes to thee . . . even as to the old . . . say not to him: 'I am young' . . . death comes and takes as first-offering the child from the mother's breast, as well as the man who has grown old."[5] In this case it

[1] Ä. Z., 1882, 6.
[2] Mar. Mast., 200.
[3] Mar. Cat. d'Ab., 702, cp. with 703.
[4] From my own copy.
[5] Pap. de Boul., i. 17, 14-18, 4.

was the most sacred duty of those who were left, to fulfil that which the father was unable to perform for the safety of his soul, and to erect his tomb "according to that which he had said while he yet stood upon his feet."[1] This happened more often than we might expect, for many stelae, especially those of later ages, bear the statement that they were erected to a father "by his loving son, who maintains his name in life."

One circumstance that might tend to the postponement of the building of the tomb longer than was right was its great cost. Many men, whose rank obliged them to have their own tombs, had not the means to afford this luxury. There was a simple way out of this difficulty; without further trouble many people seized upon an ancient tomb that had perhaps belonged to an extinct family and was no longer cared for. If this were a grotto tomb, the walls were if necessary replastered and repainted; if it were a mastabah, it was rebuilt so far as was needful in order to remove the compromising inscriptions.[2] But this convenient expedient was considered sinful to a certain degree, and a really pious man preferred to build his tomb "on a pure place, on which no man had built his tomb; he also built his tomb of new material, and took no man's possession."[3] Others obtained help from the munificence of the Pharaoh for the proper construction and equipment of their tombs. Thus, apparently at the same time as the building of his own pyramid, king Menkerê' caused fifty of his royal workmen, under the direction of the high priest of Memphis, to erect a tomb for Debḥen, an officer of his palace. He also had a double false door brought for him from the quarries of Turah, which was then carved for him by the royal architect.[4] King Sehurê' also presented his chief physician Sechmetna'e'onch with a costly false door,[5] which was carved under the eyes of the Pharaoh by his own artists and painted in lapis-lazuli colour. The fate of this present was the same as that of many royal presents; the very modest tomb, which was all this learned man could afford to build for himself, looks all the poorer for this munificent royal gift. To others of his faithful servants the Pharaoh would send by the "treasurer of the god," with the "great transport ships of the court," a coffin together with its cover, which he had cut for them in the quarries of Turah.[6] Under the Middle and the New Empire the *good god* not infrequently presented the statues which were placed in the tomb or in the temple for the funerary worship. On many of these we can still read that they were "given as a reward on the part of the king."

It was natural that a people who thought so much of a suitable tomb should celebrate with special pomp the day on which the deceased was carried thither. With regard to those historical periods with which we are concerned, we are not certain how long a time intervened between the day of death and that of the funeral; at all events it was a long interval,

[1] L. D., ii. 34 d.

[2] Cases also exist however of ancient date, in which nothing in the tomb has been changed.

[3] Mar. Mast., 342. [4] L. D., ii. 37 b. [5] Mar. Mast., 204, 205.

[6] Ä. Z., 1882, 6-7; similarly in the injured inscription, L. D., ii. 76.

for whichever method of embalmment was followed, that process always occupied a considerable time. Even when the mummification was complete, the funeral of men of rank was often delayed in consequence of a curious custom; the mummy had first to take a journey. This may seem absurd to us, but to the Egyptian it was quite a serious matter. As I have remarked before, Abydos, the burial-place of the head of Osiris, was considered as the special grave of this god, and as Osiris was the divine prototype of all the faithful deceased, there could be no better spot for them to rest than in this sacred place. From the time of the 6th dynasty, countless numbers from all parts of Egypt were buried there in the hope that thus they would approach nearer to the god; "that they would receive the gifts of incense and divine offerings on the table of the king of the gods; that the great ones of Abydos would bid them 'welcome'; that a place would be granted them in the bark Neshmet on the festival of the necropolis."[1] Inasmuch as every one neither could nor would join this retinue of the god, they resorted to the expedient of causing the deceased to pay a personal visit to Osiris before he was laid to rest in the burial-field of his home. The mummy was wrapt in embroidered linen and brought on board a boat to Abydos; his friends escorted him in a second boat. We know nothing of what took place after the mummy "had arrived in peace at Abydos, in order to serve Osiris Uennofre"; probably the body assisted at the offerings to Osiris, for when the deceased "had returned in peace from Abydos," he boasted that he had there received offerings of bread, and "had breathed the breath of myrrh and incense."[2]

The day at length arrives when the mummy is to be laid to his eternal rest; the relations and friends assemble to escort it for the last time; though we can scarcely call it a funeral procession, for the mummy had to be taken across the Nile. The coffin, contained in a great painted case, covered with flowers, is placed on a richly decorated bark. Squatting near the body are the women relations of the deceased with their breasts bare, lamenting him; the funerary priest makes offerings and burns incense before the mummy. His official recitation, "an incense offering to thee, O Harmachis-Chepr'e, who art in the bark of Nun, the father of the gods, in that Neshmet bark, which conducts thither the god and Isis and Nephthys and this Horus, the son of Osiris," contrasts strangely with the lamentations of the women who, while they grieve that their husband and father has forsaken them, have no understanding of the subtle mysticism of these ceremonies. The boat in front of the funerary bark also contains women, who sit on the deck and make their lamentations towards the mummy; a near relation of the deceased stands in the bows of this boat and calls out to the helmsman: "Steer to the west, to the land of the justified. The women of the boat weep much, very much. In peace, in peace to the west, thou praised one, come in peace. . . . When time has become eternity then shall we see thee again, for behold, thou goest away to that

[1] Stele of 'Enḥer-necht of the seventh year of Usertsen II. (L. A.), and many similar examples.
[2] Journey to Abydos—M. E.: L. D., ii. 126, 127; N. E.: W., iii. lxvi.

FUNERAL PROCESSION A

NO. I. FROM THE TOMB OF NEFERḤÔTEP AT THEBES, OF THE TIME OF

NO. 2. FROM THE TOMB OF ROY, THE ESTATE-SUPERINTENDENT, OF THE TIME OF THE BEGINNING OF

the panther-skin is the Sem; the priest holding the mummy is dressed as An

ꞮEMONIES AT THE TOMB.

ꞮE OF THE 18TH DYNASTY. AFTER W., III. PL. 67. (Cp. the explanation, p. 320 f.)

H DYNASTY. AFTER W., III. PL. 68. (The priest with the book is the reciter-priest; the bald-headed priest with tomb is situate at the slope of the mountain; before it stands the funerary stela.)

country in which all are equal." In a third boat are the male relations, whilst the fourth is occupied by the colleagues and friends of the deceased, who carry the insignia of their office, and are come to render the last honours to him who is gone, and to lay in his tomb their presents, which are borne before them by their servants. The words of these prophets, princes and priests are of course less impassioned; they admire the crowd of followers: "Oh how beautiful is that which befalls him. . . . Because of the great love he bore to Chons of Thebes he is allowed to attain to the West followed by tribe after tribe of his servants." When these boats and the little barks containing the servants with bouquets of flowers, offerings of food, and boxes of all kinds, have all arrived at the western shore, the real funeral procession begins.[1] The bark with the coffin is placed on a sledge and drawn by oxen; the men walk in front followed by the women; thus in the same order that they had crossed the Nile, they wind along all the long way to the grave. We will pass over the necessary ceremonies which were performed here before the mummy, the mystical opening of the mouth of the deceased with the crook, the pouring out of water before him, the recitations of one priest from his book, the offering of incense by other priests,[2]—for it is necessary to be an Egyptian to feel much interest in these matters. It touches even our hearts however, when we hear the wife lament as she throws her arms round the mummy:[3] "I am thy sister, Meryt-Rê'; thou great one, forsake me not. Thou art so beautiful, my good father. What does it mean that I am now far from thee? Now I go alone. . . . Thou who didst love to talk with me,—thou art now silent and dost not speak." With the grief of the wife mingles the wailing of the mourners, who put dust on their heads and call out, "Alas the misfortune!" They cannot understand why he who had so many friends is now in the country where he knows but a few; why he who was so active should now be fettered and bound; why he who had such beautiful clothes should now wear the dress of yesterday for ever. In the rear there stands a group whose lamentations for the deceased do him most honour, the poor widows and orphans whom he had provided for during his lifetime.

The above description gives the essential characteristics of the funeral procession at all periods, except that sometimes one ceremony, at other times another ceremony, was the more minutely carried out. Under the New Empire the most important part was played by the acquaintances and friends of the deceased,[4] "the princes and friends of the palace,"[5] who escort the "praiseworthy good man"[6] and place the lordly *household goods*[7] near the coffin as their last gift. Under the Old and the Middle

[1] All the above remarks, after W., iii. lxvii., which is repeated (without the inscriptions) in the upper part of the accompanying plate.

[2] The above, after W., iii. lxviii.; cp. the lower part of the accompanying plate.

[3] The following again, after W., lxvii.

[4] Thus the "prophets, princes and priests" followed a priest (W., iii. lxvii.); the various artists of the *house of silver* follow a high official of the treasury (L. D., iii. 242).

[5] L. D., iii. 242. [6] W., iii. lxvii.; L. D., iii. 242 b. [7] Amh., 2, 9; Abb., 4, 3.

Empire[1] however, the transport of the statues of the deceased was the more important feature of the funeral;[2] and whilst the workmen dragged these statues on sledges to their appointed places, the reciter-priest offered incense before each; meantime dancing and singing girls gave a festive appearance, as the Egyptians thought, to the procession. These statues were not all taken to the *serdab* of the tomb; whoever was allowed to do so placed a statue in the temple of the god of his home[3] and others in a chapel on the roof of his house[4] as well as in his garden,[5] where many prepared a place in which their *Ka* should be honoured.

It is not our intention to describe this worship in detail; it consisted of offerings and burning of incense on festival days; in certain cases other ceremonies were added as well; for instance at Siut under the Middle Empire,[6] lamps were lighted before the statue of the deceased on the first and last days of the year, and on other festivals; also on the same days the friends came to the temple singing songs in praise of the departed. One scene only of these festivities shall be described here more fully, for it seems to have been of particular interest to the Egyptians and indeed especially to those of the Old Empire, as we gather from the countless representations in which it is depicted. This scene is the slaughter of the sacrificial animal, an ox or a great antelope.

The patient animal is led to the place of slaughter, and two practised slaughterers throw him down with ease.[7] The hind and fore legs are bound together, a string is tied round the tongue, and when this is pulled the poor animal falls at once helpless to the ground. Sometimes exciting scenes take place. A powerful animal sometimes rebels against his tormentors in a *very fighting* manner, and rushes madly upon them. But it is of no use,—whilst some avoid his thrusts in front, others boldly seize him from behind; they hold on to his legs, they hang on to his tail, two of the most courageous even spring madly on his back and wring his horns with might and main. The bull is unable to withstand their united efforts; he falls down, and the men succeed in binding his fore and hind legs together. They then fearlessly give him his death stroke; they cut his jugular vein, and, as they ironically say, they "allow him to yield." When the blood has been carefully collected they begin the chief business, the scientific cutting up of the animal. According to very

[1] O. E.: L. D., ii. 64 bis, 78, 104 c; Mar. Mast., 342 f; M. E.: L. D., ii. 126-127; N. E: (Memphis) L. D., iii. 242, I do not remember it in any Theban pictures.

[2] Representations of funerals under the Old Empire, besides those quoted in the previous note: L. D., ii. 14 a, 35, 101 b.

[3] L. D., ii. 124, 83; Ä. Z., 1882, 166, 173. Thus the statues of men of rank have been found at Karnak and in the temple of Memphis.

[4] L. D., ii. 35; it is doubtful, nevertheless, whether it may not be the roof of the mastabah.

[5] Ä. Z., 1882, 182.

[6] Ä. Z., 1882, 164.

[7] The throwing down of the ox—O. E.: Bädeker, 404; L. D., 14 b; M. E.: L. D., ii. 129; Ros. Mc., 29, 1. Stabbing the animal—O. E.: Brugsch, Gr. W., 97; N. E.: Ros., Mc., 86. Cutting up of the animal represented continually, remarkable examples—O. E.: Düm. Res., 11; L. D., ii. 24, 52, 66-68 (=Ros. Mc., 83), 73, 78; Brugsch, Gr. W., 92-100; Perrot, 145-281; M. E.: L. D., ii. 128-129 (with other words), Ros. Mc., 119, 3; N. E.: Ros. Mc., 86.

ancient custom, which we often find retains its authority at sacrificial ceremonies, the slaughterers use flint knives for this purpose; but as these knives would soon become blunt, the men wear a metal sharpener (like our modern steel) tied to the corner of the apron, with which they sharpen the knife, striking off splinters of the stone.

The legs, which the Egyptians considered the best part of the animal, are cut off first; one man holds up the hoof of the animal, and with his arm round it draws it back as firmly as he can, the other cuts it off at the joint. The following conversation takes place between the two men: "Draw it as far as you can"; "I am doing so." The belly is then slit up, and the heart of the animal taken out, this being also esteemed as such a choice piece for sacrificial purposes, that the one man takes much interest in showing the beauty of it to the other.

The disjointed pieces however cannot yet be made use of for the offering, for the most important personage has not yet appeared on the scene of action; the slaughterer already remarks in a vexed tone, "Will not the priest come to this leg joint?" At length he comes; he is the superintendent of the Ue'bs of the Pharaoh, who must declare the sacrifice to be pure. He gravely smells the blood of the animal and examines the flesh carefully, he then declares all to be good and pure. Now the legs can be laid upon the table of offerings; afterwards at the close of the festival they will be used to satisfy the hunger of the mourners.

These bulls, as well as the offering of bread and beer, are said to be the "offering that the king gives,"[1] for, according to ancient custom, it was the duty of the Pharaoh to provide the funerary offerings. Under the Middle Empire a "steward of the provision-house and superintendent of the horns, feathers, and claws" (see p. 96) boasts that he had "caused the offerings for the gods and the funerary gifts for the deceased to be brought, according to the command of Horus, the lord of the palace," *i.e.* the king.[2] This custom probably only existed in those early ages when there were but a few men of high station who were allowed by the gracious permission of the king to construct their tombs near the tomb of the monarch. Later, the number of tombs increased to such an extent that the custom fell into disuse of itself; the funerary offering however was always called "the offering that the king gives," though it was brought, as was natural, by the relations of the deceased. It was the most sacred duty which the latter had to fulfil, to present the offerings regularly to their ancestors, to keep up their tombs, and thus to "cause their names to live." As it was impossible however to know what might happen to a family after many centuries, whether indeed it might be in existence or whether the property might suffice to pay for the necessary offerings, most men of rank even under the Old

[1] L. D., ii. 35.

[2] Leyden, v. 7 (L. A.). Cp. also L. D., ii. 22 b, where in addition to the funeral offerings, the *treasure* (*i.e.* the clothes, rouge, and oil) is also given from the royal house; see also R. J. H., 93, where the funerary offerings are supplied by the royal barns, houses of silver, workshops, etc.

Empire established special endowments for the cost of their funerary offerings, and for the maintenance of a special priest, the *servant of the ka.* Sometimes certain villages or plots of ground were put aside with their taxes or produce for the *house of eternity,—i.e.* for these endowments;[1] sometimes contracts were concluded with the priesthood of a town, who, in consideration of a higher remuneration, undertook to supply the necessary offerings to the tomb for ever.[2] Special deeds were drawn up for the administration of these endowments; and from the way in which provision was made for various casualties, it is natural to conclude that these endowments often met with mischances. For instance, if a tomb possessed but one funerary priest, he would be able alone to dispose of the endowed property, and he might prefer at his death to divide it amongst his children, instead of making it over to the one of his sons who was to succeed him in his office.[3] If, on the other hand, as was usually the case with the great men of the Old Empire, many funerary priests were appointed, disputes often arose about the revenues of the endowment.[4]

It would be very interesting to find out how long these provisions lasted, and for what length of time the tomb endowments were respected. I fear not for very long. Under the Middle Empire the nomarchs of Beni Hasan and Bersheh were obliged to re-establish the tomb-abodes of their ancestors.[5] Thus the length of time between the 6th and the 12th dynasty had sufficed for the provision for the regular maintenance of these tombs to lapse. In the same way the tomb of the oft-mentioned Chnemḥôtep at Beni Hasan was certainly left unguarded at the beginning of the New Empire, otherwise it would have been impossible for four scribes of that time to have immortalised themselves with the remark that they had here admired the temple of king Chufu;[6] visitors do not scribble upon the walls of a chapel that is being regularly used for worship. Probably therefore the tomb of this mighty ruler was at that time empty and forsaken, and the endowment which had been made for eternity had already come to an end. This will not surprise us when we remember that important estates were tied up in endowments to serve this most useless purpose. This was such an unnatural state of affairs that from time to time a reaction was sure to set in against it. This reaction need not have been a violent one; when a family became extinct or went down in the world so much that the members were unable to threaten the administrators of the endowment and to insist that they should perform their duty, the latter gradually dropped the maintenance of the offerings. Even if a family maintained their power and their riches for centuries, they would be obliged after a time to be faithless to the ordinances of their fathers; for

[1] The lists of villages found in the mastabahs may refer simply to this endowed property; they would not then represent the whole property of the deceased. The remarkable list of lands at Beni-Hasan is certainly a list of the endowments (Champ. Not., ii. 336 ff.).

[2] See the instances given, p. 145. [3] Mar. Mon. div., 64, 9-12. [4] R. J. H., i.; Mar. Mast., 318.

[5] Dḥutnacht of Bersheh restored three tombs in Sheikh Said (L. D., ii. 112 e, 113 b, c). Chnemḥôtep of Beni Hasan restored the "injured" tombs of his fathers (ib. 125, 161 ff.).

[6] L. D., vi. 22.

each generation constructed at least *one* new tomb for which it was necessary to provide an endowment out of the estates. Under these conditions we cannot blame even the richest families when they transferred an endowment belonging to the tomb of a long-forgotten ancestor to the tomb of one they had lately lost.

When once the maintenance of the funerary worship of a tomb ceased, its doom was certain. It was closed and left to its fate, and I need not add, after what I have said in the seventh chapter, that its fate was robbery and violation. The state did what it could to protect the tombs, but these small uninhabited buildings, situated far from the town, in an extensive and often hilly region, were difficult to guard in spite of the walls which surrounded them and the police who had charge of them. Even if robbers were kept off from outside, there were thieves in their midst who were still more dangerous. The workmen who built and decorated the new tombs plundered the old ones; the art of cutting passages in the rock, which was carried to such perfection in the service of those lately deceased, was turned to account by them in making subterranean ways from an open tomb into the interior of one strictly closed. Whether the state gave them their wages or not, we can easily understand, from what we have already related (p. 125), how difficult it was for these starving people to withstand the temptation of appropriating the treasures hidden in the ground all round them—treasures also which were greatly exaggerated by report. They did their work of clearance so well that it is rarely we find a tomb inviolate; they were all plundered in old times.

The class of tombs most in danger were of course those of the royal families. A few ornaments might be found on the bodies of private individuals, but, according to popular tradition, the body of a Pharaoh would be a real gold mine. Special precautions were therefore taken with regard to the tombs of the kings. Over the bodies of the rulers of the Old and Middle Empires were erected the mighty pyramids, and their massive walls were of such immense strength that it was impossible to break through them by violence, whilst the small passage through which the coffin was introduced into the inner chamber was plugged up in the most ingenious manner with great blocks of granite. Difficulties of this kind were of course impracticable for the common thieves of the necropolis, and the robbers, who overcame them and made their way into the pyramids, did so by destructive works on a vast scale, which were certainly carried on with the knowledge of the rulers of the state.

The method by which the government tried to protect the bodies of the Theban Pharaohs was not so successful. The tombs of those kings who ruled after the 18th dynasty were situate outside the necropolis in the rocky valley of Biban el Moluk, separated from the Theban City of the Dead by the high mountain Asâs. The sides of this valley are steep and rocky, and it is entered by but one good road, a circuitous route of two hours, with such a narrow opening into the Valley of the Tombs that it can be easily guarded by a few men. Direct from western Thebes it was possible to cross the rocky steep walls of the Gebel Asâs at two points only; there was also another difficult entrance from the valley behind Biban el Moluk. These three footpaths over the mountains were guarded by military outposts, and the ruins of their stone huts are still to be seen; another outpost was stationed at the entrance to the valley. Thus, according to human calculations, it seemed that the Valley of the Tombs of the Kings was safe from the entrance of all unauthorised persons. Did thieves succeed in crossing the rocky mountain at an unguarded part, it would be scarcely possible in that narrow valley for them to escape the eyes of the watch. The greed of man, however, can always find ways to overcome difficulties which in the natural course appear unsurpassable, and the tombs in the Biban el Moluk fell victims to the thieves of the 20th dynasty. We have already shown in the seventh chapter how thoroughly they carried out their work.

It was not necessary that the funerary worship of the Pharaohs should suffer because their tombs were injured. Under the Old Empire as well as under the New Empire, the funerary services were held, not in a chamber of the king's tomb, but in a great temple built for the purpose. At Memphis these temples were situate quite close to the pyramids, but at Thebes they were built far away from the tombs in the general necropolis proper, there being no room for buildings in the narrow Biban el Moluk. Under the New Empire the king alone was not worshipped in these temples; they were dedicated also to Amon and his co-deities; the Pharaoh was one amongst these gods, an exceeding great honour being thus paid to him. At this time therefore we no longer hear of the priests of the kings, for the clergy of these temples, being in the first place priests of Amon like other clergy, would only take the former title in addition.

Under the Old Empire it was otherwise; many men of rank of that time were called priests of the kings, some even who held six different priestly offices together with their previous charge.[1] These priests are generally called "Prophets of the pyramid of the king," seldom prophets of the king himself—the latter title seems to indicate that the monarch enjoyed purely divine honours in addition to the adoration paid to him as a deceased king in the pyramid temple. This worship of the kings lasted a long time, for even as late as the time of Psammetichus we find priests of Menes and of D'eser. Thus these celebrated kings of antiquity were revered for more than two thousand years, though there were probably long periods when their worship was interrupted owing to political circumstances. Political hatred in Egypt stood in no awe of the tombs, even when they belonged to a past age. Prof. Petrie has conclusively shown that all the funerary temples of the kings of the Old Empire were ruined in an outbreak of political rage. The destruction of these temples is such as can be explained by no other hypothesis. For love of gain, treasure-seekers might break into pyramids and smash granite sarcophagi, but men who threw the statues of kings into wells or broke them into atoms, could only

[1] Mar. Mast., 198-199.

be actuated by fanaticism. In later times in Thebes we see an instance of a similar though less barbarous act of revenge perpetrated on a hated form of government. It must strike every one who goes through the tombs belonging to the second half of the 18th dynasty, that there is generally a hole in the wall of the tomb in the place where the name of the deceased ought to be inscribed, so that a long search is often required in order to find the name perhaps in some dark corner of the ceiling. After the victory of the heretics under Chuen'eten, these fanatics revenged themselves thus on the adherents of the orthodox government they had overthrown.

TOMBS IN THE NECROPOLIS, FROM A STELE AT GIZEH.

FROM A BOOK OF PRESCRIPTIONS OF THE BEGINNING OF THE NEW EMPIRE (Eb. 88, 13).

CHAPTER XIV

LEARNING

WHEN the wise Dauuf, the son of Chert'e, voyaged up the Nile with his son Pepy, to introduce him into the "court school of books," he admonished him thus: "Give thy heart to learning and love her like a mother, for there is nothing that is so precious as learning."[1] Whenever or wherever we come upon Egyptian literature, we find the same enthusiastic reverence for learning (or as it is expressed more concretely, for books). If however, we expect to find ideal motives for this high estimation of learning, we shall be disappointed. The Egyptian valued neither the elevating nor ennobling influence which the wise men of antiquity imputed to him, and still less the pure pleasure which we of the modern world feel at the recognition of truth. The wise Dauuf himself gives us the true answer to our questions on this subject; after he has described in well-turned verses all the troubles and vexations of the various professions, he concludes in favour of wisdom in the last two lines, which have been frequently quoted by later writers:

"Behold there is no profession which is not governed,
It is only the learned man who rules himself."[2]

The Egyptians valued learning because of the superiority which, in matters of this life, learned men possessed over the unlearned; learning thus divided the ruling class from those who were ruled. He who followed learned studies, and became a *scribe*, had put his feet on the first rung of the great ladder of official life, and all the offices of the state were open to him. He was exempted from all the bodily work and trouble with which others were tormented. The poor ignorant man, "whose name is unknown, is like a heavily-laden donkey, he is driven by the scribe," while the fortunate man who "has set his heart upon learning, is above work, and becomes a wise prince."[3] Therefore "set to work and become a scribe, for then thou shalt be a leader of men.[4] The profession of scribe is a princely profession, his writing materials and his rolls of books bring pleasantness and riches."[5]

[1] Sall., 2, 4, 2-5.

[2] Sall., 2, 9, 1 = An., 7, 4, 6. Quoted, e.g. Sall., 1, 6, 8.

[3] Ä. Z., 1880, p. 96.

[4] An., 3, 6, 3.

[5] An., 5, 10, 8 ff.

The scribe never lacks food, what he wants is given to him out of the royal store: "the learned man has enough to eat because of his learning."[1] He who is industrious as a scribe and does not neglect his books, he may become a prince, or perhaps attain to the council of the *thirty*, and when there is a question of sending out an ambassador, his name is remembered at court.[2] If he is to succeed, however, he must not fail to be diligent, for we read in one place: "the scribe alone directs the work of all men, but if the work of books is an abomination to him, then the goddess of fortune is not with him."[3]

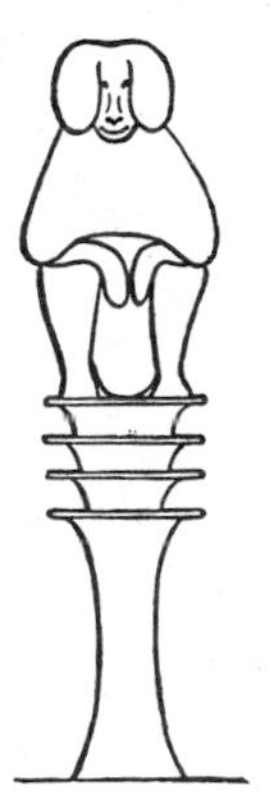

THE GOD THOTH IN THE FORM OF HIS SACRED ANIMAL. (After L. D., iii. 171.)

Therefore he who is wise will remain faithful to learning, and will pray Thoth the god of learning to give him understanding and assistance. Thoth is the "baboon with shining hair and amiable face,[4] the letter-writer for the gods,"[5] he will not forget his earthly colleagues if they call upon him and speak thus to him: "Come to me and guide me, and make me to act justly in thine office. Thine office is more beautiful than all offices. . . . Come to me, guide me! I am a servant in thine house. Let all the world tell of thy might, that all men may say: 'Great is that which Thoth hath done.' Let them come with their children, to cause them to be marked as scribes. Thine office is a beautiful office, thou strong protector. It rejoices those who are invested with it."[6]

The boy who was intended for the profession of scribe was sent when quite young into the *instruction house*, the school, where, even if he was of low rank, he was "brought up with the children of princes and called to this profession."[7] In old times the *school for scribes* was attached to the court;[8] the schools of the New Empire must have been organised differently, for it seems that the various government departments, *e.g.* the house of silver, etc., had their own schools, in which the candidates for the respective official positions were educated. From various passages in the school literature we know that the individual training of the young scribes was carried on by one of the higher officials of the department to whom they were assigned as pupils and subordinates. One of these pupils writes to his tutor: "I was with thee since I was brought up as a child; thou didst beat my back and thy instructions went into my ear."[9] From this we may assume that there was no disconnection at all between the early teaching and the later higher instruction; it seems that the same old official who initiated *his disciple*[10] into his duties, had also to superintend his work when he had to learn the first elements of knowledge.

[1] Prisse, 15, 13. [2] An., 5, 9, 5; ib. 17, 7.
[3] Sall., 1, 6, 8. [4] An., 3, 4, 12. [5] An., 5, 9, 7.
[6] An., 5, 9, 2-10, 2. I have amended the text in one place, where it was injured.
[7] An., 5, 22, 6 ff. Cp. also Sall., 2, 4, 1. [8] Sall., 2, 3, 9 ff. [9] An., 4, 8, 7.
[10] An., 5, 18, 1. An. 5, 22, 8.

It was quite possible for a boy to enter a different profession from that for which he was educated at school; Bekenchons the high priest of Amon relates that, from his fifth to his sixteenth year, he had been "captain in the royal stable for education,"[1] and had then entered the temple of Amon in the lowest rank of priesthood. After serving as a cadet, as we should say, he entered the ecclesiastical profession. The *stable for education* must have been a sort of military school, in which boys of rank who were intended to be officers in the army became as a rule "captains of the stable."[2]

Fortunately our sources of information enable us to follow the broad outlines of the form and kind of instruction which was given in this ancient period. The school discipline was severe. The boy was not allowed to oversleep himself: "The books are (already) in the hands of thy companions, take hold of thy clothes, and call for thy sandals," says the scribe crossly as he awakes the scholar.

Lesson time, the results of which were said to "endure for ever like the mountains,"[3] took up half the day, when "noon was announced" the children left the school *shouting for joy*.[4] The food of the school children must have been rather sparing—three rolls of bread and two jugs of beer had to suffice for a schoolboy;[5] this was brought to him daily by his mother from home.[6] On the other hand there was plenty of flogging, and the foundation of all the teaching was: "The youth has a back, he attends when it is beaten."[7] A former schoolboy writes thus to his old tutor, from whom he has received yet severer punishments: "Thou hast made me buckle to since the time that I was one of thy pupils. I spent my time in the lock-up; he bound my limbs. He sentenced me to three months, and I was bound in the temple."[8]

The Egyptians justified this severity in theory. The usual argument was that man was able to tame all animals; the Ka'ere, which was brought from Ethiopia, learnt to understand speech and singing; lions were instructed, horses broken in, hawks were trained, and why should not a young scribe be broken in in the same way?[9] As however he was not quite on a par with lions or horses, these pedagogues used admonishment also as a useful expedient. This was applied unceasingly; whether the schoolboy was "in bed or awake" he was always instructed and admonished.[10] Sometimes he hears: "O scribe, be not lazy, otherwise thou wilt have to be made obedient by correction. Do not spend thy time in wishing, or thou wilt come to a bad end.

"Let thy mouth read the book in thy hand, take advice from those who

1 (statue of Bekenchons at Munich); is often used in this sense.

2 We must not therefore conclude that each captain of the stable was a boy.

3 M. E.: Sall., 2, 9, 4. 4 M. E.: Sall., 2, 10, 2. 5 M. E.: Sall., 2, 10, 6.

6 Pap. de Boul., I. 20, 20. 7 An., 5, 8, 6.

8 An., 5, 18, 1-3. The *temple* doubtless signifies here the prison of the temple.

9 Bol., 3, 9 f.; An., 5, 8, 7 ff. = An. 3, 4, 1 ff. 10 Bol., 3, 7.

know more than thou dost. Prepare thyself for the office of a prince, that thou mayst attain thereto when thou art old. Happy the scribe who is skilled in all his official duties. Be strong and active in thy daily work.

"Spend no day in idleness, or thou wilt be flogged. For the ears of the young are placed on the back, and he hears when he is flogged.

"Let thy heart attend to what I say; that will bring thee to happiness. . . . Be zealous in asking counsel — do not neglect it in writing; do not get disgusted with it. Let thy heart attend to my words, thus wilt thou find thy happiness."[1]

As soon as the scholars had thoroughly mastered the secrets of the art of writing, the instruction consisted chiefly in giving them passages to copy, so that they might at the same time practise their calligraphy and orthography and also form their style. Sometimes the teacher chose a text without much regard to the contents — a fairy-tale,[2] a passage from some religious or magical book,[3] a modern[4] or an ancient poem[5] — the latter was especially preferred, when it would impress the youth by its ingenious enigmatical language. More frequently, however, he chose his specimen, so that it might tend to the education of his pupil; he gave him a *sbayt*, that is an *instruction*, to copy. These *instructions*, which we shall consider more closely in the next chapter, are of two kinds. In the first place most of those of the time of the Middle Empire contain rules for wise conduct and good manners, which are put into the mouth of a wise man of old times.[6] The others, which are of later date, are instructions in the form of letters, a fictitious correspondence between tutor and pupil,[7] in which the former is supposed to impart wisdom and at the same time a fine epistolary style. It was of course only exceptionally that the teacher would compose these letters himself, he preferred to take them word for word out of books, or sometimes to paraphrase some other person's letter.[8] This did not however prevent many tutors and pupils from signing their own names to these old letters, as if they were really carrying on a correspondence with one another.

The number of these letters which have come down to us in these copy-books and stelae is comparatively speaking very great; a much greater number than we have of any other literary composition. This need not surprise us, for it was more important to the young scholar to have

[1] An., 3, 3, 9 ff. = An., 5, 8, 1 ff.

[2] E.g. that of the d'Orbiney and Sall., I.

[3] Religious: L. D., vi. 115 ff. Magical: Sall., 4.

[4] Sall., 3.

[5] E.g. the hymn to the Nile, Sall., 2; An., 7.

[6] Proverbs of Ptaḥḥôtep and of Kagemn'e in the Pap. Prisse; teaching of Dauuf in Sall., 2, An., 7; teaching of Amenemḥê't, ib. Pap. Millingen at Berlin; Proverbs of 'Eney, on papyri at Gizeh and stelae at Berlin.

[7] It is evident that these letters are mostly fictitious, partly from their contents, which are usually couched in general terms, and partly from the fact that where special circumstances are mentioned, round numbers are always employed.

[8] Therefore we find the same letter repeated in the various school copy-books under different names, e.g. An., 3, 5, 5 ff. = An., 4, 9, 4 ff. An., 4, 11, 8 ff. = Sall., 1, 9, 9 ff. etc. Sometimes, as an exception, of course a tutor may have given a real letter instead of a fictitious one as a copy.

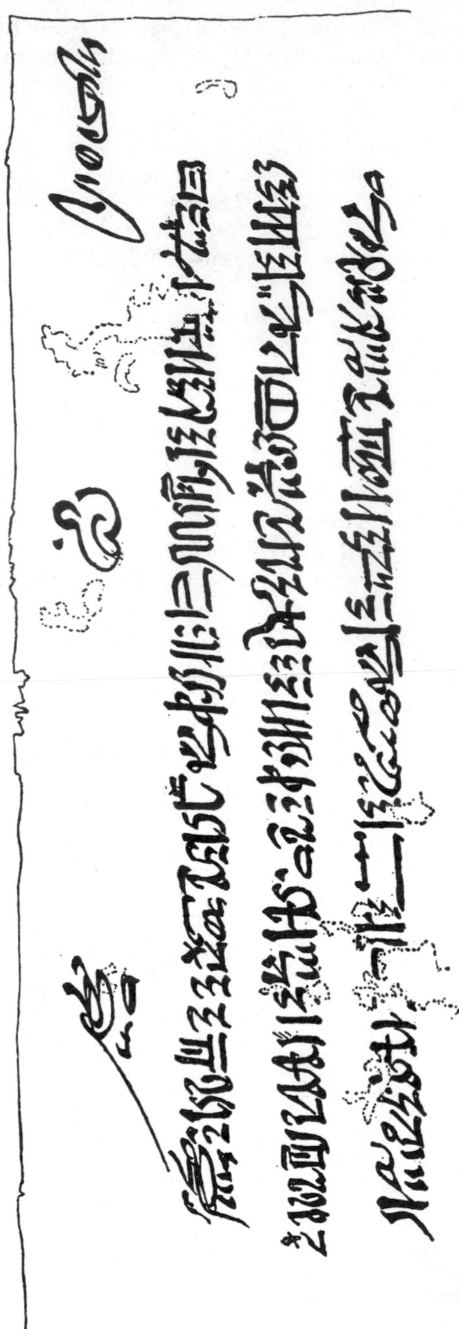

UPPER PART OF A PAGE OUT OF A SCHOOL COPY-BOOK.

The text runs: "Harvest. The worm took half of the food, the hippopotamus the other half. Many mice were in the field, the locusts, the cattle ate; the sparrows stole. Woe (?) to the farmers! The remainder, which is in the threshing floor, the thieves made an end of for him. . . ." The word '*asha* = much, at the end of the first line, is corrected, as well as the sign *te* in the middle of the third line, both of which were not written well enough by the otherwise not unskilful scribe. (After An. 5, 16.)

in his tomb his copy-book, the only achievement of his youthful powers, than for the man to have his favourite book, apart from the fact that the friends and relations would find it easier to part with a worthless copy-book than with a really serviceable writing, which might be of further use to the living. An Egyptian copy-book is easily recognised; its size is peculiar as well as its shape; the pages are short, and contain a few long lines, while on the upper edge of these pages there are usually the tutor's corrections, which are generally of a calligraphic nature. It is interesting to find on one of these school papyri the date, the 24th of Epiphi written in on the right-hand side; three pages before we find the 23rd of Epiphi, and three pages after, the 25th Epiphi; evidently three pages was the daily task the pupil had to write. This may not seem much, but we must remember that these pupils had at the same time to do some practical work in the department. We learn this also from their copy-books, not from that part which was shown to the teacher, but from the reverse sides. The back of the papyrus rolls, which was supposed to be left blank, was often used by the Egyptians as a note-book ; and a few hasty words jotted down there by the young scribe are often of more interest to us than the careful writing on the other side. There are many of these scribbles on the backs of the copy-books, and the little pictures of lions and oxen, specimens of writing of all kinds, bills of the number of sacks of corn received, or drafts of business letters and the like, show us the sort of practical work the owners of these rolls of books did for the department in which they had been entered. When we observe the astonishing early maturity of the modern Egyptian boy, we need not be surprised that these twelve- or fourteen-year-old scribes of antiquity had already learnt to be really useful to the authorities.

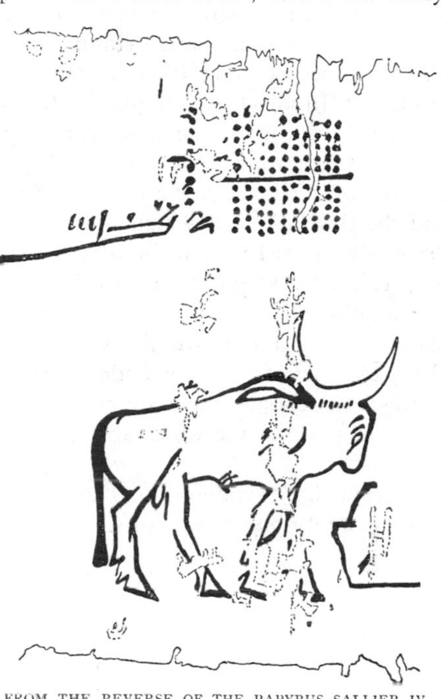

FROM THE REVERSE OF THE PAPYRUS SALLIER IV. (PAGE 14).

Below is a bull, above him a sum—109 dots, one group of which (as we see by the writing at the side—"together 511") signifies the addition of five sacks of corn, bread, or such like, at a time ; the second, of eight at a time ; the third, of one at a time.

From the earliest ages the Egyptians had the greatest veneration for their writing, which they considered to be the foundation of all education. They called it the *divine words*, and believed it to have been an invention of the god Thoth, who had taught it to the inhabitants of the Nile valley. In fact, though hieroglyphs may not have been invented by an Egyptian god, they were especially an Egyptian invention, and one of which that nation had every reason to be proud. For in spite of its complexity the Egyptian is one of the best and the easiest to be read of all the various kinds of writing that have ever been current in the world. The form which we find in historical times is certainly not the original one. It is now pretty well proved that the most ancient hieroglyphic writing was purely phonetic, somewhat like the Phoenician. It possessed the same peculiarity as the Phoenician and various Semitic styles of writing, viz. as a rule the consonants only of the words were written. *Chôdeb*, to kill, was written *chdb*, and *mosd'ed'*, to hate, was written *msd'd'* ; the reader had to guess from the context whether the word was *chdb* or *msd'd'*, as written, or perhaps *chadbi*, I killed; *masdedi*, I hated.

It may seem strange to us that all these nations stopped half-way as it were, and did not go on to indicate, by other signs, how the consonants were to be respectively vocalised, or whether they were to remain without vowels. When we understand however the construction of these languages, we see how it came to pass that the vowels had a secondary position. In all these languages the meaning of the word is generally contained in the consonants, whilst the vowels are added as a rule to indicate the grammatical forms. If we take for instance the Arabic word *qatala*, he killed, the meaning of *killing* rests in the three consonants *qtl*, and the three *a*s, with which these consonants are united, serve merely to designate the 3rd person singular of the active perfect. The passive form, he was killed, is expressed by the vowels, *u*, *i*, *a*, and is therefore *qutila*, the infinitive is *qutl*, the imperative *qtul*, the participle *qâtil*, etc.—the consonants of the word always remain the same, whilst the vowels are changed. We can easily understand that a nation, speaking a language of this kind, should naturally come to consider the consonants as the only essential part of the word, and to find it sufficient if these alone were written.

Originally, therefore, the Egyptian writing consisted only of the following twenty-one consonants:

b — p — f

k — q (a kind of k, the ק) — g

t — t′ (a kind of t)

d — d′ (a kind of d)

m — n

h — ḥ (a hard h) — r and l

s — sh — ch

w — the א of the Hebrew or an allied sound

a weak, and a strong peculiar sound (somewhat like the ע of the Hebrew).

Each of these signs stands for a short word with similar sound, from which it derives its phonetic worth; thus *t* is probably a roll of bread *ta*, *r* is properly the mouth *ro*, *n* is the water *nu*, *d* the hand *dot*, etc.

The god Ptaḥ is written, the thigh, *chôpesh*, , the name, *ran*, , the father, *'ôt*, , the vowels of these words being simply omitted.

In a few cases only, in which the vowel was really important for the right reading of the word, the Egyptians tried in a way to indicate the same in their writing. For this object they made use of the three consonants , just as the Hebrews used ה *h*, י *j*, ו *w*; at the same time these vowels always remained uncertain, being exceptional to the language. It was not the vowels alone which were suppressed by the Egyptians; in many words an *m*, *n*, or *r* was omitted, with apparently no reason for the omission. Thus for instance they wrote as a rule , *rt'*, for , *rômet'*, many (Coptic *rôme*): other examples might be given.

A method of writing such as we have described is in itself both readable and comprehensible, at any rate by the people who write it. Nevertheless the Egyptians were not content with this simple system, but even in prehistoric times they developed it in quite a peculiar manner. They endeavoured to make the language clearer and more concise by the introduction of word symbols. In order to express the word *nefer*, the lute, the three letters would rightly be necessary, but for the sake of simplicity they drew the lute, , itself instead of writing the three consonants; the advantage of the latter plan was that the reader knew exactly what word was meant, which was not so apparent by the letters . If they wrote *sa*, the goose, with only, and *cha*, the flower, with only, or with , it would still remain doubtful whether the reader would immediately connect the right idea with those signs; if on the other hand they drew the goose, , or the flower, , all ambiguity would be avoided. A great number of these picture signs being introduced into the writing, give the hieroglyphs their peculiar character. In many cases they have quite superseded the purely phonetic writing of the word; it would occur to no one for instance to write *per*, the house, ; the house itself, , was always drawn instead. There were however a great number of words which could not be drawn, *e.g. good*, *son*, or *to go out*; they therefore went a step further and substituted words with a similar sound which could be easily drawn. In order to write *nôfer*, good, they had recourse to *nefer*, the lute, ; *sa*, the son, was replaced by *sa*, the goose, ; and for *per*, to go out, they substituted *per*, the house, . Further, as words such as *good* and *son* occurred much more frequently than *lute* or *goose*, the signs and were in a great measure turned aside from their primitive signification, and if possible the words which they originally represented were written in some other fashion. Finally, many short words, the signs for which were often used variously, lost their meaning, and became mere syllabic signs which could be employed in any word in which that syllable occurred. For instance, with the signs or or , no one thought of the words *cha*, the flower, or *pa*, to fly, or *nu*, the jar, which they originally represented; they became mere phonetic syllabic signs without any special signification. In the same way , the draughtboard, became the sign for the syllable *mn*; and , the fan, a sign for the syllable *ms*, etc.

In picture-writing of this kind it was impossible to guard against all misunderstandings, and the reader might often feel doubtful as to what idea was intended by a certain sign. For instance, with the sign of the ear, , it might be impossible to know whether it stood for *masd'rt*, the ear, or for *sôd'm*, to hear, or *'edn*, the ear, or *'ôdn*, to substitute, for it was used as a sign for all these words. A simple expedient was then adopted—these various words were defined in the following manner: the sign was used as the final or initial consonant of one or the other word. Thus they wrote *'edn*, the ear, ; *'ôdn*, to substitute, , and *sôd'm*, to hear, . In words which rarely occurred they might write out all their consonants also, *e.g.* , *sôd'm*, to hear, or , *pet*, heaven.

Whether a sign was to be used for the whole word, whether consonants were to be added, or how many of these there ought to be, was decided in each word by custom. *Ḥqt*, beer, was written phonetically only, , whilst *ḥqat*, dominion, was written with the sign for the word and the two terminal consonants . *Per*, to go out, retained the final *r*, , whilst the *p* was not written; in *pr*, house, , on the contrary, neither consonant was added.

One point still remained which might lead to many errors. The Egyptians wrote, like nearly all the nations of antiquity, without any division of the words, and there was therefore the danger of not recognising the words aright. It would be possible, for instance, to read , *rn*, name, as *ro n*, the mouth of, or , *masd'rt*, the ear, as *mes d'rt*, born of the bird, or \\, *chaui*, night, as the dual form of *cha*, flower, signifying simply two flowers. This danger was avoided in a most ingenious manner. At the end of the various words were added the so-called determinatives, signs indicating the class of idea to which the words belonged. Thus after all words signifying man, they wrote , after those in which the mouth was concerned 𓀁, after abstract ideas 𓏛, and so on. All ambiguity was thus avoided. If after 𓂋𓈖 there followed 𓀀𓏤, it would signify name; with 𓇯 signified night, because there followed the determinatives of the sky and the sun; and was determined with certainty by the figure of the ear to be the word *masd'ert*, the ear.

These determinatives are the latest invention of Egyptian writing, and we are able to observe their gradual introduction; in the oldest inscriptions they are used but rarely, whilst in later times there is scarcely a word which is not written without one or even several determinatives. Which determinative ought to belong to a certain word, or in which line it ought to be written, is again decided by custom; 𓂻, to go out, receives the determinative of going; 𓂻, *'eu*, to go, is written in the older inscriptions without that sign; while 𓂻, *wð'er*, to fly, takes the determinative of going as well as that of marching, and so on.

We see that the hieroglyphic writing was very complicated (it contains

EXAMPLES OF HIEROGLYPHS DRAWN IN FULL.
Below are the same in the simpler form, as we use them (in reverse direction) for printing.

altogether about 500 signs in general use), but it is at the same time one of the best and most intelligible of the Eastern languages. When the orthography of the various words has been learnt by practice, it is easy to read a hieroglyphic text. The determinative shows throughout how the words are to be divided, and it enables us also at the first glance to recognise approximately with what sort of word we have to do. We must not underestimate this advantage in a language where the vowels are usually omitted.

The appearance of the hieroglyphs is also much more pleasing than that of the cuneiform; when the signs are carefully drawn and coloured with their natural colours, they present an aspect both artistic and gay.

Broad spaces of architecture were often brightened up by this form of decoration, and we may even say that most of the inscriptions on the walls and pillars of the Egyptian buildings are really purely decorative. This is the reason of the empty character of the contents of these inscriptions; with the object merely of decorating the architecture with a few lines of brightly-coloured hieroglyphs, the architect causes the gods to be assured for the thousandth time that they have put all countries under the throne of the Pharaoh their son, or he informs us a hundred times that his Majesty has erected this sanctuary of good eternal stones for his father the god.

It is evident, from the carefulness with which the Egyptians considered the arrangement and order of the hieroglyphs, that they regarded these monumental inscriptions chiefly as decorative. It is an inviolable law in Egyptian calligraphy that the individual groups of hieroglyphs forming the inscription must take a quadrangular form. If, for instance, we have the three signs *p*, *t*, and (determinative of the sky), which together make the word *pet*, the sky, they can only be written , not , nor . The word *secher*, the custom, was written or , not nor ; *dôr*, to constrain, was written , not nor . They carried this endeavour so far that with words in which the consonants would not make a quadrangular form in their right order, they preferred to write them incorrectly rather than to make the group ugly. Thus, for instance, the word *χaft*, in sight of, is rarely written , but almost always . The same desire for decorative effect is seen in the fact that when two inscriptions are placed as pendants to each other, the writing runs in opposite directions. As a rule the characters run from right to left, so that the heads of the hieroglyphs look towards the right; in the above case however the signs in the inscription on the right have to be content with following the reverse direction.

The ornamental character of the hieroglyphs was in no way an advantage for the sense; the scribe, when making his pretty pictures, forgot only too easily that the individual signs were not merely ornamental, but that they had a certain phonetic value. The indifference to faults which thus arose was increased by another bad peculiarity of Egyptian writing. The frequent use of signs for whole words, which was allowed by the language, rendered the scribe more and more indifferent to the use of an insufficiency of phonetic signs. They often wrote, for instance, , *ḥmt nb*, instead of , *ḥimet nibet*, every woman; every one who understood the connection, would read the words *ḥimet nibet* whether the feminine termination were added to the second word or not. They would also write both the active participle, *mrr*, as well as the passive, *mry*, simply, *mr*; the reader could easily see from the context whether *loving* or *loved* was intended; thus we see that the more ambiguities the writing admitted, so much the more did the scribes aggravate the evil by their feeling for sufficiency merely.

The inconveniences however, which sprang from the gradual wider development of the language, were still worse. Even in the time of the Old Empire the standpoint of the language was not the same as that represented by the oldest religious texts, and under the Middle Empire the difference had become very sensible between the language actually spoken and that of the sacred writings, which were still considered as the standard of good language.

As the writing consisted merely of consonants, the old orthography still held its own. Great confusion began however, when from the beginning of the New Empire many of the final consonants of the spoken language were either dropped or changed, without the people being courageous enough to forsake the former orthography, which had become quite obsolete. From this time, as centuries elapsed, the scribes more and more lost the consciousness that the letters which they wrote ought to signify certain phonetic signs. When for instance, *ḥmt*, woman, and, *prt*, winter, were read *ḥime* and *prô* in spite of the two final *t*s, they concluded that the *t* at the end of the word was merely a sign with no value, which might be added indifferently to other words. As there were many words with a final *t*, which were written also either with the determinative of the house, ⊏⊐, or with that of going, Λ, as for instance, *'et*, house, *ḥt*, building, *shmt*, to go, *prt*, to go out, the scribes of the 19th and 20th dynasties began to place the *t* always above these two signs, so that these determinatives of the house and of going became and. In many words the confusion became so great, and in individual cases the contradictions which ensued were so manifold, that for instance they wrote the words *ḥrêre* (old *ḥrêret*), the flower, and *sim*, the weed, not, as under the Old Empire, *ḥrrt* and *sm*, but, horrible to say, *ḥururu* and *stimu*.

In the above pages I have always spoken of *hieroglyphs*, but this term may include, not only the carefully-drawn signs which usually occur in our inscriptions, and which we print, but also two other forms of writing. Even under the Old Empire a special cursive hand had already been invented for daily use, the so-called hieratic, in which the various hieroglyphs were gradually abbreviated more and more so as to be easily written

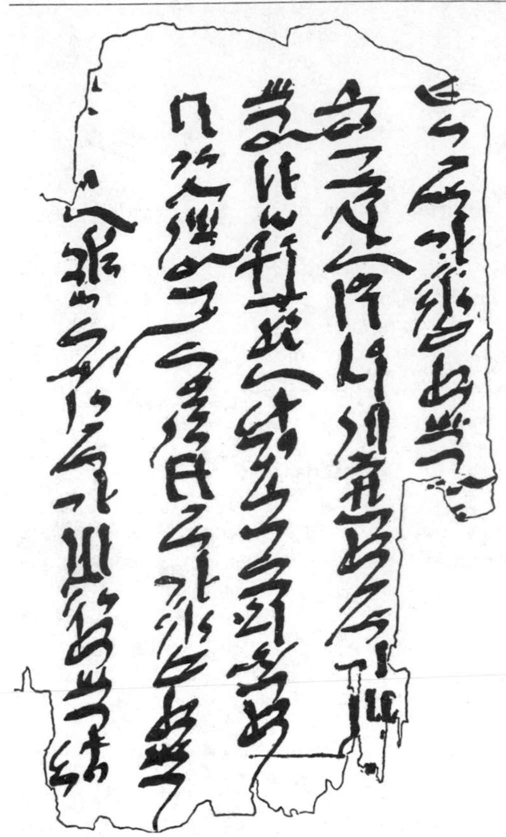

TEXT.

nbt. ‘D'd-'en . . . te pn : . . . 'n chndk ḥr ḥbsu'e. D'd-'en sechte pn : 'ery'e ḥstk, nfr mtnu'e. Prt pu 'ernf r ḥrt. D'd'en . . te pn : . . . . r uat. D'd-'en sechte pn : nfr

TRANSLATION.

. . . all. This . . . . official said : . . . . . go not over my clothes. This marshman said : I do what thou dost wish, my way is good. He went out upstairs. This . . . . official said : . . . . on the way. This marshman said : good.

HIERATIC BOOK-WRITING FROM THE BEGINNING OF THE NEW EMPIRE
(Eb. 88, 13.)

TEXT.

(The parts that are spaced are written in red ink.)

R r t n t d r ‘a b r - s a. Chpr ‘a, ŝ‘ad d'ad'af dnḥfe, ub | d, rda ḥr mrḥt, da rf. 'er m c h t m r k (inserted afterwards: d r) st, snuch | chrk d'ad'af dnḥfe, rda ḥr mrḥt ‘apnnt, u — | bd, rda sur'e st s

TRANSLATION.

Remedy to drive away all kinds of bewitchment (?) A large beetle, cut off his head and his two wings, war- | m (him), put into fat, apply (him) (?). *If then thou dost wish to (drive) it away*, then warm | his head and his two wings, put into snake-fat, war- | m (it), let the man drink it.

HIERATIC BUSINESS-WRITING OF THE TIME OF THE TWENTIETH DYNASTY.

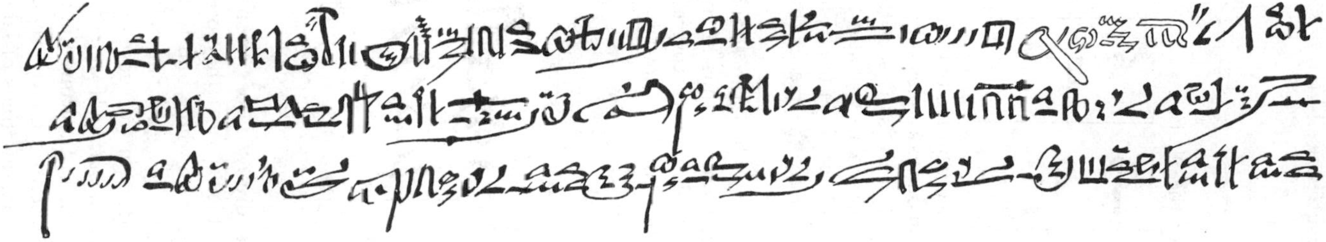

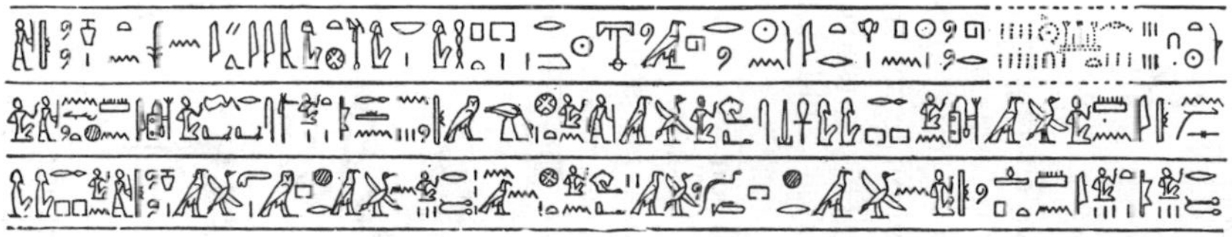

TEXT.

(The part spaced is written in red.)

R n p t 16, 'ebd 3 s h a t, h r u 19. Hru pa ḥr tr'e n ruhau r ma pr Ptḥ nb Ust. 'ey,'en 'abuu stn Ns'emn, pa 'an (?) n Pr 'a ('anch ud'a snb), ḥ'a Pasr n nt. Gmnu 'a n 'est Usrchpsh, 'an (?) 'mnncht, rmt' 'est 'emnḥtpu n·pa chr. D'du pae ḥ'a n nt n na rmt' n pa chr m bḥ pa 'abuu n Pr'a.

TRANSLATION.

Y e a r 16, 3rd s u m m e r m o n t h, 19th d a y. On this day, towards evening, near the temple of Ptaḥ, the Lord of Thebes, Nesamun, the vassal of the king, the scribe of the Pharaoh (Life, Health, Power!) and Paser, the prince of the town, came. They found (*i.e.* held judgment over) the chief workman Userchopesh, the scribe Amennacht, and the workman Amenḥôtep of the necropolis. The prince of the town spake to the people of the necropolis before the vassal of the Pharaoh.

by the reed pen of the scribe. We will take a few well-known signs as examples:

Hieroglyphs:

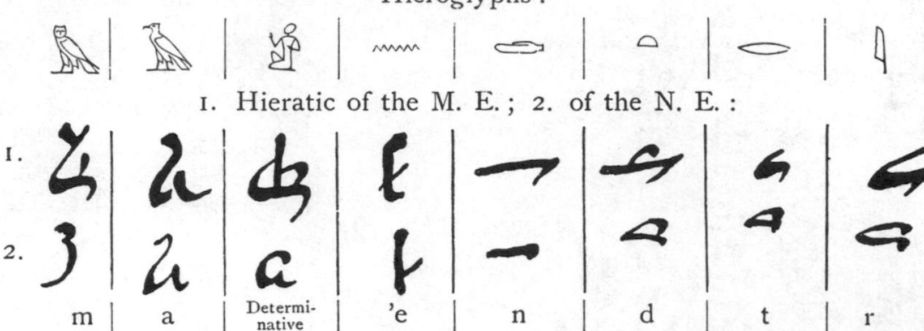

As we see, the cursive characters have this disadvantage that they often obliterate the characteristic forms of the signs; in our examples, for instance, the letters *d*, *t*, and *r* are so much alike that most of the scribes of the New Empire failed to distinguish the one from the other. This was also the case with many other signs. Thus mistakes of all kinds crept in freely, and the Egyptians themselves often could not read correctly the pieces that they were copying.

The height of confusion was reached however, when the scribes who were employed in rapid business-writing began, from the time of the 20th dynasty, to cut short to a few strokes those words which occurred most frequently. The following examples will suffice to show how much this writing differed even from the older cursive hand.

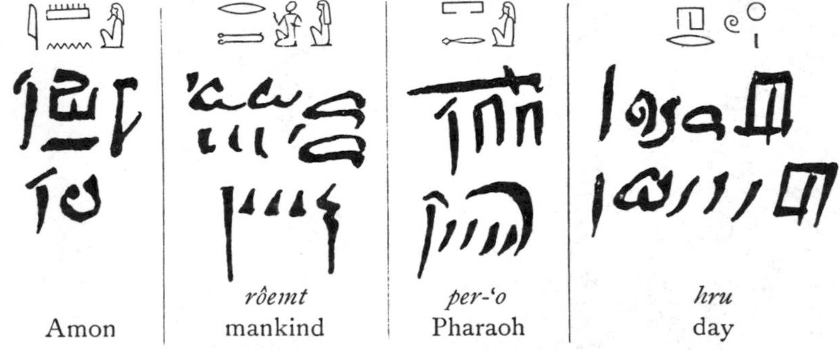

These signs of course can be no longer really *read*, for no one could make out from these strokes and dots which hieroglyphs they originally represented. We have to take a group of signs as a whole, and to bear in mind that a perpendicular stroke with four dots is the sign for mankind, and so on. A few centuries later and this shortened form was developed into a new independent style of writing, the so-called *demotic*. If we reflect that the writing underwent this complete degeneration at the same time as the orthography also degenerated in the manner described above, we shall be able to imagine the peculiar character of many handwritings of later time.

A third circumstance contributes to make the time of the New Empire unsympathetic to a philological mind, viz. the barbarism of the language of the religious and official texts. Whilst the spoken language of the time (the New Egyptian) was commonly used from the beginning of the 18th dynasty for the writing of everyday life, it was thought necessary that the official and religious texts should be kept in the ancient language. The Old Egyptian plays the same part under the New Empire as Latin did in Europe during the Middle Ages, with this difference that the former was misused in far worse manner than the latter. The barbarism which reigns in many of these texts defies all description; it is so bad that it strikes even us, who know so little of the old language. This applies not only to those Egyptian texts, which were composed under the New Empire, but also to the far more ancient religious books in the handwriting of the New Empire, which are often so bad that we can only conclude that the scribes did not at all understand what they were copying. Other nations have succeeded comparatively well in the experiment of employing and carrying on an ancient language, because they sought the assistance of grammars and lexicons; we are forced to conclude on the other hand that the Egyptians, who failed so completely, studied little or no grammar. In fact, no fragment of a lexicon or of a grammar has yet been found in any Egyptian papyrus. They did indeed write expositions of the sacred books, but as far as we can see from the commentaries that have come down to us, these were concerned merely with the signification of the matter of the contents, and did not discuss the meaning of the words; it was indeed impossible to do so, for the words appeared differently in every manuscript. The Egyptians never succeeded in making a final definite text of their sacred writings, a text which in no point ought to be changed. Their sacred books, which were supposed only to be touched by the gods after they had purified themselves, were really, in spite of their sacred character, at the mercy of every scribe. The learned body of religious men had more important matters to do than to protect them, they had to explain them; and the manner in which this was done is so characteristic of the Egyptians that I will give the reader a specimen of the above-mentioned commentary.

Amongst the earliest conceptions of the life of the soul after death (see the preceding chapter) was one particularly widespread, according to which the soul left the body behind and went up into heaven. All impurities were taken away, the divine part alone remained, and the soul became a god like the other gods; was welcomed by the glorified, and entered proudly through the gate of heaven, in order to remain in everlasting glory with the sun-god Atum and the stars. The triumphal hymn, as it were, which the soul sang on entering into heaven, is contained in the very ancient "Chapter of the coming forth by day out of the netherworld." The beginning runs somewhat in the following manner:

"I am the god Atum, I who was alone.

"I am the god Rê' at his first appearing.

"I am the great god, who created himself, and created his name, lord of the gods, to whom not one of the gods is equal (?).

"I was yesterday, and I know the morrow; the place of combat of the gods was made when I spoke. I know the name of that great god who dwells within him.

I am that great Phœnix who is in Heliopolis, who there reckons up everything that is and that exists.

"I am the god Min at his coming forth, whose feathers I place upon my head.

"I am in my country, I come into my town. I am daily together with my father Atum.

"My impurities are driven out, and the sin which was in me is trodden under foot. I washed myself in those two great tanks which are in Herakleopolis, in which the sacrifices of mankind are purified for that great god who dwells there.

"I go on the way, where I wash my head in the lake of the justified. I reach this land of the glorified and enter through (?) the glorious gate.

"You, who stand in front, reach out to me your hands, I am so, I am become one of you—I am together daily with my father Atum."

So much for the old text, which even now does not need much commentary to enable us to gather the general sense. The deceased stands at the gate of heaven, he feels that he has become a god, and boasts of his divine nature. He esteems himself the equal of each of the ancient gods, of Atum, of Rê', and of that god at whose word the gods once fought. He has forsaken his earthly house in order to enter the heavenly one; he has cleansed himself from all impurities, and now enters the gate of heaven, and the glorified spirits reach out to him their hands, and conduct him to his father the sun-god.

The learned men of Egypt were however of a different opinion. The words of the ancient poet in praise of the happy fate of the deceased did not touch their hearts, but only incited their heads so much the more to invent difficulties, and for those who as they thought really understood the religion there was not a line in which there were not problems to solve. In early times therefore the old hymn was provided with a commentary, which in the course of centuries became more and more voluminous. Many passages that the learned men of the Middle Empire had considered clear appeared to those of the New Empire to need explanation, and on the other hand many old elucidations appeared incorrect to later commentators, and they felt themselves bound to add a better explanation. We can easily conceive, after the previous remarks, that they did not content themselves with amending the commentary, but sometimes endeavoured to improve the ancient text itself.

The commentary to the "Book of the coming forth by day" was certainly considered a masterpiece of deep learning; to us of the modern world it will often appear nonsense, for in every harmless word the commentators scented a hidden meaning. When the poet said: God knows "that which is, and that which exists," he naturally meant that God knew all things; this explanation, however, was too simple for the learned men of Egypt; "that which is, and that which exists" is, according to the older commentators, "eternity and the endless existence," whilst according to the later ones, we are led to understand that what is meant is "day and night." We must add one more thought. When the poem was composed the descriptions of the gods and of the life after death were as obscure as such matters are in the lore of all primitive people. This obscurity had long vanished. The details of the lives of the gods had been evolved, as well as the history of what should happen to the soul after death, and in particular that doctrine had been formulated which treated of the particular relations of the deceased to Osiris, the god of the dead. It appeared of course incomprehensible to the learned that this sacred hymn should mention nothing of all this; evidently it was only necessary rightly to understand it in order to find all they wanted. Thus in fact everything that they sought in it was found, especially when they helped out the text a little.

When at the beginning of the old song the poet said: "I am Atum, I who was alone," he meant, of course, that this god existed before all the other gods; the later writers preferred to say: "I am Atum, I who was alone on the ocean of heaven," they thus foisted in the conception that with the god an ocean, a chaos, already existed. Further on we read: "I am Rê' at his first appearing." The beautiful idea of the sun-god suddenly enlightening the hitherto dark world was not sufficient for the learned men of the New Empire; they changed the text into "I am Rê' at his appearing, as he began to rule over what he had created." Then they added further the following gloss; "Explain it—This Rê', who began to rule over what he had created, this is Rê' who shone as king before the supports of Shu were created. He was on the terrace of the town Chmunu when the children of the rebels were given to him on the terrace of Chmunu." Here they succeeded therefore in interpolating into the old text the legend that Rê' formerly ruled as king over the earth, before he withdrew to rest on the heavenly cow supported by the god Shu. According to the commentators the poet was even supposed to have in his mind a particular event in this reign which took place in the famous town of Chmunu, when he compared the deceased, who had become like a god, with the sun-god.

The following portion of the text then mentioned a "great god, who created himself, created his name, the lord of the circle of gods, to whom not one amongst the gods was equal"; these remarks are couched in terms too general to understand which god was in the poet's thoughts. At all events however he was certainly thinking of *one* god, not, as the commentators insist, of three different gods. The learned of the New Empire explained the passage in the following manner:

"I am the great god, who created himself.

"Explain it: The great god who created himself is the water; that is the heavenly ocean, the father of the gods.

"Another says: it is Rê‘.

"Who created his name, the lord of the circle of gods.

"Explain it: That is Rê‘ who created his names for his limbs, and created those gods who attend him.

"To whom not one is equal amongst the gods.

"Explain it: That is Atum in his sun's disk. Another says: that is Rê‘, who rises in the eastern horizon of heaven."

From the variants we have quoted, we see that though some scholars liked to interpret the passage as applying to the *one* god, Rê‘, official opinion was certain that the three gods mentioned in the first passage, namely Nun, Rê‘, and Atum, were here intended. The interpretation of the next passage: "I was yesterday, and I know the morrow," was still more involved. When the deceased thus boasted about himself he only meant that like the other gods he was removed from the limits of time, and that the past and the future were both alike to him. Yet the commentators of the Middle Empire were minded to see here a reference to one particular god; according to them the god who was yesterday and knows the morrow was Osiris. This was no doubt an error, but was a more reasonable supposition than the view of later scholars, who declare that *yesterday* is here a name of Osiris and *the morrow* a name of Rê‘.

We see that however simple a passage might be, and however little doubt there ought to have been concerning its meaning, so much the more trouble did these expositors take to evolve something wonderful out of it. They sought a hidden meaning in everything, for should not the deepest, most secret wisdom dwell in a sacred book? From the passage: "I am the god Min at his coming forth, whose double feathers I placed on my head," every child would conclude that reference was made to the god Min, who was always represented with two tall feathers on his head; yet this was too commonplace and straightforward for it to be the possible meaning of the text. Evidently something quite different was intended; by Min we must not understand the well-known god of Coptos, but Horus. It was true that Horus did not usually wear feathers on his head; yet for this they found a reason. Either his two eyes were to be understood by the two feathers, or they might have some reference to the two snakes, which not he but the god Atum wore on his head. Both these interpretations of the feathers, especially the latter, were rather too far-fetched to be reasonable, and therefore a welcome was accorded to the ingenious discovery of a scholar of the time of the 19th dynasty, who succeeded in proving from the mythology that there was something like feathers on the head of Horus. His gloss ran thus: "With regard to his double feathers, Isis together with Nephthys went once and placed themselves on his head in the form of two birds—behold that then remained on his head."

I will spare the reader any further specimens of this curious learning; they all show the same foolish endeavour to insert things in the text of which the composer had never even thought. In this respect the Egyptian scholars did but follow the same course as the mystical writers of the

Middle Ages, who made out that both the Bible and Virgil were *allegorical;* the Rabbis and many interpreters of the Koran have done the same; reverence for ancient literary works, if carried too far, always bears the same fruit. The religious teachers of Egypt must have shared not only the harmless pleasure, which all those who trace out similar subtle questions feel in their work, but also their characteristic annoyance with colleagues who insist upon a different solution to any of these interesting problems; who knows, for instance, whether the various glosses about the name

RAMSES II. SEATED BEFORE THE SACRED TREE ON WHICH THE GODS ARE WRITING HIS NAME. After L. D. iii. 169.

which the lake of Natron at Chenensuten ought to bear, were not the subject of embittered controversy between the individual heads of the various schools? Some called it "Eternity," others the "Guide of Eternity," others the "Begetter of Eternity." This wonderful wisdom does not seem to have been within the reach of all learned men, for the great and wise man Amenḥôtep, the son of Ḥapu (see pp. 103, 148, 149) expressly relates of himself that after he had attained to a certain rank, he "went in to the divine book, and saw the excellent things of Thoth." If this is the right translation of the passage, it means that he understood the signification of difficult passages, and that people sought his counsel about them.[1]

[1] Mar. Karn., 36, 27; this explanation is due to Brugsch, cp. Ä. Z., 1876, 96 ff.

If the Egyptian contributions to learning were of such little value on a subject which appeared to them of such great importance, it is natural to suppose that on subjects of wider scope they have not rendered much service to science. The more we come to understand the monuments, the more inclined we are to join issue in the much-debated question as to whether the Egyptians possessed a complete written history. Various kings have left us a short account of their achievements, and these may have been taken from official year-books ;[1] we also have a list of kings on the reverse side of a Turin papyrus,[2] and this may of course be designated as an historical work. But this is all ; other descriptions of historical events that have come down to us are more or less of a legendary character. The point of view from which the Egyptians wrote scarcely embraced more than the annals of the kings and of the temples, their only object

STAR-CHART OF THE NORTH POLE OF THE SKY.
(From the Tomb of Sety I. After L. D., iii. 137).

being to hand down to posterity the name of the Pharaoh and his mighty deeds. The gods also were supposed to write histories of this kind. In the *great hall* at Heliopolis stood a very ancient sacred tree. Thoth and the goddess Sefchet, "the lady of writing, the ruler of books," wrote the name of the monarch on its leaves, and the god Atum, as our picture shows, followed her example, and "wrote the name on the noble tree with the writing of his own fingers."[3]

In the clear Egyptian sky the stars are wonderfully bright, and the inhabitants of the Nile valley must have observed them in very early ages. Though they did not, like the dwellers in Mesopotamia, regard them as divinities, yet they looked upon them as the abode of pious souls ; *e.g.* the dog-star, the so-called Sothis, was regarded as the soul of Isis, Orion as that of Horus. Other stars were the genii with whom the

[1] These must be the [hieroglyphs], spoken of Mar. Karn., 52, 20.

[2] That it is only on the reverse side—an important fact when we come to criticise it—has been observed by Wilcken.

[3] L. D., iii. 37a, 169.

sun was connected in his course; they thus especially regarded the thirty-six constellations situated on the horizon, the so-called decan stars.

But besides this semi-poetical view of the stars, the Egyptians of the New Empire, if not those of earlier date, possessed the elements of real astronomy. On the one hand they tried to find their way in the vastness of the heavens by making charts of the constellations according to their fancy, charts which of course could only represent a small portion of the sky. On the other hand they went further, they made tables in which the position of the stars was indicated. The plan of these was so curious that we must describe them in more detail. They imagined that under the centre of the sky a human figure sat upright, and that the top of his head was placed below the zenith. The stars which were approaching

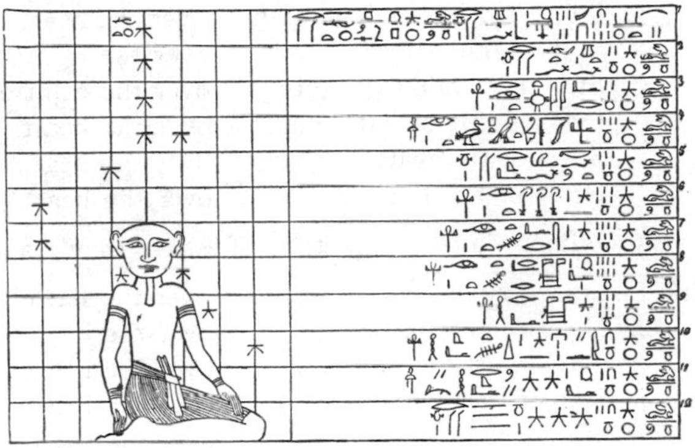

LIST OF STARS ON THE 16TH OF PAOPHI. (After L. D., iii. 227.)

the zenith were situate over a portion of this figure, and their position was indicated in the lists of stars. There are several of these kinds of lists in the tombs of the kings of the 20th dynasty,[1] they give the position of the stars during the twelve hours of the night, at intervals of fifteen days. Unfortunately, as they only served as pieces of decorative work for the tomb, they were very carelessly done, and it is therefore very difficult to make them out.

On the 16th of Paophi, for instance, they thus indicated the position of the stars during:

"The 1st hour the leg of the giant over the heart.
„ 2nd „ the star Petef over the heart.
„ 3rd „ the star 'Ary over the left eye.
„ 4th „ the claw of the goose over the left eye.
„ 5th „ the hinderpart over the heart.
„ 6th „ the star of thousands over the left eye.
„ 7th „ the star S'ar over the left eye.
„ 8th „ the fingerpoint of the constellation S'ah (Orion) over the left eye.

[1] L. D., iii. 227-228, bis.

The 9th hour	the star of S'aḥ (Orion)	over the left elbow.
„ 10th „	the star that follows Sothis	over the left elbow.
„ 11th „	the fingerpoint of both stars	over the right elbow.
„ 12th „	the stars of the water	over the heart."

After fifteen days, on the 1st of Athyr, the stars have changed their positions as follows:

"Hour 1.	Star Petef	over the heart.
„ 2.	Star 'Ary	over the left eye.
„ 3.	Head of the goose	over the right eye.
„ 4.	Hinderpart of the goose	over the heart.
„ 5.	Star of the thousands	over the heart.
„ 6.	Star of the S'ar	over the heart.
„ 7.	Point of finger of the S'aḥ	over the heart.
„ 8.	Star of the S'aḥ	over the right eye.
„ 9.	Star that follows Sothis	over the right eye.
„ 10.	Fingerpoint of both stars	over the heart.
„ 11.	Stars of the water	over the heart.
„ 12.	Head of the lion	over the heart."

And again after fifteen days on the 16th of Athyr they stand thus:

"Hour 1.	Star 'Ary	over the left eye.
„ 2.	Head of the goose	over the heart.
„ 3.	Hinderpart of the goose	over the heart.
„ 4.	Star of the thousands	over the heart.
„ 5.	Star of the S'ar	over the left eye.
„ 6.	Star of the S'aḥ	over the heart.
„ 7.	Star of the S'aḥ	over the left eye.
„ 8.	Star that follows Sothis	over the left eye.
„ 9.	Fingerpoint of both stars	over the heart.
„ 10.	Stars of the water	over the heart.
„ 11.	Head of the lion	over the heart.
„ 12.	Tail of the lion	over the heart.

These lists were probably used for practical purposes; for though it has not been proved that astrology, *i.e.* the use of the stars in a superstitious way, was practised in Egypt, yet the stars were of great service in questions of the calendar,[1] in the elaboration of which the Egyptians were very successful. The old problem of how to divide time in accordance with the course of the sun into periods of about 365¼ days, and these again in accordance with the course of the moon into periods of about 29¼ days, was solved by the Egyptians in such a satisfactory manner that their solution forms even now the foundation of our own calendar. In the division of time into months they ignored the moon and made it an arbitrary division of time containing 30 days; 12 of these months, that is 360 days, formed a year; and as the real year contained 365¼

[1] Thus the beginning of the inundation was originally dated from the early rising of Sothis.

days, the deficit was made good by five intercalary days, which, as the "five surplus days of the year," were added on to the end of the year. The twelve months were then again divided into three seasons consisting each of 120 days, which were named after the three chief periods of Egyptian agriculture, the *Inundation*, the *Growing* of the seed, and the *Harvest*. The beginning of the time of the inundation was about the 20th July, which was therefore rightly considered to be the Egyptian New Year's Day.

This calendar however, which existed in this form even under the Old Empire, had one disadvantage,—its year of 365 days was still a $\frac{1}{4}$ of a day too short, and thus every fourth year was a day behind the true year. If in the year 2782 B.C. New Year's Day fell at the beginning of the inundation, in the year 2542 B.C., it would fall two months before the inundation, and in the year 2302 B.C. the difference would have become so great that the period which they called the inundation would correspond with the four months in which they gathered the harvest. It would require the long period of 1460 years to equalise these errors, and it was not till the year 1322 B.C. that New Year's Day would again coincide with the 20th of July, the official beginning of the inundation. They had thus a changing year, the periods and months of which did not as a rule agree with the periods of nature, but which, owing to its practical advantages, was generally accepted. The real natural year was quite thrown into the background, and played the same part with regard to the changing year as the actual month from new moon to full moon does with regard to our conventional month. The peasants and the priests, on account of agriculture and of certain festivals, alone cared for the Year of Nature; they maintained the old tradition that the day to be regarded as the beginning of the year, and of the inundation, was that on which Sothis first reappeared in the morning sky.[1]

Though the Egyptians thus laid the foundations of our calendar, yet on the other hand they were not at all exempt from the superstitious beliefs connected with the calendar regarding the so-called lucky or unlucky days. The idea, so widespread throughout the ages of antiquity, prevails even in modern times that it is lucky on some days, but unlucky on others, to undertake any affair. This idea appears, as far as we can judge from a book of the time of the New Empire, to have been very prevalent in Egypt. Here as everywhere religious reasons were brought forward in favour of this superstition. One day was lucky or unlucky according as a good or bad mythological incident took place on that day.[2] For instance, the 1st of Mechir, on which day the sky was raised, and the 27th of Athyr, when Horus and Set concluded peace together and divided the world between them, were lucky days; on the other hand the 14th

[1] Therefore this natural year of the Egyptians was called the Sothic year, and the periods of 1460 years, which it took to coincide with the variable year, was called a Sothic period.

[2] The following is after Sall., 4. The text of this document, which is most important for the mythology, has unfortunately suffered much injury, which prevents the comprehension of many passages.

of Tybi, on which Isis and Nephthys mourned for Osiris, was an unlucky day. With the unlucky days, which fortunately were less in number than the lucky days, they distinguished different degrees of ill-luck. Some were very unlucky, others only threatened ill-luck, and many like the 17th and the 27th of Choiakh were partly good and partly bad according to the time of day. Lucky days might as a rule be disregarded. At most it might be as well to visit some specially renowned temple, or to "celebrate a joyful day at home," but no particular precautions were really necessary; and above all it was said: "what thou also seest on the day is lucky." It was quite otherwise with the unlucky and dangerous days, which imposed so many and such great limitations on people, that those who wished to be prudent were always obliged to bear them in mind when determining on any course of action. Certain conditions were easy to carry out. Music and singing were to be avoided on the 14th Tybi, the day of the mourning for Osiris, and no one was allowed to wash on the 16th Tybi; whilst the name of Set might not be pronounced on the 24th of Pharmuthi. Fish was forbidden on certain days; and what was still more difficult in a country so rich in mice, on the 12th Tybi no mouse might be seen. The most tiresome prohibitions however were those which occurred not infrequently, namely, those concerning work and going out: for instance, four times in Paophi the people had to "do nothing at all," and five times to sit the whole day or half the day in the house; and the same rule had to be observed each month. Even the most cautious could not avoid all the ill-luck that unlucky days could bring, so that the knowledge of them was ever an anxiety to them. It was impossible to rejoice if a child were born on the 23rd of Thoth; the parents knew it could not live. Those born on the 20th of Choiakh would become blind, and those born on the 3rd of Choiakh, deaf.

The book from which I have taken these examples does not belong to the same class of literature as the superstitious books of other times and nations. No nation is entirely without these intellectual productions, and by some people they are highly esteemed; they form however at most a valuable addition to literature, which wise men may study at will, but are not quite the sort of educational material most suitable for young people. It was otherwise in Egypt, and the strange manual relating to the selection of days has really come down to us in a school copy-book. Superstition with this people was not an interesting by-product of their civilisation; it was, as in Babylonia, one of the most mighty influences of their intellectual life. The belief that there were words and actions by which they could produce an effect on the powers of nature, upon every living being, upon animals, and even upon gods, was indissolubly connected with all the actions of the Egyptians. Above all the whole system of the funeral ceremonies and worship was ruled by superstition; the wooden figures who were supposed to do the work or prepare the food for the deceased; the formula of the offerings, the repetition of which would, they thought, create food for him,—these and similar customs are neither more nor less than magical. Neither men nor gods could get on without magic; even the latter wore amulets as a protection, and used magical formulae to *constrain* each other. Isis was above all other divinities the mistress of magic, and famous as "great in magic words."

The magical formulae used by the Egyptians were founded chiefly on the following idea. The magician would recollect some incident in the history of the gods, which had brought good luck to one of the heavenly beings. In order to reproduce the same good luck he would imagine that he himself represented that god, and he would therefore repeat the words the god had spoken in that incident; words which had formerly been so effective would, he felt sure, be again of good service. For instance, if he desired to cool or heal a burn, after using as a remedy "the milk of a woman who had borne a son," he would say over it the following formula: "My son Horus, it burns on the mountain, no water is there, I am not there, fetch water from the bank of the river to put out the fire."[1] These words were evidently spoken by Isis in a divine legend. A fire[2] had broken out, and the goddess called anxiously to her son Horus to fetch water. As this cry for help had formerly produced the means whereby the fire on the mountain was extinguished, it was to be hoped that the same words in the mouth of the magician would stop the burning of the wound. It was the same with the following exorcism, which was spoken over the *smell-seeds* and over the inevitable "milk of a woman who has borne a son," in order to make these medicaments effective against a cold. "Depart cold, son of a cold, thou who breakest the bones, destroyest the skull, partest company with fat, makest ill the seven openings in the head! The servants of Rê beseech Thoth—'Behold I bring thy recipe to thee, thy remedy to thee: the milk of a woman who has borne a son and the smell-seeds. Let that drive thee away, let that heal thee; let that heal thee, let that drive thee away. Go out on the floor, stink, stink! stink, stink!'"[3] This *catarrh incantation* is taken from a myth concerning the old age and the illnesses of the sun-god. Rēʿ is suffering from a cold, which confuses his head; his attendants beseech the god of learning for a remedy; the god brings it immediately and announces to the illness that it must yield to it.

In these magical formulae the magician repeated the words of the god, and through them he exercised the magic power of the god; in other cases it would suffice for him to designate himself as that god, whose power he wished to possess. For instance, whoever recited the following words over the water:

> "Thou art not above me—I am Amon.
> I am Anḥor, the beautiful slayer.
> I am the prince, the lord of the sword.
> Raise not thyself—I am Mont, etc."[4]

caused the crocodiles to be as terrified by this formula as if those gods

[1] Eb., 69, 6, similarly 69, 3.

[2] Perhaps that mentioned in Ä. Z., 1879, 3.

[3] Eb., 90, 16.

[4] Pap. mag. Harris, 8, 5.

themselves had passed by that way. It was of course especially effective if instead of using the usual name of the god, the magician could name his *real name*, that special name possessed by each god and each genius in which his power resided. He who knew this name, possessed the power of him who bore it, and as we saw in the 12th chapter (p. 265), from the time that Isis the great enchantress constrained the sun-god to reveal to her his secret name, she became as powerful as he was himself. Therefore the following incantation, which refers to this name, would work even better against the crocodiles than that quoted above :

"I am the chosen one of millions, who proceeds from the kingdom of light,
Whose name no one knows.
If his name be spoken over the stream
It is obliterated.
If his name be spoken over the land
It causes fire to arise.
I am Shu, the image of Rê',
Who sits in his eye.
If any one who is in the water" (*i.e.* a crocodile) "open his mouth,
If he strike (?) his arms,
Then will I cause the earth to fall into the stream
And the South to become the North
And the earth to turn round."[1]

As we see, the magician guards himself from actually pronouncing the real name of Shu ; he only threatens to name it, and therewith to unhinge the world. Incidentally indeed he even threatens the god himself with the mention of his secret name, to whom the revelation would be fatal. Further, he who in terror of the monsters of the water should repeat the following incantation four times :

"Come to me, come to me, thou image of the eternity of eternities !
Thou Chnum, son of the One !
Conceived yesterday, born to-day,
Whose name I know,"

the divine being whom he called, who "has seventy-seven eyes and seventy-seven ears,"[2] would certainly come to his help.

It is no real loss that the actual mention of the name is rarely made, and that therefore we do not know how the real names of Rê' or of Amon were pronounced, for what we know of these names shows us sufficiently how childish they were. It is impossible to discover any sense in the wonderful words they used, *e.g.* in the secret name which the Pyramid texts disclose to us in a snake-incantation, "He'te'tebe'te'shes, son of Ḥe'fget,"[3] or in the name with which the genius of a wild animal is addressed under the New Empire, "Shat'ebut'e, 'Art'ebuhaya,"[4] or finally in the appellation of a god, which was ascribed later to our oft-mentioned Amenḥôtep, son of Ḥapu ; "O Shauagat'eennagat'e, son of the 'Erukat'e ! Kauarushagat'e !"[5] They are nothing but senseless noises making a

[1] Pap. mag. Harr., 7, 1. [2] Pap. mag. Harr., 7, 4. [3] Un'es, 325.

[4] Pap. mag. Harr., B. 8. They have the determinative [hieroglyph], and are therefore names of this animal. [5] Maspero, Mémoire sur quelques papyrus du Louvre, p. 58.

strange sound. Magical effect was always ascribed to similar curious words: P'ap'aruka p'ap'araka, p'ap'arura [1] is the beginning of an incantation, and another runs thus:

" 'Edera 'edesana,
'Ederagaha 'edesana,
Together: matmu 'edesana,
Together: 'emuy 'edesana,
Together: ducha'eryna 'edesana,
Together: degaksana 'edesana,
Together: t'akarut'a 'edesana
Given: uaraha'ea,
Qena,
Hamu." [2]

Magical formulae of this kind are in use amongst all nations, and the explanation which has been given of this nonsense may apply to them all: these words are all said to belong to some foreign, or some unknown tongue. Arab magicians call their magic words "Syrian," Germans explain theirs as "Hebrew," the Egyptians declared that "Sant'ekapupeuay 'eyment'erakakara" belonged to the Phoenician language.[3] I am afraid it would be lost trouble if we were to try to identify these words out of the Phoenician. A few words of that language may really have found their way into the magical literature of Egypt, as many of the Hebrew names of angels have into ours, but most of these *Phoenician* words were certainly pure inventions.

The magic formulae were naturally most effective when they were said aloud, but they were of use also even when they were written; this accounts for the zeal with which the magic formulae for the deceased were written everywhere in the tomb, and on the tomb furniture,—the greater the number of times they were written, the more certainly they took effect.

There was another way of perpetuating the power of the magic formulae; they were recited over objects of a certain kind, which were thus invested with a lasting magical virtue. Thus the above crocodile incantations might be recited over an egg made of clay; if then the pilot of the boat carried this egg in his hand, all the terrible animals that had emerged from the stream would again sink immediately into the water.[4] In the same way it was possible to endow figures of paper or of wax with magical efficacy; if such were brought secretly into the house of an enemy, they would spread sickness and weakness there.[5] We have already related in the preceding chapter how they made use of other small figures as servants of the deceased; these, with the stone geese and the wooden models of kitchens, and all similar adjuncts of the tombs, had all been filled with magical power by the recitation of formulae. We know this was also certainly the case with the numberless little ornaments in stone and china which

[1] Pap. mag. Harr., 7, 12. [2] Ditto, C. 1.

[3] London medical papyrus from a duplicate of Golenischeff's. A Semitic tongue is probably intended, the reading Phoenician is very hypothetical. Amongst these nonsensical words the name of Ba'al occurs: Pap. mag. Harr., C. 4.

[4] Pap. mag. Harr., 6, 12. "Clay" is only hypothetical. [5] Lee, 1, 4; Rollin, 1.

have been found with the mummies, and with which our museums are filled. For instance, over the little figure of the pillar *Ded* 𓊽, representing the sacred backbone of Osiris, the following words had to be spoken: "Thy back belongs to thee, thou with motionless heart: thy vertebrae belong to thee, thou with motionless heart. Thou dost lie upon thy side, I put water underneath thee. Behold, I bring thee the *Ded* and thou dost rejoice therein." Through this formula the *Ded* ensures to the deceased, round whose neck it is hung, a safe entrance into the gate of the nether world.[1] Over a similar amulet however made of carnelian, these words were spoken: "O blood of Isis, O splendour of Isis, O magic power of Isis, O amulet for the protection of this great man, beware of doing harm to him." If the deceased wear this amulet, Isis will protect him, and Horus will rejoice when he sees it.[2]

Amulets such as these were worn as a protection not only by the dead, but by the living, and even the gods and the sacred animals could not manage without safeguards of this kind. Under the Old Empire one amulet appears to have consisted merely of two stones or pieces of wood stuck through each other,[3] later it took the form of a heart,[4] or it consisted of a four-cornered shield with mystic figures, decorated at the top with a little hollow.[5]

This dominating belief in magic certainly hindered the intellectual progress of the nation, for who would take the trouble to follow the long wearisome ways of nature when they thought the same result might be obtained in a superhuman and much shorter manner? The Egyptians believed this especially with regard to medicine. They followed this science with great zeal, and from the practical side at any rate they were able to boast of good results, but their doctors were never able to shake themselves free from the influence of magic. For besides the specially wonderful incantations, which were to be spoken over various remedies in order to endow them with the right power, the following formula had to be recited at the preparation of all medicaments. "That Isis might make free, make free. That Isis might make Horus free from all evil that his brother Set had done to him when he slew his father Osiris. O Isis, great enchantress, free me, release me from all evil red things, from the fever of the god and the fever of the goddess, from death, and death from pain, and the pain which comes over me; as thou hast freed, as thou hast released thy son Horus, whilst I enter into the fire and go forth from the water," etc.[6] Again, when the invalid took his medicine, an incantation had to be said which began thus: "Come remedy, come drive it out of my heart, out of these my limbs, strong in magic power with the remedy."[7] There must however have been a few rationalists amongst the Egyptian doctors, for the number of magic formulae varies much in

[1] Totb. Chap. 155.
[2] Totb. Chap. 156.
[3] Düm. Res., 8; L. D., ii. 48, 73; Perrot, 91. Variation, L. D., ii. 3, 5.
[4] E.g. see p. 222.
[5] E.g. see p. 208, that in the hand of the central figure.
[6] Eb., 1, 12 ff.
[7] Eb., 2, 1 ff.

the different medical books. The book that we have specially taken as a foundation for this account of Egyptian medicine—the great papyrus of the 18th dynasty edited by Ebers—contains, for instance, far fewer exorcisms than some later writings with similar contents, probably because the doctor who compiled this book of recipes from older sources had very little liking for magic.

The science of medicine even under the Old Empire was already in the hands of special physicians called [hieroglyph] *snu* (Coptic sajn).. We still know the names of some of the royal body-physicians of this time; Sechmetna'e'ônch, the "chief physician of the Pharaoh," served the King Sehurê',[1] while of somewhat earlier date perhaps,[2] are Ra'na'e'ônch the "physician of the Pharaoh," and Nesmenau his chief, the "superintendent of the physicians of the Pharaoh." The priests also of the lioness-headed goddess Sechmet seem to have been famed for their medical wisdom,[3] whilst the son of this goddess, the demigod Imhôtep, was in later times considered to be the creator of medical knowledge. These ancient doctors laid the foundation of all later medicine;[4] even the doctors of the New Empire do not seem to have improved upon the older conceptions about the construction of the human body. We may be surprised at this, but their anatomical knowledge was very little,—less than we should expect with a people to whom it was an everyday matter to open dead bodies.[5]

Besides the structure of the bones and of the large viscera such as the heart, stomach, spleen, etc., the ancient Egyptians knew barely anything of the human body, and their teaching concerning the *vessels* is mostly characterised by pure invention; this teaching however was considered by them as specially important, it was the "secret of the doctor."[6] These *vessels* correspond essentially with the great veins or indeed preferably with the arteries, but as they thought that they carried water, air, excretory fluids, etc.,[7] we must understand their words in a very broad sense, unless we prefer to consider the statements about their activity as pure fancy. The Egyptians realised at any rate that the vessels took their course from the heart to the various members of the body. The heart is the centre, "its vessels lead to all the members; whether the doctor . . . lays his finger on the forehead, on the back of the head, on the hands, on the place of the stomach (?), on the arms, or on the feet, everywhere he meets with the heart

[1] Mar. Mast., 203 f.

[2] L. D., ii. 91 a, 92, d, e. They may be contemporaries, for the former makes offerings in the tomb of the latter.

[3] Eb., 99, 2. Cp. also the name there quoted "Sechmet is my life."

[4] Of course I do not maintain that we can believe the statements concerning the composition or the discovery of medical writings under certain kings of the Old Empire. They show at the same time that the nucleus of this literature is of a great age. The language of these books teaches us the same lesson.

[5] We must indeed not overlook the fact that in the art of mummifying, the abdomen alone was opened.

[6] Eb., 99, 1.

[7] Water: Eb., 99, 9, 19, 100, 10. Mucus: 99, 6. Air: 100, 3, 10. Other fluids: 100, 7, 103, 18. Excrement: 100, 14. The vessels of the face twitch: An., 4, 13, 6.

(*i.e.* the pulse), because its vessels lead to all the members." The heart was therefore called also the "beginning of all the members."[1] The Egyptians knew little, however, about the position of the various vessels. An ancient manual on this subject declares that there were twelve of them, which went in pairs to the breast, to the legs, to the forehead, and to other exterior parts of the body.[2] In another manual however, more than forty of them are mentioned, some of which lead to the viscera; this manual evidently represents an amended edition of the old teaching; it remains however very doubtful how much is based upon observation.[3] This theory of the vessels is of special importance in Egyptian medicine, for many neuralgic or rheumatic affections were dependent, according to Egyptian ideas, on the vessels. They were stopped up, they were heated, they grew stiff, they itched, they had to be strengthened or pacified, they would not absorb the medicine—troubles which the doctor had to counteract by poultices and ointments.[4]

As a rule the Egyptian doctors thought they could *see*, without further examination, what was the matter with their patients. Many, however, were conscious that an exact knowledge of any disease is the foundation of a cure, and therefore in their writings,[5] directed such straightforward diagnoses as for instance the following: "When thou findest a man who has a swelling in his neck, and who suffers in both his shoulder-blades, as well as in his head, and the backbone of his neck is stiff, and his neck is stiff, so that he is not able to look down upon his belly . . . then say: 'He has a swelling in his neck; direct him to rub in the ointment of stibium, so that he should immediately become well."[6] Or with one ill in his stomach: "If thou findest a man with constipation . . . with a pale face and beating heart, and dost find, on examining him, that he has a hot heart and a swollen body; that is an ulcer (?) which has arisen from the eating of hot substances. Order something that the heat may be cooled, and his bowels opened, namely, a drink of sweet beer to be poured over dry Neq'aut fruit; this is to be eaten or drunk four times. When that which comes from him looks like small black stones, then say: 'This inflammation departs.' . . . If after thou hast done this thou examinest him and findest that that which he passes resembles beans, on which is dew . . . then say: 'That which was in his stomach has departed."[7] Other obstructions in the abdomen gave rise to other symptoms, and required different treatment, thus when the doctor put his fingers on the abdomen and found it "go hither and thither like oil in a skin bottle,"[8] or in a case when the patient "vomits and feels very ill,"[9] or when the body is "hot and swollen."[10]

If the illness were obstinate, the question arose which was to be employed out of many various remedies, for by the beginning of the New

[1] Eb., 99, 1 ff.

[2] Eb., 103, 1 ff. In the text before us eighteen are certainly enumerated.

[3] Eb., 99, 1 ff.

[4] Eb., 79, 5—86, 3.

[5] Above all the book of diseases of the stomach: Eb., 36, 4—43, 2.

[6] Eb., 51, 19 ff.

[7] Eb., 42, 8 ff.

[8] Eb., 40, 1.

[9] Eb., 40, 15.

[10] Eb., 42, 10.

Empire the number of prescriptions had increased to such an extent, that for some diseases there were frequently a dozen or more remedies, from amongst which the doctor could take his choice. When we examine them more closely, this superfluity of recipes becomes more limited. Some medicines were supposed to act at once, others more slowly but at the same time more surely: "remedies" and "momentary remedies." Many remedies again might only be used at certain seasons of the year. Thus amongst the prescriptions for the eyes, we find one that is only to be employed during the first and second months of the winter, whilst another is to be used during the third and fourth months, and of a third it is expressly stated that its use is allowed during all the three seasons of the year.[1] In the same way the doctor had often to consider the age of his patients. In cases of ischury for instance, adults might take a mixture of stagnant water, dregs of beer, green dates, and other vegetable substances, the dose to be repeated four times; children however might not take this remedy, the latter were to have an old piece of writing soaked in oil placed as a compress round the body.[2] A difference was also to be observed between child and child; we read in one place: "if it be a big child, it shall take the pills, if however it be still in its swaddling clothes, the pills shall be dissolved in its nurse's milk."[3] In other cases, where these distinctions were not to be made, the doctor had not often much difficulty of choice, for the prescriptions were of various degrees of excellence. He might have tried many in his own practice, and written *good* by the side of them in his own prescription book;[4] older colleagues might already have made similar remarks in the margin of others, *e.g.* "excellent, I have seen it, and also have often made it";[5] or again: "Behold this is a real remedy. It was found in an examination of the writings in the temple of Uennofre."[6] Other remedies may have owed their great reputation to the recovery of some famous person of antiquity,[7] others again to their foreign origin. Thus there was an eye-salve, said to have been discovered by a "Semite of Byblos"—it was valued by the Egyptians as a *Phoenician* remedy, in the same way as many esteem an *American* nostrum in our days.[8]

There were of course many panaceas, which in this curious rhetoric were said to "drive out the fever of the gods, all death and pain from the limbs of man, so that he immediately becomes well."[9] These wondrous remedies were not invented by human wisdom, but by the various gods for the sun-god Rê', who had to suffer from all kinds of diseases and pain before he withdrew to his heavenly repose. Yet in spite of their supernatural origin, they are composed very much in the same way as the earthly prescriptions. One for instance consists of honey, wax, and fourteen vegetable substances, to be mixed in equal parts; poultices were to be made of the mixture.

[1] Eb., 61, 4, 6, 15. [2] Eb., 48, 22, 49, 15. [3] Eb., 49, 22.
[4] Eb., 35, 18, and frequently. [5] Eb., 69, 17; it may perhaps be construed otherwise.
[6] Eb., 75, 12. [7] Eb., 63, 4, 66, 15. [8] Eb., 63, 8. [9] Eb., 46, 10—47, 10.

Many believed also that the remedy for all ills was to be found in some particular plant, *e.g.* the tree *Dgam*, *i.e.* probably the olive tree.[1] In an "ancient book of wisdom for mankind," amongst other things we find the following remarks about this tree: "If the boughs are crushed in water and put upon a head which is ill, it will become well immediately, as if it had never been ill. For the complaint of indigestion (?) let the patient take some of the fruit in beer and the impure moistness will be driven out of his body. For the growth of a woman's hair let the fruit be pounded and kneaded into a lump; the woman must then put it in oil, and anoint her head with it."[2] In spite of these virtues vouched for by *the ancient book*, the tree does not appear to have played a great part in medicine,—we meet with it comparatively seldom in the prescriptions.

By far the greater number of the drugs employed were of vegetable origin; so numerous indeed were the fruits and herbs in use, that a good knowledge of botany was essential to every Egyptian physician. Many plants were indeed so rare that they were unknown to the doctor. The recipe then gives a description like the following: "the herb called *Smut;* it grows on its belly (*i.e.* creeps) like the plant *Q'edet*, it has blossoms like the lotus and its leaves look like white wood."[3]

Ingredients of animal origin were more rare; amongst these preference seems to have been given to substances most repulsive to us. The idea prevailed in Egyptian as in all folk-medicine, that a remedy ought not to be too simple or too commonplace. A prescription ought if possible to contain many ingredients—there was in fact a poultice which was composed of thirty-five different substances;[4] it was also necessary that the ingredients should be rare and also if possible disgusting. Lizards' blood, the teeth of swine, putrid meat and stinking fat, the moisture from pigs' ears and the milk of a lying-in woman, and a hundred other similar things, were favourite ingredients. Above all, certain substances valued for the healing craft were the same that were also revered so highly by the apothecaries of our 17th century, viz. excreta of all kinds. The excreta of adults, of children, of donkeys, antelopes, dogs, pigs, cats, and other animals, down to the "dirt of flies found on the walls"; all this is enough to disgust any one.[5]

It would not however be right to deny the possibility of results to Egyptian medicine because of this admixture of absurdity. Even with the recipes described above, good cures would be possible supposing that combined with senseless but harmless ingredients they contained even one substance that was efficacious. In many recipes we can discover one such useful ingredient,—as a rule something quite common, like honey, beer, or oil. It would have been sufficient to use that alone, but as no special good result could be expected from anything so commonplace, it was thought

[1] Br. Wb. Suppl., 1378. [2] Eb., 47, 16 ff.
[3] Eb., 51, 15. [4] Eb., 82, 22.
[5] A good summary of these details is to be found in Stern's glossary to the Pap. Ebers.

better to add to it all manner of possible and impossible things. In consequence, many recipes against ills of one class contain several identical substances, though the others vary; the efficacy depends on the former. This explains also the astonishing number of recipes; doctors in search of novelties might change the various indifferent ingredients as they liked, whilst the remedy itself was neither the better nor the worse.

The outward form of some of these old recipes is more satisfactory than the contents we have described. In perspicacity and brevity there is nothing to be desired. In the first place there is a superscription giving the object of the prescription:

"Remedy to draw the blood from a wound"; then come the ingredients with the statement of the quantities:

"Wax	1
Fat	1
Date-wine (?)	1
Honey	1
Boiled horn	1"

then (generally in abbreviated form) some necessary remarks about the preparation and use of the remedy: "boil, mix together, make fomentations therewith four times."[1] All manner of fine distinctions were observed; there were distinct terms for *pound* and *triturate*, for *mix* and *mix together*, for *fomentations* and *embrocations*, for *anoint* and *apply to*, and in his prescription-book the doctor would carefully correct a somewhat ambiguous term into one more exact.[2]

The medicine was supposed to enter the *vessels* of the body mentioned above, and this could be effected in various ways, either as a drink, or in the form of pills, or in embrocations or fomentations. Inhalation was also employed; thus in the illness *setyt*, a common complaint of the stomach, the remedy for which was generally warm milk with various additional substances, it was also useful to take the plants *T'e'am* and *'Amamu* in equal parts, "to reduce them to fine powder, to put them on the fire, and to inhale the rising steam through a reed."[3] The following recipe was more complicated but more efficacious; it was to be employed in the same illness:

"The seeds of the sweet woodroof
The seeds of *Mene*
The plant *'A'am*

reduce to powder. Then take seven stones and warm them at the fire. Take one of the same, put some of the remedy on it and put a new pot over it. Knock a piece out of the bottom of the pot and stick a reed into the hole. Put thy mouth to this reed so as to inhale the rising steam. Do the same with the other six stones. Afterwards eat some fat, *e.g.* fat meat or oil."[4]

[1] Eb., 70, 5.   [2] Eb., 70, 3.   [3] Eb., 54, 8 ff.   [4] Eb., 54, 18 ff.

It is particularly interesting to compare the number of recipes in the separate sections of the medical books, for in this way we can judge pretty well of the comparative frequency of the various diseases. The remedies for diseases of the eyes occur so frequently as to form a tenth part of the whole; this shows how common were such complaints. Probably in old times ophthalmia was as prevalent in Egypt as it is at the present day, and as this terrible scourge is now due in great measure to the want of cleanliness amongst the people, we may assume that the same conditions probably existed in old times. The same unwashen children with their eyes discharging, and their faces literally covered with flies, probably formed the same inevitable figure-groups in the street scenes as they do now.

The remedies are also very numerous "to kill worms" or "to drive out the disease which gives rise to worms."[1] The latter expression is due to the singular idea that worms are not the cause but rather the effect, the symptom of the disease. They thought that (in consequence, perhaps, of an obstruction) a gathering formed inside the human body, "which could find no way to discharge; it then became corrupt and was transformed into worms."[2]

The department of women's diseases was of course as extensive in Egypt as it has been and is in all countries, and in addition to the mother, the child at her breast was not forgotten. We learn that from the first cry one could foretell its chance of life; if he cried *ny*, he would live, if he cried *mbe'*, he would die.[3] We learn also how it was possible to tell the goodness of the mother's milk from the smell,[4] and a recipe is given for quieting the immoderate crying of children. The remedy which worked this miracle[5] was a mixture of the seeds of the plant *Shepen*, and of the everlasting fly-dirt; the second ingredient was of course useless, the first may have been most efficacious, especially if the plant *Shepen* was the same as that now used to quiet children in Upper Egypt, viz. the poppy.

We now come to the household remedies, which in Egypt formed a strange appendage to medicine. The doctor was not only required to furnish cosmetics, to colour the hair (cp. p. 232), to improve the skin,[6] and to beautify the limbs,[7] but people entreated his assistance against house vermin. He was ready to give advice. In order "to drive" fleas, that plague of Egypt, "out of the house," he would order the house to be sprinkled with natron water, or he would cause it to be "properly swept out"[8] with charcoal mixed with the powdered plant *Bebet*. As a protection against fly-stings he might order the fat of the woodpecker, while fresh palm-wine would protect against gnat-stings.[9] A dried fish or a piece of natron, if laid upon a snake's hole, would prevent this dreaded invader of Egyptian houses from venturing out.[10] Supposing however they

[1] Eb., 20, 16, 23; 21, 14. [2] Eb., 25, 3 ff. [3] Eb., 97, 13.
[4] Eb., 93, 17; 94, 9. [5] Eb., 93, 3. [6] Eb., 87, 3.
[7] Eb., 87, 4. [8] Eb., 97, 15. [9] Eb. 97, 20. [10] Eb., 97, 17.

wished to protect something in the house from the mice, a piece of cat's fat had to be laid upon it, for then the mice would not *approach* it, evidently they were supposed to imagine that the cat was at no great distance.[1] It is more difficult to explain the antipathy which rats were supposed, according to Egyptian belief, to have to the excreta of gazelles. In order to keep these dreaded visitors away from the granaries, they were to take "excreta of gazelles, put it on the fire in the granary, then scour with water the walls and floor where traces of rats were to be seen; the consequence will be that no more corn will be eaten."[2]

I cannot conclude this sketch of Egyptian medicine without referring to one other point.

It is wonderful how faithful the modern inhabitants of Egypt have remained to much of this strange medicine. Centuries have elapsed, the country has passed through the most terrible revolutions, the language is different, the religion has twice been changed, the people have lost all remembrance of their former greatness, but yet they have not forgotten that the excreta of dogs and the bones of fish are excellent remedies. "Against all kinds of witchcraft," the ancient Egyptian employed the following as a good preventive: "a great scarabaeus beetle; cut off his head and his wings, boil him, put him in oil, and lay him out. Then cook his head and his wings, put them in snake-fat, boil, and let the patient drink the mixture."[3] When the modern Egyptian wishes to cure haemorrhoids, he takes a black beetle, bakes it in oil, he then removes the wing-cases and the head, and softens them in oil over a gentle fire.[4] It is the same recipe, except that the snake-fat is replaced by ordinary oil.

Still more remarkable than these examples are other superstitions which have spread into Europe. In a medical papyrus in the Berlin museum, the following artifice is described, by which one might be certain as to the prospect of a woman having children or not. "The herb *Bededu-Ka*, powdered and soaked in the milk of a woman who has borne a son. Let the woman eat it . . . if she vomits it, she will bear a child, if she has flatulence, she will not bear." The same curious recipe is given by Hippocrates: Take figs or the plant Butyros and the milk of a woman who has borne a boy, and let the woman drink it. If she vomits, she will bear a child, if not, she will have no child.[5] The same old papyrus tells us a simple way of knowing whether a woman will bear a boy or a girl. It is only needful to steep some wheat and some spelt in some water she has passed; if the wheat sprouts, it will be a boy, if the spelt sprouts, it will be a girl. This recipe is not indeed to be found in Hippocrates, but by some means it came into Europe, for in an ingenious book of the seventeenth

[1] Eb., 98, 1. [2] Eb., 98, 6. [3] Eb., 88, 13.

[4] Klunzinger, 390. Cp. also ib., 391 with Eb., 63, 14 (inflexion of the eyelashes).

[5] Le Page Renouf, Ä. Z., 1873, 123. The papyrus is in the Recueil II., published by Brugsch; the passages quoted here are in pl. 106, 107.

century,[1] Peter Boyer thus speaks: "Make two holes in the ground, throw barley into the one and wheat into the other, then pour into both the water of the pregnant woman, and cover them up again with earth. If the wheat shoots before the barley, it will be a boy, but if the barley comes up first, thou must expect a daughter." There is also a little English book, called *The experienced Midwife*, in which this recipe appears in a somewhat modified form.[2] We see that the wisdom of the Egyptians has found its last refuge with the old herbalists and fortune-tellers.

Every department of Egyptian intellectual activity that we have as yet examined, we have found to be overgrown with superstition and magic. One branch of science, viz. mathematics, remains however untouched, so far as we know, by these noxious weeds. Thanks to a papyrus in the British Museum,[3] we are now pretty well informed on this subject. This book, which is a copy made under one of the Hyksos kings of an older work, is a collection of specimen examples of all kinds of arithmetical and geometrical problems, and thus it gives us a good idea of the proficiency the Egyptians had then attained. Their knowledge of this science at that time was not very great, and we doubt whether they carried their studies much further even under the New Empire, for, more than a century and a half later, we find in the agricultural lists of the temple of Edfu the same primitive ideas of geometry which are contained in our old book. Mathematics as well as medicine seems to have remained stationary at the same stage that it had reached under the Old Empire; progress was made in certain details, but a genius seems never to have arisen to give a fresh impetus to this science. There was indeed no need. The problems presented to the skill of the arithmetician were ever the same, and if the solution, which was often only an approximate one, had contented the government of the Old Empire, it sufficed also for that of the New Empire. Mathematics served merely a practical purpose for the ancient Egyptians,—they only solved the problems of everyday life, they never formulated and worked out problems for their own sake. How certain eatables were to be divided as payments of wages; how, in the exchange of bread for *beer*, the respective value was to be determined when converted into a quantity of corn; how to reckon the size of a field; how to determine whether a given quantity of corn would go into a granary of a certain size—these and similar problems were taught in the arithmetic book.

In pure arithmetical examples there are no errors as far as I can see, at most a small fraction is sometimes purposely disregarded. Everything is worked out in the slowest and most cumbrous manner—even the

[1] Paullini, Neu-vermehrte Heilsame Dreckapotheke. Frankfurt a. M., 1697, p. 248. A careful perusal of this literature would doubtless give many similar instances in proof.

[2] Le Page Renouf, Ä. Z., 1873, 124.

[3] Pap. Rhind (a mathematical handbook of the ancient Egyptians, Leipzig, 1877), utilised by me in accordance with Eisenlohr's explanatory publication. I have followed throughout Eisenlohr's explanation of the calculations, without always agreeing with his interpretation of the words of the text.

multiplication of the most simple numbers. If, for instance, the schoolboy had to find out in his sum the product of 8 times 8, this difficult problem would be written out thus:

1 8
2 16
4 32
—8 64

Evidently in mental arithmetic, he was only equal to multiplication by 2.[1] Strange to say also, he had no proper method for division; he scarcely seems to have had a clear idea of what division meant. He did not ask how many times 7 was contained in 77, but with which number 7 was to be multiplied that the product might be 77. In order to discover the answer he wrote out the multiplication table of 7, in the various small numbers, and then tried which of these products added together would give 77:

—1 7
—2 14
4 28
—8 56

In this instance the multiplicators belonging to 7 and 14 and 56 are marked by the pupil with a stroke and give the numbers wanted. Therefore it is necessary to multiply 7 by $1 + 2 + 8$, *i.e.* by 11, in order to obtain the 77, ∴ 7 goes 11 times in 77. If the question were how often is 8 contained in 19, or in other words what number must 8 be multiplied by to obtain 19, the result of the sum:[2]

1 8
—2 16
$\frac{1}{2}$ 4
—$\frac{1}{4}$ 2
—$\frac{1}{8}$ 1

would be that 2 and $\frac{1}{4}$ and $\frac{1}{8}$ are the desired numbers, for the addition of the numbers belonging to them would exactly make 19. We should say: 8 goes $2\frac{3}{8}$ times in 19.

In connection with this imperfect understanding of division, it is easy to understand that the Egyptian student had no fractions in our arithmetical sense. He could quite well comprehend that a thing could be divided into a certain number of parts, and he had a special term for such a part, *e.g.* *re-met* = mouth of ten, *i.e.* a tenth. This part however was always a unit to him, he never thought of it in the plural; they could speak of "one tenth and a tenth and a tenth" or "of a fifth and a tenth," but our familiar idea of $\frac{3}{10}$ did not exist in the mind of the Egyptian. Two

[1] Math. Handb. Nr. 50 (Pl. 17).

[2] Math. Handb. Nr. 24 (Pl. 11).

thirds was an exception ; for $\frac{2}{3}$ he possessed a term and a sign,—it was his only fraction which was not of the most simple kind. When he had to divide a smaller number by a greater, for instance 5 by 7, he could not represent the result as we do by the fraction $\frac{5}{7}$, but had to do it in the most tiresome roundabout fashion. He analysed the problem either by the division of 1 by 7 five times, so that the result would be $\frac{1}{7}+\frac{1}{7}+\frac{1}{7}+\frac{1}{7}+\frac{1}{7}$, or more usually he took the division of 2 by 7 twice and that of 1 by 7 once. There were special tables which gave him the practical result of the division of 2 by the odd numbers of the first hundred.[1] He thus obtained $\frac{1}{4}$ $\frac{1}{28}$, $\frac{1}{4}$ $\frac{1}{28}$, $\frac{1}{7}$, which he then knew how to reduce to $\frac{1}{2}+\frac{1}{7}+\frac{1}{14}$.

If by this awkward mechanism they obtained sufficiently exact results, it was owing exclusively to the routine of their work. The range of the examples which occurred was such a narrow one, that for each there was an established formula. Each calculation had its special name and its short conventional form, which when once practised was easily repeated. The following example giving the calculation of a number may illustrate what has been said :[2]

a.	A number together with its fifth part makes 21.
b.	1 5
	5 1 together 6.
c.	—1 6
	—2 12
	—$\frac{1}{2}$ 3 together 21.
d.	—1 $3\frac{1}{2}$
	2 7
	—4 15 (read 14)
e.	The number $17\frac{1}{2}$
	$\frac{1}{5}$ $3\frac{1}{2}$ together 21.

I scarcely think that the most expert arithmetician will grasp what these figures mean ; it is only by the comparison of similar calculations that we can understand all these abbreviations. The proposition formulated by *a* corresponds to the equation $x+\frac{1}{5}=21$, the result of which $x=17\frac{1}{2}$ is given quite correctly in *e*. As the Egyptian could not very well calculate in fractions, he had next to create this wretched $\frac{1}{5}x$; this he did thus : in *b* he multiplies the number and the fifth of the number by 5, which together makes 6. In *c* 21 is divided according to the cumbrous Egyptian method by this 6, the result being $3\frac{1}{2}$. This $3\frac{1}{2}$ would have been the desired number if we had not beforehand in *b* changed the fraction $\frac{6}{5}$ into the number 6 by multiplication with 5 ; the result of our division must therefore be made five times greater. This multiplication takes place in *d*, and gives the final result $17\frac{1}{2}$. In *e* we

[1] Math. Handb. (Pl. 1-8).

[2] Math. Handb. Nr. 27 (Pl. 11).

find the example is proved by adding together this $17\frac{1}{2}$ with the $\frac{1}{5}$ obtained above, namely $3\frac{1}{2}$, which correctly gives the 21 of our problem. Written after our fashion, the whole would stand thus:

$$(a)\ \tfrac{6}{5}\,x = 21$$
$$(b)\ 6\,x = 21 \times 5$$
$$(c)\ x = \tfrac{21}{6} \times 5$$
$$(d)\ x = 3\tfrac{1}{2} \times 5$$
$$(e)\ x = 17\tfrac{1}{2}.$$
$$\text{Proof: } 17\tfrac{1}{2} + 3\tfrac{1}{2} = 21.$$

The Egyptians knew still less of geometry than they did of arithmetic, though surface-measurement was most necessary to them, because of the destruction of so many field boundaries in the inundation every year. All their calculations were founded on the right angle, the content of which they correctly determined as the product of the two sides.[1] But in the strangest way they quite overlooked the fact that every quadrilateral figure, in which the opposite sides are of the same length, could not be treated in the same manner. Now as they treated each triangle as if it were a quadrangle, in which two sides are identical, and the others are half the size, they carried this error into the calculation of triangles also. To them also an isosceles triangle equalled half the product of its short and its long side,[2] because they would in all cases determine the quadrangle corresponding to it by the multiplication of its two sides, though it were nothing but a right angle. The error which would arise from this kind of misconception might be considerable under some circumstances.

The calculation of the trapezium [3] suffered also from the same error; in order to find its content, they would multiply the oblique side by half the product of the two parallel sides. As we see, the fundamental mistake of these students of surface-measurement was that they never realised the value of the perpendicular; instead of the latter they used one of the oblique sides, and therewith from the outset they excluded themselves from the correct manner of working. It is remarkable that, with such errors, they should have rightly determined approximately the difficult question of the area of a circle; in this case they deducted a ninth of the diameter, and multiplied the remainder of the same by itself. Thus if the diameter of a circle amounted to 9 rods, they would calculate its area to be $8 \times 8 = 64$ square rods, a result which would deviate from the correct result by but about $\frac{2}{5}$ of a square rod.[4]

Amongst the volumetric problems which they attempted, they would calculate, for instance, the quantity of corn which would go into a granary of a certain size; the little that we can as yet understand with any certainty of these problems seems to indicate right conceptions, but the conditions are here too complicated for us to give a decided opinion.

[1] Math. Handb. Nr. 49 (Pl. 17).
[2] Math. Handb. Nr. 51 (Pl. 17).
[3] Math. Handb. Nr. 52 (Pl. 17).
[4] Math. Handb. Nr. 50 (Pl. 17).

Probably however if we understood them, it would not much alter our general impression as to the mathematics of the ancient Egyptians: our conclusion on this subject is that there is little to be said for their theoretic knowledge of this science, but their practical knowledge sufficed very well for the simple requirements of daily life.

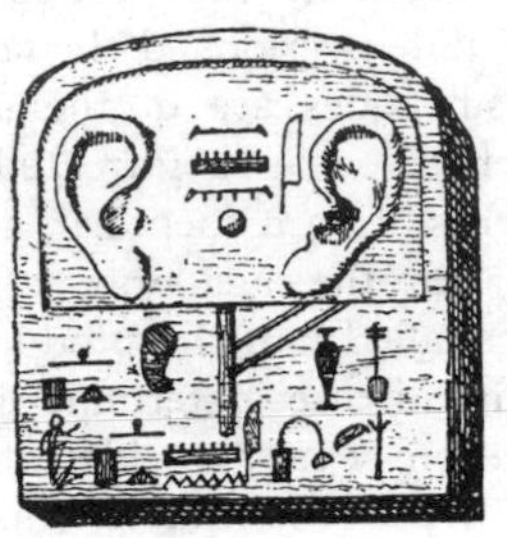

SMALL STELA, DEDICATED BY AMENHÔTEP, A SCRIBE, TO AMON RÊ', PROBABLY FOR THE CURE OF A BAD EAR.

(Wilk. ii. 358, from Thebes.)

THE WOLF AS GOAT-HERD AND THE CAT AS GOOSE-HERD.
From the satirical pictures in a London papyrus. (After the restoration in Lepsius, Auswahl, pl. 23.)

CHAPTER XV

LITERATURE

FAIRY tales have always rejoiced the heart of the Egyptian, both of ancient and modern days, and when the treasury of the fairy lore of the fellahin was brought to light, the learned discoverer conjectured at once that these tales were to a large extent of very early origin.[1] In fact a comparatively large number of tales of very similar character have come down to us from the various periods of Egyptian history; hence we learn the delight the old Egyptians found in story-telling. These slight poetical compositions were doubtless favourites with the Egyptian peasantry of all ages, though they may not always have enjoyed the same repute in their literature. We know nothing of the literary conditions that existed before the time of the Middle Empire; several tales of that period have however come down to us, and the contents of these show that they were of popular origin. A remarkable fragment contained in a Berlin papyrus is also, comparatively speaking, of homely form. It relates that a shepherd caught a glimpse of a *goddess* in the marshes, and fell deeply in love with her: "he had never spoken to her, (but) her power pursued his body." He then caused the wisest of the magic formulae of the shepherds to be read, and "as it dawned quite early . . . and he had placed himself before the lake, then she came divested of her clothes and with disordered hair."[2] What she said to him the reader must imagine for himself, for unfortunately an old proprietor of the book thought well to wash off the end as well as the beginning of the papyrus, in order to provide himself in a cheap way with clean paper.[3]

The Egyptians of the Middle Empire seem to have been especially fond of stories of travel, in which the hero relates his own adventures. Out of the half-dozen books which we possess of this period, two at

[1] Cp. the remarks of Spitta in his Contes arabes.
[2] Berlin Pap., 24, E—F.
[3] Examples of this economy are frequent under the M. E. and the N. E.

least contain narratives of this kind, whilst we have not a single one of later date. In the first (which we shall treat in more detail in the 19th chapter) a shipwrecked sailor narrates his wonderful experiences on the fabulous snake-island ; the other story has less the character of a romance, —it describes the fate of an exile amongst the Syrian Beduins. The tale is simple and homely, there is nothing remarkable in the contents, and the fame that the book enjoyed for centuries must have been due to the charm of its half poetic style.[1] Sinuhe, a distinguished courtier of King Amenemhê't I., accompanied the heir and co-regent of this king in an expedition against the Libyans ; in the meantime the old king died ; the news of his death reached the camp, and Sinuhe, whose life—we know not why—was endangered by this circumstance, immediately took to flight. He escaped safely to the eastern frontier of Egypt, but it was dangerous to pass this frontier, because it was fortified by defences—" the princely wall erected for defence against the Beduins." " I then crouched down in the bushes," so he relates, " for fear that the watchmen on the roof of the tower should see me. I went on by night, and by daybreak I reached the country of Peten. When I approached the lake Qem-uêr (evidently one of the Bitter Lákes) thirst seized me—and my throat burned. Then I said : 'This is the taste of death.' (All at once) my heart revived, I roused myself : I heard the lowing of a herd. I caught sight of an Asiatic. . . . He gave me water, and I boiled myself some milk. Then I went with him to his people . . . and one tribe passed me on to the next. . . . I left Beḥt (?) and came to Qedem, and spent a year and a half there. Then 'Amu-'en-sh'e, the prince of the upper land of Tenu, took me to him and said to me : 'Remain with me, then shalt thou hear something of Egypt.' He said that because he knew who I was ; he had heard of my valour, and the Egyptians who were with him testified of the same. Then he said further to me : 'Why hast thou come hither ? What has happened ? Something must have happened at the court of King Amenemḥê't, who has gone to heaven, without its being known moreover what had happened.' I answered : 'That is false.' " Then Sinuhe launches forth in long eulogies of the late and of the reigning king, and of their great power against all countries ; and hints (if I rightly understand) to the barbarians, that it would be well for them to secure him as a mediator for future occasions, for King Usertsen would probably carry his arms into this part of the country again. This seemed good to the Beduin, and he kept Sinuhe to live with him. " He placed me," relates our hero, " at the head of his children, and married me to his eldest daughter. He let me choose from amongst his lands, from amongst his choicest possessions on the frontier of another country. This was the beautiful country of 'Eaa ; figs and vines grew there, there were many

[1] Two ostraca show that even under the New Empire these tales were considered classical literature. In the beginning of 1886 one ostracon was found in a Theban tomb of the 20th dynasty containing the beginning of the book, though in a badly arranged text ; the other is in London and contains the last few lines.

sorts of wine and it was rich in honey, its olive trees were plentiful, and all kinds of fruits grew on its trees. There was corn there, and barley, and herds without number. And there was yet more that happened to me from love to me (?), for he made me prince of a tribe of his country. Then I had as much bread as I wanted, and wine for every day, boiled meat and roast goose, irrespective of the game of the country that I caught and carried off as spoil, and irrespective of what my greyhounds brought me. . . . Thus I spent many years, and my children became heroes, each the protector of his adopted tribe. The messenger who came from the court or went thither stayed with me, I gave hospitality to every one, and I gave water to the thirsty." . . . Opportunities for warlike deeds were also not lacking in the country of Tenu,—"I subdued each people against whom I marched, I drove them from their pastures and from their wells. I captured their cattle, and carried off their children ; I robbed them of their food ; I killed their people with my sword, with my bow, with my marches, with my wise designs. . . . A hero of Tenu came and challenged (?) me in my tent. He was a daring man (?) he had no equal, he had subdued everybody. He said : 'Let him fight with me' ; he thought (?) he would slay me, he imagined he would carry off my cattle. . . ." After much speaking, in which *e.g.* the warriors are compared to bulls who are fighting for their cows, it comes at last really to a hand-to-hand fight : "I shot at him, and my weapon stuck in his neck ; he cried out, he fell on his nose." The victory was decisive, and "all the Beduins cried out. Then I took away his possessions, I carried off his cattle ; what he thought to have done to me, that did I to him."

Life amongst the Beduins however did not content this distinguished Egyptian for ever ; as he grew old and felt his end approaching, he could bear it no longer, and wrote a piteous letter to the king, praying for the favour of the monarch and of his consort. The second half of the book relates to us how graciously the king answered, and the graceful reply of Sinuhe to this *royal command ;* next, how a messenger was sent to fetch him, how he bequeathed his property to his children, how at the court he besought the king for favour, and how the royal children interceded for him. All this account gives the author ample opportunity to show himself a master of fine language. We will leave these high-flown and rather obscure sentences, and consider the conclusion : "His Majesty said : 'Let him not be afraid . . . he shall be a *friend* amongst the princes, and he shall be received amongst the courtiers. Go to the chamber of adoration, in order to show him his rank.'[1] When they now came out of the chamber, the royal children gave him their hands, and they then went to the great double outer hall.[2] He was received into a house in which an honourable son of the king dwelt." . . . There servants attended to his toilet, and "they caused the age of his body to pass away." His hair was brought into order, and fine robes were put upon him : he "forsook the vermin of the desert and the (rough) clothes of the Beduins." He was anointed

[1] Cp. the "house of adoration," see pp. 69, 70. [2] Cp. p. 58.

with the finest oil, and laid to rest on a beautiful couch. A new house was erected for him, and "three times and four times in the day food was brought to him, irrespective of that which the royal children gave him unceasingly." Then the royal artisans and architects built him a tomb, "a pyramid of stone amongst the pyramids," which was furnished with all that was necessary. Sinuhe closes his story as follows: "Thus my life is crowned with the rewards of the king, till the day shall come for me to go hence."

It stands to reason that for the educated Egyptian the charm of the above story lay rather in the elegance of its language than in its contents merely; the long letters and speeches, which continually interrupt the narrative, and in which one thought is wearisomely played upon and spun out, were evidently considered the chief value of the book.

The latter remark applies still more to another contemporary writing, the history of a poor man of the marsh and of Meruetense the estate superintendent. In this story romance disappears. The donkey of the poor man has been unjustly confiscated, and he turns for help to the rich official; long endless speeches from both parties follow; they all probably relate to the confiscated donkey. I say *probably*, for it is difficult to see exactly what is the object of these difficult, incomprehensible, bombastic phrases. This constituted, however, the wit of this bulky book; it was intended to show what beautiful thoughts and what fine language a clever man could weave round any ordinary subject. The rhetoric which here seems launched forth with such ease was much admired, and it is doubtless not accidental that we meet with it continually in other writings also belonging to the Middle Empire. The reader will observe it for instance in the quotations from the tomb inscriptions of this epoch given above (see p. 88), but this rhetorical style is chiefly to be seen in the didactic literature,[1] to the consideration of which we shall return later. One example only is given here of this kind of artificial writing, which I believe I have translated with tolerable certainty, though as a rule this fine style renders the sense quite unintelligible to us. "A son hears, it is splendid. The hearer enters (into the palace). If a hearer hears, then the hearer becomes a good servant, good in hearing, good in speaking. Each one who hears is something splendid. It is splendid, a hearer hears. Hearing is better than all things that exist; it creates beautiful love. How beautiful it is when a son receives what his father says; that creates for him a good old age with her (*i.e.* love). He who loves God, hears; he who hates God does not hear. The heart causes its master to hear or not to hear."[2] In the original almost every sentence in this example begins with the same word with which the preceding one ends.

The literature of every country has to pass through an unnatural stage of this kind, but finally common sense always gains the victory, and even the Persians, who went to the greatest extremes in this foolish artificial

[1] This defect is specially observable both in the Pap. Prisse and in the "Instructions of King Amenemḥê't.

[2] Prisse, 16, 3-8.

style, learned after the time of Wassêf, to express their thoughts in a comprehensible form. In Egypt also a revulsion of thought ensued, and indeed the great catastrophe which overtook the Middle Empire seems also to have made an end of this bad literary style. Instead of the subtle refinement which in previous times had predominated in light literature, the stories became, after the time of the Hyksos, quite simple both as regards their contents and their form. Nothing can be more homely than the tales of the New Empire with their monotonous though popular language destitute of all rhetoric and exaggeration.

The subject of the most ancient of these stories, which, judging from the language, seems to have been written in the Hyksos' time, is connected with old historical incidents—incidents that had lived in the memory of the nation because the pyramids, the greatest monuments in the country, served ever to call them to mind.

This papyrus, which was lately purchased by the Berlin Museum, relates that once upon a time King Chufu ordered his sons—they were all *first reciter-priests* to the king—to relate tales of the wonderful deeds of certain great magicians at the court of his predecessor.[1] One had caused a faithless wife and her lover to be seized by a small crocodile of wax; another had by a magic formula fetched up from the depth of the water a jewel which a lady had dropped there, etc. Chufu admired exceedingly the *learning* of these ancient wise men, and at the end of each story he ordered an offering to be made to the hero of the tale.

When it came to the turn of Prince Ḥardadaf, he produced no story of an ancient magician, but preferred to relate to his father a tale of a man still living in his own time. "This man is called Ded'e and lives in Ded-Snefru. He is a young man of 110 years and eats 500 cakes of bread together with a joint of beef, and drinks 100 jugs of beer, even at the present day. He knows how to set on a head that has been cut off, and he can cause the lions of the desert to walk behind him." One other thing Ded'e knew which would be sure to interest King Chufu. He knew where certain secret things out of the house of the god Thoth were hidden, which the king had long wished to use *for his horizon* (*i.e.* either for his palace or for his pyramid).

Chufu immediately sent Ḥardadaf to fetch the wise man to his court; boats were equipped, and the prince went up-stream till he came near Ded-Snefru. There he landed, and was carried in his ebony sedan-chair to the house of the aged learned man, whom he found stretched on his couch. After a few general remarks on health in old age, the prince gave his message as follows: "I have come from afar as a messenger from my father Chufu, to summon thee to eat of the excellent food that he gives, and of the meats of his attendants, that he may conduct thee by a beautiful life to thy fathers, who are in the city of the dead." Ded'e declared himself ready to follow the summons of the king, and "the prince Ḥardadaf gave him his hand and raised him up. Then he went with him to the

[1] See pp. 76, 90.

bank of the river, whilst he gave him his arm." Then they went downstream in the same boats; the learned man stipulated however (if I rightly understand) for a special boat for the transport of his books. "When he had now arrived at court, Prince Ḥardadaf went in to announce the news to King Chufu. Prince Ḥardadaf said: 'O king, my lord, I have brought Ded'e.' The king answered: 'Run and bring him in.' His Majesty then went into the hall of the palace, and Ded'e was led in to him.

"His Majesty said: 'How is it, Ded'e, that I never see thee?' Ded'e answered: 'He who is called, comes; the king calls and behold here I am.' The king said: 'Is it true what they say, that thou canst set on a head that has been cut off?' Ded'e answered: 'Yes I can, O king, my lord.' The king said: 'Let them bring in a prisoner from the prison . . .' Ded'e answered: 'Not so, not a man, O king, my lord. Behold, let the order be given that this shall be carried out on an excellent animal." Then they brought a goose and cut off its head; the goose was then laid in the western corner of the hall, and the head in the eastern corner, and Ded'e said his magic formula. Then the goose stood up and tripped along and the head did likewise. When now one part had come to the other, the goose stood there and cackled. They then brought a duck (?) and the same happened to it. Then the king caused a bull to be brought and his head to be thrown on the ground. Ded'e said his incantation, and the bull stood there behind him." . . . These miracles convinced the king that he might really trust to the wisdom of Ded'e, and he now asked him openly about the subject which he had at heart, viz. as to the hiding-place of certain secret things, which had been originally in the house of the god of wisdom. But the king received no satisfactory answer; the wise man acknowledged indeed that he knew the house at Heliopolis, in which they were, "but," he added, "I will not bring them to thee." "Who then will bring them to me?" asked the king, and the wise man answered: "The oldest of the three children, whom Reddedt will bear, shall bring them to thee." When Chufu asked in amazement who this Reddedt might be, Ded'e explained: "She is the wife of a priest of the god Rê', in the town Sachebu,[1] who is now pregnant with three children by Rê' of Sachebu. He has told her that they will exercise that excellent dignity over this whole country, and the eldest of them shall be high priest of Heliopolis." "Then was his Majesty very sad." Well might he be so. He knew well what the wise man had meant by *that excellent dignity*. What Ded'e had prophesied was the future birth of three kings of a new race. All the Pharaohs boasted that they were descendants of the sun-god, who had now begotten himself a new race, and had rejected the old one.

What Chufu decided to do to turn aside this threatened disaster remains uncertain. Our book passes on to the climax, the birth of the three sons of the god. When the hour of the delivery of Reddedt drew near, Rê' called to the goddesses Isis, Nephthys, Mesechent, and Ḥeqt, as

[1] The reading of the name of the town is uncertain.

well as to the god Chnum, and said: "Come, hasten and deliver Reddedt of her three children, who shall at a future time exercise that most excellent dignity over this whole country. They shall build your temples, care for your altars, increase your drink-offerings, and cause your temple revenues to be great." The divinities followed his bidding, and repaired in human form to the house of the woman, where they presented themselves to the anxious earthly husband the priest Raʿuoser, as experienced women, who "understood how to deliver." He admitted them into the house, they closed the door behind them and began their work. They brought three children into the world, each measured a cubit and had powerful bones; Isis gave a name to each, and Mesechent prophesied of each, that "he would become a king over this whole country." This prophecy was fulfilled later, in fact the three children became, as we know by their names, the first three kings of the 5th dynasty.

When the goddesses left the house and announced to the husband of Reddedt the birth of the triplet, he was full of gratitude and presented them with some corn, which they gladly accepted. Chnum, who played the part of their servant, had to lade himself with it. "When they were now returned to the place whence they had come, Isis spoke to those divinities: 'How is it that we have come away without working a miracle for those children, a miracle to announce to their father who sent us thither?'" After much consideration they formed diadems and laid them in the corn that they had received as a reward; they then raised a storm, which carried this grain back into the house of Reddedt. When now, after a fortnight, Reddedt began again to see after her household affairs, she learnt to her astonishment from her maid that the corn which had been given away was still there. She sent the girl to fetch some of it, but the girl returned frightened, for as soon as she had opened the house in which the corn lay, she had "heard the sound of song, music, and dancing, as if to do honour to a king."

This miracle, by which the new-born children were greeted as kings, brought them into much danger, for on one occasion, when the servant girl was punished by Reddedt, she said to the people: "Ought she to do that to me, she who has borne three kings? I shall go and tell it to King Chufu." And in fact she set off to travel to court.

What King Chufu said to her message; what he attempted against the children; how the latter escaped his persecution, until at last, when they reached man's estate, they thrust his race from the throne—all this we must imagine for ourselves, for unfortunately the end as well as the beginning of the papyrus is missing.

When this tale was written, a thousand years and more had passed away and yet the disputes about the throne under the Old Empire which form the foundation of the story were not forgotten. Sometimes, however, legend grafted her wonderful leaves and blossoms on incidents which were not so long past. We have a story written about the close of the 19th dynasty which, in the form of a romance, describes the beginning of the

Hyksos wars; and to about the same date belongs the account of the taking of the town of Joppa by Thothmes III. The latter incident had occurred scarcely 200 years before, and yet, amongst other things, they related of one of the generals of the king how he had packed up 600 soldiers in sacks or baskets and by a stratagem had them carried into Joppa by 600 of their fellows. Historical romances of this kind seem to have been very common in ancient times, for the Greek tales that have come down to us concerning the older Egyptian history seem to have been taken from similar writings.

Besides these stories founded on history, there were others, the scenes of which took place in the happy period of "once upon a time." We will take as an instance the following pretty tale,[1] the motive of which is common to the whole world.

"There was once a king, who had no son. He therefore prayed the gods to give him a son, and they ordered that a son should be born to him. He slept at night with his wife and she became pregnant. When her months were accomplished, behold she bore a son. When now the Ḥatḥors came to decide upon his fortune, they said: 'He shall die by a crocodile, a snake, or a dog.' The people who were with the children heard these words. They related them to His Majesty. Then was His Majesty very very sad. Then His Majesty caused a castle to be built in the mountains; this castle was provided with servants and with all good things from the palace, and the child was never allowed to go out of the castle.

"Now when the child had grown tall, he went up on the roof and saw a greyhound running after a man, who was walking along the road. He said to the servant who was with him: 'What is that following the man, who is walking along the road?' He answered him: 'That is a greyhound!' The child said to him: 'Let them bring me one.' Then the servant went and told the king. The king then said: 'Let them take him a pup,[2] that his heart may not grieve about it.' Then they brought him the greyhound.

"Now after many days were gone, the child waxed great in all his members, and sent to his father to say: 'Why should I remain here? Behold I am predestined to the three fates, and whether I do according to my will or not, God will do as He wills.' Then they gave him weapons of all kinds . . . they brought him to the eastern frontier and said to him: 'Go then according to thy wish.' His dog was with him, and he travelled according to his heart's desire in the mountains, and lived on the best mountain game. Then he came to the prince of Naharanna. The prince of Naharanna had an only child, a daughter. He had built a house for her with a window more than seventy cubits from the ground. He ordered all the children of all the princes of Charu to be brought before him, and said to them: 'Whoever shall climb to the window of my daughter, shall have her for wife.'

[1] Cp. Records of the Past, vol. ii. p. 153.

[2] In the text a special breed is spoken of.

"Now after many days had passed, and the princes were making their daily attempt, the youth came past. Then they brought the youth to their house, they washed him and gave his horse food. They did all manner of good to the youth, they anointed him, they bound up his feet, and gave him of their own bread. They then talked to him and said: 'Whence comest thou, thou beautiful youth?' He answered them: 'I am the son of an Egyptian officer, my mother died, and my father took to himself another wife. . . . Thereupon she hated me, and I ran away and fled before her!' Then they embraced him and kissed him."

The prince then learnt from his hosts, what had brought them hither, and naturally he also became desirous to win the king's daughter. "Then they went to climb, as was their daily endeavour, and the lad stood afar from them and watched, and the eyes of the daughter of the prince of Naharanna rested upon him.

"Now after some time had passed, the youth went to climb with the children of the princes. He climbed and reached the window of the daughter of the prince of Naharanna. She kissed him and embraced him in all his limbs. Then they went to rejoice the heart of her father, and said to him: 'A man has reached the window of thy daughter.' The prince then asked: 'The son of which prince is it?' and they answered him: 'It is the son of an officer, who has fled from his stepmother in Egypt.' Then the prince of Naharanna was exceeding angry. Then he said: 'I give my daughter to no Egyptian fugitive; he may return to his house again,' and they went and told him: 'Go back again to the place whence thou hast come.' But the daughter seized him and swore; 'By Rê'-Harmachis, if they take him from me, I will neither eat nor drink until I die.' Then the messenger went and told her father what she had said. The prince sent people to kill him whilst he was in his house. But the daughter said: 'By Rê', (if they kill) him, then I (also) shall be dead by sunset—I will not live an hour without him.' . . . Then the messenger told this to her father."

The father could not understand such love, and he gave his daughter to the youth. "He embraced him and kissed him in all his limbs, and said to him: 'Tell me then who thou art; behold, art thou not now my son?' He answered him: 'I am the son of an Egyptian officer, my mother died, my father took to himself another wife, thereupon she hated me, and I fled before her.' Then he gave him his daughter to wife, and gave him (servants) and fields together with cattle and all good things.

"Now after some time the youth spake thus to his wife: 'I am predestined to three fates, to the crocodile, the snake, and the dog.' Then she said, 'Let then thy dog, who runs before thee, be killed'; he answered: 'I will not allow my dog, whom I have brought up from a pup, to be killed.' Then she feared much for her husband, and would never let him go out alone."

Thus far the tale goes. From the mutilated pages of handwriting that follow we next gather that, thanks to the watchfulness of his wife, the prince escapes from the danger which threatens him through the snake and the crocodile. It is probable that his faithful dog afterwards involuntarily takes his life, and thus his fate is fulfilled.

Each of the above tales springs throughout from the same source; a definite scheme is followed consistently in each. At the same time there were other tales in which various old legends were mixed together, and which are therefore destitute of any consecutive cohesiveness, a quality common to the folklore of all nations, and especially to that of modern Egypt. The following confused though pretty tale of the 19th dynasty gives an excellent example of a story of this description.

"Once upon a time there were two brothers, born of one mother and of one father; the elder was called Anup, the younger Bata. Now Anup possessed a house and had a wife, whilst his younger brother lived with him as a son. He it was who weaved (?) for him, and drove his cattle to the fields, who ploughed and reaped; he it was who directed all the business of the farm for him. The younger brother was a good (farmer), the like of whom was not to be found throughout the country." The affectionate relationship between the two brothers was disturbed, however, by the fault of the wife. One day when Bata came back from the field, where he had been ploughing with Anup, to the house to fetch some seed for sowing, the desires of his sister-in-law awoke in her, and she sought to seduce him. But he thrust her away angrily, and hastened back to his cattle in the field, but he told Anup nothing of what had occurred. This forbearance was his ruin. "Now when evening was come, the elder brother returned to the house, and the younger brother went along behind his cattle. He had laded himself with all the herbs of the fields, and drove his cattle before him, to bring them to the cattle-pen. Then the wife of the elder brother feared because of what she had said. She therefore pretended that she had been ill-treated with violence, in order to say to her husband: 'Thy younger brother has ill-treated me.' In the evening her husband came back as he did every day; he reached his house, there he found his wife lying, ill through violence. She did not pour water over his hands as was her custom, she had not lighted the lights for him, his house was in darkness, and she lay there ill. Her husband said to her: 'Who has spoken with thee?' Then she answered him: 'Nobody has spoken with me except thy younger brother.'

"Then the elder brother became raging like a panther; he sharpened his knife, and took it in his hand. And the elder brother stood behind the door of his cattle-shed, in order to kill the younger, when he came back in the evening to bring the cattle into the shed.

"Now when the sun was setting and he had laden himself with all the herbs of the field as was his custom, then he came. His first cow entered the cattle-shed and said to her herdsman: 'Beware, there stands thy elder brother before thee with his knife, in order to kill thee; run away from him.' Then he heard what the first cow had said. The second entered and said likewise. He looked under the door of the cattle-shed, he caught sight of the feet of his brother, who was standing behind the door with his knife in his hand. He threw his burden on the ground and began to run away quickly. His elder brother ran after him with his knife in his hand." Thus Anup followed him in a rage, but Rê' caused a stream of water to come between them, and thus placed the poor Bata in a safe place from his pursuer. Throughout the night they stood on either side of the water; in the morning however Bata expostulated with his brother and swore to him before the sun-god, that he was innocent, and reproached him that he could so easily doubt his sincerity. "And," he added, "now go home and see after thy cattle thyself, for I will no longer stay with thee. I shall go to the acacia valley. This is however what shall happen to me: I shall take my heart and put it on the flower of the acacia. And when they give thee a jug of beer and it froths—that shall be a sign to thee, then come and seek the heart." Then Anup went back and killed his wife and sat there in sadness; Bata however went to the acacia valley.

Thus we see the story begins in a simple and purely human manner, but afterwards a motive breaks in, the connection of which it is difficult to understand. Bata is metamorphosed from the pious young herdsman into a hero, whose life is bound up in a mystical manner with the flower of a tree. He lives under the tree, the gods hold intercourse with him, they present him with a wife that he may not be alone. But this divine maiden becomes his misfortune. The king of Egypt, to whom the sea has carried a lock of her hair, sends his messengers to her, and she allows herself to be carried off. She betrays to the king the secret on which the life of her husband depends; the acacia is felled and Bata sinks to the ground dead. Now there happens what Bata had foretold. Anup at home recognises, by the frothing of the beer in his jug, that something has happened to his brother; he goes to the acacia valley and finds his body. Then for seven long years he seeks his heart; when at last he finds it, Bata awakes from the dead. But he is immediately transformed into a sacred bull, which Anup has to lead to the king. When this bull approaches the queen, he causes her to recognise him as her husband. She causes him to be slaughtered, but from his blood there spring two sycamores; she causes these to be cut down, but a splinter of the wood enters her mouth. Then she bears a son, whom the king acknowledges as his heir. The boy, however, is Bata himself, who when he has grown up causes the queen to be killed and reigns as king with his brother.

Thus the tale closes; but by the boldest interpretation we can scarcely discover any internal connection between the individual parts. Apparently they are fragments of different legends, which have been welded to a whole in the mind of the narrator; one small feature can even now be identified with certainty as a reminiscence of the Osiris myth.[1]

The simplicity of the style, which distinguishes these stories of the New Empire from those of the Middle Empire, is also a characteristic of

[1] D'Orbiney, 7, 9.

the later literature; evidently fashion had reverted to a great extent to the truth of nature. Yet we must not imagine this rebound to have been of a very deep nature, the books of the Middle Empire were always considered by scholars to be patterns of classical grace,[1] and in the official texts they imitated their heavy style and antique phraseology without producing, according to our opinion, anything very pleasing. A story like the above, simply related in the conversational manner of the New Empire, appeals to us far more than the elegant works of the learned litterateurs, who even when they made use of the spoken language, always believed themselves obliged to interlard it with scraps from a past age.

The interesting book which is preserved to us intact in the first Anastasi papyrus gives us a wonderful glimpse into the taste and life of the literary circle under the New Empire. It consists of the epistles sent by the scribe N. N. (the name is destroyed) the son of Nennofre, holding an appointment in one of the royal stables, to "his friend Nechtsotep, the royal scribe of the commands for the army."[2] These letters were not intended to convey news, but merely to show off the writer's fine wit and graceful style in a literary dispute. The author is supposed to be a learned man and a wit; he calls himself a "proficient in the sacred writings, who is not ignorant; one who is brave and powerful in the work of the (goddess of wisdom) Sefchet; a servant of the lord of Chmunu (the god Thoth) in the house of the books." He is "teacher in the hall of the books," and is "a prince to his disciples" (*i.e.* his pupils).[3] His opponent Nechtsotep has little to boast of in comparison with such advantages; he is indeed "of a wonderful good heart . . . has not his equal amongst all the scribes, wins the love of every one; handsome to behold, in all things he is experienced as a scribe, his counsel is asked in order to know what is most excellent,"[4] but with all these good qualities, he lacks that eloquence in which the author so greatly excels. The latter is able indeed to boast that "whatever comes out of his mouth is dipped in honey."[5] This superiority of his own style over that of Nechtsotep forms the chief subject of the book.

"Thy letter reached me," writes the author to Nechtsotep, "just as I had mounted the horse that belongs to me, and I rejoiced and was glad over it." His pleasure however was not of long duration, for on examining it more closely, he says: "I found it was neither praise- nor blameworthy. Thy sentences confuse one thing with another, all thy words are wrong, they do not express thy meaning.[6] It is a letter laden with many periods and long words.[7] What thy tongue says is very weak, thy words are very confused; thou comest to me involved in confusion and burdened with faults."[8]

It seems that the author now intends to contrast this circumstantial misshapen letter with his answer; he wishes to show how Nechtsotep ought to have written, and for this purpose he repeats to him a part of his letter

[1] We gather this from the many excerpts found in the school copy-books of the N.E.
[2] An., 1, 2, 3. [3] Ib., 1, 1-3. [4] Ib., 2, 3 ff. [5] Ib., 1, 7.
[6] Ib., 4, 6 ff. [7] Ib., 18, 3. [8] Ib., 28, 2, f.

in more elegant form.[1] He manages of course to take his choice out of the many rolls[2] Nechtsotep had sent, so as to be able at the same time to direct all manner of little sarcasms at his opponent. The latter had boasted of his warlike deeds, and described with pride his expeditions through Syria; in the author's repetition these deeds are also related, but as a rule rather ironically.

Before the author touches upon this subject which forms the main part of his book, he considers it necessary to defend himself from two personal attacks, which his *friend* had ventured to make against him. He had reproached him that he was a bad official, "with broken arm, and powerless." The answer to this is: "I know many people who are *powerless* and whose *arm is broken*, miserable people with no backbone. And yet they are rich in houses, food, and provision. No one can thus reproach me."[3] Then he cites to him examples of lazy officials, who nevertheless have made a career, and as it appears are the good friends of his antagonist: he gives their names in full as proof. The other attack is easier to parry; Nechtsotep had reproached him with being neither a scribe nor an officer, his name not being recorded in the list. "Let the books but be shown to thee," the author answers him, "thou wilt then find my name on the list, entered in the great stable of King Ramses II. Make inquiries only from the chief of the stable; there are incomings that are entered to my name. I am indeed registered, I am indeed a scribe."[4]

The author then begins the promised recapitulation of the deeds of Nechtsotep, the deeds of "that most excellent scribe, with an understanding heart, who knows everything, who is a lamp in the darkness before the soldiers and enlightens them."[5] He reminds him how well he had transported the great monuments for the king,[6] and had quarried an obelisk 120 cubits long at Syene,[7] and how afterwards he had marched to the quarries of Ḥammamât with 4000 soldiers that he might there "destroy that rebel."[8] Now however he is striding through Syria as a *mahar*, as a hero, a *maryna*, a nobleman styling himself with pleasure by these foreign titles.[9] The author has here come to the subject which affords him the best opportunity for his raillery.

In thought he accompanies his opponent through all the stages of his journey: "I am a scribe and a *mahar*, so thou dost say repeatedly. Now then, what thou sayest is true. Come along. Thou dost see after thy team, thy horses are as swift as jackals; when they are let go they are like the wind of the storm. Thou dost seize the reins, thou takest the bow—we will now see what thy hand can do. I will describe to you how it fares with a *mahar*, I will relate to you what he does.

"Dost thou not come to the Cheta country, and dost thou not see the 'Eupa country? Knowest thou not the shape of Chaduma? and Ygad'ay also; how is it formed? The D'ar of King Sesetsu—on which side of him lies the town of Charbu? and how is his ford constituted?

[1] An., 7, 4 ff. [2] Ib., 7, 8. [3] Ib., 9, 3 ff. [4] Ib., 11, 8 ff. [5] Ib., 17, 2 ff. [6] Ib., 14, 1 ff. [7] Ib., 15, 3. [8] Ib., 17, 3. [9] *Mahar*: Ib., 18, 4; *maryna*: Ib., 23, 2; 28, 1.

"Dost thou not march to Kadesh and Tubache? Dost thou not come to the Beduins with mercenaries and soldiers? Dost thou not tread the road to the Magar? where the sky is dark in the daytime, for the country is overgrown with oaks and acacias (?) which reach to the sky, where the lions are more numerous than the jackals and hyenas, and where the Beduins surround the road.

"Dost thou not ascend the mountain Shaua? . . . When thou returnest at night, all thy limbs are bruised and thy bones are worn out, and thou dost fall asleep. When thou dost awaken, it is the time of gloomy night and thou art quite alone. Has not a thief come to rob thee? . . . The thief has made off in the night, and has stolen thy clothes. Thy groom awaked in the night, saw what had happened, and took away with him what was left. He then went off to some bad fellows, joined the tribes of the Beduins, and transformed himself into an Asiatic. . . .

"I will relate to you of another mysterious town, called Kepuna. How is it with her? her goddess—another time. Hast thou not come across her?

I call: Come to Barut'e (Beyruth), to D'i(du)na (Sidon) and D'arput'e (Sarepta), where is the ford of Nat'ana? How is it with 'Eutu? They are situate above another town on the sea, D'ar (Tyre) of the coast is her name; water is brought to her by ship, she is richer in fish than in sand. . . . Whence leads the road from 'Aksapu? to which town?

"I call: Come to the mountain User. How is its summit? Where is the mountain Kama? Who will take it? the *mahar*.

"How does he march towards Ḥud'aru? where is the ford? Show me how one goes to Ḥamat'e (Hamat), to Degar and Degar-'ear, to the place where the *mahar* betakes himself."[1]

It goes on in this same tone; a wearisome series of empty rhetorical questions and a confused accumulation of barbarous-sounding names, with here and there a little description of the sufferings of a traveller, which though only moderately clever, seems to the reader like an oasis in the surrounding desert. Thus after the usual question as to where the ford of the Jordan may be, where Megiddo is situate, and whether there could exist anywhere else such a brave *mahar*, suddenly the letter continues: "Beware of the gorge with the precipice two thousand cubits deep, which is full of rocks and boulders. Thou dost make a *détour*. Thou dost seize thy bow . . . and showest thyself to the good princes (*i.e.* to the allies of Egypt), thus their eye is wearied at thy hand. *'Ebata kama 'ear mahar n'am u'* they say, so dost thou win to thyself the name of a *mahar*, and of one of the best officers of Egypt. Thy name becomes as famous to them as the name of Qad'ardey, the prince of 'Esaru, when the hyenas found him in the thicket, in the defile which was shut in by the Beduins: they were hidden under the bushes, and many of them measured 4 cubits from the nose to the heel, they had wild eyes, their hearts were unfriendly, and they would listen to no flattering words.

[1] An., 18, 4-21, 8, with a few excerpts.

"Thou art alone, no spy is near thee, no army follows thee, and thou canst find no one to show thee the right way. Thou must go alone and thou knowest not the way. Fear then seizes thee, thy hair stands on end, and thy heart is in thy mouth. Thy road is full of rocks and boulders, thou canst not get along because of the *'eshbururu* and *qad'a* plants, because of the *naḥa* plants and the wolf's-bane. On one side of thee is the precipice, on the other the side of the mountain, thus thou goest up the hill."[1]

The end of this difficult journey is that the horses take fright, and break their traces, the poor *mahar* has to go on foot in the heat of the sun, suffering from thirst and from fear of enemies in ambush. Misfortune follows him all along the way. "When thou enterest Joppa," the author relates mockingly, "thou dost find a garden green as the spring. Thou dost enter in order to get food, and findest there the lovely maiden who takes care of the vines ; she becomes thy companion, and charms thee with her beauty."[2] A thief naturally makes the best of this hour of romance to cut loose the horses from the *mahar's* carriage, and to steal his weapons.

We see that, in the principal part of the book, the attack of the author on Nechtsotep merely consists in harmless teasing, and as a proof that he really does not mean to wound, he adds the following gracious conclusion to his epistle: "Regard this in a friendly manner, that thou mayest not say that I have made thy name to stink with other people. Behold I have only described to thee how it befalls a *mahar;* I have traversed Syria for thee, I have described to thee the countries and the towns with their customs. Be gracious to us and regard it in peace."[3]

Thus our book closes. The kindest critic will scarcely maintain that it is distinguished by much wit, and still less will he be inclined to praise it for the virtues of clear description and elegant style. Yet in Egypt it enjoyed great repute, and was much used in the schools,[4] and as it had no moral nor didactic purpose, this wide circulation must have been due to its intellectual style. What seems so prosy to us, appeared to the educated literary Egyptian of the time of the New Empire charming and worthy of imitation, "dipped in honey," to retain the strong expression of our author.

The school-books proper are easily recognisable by their title *sbot*, teaching or lesson books. They are necessarily dominated by a striving after a certain style. The older books, all of which seem to date from the Middle Empire, are intended not only to teach wise living and good manners, but also to warn from a frivolous life ; the instructions they contain are always couched in the following form: some ancient sage of former days—the great king Amenemḥê't I., or a learned governor of the Old Empire, imparts to his son as he is growing up the wisdom which has led him so happily through life. Even in their outward form these maxims

[1] An., 23, 3-24, 4. [2] Ib., 25, 2 ff. [3] Ib., 28, 7.

[4] The whole is preserved in An., i. ; Extracts : Tur., 62, and the Caillaud ostrakon (in Chabas' Voyage).

show that they emanate from a man who does not care for idle chatter; they either approach the impossible in laconic expression, or they conceal thoughts under a multitude of illustrations, or again they are remarkable for the artificial composition of the sentences. An example of this obscure language, which as a rule is quite incomprehensible to us, has already been given in the earlier part of this chapter.[1]

There exist, however, two pleasant exceptions in this literature. One is the admonition which 'Eney bequeathed to his son Chensḥôtep, a set of short proverbs in comparatively simple style, in which even we who are not Egyptian scribes may take pleasure. The passages quoted in various places above may vouch for this fact.[2] The other is the didactic poem of Dauuf, in which this wise man warns his son Pepy of the unhappiness of any occupation that is not literary, and represents to him that each of the other professions is a source of misery, whilst he exalts and exaggerates the happiness which attends the life of a learned man.[3]

The *instructions* of the New Empire, which are couched in the form of letters from the teacher to the pupil, harp wearisomely upon the same idea. It is a misfortune to be a soldier, and a misery to till the ground, for the only happiness for mankind is to "turn the heart to books during the daytime and to read during the night."[4] The fool who does not strive after the "service of Thoth,"[5] who in spite of all warnings "flies from his books as quickly as his feet will carry him, as the horse on the racecourse (?) or as a gazelle when it flies," has as stubborn a mind "as a donkey when it is beaten," he is no more docile than "a deaf man who does not hear, and to whom one must speak with the hand"; he is like a bad sailor who knows not how to steer his boat.[6]

According to Egyptian ideas there was good reason for teaching the student of wisdom by fictitious letters, and tormenting him with the copying of pattern letters; for correct letter-writing was an art that had to be learnt, in order that each superior and each inferior might address each other with the etiquette due to their rank. To a relation or a friend, for instance, when asking after his health, one might write assuring him: "I say daily to Rê' Harmachis at his rising and setting, and to Amon Rê and Ptaḥ, and to the other gods and goddesses: Mayst thou be in health! Mayst thou live long! Mayst thou be happy! O that I might see thee again in health and embrace thee in my arms." The suitable phrases however, whereby an inferior might address a superior, ought to be full of humility, as has already been shown in the sixth chapter (p. 115). A letter should also be well considered, for he who understood how to write an elegant poetical style would be able, as we have seen by the specimen letters, to give a graceful turn to the most unimportant matter. For instance, in reclaiming geese that have not been delivered, one could speak of "that white bird," or "that cool tank";[7]

[1] Cp. also p. 165 for the contents of a similar book.

[2] Pp. 155, 165, 166, 256, 318, 394, 395. I now think I was wrong in attributing the text to the New Empire; it probably belongs to the Middle Empire.

[3] Examples will be found in the beginning of chapters 14 and 18.

[4] Sall., i. 3, 6. [5] An., 5, 6, 2. [6] An., 4, 2, 4 ff. = Koller, 2, 2 ff. [7] See p. 122.

or in saying that one had arrived safely at home, one might append a long poetical description of its beauty.[1]

In our first chapter we touched upon the unimaginative character of the ancient Egyptians as well as of their modern descendants, and we strove to explain this characteristic by the pleasant yet monotonous surroundings of their home. It stands to reason that this quality would make itself felt especially in their poetry and in their plastic art. In both they give us nothing but what is good, so long as they only attempt realistic work. The homely character of their natural surroundings, and the simple conditions under which they lived, presented the right material for their sculptors and their poets. Therefore in the consideration of Egyptian poetry, if we take the ballad as our starting-point, we begin with their best achievement.

One of the greatest pleasures of the fellahin of the present day, when working the shadoofs or water-wheels, is to drone their monotonous song; their ancestors also probably accompanied their work with the same unending sing-song. A happy chance has preserved two such songs for us. One, of the time of the 5th dynasty, was sung by the shepherd to his sheep when, according to Egyptian custom, he was driving them after the sower over the wet fields, so that they might tread in the seed into the mud. It runs somewhat as follows:

"Your shepherd is in the water with the fish,
He talks with the sheath-fish, he salutes the pike
From the West! your shepherd is a shepherd from the West."[2]

The meaning is (if I understand it rightly), that the shepherd is making fun of himself for having thus to wade through the puddles, where the fish call out good-day to him. Of the time of the 18th dynasty, however, we have the following little song, sung to the oxen by their driver, as he drove them ever round and round the threshing-floor:

"Work for yourselves, work for yourselves,
Ye oxen,
May you work for yourselves,
The second corn for yourselves!
The grain for your masters!"

These words sound very devoid of sense, and have evidently been garbled. In fact, the song as a genuine national song is worded in several different ways; the following, which has also come down to us, is certainly more comprehensible:

"Thresh out for yourselves, thresh out for yourselves,
Ye oxen, thresh out for yourselves!
Thresh out the straw for yourselves for food,
And the grain for your masters.
Give yourselves no rest,
It is indeed cool to-day."[3]

---

[1] An., 3, 1, 11 ff.

[2] Bädeker, Lower Egypt, 427. "Salutes" and "pike" are both hypothetical.

[3] L. D., iii. 10 d, and ib. c; the last line is to be understood by the words of the ploughman, ib. a.

One of our versions of this song may have been really sung by the Egyptian peasant; we have also, at any rate in a revised form, another old national song belonging rather to the educated classes. This is a drinking song of the Egyptians, which seems also to have been known to the Greeks. The latter relate that at a feast the figure of a mummy was carried round with the wine, in order to remind the guests of death, while in the enjoyment of this fleeting life;[1] the subject-matter of our song agrees as nearly as possible with this custom.

The oldest version that has come down to us is the "Song of the house of the blessed King 'Entuf, that is written before the harper";[2] it was a song therefore that was written in the tomb of this old Theban monarch near the representation of a singer. It has also come down to us in two versions of the time of the New Empire, and must therefore have been a great favourite:

"It is indeed well (?) with this good prince!
The good destiny is fulfilled (?)
The bodies pass away and others remain behind,
Since the time of the ancestors.
The gods (*i.e.* the kings) who have been beforetime,
Rest in their pyramids,
The noble also and the wise
Are entombed in their pyramids.
There have they built houses, whose place is no more,
Thou seest what has become of them.
I heard the words of Ymḥôtep and Ḥardadaf,
Who both speak thus in their sayings:
'Behold the dwellings of those men, their walls fall down,
Their place is no more,
They are as though they had never existed.'
No one comes from thence, who tells us what has become of them,
Who tells us how it goes with them (?), who nerves our hearts,
Until you approach the place, whither they are gone.
With joyful heart, forget not to glorify thyself
And follow thy heart's desire, so long as thou livest.
Put myrrh on thy head, clothe thyself in fine linen,
Anointing thyself with the true marvels of God.
Adorn thyself as beautifully as thou canst
And let not thy heart be discouraged.
Follow thy heart's desire and thy pleasures
So long as thou livest on earth.
Let not thy heart concern itself
Until there comes to thee that day of mourning.
Yet he, whose heart is at rest, hears not their complaint,
And he, who lies in the tomb, understands not their mourning.
With beaming face celebrate a joyful day
And rest not therein.
For no one carries away his goods with him
Yea, no one returns again, who is gone thither."

---

[1] Plut., Isis and Osiris, cap. 17; Herodot., 2, 9. Our song corresponds essentially to the Maneros song.

[2] Harr., 500, 6, 2—7, 3; and in an inscription of the Leyden Museum. Cp. Maspero, Études égypt., 178 ff., and Records of the Past, vol. iv., p. 115 ff.

A later version runs in similar fashion; it was sung by the harper at the funerary feast of the priest Neferḥôtep:[1]

"How beautiful is this righteous prince!
The beautiful destiny is fulfilled.
The bodies pass away since the time of Rê',
And the younger ones step into their places.
The sun reappears each morning
And the evening sun sets in the west.
Men are begetting, women are conceiving,
Every nostril breathes the breath of the morning.
But those who are born there, all together,
They go to the place, which is ordained for them.
Celebrate a joyful day, O priest!
Place oils and sweet odours for thy nostril.
Wreaths of lotus flowers for the limbs,
For the body of thy sister, who dwells in thy heart,
Who sits beside thee.
Let there be music and singing before thee,
Cast behind thee all cares, and mind thee of joy,
Till there cometh that day, when we journey to the land that loveth silence.
Celebrate a joyful day, O Neferḥôtep,
Thou wise man, with pure hands.
I have heard all that has happened to the ancestors,
Their walls fall down,
Their place is no more,
They are as though they had never existed."

Therefore (such is the ever-recurring moral of these songs) enjoy thy life, as long as thou canst, before thy heart is still for ever; the day of death comes before thou thinkest, and all thy lamentations, all thy sacrifices, will not call the dead back to thee. The treasures thou hast won here thou must leave behind thee; what thou hast built upon earth falls down; only the pleasures which thou hast enjoyed dost thou really possess. Yet there is one thing thou canst win, which will never be lost to thee:[2]

"Give bread to him who has no field,
And create for thyself a good name for posterity for evermore."

I think that these poems would appear worthy of attention, even if they belonged to another country richer in the poetical art: here in the barren desert of Egyptian literature, where most of the vegetation dries up even as it buds, they are doubly delightful to us. The love songs of the time of the New Empire are almost as charming.

There is a collection called "the beautiful, gladsome songs of thy sister, whom thy heart loves, who walks in the fields";[3] they describe to us the love-sick maiden, as she looks out in vain in the fields "for the brother whom her heart loves." No joys comfort her any longer, neither cakes nor wine: "what is sweet to the mouth is to me as the gall of birds;

[1] Beginning of the song from the tomb of Neferḥôtep; first translated by Stern, Ä. Z., 1873, 58 ff., 72 f., afterwards by Maspero, Études égypt., 172 ff. Cp. also Records of the Past, vol. vi., p. 127 ff.

[2] From the Song in the tomb of Neferḥôtep, towards the close.

[3] Harr., 500, 12, 1 ff. My translation of these songs follows essentially that of Maspero (Études égypt., 217 ff.); though in a text of this kind many details are of course doubtful.

thy breath alone can comfort my heart."[1] The occupations with which she had formerly busied herself can interest her no longer to-day; in everything she misses her friend:

> "I say to thee: see what I do.
> I go and set my snare with my hands . . .
> All the birds of Arabia flutter over Egypt,
> Anointed with myrrh;
> The one that comes first, seizes my worm.
> He brings his fragrance from Arabia,
> His claws are full of incense.
> My heart longs for thee, that we may open the snare together,
> I with thee together, alone.
> That thou mayest hear the wailing cry of my beautiful one anointed with myrrh,
> There, thou together with me.
> I set the snare:
> How beautiful is he who comes into the field, because one loves him."[2]

But the lover does not come to help her:

> "The cry of the goose wails,
> It is caught by the worm.
> Thy love makes me tremble
> And I cannot loose the snare.
> I will carry my net away.
> What will my mother say when I come to her?
> Every day I return laden with my spoil,
> But to-day I have set no snare,
> For thy love has taken possession of me."[3]

Soon she speaks out her wishes more openly:

> "Thou beautiful one, my wish is (to be with thee) as thy wife,
> That thy arm may lie upon my arm.
> Will not my elder brother (come) to-night?
> Otherwise I am as one who lies in the grave.
> For art thou not health and light?"[4]

At last, after a wakeful night, she finds him:

> "The voice of the dove speaks,
> She says: 'the world is light, observe it.'
> Thou, thou bird dost entice me.
> Then I find my brother in his room,
> And my heart is joyful . . .
> I will not turn from thee,
> My hand remains in thy hand,
> When I go out I am with thee in all beautiful places."[5]

Grief and jealousy seem, however, to make their way into the heart of the maiden, as she leans her face out of the outer door of the house, and looks anxiously down the road to see if her lover may not be coming; she hears steps indeed, but it is only "a swift-footed messenger," who has to excuse his remaining out. "Say only, another has found thee,"[6] she answers him.

[1] Harr., 500, 13, 1 ff.
[2] Ib., 12, 2 ff.
[3] Ib., 12, 7 ff.
[4] Ib., 13, 3 ff.
[5] Ib., 13, 6 ff.
[6] Ib., 13, 8 ff.

Again the youth complains:

"I will lie down in my room,
I am ill indeed through violence.
My neighbours come to visit me,
Yet if my sister came with them,
She would put all the doctors to shame (?)
For she understands my sickness."[1]

But the sister does not come, though he would give all he possesses for her only to speak to him:

"The castle of my sister—
Her tank lies before her house,
Her door stands open . . . . .
Then my sister comes out angrily.
Ah, if I were only her doorkeeper,
That she might scold me,
Then should I hear her voice even though she were angry,
As a boy full of fear before her."[2]

I have already shown in the ninth chapter that to the Egyptian the garden with its flowers was the right place for love scenes. We may here quote, in addition to the pretty song cited above (p. 194), a couplet from another poem, which is also of interest from its form. For, like the Italian ritornelles, each couplet in it begins with the name of a flower, with which the rest is lightly connected by a play upon the word: we have to remember that the maiden is weaving a wreath, and that each flower she adds to it serves to remind her of her love. Thus, if we may be allowed to replace the Egyptian word-play by one of like import, we may render it as follows:

"*Blush* roses are in it (the wreath), one *blushes* before thee.
I am thy first sister,
And thou art to me as the garden,
Which I have planted with flowers
And all sweet-smelling herbs.
I directed a canal into it,
That thou mightest dip thy hand in it,
When the north wind blows cool.
The beautiful place where we take a walk,
When thine hand rests within mine
With thoughtful mind and joyful heart,
Because we walk together.
It is intoxicating to me to hear thy voice,
And my life depends upon hearing thee.
Whenever I see thee
It is better to me than food and drink."[3]

We must now turn our attention to the more lofty style of lyric poetry, though this branch of poetical art contains nothing very pleasing. The hymns which have come down to us in such great numbers are mostly in the form of litanies in praise of the power of the gods; there seems to be no question of devotional feelings on the part of the singer,

[1] Harr., 500, 10, 9 ff. [2] Ib., 10, 11 ff. [3] Ib., 15, 7 ff.

in fact the greater part consists of stereotyped phrases, which could be adapted to any of the mighty gods, and could also be used in adoration of the king. "The two countries together show him honour—to him whose fear is impressed upon all countries—great in fame, who has subdued his enemy—praised by the great cycle of gods—to whom the dignity of his father is given—he has received the lordship of the two countries—all creatures are full of delight, their hearts are full of joy, all men rejoice and all creatures adore his beauty"—these are examples of this phraseology; if the name of one of the gods is added, and a few allusions to the myth of the god, his temple, or his crowns, are put in, the hymn in its usual form would be complete. Is it possible, for instance, to imagine anything more unmeaning than the following hymn to Osiris, which describes his statue and enumerates his temples? "Adoration to thee, Osiris, son of Nut! Lord of the horns with the high pillar, to whom the crown is given, and the joy before the gods! Created of Atum! Whose power is in the hearts of men and gods and spirits! To whom was given the lordship in Heliopolis; great in existence at Busiris! Lord of fear at 'Eadte, great in manhood at Resetu! Lord of might in Chenensuten, Lord of the sistrum in T'enent! Great in love in every country, of beautiful memory in the palace of the god! Great in splendour at Abydos, to whom was given the triumph before the gods. . . .[1]

Comparatively speaking, the best amongst these religious poems are some that formerly enjoyed a very wide circulation: the "Adorations of Rê'." When the sun rises in the east, the *divine land*, and drives away the darkness, then all living creatures shout for joy, especially the baboons, who, as the Egyptians believed, were wont then to raise their paws in adoration to that beneficent day-star.[2] Mankind they thought ought also to act like these pious learned animals, and thus to say to the rising sun:

"Adoration to thee, O Rê' at thy rising, to Atum at thy setting! Thou dost rise, dost rise and shine, thou shinest, crowned the king of the gods. Thou art the lord of Heaven and the lord of the earth, who hast made those above and those below.[3] Thou only god, who art from the beginning! Thou who made the world, and created man, who made the river of heaven and created the Nile, who made the water and gave life to what therein is! Who piled up the mountains and caused men and cattle to exist. . . ."[4]

Or again:

"Adoration to thee, who rises in the river of heaven and enlightens the two countries after he has come forth. All the gods together praise thee . . . thou young man, beautiful in love! When he rises mankind live and the gods shout with joy to him. The spirits of Heliopolis glory

[1] Louvre C. 30 (from the M. E.).

[2] Cp. e.g. Totb. ed. Naville, cap. 16. Puchstein has drawn my attention to the fact that Horapollo was cognisant of this.

[3] I.e. according to the explanation: the stars and mankind.

[4] Totb. ed. Naville, 15 A III.

in him, and the spirits of Buto exalt him.[1] The baboons adore him, and all wild animals praise him together.

Thy uraeus-snake beats down thine enemies. Those who are in thy bark rejoice over thee, and thy sailors are content. The bark of the morning sun has received thee, and thy heart, O lord of the gods, is joyful over that which thou hast created ; they show thee adoration. The goddess of heaven shines like lapis lazuli by thy side, and the god of the river of heaven dances (?) before thee with his rays of light."[2]

These hymns to the sun are found in a hundred variations for the morning and for the evening—as a rule they give us more satisfaction than the "adorations" to other gods, probably because the rising and setting of this mighty life-giving luminary awakens in man deeper and truer feelings than a figure of Osiris, or a representation of Ptaḥ. The same may be said of the hymns to the Nile ; the flowing stream laden with blessing is a visible sacred being, and when the Egyptian treats of the real, and describes the things he daily sees, his art always succeeds the best. This is plainly to be seen in these poems ; if we ever find that a pleasing passage has made its way into the monotonous phrases, we may wager ten to one that it has been called forth by some mention of nature.

Thus the compiler of a hymn to Amon may interrupt his recapitulation of the epithets of the god, and after the following hackneyed phrases :

"Who has made all that is and that exists,
From his eyes mankind came forth
And the gods from his mouth,"

he goes on to add the following verses :

"Who makes the herb for the cattle
And the fruit tree for mankind,
He gives life to the fish of the river
And to the birds under the heaven.
He gives breath to the being in the egg,
And preserves the son of the worm, (?)
He creates that whereon the fly lives,
The worms and the fleas, as many as they are.
He creates what the mice need in their holes,
And preserves the birds (?) on all the trees."[3]

This is naïve and pretty; it shows the same loving observation of nature which is the cause of the great success of the animal representations on the Egyptian reliefs.

What we have said above about the religious hymns applies also essentially to those that refer to the king, the style of which the reader will remember from several passages that have been quoted.[4] These also

[1] These spirits are daemonic beings with heads of jackals or hawks, who are often mentioned, and must have played a part in the mythology.

[2] Totb. ed. Naville, 15 A. II.

[3] Pap. 17 de Boul., 6, 3. The *son of the worm* is perhaps a corruption of the word for *locust*.

[4] Pp. 66, 67, 71, and the specially characteristic passages pp. 57, 68.

consist mostly of a string of phrases, and are full of big words and bold hyperboles that have become hackneyed by frequent use. For instance, in an ode, which was much admired in Egypt,[1] Amon Re' addresses Thothmes III. the great conqueror:

"I come and cause thee to destroy the great men of D'ah,
I throw them beneath thy feet, which pursue their people.
I cause them to see thy Majesty as the lord of light,
Thou shinest over them as my image.
I come and cause thee to destroy those who are in Asia,
The chiefs of the Asiatics of Syria thou dost take captive.
I cause them to see thy Majesty adorned with thy splendour,
Thou dost seize the weapons and dost fight on thy chariot";

and so on in the same tone for ten double verses; all these high-sounding words, however, do not impress the reader, who remains untouched by these continually-repeated assurances that the king "is leading the rebels captive to Egypt, their princes with their tribute to his palace," that "the fear of him is in their body, and their limbs tremble at the time of his fear," that "the country of Cheta is pierced to the heart, and become a heap of corpses,"[2]—how willingly would we exchange these for one verse of genuine feeling. It is a bad sign, and shows the worthlessness of these pretentious poems, that scarcely a passage remains in the memory of the reader. We have *one* feeling only about these high-flown words, namely, that we have read them dozens of times before in other places. Yet even in these odes the descriptions of nature form an exception now and then; these are generally figurative passages, in which the king may be compared to "a lion victorious when he comes and goes, when he roars, when his cry resounds through the rocky valley of the antelopes; a jackal hastily seeking his prey, roving all round the world in no time . . . a fire fed with the oil of herbs, with the storm in its rear, like a flame which has tasted the heat . . . a terrible storm, raging on the sea, the waves rise like mountains, no one approaches him, and he who chances to be therein, sinks in the deep."[3]

The fairy tales which, as we have seen, often contain the plot of historical events, convince us that the mighty deeds of the kings, their great buildings, and their wars, could rouse the imagination of the Egyptians to nobler compositions than these hymns. As a nation, however, they seem scarcely to have risen above these unpretending tales to the higher step in poetic art, to epic poetry, for in the literature that has been preserved to us there is only one example of an attempt to relate the deeds of the Pharaoh in true poetic form. This is the poem on the great battle which Ramses II. fought with the Cheta at Kadesh. This poem must have been most gratifying to the king who was extolled, for in several instances he caused it to be inscribed on the walls of his newly-built temples. With the people also it seems to have been in great repute, for about seventy years

[1] A century and a half later the same ode was dedicated to Sety I.

[2] L. D., iii. 195 a.

[3] L. D., iii. 195 a.

later, in the reign of Merenptaḥ, we meet with it in a school copy-book.[1] Yet it makes little impression on us, the spoilt folk of modern days, and the reader will hardly be inclined to join in the admiration of those enthusiastic Egyptologists who have compared it with the *Iliad*.

In the first place we are exactly informed in an absolutely prosaic manner where and how the two armies stood before the battle. The poem then continues : " His Majesty hastened forward, and broke the ranks of the Cheta, he quite alone, and nobody was with him. When his Majesty then looked behind him, he saw that his retreat was cut off by 2500 chariots, which were manned by all the heroes of the miserable prince of the Cheta, and of the many countries in confederation with him, 'Ertu, Masu, P'atasa, Keshkesh, 'Erun, Qad'auadana, Cherbu, 'Ekatere', Kadesh, and Ruka. On each chariot there stood indeed three of them. . . . No prince was with him, and no chariot-driver, no officer of the infantry, nor of the chariot force ; his infantry and his chariot force had forsaken him, and not one of them was there to fight beside him.

" Then spake his Majesty : ' How is this, my father Amon ? Does a father then forget his son ? I have done indeed nothing without thee. Did I not for thy sake go forward or stand still ? without ever overstepping thy plan, and I never turned aside from thy will. . . . What do these Asiatics, indeed, want before Amon ? He is miserable who knows not God. Have I not erected to thee many monuments, in order to fill thy temple with my spoil ? I have built for thee the house of millions of years, and have made offerings for its endowment. All countries together bring thee their first fruits, in order to increase thy sacred revenues ; for thee ten thousand oxen are slaughtered, with all manner of sweet-smelling herbs. I did not withdraw my hand until I had established thy hall of pillars, and built to thee stone pylons . . . and erected eternal flag-staves to thee ; I brought also obelisks from Elephantine. I am he who causes eternal stones to be brought for thee, and who causes the ships to voyage on the sea, in order to bring thee gifts from all countries. Has this indeed ever happened once before ?

" ' Shame upon those who defy thy will ! well for him who understands (?) thee, Amon ! . . . I call to thee, my father Amon. I am in the midst of many people, I am quite alone, no one is with me, and my foot soldiers and my chariot force have forsaken me. When I cried to them, not one of them heard me. When I called to them I found that Amon was better to me than millions of foot soldiers and hundreds of thousands of chariots, of brothers or of sons united together. The works of men are as nothing ; Amon is more precious than they. I have come hither, according to the word of thy mouth, O Rê', and have not overstepped what was thy design.

" ' Do I not call from the ends of the world ? And yet my voice has indeed reached to Hermonthis. Rê' has heard me, he comes to me when

[1] Sall., 3. The scribe of this manuscript, a certain Pentauert, who has been erroneously thought to be the author of the poem, was still alive, as Sall. I. informs us, in the tenth year of Merenptaḥ.

I call to him. He reaches his hand to me, I rejoice—he calls from behind me: 'Thou art not alone, I am with thee, I thy father Rê', my hand is with thee. I am worth more to thee than hundreds of thousands together, I am the lord of victory who loves valour.'

"'I take heart again (?), my breast is full of joy. What I desire to do, that happens. I am as Mont, I shoot to the right and hurl (?) to the left. I am as Ba'al, as a plague upon them; I find the 2500 chariot force of their army lying slaughtered under the feet of my horses. Behold none of them are able to fight before me, their hearts melt in their bodies, their arms fall down, they cannot shoot, and they have no courage to grasp the dagger. I make them rush into the water even as the crocodiles rush into the water. They fall over each other and I slay them according to my will. Not one of them looks behind him and not one of them turns round. He who falls of them rises not up again.'"

If the poem came to an end here, we might rejoice in the really beautiful thought that the god should hasten into a far country to the help of the king, when he firmly trusted in him. Unfortunately the poem is spun out interminably, though in the part that follows, which is three times as long, the action scarcely advances at all. The king expatiates unweariedly on his heroic courage and his great victory, on the faint-heartedness of his soldiers, and the discomfiture of the enemy. Thus in this so-called *epic* there is little action and much discourse.

This history of the battle of Kadesh is termed a poem, merely on account of the style, which has poetic colour, though it appears to be wanting in poetic form. This is as a rule the same form with which we are familiar from Hebrew poetry, the so-called parallelism of the phrases; two short sentences following each other, and corresponding in arrangement and also as a rule in purport. The following description of a king is an exact case in point:[1]

"His eyes, they see through every creature,
He is Rê', who beholds with his rays.
He enlightens Egypt more than the sun,
He causes the country to flourish more than a high Nile,
He gives food to those who follow him,
He nourishes him who follows him in his way."

Somewhat freer is the parallelism in the graceful comparison of the mutability of fortune with the yearly change of the bed of the stream:

"The ford of the water of the past year has gone,
Another passage this year has come.
Great oceans become dry paths,
And a bank becomes an abyss."[2]

The parallel phrases may group themselves in strophes often of very artificial arrangement, as is shown by the various poems quoted in this as

[1] Mar. Abyd., ii. 25. [2] Pap. de Boul., i. 21, 8 f.

well as in previous chapters (see pp. 194, 256, 257). These parallel phrases are, moreover, frequently arranged in different order:

"I come, and cause thee to trample underfoot the West.
Phoenicia and Cyprus lie beneath thy power,
I cause them to see thy Majesty as a youthful, powerful, hornèd bull,
Whom one does not approach.
I come, and cause thee to trample underfoot those that are in their harbours,
The islands of Met'en tremble beneath thy fear.
I cause them to see thy Majesty as a crocodile, the terrible lord of the water,
Whom one dares not approach."[1]

Here the arrangement is *a b a b*, and *a* as well as *b* divide on their part again into parallel divisions, so that the scheme proper is $a^1a^2b^1b^2a^1a^2b^1b^2$. Yet the poet, not content with these two strophes, which are parallel to each other, has constructed eight others in like manner. It often happens also that the parallel verses are intentionally intercepted at a certain place by a single line standing alone.

Hand in hand with this antithetical style of poetry there seems to have been poetry of metrical nature, poetry divided into short lines, which under the New Empire were also distinguished in the manuscripts by red dots.[2] These little verses are punctuated, not merely so as to denote the sense, but also the divisions that are to be observed in recitation; we are ignorant however of further details. I would only add the following conjecture: each verse was probably supposed to contain a certain number of primary accents—in fact, usually two; it appears to me that the peculiar law of accentuation in the Egyptian language, viz. that several words closely allied in syntax should be invested with *one* primary accent, lies at the root of this verse-construction.

It was most natural that the Egyptians should seek the aid of all manner of artificial means to help out their poetry, the subject-matter of which was often so poor. For this object a very favourite device was alliteration, as is shown for instance in a verse already quoted (see p. 250), in which seven words out of the ten begin with *m*:

"'cu *m*eru *m*eḥ e*m* *m*ou *m*aut
ta b'aḥ e*m* *m*erutf"
(When the tanks are full of fresh water
And the earth overflows with his love).

In the same way the author of a dedicatory inscription to Queen Chnemtamum[3] imagined the following to be the most graceful style he could use:

"se*ch*epernef er utes *ch*'auf
*ch*epert chepru m'e *Ch*epr'e
ch'at *ch*'au m'e 'E*ch*ute"

[1] Mar. Karn., 11.

[2] There was no rule as to the marking of the verse-divisions; in several instances we have the same text with and without this punctuation. Under the Middle Empire the manuscripts are not yet punctuated.

[3] L. D., iii. 24 s.

(He has created (her) in order to exalt his splendour,
She, who creates beings like the god Chepr'e,
She, whose diadems shine like those of the god of the horizon).

In the great ode to King Thothmes III.[1] the poet also says:

"da'esn em sa *ḥ*ak,
'aue *ḥ*en'e *ḥ*er *ḥ*ert *ḥ*er se*ḥ*er chut"
(I place them behind thee as protection;
The arms of my Majesty are raised and chase away evil).

In the period however of which we are treating, this alliterative style had not taken a definite poetic form, it was only used occasionally as ornamentation, like the puns we meet with so frequently in Egyptian texts. The Egyptians took great delight in puns,—for instance, there is a poem on the chariot of the king, consisting entirely of these witticisms; all the parts of the chariot are enumerated, and a pun, describing the might of the king, is made on the name of each part. Thus, if we might attempt a modern equivalent, as far-fetched in sound as the old Egyptian, it might perhaps run somewhat as follows:

"The *wheels* of thy chariot—
Thou *wieldest* thy battle-axe.
The *scythe* of thy chariot—
Draws *sighs* from all nations."

It is interesting to perceive how much trouble the author has often taken with these devices; where they occur, the sense is almost always obscure or ambiguous, and frequently indeed quite incomprehensible, at any rate to us. For instance, no one has as yet determined the signification of the words: "*suten sut en suhanef er d'aut, 'auef em red'aut,*"[2] though the rest of the inscription is perfectly clear; the reason doubtless being that the author, in order to make his double pun, has unduly strained the language.

[1] Mar. Karn., 11.

[2] L. D., iii. 65 a.

THE GOD BES, PLAYING THE LYRE.

CHAPTER XVI

THE PLASTIC ARTS

WE are so much accustomed to regard the limits of the various branches of the plastic arts as self-evident and natural, that it will seem strange to many readers that it is only to a certain degree that we can recognise these limitations as regards Egyptian art. In Egypt we cannot, as we usually do now, reckon the art of relief as sculpture; it belongs from its nature to the art of painting or rather to that of drawing purely. Egyptian *relief*, as well as Egyptian *painting*, consists essentially of mere outline sketching, and it is usual to designate the development of this art in its various stages as painting, *relief en creux*, and bas-relief. If the sketch is only outlined with colour, we now call it a painting, if it is sunk below the field, a *relief en creux*, if the field between the individual figures is scraped away, we consider it a bas-relief. The style of drawing however is in all these cases exactly the same, and there is not the smallest difference in the way in which the figures are coloured in each. At one time the Egyptian artist went so far as to seek the aid of the chisel to indicate, by modelling in very flat relief, the more important details of the figure; yet this modelling was always considered a secondary matter, and was never developed into a special style of relief.

Moreover the Egyptians themselves evidently saw no essential difference between painting, *relief en creux*, and bas-relief; the work was done most rapidly by the first method, the second yielded work of special durability, the third was considered a very expensive manner of execution. We can plainly see in many monuments how this or that technique was chosen with regard purely to the question of cost. Thus, in the Theban tombs, the figures which would strike the visitor first on entering are often executed in bas-relief, those on the other walls of the first chamber are often worked in *relief en creux*, while in the rooms behind they are merely painted.

The royal tombs were supposed to be decorated entirely in *relief en creux*, but it is seldom that this system of work is found throughout, for if the Pharaoh died before the tomb was finished, his successor generally filled up the remaining spaces cheaply and quickly with painting. The same may be observed with regard to the temples. For instance, the sanctuary of Gurnah was begun by Sety I. on a small scale, and was therefore decorated in bas-relief; but when afterwards his son Ramses II. determined to finish it on a much larger scale, he was obliged to drop this laborious style of decoration and content himself with *relief en creux*. In the same way Ramses III. decorated his little palace of Medinet Habu with bas-relief, but when it came to the enormous requirements of the immense temple which he built in the rear at the same time, he was again obliged to substitute the cheaper method. When also, as we mentioned above, the details of a figure are worked out by the modeller, this is evidently considered a great extravagance, and is often restricted to the chief figure in a representation. Thus, for instance, in the tomb of Sety I., the face of this king alone is modelled, while his body and all the other numerous figures are given in mere outline.

The art of drawing in Egypt was ruled by fashion, and the curious way in which it was customary to treat the human figure appears most strange to us. In the endeavour to show every part of the body, if possible in profile, as being the most characteristic point of view, the Egyptian artist designed a body, the incongruities of which were quite contrary to nature. As a whole we may consider it to be in profile, for this is the usual position of the head, the arms, the legs, and the feet. In the profile of the head, however, the eye is represented *en face*, whilst the body comes out in the most confused fashion. The shoulders are given in front view, whilst the wrist is in profile, and the chest and lower part of the body share both positions. With the chest, for instance, the further side is *en face*, the nearer in profile, the lower part of the body must be considered to be three-quarter view, as we see by the position of the umbilicus. The hands are usually represented

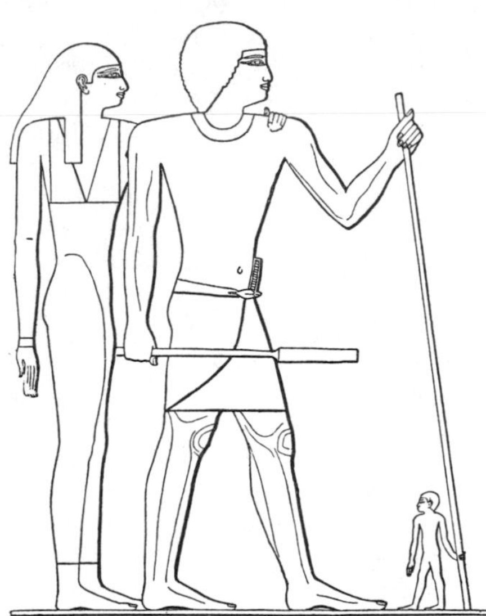

SPECIMEN FIGURES IN THE STYLE OF THE OLD EMPIRE.

As in a similar relief at Berlin, the muscles are filled in, and show that the artist made a difference between the inner and outer side of the leg. The right hand of the woman is, as is almost always the case, twisted round in an impossible manner (after L. D., ii. 29a).

in full and from the back,[1] hence we find that in cases where the hands are drawn open or bent, the thumb is almost always in an impossible position. The feet are always represented in profile, and probably in order to avoid the difficulty of drawing the toes, they are always drawn both showing the inner side, though in finished pictures, when the calves of the legs are drawn, the inner and outer sides are rightly distinguished from each other.

In addition to these peculiarities, the Egyptians usually observed

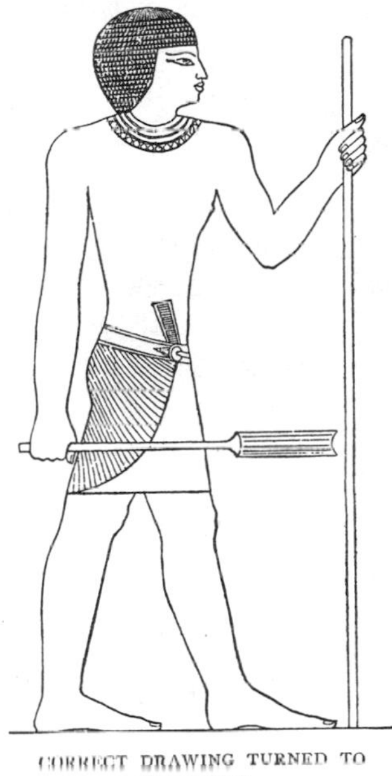

CORRECT DRAWING TURNED TO THE RIGHT.

REVERSED DRAWING TURNED TO THE LEFT.

Two representations of Prince Mer'eb (after L. D., 20, 21).

two general laws, both of which had a great influence on the drawing of the human figure. The first enacted that when one arm or foot was in advance of the other, it must always be the further one from the spectator; a figure therefore which looked towards the right could only have the left arm or foot in advance, and *vice versa*. The reason of this law is self-evident; if the right arm were extended, it would cut across the body in an ugly and confusing manner.

It is more difficult to find an explanation for the other law, by which all figures in their rightful position were supposed to look to the right, thus turning the right side to the spectator. This position was a fundamental rule with the Egyptian artist,[2] and whenever he was at liberty to represent

1 This is proved by the fact that in all representations where the details are given the nails of the fingers are shown.

2 The hieroglyphs are also usually drawn in this direction.

the figure as he pleased, he always made it turn to the right; when for any reason he was obliged to draw it looking toward the left, he contented himself with simply reversing his design, regardless of the contradictions to which such a course gave rise. The statues of the Old Empire show us (see for instance p. 204) that the pleated part of the gala skirt was always on the right side, and in all the drawings in which the figure is turned to the right it is also represented thus. From the statues we see further that the long sceptre was always held in the left hand, and the short one in the right; this is also correctly shown in all figures that are drawn looking towards the right. On the contrary, in the figures which are only mechanical inversions of those turned to the right, the sceptres as well as the sides of the skirt always change places. I cannot go into further detail as to the confusion that resulted in the drawing of the hands of these reversed figures, and of the wonderful ways in which many artists sought to extricate themselves from this tangle.[1]

The same rules were observed in the drawing of animals, which were represented in profile with the exception usually of a few parts of the body, like the eyes and sometimes the horns,[2] which would be more characteristic drawn *en face*. Animals also always advance that foot or arm which is the further from the spectator; birds even are not excepted from this rule.

The peculiar aspect of Egyptian pictures is due to the development of the above laws, which must have been invented in prehistoric times, for they are followed inviolably in the oldest monuments that we possess, and they ruled Egyptian art as long as that art existed. Even with ourselves it is not difficult to accustom our eyes to these peculiarities, so that they no longer offend us, and of course they were quite unobjectionable to the Egyptians, who doubtless believed that this was the only right way of regarding and of representing the human form.

They did not however consider this style as the only *possible* way of drawing; for even under the Old Empire they emancipated themselves to a certain extent from this traditional style. In a tomb of the 4th dynasty, for instance, we meet with individual figures which are treated in a perfectly natural manner,—they turn their backs to us, or advance the wrong leg and commit similar crimes allowed indeed by nature but not by Egyptian art. These figures are also drawn with such certainty of touch that we cannot regard them as mere experiments or isolated attempts; the artists who sketched them were evidently accustomed to work in this free style. In this ancient period therefore, there must have been, besides the strict old-fashioned style, a younger freer school of art, though the latter was evidently not regarded with so much respect as the former. Whoever liked might have his house decorated in this style, but it was not considered suitable for the tomb of a man of rank. Here it

[1] A few artists (L. D., ii. 18, 19, 21, 32) evidently imagine that when the figure is turned to the left, the body is seen from the back.

[2] E.g. the horns of oxen or gazelles *en face*, but those of the ibex in profile (L. D., ii. 6, 23, 54).

was only right that the formal traditional style should have undivided sway, and if an artist sometimes allowed himself a little liberty, it was at most with one of the unimportant figures. In fact, whenever we meet with one of these unconventional figures in a tomb, it is generally in the case of a fisher or a butcher, or perhaps of an animal such as a gazelle,

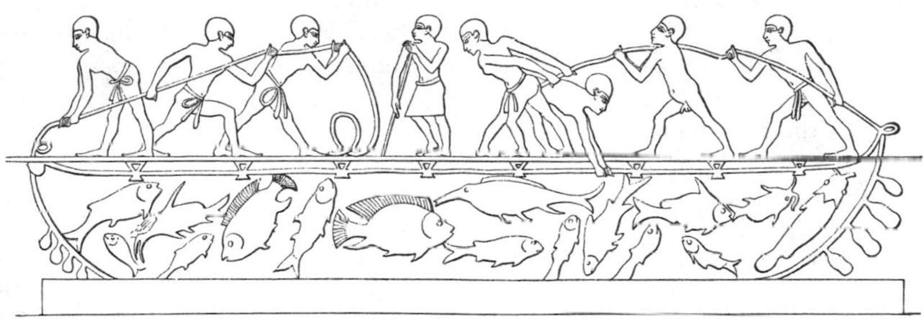

FREE REPRESENTATION OF A CATCH OF FISH, SPECIALLY REMARKABLE FOR THE FIRST MAN AT THE RIGHT-HAND END OF THE ROPE (after L. D., ii. 9).

etc.[1] It would have been considered a most unsuitable way to represent the deceased or any other important personage.

Thus under the Old Empire we meet with a realistic school, which was never of much account, side by side with the official conventional art, and in later times also we find the same conditions everywhere—they are as it were the sign manual of the whole history of Egyptian art.

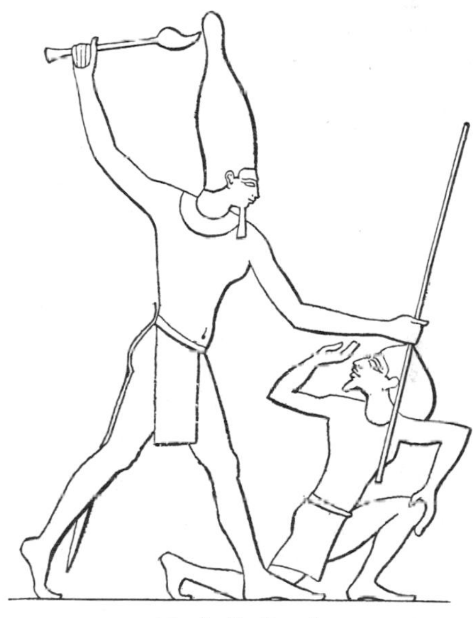

After L. D , ii 39 f.

The pictures of the Old Empire have one conspicuous merit, viz. the clearness of the drawing. This result is evidently obtained by the artist placing his figures close together in horizontal lines. Even the most complicated scenes, the confusion of the hunt, a crowded herd, are rendered distinct and comprehensible, thanks to this division into lines one above the other. The ancient artist was always conscious of the extent of his power. He moreover preferred to walk in the old ways, and

[1] E.g. figures seen from the back, L. D., ii. 9, 64; shoulders in profile, ib. 4; animals drawn unconventionally, ib. 12, 47.

to follow the same lines as his predecessors. Almost every picture that we meet with under the Old Empire—and the range of the scenes represented is not very large—has its typical mode of representation, to which all the artists adhere, though they may allow themselves to make certain slight improvements or additions. For instance, if a victory of the Pharaoh is to be represented, the king is drawn swinging his club and striding forward to slay an enemy who, pierced by a javelin, has fallen on his knee before him. The composition of the group is always the same even to the smallest detail,—the foe turns his head and right arm towards the king craving mercy; with the left arm he supports himself on the left knee, whilst with the right foot the poor wretch has already lost his footing on the ground.[1] A certain amount of liberty is allowed to the artist with regard to the costume of the king and of the barbarian, as well as with regard to the gods who are spectators of this scene, but the incident itself must always be depicted in the same manner.

In the tombs, on the other hand, the favourite subject of the slaughtering of the animals might be arranged by the artist in nine or ten different ways. The sacrificial animal might lie on the ground and the servants be busy in cutting it up. In this picture they would be represented in the act of cutting off one of the fore legs; one would be holding it straight up, the other cutting it off. A third would be standing close by, having paused in his work in order to sharpen his flint knife anew. Even the superscriptions, which always accompany this and other Egyptian pictures, are as a rule the same; over the man sharpening his knife must be written "the sharpening of the knife by the side of the slaughterer"; the one cutting off the leg must admonish his companion to "pull firmly"; and the other must answer—"I do as thou thinkest right." In the same way amongst the pictures of agriculture, those of sowing and threshing, and that of leading out the cattle, are most frequently repeated, while the representations of peasants bringing tribute, and of the deceased and his wife before the table of offerings, recur again and again. The religious pictures also which we find on all the walls of the temples of a later period, have doubtless originated from a few typical representations of the Old Empire, though the latter do not chance to have been preserved to us.

The art of the Old Empire had its centre at the Memphite court; the artists of that town having raised it to an eminence which wins our admiration even at the present day. In the provinces however, where there was little demand for works of art as long as the whole state was concentrated in the court, art had no chance to develop, and the tombs of Upper Egypt, which date from the time of the 6th dynasty, are mostly curious barbarous structures.[2] After the fall of the Old Empire this provincial art developed further in its own way, as is proved by the works

[1] Thus under Dyn. IV.: L. D., ii. 2 a, c; Dyn. V.: ib. 39 f; Dyn. VI.: ib. 116 a.

[2] There are of course exceptions, as e.g. the tombs of Zawijet el meitin, which are perhaps the work of Memphite artists, but as a rule everything that originates in Upper Egypt is very rough.

of art of the 11th dynasty period found at Abydos, which are smooth and pretty though very unskilful.

The reunion of the kingdom under Amenemḥê't I. gave a great impulse to art. The pictures which we have of the time of the Middle Empire, especially those of Beni Hasan and Siut, are equal to those of the old Memphite city of the dead, and are evidently by their style the lineal descendants of the latter. All the conventional laws of style which we noticed in the older works are still observed,[1] and in the same way freedom of drawing is only allowed in secondary figures. In the richer and more lifelike compositions however, a greater difference manifests itself, though the conventional types are adhered to as a rule. For instance, a representation of the felling of trees is given in the customary manner, with goats who are allowed to eat the foliage, but instead of the conventional sycamores with two animals stretching upwards on either side, as in the pictures of the Old Empire, the artist has made a pretty group of swaying palms, with the sportive goats eagerly jumping up at them.[2]

After L. D., ii. 126. Cp. the analogous picture of the Old Empire in chap. xviii.

Though the art of the New Empire was occupied chiefly with the decoration of large expanses of wall surface, yet it followed in a great measure the old paths. One innovation indeed we find,—the artist was now allowed to represent a figure with that arm in advance which was nearest to the spectator. This was directly contrary to the ancient law of official art.[3] But in other respects art rather retrograded than advanced, for the effort to keep to the old conventional style and to forbear following the ever-growing impulse in a more naturalistic direction, induced artists to lay more stress than was really needful on the stiffness and unnaturalness of the ancient style. We may remark, for instance, in the temple pictures of the New Empire, how, in the drawing of the hands, the points of the fingers are bent back coquettishly, and how the gods and the kings are made to balance whatever they present to each other on the edge of their hands.[4] This is intentionally and wilfully contrary to nature, a mannerism in art; to the artist it may have appeared a higher and more ideal form than any other; we of the modern world, however, have no reason to go into raptures over it.

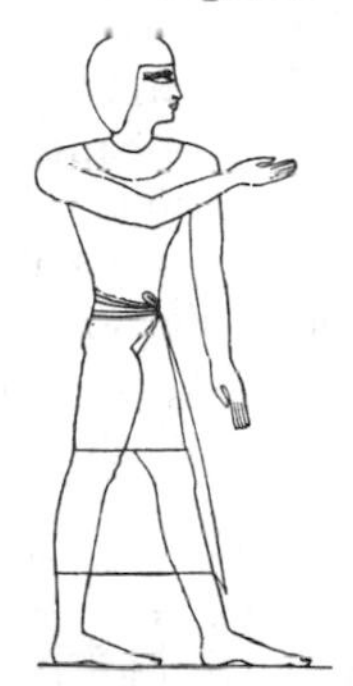

After L. D., iii. 12 a.

[1] The position of the hands however in the figures looking to the left, is now rightly given. L. D., ii. 121.

[2] Dyn. VI.: L. D., ii. 108, 111; Dyn. XII.: ib. 126.

[3] L. D., iii. 9 f, 11 a, 14, 15, etc.

[4] E.g. L. D., iii. 7 b, e, 14, 15, 17 c, 20 c, 67 a, etc.

It was quite otherwise with art which was not officially recognised; the development of the latter we can admire in many pictures in the Theban tombs. In them we meet with fresh bright figures boldly drawn, though, as under the Old and the Middle Empire, merely amongst the servants and slaves. Asiatic captives may be represented according to the will of the artist, but their Egyptian overseer must stand there in stiff formality.[1] The half-nude maiden who is serving the guests may be represented with her back to the spectator, with realistic hair, with arms drawn in perspective, and legs which set at nought every conventional rule, but the lady to whom she presents the wine must be drawn like a puppet of ancient form, for she belongs to the upper class.[2] If the reader will turn back to the picture of the feast on p. 250 he will admire the freedom with which the singers and the dancing girls are drawn; the artist was evidently allowed a free hand with these equivocal characters; in fact the superstition of "good manners" did not here constrain him to do violence to his art.

KING MAKING AN OFFERING. Style of the New Empire.

Fortunately official art was unable always entirely to withstand the influence of this freer tendency, and in pictures which otherwise follow the old rules we find little concessions to the newer style. This impulse was not only strictly forbidden, but repressed and stifled in the same way as the religious movement which stirred the people at the time of the 18th dynasty. Once indeed an attempt was made to push forward this freedom in art and to replace the strict monumental style of old times by one more realistic. It is doubtless not accidental that this attempt at reforming art should coincide with the religious reform; the same king who, by inculcating his new doctrine, tried to remove the unnatural oppression which burdened the religion of the country, attempted also to relieve the not less unnatural tension under which art languished. A right conception lay at the root of both attempts, but neither had any permanent result. The violence of the proceedings of the monarch doubtless was the greatest impediment to them; on the one hand he desired entirely to exterminate the old gods, on the other hand he would have done away with all the dignity and restfulness of the old art, and allowed it even to verge upon caricature.

The tendency of this revolution in art was to put new lifelike pictures in the place of the former worn-out representations which were ever being dished up anew. Individual figures also were now supposed to be drawn from life so that in that way their positions became more natural, and the drawing of their limbs more correct.

Formerly the king had been represented as a demigod, either as he stood making offerings before the gods of his country, or as he stabbed a

[1] L. D., iii. 40.

[2] L. D., iii. 42; cp. the illustration on the opposite page.

prisoner, or seated conventionally on his throne under a canopy ; now the artists gladly emphasised in the pictures his purely human side. His wife and children are always around him even when he is driving to the temple or praying ; they are by his side when he looks out of the window of his palace ; they mix his wine for him as he rests on his seat. The children of the Pharaoh play together or with their mother, as if their divine origin were completely ignored. The details of these pictures are still more remarkable. It is true that there may not have been much

SCENE FROM A FEAST.

The lady in strict formal style : the maid (who is filling her ointment bowl, and saying to her : "For thy *ka!* celebrate the joyful day") is drawn unconventionally (after L. D., iii. 12).

beauty in the royal family of Amenḥôtep, and the king and queen—who probably were brother and sister—may really have possessed consumptive faces and elongated necks, pointed elbows, fat bodies, thick ankles, and thin calves, but the artists who had to draw their figures need not have emphasised these unlovely peculiarities as so many of them have done. There was a happy medium between the old conventional royal pictures and these caricatures ; it was a fatal misfortune that most of Chuen'eten's artists failed to find it.

They often overshot their mark also with regard to the positions in which they represented their figures. It was not necessary to represent individual figures in rapid movement without any reasonable cause, nor to make their limbs move in wavy lines.[1] In the same way it was not necessary to represent the king and queen seated so close to each other, that the outlines of their figures are almost identical, and it is only from the arms, which are placed round each other, that we can understand the meaning of the picture.[2] It cannot be denied that finally they only substituted one affectation for another; they drove out the devil, but through Beelzebub, the chief of the devils. Moreover they were not able to break with all the evil prejudices of the old art, and we observe with astonishment that persons of the lower orders still maintain their prior claim to naturalistic treatment: they alone, when it is a question of figures in profile, have their arms correctly drawn.

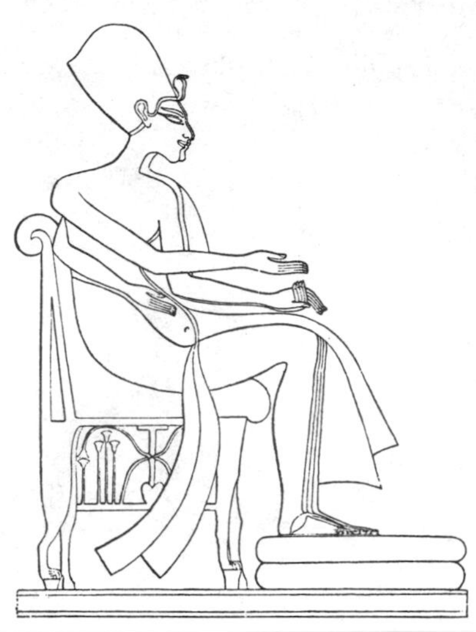

CHUEN'ETEN AND HIS CONSORT SEATED SIDE BY SIDE ON TWO CHAIRS.
After L. D., iii. 99 b.

Notwithstanding our sympathy with this new impulse, we cannot give an entirely favourable opinion with regard to the revolution in art under Chuen'eten, though we must acknowledge that real progress was made in some respects. For the first time in the history of Egyptian art we meet with a hand drawn correctly, which will bend from the wrist,[3] and with a foot seen from the outer side with toes which belong to it.[4] It is a characteristic fact that these innovations survived the reformation of the heretic king, and are often to be seen in the work of later times.[5]

In the sphere of art as in that of religion, the victory of the reaction was equally complete, and the artists of later times returned religiously to the old traditions. It would indeed have been natural, after the fall of the dreadful heretic, if they had been the more anxious not to swerve from true orthodoxy in art. Yet soon afterwards a new spirit entered the Egyptian artists, and they went to work with what would have been considered in earlier times unprecedented boldness. This renaissance did not spring from an individual fanatic, but was due to the tasks imposed upon the artists by a victorious race of monarchs, ambitious to erect vast buildings. I refer to the art of the 19th dynasty, which, though following to a great extent the old lines, yet created some works of real importance in the immense battle reliefs.

The type of these battle pictures originates in those which celebrate

[1] Cp. e.g. L. D., iii. 104, 108, 109; also ib. 98, 99.
[2] L. D., iii. 99 b.
[3] L. D., iii. 106.
[4] L. D., iii. 97 e, 99 b, 100.
[5] Hands: L. D., iii. 147 a, 206. Feet: ib. 153, 169, 172 e, 201 a.

the victories of Sety I. The composition in all is alike. At the side of the picture stands the gigantic form of the Pharaoh, on his chariot of war drawn by his prancing steeds. Before him is a wild confusion of little figures, fugitives, wounded men, horses that have broken loose, and smashed chariots, amongst which the monarch flings forth his arrows. Behind, on a hill, stands the fortress close to which the battle takes place. The effect of this picture lies undeniably in the contrast between the powerful form of the victor, represented by the artist in all the splendour he could command, and the confused crowd of the conquered foe. The calm attitude of the Pharaoh by the side of the rapid movement of the enemy, illustrates in, I might almost say, an ingenious way, the irresistible power of the king, who drives the crowd of his feeble enemies before him as a hawk drives a swarm of sparrows. If we consider the subject closer, we shall have somewhat to modify our favourable decision, for, however pleasing we find the easy composed bearing of the king,[1] it is scarcely possible to admire the representations of the enemy. If we look at the details, the false anatomy of the figures is only too obvious, while considered as a whole, the impression produced has been cynically compared to a ragoût of frogs. The essential reason of this confused impression is that the artists of the 19th dynasty no longer observed the careful procedure of their predecessors, who arranged any complicated incident in a row of parallel lines ; they wished on the other hand to draw a medley as a medley, and even if they succeeded in this difficult experiment when they attempted to draw a hunt (e.g. that given above, p. 241), yet a battle scene was beyond their powers.

Ramses II. gave the artists who had to perpetuate his deeds a yet harder task to perform. They had not only to show in half-symbolic manner the king and his foes, but faithfully and historically to portray for posterity special events in real battles. We cannot be surprised that the execution of these pictures is far behind the conception. Many details are however quite worthy of our admiration—for instance, there is a dying horse which is excellently drawn ;[2] a representation of camp-life that is full of humour,[3] but there is no attempt at unity of composition. Again and again we may see soldiers marching and soldiers formed in square, enemies who have been shot and enemies drowning, chariots attacking and chariots at rest, yet no uniform picture. The fine contrast also between the Pharaoh storming forward, and the king of the Cheta hesitating in the midst of his troops, which occurs in the most extensive of these pictures,[4] does not impress us much in the midst of all this confusion of detail.

It was, nevertheless, a great step in advance for Egyptian art when these battle pictures, and the smaller representations of like nature and style,[5] were admitted into the official cycle of pictures. We might also

[1] L. D., iii. 127 a, 130 a, and other examples.
[2] L. D., iii. 164-165.
[3] Ib. 153-155.
[4] Ib. 157-161.
[5] E.g. the favourite representation of the presentation of the captives : L. D., iii. 156, 188 a, ib. 211.

BATTLE OF SETY I. WITH THE CHETA.

Above the king are three divinities, who protect him; Horus as a hawk, the same god as the sun-disk, and the goddess of the south as a vulture. Behind him marches the hieroglyph of life as fan-bearer. The inscription extols in the usual terms the might of the victorious king (after L. D. iii., 130 a).

expect that as the realistic impulse in the country was stronger than it had ever been before,[1] art itself would now at last finally break the fetters she had worn for 2000 years. This was not however the case; on the contrary, this naturalistic impulse soon died out, and after the time of the twentieth dynasty all the figures are again modelled according to the old traditions. There were political reasons for this retrogression of art; the high priests of Amon, who seized the power after the fall of the Ramessides, established anew the orthodoxy of art as well as the orthodoxy of religion. Pious artists of their time doubtless considered it sinful even to wish to draw otherwise than the faithful of old times—in modern days we also find a similar superstition in many churches.

The history of the development of the one half of Egyptian art, as we have sketched it above, is also typical of that of the other half. The art of sculpture also had to go through the same troubles as that of drawing, except that the process of development was more simple on account of its being less widely practised, and having less important works to produce.

The art of sculpture in Egypt was, broadly speaking, required to produce two classes of works of art—portrait statues for the worship of the deceased, and statues of gods, kings, and sacred animals, for the decoration of the temples. In both cases therefore the figures in question had to be in solemn, formal positions, and as there is not much variation in these positions, the Egyptian sculptor from the outset had a very narrow scope. Even within this sphere his freedom of action was much limited, for from the time of the first artistic attempts, there existed hard-and-fast conceptions about the right way to sculpture a standing or a seated figure—conceptions which concerned even the smallest details, and were considered as the standard. Amongst the oldest statues therefore, we rarely find more than two types. The first represented the figure seated stiffly on a solid square seat; the eyes look straight forward, the hands are placed on the knees, the right one closed, the left spread out flat. In the other position also the figure is standing in the stiffest attitude; the left foot is advanced,[2] the arms hang straight down by the sides with the fists clenched, or the hands may hold the short and the long sceptre. From technical reasons the Egyptians rarely ventured to sculpture their statues quite free;[3] seated figures are generally made to lean against a slab, and standing ones always have a pillar at the back as a prop. In the same way they did not dare quite to separate the arms and legs from the body, but left connecting pieces which were painted black between the body and the pillar behind. A little piece

[1] We may compare pictures such as L. D., iii. 2 b (which insist upon the contrast between the men who are boldly drawn and the puppets of gods); the beautiful singers, ib. 236; the palace reliefs, ib. 208, the Turin obscene papyrus, and others besides.

[2] Women and children however stand with their feet together; this was probably considered the more modest position.

[3] The wooden statues are almost the only exceptions; they are made quite free, and their arms and legs are not joined together.

was also left in the hollow of the loosely-closed hand,—this has often erroneously been supposed to be a short stick.

The treatment of the detail was as strictly determined as that of the whole. Almost every part of the body had its conventional style of reproduction, which does not at all always seem to us to be the best. The calves of the legs were indicated by a succession of smooth surfaces which give their form very imperfectly ; the collar-bone, which was rarely omitted even in the most hasty work, is generally in the wrong place, the fingers of an outstretched hand always resemble four smooth little sticks, and there is no indication whatever of the joints. These forms were as deeply engrained in the heart of the Egyptian artist as the conventional forms in drawing ; in the statues the hand and the calf of the leg had to be thus carved, and thus only, and the slightest deviation would have been felt to be wrong.

Originally the head was also included in this conventional treatment, for in the faces of many of the statues there can be no question of portraiture. Here however individual treatment first forced its way, and in many of the statues of the fourth dynasty we find an entirely conventional body with a head which is evidently intended to have individual features. A little later many artists began to treat the body also from the portrait standard ; they would represent for instance, in a few touches, the hanging paunch of a fat old man. In the works of the fifth dynasty especially, the reproduction of the forms of the body is brought to such perfection, and at the same time the face is so lifelike through the special accentuation of its characteristic features, and through the introduction of crystal eyeballs, that these works of art rightly belong to the *chefs d'œuvre* of all times and nations. Statues like the so-called *Sheikh el beled* (p. 30) and that of his wife at Gizeh, that of the Red Scribe (p. 33), and that of Peḥ-er-nefr at Paris, or that of the little figure of a dwarf at Gizeh (a representation of which is given here), strike every unprejudiced person with wonder.

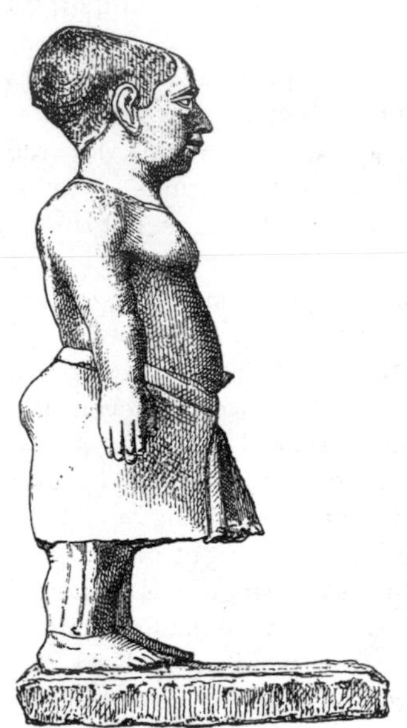
THE DWARF CHNEM(?)ḤÔTEP
(after Perrot-Chipiez).

The above-mentioned figure of the scribe shows that the artists of the fifth dynasty were no longer bound down by the two conventional types of the standing and seated figure. From the time of the 5th dynasty the artist was allowed to represent the deceased as he squatted on the ground with his legs crossed underneath him, or, as in the above example, in the usual posture of an official writing down a deed on a roll of papyrus.

Groups were even attempted; these generally represented the deceased embraced by his wife and son. The custom of placing figures of domestic servants in the tomb with the deceased gave artists a good field for their art as regards figures from the life; we may quote as examples the figures of the women pounding grain and kneading dough (p. 190).

As regards the period of the Old Empire, we have only two examples of that other branch of Egyptian sculpture which played such an important part in later times, viz. royal statues. These are two statues of King Chafrê' the builder of the second pyramid, which were found by Mariette in a very old temple situate not far from the great Sphinx. They represent (as the reader may see from the illustration p. 38 of the larger of the two) the monarch in the conventional attitude of seated figures; the head-gear and the throne adorned with lions alone show that the figure represents the Pharaoh. The face is evidently a portrait, and indeed one statue represents the king as an older man than the other; we can scarcely say the same of the body, for though it is indeed most excellent as a work of art, it is treated in the usual conventional manner. One of these statues is also remarkable for its size; it is larger than life-size, whilst all the statues of private individuals of that time are at most life-size, and indeed as a rule much smaller.

Though as a whole we estimate the sculpture of the Old Empire very highly, especially in its freer development under the 5th dynasty, yet we would guard ourselves on the other hand from an over-appreciation of its worth. We must not, as is so often the case, judge this art merely from the masterpieces, which really form the exceptions. The bulk of the statues of this time deserve only moderate admiration, and many are decidedly bad; even in those old days good artists were evidently few and far between.

The sculpture of the Middle Empire followed essentially the same lines, in fact the development of the statuary art in Egypt evolved itself within very narrow limits. The statues of private individuals remind us of the realistic figures of the 5th dynasty; we also find during this period figures with dense unimaginative faces and thick bodies, as well as groups of three or four figures, mostly worked in very hasty style. The royal colossi, on the contrary, keep to the strict idealistic type and make no concession to the truth of nature. They were intended to serve merely as part of the architecture of the temples, and were executed from a purely decorative point of view, as we see from the intentional false position of the ears. We must except from this decision one remarkable group of royal statues, viz. the figures we mentioned above (p. 40) with the un-Egyptian faces. The manner in which the artist has given these foreign features, without falling into the impending danger of caricature, deserves our unqualified admiration, as well as the remarkable way in which the no less foreign style of wearing the hair and beard is represented.

The number of works of sculpture extant belonging to the New Empire is enormous; they are for the greater part sculptures of the decorative kind. The colossi, which were erected at this time in front of the temples, were of immense size—one is 55, another 42 feet high—and the numberless statues with which the sanctuaries were peopled—a temple at Karnak built by Amenḥôtep III. contained several hundred life-size statues of the lioness-headed goddess Sechmet—all these are almost more the work of the artisan than of the artist. The ease with which these immense blocks of stone were mastered is certainly marvellous, but it is rather the technical work of the sculptor which astonishes us than the spirit of the artist, which indeed is almost absent. The head of the colossus was certainly a portrait, but as a rule so idealised and confused that it makes little impression on us. The body was sculptured quite in the old traditional style, with bad calves to the legs, and still worse hands, and, what strikes us as especially disagreeable in a colossus, the modelling of the body was not carried out throughout. If we now turn aside from these works, which were made by the dozen as the architect required them, and consider the comparatively small number of real works of art which have come down to us from the time of the New Empire, our opinion of the art of that period will be far more favourable.

The colossal head of Amenḥôtep III. in London, which expresses the coarse features of this monarch ; the pleasing smiling head of a queen at Gizeh, which is now thought to represent the consort of Ḥaremḥêb ; the beautiful statue of Ramses II. at Turin (see p. 48), which from the non-archaistic costume was evidently taken from life ; these are works of art which are not valuable merely as pieces of decoration. We have also one small statue of the time of the attempted reformation under Chuen'eten, (see p. 45) which shows us that a true artist could discern the good qualities of this new royal style.

Amongst the statues of private individuals under the New Empire, apart from the number of mechanical works, there are a few figures at any rate, especially amongst the wooden statues, that are very interesting. The group of parents and children is again a favourite subject ; a new motive also came in under the 18th dynasty for single figures : the man squats on a footstool on the ground, and wraps himself up in his garment in such a way that the head and hands only are visible. We cannot deny however, that even in these good statues of the New Empire, the rich clothes and complicated coiffures are often worked out with even more care than the face ; and we must not let the fact pass uncensured, that the traditional faults of the Egyptian sculptors, especially the wretched hands, are still to be found even in the otherwise good work of this period.

It is really necessary to have a certain education of the eye in order to estimate Egyptian works of art at their real value, owing to the peculiarities of style that are inherent in most of them. The most inexperienced of us however can appreciate one of their qualities—the technical. The Egyptians carried the mastery of material further perhaps than any other nation ; they knew how to conquer stone that gave the greatest resistance, viz. the red and black granite and even the diorite, which is as hard as iron.

The sharply-cut details and the softness of the surfaces which these sculptors attained in such a material, and the splendid polish which they gave it, can scarcely be emulated by us modern folk, even with all the means at our command. This technical skill rose perhaps to its highest point of excellence under the New Empire, though many artists under the 4th and 5th dynasties were able to work wonders in this respect, as is shown by the diorite statue of King Chafrê and a little statue of the same material in the Berlin collection.

Nevertheless, material was not a matter of indifference to the Egyptian sculptor. It is not an accident that by far the best statues which we possess are executed in wood and limestone ; in the long and wearisome work of mastering granite and diorite, much of the artist's spirit was expended and lost. The Egyptian knew this himself, and when, especially for public monuments, he nevertheless chose the hardest stone, it was for reasons of another kind. On the one hand he wished to employ "eternal stones," which would ensure unlimited duration to the monument, and therewith to the name and image of the monarch it commemorated ; on the other hand he rejoiced in the beautiful colour which these noble species of stone exhibited when well polished. The Egyptians showed their appreciation of this quality by excepting this hard stone from the universal rule to which other materials were subject. The former alone remained unpainted.[1] The painting of all statues, reliefs, and decoration appeared to the Egyptians to be a matter of course, and, with the exception of the above valuable species of stone, they scarcely allowed any material to go unpainted. The Egyptian sculptures and buildings in their present uncoloured state give us therefore a very different impression from that which was originally intended by those who designed them ; it remains a question whether the change is to their disadvantage.

I have already remarked that even modern artists scarcely understand the treatment of stone as well as the Egyptians. This is the more remarkable as the latter worked with the most primitive tools ; their execution was due entirely to their inexhaustible patience. All the reliefs as well as the statues were executed with a little metal chisel fixed into a wooden handle, and with a wooden mallet,[2] whilst the polishing was produced by beating and rubbing with pieces of quartz.[3] Even if they supplemented these imperfect tools by all manner of contrivances, the work must still have been very troublesome and lengthy. A few unfinished statues prove to us that this was the case ;[4] for limestone alone they could use larger mallets in order to obtain the desired form, but with the hard stone they had to detach tiny little pieces with a pointed chisel.

The Egyptian sculptors also showed great skill in the way in which they helped out the deficiencies of a bad material. They had plenty of

[1] As a rule, with these hard materials, at most the drapery alone might be coloured.

[2] Perrot, 755 ; Ros. mon. civ., 46, 4, 9, 11 ; 48, 2, 49, 2.

[3] Beating with two stones : L. D., iii. 41 (= Ros. mon. civ., 47) ; Polishing : Perrot, 755, and frequently.

[4] Gizeh, 5005, 5008, and two others also there.

opportunity to do this, for a mastabah had frequently to be built of the coarse Memphite limestone, or a tomb had to be excavated in the side of a rock where the stone was too crumbly to take any fine carving. In such cases the sculptors chiselled their reliefs or their statues in the roughest fashion, and then overlaid this rough carving with a layer of fine stucco, which would take the detail of the forms. They covered the larger wooden sculptures also with a similar stucco, as it was difficult to get as good a surface on the knotty sycamore wood as was required for the reception of the colouring matter.

The history of art in Egypt will always be deficient in one respect. It is true that we can recognise which works belong to one period or to one school, and that now and then we may think we recognise one hand in two different works,[1] but more than this we can scarcely ever hope to

SCULPTORS OF THE TIME OF THE 5TH DYNASTY.
From the tomb of T'y. (After Perrot-Chipiez.)

know; the artists themselves are quite lost to us. In a few cases only we find painters or sculptors with their names annexed, represented amongst the secondary figures in a tomb, and we then suspect that these people were the artists of that tomb itself, and have thus perpetuated themselves in it. Thus for instance, in the tomb of the superintendent of the property of the mother of Chuen'eten, 'Eute the *chief sculptor* of this lady is represented in the act of finishing the painting of a statue of the princess Bekt'eten.[2] If we may take for granted that he was employed to decorate this tomb, we then know the name of the artist of a very characteristic piece of work. As we have said however, these conclusions are but hypotheses, and in Egypt the names of the artists with their distinctive works of art are not to be found.

It would be wrong to conclude however, that the Egyptians took less pride in their works of art than the Greeks. In the school-books of the learned scribes much contempt is indeed expressed for this foolish

[1] Thus the representations in the Manofer tomb at Berlin are evidently related to those of the same period in the tomb of Ptaḥḥôtep.

[2] L. D., iii. 100 a.

business,[1] but in real life the social position of artists was not, as a rule, at all a humble one. Under the Old Empire the high priest of Memphis was considered as their chief, in fact he bore the title of "chief leader of the artists," and really exercised this office.[2] It is quite explicable that the duties of this high ecclesiastic comprehended the care of art, for as his god was considered the artist amongst the gods, so the chief servant of Ptah would also necessarily be the chief artist, just as the priests of the goddess of truth were at the same time the guardians of justice. The artists of lower rank under the Old Empire also gladly called themselves after their divine prototype.[3] If we could deduce any facts from the priestly titles of later times, we might conclude that this was also the case at all periods, for as long as there existed a high priest of Ptaḥ, he was called the "chief leader of the artists." We can scarcely believe however that this was so; the artists were differently organised in later times, although Ptaḥ of Memphis still remained their patron genius.[4]

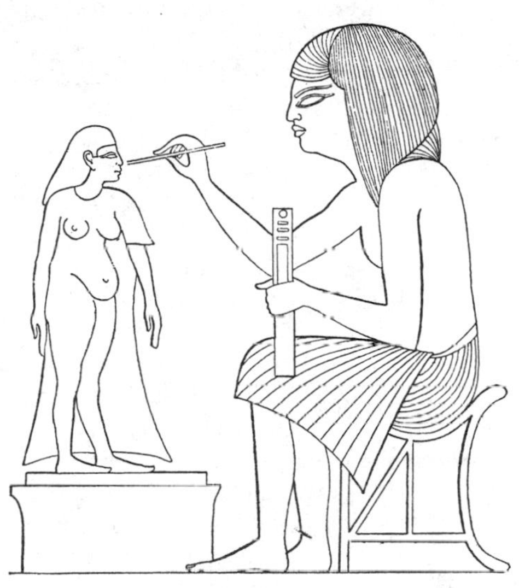

'EUT'E, THE CHIEF SCULPTOR OF THE QUEEN-MOTHER TEY. (After L. D., iii. 100.)

In the Middle Empire, under the eleventh dynasty, we meet with Mertesen, "superintendent of the artists, the painter, and sculptor,"[5] who boasts of his special artistic power. He was "an artist, wise in his art, and appearing as first in that which he knew"; he understood how to indicate that his figures were walking or standing still, and was possessed of secrets of technical skill.[6] In addition to Mertesen, we hear of several painters of about this period,[7] for instance, a special "painter in the royal

1 Sall., 2, 4, 6, 8; ib. 5, 1.

2 Cp. p. 291.

3 Cp. e.g. the lists of artists: L. D., ii. 115 b, c, g.

4 In the tomb of Paser, and therefore at Thebes, an artist prays to Ptaḥ for his assistance, and Paser himself, at the sight of a finished statue, cries, "praised be Ptaḥ." (From my own copy.) On the painter's palette of Amenuaḥsu, artist of the temple of Amon, found at Thebes, the owner prays to the Ptaḥ of Menes and to the Ptaḥ of Ramses II. (Berlin, 6764). This can scarcely be accidental.

5 A sculptor is called [hieroglyphs], cp. the superscription of the pictures: Ros. mon. civ., 46, 4, 9, 11; 47, 1; 49, 2. Another term, [hieroglyphs] (L. D., ii. 100 a, 132 r, and in other places), seems to signify the same.

6 Louvre, C. 14.

7 [hieroglyphs] Mar. Cat. d'Ab., 574, 699. The signification of this word and of others

house,"[1] and another who calls himself the superintendent of the necropolis of Abydos; this place was therefore probably the sphere of his work.[2] Under the New Empire we find a "superintendent of all the artists of the king," and in his tomb are represented all the workshops in which all the necessary architectural parts were carved and painted "for all the buildings which were under his superintendence."[3] As a rule, the artists of this time belonged to the department of the treasury,[4] and the chief royal "superintendent of the house of silver" reckoned amongst his officials two "deputies of the house of silver," and with them also two "deputies of the artists of the house of silver," also a "superintendent of the works in the place of eternity" (*i.e.* in the necropolis)—who was at the same time "superintendent of the sculptors,"—a "scribe of the painters," a "chief of the painters," and an "architect in the royal house of silver."[5] The administration of the great temple of Amon comes forward prominently by the side of that of the state; in this department, as in all others, the Theban god had his own "painters,"[6] and "chief of the painters,"[7] "sculptors," and "chief of the sculptors,"[8] and a crowd of other artists, who, as we have seen above (p. 294), were under the supervision of the second prophet. As I have already remarked, many artists belonged to the upper classes; at the beginning of the eighteenth dynasty two "painters of Amon" were members of the distinguished nomarch family of El Kab,[9] and under the twentieth dynasty a painter was father-in-law to a deputy-governor of Nubia.[10] It is also interesting to see how tenaciously many families kept to the artistic profession. The office of "chief of the painters of Amon" remained for seven generations in one family,[11] and that of his "chief sculptor" was certainly inherited from the father by the son and the grandson;[12] in both cases the younger sons of the family were also painters and sculptors. The inheritance of a profession was specially an Egyptian custom, but I know of no example on record in which it was carried on for such a length of time as in the case of the painter mentioned above, at any rate it is never brought so prominently forward in other examples. It cannot be purely accidental that the oldest of the long genealogies that we possess belongs to a family of artists; the members of this family evidently attached importance to the fact that pure art—*i.e.* the art described above, the art of rigid tradition—was hereditary in their family.

To the above sketch of sculpture and painting I wish to add a few further remarks on Egyptian architecture and objects of art. The

is elucidated by the inscriptions about painting in the tomb of Paser at Thebes, and by those above the pictures: Berend, Princip. monum. du musée Eg. de Florence, I. pl. x., as well as Ros. mon. civ., 63. Nevertheless we can also say alone, Ros. mon. civ., 46, 49.

[1] Mar. Cat. d'Ab., 567. [2] Ib. 366. [3] L. D., iii. 26. Another: Liebl., 944.

[4] Cp. the letter An., 4, 16, Rs. about the works of repair in the palace.

[5] L. D., iii. 241, 242. The *smn* evidently stands for *msn* "sculptor."

[6] L. D., iii. 12 d; Liebl., 553, 558, 720. "Painters of Amon for the necropolis," ib. 689.

[7] Liebl., 553. [8] Liebl., 623. [9] L. D., iii. 12 d; Liebl., 558.

[10] L. D., iii. 229 a, at the same time a priest.

[11] Liebl., 553, probably, nevertheless, of the New Empire? [12] Liebl., 623.

limits of this work do not allow me to enter fully upon the wide subject of Egyptian architecture, and the most important matters concerning the plans of houses, temples, and tombs have already been treated (see pp. 171 ff., 280 ff., 285 ff., 310 ff.). What remains to be described is principally the ornamental branch of this art.

The natural building material of Egypt is the Nile mud; this substance can be easily fashioned into any shape, and when dried in the sun possesses no little strength, and is the more enduring as under that happy sky it is rarely exposed to any rain. In Egypt little mud huts are still to be seen in country places, and there seems no doubt that a similar barbaric, rough style of building was that most anciently practised in Egypt. In historic times Egyptian architecture possesses, at any rate, some forms which are apparently derived from mud buildings of this kind. The outer walls of the buildings diminish in size towards the top, evidently because in a mud wall greater strength is required in the lower part to give due

After L. D., iii. 40.

support. The corners of the building are formed by round posts; these were to protect it from crumbling, a danger which, without this precaution, would be inevitable at the corners of a mud building. In the same way the upper edge of the wall is protected by a similar beam, without which the rafters would crush in the soft walls. The roof itself however, with its hollow recess, was generally constructed, as in modern days, of trunks of wood, covered in on the outside with a layer of mud. The short marks which we see side by side in the hollow recess, may possibly represent the sloping ends of the beams,[1] just as the horizontal frame which encloses them above represents the coating of mud.

In very early times the Egyptians discovered that they could construct the walls with far greater ease and safety, if they converted the mud into rectangular pieces of a definite size, *i.e.* into bricks. Brick buildings, belonging to all ages of Egyptian history, still exist, but as yet they have not attracted due attention. With few exceptions the bricks are unburnt, and are mixed with short pieces of straw; in the periods with which we are concerned their size is always a matter to be taken into account—they are generally 15 inches × 7 inches × 4½ inches.[2]

[1] They do not form a complete circle, for in order to rest firmly on the corner beam, their under sides had to be cut off.

[2] The small bricks generally belong to quite late times, and the earliest burnt bricks as a rule to the Middle Ages.

The above interesting representation[1] of the time of the 18th dynasty shows us how they prepared the bricks. The storehouses of the great temple of Amon could no longer contain the royal gifts; Thothmes III. therefore ordered a new building to be constructed. The high official who was entrusted with this commission has represented for us in his tomb how

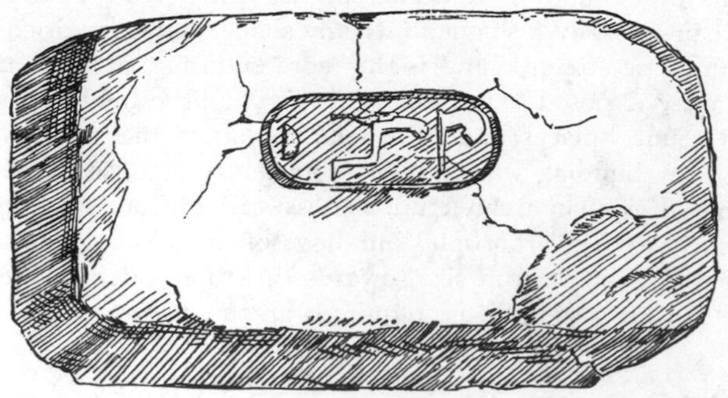

BRICK WITH THE NAME OF QUEEN CHNEMTAMUN (after L. D., iii. 26).

the necessary number of bricks were made; they were, as was usually the case, the work of the captive Asiatics, whom the king had presented to the temple. As we see, the Nile mud is first moistened—two men are drawing the water from a tank for this purpose—it is then worked through with the common Egyptian hoe. It is next placed in wooden moulds which, as is proved by many bricks we possess, were stamped with the name of the reigning king. When ready, the bricks were placed in the sun to dry; the dried bricks, which can be recognised in our representation by

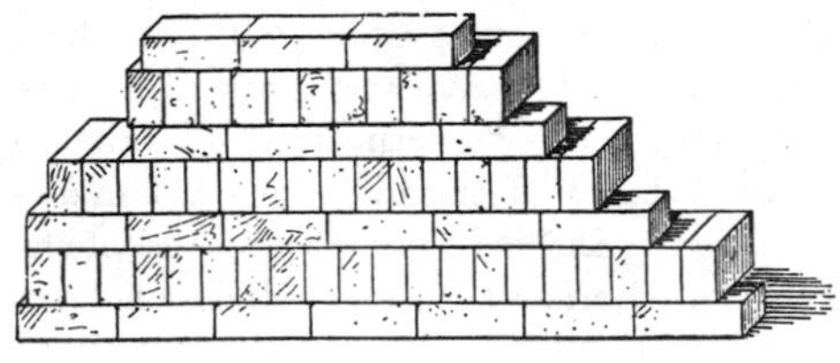

EGYPTIAN BRICK-WORK.

EUROPEAN BRICK-WORK.

their small size, were then placed in heaps ready for the builders to fetch them away for their work. Further on in our picture the process of building is represented, and one fact that we observe here we also learn from every brick building which has been preserved to us, namely, the curious way in which the bricks were built up. In old times, as in modern days, the Egyptian rarely placed his bricks as we do now, with all the bricks in each row resting on the broad side. It was the Egyptian custom, on the contrary, to place the bricks alternately in one or two layers, first on the broad side and then on the narrow side.

[1] L. D., iii. 40.

The Nile mud served also as mortar in the brick buildings; for this purpose it was generally mixed with potsherds. I must add that in very early times they understood how to build the arch;[1] in the long vaulted passages (probably used as store-rooms) which Ramses II. built round his funerary temple, the vaulting is constructed with peculiarly flat bricks, somewhat resembling our tiles, these were provided with special grooves in order to fasten them together more securely.

In the remote ages, when Egypt was not so destitute of trees as in historical times, wood was extensively used for building. We have already endeavoured to reconstruct an ancient wooden palace (see p. 171). We have also spoken of the old form of door, which, with its boards and laths, we recognise at once as carpenters' work. Another architectural feature owes its form evidently to wood—the material in which it was first constructed—I refer to the pillar. The pillar was originally the wooden prop which helped to support the roof, and could not be dispensed with even in a mud building, except in the narrow passage-like rooms usual in Assyrian architecture. Two supplementary features were naturally derived from this pillar: where it stood on the ground, it was necessary to heap up clay to give it a firmer hold, and where the beam of the roof rested on it, the weight was divided by means of a board which was placed between the beam and the pillar. Both these features were retained in the Egyptian column, they constitute the round base and the square abacus.

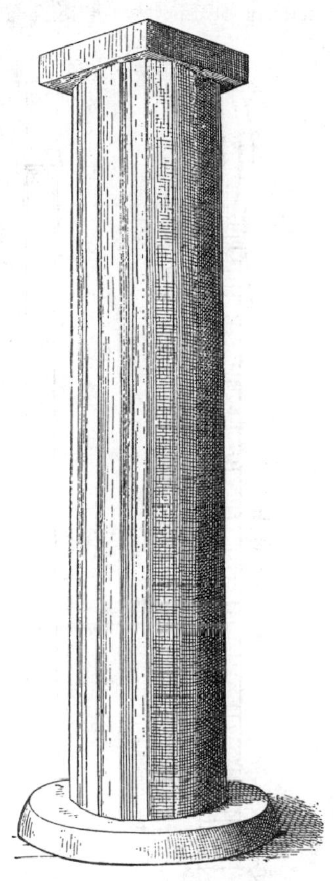

SO-CALLED PROTO-DORIC COLUMN (Beni Hasan, Middle Empire).

The most simple form of pillar in common use, if we except the plain square pillar, was the so-called proto-doric column, which occurs frequently before the time of and during the 18th dynasty. It is a simple pillar, 8 or 16 sided, with base and abacus, but no capital. The latter was always of secondary importance, and was apparently derived from the ornamentation of the pillars. The decoration of the pillars was connected with the universal love for flowers in Egypt; a special instance of which is seen in the custom of giving the pillars the form either of flowers or of bunches

[1] The oldest stone arch is represented in Perrot-Chipiez; it occurs in a tomb of the 6th dynasty at Abydos.

of flowers. Hence there arose in old times two principal types, which we may designate as flower-pillars and bud-pillars. In its oldest form the latter represents four lotus buds, which are bound together so that their stalks form the shaft and their buds the capital ;[1] in later times the general scheme of this pretty idea is alone retained, and the detail is often replaced by

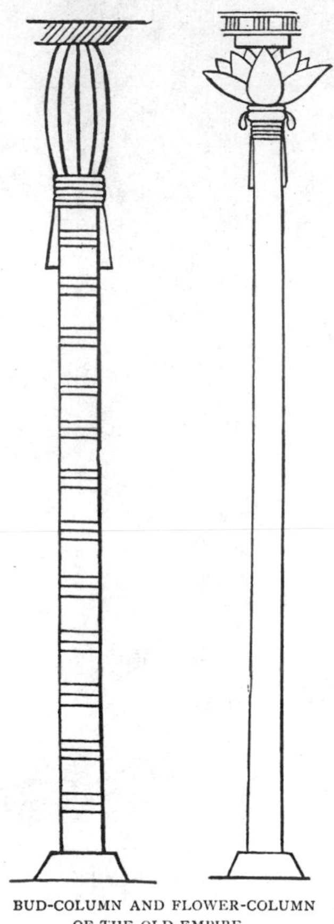

BUD-COLUMN AND FLOWER-COLUMN OF THE OLD EMPIRE.

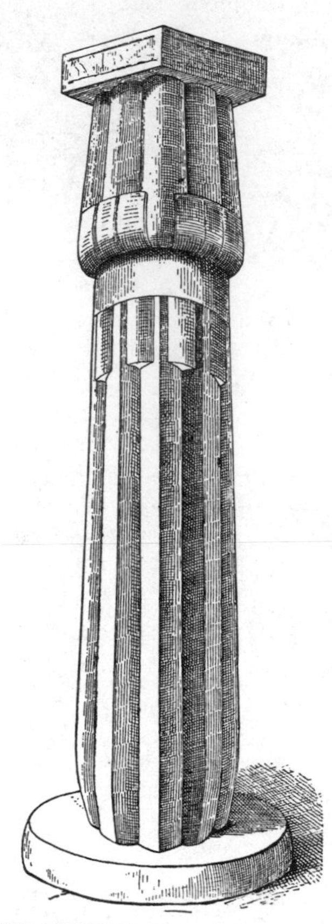

BUD-COLUMN OF STONE ARCHITECTURE IN ITS ORIGINAL FORM.

other favourite ornamentation. The flower-pillar is more difficult to understand, it represents the calyx of a large gay flower placed as a capital on a round shaft ; under the New Empire this form was often treated very arbitrarily.[2] A third form of pillar occurs more rarely, but may be traced back as far as the Middle Empire ;[3] from later examples we judge

[1] Bud-pillars under the O E.: L. D., ii. 61 a 111 e; under the M. E.: L. D., ii. 134 b. Originals of the time of the M. E. are also still in existence (Beni Hasan and Berlin Museum).

[2] Flower-pillars under the O. E. : L. D., ii. 41, 111 e c (with bands under the flower, as if here also the shaft was supposed to consist of stalks tied together).

[3] L. D., ii. 127 ; in one example bands are also found here below the capital.

that this pillar was intended to represent a palm with its gently-swaying boughs.

A new development of the pillar is found in the so-called Ḥatḥor capital, which was certainly in use before the time of the New Empire, though, as it happens, we cannot identify it in the scanty materials we

LATER BUD-COLUMN IN ITS DEGENERATE FORM.

LATER FLOWER-COLUMN IN ITS DEGENERATE FORM.

possess. The upper part of the pillar is adorned, in very low relief, with a face recognisable by the two cow's ears as that of the Egyptian goddess of love, who may have been revered in some Egyptian sanctuary as a pillar carved in this fashion. In the same way in early times the pillar 𓊽, the sacred emblem of Osiris of Dedu, was employed in architecture, and by the combination of this pillar with the round arch, flat mouldings and other ornaments, the Egyptians were able to create very charming walls with carved open work.[1]

All these pillars and columns, and even all the small painted details of ornament in the brick buildings—the gay bands and the surfaces covered with patterns, which were apparently derived in great measure from the custom of covering the walls with gaily-coloured mats—were then directly assimilated into stone architecture, and for the greater part only exist for us in the latter form. We cannot therefore emphasise too strongly the fact that the forms of Egyptian architecture, as we know them, were rarely intended originally for the places in which we see them. These dainty

BRONZE MIRROR WITH THE HEAD OF BESA. THE HANDLE IS FORMED BY A CONVENTIONAL FLOWER (after W., ii. 351).

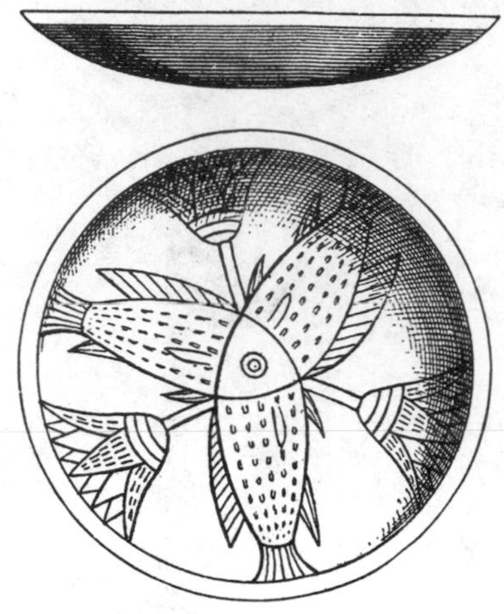

SMALL FAYENCE BOWL IN THE BERLIN MUSEUM, DECORATED WITH A PAINTING OF THREE FISH WITH ONE HEAD, AND THREE LOTUS FLOWERS (after W., ii. 42).

bud and flower pillars were not really intended to be constructed with a diameter of 12 feet and to reach a height of over 60 feet, and if, nevertheless, they exercise such an ineffaceable effect upon our minds, it is owing rather to the force of their immense dimensions than to the æsthetic beauty of their form.

We cannot here trace the details of the development of the architectural forms in the great temple buildings, though the movement was confined to comparatively narrow limits. These forms however were evidently developed in a freer fashion in the private buildings; unfortunately these are now known to us only by representations in the tombs. For instance, the pillars of the verandahs, shown in representations of the time of the New Empire, often exhibit forms of exuberant fantasy. When we see dead geese carved upon the pillars as decoration, as at Tell el Amarna,[2] or when,

[1] See a very beautiful ivory casket in the Louvre; employed as ornamentation, e.g. in the tomb of Pu'emrê' under Thothmes III. (from my own copy).

[2] L. D., iii. 106 c.

as in a chapel of the time of the 20th dynasty,[1] three capitals are placed one above the other, and connected together by a support so thin that it appears that the pillar *must* break, we are convinced that the direction followed in the architecture of private houses was not in any way subservient to the traditional rules observed in the temples. The faint remains of a painting also, which are still to be seen in a window recess in the palace of Medinet Habu (a practised eye will recognise a basket of fruit and flowers), betrays a decorative style unknown in the sanctuaries of the gods. Evidently in architecture, as in painting and sculpture, side by side with the stiff conventional style, a more living art was developed, which shook itself free from the dogmas of tradition; unfortunately it is almost unknown to us, as it was exclusively employed in private buildings which have long since disappeared.

WOODEN OINTMENT-BOWL (after Perrot-Chipiez).

The industrial arts also made good use of architectural forms and ornamentation; boxes finished off at the top with a hollow gorge, and rouge pots in the form of pillars, exist in great numbers. At the same time special forms were developed in this branch of art,—forms worthy of more attention than they have received as yet. In part, they owe their individual style to the peculiar properties of the material used, and to the technique; this is the case with the pottery and wood-carving. For instance, the well-known pattern resembling an arrow-head, used for little wooden boxes and other objects, is the natural outcome of the cutting of a piece of wood, and in the same way the so called *panelling* in the sides and covers of boxes, which appears as early as the 6th dynasty,[2] represents a peculiarity due to a joiner's mode of working.

In a great measure also imitations from the world of nature were employed for the smaller objects of art; these might either be carved in the form of animals or plants, or representations of both might be used in their ornamentation. It is very interesting to observe what manner of ideas were especially brought into play for this purpose. In the first place, connected with hunting, we find seats supported by lions, and little ointment bowls in the form of gazelles tied up. From the subject of war, we get under the New Empire the figures of the captive barbarians supporting

[1] L. D., iii. 235.

[2] On the relief of 'Ep'e at Gizeh.

the flat tops of tables, or carrying little ointment bowls as tribute on their shoulders, or, as in a pretty example in the Gizeh museum, serving as a pair of scissors. Figures of beautiful girls as well as of pet monkeys occur as a matter of course; the latter may be seen reaching up on one leg to get a look into the rouge pot, or twining themselves round this important toilet requisite. The barbaric little god Besa also, who took all perfumes under his care, would perhaps keep the rouge in his little fat body, or carry the lady's mirror on his head. These erotic subjects invaded also the domain from which the Egyptians obtained their favourite motives for ornamentation, viz. the realm of flowers and papyrus reeds, birds and fishes, the marsh scenes, and the "bird-tanks of pleasure." The lovely maiden wading through the rushes to pick the flowers, or catching a duck as she swims through the water; the lion in the reeds robbing the cow of her calf; the tank with its lotus flowers and fish; the merry pictures of the harem on the water with the master, and the rough play with him;[1] the little boxes and bowls in the shape of geese, fish, and flowers—everywhere and continually we have allusions to the pleasures of life to be enjoyed in the marshes. We have often shown in the course of this work how, from the days of the Old Empire down to the Roman time, the Egyptians thoroughly enjoyed this life; we must therefore regard the art of the New Empire, which treated of these subjects, as an especially popular development. The art of the Old Empire also, which invested the pillars with the forms of lotus-buds and water flowers, had followed the same direction; but these forms had long since either died away or been turned to stone, when the artists of the New Empire again drank from the same fresh spring whence their forefathers had drawn their inspiration in times of old.

[1] A small stone bowl at Gizeh.

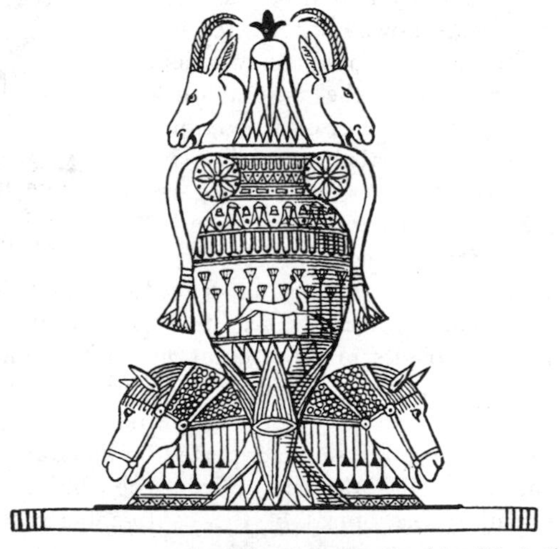

VASE WITH HEADS OF GAZELLES AND OF HORSES (after W., ii. 6).

HARVEST SCENE UNDER THE NEW EMPIRE. REAPERS, ONE OF WHOM IS DRINKING OUT OF A JUG; GLEANING; CARRYING AWAY AND HEAPING UP THE CORN (after W., ii. 419).

CHAPTER XVII

AGRICULTURE

THE reason that the little land of Egypt has played as important a part in the history of civilisation as many a large empire, is due to the wealth which yearly accrues to the country from the produce of the soil; agriculture is the foundation of Egyptian civilisation. The results which the agriculturists of the Nile valley have obtained, they owe however, not to any special skill or cleverness on their part, but to the inexhaustible fertility of the land.

REPRESENTATION OF THE NILE, BRINGING VASES OF WATER AND FLOWERS AS HIS GIFTS TO THE COUNTRY.

He is hermaphrodite, and wears a girdle like that worn by sailors and fishermen.

It is inexhaustible in the literal sense of the word, for unless quite unreasonable demands are made on the soil, the nourishment that the crops have absorbed is returned to it without any human aid. I need scarcely say that this miracle is worked each summer by the inundation of the Nile; it is the Nile which "supplies all men with nourishment and food."[1] The great river however does not bestow its gifts impartially, it may also be the cause of misfortune to the country, for whilst a "great Nile,"[2] *i.e.* a high inundation promises the richest increase to the fields, with a low Nile comes the inevitable dread of a "year of famine."[3] This stands to reason, for the inundation brings with it, not alone the fertile mud, but the needful humidity for the soil. In this rainless country plants can only grow on those spots that have

[1] L. D., iii. 175 d.

[2] L. D., ii. 122, b; Harr., i. 23, 4.

[3] L. D., ii. 122, b. We see how terrible a famine in Egypt can be from Abdallatif's description of the famine in 1201 A.D. (Abdallatif, ed. de Sacy, p. 360 ff.).

not merely been overflowed, but also sufficiently saturated with the water; where this is not the case the hard clay soil is quite bare of vegetation.

ANCIENT SHADUF. (Thebes. After W., i. 281.)

At the same time even the highest inundation does not overflow all the fields, and if these are not to be barren the peasant must undertake an artificial irrigation. The water of the Nile is brought as near as

MODERN SHADUF.

possible to his field by a trench, and he then erects a kind of draw-well, now called by the modern term *shaduf*, though it has retained its old form.[1] It is hard work the whole livelong day to raise and empty the pail of the shaduf, in fact nothing is so tiring in the daily work of the Egyptians as this irrigation of the fields. At the present time, when the system of cultivation has been so immensely improved, the fellahin use it most extensively, especially in Upper Egypt; in old times the shaduf was perhaps employed less frequently.

The inundation over, the Nile withdraws, leaving pools of water standing here and there on the fields. This is the busy time of the year for the Egyptian farmer, "the fields are out" and he must "work industriously"[2] so as to make good use of the blessing brought by the Nile. He can do this the better as the sultry heat, which during the summer had oppressed both him and his cattle, has at length given way. "A beautiful day, it is cool, and the oxen draw well; the sky is according to our desire," say the people who till the ground, and they set to work with good will, "for the Nile has been very high," and wise men already foretell that "it is to be a beautiful year, free from want and rich in all herbs," a year in which there will be a good harvest, and in which the calves will "thrive excellently."[3]

PLOUGHING, HOEING, AND SOWING UNDER THE OLD EMPIRE. (Tomb of T'y. After Bädeker, p. 414.)

The first duty of the farmer is now to plough the land;[4] this work is the more difficult because the plough with which he has to turn over the heavy soil is very clumsy. The Egyptian plough has changed but little; from the earliest period it has consisted of a long wooden ploughshare,[5] into which two slightly-bent handles are inserted, while the long pole, which is tied on obliquely to the hinder part of the ploughshare, bears a transverse bar in front, which is fastened to the horns of the oxen. Such is the stereotyped form of plough, which for centuries has scarcely altered at all; for though under the Middle Empire another rope was added to bind the pole and ploughshare together, and again under the New Empire the handles were put on more perpendicularly and provided with places

[1] The illustration in the text and a second representation, also W., i. 281, are the only ones I know of which are of early date; the water-wheels may also be old, but there is no proof of this fact as regards the periods with which we are dealing.

[2] D'Orbiney, 2, 3.

[3] After the representation in the tomb of Pa-ḥre at El Kab, L. D., iii. 10, a.

[4] Representations of ploughing—O. E.: L. D., ii. 43, 51; Bädeker, p. 414; L. D., ii. 106, 107; Ros. M. C., 32, 7; M. E.: L. D., ii. 127; W., ii. 391 (=Ros. M. C., 32, 4). N. E.: Perrot, 704 (=L. D., iii. 77 d); L. D., iii. 10 a; W., i. 372. Conventional but pleasing, W., ii. 396 (=Ros. M. C., 32, 2=Desc. de l'Eg. antiq., ii. 90).

[5] If the ploughshare is brown (Ros. M. C., 32, 4, 5) the other parts of the plough are light yellow; from this circumstance we might perhaps conjecture that they are of different wood. The darker colour might however only indicate the earth sticking to the ploughshare. This may be the case also with the hoe (see note 2 on the following page).

for the hands, yet these alterations were quite unimportant. Two men are needed for ploughing—one, the ploughman proper, presses down the handles of the plough, the other, the ox-driver,[1] is indefatigable in goading on the animals with his stick. The work goes on with the inevitable Egyptian cries; the driver encourages the ploughman with his "Press the plough down, press it down with thy hand!" he calls to the oxen to "pull hard," or he orders them, when they have to turn at the end of the field, to be "round."[2] There are generally two ploughs, the one behind the other, probably in order that the second might turn up the earth between the furrows made by the other.

If the Egyptians merely wanted to loosen the upper coating of mud, they employed (at any rate under the New Empire) a lighter plough that was drawn by men.[3] Here we see four boys harnessed to the bar, while an old man is pressing down the handles. This plough also differs somewhat from the usual form; the ploughshare consists of two parts bound together, it has also a long piece added on behind and turned upwards obliquely, by which the ploughman guides the plough.

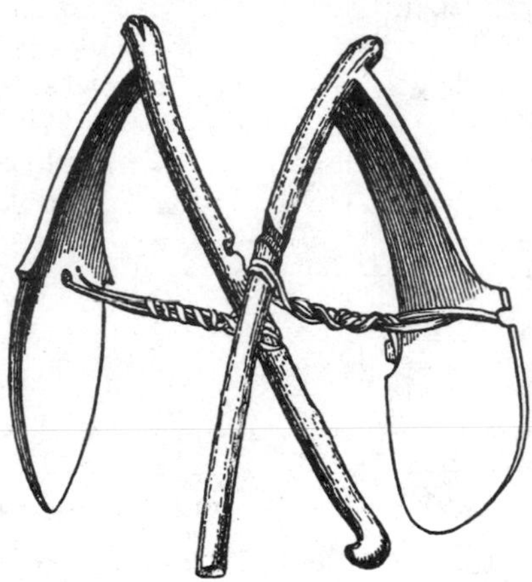

WOODEN HOE.
From a public tomb at Thebes of the time of the New Empire. (Berlin. After W., ii. 252.)

After ploughing however the great clods of the heavy Egyptian soil had to be broken up again before the ground was ready for the seed. At the present day a "cat's claw"—a roller covered with spikes—is drawn over the fields for this purpose; in old times a wooden hoe was used,[4]—the latter seems indeed to have been the national agricultural implement. We could have scarcely formed a correct idea of it from the figure [hieroglyph], which it takes in the hieroglyphs and on the reliefs; happily however we have some examples of real hoes in our museums. The labourer grasped the handle of this hoe at the lower end and broke up the clods of earth with the blade; by moving the rope he could make it wider or narrower as he pleased. In the pictures of the Old Empire, the men hoeing are always represented following the plough; later, they

[1] Horses ploughing occur in a tale of the New Empire, d'Orb, 2, 2, if the word *ḥtr* is to be translated here by horse, which is doubtful.

[2] Perhaps the great lever that (L. D., ii. 107) is carried before the plough was used to facilitate the turning; it is represented as dark coloured on the lower side; this fact would confirm this hypothesis.

[3] N. E.: L. D., iii. 10 a.

[4] Hoes—O. E.: L. D., ii. 51 (=Ros. M. C., 32, 1), 56 a (two-pronged?); Bädeker, 414. M. E.: L. D., ii. 127; W., ii. 391; Perrot, 4; Ros. M. C., 32, 6 (coloured, the handle lighter than the blade). N. E.: W., ii. 394; Perrot, 704.

appear to have gone in front as well; under the New Empire we meet with them also alone in the fields, as if for some crops the farmers dispensed with the plough and were content with hoeing the soil. In the above-named periods wooden hammers were also employed to break up the clods of earth.[1]

After the land had been properly prepared, the sowing of the seed followed.[2] We see the "scribe of the corn" gravely standing before the heap of seed, watching the men sowing, and noting down how often each filled his little bag with seed. When the seed had been scattered, the work of sowing was not complete—it had next to be pressed into the tough mud. For this purpose sheep were driven over the freshly-sown fields.[3] In all the pictures of this subject one or two shepherds with their flocks are to be seen following the sower. Labourers swinging their

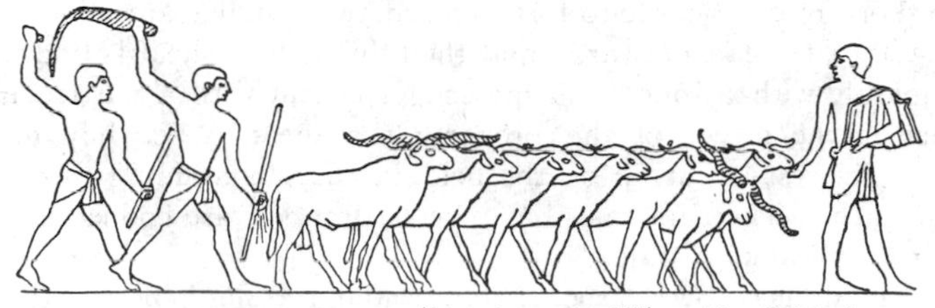

RAMS TREADING IN THE SEED (from the tomb of T'y. After Bädeker).

whips drive the sheep forward; others no less energetically chase them back. The frightened animals crowd together; a spirited ram appears to be about to offer resistance—he lowers his head in a threatening attitude; most of the creatures, however, run about the field in a frightened way, and *plough* it (to use the expression of the inscriptions) *with their feet.*

This trampling in of the seed is only represented in the pictures of the Old Empire; the custom probably continued later, but became less common. When Herodotos travelled in Egypt, he noticed that pigs were employed in the Delta for this purpose; in Pliny's time this practice was spoken of as a long-forgotten custom of doubtful credibility.

Harvest-time comes, and the corn[4] is cut by means of a short sickle,[5] with which, contrary to our custom, they cut the stalks high above the ground—sometimes close to the ears[6]—as if the straw were useless, and

[1] Hammers—N. E.: Perrot, 704.

[2] Sowing—O. E.: L. D., ii. 51, 56 a; Bädeker, p. 414; L. D., ii. 106 b; W., ii. 390. N. E.: W., ii. 394; Perrot, 704; Ros. M. C., 32, 2 (=W., ii. 396); W., i. 372.

[3] Sheep trampling in the seed—O. E.: L. D., ii. 51 (Ros. M. C., 32, 1), 56 a, 106 b (=Ros. M. C., 32, 3); W., ii. 390. In all the pictures I know, sheep are the animals represented, not goats, as has often been said.—What is the little bag and the short stick which the driver carries besides his whip?

[4] Men cutting corn under the O. E.—Dyn. IV.: L. D., ii. 51; also ib. 13. Dyn. V.: ib. 43, 47, 73 (misunderstood), 80 c. Bädeker, p. 407. Dyn. VI.: ib. 106, 107. Under the M. E.: L. D., ii. 127. Under the N. E.: W., ii. 419, 422, 424, 427.

[5] The shape of the sickle varies very much, without our being able to give a limit of time for these changes.

[6] Thus W., ii. 419 (N. E.). Under the O. E. they used to cut them off at about the height of the knee.

only added to the difficulty of threshing. The work proceeds quickly, as we see from the rapid movements of the men ; amongst them however we often find an idle labourer[1] standing with his sickle under his arm ; instead of working, he prefers to reckon up on his fingers to his comrades how many sheaves he has already cut on that day. The conversation of the other harvest-men also appears to be chiefly concerned with their own many excellent qualities ; unfortunately their witty remarks are quite incomprehensible to us.[2] Now and then there is a pause in the work, and a pointed jug is passed round amongst the thirsty labourers.[3]

REAPER (from the tomb of T'y. After Bädeker).

When the corn has been cut it is bound in sheaves ; and as the stalks are too short for one bundle to form a sheaf, two bundles are laid with their ends together, the ears outwards, and then this double sheaf is tied together in the middle with a rope.[4] A messenger is sent with a particularly fine specimen to the owner of the property, that he may see how good the crop is ;[5] the rest is put up on the field in heaps containing three or four bundles each. The ears that have been dropped are collected in little bags by the gleaning women.[6]

The corn has now to be taken to the threshing-floor, which was situate probably near the town. It was carried on the backs of those patient animals—even now the beasts of burden of modern Egypt—the donkeys. We may see quite a number of them being driven in wild career on to the fields,[7] their drivers behind them calling out to them and brandishing their sticks. On the way they meet the animals returning home with their loads ; amongst them is a donkey with her foal. With her head raised she greets the company with a loud bray ; but the sticks of the drivers admit of no delay. Soon enough any foolish resistance is over. The donkeys arrive on the harvest-field ready to be laden with the sheaves ; one of the animals then kicks up his heels, and refuses to come alongside. One of the drivers pulls him by the ears and leg, another beats him ; "run as thou canst," they cry to him, and drag him up to the lading place.[8]

In the meantime the sheaves have been tied up in a large basket[9] or sack,[10] or they may have been, as was apparently customary later, packed

[1] L. D., ii. 80 c, 106 b, 107, 127.

[2] Brugsch, Gr. W., 165-169.

[3] L. D., ii. 9 ; W., ii. 419.

[4] O. E. : L. D., ii. 51, 43, 47, 106. N. E. : W., ii. 424. After the time of the M. E. it appears as if they dispensed with the tying up of the sheaves as a rule, and collected the cut corn direct into the basket or bag in which it was carried to the threshing-floor. Cp. L. D., ii. 127 ; W., ii. 419, 420, 422.

[5] O. E. : L. D., ii. 47.

[6] M. E. : L. D., ii. 127 (superscription *srd*, i.e. Copt. ⲥⲣⲓⲧ, gleaning). N. E. : W., ii. 419, 422.

[7] L. D., ii. 51, 47, 73, 106. These scenes are still to be seen in the daily life of modern Egypt.

[8] L. D., ii. 47, 80 a.

[9] Called *'eadt*, and made of cord : Perrot, 669 ; L. D., ii. 80 c, 106. Open at the top, ib. 56 a. The saddle below has rings to which the basket is to be fastened, ib. 106.

[10] L. D., ii. 51, 43, 73 ; fastened up at the top, ib. 47. Bädeker, p. 407.

in panniers,[1] which were hung over the saddle of the donkey. When the donkeys are laden, one sheaf, for which no room could be found, is put in the basket,[2] and the procession sets off. They go slowly enough, though the men never cease calling out to their beasts to "run," but the donkeys are heavily laden, and one stumbles under his burden. The driver guides him by the tail; his boy, who has to see that the load is rightly balanced, pulls him by the ear.[3] When they arrive at the corn stack, which has been raised in the threshing-floor, the sheaves are divided, and two workmen busy themselves with throwing up the separate bundles of ears on to the stack. Great skill and strength seem to have been necessary for this work, so that by a powerful throw the stack might be made as firm as possible; a third workman is often to be seen gathering together one by one the ears that have fallen below.[4]

TRANSPORT OF CORN. (From the tomb of T'y. After Bädeker).

The threshing-floor, in the midst of which appears to have been the stack,[5] is, to judge from the pictures, a flat round area, with the sides some-

DONKEYS THRESHING IN THE THRESHING-FLOOR (after L. D., ii. 9).

what raised.[6] The corn is spread out here, and trodden by the hoofs of the animals driven about in it. Under the Old Empire the animals used for this purpose were nearly always donkeys,[7] and oxen are only met with when, as we may say, extra help was wanted;[8] after the time of the Middle Empire however, the Egyptians seem to have followed a different

[1] M. E.: L. D., ii. 127. N. E.: W., ii. 420.

[2] L. D., ii. 80, 106. Bädeker, p. 407; Perrot, 669. In one case (L. D., ii. 47) it is a bundle of weeds, evidently carried thus for food.

[3] L. D., ii. 51, 47, 56 a, 73, 80, 106-107; Bädeker, p. 407.

[4] L. D., ii. 51, 43, 56 a, 73, 80, 105. The stack is called [hieroglyphs], the throw [hieroglyphs].

[5] Cp. the picture W., ii. 424.

[6] Under the O. E. and the M. E. the floor is drawn [sign], yet as we do not see the feet of the animals standing upon it, the level must be lower in the centre. Under the N. E. we find it represented thus [sign]. Both prove the same fact.

[7] L. D., ii. 9, 43, 73, 80 a; Perrot, 669.

[8] L. D., ii. 47, 71 a, 106.

plan, for we find that in later times oxen were employed alone.[1] As a rule, when donkeys were used, ten animals were employed, but in the case of oxen three were considered sufficient. They were driven round the floor in a circle,[2] and the stick and the voice were of course in great request, for donkeys are particularly self-willed creatures. As we see, one wants to run the other way, another will not go forward at all, so that there is nothing to do but to seize him by the fore leg and drag him over the threshing-floor. We often see an ox or a donkey munching a few ears while threshing, as if to illustrate the Hebrew maxim that "thou shalt not muzzle the ox that treadeth out the corn."

HARVEST SCENE UNDER THE NEW EMPIRE.

Threshing in the threshing-floor, sweeping together of the corn, and winnowing. On a tree near the threshing-floor there hangs a skin, out of which a labourer drinks. To the left the measuring of the corn that has been threshed (after W., ii. 419).

After the corn has been threshed, it is collected, together with the chaff, by means of a wooden fork, into a big heap,[3] which is weighted at the top in order to keep it together. The next necessary work is to sift the corn from the chaff and dirt consequent on such a rude procedure. This easy work seems always to have been performed by women.[4] They winnow the corn by throwing it up quickly by means of two small bent boards. The grain falls straight down while the chaff is blown forwards.[5] The corn has already been passed through a great rectangular sieve to separate it from the worst impurities.[6]

A sample of the freshly-threshed corn is then sent for the master to see; the harvest-men also do not forget to thank the gods. They not only dedicate the first-fruits to the god specially revered in the locality,[7] and celebrate a festival to Min, the god of agriculture,[8] but also during harvest-time the peasants give thanks to heaven. In one example, for instance, we find two little altars erected near the threshing-floor between the heaps

[1] M. E.: L. D., ii. 127. N. E.: W., ii. 419, 420, 423, 424; L. D., iii. 10 c, d.

[2] W., ii. 420, there are four oxen threshing, their horns are fastened together with a stick, so that they have to keep in step.

[3] This sweeping together is called ; the fork has two or three prongs. O. E.: Perrot, 36; L. D., ii. 9, 47, 71, 80. M. E.: L. D., ii. 127. N. E.: W., ii. 422, 423.

[4] The overseer sits near them with a stick, L. D., ii. 9.

[5] O. E.: L. D., ii. 47 (very instructive), 71, 73, 80; Bädeker, p. 407; Perrot, 36. N. E.: W., ii. 419, 422, 423.

[6] Perrot, 36; Brugsch, Gr. W., 143; L. D., ii. 9, 47, 71, 80. All these pictures are of the time of the O. E.

[7] Cp. p. 272.

[8] See p. 66.

of grain,[1] and in another a little bowl is placed on the heap of grain that a woman has piled up ;[2] both are doubtless offerings to the snake goddess, Renenutet ; the altars[3] and chapels[4] that we meet with in the courts of the granaries were also probably erected to her honour.

Finally, at the close of the harvest, two officials belonging to the

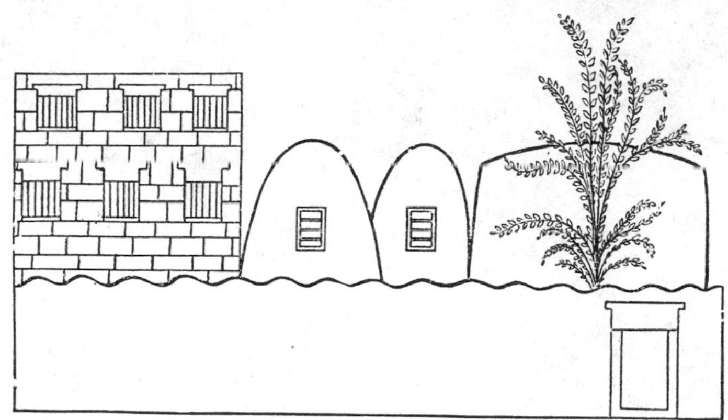

PROPERTY CONSISTING OF A HOUSE, TWO GRANARIES, AND A BUILDING OF UNCERTAIN DESIGN (Tell el Amarna. After Perrot-Chipiez).

PROPERTY, CONSISTING OF FIVE BARNS, SURROUNDED BY A BRICK WALL ; THREE BARNS HAVE ALREADY BEEN FILLED (Thebes. After W., i. 371).

estate come on the scene, the "scribe of the granary" and the "measurer of the corn." They measure the heaps of corn[5] before they are taken

[1] L. D., ii. 80.

[2] L. D., ii. 9.

[3] O. E. : Perrot, 30.

[4] N. E. : W., i. 348 ; cp. also ib. 385.

[5] The [hieroglyphs] of a domain under the O. E. consisted, according to L. D., ii. 71, of (1) the [hieroglyphs], superintendent ; (2) the [hieroglyphs], scribe ("scribe of the granary," L. D., ii. 51) ; (3) the

into the granary. These granaries were, at all periods, built essentially on the same plan. In a court surrounded by a wall were placed one or two rows of conical mud buildings about 16 feet high and $6\frac{1}{2}$ feet broad; they had one little window high up, and another half-way up or near the ground. The lower one, which served for taking away the corn, was generally closed on account of the mice, and the workmen emptied their sacks through the upper window, which was reached by a ladder.[1] Under the Middle Empire we find also a somewhat different form, which may be seen in the model represented here.[2] These granaries had all, as a rule, a flat roof reached by an outside staircase; the roof formed a good vantage ground for the scribe, from which he could keep account of the sacks that were brought up and emptied into the granary.[3] Such a granary was only suitable for a large establishment, for a property, for instance, like that of Paḥre of El Kab, who lived at the beginning of the eighteenth dynasty, where we see the harvest brought by great ships to the granary; the workmen who are carrying the heavy sacks of corn on board break out at last into complaints: "Are we then to have no rest from the carrying of the corn and the white spelt? The barns are already so full that the heaps of corn overflow, and the boats are already so full of corn that they burst. And yet we are still driven to make haste."[4]

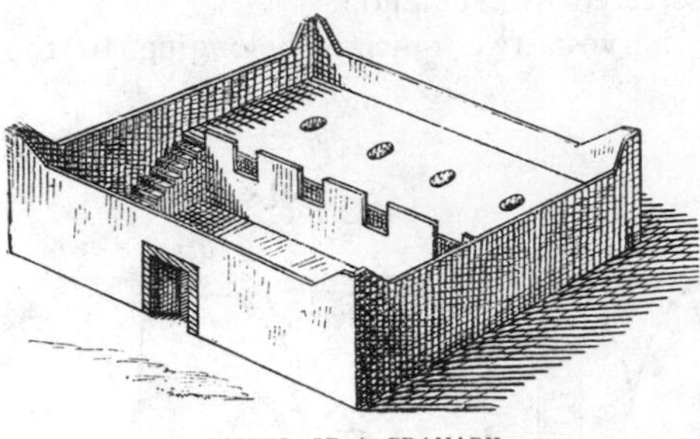

MODEL OF A GRANARY
(Louvre. After Perrot-Chipiez).

Up to this point I have spoken of corn in general, because the various species of corn are never represented in the pictures with any certainty. There are two kinds of corn which are brought to our notice in the usual representations of agriculture, barley and wheat; both were extensively cultivated in Egypt, as is proved by the straw still to be seen in the unburnt bricks.[5] On a few monuments of the time of the New Empire the harvest of another cultivated plant is represented; it has a

[hieroglyph], measurer; (4) the [hieroglyphs] strong in speech (?) of the granary (the correct reading, L. D., ii. 103). The "measurer of the corn" is often found also under the N. E. Similar representations of the N. E., W. ii. 419, 422.

[1] O. E.: Perrot, 30. M. E.: W., i. 371 (with staircase). N. E.: W., i. 371; Perrot, 48 (Prisse texte, p. 218).

[2] Also L. D., ii. 127; Perrot, 488. The staircase also, W., i. 371, in spite of the fact that the roof is not flat.

[3] The form [hieroglyph], a heap of corn raised on a stand of mud on account of the mice, must judging by the hieroglyphs, have been the usual way of keeping the corn in the earliest ages; yet the double granary at Tell el Amarna (W., i. 348) is the only one I know of, in which similar heaps are represented instead of the granary.

[4] L. D., iii. 10 a.

[5] I pass over here purposely the difficult question as to the period at which the various cultivated plants were introduced into Egypt.

stalk with a small red fruit at the top. This has been recognised with great probability as the black millet, the durra of modern Egypt.[1] As we see by the accompanying picture, the durra was not cut, but pulled up ; the earth was then knocked off the roots, after which the long stalks were tied

HARVEST OF CORN AND OF DURRA (after W., ii. 427).

together in sheaves. To get the seed off the stalks a curious instrument something like a comb was used, which is seen in the illustration below. In a similar picture the old slave whose duty it was to do the combing is seated in the shade of a sycamore ; he pretends that the work is no trouble, and remarks to the peasant, who brings him a fresh bundle of

DURRA HARVEST UNDER THE NEW EMPIRE (after W., ii. 428. El Kab).

durra to comb : " If thou didst bring me even eleven thousand and nine, I would yet comb them." The peasant however pays no attention to this foolish boast ; " Make haste," he says, " and do not talk so much, thou oldest amongst the field labourers." [2]

Besides the above crops, there is no doubt that vegetables such as onions, cucumbers, and melons were cultivated as extensively in ancient as in modern Egypt. On this point however our knowledge is very scanty, and it will therefore be best now to turn to the other department of Egyptian husbandry, viz. cattle-breeding, concerning which there is, comparatively speaking, rich material at hand. The pictures, specially of the Old Empire, represent the life of the cattle so frequently and with such great truth to nature, that we are tempted to believe that the Egyptians of old were as friendly with their animals as those of modern times are rough and cruel.

[1] Durra harvest : W., ii. 396, 427, 428 ; L. D., iii. 10 e.

[2] L. D., iii. 10 e.

This love of animals had one feature peculiar to Egypt,—of all domestic animals the ox was the dearest to the heart of the Egyptian. Cattle-breeding takes up a very large space in the representations on the monuments; in almost every tomb of the Old Empire we meet with the herdsman and his animals; the latter are either swimming through the water or are being fed or milked. The Egyptians talked to their oxen as we talk to our dogs; they gave them names[1] and decked out the finest with coloured cloths and pretty fringes;[2] they represented their cattle in all positions with an observation both true and affectionate, showing plainly how dearly they valued them. The sort of contempt that we feel for dumb oxen was unknown to the Old Egyptian; on the contrary, the cow was to him a sacred animal, in whose form the highest goddess had deigned to appear, while the bull was considered the ideal conception of heroic strength and power. Other nations have compared their most powerful gods and their greatest heroes to the lion; the Egyptians, on the other hand, compared them to the "strong bull."

The oxen of ancient Egypt were indeed, as a matter of fact, worthy of all admiration.[3] According to the pictures and the skulls that we possess, the breed belonged to that species which is still at the present day the ruling race throughout Africa, the so-called zebu; they resembled that animal in having "the forehead very receding, the little projection of the edge of the socket of the eye, the flatness and straightness of the whole profile strongly marked." The hump so fully developed in many zebus is almost entirely wanting, yet this is often the case with those animals in the interior of Africa. The Egyptians developed several species and varieties from the zebu by breeding; these differed not only in appearance, but their flesh also varied in goodness.[4] The most important species under the Old Empire was the long-horned;[5] the animals had unusually long horns, which as a rule were bent in the lyre form, more rarely in that of the crescent. Further, they possessed "a dignified neck like the bison . . . a somewhat high frame, massive muzzle, and a fold of skin on the belly." They were generally pure white, or white with large red or black spots, or they might be light yellow or brown; in one of the pictures we see a rather uncanny-looking animal of a deep black colour, with red belly and ankles. The connoisseur recognised several varieties of this long-horned race; the common *'ena* was distinguished from the rarer *neg*,[6]

[1] Cp. the cow "purest of bulls" (sic) and the calf "good ox," of the 12th dynasty in Mar. Cat. d'Ab., 742.

[2] Fringes: L. D., ii. 15 b, 57, 69, 70, etc. There are some preserved in London which are made of plaited reeds.

[3] Cp. R. Hartman in Ä. Z., 1864, p. 25, on the oxen of Egypt; he does not appear however to regard the hornless cattle as a different species.

[4] The list of offerings in Perrot, 667, differentiates between the flesh of the species *neg*, the *'eua* and the *ḥred 'eb'a*.

[5] The long-horned species is called the *'eua* "oxen" in contradistinction to other species. Representations of them are found everywhere; unusually large horns, e.g. L. D., ii. 31; Düm. Res., 9. Coloured pictures: L. D., ii. 19-21, 57, 58, 66.

[6] The *neg* is represented L. D., ii. 14 b (gigantic), 24, 54, 91 c.

though to our uninitiated eyes there is no recognisable difference between the representations of the two varieties.

In the pictures of the Old Empire, animals with short horns[1] are represented more rarely than the long-horned, though the former appear frequently in later times. Whether they were rarer in the earlier period, or whether in their reliefs the Egyptians preferred to represent the long-horned species, because they looked more picturesque and imposing, we cannot decide.

In the Old Empire reliefs there are also representations of animals which apparently remained hornless all through the different stages of their life. These may be regarded as a third species.[2] They seem to have been valued as fancy cattle, for we never find them employed in ploughing or threshing; the peasants liked to deck them out in bright cloths and bring them as a present to their master. At the same time they cannot have been very rare, for on the property of Cha'fra'onch there were said to be 835 long-horned animals, and no less than 220 of the hornless species.

HORNLESS CATTLE UNDER THE OLD EMPIRE (after L. D., ii. 9).

The Egyptians were not content with the different varieties of the original breed, which were due to their skill in breeding; they adopted also an artificial method in order to give the animals a peculiar appearance. They had a method of bending one horn of the bull downwards, and this gave the animal a most fantastic appearance.[3] This result was probably obtained by the same process which is still employed in the east of the Sudan; the horn substance was shaved off as far as the root on the side to which the horn was to bend; as it healed, the horn would bend towards the side intended, and finally the bending was further assisted by hot irons.

The care with which the different breeds are kept apart in the pictures

[1] Short-horned animals: Düm. Res., 9; L. D., ii. 70; in some degree also, 47, 74 c, 104 a. Under the M. E. fighting bulls with quite short horns: L. D., ii. 132.

[2] Hornless, generally called , *ḥred'eb'a* (?), sometimes only designated as *'eua*, L. D., ii. 9 a (with calf); 15 b, 45 d, 50 b, 60, 62, 74 c, 77 (with calf); 80 e, 91 c, 96, 102 a, b, 105. Under the M. E. they are described sometimes as *'eua* (L. D., ii. 128, 129, 132), and sometimes by the signs for the syllables *un* and *du* put together (ib. 129, 131); they frequently occur at this time. A speckled animal of this time, ib. 152 h. That the *ḥred'eb'a* are not a youthful stage of the common species we learn—(1) from the occurrence of calves; and (2) from the occurrence of "young cattle," *ren*, of this species (L. D., ii. 105); (3) from the express differentiation between the *neg* and the *'eua* in the list of offerings: Perrot, 667.

[3] Bent horns—O. E.: L. D., ii. 47, 70, 102 b; Düm. Res., 9. M. E.: L. D., ii. 129. Cp. R. Hartmann in Ä. Z., 1864, p. 26.

shows that, even under the Old Empire, the Egyptians had already emerged from the primitive stage of cattle-breeding. They were no longer content to lead the animals to their pasture and in other respects to leave them to themselves; on the contrary, they watched over every phase of their life. Special bulls were kept for breeding purposes,[1] and the herdsmen understood how to assist the cows when calving.[2] They took care that the food for the cattle was plentiful, though perhaps not quite in the way described in the fairy tale of the New Empire: "His oxen said to him: 'There and there the herbs are good,' and he heard what they said and drove them to the place of good herbs, and the cattle which he kept throve excellently and calved very often."[3] As a matter of fact, they had a much more prosaic method of fattening their cattle, namely, with the dough of bread.[4] Judging from the pictures in the tombs, this

After L. D., ii. 62.

method must have been in common use under the Old Empire. We continually see the herdsmen "beating the dough," and making it into rolls; they then squat down before the ruminating oxen and push the dough from the side into their mouths, admonishing them to "eat then." A good herdsman had also to see after the drink of his cattle; he sets a great earthen vessel before them, patting them in a friendly way to encourage them to drink.[5] He had, of course, to go more sternly to work when he wanted to milk the "mothers of the calves," or as we should say, the milch cows. He had to tie their feet together, or to make one of his comrades hold their front legs firmly; the calves who disturbed his work had also to be tied up to pegs.[6]

In modern Egypt the cows feed in the cultivated clover fields, for

[1] Cows and bulls: L. D., ii. 77, 105.

[2] Calving cows: Düm. Res., 9; and much injured: L. D., ii. 96.

[3] D'Orb., 1, 10.

[4] The fattening of cattle: Düm. Res., 9; L. D., ii. 50 b, 62, 96, 102 b; Br. Gw., 1. Under the M. E.: L. D., ii. 132. This *usha* was also employed in the fattening of antelopes and poultry; the idea that the giving of medicine is represented is scarcely credible. The "beating of the dough": L. D., ii. 66, 77, 96, 105. The twisting of the rolls: Perrot, 33; Bädeker, 405 = Prisse, Hist. de l'Art. Atlas. The dough or the rolls seem to have been boiled.

[5] Drinking: L. D., ii. 62, 96, 105.

[6] L. D., ii. 66, 77, 96, 106 a; Perrot, 39.

there are no longer any meadows with grass growing wild. Under the Old Empire it was quite otherwise; the cattle found their natural pasture in the stretches of marshy land of which we have often spoken in this book. As at the present day in mountainous countries the cows are sent up to the *alps* for the summer, so these ancient herdsmen sent their cattle for a part of each year to the marshes of the north; for though in the Nile valley proper all the land was pretty well brought under cultivation, a good part of the Delta was still wild and uncleared. In the marshy districts the cattle were kept by men who were scarcely regarded by the true Egyptian as his equals. The manner in which the sculptors of the Old Empire designated the , *marshmen*, shows that they considered them rather as pariahs. Such a man might be indispensable as a good herdsman, an excellent fisherman, an expert bird-catcher; he might make good mats and boats from the papyrus reed, his masters might enjoy his dry wit and homely wisdom, but he was all too dirty. He never thought of shaving off his hair cleanly, but contented himself with cutting it short on the forehead; many indeed went so far as to wear a beard, and even whiskers and moustache as well. That his clothing was of a very primitive description did not much matter, as the Egyptians were not very particular in this respect, but it must have looked intensely comical even to them, when the herdsman tried to beautify himself and put on a short skirt like other folk. For his skirt was not of soft white linen, but of stiff yellow matting, which would in no way bend to the right shape, and the artists enjoyed depicting the wonderful folds of the front flap of this skirt over the shepherd's legs. His skirt would take every shape except the right one.[1]

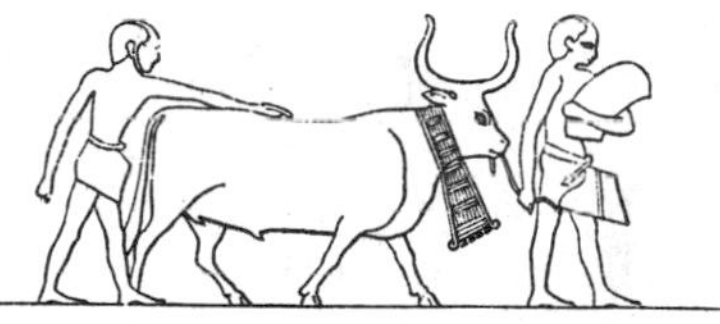

HERDSMAN LEADING AN OX
(after L. D., ii. 69).

These men lived in the marshes with the cows; they had no settled home, for their reed huts could be moved from place to place when needful. The Greek description of them in late times corresponds very nearly with the representations on the monuments of the Old Empire more than two thousand years earlier.[2] In our illustration, for instance, it is evening and the work is at an end; some of the men are squatting round the low

[1] Brugsch has already remarked that the *sochte* are not field labourers but *marshmen*. For the wise sayings of a *sochte* see p. 372. I have identified them with the herdsmen, bird-catchers, fishers, described by Wilkinson (i. 289) as "caricatures." Costume of these men: L. D., ii. 12, 50, 54, 66, 69, 70, 96 (yellow), 105. Hair: Düm. Res., 8, 9; L. D., ii. 45 c, 66, 69, 96; Perrot, 33. Beard: L. D., ii. 69, 96. Under the M. E. (L. D., ii. 127, 131, 132) the herdsmen look like ordinary Egyptians. Each herd of this time is under the "chief of a thousand," and the "superintendent of a thousand" (ib. 132).

[2] Cp. Perrot, 36 (L. D., ii. 66, 77; L. D., ii. 77, gives the continuation of the Perrot picture; in the latter the herdsman who was represented as asleep, has waked up, and his dog is also awake and is looking towards his master).

hearth roasting their geese on wooden spits at the fire; one has not got so far and is only plucking his goose. Others are occupying themselves either with plaiting papyrus reeds or cooking dough for the cattle. Another man is comfortably asleep. He sat down on his mat when he came home and fell asleep there with his shepherd's crook still in his hand; his dog with the long ears and the pointed muzzle has followed his master's

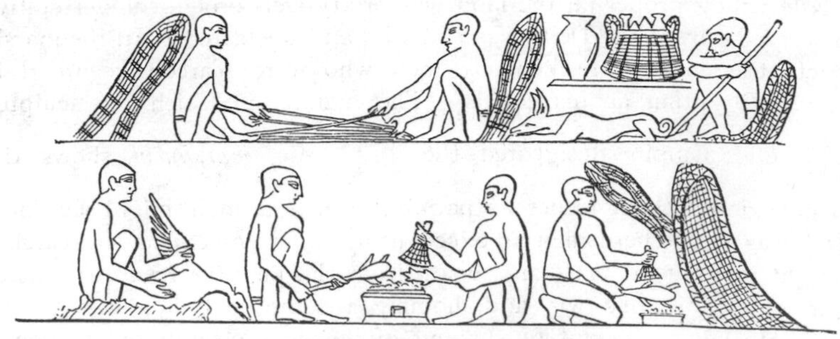

HERDSMEN OUT IN THE COUNTRY.
Relief of the time of the Old Empire at Gizeh (after Perrot-Chipiez).

example and has gone to sleep at his feet. A large jug, a basket with some small vessels, and a few papyrus mats are all the goods required for our herdsman's housekeeping.[1]

The Egyptian herdsmen seem to have had no delight in the romance of this life in the marshes; doubtless they longed for the comforts of their houses at home. It was a joyful day when they "went out of the north country" and drove their cattle "upwards." However troublesome it might be to cross the many branches of the river on their way from the

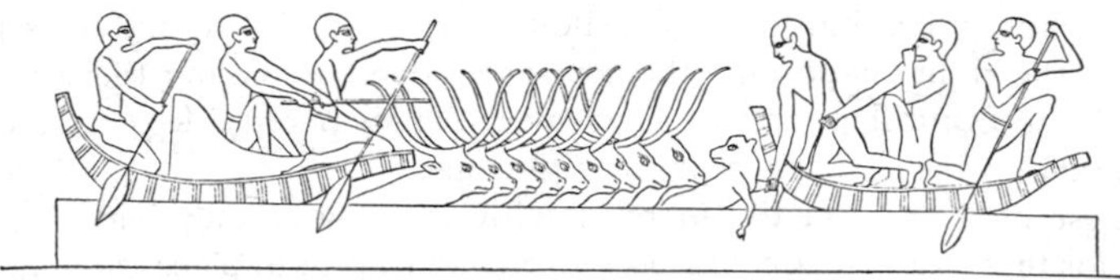

A HERD OF OXEN TAKEN THROUGH THE WATER (Old Empire picture. After L. D., ii. 60).

north country, nothing was a trouble on that day; in spite of all vexations, we are assured by an inscription that "this herdsman is very merry."[2] If the water were shallow enough it was not much trouble to wade through it with the oxen, at most the herdsman had only to carry the little calf through on his back. It was worse when a deeper stream had to be

[1] The object seen, for instance, behind each of the men who are plaiting, is a kind of reed collar which was hung with a fringe round the neck of the oxen; the crook and this collar form the attributes proper to the herdsman. Cp. e.g. the picture of L. D., ii. 132; W., ii. 84, 100, and the hieroglyphic sign [hieroglyph].

[2] Home-coming of the cattle from the north country: L. D., ii. 12, 60, 105; Düm. Res., 9; Perrot, 32-33; Bädeker, 413; Brugsch, Gr. W., 145, 146.

INSPECTION OF THE HERDS OF OXEN BY A HIGH OFFICIAL.

Above, to the left, are the herdsmen, one of whom is kissing the master's foot. Below, to the left, the scribes, together with the boxes of deeds; the foremost has a list in his hand; a young herdsman is talking to him in an animated way, but an official behind him rebukes him with the words: "Run, be off with thee, do not talk before the blessed one; he loathes a talkative man."

crossed. Then, as we see, *nolens volens*, the herd has to swim; a few herdsmen cross first in a boat, and encourage the tired animals by their cries; they drag the calves through the water by their fore-feet. Another boat follows the animals so as to keep the herd together. The herdsmen, however, are powerless to protect them against one serious danger, and if the crocodile that we see lying in the water near the cows has the courage to attack them, it will be scarcely possible to drive him off his prey.

It is doubtful whether, after all, the herdsmen will enjoy the longed-for joys of home, for there a business awaits them from which it is hardly possible to banish vexation. Scarcely have they arrived, and handed over to the master a couple of young gazelles or pretty birds as a present, when important personages appear on the scene—the scribes of the property,—"in order to look at the accounts of the herdsmen." Now follows the reckoning as to how many head of each breed and of each class, arranged according to their age, are forthcoming; of the "first cows of the herd" (*i.e.* of leading cows), of "young cattle," of calves and of their "mothers."[1] The cattle also have to be led before the master;[2] an endless succession of oxen, goats, donkeys, and sheep. The chief scribe then hands to the master a long piece of writing, and explains to him that, according to it, he may call his own no less than 835 long-horned and 220 hornless cattle, 760 donkeys, 974 sheep, and 2234 goats.

We see from this example that the proprietors of the Old Empire not only possessed large herds of oxen, but also sometimes as many as 1300 cows,[3] and also a considerable number of small stock. The ancient Egyptians however, with their great admiration for oxen, never grew weary of representing them again and again, while they rarely give us pictures of sheep,[4] goats,[5] or donkeys.[6] Yet both the buck and the ram are noble animals with beautiful twisted horns,—the latter also had the honour of representing a mighty god. Pictures of pigs are rarely found on the monuments, and had we not learned from one of the chapters of the ancient Book of the Dead that the god Set once assumed the shape of this animal, we might doubt whether they ever existed in Egypt.

In addition to the domestic animals proper, such as oxen, sheep, goats, etc., the herds of the great men in Egypt contained many kinds of wild ruminants. These were taken either by the lasso or the greyhounds in the desert or mountains, and were brought up together with the cattle; thus in all the pictures of the Old Empire we meet with the antelope and the ibex amongst the oxen; the *maud'* also, with its long sword-like

[1] "First bull of the herd": L. D., ii. 61. "Young cattle" (*ren*) of the *'eua:* L. D., ii. 61, 66, 91, 102 b, etc.; of the *ḥred'eb'a:* L. D., ii. 105; of the *neg:* L. D., ii. 91. "Mother-cows"; L. D., ii. 102 a. "Calves": L. D., ii. 31, 66, 77 (sucking), 96, 102, 105; Düm. Res., 9, etc.

[2] The herds brought for inspection: L. D., ii. 9, 31. Under the M. E.: L. D., ii. 131-132. Cp. also pictures, such as: L. D., ii. 91, 102 a, b, etc., though they really refer to the supplies for the worship of the dead.

[3] L. D., ii. 105.

[4] Sheep brought out for inspection before the master: L. D., ii. 9; M. E.: L. D., ii. 132.

[5] Goats brought out for inspection: L. D., ii. 9; Perrot, 37; M. E.: L. D., ii. 132.

[6] Donkeys brought out for inspection: L. D., ii. 9; M. E.: L. D., ii. 132.

horns, the graceful *gaḥs*, and the *nudu*, the *shes*, with its lyre-shaped horns, and the noble ibex, the *n'eafu*.[1] They are always reckoned with the cattle; like the oxen, the animals when full grown are described as "young cattle," they are also tied up to pegs and fattened with dough after the same process as that carried out with oxen.[2] The flesh of a fat antelope must have been considered as particularly good when roasted, for we nearly always find the antelope amongst the sacrificial animals.

The Egyptians provided themselves with birds in the same easy way; the bird-catchers caught the geese in the marshes in their large traps, they were then reared and fattened. The Egyptians, at any rate in the early period, had no tame birds. Why should they take the trouble to breed them when the bird-catcher could get them with so little trouble?[3] An immense number of European birds of passage "inundate Egypt with their cloud-like swarms," and winter every year in the marshes with the numberless indigenous water-birds. For this reason the birds of an ancient Egyptian property present a more brilliant appearance than would be possible were the domestic birds represented alone.[4] We find, in the first place, flocks of geese and ducks of various kinds, each of which bears its own special name. In addition, there are all manner of swans, doves, and cranes; the Egyptians evidently took a special delight in representing the different species of the latter; these birds also seem to be always fighting with each other, thus forming a contrast to the peaceful geese and ducks.

As I have already remarked, the birds were fattened in the same way as the cattle; the fattening bolus was pushed down the throat of the goose in spite of its struggles.[5] This fattening diet was given in addition to the ordinary feeding; we can scarcely believe, for instance (as in fact it is represented), that "the geese and doves hasten to the feeding," on the herdsman clapping his hands, if he had nothing to offer them but those uncomfortable fattening balls of paste. A picture of the time of the Old Empire shows us also that care was taken in "giving drink to the cranes."

The description of cattle-breeding, which I have sketched out above,

[1] Amongst the many examples we may note as remarkable: the *maud'*: L. D., ii. 14, 17, 24, 45, 50, 54, 102 b. the *gaḥs*: L. D., ii. 14, 46, 70, 102 b.; Perrot, 37. the *nudu* (?); L. D., ii. 61 b, 70, 102 b: Düm. Res., 3 (male and female). the *shes*: L. D., ii. 70; Perrot, 37. the *n'eafu*: L. D., ii. 45, 46, 61 b. According to R. Hartmann (Ä. Z., 1864, p. 22 f.; Düm. Res., p. 29) the *maud'* is the oryx leucoryx, the *gaḥs* the antilope dorcas, the *nudu* the addax nasomaculatus, the *shes* the antilope bubalis, the *n'eafu* the ibex nubianus.

[2] Fattening of antelopes: L. D., ii. 102 b. Under the M. E.: L. D., ii. 132.

[3] Pictures such as L. D., ii. 132, show us that geese were snared by the bird-catcher; the flocks of geese are not there reckoned amongst the farm animals, but form part of the picture centring round the bird-catcher.

[4] Good representations of geese of various kinds, etc., with their names attached: L. D., ii. 61 b, 70; Düm. Res., 9; Prisse Hist. de l'Art. Atlas. Doves: Düm. Res., 3; L. D., ii. 70. Cranes: L. D., ii. 17 b, 50 b, 70; Prisse, Hist. de l'Art. Atlas.

[5] The fattening of geese is represented in the tomb of T'y. Cp. Prisse, Hist. de l'Art. Atlas, and Bädeker, pp. 404, 405. The inscriptions appertaining thereto are given fully in Brugsch, Gr. W., 4-9, 11-14, 17-21, as well as those relating to the supplies of food and drink. It is not clear, however, to what the words "four times a day I feed" (ib. 15) refer. Of the time of the M. E.: L. D., ii. 132.

INSPECTION OF THE FLOCKS OF GEESE AND OF THEIR HERDSMEN BY A HIGH OFFICIAL.

Below on the left is the scribe who is presenting the list. Behind him the herdsmen, who press forward wishing to speak. They are desired to be quiet by two overseers: "Sit still and do not speak!" says one, whilst the other calls out to the man with the basket: "Do not hasten so with thy feet, thou with the geese! . . . Dost thou not know of any other time for thy discourse?" Above, the remains of a similar representation may be seen.

(Theban tomb-picture of the time of the New Empire in the British Museum.)

is founded on the reliefs of the Old and the Middle Empire, where this theme is treated with evident predilection. What we know of the subject of later date is comparatively little;[1] other matters seem to have been more interesting to the great men of the New Empire. Cattle-breeding seems however to have forfeited none of its old importance in the country, for we still hear of enormous numbers of cattle. The Egyptian temples alone, during the space of thirty-one years, are said to have received 514,968 head of cattle and 680,714 geese; this denotes, as far as I can judge, that live-stock were kept in far greater numbers than at the present day.

In addition to the principal breed of cows, viz. the old long-horned race which still exists in the Nile valley,[2] there appears to have been another variety, represented in the accompanying illustration, which seems to have come to the fore for a time under the New Empire. These animals, as we see, have rather short horns which grow widely apart, and have lost their old lyre shape; in some instances the hump is strongly developed, and the colour of the skin is often speckled.[3] It may be that this species originated from foreign parts, for when Egypt ruled over Nubia, and for a time over Syria also, oxen were often brought into the Nile valley either as tribute or as spoil from these countries. Thus the Theban Amon received from Thothmes III. a milch-cow from Palestine, and three cows from Nubia;[4] and under Ramses III., amongst the charges on his Syrian property, there were included seventeen oxen.[5] Bulls from the land of Cheta and cows from 'Ersa[6] were valued especially highly, as well as bullocks "from the West" and certain calves "from the South."[7] There is one representation of Nubian cattle, and amongst them two remarkable short-horned animals which, according to the barbarian custom, are drawing the carriage of an Ethiopian princess.[8]

HERD OF PIGS IN A THEBAN TOMB OF THE TIME OF THE NEW EMPIRE (after W., ii. 100).

Whether the breeds of any of the other domestic animals were different under the New Empire we cannot tell, on account of the scanty material at our command; it is interesting however to meet with a drove of pigs (see the accompanying illustration). Probably from religious reasons, this animal was never represented by the artists of the Old Empire. Concerning the introduction of the horse and

[1] There is, of course, much still existing at Thebes that has not been published, but at the same time pictures of farming operations of later date are always rare.

[2] Representation of long-horned cows under the N. E.: L. D., iii. 10 a; W., ii. 84. We find no examples of hornless cattle in the pictures of the N. E.

[3] W., i. 370; ii. 446.

[4] L. D., iii. 30 b, 8.

[5] Cp. p. 303.

[6] An., 4, 17, 9.

[7] An., 4, 15, 5.

[8] L. D., iii. 117. In addition, long-horned cattle and a gigantic animal with horns wide apart; the ornament with which the latter is adorned is also used by the Egyptians for their oxen, cp. ib. 94.

mule, which took place during the period between the Middle and the New Empire, I shall have to speak in the 19th chapter.

We know little of the details of cattle-breeding under the New Empire, of how the herds of Upper and Lower Egypt, with the oxen, geese, and small stock, were increased by the hundred thousand.[1] The "herdsmen take care of them and carry herbs to the oxen,"[2] they are

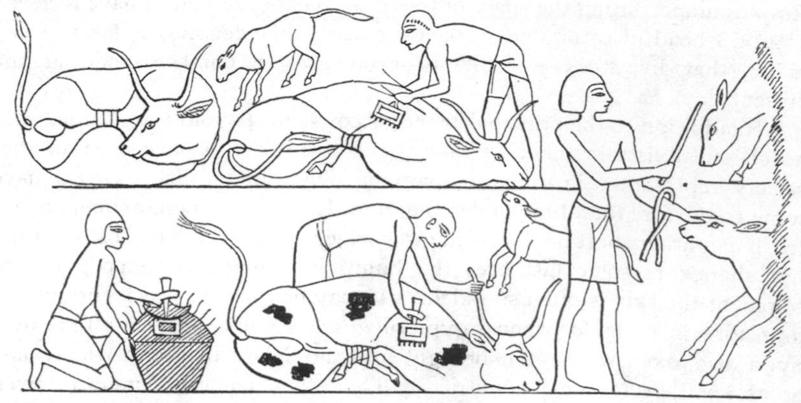

THE BRANDING OF CATTLE (after W., ii. 84).

still fattened according to ancient custom,[3] and they are branded with the stamp of the department to which they belong.[4] The *'ehay*,[5] which is often mentioned at this time as the place where the cattle were kept at night, must have been an open fold; and, in fact, a picture at Tell el Amarna shows us the oxen lying in an open yard.[6]

As regards the rearing and feeding of the domesticated water-birds, if we can rely upon the *argumentum ex silentio*, the Egyptians seem to have confined their attention to geese alone; the goose in fact held the first place amongst the farm birds, in the same way as the ox did amongst the cattle. In the texts of this period geese are frequently mentioned, and in the beautiful picture shown in the plate we have just given, we see exactly how the lists of these birds, which were very valuable for food, were brought to the proprietor. The goose was not always kept for such a material purpose, and those who are fortunate enough to come across the tomb of a certain Bek'e belonging to the beginning of the New Empire, in the necropolis of Dra-abul-nega at Thebes, may there observe that the wife of this man, instead of a pet dog or little monkey to play with, preferred a big goose.[7]

[1] Harr., i. 7, 9. In this passage the officials of the herds of Amon are called (1) the superintendent of the oxen; (2) the scribe; (3) ; (4) .

[2] Ib. [3] W., i. 370. [4] Cp. with the above illustration W., ii. 84.

[5] D'Orb., 1, 7; An., 4, 3, 11; An., 4, 13, 4 for oxen; An., 3, 6, 5 for horses. The same word is used for the camp of the army.

[6] W., i. 370, a court, at the back of which are thirteen small rooms.

[7] From my own notes; the inhabitant of the tomb bears no title.

I cannot close this description of Egyptian husbandry without referring to one curious circumstance. Everything tends to show that the Egyptians themselves felt that agriculture, together with cattle-breeding, was the most important industry for the country. Nevertheless, the prestige of this idea had no influence upon the position of the agricultural labourer, who was always looked down upon as a poor hard-worked creature. The following sad sketch of the lot of the harvestmen was written by the compiler of a didactic letter, of which many copies are extant, and implies not only a personal opinion but the general view of this matter:[1] "The worm has taken the half of the food, the hippopotamus the other half; there were many mice in the fields, the locusts have come down, and the cattle have eaten, and the sparrows have stolen. Poor miserable agriculturist! What was left on the threshing-floor thieves made away with. . . . Then the scribe lands on the bank to receive the harvest, his followers carry sticks and the negroes carry palm rods. They say, 'Give up the corn'—there is none there. Then they beat him as he lies stretched out and bound on the ground, they throw him into the canal and he sinks down, head under water. His wife is bound before his eyes and his children are put in fetters. His neighbours run away to escape and to save their corn." This is, of course, an exaggerated picture, which is purposely overdrawn by the writer, in order to emphasise the striking contrast that he draws in his eulogy of the profession of scribe; in its main features however it gives us a very true idea, for the lot of the ancient peasant very much resembled that of the modern fellah. The latter labours and toils without enjoying the results of his own work. He earns a scanty subsistence, and, notwithstanding all his industry, he gains no great renown amongst his countrymen of the towns; the best they can say of him is, that he is worthy to be compared with his own cattle.[2]

[1] An., 5, 15, 6 ff. = Sall. 1, 5, 11 ff. The text of both is in great confusion.

[2] This applies to the state of Egypt a few years ago, before the abolition of the corvée.

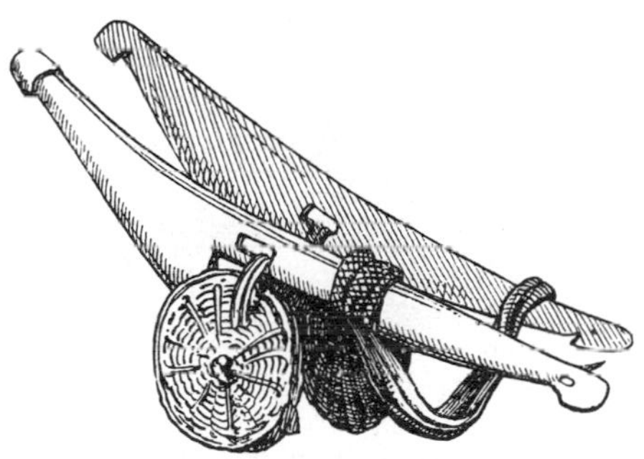

YOKE FOR OXEN (after W., ii. 392).

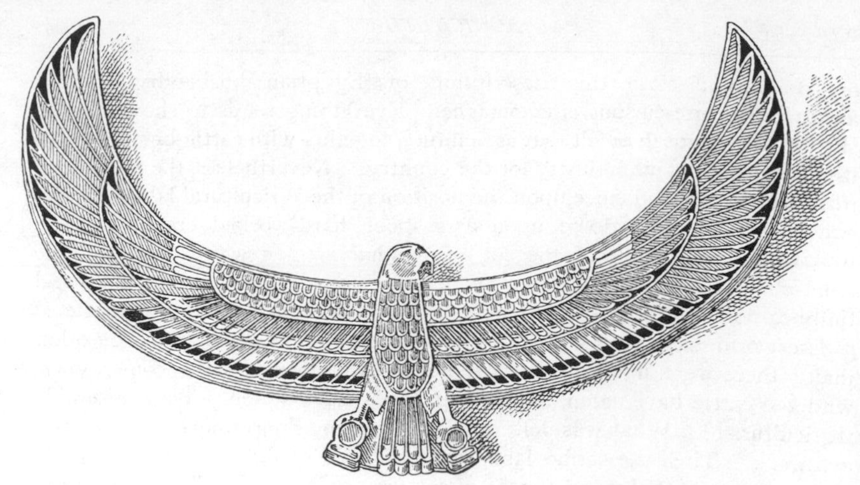

GOLDEN HAWK WITH ENAMELLED WINGS (Louvre. After Perrot-Chipiez).

CHAPTER XVIII

ARTS AND CRAFTS

THE low esteem in which the Egyptians held their agriculturists extended also to their craftsmen. According to the learned opinion of the scribes, the latter were also poor creatures who led an inglorious existence, half pitiable and half ridiculous. Thus a poet of the Middle Empire speaks, for example, of the metal-worker :—

"I have never seen the smith as an ambassador,
Or the goldsmith carry tidings ;
Yet I have seen the smith at his work
At the mouth of his furnace,
His fingers were like crocodile (hide),
He stank more than the roe of fish."[1]

The same scribe also thus describes the work of a wood-carver :—

"Each artist who works with the chisel
Tires himself more than he who hoes (a field).
The wood is his field, of metal are his tools.
In the night—is he free ?
He works more than his arms are able,
In the night—he lights a light."[2]

Fortunately we are not dependent on these gloomy sources to form

[1] Sall., 2, 4, 6 ff. [2] Sall., 2, 4, 8 ff. The translation of the fourth line is very uncertain.

our opinion of Egyptian handicrafts, for the work of the metal-workers and wood-carvers which still exists shows that these industries reached a very high standard in Egypt, a comparatively far higher one in point of fact than either learning or literature. The workmen who created those marvels of gold and ivory, of porcelain and wood, the finish of which we admire to this day, cannot have been such wretched creatures as they were considered by the proud learned professors.

The direction followed by the mechanical arts of a country is essentially determined by the materials found in that country. It was of the greatest consequence for Egyptian industrial arts that one of the most useful plants the world has ever known grew in every marsh. The papyrus reed was used as a universal material by the Egyptians, like the bamboo or the coco-nut palm by other nations; it was the more useful as it formed a substitute for wood, which was never plentiful. The reeds were pulled up by the stalks in the marshes,[1] by labourers who worked nude and who afterwards brought them to the workshops tied up in bundles. From the papyrus, boats were manufactured,[2] mats were plaited, rope was twisted, sandals were prepared;[3] but above all the papyrus supplied the material for paper. For the latter purpose the stem was cut into thin strips of the length required, and a second layer of similar strips was then placed crosswise over these; the leaves thus formed were then pressed,[4] dried, and, if a larger piece were required, pasted together. Numberless papyri, of which some are as old as the Middle Empire, testify to the perfection attained in this manufacture, even at an early date;[5] and it is well known to what an extent it was carried on in Graeco-Roman times, when it formed one of the chief articles of export. During the periods with which we are occupied, papyrus paper can never have been very cheap, for in the first place the Egyptians often made use of each roll several times by washing off the former writing, and secondly, for rough drafts or unimportant matters they made out with a cheaper writing material such as potsherds or pieces of limestone.

As I have already mentioned, the papyrus served for the preparation of rough mats and ropes, though for this purpose they also possessed another excellent material in palm bast. In the plaiting of these mats, which were indispensable to spread over the mud floors of Egyptian houses, they were evidently very skilful; this is shown by the stripes of rich ornamentation found particularly on the ceilings of the tombs, which doubtless originally represented a covering of matting.[6] The examples

[1] Papyrus harvest: O. E., L. D., ii. 106 a. Düm. Res., 8.

[2] Cp. pp. 479, 480.

[3] Cp. pp. 227, 228.

[4] Or rather made smooth by beating and pressing: hence the soldier who has to endure much beating is compared with a book, An., 4, 9, 7.

[5] The papyrus rolls still existing are of very different kinds; a comprehensive examination of them is still needed.

[6] The weaving of a carpet shows the same principle: Ros. M. C., 41, 5 (=W., ii. 170, N. E.). On the use of matting, cp. pp. 186, 187. Their style and their universal formation in rectangular stripes show, irrespective of Perrot, Pl. 14, that the well-known ornamentation in the tombs is derived from the patterns of carpeting.

already shown (pp. 79, 162, 397, 479) will give an idea of the kind of work referred to here. Bright colours were always employed;[1] the same style and colouring may also be seen in the pretty baskets brought to our museums from the Theban tombs; these are plaited in patterns of various coloured fibres.[2]

This fondness for coloured patterns was nevertheless confined to the weaving of the coarser materials; colour and pattern were almost excluded from the finer stuffs manufactured for clothing.[3] In the latter materials they lavished all their skill in the one endeavour to prepare the finest and whitest linen that was possible, and they certainly brought their linen to great perfection; I need only remind my readers of the white garments worn by men of rank, which were so fine that their limbs could be seen

TO THE RIGHT THE SPINNING AND UNRAVELLING OF THE FLAX, TO THE LEFT THE WEAVING. THE OLD FAT MAN STANDING BY THE LOOM IS THE OVERSEER OF THIS WORK (Beni Hasan. After L. D., ii. 126).

gleaming through them. Some of this very fine linen that we possess is almost comparable to our silken materials for smoothness and softness;[4] the manufacture at all periods of the stronger and coarser linens was also often most excellent. The Egyptians were conscious themselves that they excelled in weaving, for many inscriptions extol the garments of the gods and the bandages for the dead. The preparation of clothes was considered as a rule to be woman's work, for truly the great goddesses Isis and Nephthys had spun, woven, and bleached clothes for their brother and husband Osiris.[5] Under the Old Empire this work fell to the household slaves, in later times to the wives of the peasant serfs belonging to the great departments.[6] In both cases it was the *house of silver* to which the finished work had to be delivered, and a picture of the time of

[1] Cp. the coloured representations: L. D., i. 41; W., i. Pl. 8; Ros. M. C., 71; Prisse, 28.

[2] Baskets of this kind, e.g. Berlin Museum, 9631. The patterns very nearly resemble those of the modern Nubian baskets.

[3] Exceptions, cp. p. 217.

[4] Cp. e.g. the bandages of King Pepy and King Merenrê' of the 6th dynasty in the Berlin Museum, also the transparent overdress of the time of the New Empire in the same museum, No. 741.

[5] Brugsch, Wb. Suppl., 637.

[6] Cp. p. 111.

the Old Empire[1] shows us the treasury officials packing the linen in low wooden boxes, which are long enough for the pieces not to be folded. Each box contains but one sort of woven material, and is provided below with poles on which it is carried by two masters of the treasury into the *house of silver*. In other cases we find, as Herodotos wonderingly describes, men working at the loom; and indeed on the funerary stelae of the 20th dynasty at Abydos, we twice meet with men who call themselves weavers and follow this calling as their profession.[2]

The operation of weaving was a very simple one under the Middle Empire. The warp of the texture was stretched horizontally between the two beams, which were fastened to pegs on the floor, so that the weaver had to squat on the ground. Two bars pushed in between the threads of the warp served to keep them apart; the woof-thread was passed through and pressed down firmly by means of a bent piece of wood.[3] A picture of the time of the New Empire[4] however gives an upright loom with a perpendicular frame. The lower beam appears to be fastened, but the upper one hangs only by a loop, in order to facilitate the stretching of the warp. We also see little rods which are used to separate the threads of the warp; one of these certainly serves for a shuttle. A larger rod that runs through loops along the side beams of the frame appears to serve to fix the woof-thread, like the reed of our looms.

UPRIGHT LOOM OF THE NEW EMPIRE (after W., ii. 171).

As this industry in Egypt consisted entirely in the weaving of linen, the culture and preparation of flax were of considerable importance. It is again from pictures of the time of the Middle Empire that we learn the mode of its preparation.[5] The flax stalks were first *boiled* in a large curiously-shaped vessel—a process which evidently, like our *roasting*, was intended to loosen their outer covering; they were then beaten (as at the present day) with hammers, till the outside was loosed and destroyed. The flax thus obtained was still mixed with bits of the outside and with

[1] L. D., ii. 96. [2] Their wives are singers of Osiris, Mar. Cat. d'Ab., 1175, 1187.

[3] Weaving: L. D., ii. 126 (=W., i. 317=Ros. M. C., 41, 6=Champ. Mon., 381 bis); Ros., 41, 4 (=W., ii. 170). Erroneously given as originating from Gurnah, ib. 41, 5, repeated in more correct drawing. Setting up the loom: Ros. M. C., 41, 3, 42, 4, 5. According to Ros. M. C., text ii. 25, Rosellini had seen ten representations of weaving.

[4] W., ii. 171, in spite of the explanation given, ib. p. ix, obscure in many respects.

[5] Boiling and beating: Ros. M. C., 41, 1. Unravelling (Egypt. *msn*): L. D., ii. 126 (=W., i. 317), and Ros. M. C., 41, 2, 3. Spinning: L. D., ii. 126; W., i. 317; Ros. M. C., 41, 2, 4.

other impurities, and had to be separated from this rubbish before it could be used. In later times it was cleaned with a comb much after the modern method;[1] we do not find this process represented however in the old pictures; according to them the flax seems to have been cleaned by hand,—the good fibres were carefully picked out and laid together to form a loose thread. This thread was then moistened, and twisted together more firmly by means of the spindle. Close by on the ground stood the pot in which lay the rough threads; and the person spinning allowed the thread to run over his raised hand or over a fork. In the tombs of the Middle Empire we find wonderful feats performed in the way of spinning,—we see women managing two spindles at the same time and even twisting each of the two threads from two different sorts of flax. To do this they are obliged to balance themselves on a stool, and to take off every unnecessary article of clothing for fear the two spindles and the threads should get entangled.

The working up of the threads into rope is shown by two pictures, which, though belonging to different epochs, yet represent essentially the same procedure. A workman seated on the floor keeps the threads in the right position with his hand, while the rope-maker walks backwards, twisting them together. For this purpose he apparently uses a reed, through which he lets the threads run, and to which he gives a rotating movement; a weight hanging on the reed, and swinging with it, increases its power of rotation.[2] We see by a picture of the time of the Middle Empire[3] that, in making nets also, balls are tied on to the ends of the threads; these would naturally give them a quicker and more vigorous twist.

Ancient Egypt was exceedingly rich in skins, the result of the stock-breeding so extensively carried on in that country. The inhabitants were well aware of their value; they considered the skin indeed to be such an important part of the animal, that in their writing the sign of a skin indicated all mammiferous animals. Beautiful skins, especially such as were gaily spotted, were never denuded of the hair, but were manufactured into shields, quivers, and clothing (see p. 205), or were employed in the houses as coverings for seats. The "skins of the panther of the south" were valued very highly; they were brought from the upper Nile and from the incense countries.

Less valuable skins, such as those of oxen, gazelles, etc., were manufactured into leather; the leathern objects which have been found in the tombs prove to what a degree of excellence this industry attained, especially under the New Empire. Of this period our museums possess examples of every kind of leather,—coarse leather and fine leather, the former manufactured into sandals, the latter into aprons and straps; white leather made into a kind of parchment and used like the papyrus for writing

[1] Flax-combs: Berlin, 6810, 6812.

[2] O. E.: Düm. Res. 8. N. E.: Ros. M. C., 65 (=W., ii. 178), from Thebes. In the first case the weight is certainly there, though the reed seems to be absent.

[3] Ros. M. C., 41, 4 (=41, 5=W., ii. 170).

material; also fine coloured leather stamped with an ornamental pattern which was used for the ends of linen bands. Though, as far as I know, we possess no leathern articles of the older period, yet we see by the brightly-coloured patterns on the belts of the statues, that the workmen of the Old Empire understood their craft as well as those of later date. We do not know what process the Egyptians used in the dressing of skins, though pictures of all periods represent men working at the leather trade.[1] We first see how they soften the leather in great vessels, how they then beat it smooth with a stone, and finally stretch and pull it with their hands over a three-legged wooden frame until it has attained the necessary suppleness. The shoemaker now takes the prepared leather, and puts it on his sloping work-table, and cuts it into soles or straps: for this purpose he uses the same kind of knife with the curved blade and short handle which is in use at the present day. The necessary holes are then bored with an awl, and the straps are drawn through. The workman was accustomed to do this with his teeth. After being fastened with knots, the simplest form of sandal was complete. We possess small monuments erected by shoemakers of the time of the New Empire, which prove to us that these tradesmen held a certain social position. The most remarkable of these is the small statue[2] of a "chief of the shoemakers," representing this gallant kneeling, dressed in the *shend'ot* which, under the New Empire, the higher craftsmen had a right to wear.[3] The learned poet of old certainly overdrew his picture when he thus wrote of the shoemaker: "He is very wretched, he is always begging, and (alluding evidently to the custom of drawing the straps through with the teeth) what he bites is (only) leather."[4]

In various places I have alluded to the fact that the ancient Egyptians suffered from the lack of good wood in the same way as their modern compatriots. It is quite possible that the land was rather better timbered in old times, but the wood produced was always of a very unserviceable nature. Sycamore wood can certainly be cut into great blocks and strong planks; but it is so knotty and yellow that it is quite unsuitable for fine work. The date and dôm palm trees only supply long, and as a rule, crooked boards; short pieces of hard wood can be obtained from the tamarisk bushes on the edge of the desert, but the acacia, which furnished a serviceable material for ships, doors, furniture, etc., appears, even in early times, to have been almost extinct in Egypt proper.

We are not surprised therefore that the Egyptians began at a very ancient date to look about in foreign countries for better wood. Thus

[1] Leather-working—O. E.: (*a*) L. D., ii. 49 b. M. E.: (*b*) Ros. M. C., 64, 5. N. E.: (*c*) Ros. M. C., 64, 1-3 (=W., ii. 188); (*d*) Ros. M. C., 64, 4; (*e*) Ros. M. C., 65, 11; (*f*) W. ii. 187; (*g*) Ros. M. C., 44 (=W., i. 232). In the same places—manufacture of skins into shields: c, 2. Softening: e, c, 2. Beating: a, b, c, 3, d. Stretching: a, b, c, 1, d, g. Work-table: c, 1-3, d, g. Leather work for a carriage: g.

[2] Berlin Museum, 9571, from Thebes. See also Mar. Cat. d'Ab., 1174. Ib. 1080 a "royal shoemaker" belonging to a family of rank, if otherwise the reading is correct.

[3] See p. 210.

[4] Sall., 2, 8, 1=An., 7, 3, 4.

the Berlin Museum possesses three great wooden coffins,[1] belonging to the unknown period between the Old and the Middle Empire; they are made of a kind of strong pine-wood which must have been brought to Memphis from the Syrian mountains. This foreign wood must always

WOODCUTTERS (tomb of Sawijet el meitin. After L. D., ii. 108).

have been expensive, for native wood was often employed even for ornamental furniture, and was painted light yellow with red veins so as to give the appearance of the costly foreign material.[2] The native wood was never considered beautiful, and, like limestone and granite, it was almost always covered up with a layer of stucco and brightly painted; the variegated granite alone was allowed to show its natural colour.

PREPARATION OF COFFINS AND OF THE NECESSARIES FOR THE TOMB UNDER THE NEW EMPIRE (after W., iii. Pl. lxxii.). The coffins appear to be made partly of the so-called cartonage, for which purpose the workman below to the left is bringing strips of linen. The coffin below on the right is being polished and painted (?), a workman is boring a hole in the wooden footboard. Above on the left a plank is being sawn, and a leg of a stool cut with an adze. Behind lies the food for the men, close to which a tired-out workman has seated himself.

When agricultural work recommenced after the inundation, the carpenters sallied forth, simultaneously with the ploughmen, to replenish their store of wood.[3] As at the present day, flocks of goats went out with them into the fields, to eat the foliage of the trees that were felled. Thus we see that where the axes of the woodcutters have felled

[1] No. 7796. [2] E.g. the beautiful funerary couch of 'Ety at Gizeh, of the 11th dynasty.

[3] Cp. the pictures of the N. E., W., ii. 394; Perrot, 704. Thus in the modern popular calendar of Egypt the "Beginning of seedtime," is placed on the 5th of Babe; the "Felling of trees" on the 10th of Babe. Cp. Lortet, Calendrier Copte, Lyon, 1851 (from the writings of the academy there).

a sycamore or a palm,[1] goats are always represented browsing on the young leaves of the tree. They have however to pay dearly for this good food; this is a feast day with the woodcutters, and they are allowed to kill a kid. The little creature is hung up on the boughs upon which it had just been feeding, and one of the woodmen cuts it up, whilst his companion boils the water to cook the food they long for so greedily. The meal over, there is still much hard work to be done, the trunk has to be rough-hewn, and afterwards, with a good deal of trouble, carried home hanging on a pole.[2]

The tools used by the carpenters and joiners were of a comparatively simple nature; evidently it is not due to the tools that the work was often carried to such perfection. The metal part of all tools was of bronze, and in the case of chisels and saws was let into the handle, whilst with axes and bill-hooks it sufficed to bind the metal part to the handle with leather straps. For rough-hewing the Egyptians used an axe, the blade of which was about the size of a hand, and was bent forwards in a semicircular form.[3] Subsequent work was carried on with a tool that, from its constant employment, might almost be called the universal tool of Egypt. This is the adze of our carpenters, a sort of small bill-hook, the wooden part of which was in the form of a pointed angle with unequal shanks; the bronze blade was bound to the short shank and the longer served as a handle.[4] To work in the details more perfectly a small chisel was used with a wooden mallet to strike it.[5] A large spatulate instrument served as a plane, with the broad blade of which the workman smoothed off the small inequalities of the wood;[6] lastly, a fine polish was attained by continual rubbing with a smooth stone.[7] The saw, like our hand-saws, had but one handle, and it was most tedious work to cut the trunk of a thick sycamore into planks with this awkward instrument. As a rule, the wood that had to be sawn was placed perpendicularly and fastened to a post that was stuck into the ground, the part of the wood that was already sawn was tied up, so that its gaping asunder might not interfere with the work. In very early times a stick on which a weight was hung was stuck obliquely through these fastenings; this was evidently intended to keep them at the right tension, and to prevent them from slipping down.[8] For boring, a drill was employed of the shape customary in Egypt even now; the female screw in which it moved was a hollow nut from the dôm palm.[9]

[1] O. E., felling of sycamores: L. D., ii. 108 (=Ros. M. C., 28, 3-4), ib. 111. Relief in the tomb of T'y. M. E., felling of palms: L. D., ii. 126 (=Ros. M. C., 43, 1). The popularity of this scene is shown by the fact that the tree with the goats was used as a favourite motive for ornamentation in Egyptian industrial arts.

[2] E.g. Ros. M. C., 47.

[3] O. E.: Bädeker, 408; L. D., ii. 108. M. E.: L. D., ii. 126. N. E.: Perrot, 842.

[4] O. E.: L. D., ii. 49, 61, 108; Bädeker, 408, 409. M. E.: L. D., ii. 126. N. E.: Perrot, 81, 759, 842; W., i. 227, 231.

[5] O. E.: L. D., ii. 49, 108; Bädeker, 408, 409.

[6] O. E.: L. D., ii. 61. Also the instrument, W., i. 306, belongs to this class.

[7] O. E.: L. D., ii. 49; Bädeker, 409; W., i. 306. N. E.: W., ii. 178; W., iii. Pl. lxxii.

[8] O. E.: L. D., ii. 49, 108; Bädeker, 408, 409. M. E.: L. D., ii. 126. N. E.: Perrot, 842; W., iii. lxxii.

[9] O. E.: Bädeker, 409. N. E.: W., ii. 178; W., iii. lxxii. in which the hand is reversed.

By a happy chance originals of nearly all these tools, which I have enumerated from tomb-pictures, have been preserved to us. A basket was found, probably in one of the Theban temples, containing the tools employed by King Thothmes III., "when he stretched the rope over

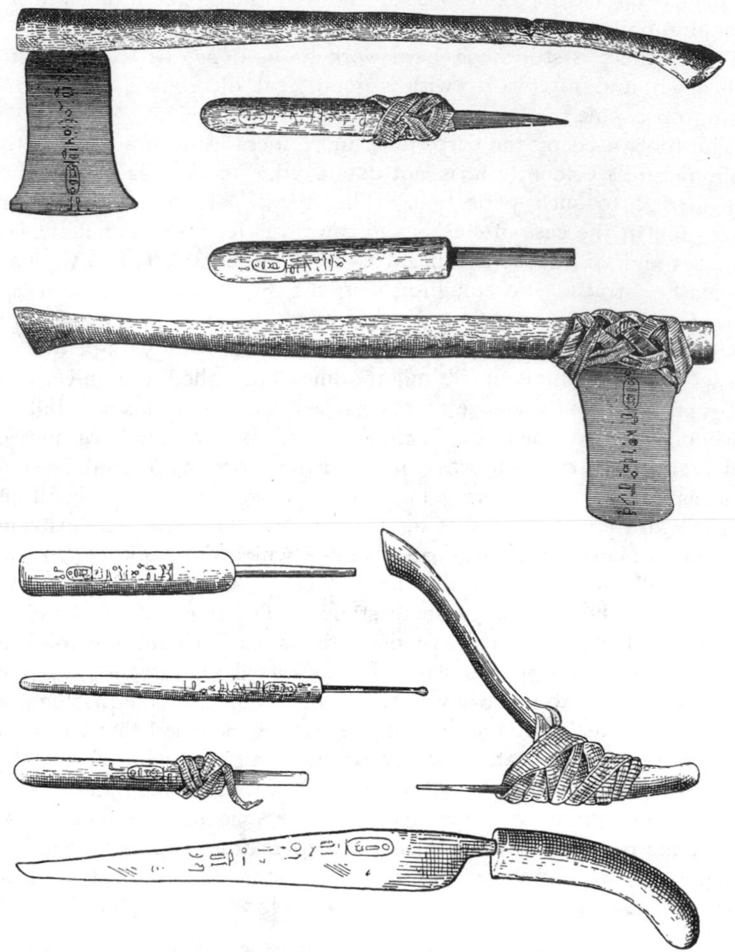

EXAMPLES OF THE TOOLS USED BY THOTHMES III.: 2 AXES, 5 CHISELS, AN ADZE, AND A SAW. (From the collections at Leyden and at Alnwick Castle.)

'Amon glorious in the horizon,'" *i.e.* when he accomplished the foundation ceremonies for the temple of this name.[1] We see that they are tools specially prepared for this ceremony, for they are not suitable for hard work; they give us however a variety of model specimens, from which we can form a very good idea of the simpler tools used by the Egyptian workman.

[1] They are now at Leyden, London, Alnwick Castle, and at Gizeh.

It is impossible here to give full details of the excellent work the Egyptian carpenters and cabinetmakers turned out, in the preparation of the boats and carriages, the portions of houses and furniture, the weapons, coffins, and other necessaries for the funerary equipment of the deceased.[1] We shall only indicate here a few of the peculiarities of Egyptian workmanship, peculiarities principally due to the poor character of their materials. If we confine ourselves to the consideration of native wood, we find a complete lack of planks of any great length; the curious art was therefore devised of putting together small planks to form one large one. In boat-making, where fine workmanship was not required, the little boards were fastened the one over the other like the tiles of a roof; this process, which is unmistakably represented in a picture of the Middle Empire,[2] was still in common practice in Egypt in the time of Herodotos, though, like other old Egyptian customs, it is now confined to the Upper Nile. In the case of coffins and furniture however, where it was desirable to conceal the joining of the boards, the wood was cut so that the edges should exactly fit together; the adjoining surfaces were then fastened together with little wooden pegs; afterwards the joint was completely hidden by painting. In the same way the Egyptian workmen understood how to make good the holes and bad places in the wood. Wooden pins were commonly used as the method of fastening, and during the periods with which we are occupied, glue was employed but rarely.[3] In the older period they seem to have joined pieces of wood at right angles to each other by the simple mitre joint; as far as I know, the so-called dovetailed work came in comparatively speaking much later.[4]

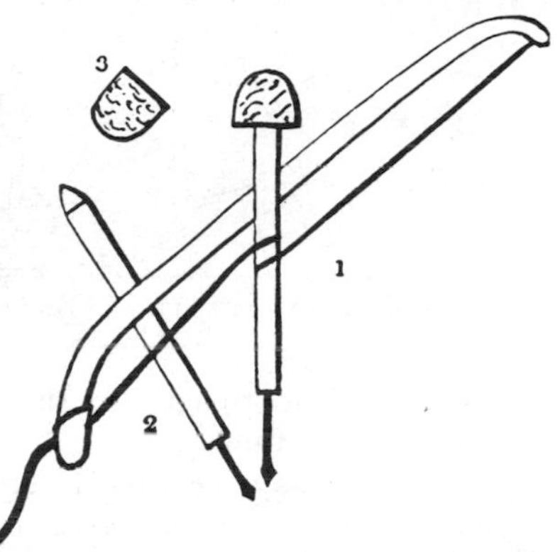

A DRILL WITH ITS BOW AND ITS DIFFERENT PARTS (2, the drill; 3, the mother). (After W., i. 400.)

The following was the method by which they gave the planks of a boat the right curve: when the boat was ready in the rough, the boat-builder of the Old Empire drove a post with a fork at the top into the middle of the bottom. Strong ropes were then fastened to the stern and the bow of the boat, and drawn over the fork; the workmen next stuck poles

[1] Boat-making—O. E.: L. D., ii. 61, 108; Bädeker, 408, 409. M. E.: L. D., ii. 126 (Ros. M. C., 44). Carriage-making—N. E.: W., i. 227, 231, 232. Making of doors and bolts—O. E.: L. D., ii. 49; Bädeker, 408. N. E.: L. D., iii. 26. Furniture-making—O. E.: L. D., ii. 49; Bädeker, 409. M. E.: L. D., ii. 126. N. E.: Perrot, 81, 759, 842; W., ii. 178. Weapon-making—O. E.: L. D., ii. 108. Coffin-making—N. E.: W., iii. lxxii.

[2] L. D., ii. 126. Ros. M. C., 44.

[3] W., ii. 198, gives a wooden box joined together by glue. The picture, W., ii. 199, may possibly represent gluing.

[4] The Berlin coffins of the time of the Middle Empire exhibit excellent ancient specimens of these various styles of workmanship.

through these ropes and then twisted them round till the boards of the boat had been curved into the necessary shape.[1] The men had of course

BENDING A BOAT INTO A CURVE; OTHER WORKMEN ARE TRIMMING IT AND BORING (?) IT.
(Tomb at Sawijet el Meitin. After L. D., ii. 108.)

to exert all their strength, so that the rope should not untwist, and all their work be in vain.

I have already mentioned that wooden furniture, etc., was generally painted; there were other styles of decoration also in use, appropriate to the character of the material in question. Thin pieces of wood, such as were joined together for light seats or were used for weapons, were left with their bark on; they were also sometimes surrounded with thin strips of barks of other colours—a system of ornamentation which has still a very pleasing effect from the shining dark colours of the various barks.[2] A second method was more artistic; a pattern was cut deeply into the wood and then inlaid with wood of another colour, with ivory, or with some coloured substance. The Egyptians were especially fond of inlaying "ebony with ivory." This inlaid work is mentioned as early as the Middle Empire, and examples belonging to that period also exist.[3] In smaller objects of brown wood, on the other hand, they filled up the carving with a dark green paste.[4]

I cannot quit this subject without mentioning a curious technique, by which they tried to create a substitute for rare wood. This substitute consists of the so-called Egyptian cartonage, which was chiefly employed for coffins carved in human form. During the periods of which we are treating it consisted of pieces of linen firmly stuck together with a sort of paste, and then covered with stucco; the pieces of cartonage, which often possess a considerable strength, were probably pressed when wet into the desired shape. I cannot say whether the real papier-maché, so common in the Greek period, was also manufactured in the earlier ages; this was prepared from old papyri in the same way as ours is from old paper.

We will now turn to the art of the potter: in contradistinction to that of the carpenter, this art was particularly favoured in Egypt by the wealth of the raw material at command. In all parts of Egypt good clay was to be found for ceramic ware, and it is not due to chance that this

[1] L. D., ii. 108.

[2] Weapons and sceptres in this style—Gizeh, 4611, 4725; Berlin, 4724. Seats made of bits of wood with their bark on, but without pieces twisted round: Gizeh.

[3] M. E.: Stele C. 14, in the Louvre. N. E.: L. D., iii. 64 a.

[4] Numberless examples exist, especially in the Louvre.

industry has even now the strength to resist the suffocating influence of the mechanical art of Europe. The obstinacy with which a nation clings to the forms of its pots and bowls is most remarkable ; nothing in Egypt is so difficult to date as pottery, for potsherds which are centuries apart in point of date, have almost identical characteristics. The modern grey ware of Keneh or the red ware of Siut might almost be mistaken for pottery of the New Empire.

Various pictures of the time of the Old and the Middle Empire show us the potter at work. It was only the simplest vessels that were formed

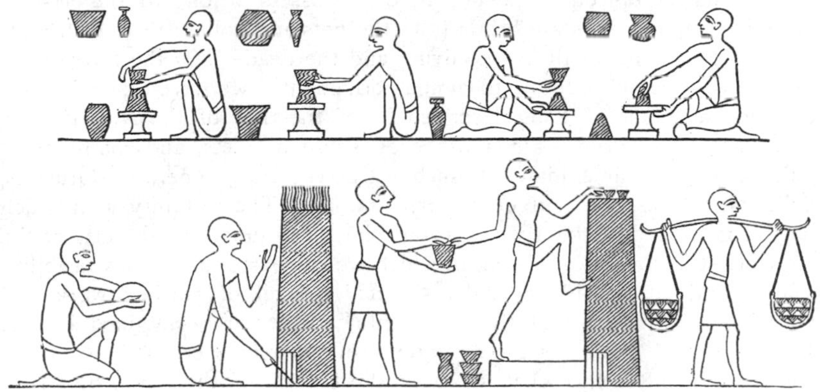

POTTERS OF THE MIDDLE EMPIRE (Beni Hasan. After W., ii. 192). Above are four men at the potter's wheel : the first one turns it, the second cuts off the pot that is finished, the third one takes it down, the fourth begins a new one. Below, the shaping of a plate with the hand, two furnaces, and the carrying away of the pottery that is finished.

entirely by the hand.[1] As a rule the potter's wheel was used, which was turned by the left hand, whilst the right hand shaped the vessel.[2] The pots were then burnt in a stove which seems to have resembled that used by the Egyptian bakers. As is shown in our illustration, the fire was below, and the pots were placed either on the top or inside ; in another picture we see the pots standing on the top apparently covered with ashes.[3]

The earthenware thus prepared by the potter was almost always of the simplest description ; the pots, bottles, and bowls were without any glaze or ornamentation of any kind, except a few lines of paint ; they made dolls also, and similar rude figures. The beautiful pottery and the artistic terra-cotta figures of Greece were quite unknown to the more ancient Egyptians.[4] The reason is apparent,—for small and beautiful objects the Egyptians understood the manufacture of a ware far better adapted

[1] This seems to be indicated by the picture L. D., ii. 74 a, also by the figure to the left of the stove in our illustration.

[2] Potters' wheels—O. E. : L. D., ii. 13. M. E. : L. D., ii. 126, W., ii. 192.

[3] Potters' stoves—O. E. : Tomb of T'y. M. E. : W., ii. 192 ; L. D., ii. 126.

[4] Of the time of the Old Empire I can only mention some rude statues at Gizeh, and the figure of a weeping female servant. Of the time of the New Empire the fragment of a statue of Isis at Berlin, and a fragment of a relief in the Louvre, placed amongst the Greek terra-cottas.

than the rough clay, viz. the so-called faïence. The achievements of the Egyptians in this branch of art stand so high that modern technical skill has barely attained to it even in part. It is therefore the more to be deplored that in this branch of art the pictures on the monuments leave us in the dark, and that we do not possess even one representation showing the preparation of faïence. Even the Egyptian name for this ware is as yet unknown,[1] a circumstance which shows us clearly the incompleteness of our knowledge, and the defective nature of the inscriptions that have come down to us.

The oldest objects in faïence that we possess belong to the close of the Old Empire; they are beads from the nets and collarettes, which were worn as ornaments, both by the living and the dead.[2] Of the time of the Middle Empire, in addition to similar ornaments,[3] we have a small vase[4] bearing the name of King Usertsen I.; of the time of the New Empire there are also various kinds of beads, small amulets, and many other objects of this same material, such as bowls, tiles, funerary statuettes, dolls, caricatures, etc., and even small statues. The certainty with which faïence is treated at this time is astonishing; the funerary statuette of the high priest Ptaḥmose at Gizeh, in which we see pastes of various fusibility sharply and clearly side by side, is a real marvel of finished work, and the same may be said of the ornamental object lately obtained by the Berlin Museum, with its pigmy figures of gods in pierced work. The colouring of the faïence changed with the fashion of the time; as a rule, however, the two colours blue and green in various grades predominated at all periods. The reason why these two colours were preferred above all others is apparent,—the blue and green *objets d'art* were supposed to look as if they were made of the most costly materials known to the Egyptians, viz. lapis-lazuli and malachite. These favourite stones were imitated in various ways in Egypt, in blue and green pastes and colouring matters.

The material that we call Egyptian faïence is only identical to a certain degree with modern faïence, for whilst in the latter the glazing is always laid on an object of refined clay, the Egyptians understood also the glazing of objects of cut stone.

The glazing of this faïence, and still more the splendidly-coloured pastes which we meet with at the beginning of the New Empire in the enamels of the goldsmith's work, show that the preparation of glass must have been familiar even in early times to the Egyptians. It is uncertain, however, when glass was first employed as an independent material. A small glass vase in the British Museum bearing the name of Thothmes III., is considered to be the oldest example known; objects in glass were doubtless manufactured before this period, but as none have been identified,

[1] I conjecture indeed that signifies faïence; at any rate the description of the objects mentioned of this material appears to me to answer to faïence rather than to glass, as is surmised by Brugsch, Wb. Suppl., p. v.

[2] Berlin, 1381.

[3] E.g. at Gizeh.

[4] Gizeh, 3893.

they were probably much rarer than the faïence. Nevertheless the two pictures which in all probability represent glass-blowing belong to the time of the Middle and the New Empire.[1] The older of the two represents two men sitting by a fire blowing into tubes, at the lower end of which is seen a green ball—the glass which is being blown. In the later picture two workmen are blowing together through their tubes into a large jug, whilst a third has the green ball at the end of his tube.

The pictures of the time of the Old Empire, on the other hand, which have been supposed to represent glass-blowing, may probably be otherwise explained.[2] In these representations five or six men are seated round a curious object which may be a small clay furnace; they are blowing through tubes which are provided with a point in front. In the inscriptions we read that the melting of a certain substance termed is here represented.[3] The blowing is merely to fan the glow of the furnace. The pictures of working in metal to which we must now turn, show us that this explanation is probably accurate.

The latter pictures represent workmen smelting the precious metal, they are sitting before the fire blowing through tubes into the flame; in one case the tube has the same point as is seen in the older pictures.[4] These metal points,[5] which are evidently intended to concentrate and increase the draught of air, are also to be seen on the tubes of the bellows represented in a tomb of the New Empire.[6] These bellows consist of two bags, apparently of leather, in each of which a tube is fastened. A workman stands with one foot on each bag; if he presses the left one down, he raises the right leg at the same time, and draws up the right-hand bellows with a string. Two pair of these bellows are being used for an open coal fire, and the glow they produce is so strong that the workmen are obliged to use long wire rods in order to take off the little crucible. When a smaller fire only was needed, it might be lighted in a deep clay bowl surrounded by metal plates[7] to protect it from draught; this fire could also be fanned by blowing through a tube.

The methods of metal-working, the melting, forging, soldering, and chasing of metal, are unfortunately rarely to be found in any representation.[8] We are confronted here by the same curious fact that the tomb-pictures, whilst showing a predilection for treating of much that is unimportant, almost ignore an art which was not only much practised, but also most highly developed. The frequent mention of workers in metal gives us a truer conception of the importance of this industry than the few

[1] M. E. and N. E.: W. ii. 140.

[2] L. D., 13, 49 b, 74 a (the stove, or whatever it may be, is apparently wanting), Perrot, 32.

[3] If we may take this drop-like substance to represent glass, which hypothesis has much in its favour, these pictures would then probably represent the preparation of this substance in connection with the glazing of faïence.

[4] M. E.: W., ii. 234. N. E.: ib. 235 (with point).

[5] W., ii. 312, remarks that the points are of metal, in order that they should not burn.

[6] W., ii. 312.

[7] W., ii. 235.

[8] The only one we can mention here is L. D., ii. 126; W., ii. 234.

representations that exist in the tombs. The workers in bronze with their chiefs, but above all the goldsmiths, are often mentioned, and were apparently held in great esteem. Under the 12th dynasty a "superintendent of the goldsmiths," whose father held like office, was "rewarded by the king (even) in his childhood," and in later life was "placed before others in his office."[1] Another "superintendent of the goldsmiths of the king," under the New Empire, is also called the "superintendent of the artists in Upper and Lower Egypt"; he relates that he knows "the secrets of the houses of gold," by which we may perhaps understand the preparation of the figures of the gods that were guarded with such secrecy.[2] In addition there were the "goldsmiths,"[3] the "chief goldsmiths,"[4] and the "superintendents of the goldsmiths";[5] as a rule fathers and brothers carried on the same craft; the goldsmiths' art therefore, like that of the painters and sculptors, was transmitted traditionally from father to son.

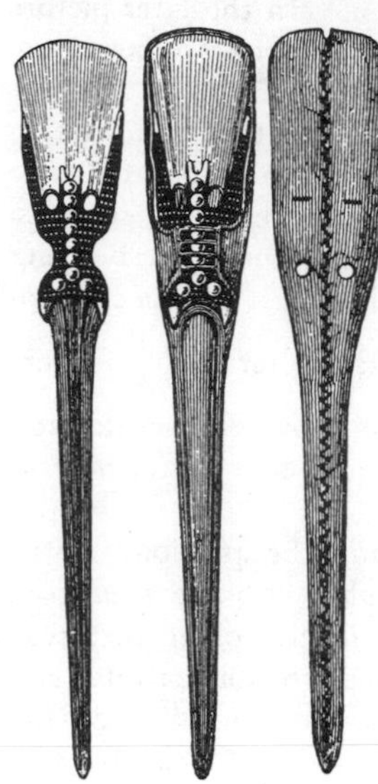

BRONZE DAGGER IN THE BERLIN MUSEUM. 1. Dagger—the handle consists of ivory and wood and is ornamented with gold nails. 2. The same in its sheath. 3. The leather sheath alone. (From a public tomb at Thebes of the time of the New Empire.)

Though the goldsmiths were held in very high esteem, owing to the fact that they had to provide the temples with figures of the gods, and that the reparation of the royal jewels and such-like duties devolved upon them, yet the bronze industry was really of far more importance for the country. Bronze was employed in Egypt for large vessels as well as for tools and weapons, and this department of metal-work was brought to very great perfection.[6] This is not the place to enter into the subject of the composition of the various bronzes which analysts have endeavoured to determine;[7] the Egyptians employed various kinds, as we learn from the texts of the New Empire, where there is frequent mention of "black bronze," and the "bronze in the combination of six,"[8] *i.e.* a six-fold alloy. It is impossible to decide at how early a period bronze was employed by artists in the making of

[1] Mar. Cat. d'Ab., 596. [2] Mar. Mast., 450.

[3] [hieroglyphs] passim, Amon possessed his own goldsmiths under the N. E.; Mar. Cat. d'Ab., 1078.

[4] *ḥre nb*, Mar. Cat. d'Ab., 1152 (N. E.).

[5] Mar. Cat. d'Ab., 596; Mar. Mast., 450. Turin stele with the name of Amenemḥê't III. (L. A.), on which two "superintendents of the goldsmiths" and four "goldsmiths" are mentioned.

[6] A workman who made knives is represented L. D., ii. 126; otherwise I know of no picture representing working in bronze.

[7] This work ought to be taken up again in a more comprehensive manner; the few older bronzes ought also to be considered by themselves, for the great number of existing bronzes belong to such a late date that they must not be included in the metallurgy of the pure Egyptian periods.

[8] Pap. Koller, 1, 7; An., 4, 16, 12.

statues,[1] the little funerary figure of King Ramses II. spoken of above (p. 137) appears to be the most ancient example of a bronze statuette. It is cast hollow, and is beautifully chased.

The fact that iron as well as bronze was used for tools from the time of the Old Empire, can scarcely any longer be considered as doubtful, for pieces of iron tools have been found at various places imbedded in masonry of very ancient date.[2] It appears to me however, that the bronze tools were always more commonly used, for in the texts bronze is continually spoken of, while iron is comparatively rarely mentioned.[3]

The Egyptians regarded silver as the most valuable of all precious metals ; it stands before gold in all the old inscriptions, and in fact, in the tombs silver objects are much rarer than gold ones. This curious circumstance admits of a very simple explanation : no silver was to be found in Egypt. The "white," as silver was called, was probably imported from Cilicia ; the Phoenicians and Syrians carried on this trade in the time of the 18th dynasty.[4] Either the brisker trade in this metal, or the discovery of new mines, led to a fall in the value of silver under the New Empire, for later texts usually mention gold first in the same way that we do.[5] In addition to gold and silver another precious metal, the [hieroglyphs], *usm*, is frequently mentioned ; Lepsius recognised this as electron, the mixture of gold and silver. Though this amalgam was in no way beautiful, it was much used for personal adornment and for ornamental vases. The proportion of the gold to the silver was apparently that of two to three.[6]

The great skill of the Egyptian goldsmiths is proved in the most conclusive manner by the wonderful jewels found on the body of Queen A'ḥḥôtep, one of the ancestresses of the New Empire ; these jewels are now amongst the treasures at Gizeh.[7] The fineness of the gold work, and the splendid colouring of the enamels, are as admirable as the tasteful forms and the certainty of the technique. Amongst them there is a dagger, on the dark bronze blade of which are symbolical representations of war, a lion rushing along, and some locusts, all inlaid in gold ; in the wooden handle are

1 The statues of the Posno collection at the Louvre do not belong to the period of the Old Empire, but are archaistic works of the 26th dynasty.

2 Cp. Maspero, Guide du Musée de Boulaq, p. 296 ; and Birch, W., ii. 251.

3 As regards the word for iron, cp. Br. Wb. Suppl., 413 ff.

4 See the representation in the tomb of Rech-m'e-Rê' ; W., i. Pl. ii. a, ii. b.

5 For the first time probably L. D., iii. 30 b, 10, under Thothmes III. ; always so in texts of the 20th dynasty, Abb. 44, Amh. 2, 6, 9, etc. That other texts retain the old original order, as is the case with many other traditional matters, is of course no argument on the other side.

6 In order to determine the component parts of *usm*, Brugsch, Wb. Suppl., has cleverly compared Harr., 26, 11, with ib. 34, a, whence it appears that in weighing *usm*, 1278 uten of gold, 1891 uten of silver, and 67 uten of copper were employed. This passage corroborates Lepsius' view ; I cannot conceive how Brugsch can infer from this small quantity of copper (which moreover may represent the nails, etc.) that *usm* is a kind of bronze. In both passages also the expression is so vague, that the conjecture is not impossible that a part of the gold might have been worked up without alloy.

7 That the jewelry of the Middle Empire was equally beautiful is shown by the wonderful jewelry of the 12th dynasty found at Dahshur by M. de Morgan in April 1894.

inserted three-cornered pieces of precious metal; three female heads in gold form the top of the handle, whilst a bull's head of the same precious metal conceals the place where handle and blade unite. The sheath is of gold. One beautiful axe has a gilded bronze blade, the central space being covered with the deepest blue enamel, on which King A'ḥmose is represented stabbing an enemy; above him a griffin, the emblem of swiftness, hastens past. The handle of the axe is of cedar wood plated with gold, and upon it the names of the king are inlaid in coloured precious stones. Gold wire is used instead of the straps which in ordinary axes bind the handle and blade together. Perhaps the most beautiful of all these precious things however is the golden breastplate in the form of a little Egyptian temple; King A'ḥmose is standing in it, Amon and Rê' pour water over him and bless him. The contours of the figures are formed with fine strips of gold, and the spaces between them are filled in with paste and coloured stones. This technique, now called cloisonné, the same which has been carried to such perfection by the Chinese, was often employed by the Egyptians with great taste. The illustration heading this chapter gives a good idea of the character of the work, but it is impossible to represent the brilliance of the enamel, and the beauty of the threads of gold that divide the partitions.

Every one however was not able, like the fortunate Queen A'ḥḥôtep, to employ gold for each and every thing; the art of gilding therefore was early developed. The Berlin Museum possesses a specimen of gilding belonging to the early period between the Old and the New Empire,[1] in this specimen the fineness of the reddish gold leaf is remarkable; in later times gilding was much used, but I believe that this industry is represented in a tomb picture as early as the time of the Middle Empire.[2]

The question so frequently asked as to whence the raw material was obtained for this highly-developed metal industry, admits as yet of an answer only in part. The problem as to whence the Egyptians obtained their tin, which they used in great quantities for the preparation of bronze, is still unsolved; we are also ignorant of the source of their iron.[3] We are better informed, however, about the origin of gold, which they procured from the so-called Arabian desert, the desolate mountainous country between the Nile and the Red Sea. The veins of quartz in these mountains contain gold, and wherever these veins come to the surface, we find, as Wilkinson has already related, that they have been worked in ancient times by the mountain folk, on account of the probability of their containing gold.

In two places especially, the quest of these gold-seekers was very successful. The first, which was probably the most ancient source of Egyptian gold, lay in the neighbourhood of Coptos,[4] and therefore presum-

[1] Mask of a mummy from the coffin of 'Ep'e-'anchu.

[2] I refer to the picture W., ii. 234, which Wilkinson explains as gold-washing, an explanation which does not quite commend itself to me. I do not give my explanation as certain.

[3] W., ii. 250, says that Burton found an old iron mine at Hamami in the Arabian desert.

[4] The "gold from the mountains" is divided into "gold from Coptos" and "gold from Nubia": Harr., i. 12 a, 6 ff. For the chart of the gold mines of this mountain (*i.e.* of the mountain Bechen) see Chabas, "Deux papyrus."

ably on the great mountain route leading from the sea and from the granite quarries to that point in the valley of the Nile where Coptos was situate. In the Wadi Foachir on this route, old forsaken gold workings have, in fact, been found; these must once have been of considerable importance, for there are still the remains of no less than 1320 workmen's huts. Even if we agree with Wilkinson's judgment as an expert, that these are as late as the Ptolemaic period,[1] yet we may reasonably conclude that the same place was worked in earlier times as well.

The greatest amount of gold, however, came from another place, from the mountains lying much further to the south, mountains belonging geographically to Nubia. Linant and Bonomi discovered one of the mines of this district. Seventeen days' journey from the southern boundary of Egypt, through a waterless, burning, mountainous desert, is a place now called Eshuranib, where the plan of the workings is still plainly to be seen. Deep shafts lead into the mountain, two cisterns collect the water of the winter's rain, and sloping stone tables stand by them to serve for the gold-washing. In the valley are perhaps three hundred stone huts, in each of which is a sort of granite hand-mill, where formerly the quartz dust was crushed. Few places on earth have witnessed such scenes of misery as this spot, now so lonely and deserted that no distant echo reaches our ears of the curses with which the air resounded in those bygone days. The people who here dug out the "gold of Nubia" for the Egyptian kings, who endured for a shorter or longer period the frightful heat of these valleys, were captives; the Wadi Eshuranib was the Egyptian Siberia. Chained, with no clothes, guarded by barbarian soldiers speaking a language unknown to them, these unfortunate wretches had to work day and night without hope of deliverance. No one cared what became of them; the stick of the pitiless overseer drove even the sick, the women, and the old men to work, till, exhausted by labour, want, and heat, death at last brought them their longed-for release. Thus it was in Greek times, and as there is no reason to believe that the Pharaohs were more humane than the Ptolemies, we may accept the terrible picture Diodorus draws[2] as applying also to the times with which we are concerned—so much the more as we cannot conceive any way in which these mines could be worked without this reckless expenditure of life.

Diodorus also describes to us the procedure followed in the working of these mines, and his account is corroborated by modern discoveries. The shafts follow the veins of quartz, for this reason winding their way deeply into the heart of the mountain. The hard stone was first made brittle by the action of fire, then hoed out with iron picks. The men who did this hard work toiled by the light of little lamps, and were accompanied by children, who carried away the bits of stone as they were hewn out. This quartz was then crushed in stone mortars into pieces about the size of lentils; women and old men then pounded it to dust in mills. This dust was next washed on sloping tables, until the water had carried

[1] W., ii. 238. Wilkinson speaks on this subject as an eye-witness. [2] Diodor., iii. 11.

off all the lighter particles of stone; the fine sparkling particles of gold were then collected, and together with a certain amount of lead, salt, and other matters, kept in closed clay smelting-pots for five whole days. Thus far Diodorus relates; the procedure of more ancient times was probably the same. Formerly however the gold was not always smelted on the spot, but was brought in bags to Egypt as at the present day.[1] For commercial purposes gold was as a rule formed into rings, which, judging from the representations, seem to have been of very variable thickness, with a uniform diameter of about five inches. Naturally these rings were not taken on trust, and whenever they were paid over, we see the master-weigher and the scribes busy weighing them and entering the ascertained weight in their books.[2] We hear of enormous sums changing hands in this way. Under Thothmes III. an official receives a "great heap" of electron, which, if we may believe the inscription, weighed 36,392 uten, *i.e.* 3311 kilos 672 grammes, which would amount to about 66 cwt.[3] This quantity of gold would now be worth about £500,000; therefore in electron, which as we have seen consisted of an amalgam of two-fifths gold and three-fifths silver, this mass would be worth at least £200,000. Moreover, under the New Empire, various kinds of gold were distinguished in commerce, *e.g.* the "mountain gold," and the "good gold," the "gold of twice," and the "gold of thrice," the "gold of the weight," and the "good gold of Katm," *i.e.* the כתם of Semitic countries.[4]

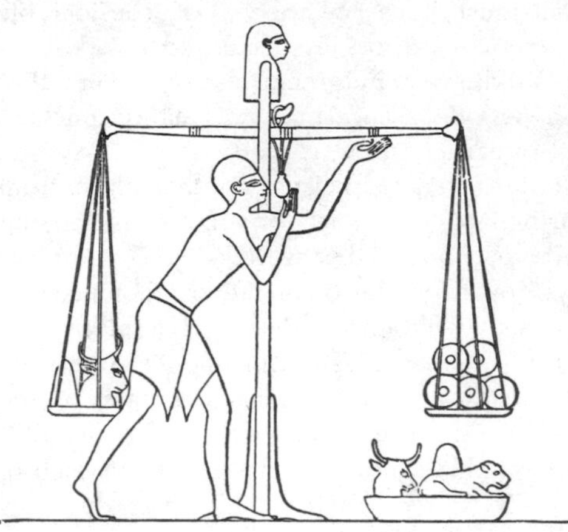

THE WEIGHING OF GOLD RINGS.
The weights are in the shape of a cow's head, of a lion, and of a cone (after L. D., iii. 39 a).

Texts are still extant describing the working of the Nubian gold-mines. They picture to us the difficulties of mining in the desert so far from the Nile valley,—each journey became a dangerous expedition, owing to want of water and to the robber nomads. But here also the *auri sacra fames* overcame all obstacles. When King Usertsen I. had subjected Nubia, Ameny, our oft-mentioned nomarch, relates that he began immediately to plunder the gold district. "I went up," he says, "in order to fetch gold for his Majesty, King Usertsen I. (may he live always and for ever). I went together with the hereditary prince, the prince, the great legitimate son of the king, Ameny (life, health, and happiness!) and I went with a

[1] Gold dust: e.g. L. D., iii. 117. [2] L. D., iii. 10 a, 39 a, d. [3] L. D., iii. 39 d.

[4] Cp. especially the distinctions made in the Pap. Harris, an enumeration of which may be found in Piehl's Index, p. v. nb. The כתם appears also in various inscriptions.

company of 400 men of the choicest of my soldiers, who by good fortune arrived safely without loss of any of their number. I brought the gold I was commissioned to bring, and was in consequence placed in the royal house, and the king's son thanked me."[1] The strong escort, which in this case was required solely for the protection of the gold, shows the insecurity of the road.

Later, under the New Empire, when Nubia was an Egyptian province, the road seems to have been safer, at any rate the inscriptions of the 19th dynasty emphasise only the other difficulty, the want of water. Thus an inscription in the desert temple of Redesieh, dated the 9th year, the 20th Epiphi, relates[2] that King Sety I. "desired to see the gold mines from which the gold was brought. When his Majesty had now ascended . . . he stood still in the way, in order to consider a plan in his own mind. He said: 'How bad is this waterless way! What becomes of those who travel along it? . . . Wherewith do they cool their throats? Wherewith do they quench their thirst? . . . I will care for them and give them this necessary of life, that they may be grateful to my name all the years that shall come.' . . . When his Majesty had spoken these words in his heart, he travelled through the mountains, and sought a fitting place. . . . The god moreover guided him in order to fulfil his request. Then were stone-masons commissioned to dig a well on the mountain, so that the weary might be comforted, and those scorched by the summer heat refreshed. Behold, this place was then erected to the great name of King Sety, and the water overflowed in such abundance as if it came from the hollow of the two cave-springs of Elephantine."

When thus the well was finished, his Majesty resolved to establish a station there also, "a town with a temple." The "controller of the royal works," with his stone masons, carried out this commission of the monarch, the temple was erected and consecrated to the gods; Rê' was to be worshipped in the holy of holies, Ptah and Osiris in the great hall, whilst Horus, Isis, and the king himself, formed the "divine cycle" of the temple. "And when this monument was now finished, when it had been decorated and the paintings were completed, his Majesty himself came thither to worship his fathers the gods."

We do not know for certain where the mine lay, to which the route of Redesieh was to lead; the inscription does not allude to the mines of Eshuranib, for, apart from other reasons, the king was endeavouring at the same time to open a way to this latter district also. We learn this from an inscription of Ramses II. his son. This king, "at whose name the gold comes forth from the mountain," was at one time at Memphis, and while thinking of the countries "from which gold was brought, he meditated plans as to how wells might be bored on the roads which were in need of water. For he had heard there was indeed much gold in the country of 'Ekayta, but the way thereto was wholly without water. When any of the gold-washers went thither, there were only the half of them who

[1] L. D., ii. 122.

[2] L. D., iii. 140 b.

arrived there; they died of thirst on the way, together with the donkeys, which they drove before them, and they found nothing to drink, neither in going up nor in coming down, no water to fill the skins. Therefore no gold was brought from this country, because of the scarcity of water.

"Then spake his Majesty to the lord high treasurer, who stood near him: 'Call then the princes of the court, that his Majesty may take counsel with them about this country,' and immediately the princes were conducted into the presence of this good god, they raised their arms rejoicing, and praised him and kissed the earth before his beautiful countenance. Then it was recounted to them how the matter stood with this country, and their counsel was asked as to how a well should be bored on the road leading thither."

After the customary long loyal phrases of the Egyptian court ceremonial, the princes answered: "'O king, our lord! The following is related of the country of 'Ekayta—and indeed the royal son of the miserable Ethiopia (*i.e.* the governor of Nubia) spake on the subject before his Majesty—it has been without water in this way since the time of Rê'. Men die there from thirst, and every king of past times has wished to bore a well there, but they did not succeed. King Sety I. also did the same, he caused a well 120 cubits deep to be bored there in his time; but it was left alone, and there came no water out of it. If however thou didst speak thyself to thy father the Nile, the father of the gods, and saidst: 'Let the water come out of the mountain,' he would then do what thou sayest, as indeed all thy plans are carried out before us. . . . For all thy fathers the gods love thee, more than any king who has been since the time of Rê'.'

"Then spake his Majesty to these princes: 'All that ye say is very true . . . since the time of Rê' no well has been bored in this country; I will however bore a well therein.'" And after the princes had expressed their astonishment at this decision, "adoring their lord, kissing the earth, lying on the belly before him, rejoicing to the heavens," the king gave the order that the work should be undertaken. This time it doubtless succeeded, otherwise the stele giving this account would scarcely have been erected; it was found at the modern Kuban in Nubia, where the route to 'Ekayta may have started.[1]

The two wonderful papyri, famous as the oldest maps in the world, relate to the gold mines of the two last-named kings.[2] One papyrus, which is only partially preserved, represents the gold district of the mountain Bechen, *i.e.* the mines situate to the east of Coptos, and belongs to the time of Ramses II. I cannot say what place is represented in the other, which may be seen in the accompanying illustration. It represents, as we see, two valleys running parallel to each other between the mountains, one of these valleys, like many of the larger wadis of the desert, seems to be covered with underwood and blocks of stone; a winding crossway valley

[1] Stele of Kuban.

[2] Published Lepsius, Auswahl, 22, Chabas, Deux papyrus. Also the reports of the Munich congress by Lauth, 1870, ii.

unites the two. The pointed mountains (the drawing of which strikes us as particularly primitive) contain the mines; that marked B bears the superscription "gold mine," whilst by the one marked A may be read "these are the mountains where the gold is washed; they are also of this red colour" (they were represented red on the papyrus). The valley M and the pass N are "routes leading to the sea," the name of the place, which is reached through the large valley marked O, or the adjoining one marked D, is unfortunately illegible. The mountain C, on which there

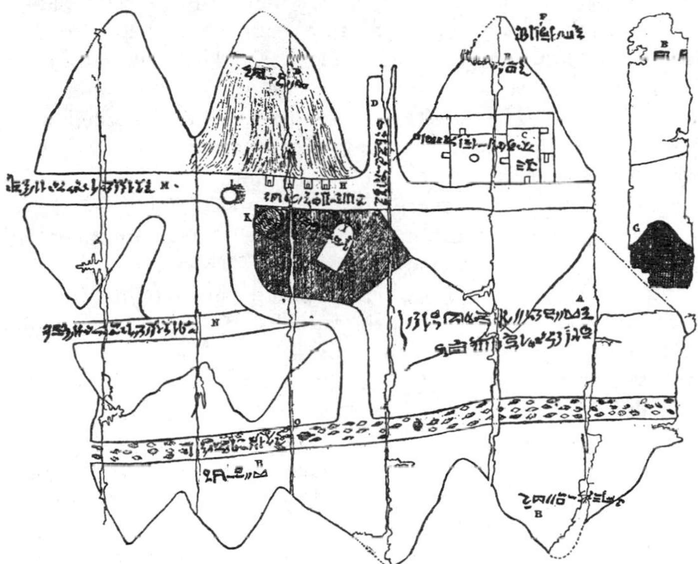

are great buildings, bears the name of the "pure mountain"; on it was a sanctuary to Amon; the small houses marked H belonged, if I read aright, to the gold miners. Finally the water tank K, with the dark cultivated ground surrounding it, represents "the well of King Sety I.": the same king who erected the great stele J, probably in remembrance of the boring of this well.

A certain poetic halo surrounded gold-digging in the mountains—we read indeed in an inscription in a mine: "gold is the body of the gods, and Rê' said, when he began to speak: 'my skin is of pure electron.'"[1] This was not the case however with the prosaic copper mines, though they were of course of more national importance; in the inscriptions relating to them there was no boasting about their daily yield. This is also the reason that the inscriptions in those mines, which were presumably copper mines, scarcely ever mention the copper;[2] but speak

[1] L. D., iii. 140 c; the allusion refers to the myth related on p. 264 ff.

[2] An exception is found L. D., ii. 137 c, where the produce is spoken of as malachite and .

rather of what is really a mere by-product of the same, the precious stone, [hieroglyphs], *mfaket, i.e.* malachite, as the yield of the mine. In Egypt, malachite was in fact considered to be one of their most valuable possessions, yet it stands to reason that it was not for the sake of malachite alone that the great mines of Sinai were worked for thousands of years. It is more likely that in official style its high-sounding name often stood for the more vulgar copper.

These copper mines lay in the mountains on the west side of the Sinaitic peninsula, chiefly indeed in the Wadi Nasb, the Wadi Maghara, and in the mountain Sarbût elchâdim; with the exception of the first, where copper ore is still obtained from one shaft,[1] they were all worked out in old times. The shafts by which they were worked are bored horizontally into the mountain, and are in the form of corridors, the roof being supported by pillars.

The most important of these mines were those of the Wadi Maghara, which were begun by King Snefru and called after him the "mines of Snefru."[2] On a hill in the midst of distant Thales there still stand the stone huts of the workmen as well as a small castle, built to protect the Egyptians stationed there from the attacks of the Sinai Beduin. For though these mountain races may have been just as insignificant as they are now, yet they might be dangerous to the miners cut off from all intercourse with their home. King Snefru and his successors, therefore, carried on a petty warfare with these nomads, which is perpetuated in triumphal reliefs on the rocks of Thales, as the "annihilation of the mountain folk." On the other hand these mountains were exempt from the other danger which generally threatened the ancient miners of the desert; there was a well not far from these mines, and the cisterns on the fortress were filled sufficiently with the rain which fell here every year. There was provision made also for the religious needs of the workmen and soldiers; amongst other divinities revered here was a "Ḥatḥor, the lady of the malachite country," she was considered the patron saint of all the mines of Sinai. Though we cannot now find a temple to this goddess in the Wadi Maghara, yet divine worship seems to have been carried on here with all due ceremony, for Ra'enuser, a king of the 5th dynasty (if I understand the representation rightly), gave to one of the gods there a great vase to be used for his libations.[3]

The mines of the Wadi Maghara were actively worked all through the period of the Old Empire, and from the time of Snefru to that of Pepy II. the kings sent their officials thither with a "royal commission." These delegates were some of them treasury officials, and some ship captains (two offices which, under the Old Empire, had duties in common, for instance, both had to fetch the same precious things for the

[1] Rüppell in Bädeker, p. 548.

[2] L. D., ii. 137 g. On the present condition of Thales and its ruins see Brugsch, Türkis minen, p. 71.

[3] L. D., ii. 152 a.

treasury); some were also officers of the army with their troops. After a long suspension of the work, the later rulers of the 12th dynasty, especially Amenemḥê't III., seem to have taken it up again energetically. Thus, *e.g.*, in the second year of his reign the latter sent one of his treasurers, "Chentchetyḥôtep, the treasurer of the god, the great superintendent of the cabinet of the house of silver," with 734 soldiers to the Wadi Maghara to pursue mining operations there. Under the New Empire also, many of the Pharaohs carried on the work of these mines, the last of these kings who we know did so being Ramses III.;[1] he relates that he sent his prince-vassals thither, to present offerings to the Ḥatḥôr, and to fetch many bags of malachite.

The mines also now called Sarbût elchâdim, the *servant mountain*, which in early times were called after an unknown personage, *the mines of the Ka*,[2] seem also to have been worked as early as the time of King Snefru, for he is represented there in a relief standing between two gods.[3] A certain Amenemḥê't also relates to us later that he, the "treasurer of the god, the superintendent of the cabinet, the leader of the young men, and the friend of the Pharaoh," rendered such great services there as "had not been known since the time of King Snefru."[4] The work was, however, first taken up in earnest by the kings of the 12th dynasty, under whom Sarbût elchâdim seems to have become the centre of the whole mining district. Amenemḥê't III. built a small temple here to the Ḥatḥôr; it stood on a high rocky terrace which dominates the valley in an imposing manner. This temple was afterwards enlarged by the kings of the New Empire, especially by Thothmes III. Round about this sanctuary were erected numberless stelæ, on which the names of many of the distinguished directors of the mines there have been passed down to posterity. These mines, like those of the Wadi Maghara, seem to have been exhausted under the New Empire, for none of the inscriptions there are later than the 20th dynasty.[5] Finally, there were also great "copper mines" in the mountain 'At'eka, which could be reached both by sea and land; Ramses III. carried on mining operations here with great success.[6]

The quarrying of "eternal stones" is even more frequently mentioned on the Egyptian monuments than mining; the indefatigable energy of the Egyptians in building caused the demand for stone to be unusually great. The cheapest material, the common limestone, was indeed to be obtained everywhere on the edge of the desert with very little trouble; but this limestone scarcely admitted of fine treatment. The really good kinds of stone which were used for sculpture were not found in very many places, that is, if we consider those places only where it could be easily quarried.

[1] Inscriptions of the Wadi Maghara—O.E.: L. D., ii. 2, 39, 116. M.E.: L. D., ii. 137, 140, 152 a. N.E.: L. D., iii. 28. Ramses III.: Harr. i. 78, 6.

[2] L. D., ii. 144 q. [3] Ib., 144 p. [4] Ib., 144 q.

[5] For Sarbût elchâdim, see Bädeker, p. 546; Lepsius Reisebriefe, 337. Inscriptions there M.E.: L. D., ii. 137, 140, 144. N.E.: L. D., iii. 29 a, 71 c d.

[6] Harr., 78, 1 ff. This must be one of the Sinaitic mines.

The fine white limestone, such as was used for instance for the better mastabahs and pyramids, and for many statues, was brought from the great quarries of Terofu, nearly opposite Memphis; these are now called the quarries of Turah, and are still worked. Frequent mention is made at all times of these quarries; they consist of immense halls quarried in the rock; and when we consider what enormous masses of stone were cut here, we cannot overestimate their importance. Notwithstanding the fact that there are fewer inscriptions preserved at Turah than, *e.g.*, in the less important mines in Sinai, yet this circumstance is to be explained by the great extent of the operations at the former place. To fetch stone from the Turah quarries, which lay close to the Nile, was such an everyday matter that it was not thought necessary to immortalise the work, however arduous it might be. It was only when a new cutting in these stone quarries was solemnly opened, in order to "cut beautiful white limestone," to build "houses that should last for millions of years," that the fact was narrated in an inscription intended for posterity. This happened under the Middle Empire in the reign of an Amenemḥê't, and in the time of the New Empire under A'ḥmose, and under Amenḥôtep III.; in the latter case "his Majesty found that the quarries which are in Turah had fallen into decay since earlier times."[1]

Under the Old Empire, alabaster was obtained from the same part of the desert. A little southward of Turah nearly opposite Dahshur, surrounded by steep limestone cliffs, the Wadi Gerraui stretches into the mountains. In this valley the old alabaster quarries were discovered in modern days by Schweinfurth; they lie three or four hours' journey from the Nile valley, with which they were connected by a road which can still be traced in places. About an hour's journey below the quarries proper are the ruins of the stone huts of the workmen. A very strong wall, formed of blocks of stone piled up, and covered on the outside with squared stone, forms a dam across the valley at this point, and presumably served to intercept the stream formed by the winter rain, and thus to store the water for both workmen and draught cattle. The greatness of this work—the dam is about 30 feet high, 216 feet broad, and nearly 140 feet thick—shows that at one time great importance was attached to the quarries of the Wadi Gerraui.[2] This may have been during a period when the finer alabaster afterwards obtained from the town of Ḥat-nub, the *gold house*, was as yet unknown.[3] Even the latter quarries were undoubtedly exhausted under King Pepy of the 6th dynasty.[4]

[1] L. D., ii. 143 i; L. D., iii. 3 a, b, 71 a, b. Such a section of the quarries is called by the plural term .

[2] The great age of this work is proved by the degree of weathering of the square stone of the dam, which is exactly like the weathering that can be observed in the blocks used for the pyramid temples.

[3] The quarries of Ḥat-nub were discovered in December 1891 by Mr. Percy Newberry of the Egypt Exploration Fund. See the Proceedings of the Bib. Archae., January 1894.

[4] Inscription of Un'e, Ä. Z., 1882, 24.

Sandstone, which was valued as the least destructible building material, was chiefly obtained, as we might surmise, from that place which was most conveniently situate for Egypt proper, the most northerly point of the sandstone plateau, Gebel Selseleh. The mountains here approach the river on both sides so closely as to render quarrying an especially easy matter, yet I doubt whether sandstone was used for building in Lower Egypt under the Old Empire; even in later times it was employed preferably in the towns of Upper Egypt. Under the New Empire the quarries of Silsilis must have been the scene of very great activity in consequence of the immense quantity of material required for the building of Karnak, Luxor, Medinet Habu, and other temples; yet here, probably for the same reason as at Turah, inscriptions having any reference to quarrying are strangely few in number. Amongst these one of the most instructive is that of a certain Set(?)-emḥeb, who was "superintendent of the house of silver" of the temple of Amon under Ramses II. He superintended the quarrying of stone here for the building of the Ramesseum. For this purpose he employed 3000 men, amongst whom were 500 masons.[1]

The quarries of Assuan, from which was obtained the beautiful red Egyptian granite, were worked even under the Old Empire. We learn this from the autobiography of Un'e, the oft-mentioned favourite of King Pepy. Merenrê', who succeeded Pepy, required this costly stone for the adornment of his pyramid, and commissioned Un'e, who was superintendent of the south at that time, to obtain it for him. Un'e went first to a part of the quarry district called 'Ebhat, and brought thence the coffin of the King and the point for his pyramid. He then went to Elephantine and from the island opposite Assuan he fetched the red granite that was further required for the furnishing of the pyramid; the stele, with the table of offerings belonging thereto; the door frames for the "upper chamber," etc. In connection with this latter journey the fact that is emphasised as most remarkable, and as never having occurred before "under any king whatsoever," is that Un'e, who had to employ for his work twelve ships for freight, required the escort of but one single warship; in former times, therefore, the country near the frontier had evidently been far from safe for Egyptian officials.[2] Later, when the cataract district had been long under Egyptian government, the military importance of this frontier was very great, and the numberless inscriptions on the rocks are due perhaps more to this fact than to the proximity of the granite quarries.

We possess still further evidence of the great importance of these granite quarries. In all the Egyptian ruins we find immense blocks of this Assuan stone, and in the neighbourhood of that town we can still see the places where they were cut. The procedure by which the old Egyptian stone masons extricated the blocks can be distinctly recognised. At

[1] Inscriptions in the quarries at Silsilis: L. D., iii. 110 i.; L. D., vi. 23, 6-8.
[2] Ä. Z., 1882, 22 ff.

distances generally of about 6 inches they chiselled holes in the rock, in the case of the larger blocks at any rate, to the depth of 6 inches. Wooden wedges were forcibly driven into these holes; these wedges were made to swell by being moistened, and the rock was thus made to split. The same process is still much employed at the present day.

The hardness of the red granite permitted its employment in great masses, and as the quarries were close to navigable water, the Egyptian architects and sculptors made good use of this happy circumstance. Some of the blocks in the temple of King Cha'frê' not far from the great Sphinx measure 14 feet in length, and those under the architraves in the sanctuary of the crocodile-god Sobk in the Feyum, built by Amenemḥê't III., are even more than 26 feet long. Amongst the Theban obelisks there is one more than 107 feet high, whilst a papyrus speaks of an obelisk of some kind from the quarries of Assuan, which measured 120 cubits, *i.e.* nearly 200 feet.[1] These again are surpassed in bulk by the colossal seated statue of red granite which lies shattered in the Ramesseum at Thebes; this colossus was hewn out of a single block 55 feet high and correspondingly broad.

As we have said, the convenient proximity to the water was the reason that the Assuan granite was constantly employed for these colossal works; the black granite, which might have been used perhaps for even larger architraves and for more slender obelisks, owing to its iron hardness, was only employed in comparatively small pieces, on account of the difficulty of transporting it from the quarries in the heart of the desert. The "valley Rehanu," or according to its modern appellation the Wadi Ḥammamât, lay on the desert route between Coptos and the Red Sea, and thence was obtained the "splendid rock the beautiful Bechen stone," from which were made nearly all the dark-coloured statues and coffins that excite our admiration in the Egyptian departments of our museums. The working of these quarries must have been very difficult, for Ḥammamât lies two to three days' journey from the Nile, and the supply of provisions for the host of labourers necessary for the transport of the blocks can have been no easy matter. Numberless beasts of burden were required to fetch the necessaries of life; for instance, we read that 50 oxen and 200 donkeys carried the supplies for 350 men,[2] thus to find water and food for these animals must again have been an arduous undertaking in the desert. In view of these difficulties, it seems to have been considered most meritorious to work there; it was indeed quite another matter to fetch stone from Ḥammamât than from Assuan or from Turah. To this cause we owe the number of inscriptions in existence at Ḥammamât, inscriptions which give us a very interesting glimpse of the working of these quarries, especially during the older period.

The officials who, under the Old and the Middle Empire, directed the works at Ḥammamât, were (as in the mines) mostly treasurers and ship captains; but at the same time there were in addition royal architects and

[1] An. 1, 15, 3. The satirical character of the book causes it to be a questionable authority.
[2] L. D., ii. 115 h.

artists, who also came hither to fetch this precious stone for the coffin or the statue of the Pharaoh. The higher officials—for there were men of the highest rank amongst them, "nearest friends of the king, hereditary princes and chief prophets," and even a "great royal son"[1]—came here probably only as inspectors, whilst the real direction of the quarrying work was placed in the hands of persons of somewhat lower standing. Thus, under the ancient King Pepy, the treasurer 'Ech'e was evidently the actual director of the quarries, and as such he once appears independently.[2] The inscriptions however only mention him as a subordinate, while they give the place of honour to Ptaḥ-mer-'anch-Meryrê', "the superintendent of all the works of the king, the nearest friend of the king, and the chief architect in the two departments." This great man twice paid a visit of inspection to Ḥammamât, once accompanied by his son, and once, when it was a question of the decoration of a temple, with a "superintendent of the commissions of the sacrificial estates of the two departments."[3] Moreover, the treasurer 'Ech'e himself also had subordinates, to whom he could occasionally delegate his office; there were five "deputy artists," and one or two architects, who were as a rule subordinate to him, but who are also mentioned in one place as acting independently.[4]

The most ancient "royal mission" mentioned in the Ḥammamât inscriptions took place under King 'Ess'e of the 5th dynasty.[5] In the confusion which ensued after the 6th dynasty, the works seem to have been in abeyance. Under the rule of a King Mentuḥôtep of the 11th dynasty a new epoch commenced. A miracle took place: "A well was discovered in the midst of the mountains, 10 cubits broad on every side, and full of water up to the brink." It was situate, if I rightly understand, "out of reach of the gazelles, and hidden from the barbarians. The soldiers of old times and the early kings had passed in and out close by it, but no eye had seen it, no human face had glanced upon it," till through the favour of the god Min, the protector of desert paths, it was granted to King Mentuḥôtep (or rather to his people) to find it, and thus "to make this country into a sea."[6] This discovery was made in the second year of the king's reign, when he had sent his highest official the *governor* to Ḥammamât, to direct the quarrying of "the splendid great pure stone which is in that mountain"; that the coffin with the name of "eternal remembrance" might be prepared for the tomb of the monarch as well as monuments for the temples of Upper Egypt. "Thither resorted Amenemḥê't, the hereditary prince, the chief of the town, the governor and high judge, the favourite of the king, the superintendent of works—who is great in his office and powerful in his dignity—who occupies the first place in the palace of his lord—who judges mankind and hears their evidence—he to whom the great men come, bowing themselves, and

[1] L. D., ii. 115 h. [2] L. D., ii. 115 c. [3] L. D., ii. 115 g, k.

[4] Ib., b, c, g. In one place we read of a father with his four sons; later they appear again separately. [5] Ib., l. [6] L. D., ii. 149 f, g.

before whom all in the whole country throw themselves on the earth—who is great with the king of Upper Egypt and powerful with him of Lower Egypt, with the white crown and the red crown . . .—who judges there without partiality—the chief of all the south country—who makes a report upon all that exists and that does not exist—commander of the lord of the two countries, and of understanding heart of the commission of the king . . . he resorted to this honourable country, accompanied by the choicest soldiers, and the people of the whole country, the mountain folk, the artists, the stone-hewers, the metal-workers, the engravers of writing, . . . the gold-workers, the treasury officials—in short, by all the officials of the Pharaonic treasury and by all the servants of the royal household." He carried out his commission successfully, and more especially he obtained a sarcophagus 8 cubits long, 4 cubits broad, and 2 cubits high. Calves and gazelles were sacrificed as thank-offerings to Min of Coptos, the protector of this desert, incense was offered up to him, and 3000 men then dragged the great block into Egypt. "Never had such a block been transported into that country since the time of the god. The soldiers also suffered no loss, not a man perished, not one donkey's back was broken, not one artisan was killed."[1]

It stands to reason that the powerful monarchs of the 12th dynasty, who were such great builders, did not neglect the Ḥammamât quarries. Under the first of these kings, for instance, 'Entef, the lord high treasurer, succeeded, after searching for eight days, in finding a species of stone, "the like of which had not been found since the time of the god." No one, not even the hunters of the desert, had known of this quarry.[2] Under Amenemḥê't III. also, no fewer than 20 men of the mountains, 30 stone masons, 30 rowers (?), and 2000 soldiers were employed for the transport of the monuments from Ḥammamât.[3] During the period subsequent to this account the inscriptions almost cease or contain no particulars.[4] Yet we must not therefore conclude that from this time the quarries were little worked; numberless proofs of the contrary are to be found in the buildings of the 13th dynasty, as well as in those of the New Empire. It was again the business-like everyday character that the work assumed, that led to the cessation of the inscriptions. Ḥammamât, at this epoch, when nothing in the way of building was considered too difficult, was placed almost in the same rank as Turah and Silsilis. Though we hear no more of the want of water or of the difficulty of communication, yet a new danger seems now to have arisen. From the above-mentioned (p. 380) satirical writing—certainly an untrustworthy source of information—we hear of a military expedition[5] being sent to Ḥammamât "in order to destroy those rebels"; exclusive of officers, the number of troops employed is given as 5000, the text therefore cannot refer to one of the petty wars frequently

[1] L. D., ii. 149 d, e. [2] L. D., ii. 118 d.

[3] L. D., ii. 138 c. Other inscriptions of the time of the M.E.: L. D., 136, 138, 151; L. D., vi. 23, 9.

[4] Inscriptions of the N.E.: L. D., iii. 219, 222; L. D., vi. 22, 5; Murray, Egypt, p. 326.

[5] An., 1, 17, 2 ff.

carried on with the wretched Beduins of these mountains. If in other respects we may believe the account, there must have been a mutiny amongst the workmen to necessitate the employment of so great a number of soldiers.

Towards the close of the New Empire under the reign of Ramses IV.,—a king who, though he has left but few monuments, seems to have planned the most magnificent ones,—we again hear of an expedition to Ḥammamât which was carried out in grand style.[1] In the first place the king commissioned three of his most trusted attendants, "Ramses-'aša-ḥeb, the scribe of the house of life," and "Ḥar'e, the scribe of the temple," and Ra'-user-ma't-nachtu, the priest of the gods Min, Horus, and Isis of Coptos," to seek for the best blocks on the mountain of Bechen, *i.e.* in Ḥammamât. This commission, the last member of which was a native of Coptos, and evidently owed his appointment to his intimate knowledge of the desert, gave in their reports as follows: "They are wholly good, there are wonderful great monuments." Thereupon the king gave command to Ramses-nachtu, the high-priest of Amon, "to fetch them to Egypt." The conduct of this expedition was entrusted to this personage, because he was officially the "superintendent of the works" of Amon, and the monuments in question were intended for that god. The men under his command were chiefly military officers, for according to the ideas of those times, work of this kind devolved on the army. No fewer than 110 officers of each rank were ordered out on this expedition. With them were associated more than fifty civil officials and ecclesiastics, and as distinguished members, two of the king's vassals—without whom at this period nothing seems to have been done—and further, the governor of Thebes, and the superintendents of oxen and high priests of various temples, etc. The technical work was given into the hands of 130 stone-masons, 2 painters, and 4 engravers, who worked under three chiefs of the stone-masons, and "Nechtamon, the superintendent of the artists." The work of transport was carried out by 5000 common soldiers, 200 officers of the troop of the fishers of the court," 800 men of the barbarian mercenaries, and 2000 bondservants of the temples. Altogether the expedition consisted of 8368 souls. It is interesting to hear how the commissariat for such a number of men was managed. Ten waggons, each drawn by 6 pair of oxen, and laden with bread, meat, and cakes, "hastened from Egypt to the mountain Bechen"; the offerings for the gods of the desert however, for Min, Horus, and Isis of Coptos, were procured from the "city of the south," *i.e.* probably from Luxor.

From the above accounts the reader will understand how the Egyptians were able to move even the weightiest of their monuments. The weights concerned were immense. The statue of Ramses II. in the Ramesseum weighed, according to one reckoning, more than a million kilogrammes (*i.e.* more than 20,000 hundredweight,[2] and in consequence it has been

[1] All that follows is after L. D., iii. 219.

[2] Murray gives the weight as more than 1000 tons.

conjectured that the architects of the Pharaohs possessed highly-developed mechanical appliances to facilitate the transport of such enormous masses. Nothing of the kind has been found to corroborate this view, and no Egyptologist now doubts that all these marvels were worked by *one* power alone, viz. by the reckless expenditure of human labour. Great things can be accomplished with the most primitive means by those who have no compunction in working hundreds and thousands of workmen to exhaustion, unconcerned as to how many fall by fatigue. To us modern Europeans, who are accustomed, at any rate in time of peace, to consider each human life as priceless, such conduct appears most criminal; to the eastern mind however, there seems nothing particularly wicked in it. Even in recent times the Egyptian fellahin were employed by the system of forced labour on the canal-works, and their strength was used as mercilessly as if they had been cattle. For instance, when the Suez canal was begun, Saîd Pasha had 25,000 peasants at his disposal for the undertaking, and in five years they dug the Sweet-water canal. The Maḥmudijeh canal was taken in hand in the same cheap way: 250,000 peasants worked at it during a whole year, and it is computed that not fewer than 20,000 were sacrificed to the undertaking.

If we accept the fact that the ancient Egyptians were not less scrupulous in this respect than their modern compatriots, we shall comprehend how they could transport the greatest weights without employing any but the most simple means. The Pharaohs of the Old Empire had

TRANSPORT OF A BLOCK DESTINED FOR THE BUILDING OF A TEMPLE AT MEMPHIS, IN THE 22ND YEAR OF A'ḤMOSE (18TH DYN.).
According to the inscription the bearded workmen are Phœnicians (L. D., iii. 3).

no scruple in making use of their own subjects for work: the later rulers, who always had captives taken in war at their disposal, naturally employed the latter for the same purpose. For instance, under Ramses II. we find foreigners of the race of 'Apury dragging stones for the royal buildings at Memphis;[1] and Ramses IV. employed, as the above-mentioned inscription relates, 800 men of the same race for the transport of his blocks from Ḥammamât. When blocks of moderate size had to be conveyed along comparatively good roads, oxen were harnessed into the sledge, as is seen in the accompanying illustration taken from the stone quarries of Turah; as a rule however, as far as we can judge from the statements of the Egyptian texts, men were employed for this heavy work. A famous picture of the time of the Middle Empire shows us plainly the manner of procedure.[2]

[1] Leyden, 349, 15; similarly, ib. 348, 6, 6.
[2] L. D., ii. 134. The beginning of the inscription ought to read *shms tut.*

An alabaster statue 13 cubits high (*i.e.* about 20 feet), representing Dḥuthôtep, a prince of the Nome of the Hare, had to be conveyed to his tomb or to the temple of his town. As we see, it is fastened by a very strong rope to an immense sledge; sticks are thrust through this rope to prevent it from slipping off, and pieces of leather are placed underneath to protect the statue from being chafed by the rope. No fewer than 172

After L. D., ii. 134. It was necessary here to leave out the right-hand side of the picture.

men are harnessed by four long ropes to this enormous load; they are so arranged that two should always grasp the rope at the same point; the further end of each rope is borne by a man on his shoulder. The overseer stands on the knee of the colossus, and gives commands to his workmen by clapping his hands and calling out to them; another stands on the base sprinkling water on the road, a third offers incense before the image of his lord. Accompanying the statue are men carrying the necessary water and a great plank, together with overseers with their sticks. At the end of the procession come the relatives of the lord, who escort him on his way. On the other hand, groups of people come to meet the procession, carrying green branches; each ten men have a leader and are dressed alike—these are the subjects of the prince, who come to greet the image of their chief. The arrival of such a great statue was in no way an everyday matter; for this town at any rate it was quite unprecedented, and not one of the past governors who had ruled over them either under the later *princes*, or under the ancient *judges and district-chiefs*, had ever "conceived such a thing in his heart." Ḍhuthôtep describes in a spirited way the difficulties of the undertaking: "As the way by which the statue was brought was exceedingly difficult, and as it was a most arduous work for the men to draw the precious block along the way because of the difficult rocky ground of sandstone,[1] I therefore ordered numbers of boys and young men, as well as the companies of masons and stone-cutters, to come and prepare a way for it. . . . The people who possessed strength called out: 'We come in order to bring it along'; my heart rejoiced; all the inhabitants of the town shouted for joy. It was an extraordinarily great sight." Thus all vied with each other to help their beloved chief, even the old men and the children, every one in his zeal redoubled his efforts, "they were strong, one man put forth the strength of a thousand." The citizens of the town came to meet the procession and to praise Ḍhuthôtep; his children followed him in festive garments; the people of the nome adored him. Thus amidst universal rejoicings they reached at last the boundaries of the town.

[1] I am doubtful about the translation "because of the difficult rocky ground of sandstone," because it is curious that there should be any mention of sandstone. It is indeed possible that the word in question, "stone of growth," originally did not specially signify sandstone. It is also strange that a statue of such dimensions should consist of alabaster.

HAWK WITH A RAM'S HEAD.
Gold inlaid with enamel. (Louvre. After Perrot Chipiez.)

EGYPTIAN ORNAMENTATION FOR A CEILING.

CHAPTER XIX

TRAFFIC AND TRADE

IN all countries consisting of the narrow valley of a great river, that river becomes the natural highway for all communication, especially when, as in Egypt, the country is difficult to traverse throughout a great part of the year. The Nile and its canals were the ordinary roads of the Egyptians; baggage of all kinds was carried by boat, all journeys were undertaken by water, and even the images of the gods went in procession on board the Nile boats—how indeed should a god travel except by boat? This was such an understood matter that it is difficult to find a word in the language that signifies to *travel;* the terms used were *chont* = to go up stream, and *chod* = to go down stream. The first word was used in speaking of any journey southwards, the latter of any journey northwards—even when it might signify travelling through the desert.[1] Under these circumstances it was natural that the building of river boats should be early developed as a national art.

The oldest form of boat used by the Egyptians was doubtless that of the little barks made of papyrus reed, such as were much admired by the Greeks of later times, and the like of which are used even at the present day in the Sudan. These boats had no deck, they were in fact little rafts formed of bundles of reeds bound together. They were rather broader in the middle than at the ends, the hinder part was generally raised up high whilst the front part lay flat on the water. The smaller of these boats, in which there was scarcely room for two people, consisted of one length only of papyrus reed; the larger (some were even big enough to carry an ox) were formed of several lengths cleverly put together. In the building of these boats,[2] every endeavour was made of

[1] Harr., 500, 5, 2.

[2] Papyrus boats in most of the pictures of the O. E.: e.g. L. D., ii. 60, 77. M. E.: L. D., ii. 127, 130; Ros. M. C., 24, 1. N. E.: W., ii. 104, 107, 108. Building of the same: Dum. Res., 8

course to join the reeds firmly together; a threefold rope was fastened round them at distances of about nine inches. When a boat of this kind was intended for the master's use, a thick mat was spread over the floor as a protection from the damp.

These papyrus boats drew very little water, and were therefore exclusively used by shepherds, huntsmen, and fishermen in the shallow waters of the marshes. They were easy to guide on account of their lightness and their small size; and even where the water was too shallow, they could be carried without any difficulty to deeper water. These little skiffs never had sails, nor were they ever rowed properly; they were either propelled along with poles provided with two points to catch the bottom, or by short oars with broad blades, with which the rower lightly struck the surface of the water; the latter could be used equally well standing or squatting. This primitive style of rowing, which is still in use amongst some of our river fishermen, sufficed very well for the little papyrus barks, especially as they only carried light weights; a touch was enough to send them gliding over the smooth water. Papyrus boats were occasionally built of larger dimensions,[1] thus, *e.g.*, in the time of the 6th dynasty we find one which required at least thirty-two rowers and a steersman. This was a foolish innovation and did not last long; as a rule, the larger boats, even in early ages, were all built of wood, though, as we have seen in the preceding chapter, Egypt was very badly off for that material. Under the pressure of necessity however the Egyptians used their bad material to great advantage; and it seems that, even in very early times, boat-building was carried on most extensively. Even under the Old Empire boats were built of large dimensions and of considerable port,—thus we hear of a "broad ship of acacia wood, 60 cubits long and 30 cubits broad," *i.e.* nearly 100 feet long and 50 feet across, and a boat of this immense size was put together in 17 days only.[2] The number of various forms of boats in the pictures of the Old Empire shows how highly developed was this branch of handicraft.[3]

The characteristic form of the modern Nile boat, in which the hinderpart rises high out of the water, is also to be seen in the boats of the Old Empire; it was doubtless due to practical reasons. In the first place, in the small boats and papyrus skiffs, which were not rowed but rather pushed along, this hinderpart gave the man who propelled them a good hold; a more important matter on the other hand was that it enabled the boat to be easily pushed off from the many sandbanks, on which even the boats of the present day are continually stranded. The channel of this sacred stream was constantly changing; even large boats were therefore built with

(in detail: the workmen have their provisions with them, and therefore are out in the fields); L. D., ii. 106 a, ib. 12; W., ii. 208.

[1] Papyrus boats of unusual size: L. D., ii. 106 a; and Düm. Res., 3 d. Observe also that in both examples the rowers sit with the face forwards, which is rarely the case in wooden boats, but always so in the little papyrus skiffs.

[2] Ä. Z., 1882, 24.

[3] I do not give an exhaustive description of all the various forms; much information on this subject may be found in Glaser's treatise (Düm. Res.), a very good practical work.

very little draught, so that as a rule they only skimmed the water, scarcely a third of their length touching the surface ; we must except the transport boats, which drew more water and were therefore built unusually flat. A boat about 50 feet long would have sides scarcely 3 feet high,[1] and had not another plank been laid along the edge, the water would certainly have beaten into the boat.

Under the Old Empire the oars[2] belonging to the wooden boats had sometimes a very narrow pointed blade ; they were used quite in the modern fashion, and not like those of the papyrus skiffs. The oars were put into rowlocks or through the edge of the boat ; the rowers sat facing the stern and pulled through the resisting water. To prevent the oars from being lost, each was fastened to the boat by a short rope, and when the oar was not being used, it was drawn out of the water and made fast to the edge of the boat.

The rudder[3] was unknown under the Old Empire, and long oars were used to guide the boat ; one steering-oar was enough for a small boat ; for a large one however, several oars were required on each side of the stern to guide it aright. These large steering-oars did not differ in shape from the other oars ; they were also put into rowlocks, and were secured by a rope to prevent their being lost. The helmsman usually steered standing.

Nearly all the boats seem to have been adapted for sailing as well as for rowing, except under the Old Empire, when sailing seems to have been an art that was little developed. We know of *one* sail only, and that is a rectangular square sail which was probably made of papyrus matting.

The mast is very curious, for as one piece of wood was not strong enough alone, the Egyptians used two comparatively slender masts bound together at the top. A strong rope went from the top of the mast to the bows, and another to the stern—these correspond to our *shrouds, i.e.* the ropes which keep the mast in place. In addition, six to twelve thinner shrouds were fastened from the upper part of the mast to the back part of the boat.

The yard-arm rested on the point of the mast ; the sailors were able to turn it to the right or left by two ropes which passed backwards from the ends of the yard. The sail hung down to the edge of the boat, and was provided in some cases at any rate with a second yard below ; it was of considerable size in comparison to the size of the boat. Thus a boat of perhaps 52 feet in length, with oars 10 feet and steering-oars 16 feet long, would have a mast of 33 feet and a yard of 20 feet, so that the sail would contain from 600 to 700 square feet of canvas.[4] When the wind dropped and the sail was lowered in order to row, the yard was taken off

[1] Düm. Res., 4.

[2] Pointed oars : Düm. Res., 5. Broader : Düm. Res., 3 ; L. D., ii. 22, 32, 45 a, b. In rowlocks : Düm. Res., 35. Stuck through the edge : Düm. Res., 4. Provided with a line : Düm. Res., 3, 4 ; L. D., ii. 45 b.

[3] Rudders—especially important : Düm. Res., 3, 4, 5 ; L. D., ii. 28, 32, 45, 62, 103 b.

[4] Düm. Res., 5.

and the mast taken down; the sail was then wrapped round both, and the whole laid on the top of the cabin or hung on forked posts.[1]

As I have already remarked, the pictures under the Old Empire represent several different sorts of boats, the inscriptions also do not speak of *boats* simply, but of "square-boats, stern-boats, tow-boats," etc. In the following pages I shall only speak of the more striking variations in the form of these ancient boats. There is no doubt that the best and quickest craft under the Old Empire were the long flat sailing-boats used

LARGE BOAT FOR TRAVELLING OF THE TIME OF THE OLD EMPIRE.
The master is standing before the cabin, his scribes are bringing their reports to him (after L. D., ii. 45 b).

by men of rank for their journeys.[2] They were built of a light yellow wood, doubtless a foreign pine wood. As we see, they differ from the other boats in that the fore and hind parts are shorter and lower than is otherwise customary; these are also frequently thrown into relief by decoration; they may be painted dark blue, or the prow may end in the carved head of an animal; this head is always turned backwards, contrary to the direction of the figure-heads in our modern ships. On the black

[1] Concerning the masts, sails, and rigging of the O. E., cp. especially Düm. Res., 4, 5; L. D., ii. 28, 43 a, 64 bis a, 96. Sail rolled up: L. D., ii. 45 a. Mast and yard lying down: L. D., ii. 103 b. The foot-rope yard, the occurrence of which under the O. E. Glaser denies: L. D., ii. 28. In the same example there is a rope between the two halves of the mast, which probably served to raise the foot-rope yard.

[2] Large sailing-boats for travelling (generally represented two together): L. D., ii. 22, 28, 43 a, 45 a, b, 64 bis a, 96; Düm. Res., 4, 5. Similar row-boats: L. D., ii. 22, 24, 43 a; Düm. Res., 3.

wooden deck behind the mast stands the cabin, the sides of which consist of prettily plaited matting, or of white linen, that can be wholly or partly taken down. During the journey the cabin is the home of the master, for even if he holds the rank of an admiral he takes no part of course in the management of the boat. We have not yet mentioned the pilot, who, with a pole in his hand to sound the depth, stands in the bows and gives directions to the steersmen. When they approach the bank in order to disembark, the pilot has to call to the men who are to help with the landing, and as he has to do this when at some distance from shore, we find that (even as early as the 4th dynasty) a speaking trumpet was used for this purpose.[1] The sailor squatting behind on the roof of the cabin has a responsible position ; he looks after the sail, and with quick gestures repeats the commands of the pilot. In addition to the sail, these vessels

SMALL BOAT FOR TRAVELLING OF THE TIME OF THE OLD EMPIRE, BUILT IN A DIFFERENT WAY FROM THE LARGE BOAT, WITH HIGH STERN, AND WITHOUT ANY OARS (after L. D., ii. 43 a).

almost always carry oars, generally about a dozen on either side. The number of rudder-oars to steer the vessel varies according to the number of oars,—to nine oars on a side there belong two rudder-oars ; to fourteen, three ; to twenty-one, four.

The large row-boats are nearly related to the above splendid class of vessel ; they also have flat stern and bow ; the cabin however takes up nearly the whole length of the vessel. These boats do not seem to be intended for sailing,—in fact there would be no room for a mast on account of the size of the cabin.

The space on board the larger transport vessels was still more restricted ;[2] all the room was utilised for stowage, so that the space allotted to the rowers and steersmen was insufficient and uncomfortable. The

[1] L. D., ii. 28.

[2] Large transport vessels : L. D., ii. 62, 104 b ; Düm. Res., 3. Similar ones, but arranged for sailing also : L. D., ii. 103. Small transport vessels : L. D., ii. 96, 103.

outer edge was high, so as to give more ship space, while in the middle of the vessel stood the large main cabin, and just behind it a second cabin, the roof of which sloped downwards to the stern. Nevertheless, it was not enough that thus four-fifths of the length of the vessel should be taken

LARGE CARGO-BOAT OF THE TIME OF THE OLD EMPIRE.
The rowers appear to have hung their oars to the neck of the calf (after L. D., ii. 62).

up with the cabins, even the remaining fifth was not left for the rowers, but had to serve as space for the cattle for transport. The three or four men, therefore, who rowed a freight vessel of this kind, had to balance themselves on a balustrade erected in the stern, whilst the two steersmen had to manage their rudder-oars from the sloping roof of the stern cabin.[1]

Besides the freight vessels proper, there were special small boats that were used for carrying lesser weights; these could be rowed and steered

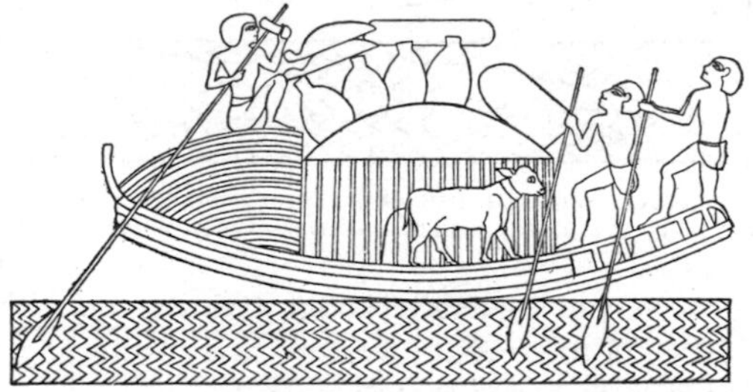

SMALL CARGO-BOAT OF THE TIME OF THE OLD EMPIRE (after L. D., ii. 104 b).

at the same time by one man, and might, for instance, accompany the large sailing boat of a gentleman and his suite as provision boats.

When sailing was impossible owing to contrary winds, or, as is too often the case on the Nile, when a dead calm ensued, the sailors had to resort to the tedious work of towing, owing to the strong current.[2] In the pictures of the vessels therefore, even of the Old Empire, we see that most of them have a strong post round which the tow-rope can be

[1] They fastened a cross piece to their rudder-oar, which afforded them a firmer grip.

[2] The towing of a funerary vessel by tow-lines and by small boats: L. D., ii. 101 b. The towing of the bark of the sun in the Book of the Dead. Concerning the vessel called the Sat', cp. also the inscription of Un'e.

twisted. In travelling by boat the Egyptians of old times were so accustomed to this wearisome expedient that they could not even imagine that their gods could do without it, and according to their belief the bark of the sun-god had nightly to be towed through the netherworld; it was only by day it could go forwards on the ocean of the sky by means of its sails and oars.

Vessels that were intended to carry a large freight seem to have been always towed either by men or by other vessels; they were too heavy for independent movement. We must here mention the boat called the *Sat'*, the name of which probably signifies *tow-boat.* Neither the prow nor the

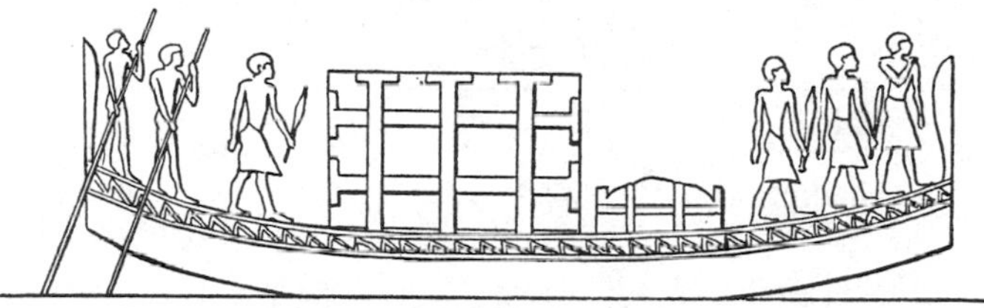

TOW-BOAT OF THE TIME OF THE 5TH DYNASTY.
The lath-crate is worthy of notice, in which the coffin is enclosed during transport (after L. D., ii. 76 e).

poop was specially characteristic, except that at both ends there was a short perpendicular post for the tow-line. They were steered, like all vessels of the Old Empire, by means of long oars. This kind of vessel was employed in the transport of blocks from the quarries on the eastern bank to the pyramids and tombs of the Memphite necropolis. The vessel represented here, which is expressly stated to be unusually large, belonged to King 'Ess'e of the 5th dynasty, and bore the name of "Fame of 'Ess'e." In our picture she is laden with the sarcophagus and the sarcophagus cover, which the king presented as a gift to his faithful servant, the chief judge, Send'em'eb.

The vessels of which we have hitherto spoken all belong to the time of the Old Empire. During the obscure period at the close of this epoch,[1] great improvements were probably introduced, for the vessels of the Middle Empire are considerably better than those of earlier date.[2]

In our illustration the clumsy steering-oars used under the Old Empire have been replaced by a large rudder, which is easily managed with a rope by the helmsman. The two laths used formerly as a substitute for a mast have also been replaced by a strong pole-mast. From this time also the

[1] We first see the mast formed of one trunk, and the shorter sail provided with a double yard, and richer rigging, in the relief of a certain [hieroglyphs] (Dyn. VI.), brought to Boulak in 1885; unfortunately I made no notes as to the manner of steering.

[2] Vessels of the M. E. (all from Beni Hasan)—sailing vessels: L. D., ii. 127, ib. 126 (Ros. M. C., 109, 1); the latter have still the old-fashioned mast. Vessel for the women: L. D., ii. 126 (=Ros. M. C., 109, 2); Ros. M. C., 105, 1. Vessel disembarking: Ros. M. C., 106, 2.

sail is always provided with a lower yard, and the upper one, instead of being fixed to the top of the mast, is fastened to it by movable rope-rings, so that it can be raised or lowered at will. The rigging has also been very much improved, so that altogether the vessels are far more easy

BOAT OF THE TIME OF THE MIDDLE EMPIRE (after L. D., ii. 127).

to navigate than they were under the Old Empire. Even the large row-boats have their share in these improvements; they also have now a true rudder, and the rowers sit on trestle seats placed on the deck of the vessel; there is also a beautiful cabin with sides of gay matting, with windows, and with a pleasant airy roof, where the women and children of the master can enjoy a cool resting-place during the journey.

For a long time the Egyptian boats did not advance beyond this stage of development, and there is not really much worthy of mention amongst the innovations introduced under the New Empire.[1] The most

BOAT FOR TRAVELLING OF THE TIME OF THE NEW EMPIRE (after W., ii. 224).

important is the abnormal breadth of the sail. Under the Old Empire the sail was considerably higher than it was broad; under the Middle Empire the breadth somewhat exceeded the height; but under the New Empire it sometimes attained such an immense breadth that no pole was long enough to serve as yard, and it became necessary to join two poles

[1] Many kinds of vessels are mentioned in the literature of the New Empire: for a picture of the *usech*, see L. D., iii. 10 a, of the *'aḥ'a*, Düm. Flotte, 2. Representations of "vessels for travelling": L. D., iii. 10 (=Ros. M. C., 110), ib. 116; W., ii. 224. State vessels, royal vessels: L. D., iii. 17 a. From the tomb of Ramses IV.: Ros. M. C., 105-108. "Transport vessels": L. D., iii. 10, 76, 116; W., ii. 213. A "fishing craft" in full sail: W., ii. 102.

together for this purpose. For instance, under the Old Empire a large vessel, perhaps 52 feet long, would have a mast of about 33 feet high and a yard 20 feet long. Under the Middle Empire the mast would be reduced to the height of 16 feet, whilst the yard retained its length of 20 feet. Under the New Empire the yard would be lengthened to perhaps 32 feet, thus double the height of the mast. These immense sails naturally required an increase of rigging, which necessitated a fresh arrangement, consequently the mast was furnished with a kind of round head, a lath-box fastened to the top. Under the New Empire we find in the bows and often also in the stern of the larger sailing vessels, a wooden boarding half the height of a man; this serves as a place for the pilot or the captain "who stands in the bows and does not let his voice be wanting."[1] The cabin itself is higher than in the older period,[2] and in outward appearance somewhat resembles a house with doors and windows. The baggage of the master is piled up on the flat roof; room must be found there even for his carriage, for no grandee of the New Empire travelled without this newfangled means of transport with him.

The tendency to luxury, which is so characteristic of all the later epochs of Egyptian history, naturally had its effect on the adornment of their vessels. Under the Old Empire the vessel used by the princes in travelling was a simple narrow boat, adorned merely with the head of a ram at the bows; under the New Empire, on the other hand, the vessel of a man of rank had to be decorated in the most sumptuous manner.[3] The cabin has become a stately house with a delightful roof and an entrance adorned with pillars; the sides of the vessel gleam with the brightest colours, and are adorned in the fore part with large paintings; the stern resembles a gigantic lotus flower; the blade of the rudder-oar resembles a bouquet of flowers, whilst the knob at the top is fashioned into the head of a king; the sails (of the temple-barks at any rate) consist of the richest cloth of the most brilliant colours. A good example of the extent to which luxury was carried in this particular, under the New Empire, is seen in the royal vessel of Thothmes III. This vessel bears the very same name as it bore under the Old Empire, viz. "Star of the two countries";[4] it is therefore nominally the same royal vessel as carried King Chufu fifteen centuries before,[5] but how different is its appearance compared with the ancient simplicity. The cabin is now a building with a front door and tapestried walls of gay colours; the boardings for the helmsman and the captain resemble chapels, and near the latter there stands, as figure-head, the statue of a wild bull trampling men underfoot, evidently in allusion to the "victorious bull," *i.e.* the king.

[1] L. D., iii. 10 a.

[2] L. D., iii. 10 a, 116.

[3] A travelling vessel of this kind (*e.g.* for the official journeys of the great lords—An., 4, 6, 11; to convey them to their country houses: An., 4, 3, 6) is called *Bair*. The same vessels are also used on the sea—Harr., 77, 8.

[4] L. D., iii. 17 a.

[5] L. D., ii. 18 ff.

This luxury only extended, as I need scarcely observe, to the vessels used for travelling by rich people. The transport vessels under the New Empire remained as unadorned as before. They were merely furnished

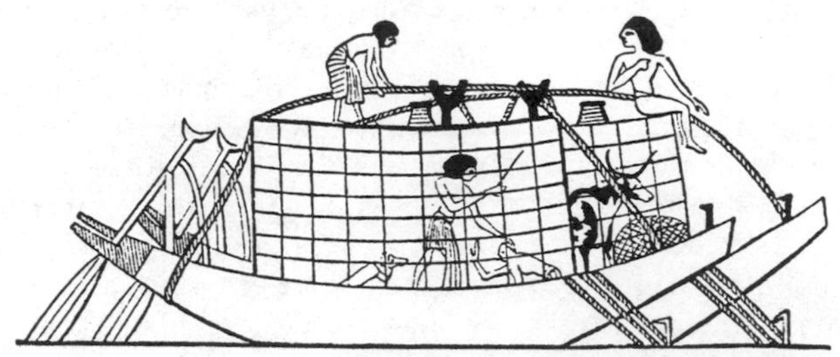

TWO CARGO-BOATS OF THE TIME OF THE NEW EMPIRE: THEY ARE ONLY ADAPTED FOR TOWING. They are moored to the bank (after W., ii. 213).

with a rough latticed partition on the deck for the cattle or for other freight.[1]

Besides their river-travelling, the Egyptians, even in early times, made sea voyages, though indeed only in a modest way. The sea ships [2] of Queen Chnemtamun, the only ones of which we possess any representation, exactly resemble the large river-boats of her time; in addition to an immense sail, they have thirty rowers.[3] These vessels did very well for coasting expeditions to the incense countries or to Syria, and the Egyptians rarely if ever undertook longer voyages.

As I have already remarked, travelling by land in Egypt was quite an unimportant matter compared to river travelling. Every journey was really made by water; it was only for the short distances from the Nile to their destination that the Egyptians required other means of conveyance. Men of rank of the Old Empire made use generally of a litter,[4] consisting of a seat with a canopy over it, which was carried on the shoulders of twelve or more servants; men walked by the side with long fans,[5] and waved fresh air to the master, whilst another servant carried a

[1] What is the purpose of the rope which passes above over the vessel?—These transport vessels of the New Empire are called *oxen ferry-boats*, and serve, for instance, for the transport of wine: An., 4, 6, 11.

[2] Under the New Empire a sea ship is called An., 4, 3, 10; Harr., i. 48, 6, 77, 8; also ib. 48, 6, as sea ship the , and ib. 77, 8, the *bpayr*; yet compared with the *menesh*, the two latter are rather ships for escort. Under the Middle Empire the Egyptians made voyages on the sea in the *'aḥ'a* (Ä. Z., 1882, 203); we find the same under the New Empire as Nile boats, Harr., i. 77, 13.

[3] Here also a rope runs horizontally over the vessel about 6 feet above it.

[4] L. D., ii. 50 a, 78 b. Relief of 'Ep'e at Gizeh.

[5] I stated erroneously that under the Old Empire these fans were used as standards (see p. 100). They consist of a long handle, to which is fastened a rectangular framework covered with linen, on the narrow side of which is a large movable flap (of feathers?), which played backwards and forwards when the fan was used.

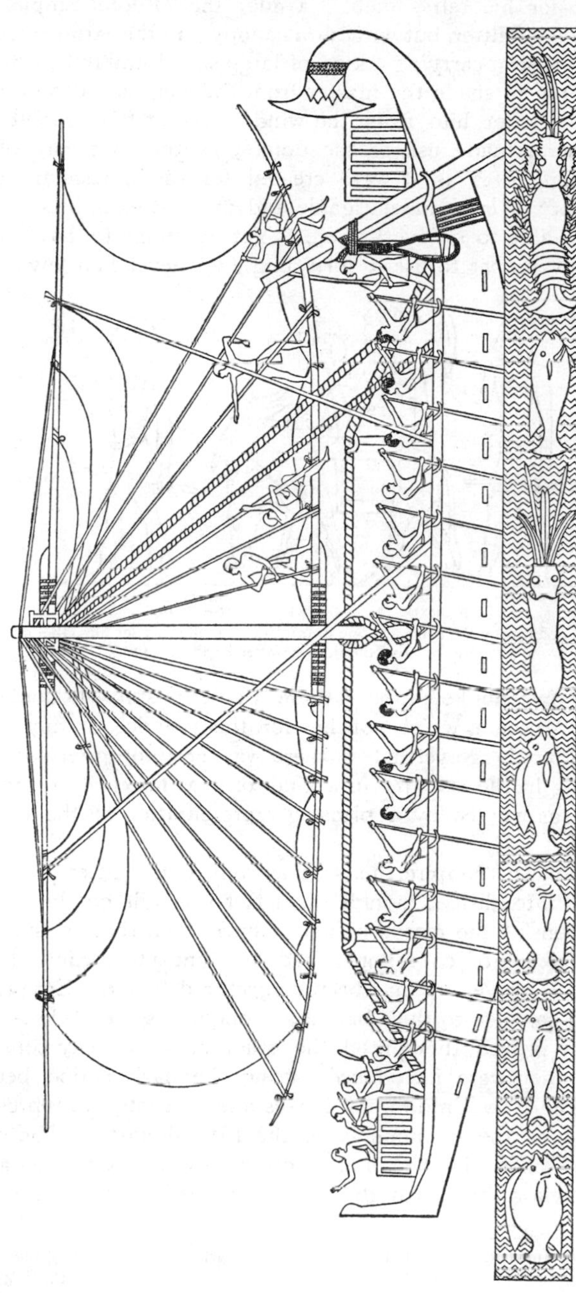

SAILING BOAT OF QUEEN CHNEMTAMUN ON THE VOYAGE TO THE INCENSE-COUNTRIES
(after Düm. Flotte, Pl. I. Cp. also the picture, p. 513).

skin of water for his refreshment. Under the Middle Empire also we meet with a similar litter, but without a canopy; in the latter picture, however, a servant is seen carrying a kind of large shield-umbrella, which might be used not only to shade the master from the sun, but also on a stormy spring day to shelter him from the wind.[1] As at the present day, the people in general made use of the donkey as the best way of getting about; the donkey is as it were created for the particular conditions found in Egypt; it is an indefatigable and, in good examples, also a swift animal, and is able to go everywhere. Yet it seems to have been considered scarcely proper to use it for riding; we never find any one repre-

JOURNEY IN A DONKEY SEDAN-CHAIR.
Two runners accompany their master, one in front to clear the way for him, the other to fan him and to drive the donkey (after L. D., ii. 43 a).

sented riding on a donkey, though there is an unmistakable donkey-saddle in the Berlin Museum, which vouches for this practice, at any rate under the New Empire.[2] Nevertheless there was no impropriety in a man of rank travelling in the country in a kind of seat fastened to the backs of two donkeys, as we see by a pleasing representation of the time of the Old Empire.[3]

Under the New Empire this seat, as well as the litter proper, appear to have fallen into disuse, though the latter was still employed on ceremonial occasions;[4] the reason seems to have been that in the meantime a far better means of conveyance had been introduced into Egypt, viz. the horse and carriage. It has been conjectured that the Egyptians owed the horse and carriage to their barbarian conquerors the Hyksos; but this has not been proved, though, on the other hand, we may consider it as certain that they were introduced during the dark period between the Middle and the New Empire, for horses and chariots are represented for the first time on the monuments of the 18th dynasty. The word *ḥtor*, which in later times signified horse, occurs once at any rate as a personal name on a stela of the 13th dynasty;[5] but as the original meaning of

[1] L. D., ii. 126=W., i. 421.

[2] Berlin, 789. Incidentally in a letter of the New Empire (Ä. Z., 1881, 119) there is the mention of the shoeing of a donkey with bronze.

[3] L. D., ii. 43 a.

[4] By the king: L. D., iii. 100, 121 a; by a high priest: L. D., iii. 97 b.

[5] Mar. Cat. d'Ab, 364.

this word signifies two animals yoked together (somewhat like our word *team*), it might therefore be used in the older period to indicate two oxen ploughing, as well as in later times in speaking of the horses of a carriage. We cannot therefore determine to which nation was due the introduction of the horse into anterior Asia and into Egypt, until we know from what language the word was derived, which became in Egyptian *ssmt* and *smsm*,[1] and in the Canaanite and Aramaic tongues סוס; this word being used in both countries for horse.

On the other hand it was certainly from the Semites, and indeed from the Canaanites, that the Egyptians borrowed the two forms of carriage, which became the fashion under the New Empire, and were used till quite late times,[2] viz. the *merkâbâ* and *'agâlâ*, or rather as they were called by the Egyptians, the *merkobt* and the *'agolt*. Whether there were vehicles of any kind in Egypt before the introduction of the above must remain uncertain.[3]

Concerning the *'agolt*, we only know that it was drawn by oxen, and used for the transport of provisions to the mines;[4] it was therefore a kind of baggage waggon. More is known about the *merkobt*, which was used for driving for pleasure,[5] for travelling,[6] for hunting in the desert,[7] and in war. It was a small very light vehicle, in which there was barely room for three persons to stand, so light in fact that it was said by an Egyptian poet[8] that a carriage weighed five uten and its axle weighed three—this must of course be a gross exaggeration, for the very lightest carriage would weigh more than eight uten (728 g. or about 1½ lbs.).

The *merkobt*[9] (cp. the illustrations, pp. 75, 408, 547) never had more than two wheels; these were carefully made of different wood or metal, and had four, or more usually six spokes. The axle carried the body of the carriage, which consisted of a floor, surrounded in front and at the sides with a lightly-hung wooden railing. The pole was let into this flooring, and for better security was fastened by straps to the railing; at the end of the pole there was a cross-bar, the ends of which were bent into a hook form, and served for the fastening of the harness. The harness was of a remarkable simplicity. Traces were at this time unknown to the Egyptians; round the breasts of the two horses there passed a broad strap, which was fastened to the transverse bar of the pole, and by this alone the carriage was drawn. In order that this strap should not rub the necks of the horses, the Egyptians put behind it underneath a broad

[1] The manner of writing this foreign word leads us to infer that it was introduced into Egypt earlier than מרכבה or עגלה, the terms for carriage.

[2] Both words are found in the Coptic.

[3] There is a third word for carriage *ureryt*, which *may* be of Egyptian origin. If from a foreign source, judging by the way it is written, it must have been introduced into the language earlier than the other two words, in the same way as one word for horse.

[4] L. D., iii. 219 e.

[5] Tur., 16.

[6] L. D., iii. 10 a.

[7] Tomb of at Thebes.

[8] An., 3, 6, 7.

[9] The following is after L. D., iii. 10 a bis, and many similar pictures. Cp. also the representations of carriage-building, Ros. M. C., 44; and also carriages still in existence (=W., i. 227-231, 232, 234, 236).

piece of leather, to the metal covering of which the strap was fastened; a smaller strap was passed from the back piece under the belly to the pole, to prevent the broad strap from shifting from its place. Reins were used to guide the horses; they passed over a hook in the back piece to the bits in the mouths of the horses. The fashion of head-gear resembled that used everywhere at the present day, and from the time of the 19th dynasty blinkers also were employed.[1]

All Egyptian carriages were built in the above manner, and were only distinguished from each other by the greater or less luxury of the equipment. In many the straps of the harness and the leather covering of the frame of the carriage were coloured purple; all the metal parts were gilded; the plumes of the horses were stuck into little heads of lions, and even the wheel-nail was carved into the shape of a captive Asiatic.

This rich equipment alone shows what value the Egyptians put upon their carriages and horses. Wherever it is possible they are represented, and it is a favourite theme of the *littérateurs* of the time to describe and extol them. The coachman, the *Kat'ana* (a foreign term by which he was called), is found in every household of men of rank;[2] and at court the office of "first Kat'ana to his Majesty" was such an important post that it was held even by princes. The favourite horses of the king, the "first great team of his Majesty," bear high-sounding names; thus, for instance, two belonging to Sety I. are called "Amon bestows strength," and "Amon entrusts him with victory," the latter bears also the additional name "Anat (the goddess of war) is content."[3] We learn from these names that the horses were trained to go into battle; and consequently fiery high-spirited horses were preferred. Thus the horses of Ramses II. required, in addition to the driver, three servants to hold them by the bridle,[4] and in other places Egyptian horses are usually represented rearing or pawing the ground impatiently. As a rule stallions were used rather than mares;[5] the colour of the animals was generally brown,—in a few instances however we meet with a team of fine white horses.[6] As far as I know geldings were not in use at this period. Those who required quiet animals preferred to employ mules; in a pretty Theban tomb-picture we see the latter animals drawing the carriage of a gentleman who is inspecting his fields; they are so easy to manage that a boy is acting as coachman.[7]

The horse was also used for riding in Egypt, but as with other nations of antiquity, riding was quite a secondary matter. We have no representations of Egyptians on horseback,[8] and were it not for a few

[1] L. D., 153 and often.

[2] In a private house, L. D., iii. 10 a bis.

[3] L. D., iii. 128 a, 130 b; ib. 126 b; a third, ib. 126 a. Those of Ramses II., ib. 153, 165, and frequently ib. 160, 166.

[4] L. D., iii. 153.

[5] L. D., iii. 153.

[6] E.g. in the above-mentioned tomb of 'Em-nud'em.

[7] From a photograph of a wall-picture in the British Museum.

[8] Barbarians in flight on horseback, Ros. M. C., 120. The Semitic goddess of war is also represented on horseback, L. D., iii. 138o.

literary allusions, we should not know that the subjects of the Pharaoh understood at all how to ride. Thus in one place we hear of the "officers (?) who are on horseback" pursuing the vanquished enemies,[1] and one of the didactic letters speaks of "every one who mounts horses."[2] In one story we read that the queen accompanied the Pharaoh on horseback,[3] and the satirical writer mentioned above (p. 380) says that he received the letter from his opponent when "seated on horseback."[4] At the same time we must repeat that the use of horses for riding was quite a secondary matter: the chief purpose for which they were used was driving.

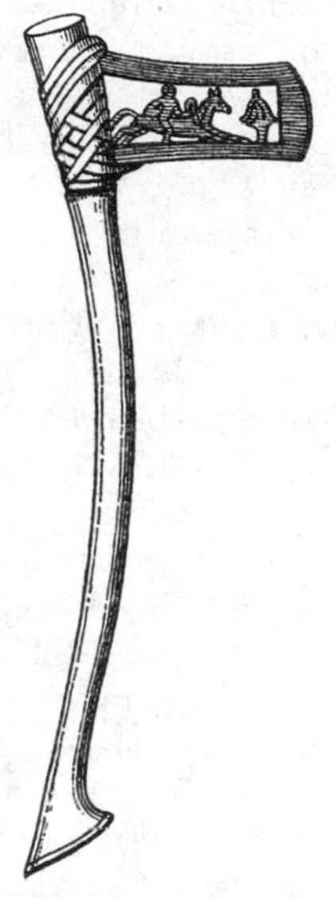

BATTLE-AXE, THE REPRESENTATION OF A MAN ON HORSEBACK IN PIERCED WORK ON THE BLADE (after W., i. 278).

Before I leave this subject I must touch upon a question that has been much discussed, viz. the introduction of the camel into Egypt. It may be considered as a proven point that this animal, which seems now so indispensable for desert-travelling, was first introduced into Egypt after the periods with which we are concerned. The camel does not appear in any inscription or picture before the Greek period,[5] and even under Ramses III. the donkey is still expressly mentioned as the beast of burden of the desert.[6]

These facilities for locomotion, the development of which we have traced above, naturally rendered the intercourse between the individual provinces of Egypt practicable. Yet owing to the long serpent-like form of the country, the distances between most of the towns were of a disproportionate length; this intercourse was therefore always of a limited nature. The distance from Thebes to Memphis was about 340 miles, from Thebes to Tanis about 430, and from Elephantine to Pelusium as much as 585 miles,—distances corresponding to those between London and Dublin, London and Perth, and between Brighton and Aberdeen. It is quite true that in other countries of antiquity, the chief towns were often situate as far apart, but the latter had facilities of intercourse on all sides, while the Egyptian towns, from the nature of the country, possessed neighbours on two sides only. These conditions did not of course tend to incite brisk intercourse between the various parts of the country, and the inhabitants of ancient Egypt (like those of modern date) were generally content with journeys to the neighbouring provinces.

Facilities for correspondence by letter seem, on the other hand, to have been early developed; these were doubly valuable on account of the

[1] Mar. Karn., 53, 38. [2] An., 4, 3, 4. [3] Orb., 17, 5. [4] An., 1. 4, 6.

[5] The attempts to prove that a foreign term in Egyptian corresponds to the word camel rest upon incorrect readings, and may therefore be considered as erroneous.

[6] Harr., i. 77, 12; 78, 3.

long distances we have alluded to above. We have already mentioned (p. 384) that the art of polite letter-writing was considered one of the most necessary accomplishments to be acquired in the schools; we must here add the little that is known concerning the despatch of letters. When, for instance, we read that the writer is disappointed of the answer he had been expecting to his letter, and finally writes to his friend that he is doubtful whether his boy by whom he had sent the letter had arrived,[1] reference is evidently made to a private messenger. There are however passages which seem to indicate that there was an established communication by messengers regularly and officially sent out; we read for instance: "Write to me by the letter-carriers coming from thee to me," and "write to me concerning thy welfare and thy health by all those who come from thee; . . . not one of those whom thou dost send out arrives here."[2] The same letter from which we have quoted the latter passage gives us also a possible indication of the manner in which small consignments were sent from one to another. The writer excuses himself for only sending fifty loaves of bread to his correspondent; the *shed* had indeed thrown away thirty because he had too much to carry; he had also omitted to inform him in the evening of the state of things, and therefore he had not been able to arrange it all properly.[3]

The same conditions which rendered personal intercourse difficult, prevented trade from assuming its due importance. For instance, the texts never speak of merchants,[4] which is a certain indication that trade had really an insignificant part to play. In ancient Egypt business was transacted for the most part in much the same way as it is in the bazaars and markets of the modern Egyptian provincial towns.

The remarkable pictures in a tomb at Sakkarah[5] show us the scenes of daily life in a market of the time of the Old Empire; they represent a market such as would be held on the estate of a great lord for his servants and his peasants. The fish-dealer is sitting before his rush basket, he is busy at this moment in cleaning a great sheath-fish, while he haggles about the price with his customer. The latter carries her objects for barter in a box, and is very far from being silent—she is holding a long conversation with the salesman as to how much she "will give for it." Near this group another tradesman is offering ointment or something similar for sale. Another is selling some objects that look like white cakes; the collarette which is offered him for one of these does not seem to him to be enough. "There (take) the sandals (as well)," says the buyer, and

[1] Bol., 1086, 7.

[2] An., 5, 12, 7, ib. 21, 1. The reader will observe the significance of the expression, *nte 'ey de mdak*, from which we conclude that reference is made to an established custom.

[3] An., 5, 21, 4.

[4] In Coptic a merchant is termed *eshôt*, a term which is not to be considered as identical with the title *shuyte*, though they are generally considered as equivalent. On the other hand, the Coptic word *eshôt* is probably descended from the above-mentioned word *shd*.

[5] L. D., ii. 96. The similar picture, L. D., ii. 103, represents rather the delivering up of the weaving to the overseer.

thus the bargain is brought at last to a conclusion. Brisk business is being carried on round the greengrocer. Onc customer is buying vegetables in

MARKETING UNDER THE OLD EMPIRE (after L. D., ii. 96).

exchange for a necklet, and the dealer assures him: "See I give the (full) value"; another customer comes up at the same moment, in the hope of buying his meal of onions in exchange for a fan. Eatables, however, are not the only things sold here; there is another dealer squatting before his basket of red and blue ornaments, he is bargaining with a woman who wants to buy one of his bright strings of beads. By her side is a man

MARKETING UNDER THE OLD EMPIRE (after L. D., ii. 96).

with fish hooks (?) who seems to be vainly pressing his wares on another man standing by.

In the tomb of the oft-named Cha'emḥê't, the superintendent of the granaries under Amenḥôtep III., there is a picture of marketing in the same small way under the New Empire. The great ships which have brought in the import of corn-provision for the state are disembarking in the harbour of Thebes, and whilst most of the sailors are busy discharging the freight, a few slip away quietly to the salesmen who are squatting on the bank before their jars and baskets.[1] Two of these dealers are evidently foreigners, perhaps Syrians; one of the latter is helping his wife to sell her goods, and the very primitive toilette of this lady leads us to conclude that their business is not very flourishing. They seem to be selling food of some kind, while in exchange the sailors are probably giving the corn that they have received out of the cargo as their wages. Goods of some kind at all events are being exchanged, for all the trade of Egypt was carried on by barter, and nothing was given in payment except goods or produce.

It seems strange to us of the modern world that a nation should hold markets, sell cattle, lend on interest, pay salaries, and collect taxes without even knowing the use of small coin; but this is really not so difficult as we might imagine, and the Mahommedans of the negro countries in Africa may be cited as a proof that a comparatively high standard of civilisation is compatible with trade by barter.

Barter of this kind never indeed remains purely as such for any length of time; the exigencies of trade soon require that some object should be set aside as an arbitrary standard by which the value of the various objects for exchange can be measured and compared. Thus at the present day in the Sudan, if a man buys gunpowder, he may perhaps pay the

[1] L. D., iii. 76 a.

merchant for it in fowls, but in order to know how much powder the one has to give, and how many fowls the other has to pay, they both reckon the present market value of their goods in a third commodity in common use, perhaps in amber beads. They may not make use of any amber beads in payment, or merely of a few to adjust some slight difference in value, but the beads have become an arbitrary measure of value in the market by which the price of goods can be reckoned. We see that in this case amber beads really play the part of money.

Measures of value of this kind are still common in Africa, and the merchants who carry on trade with the interior have to acquire exact knowledge of the usages of the various markets and towns. In one place beads may be used, in another blocks of salt, in another iron spades or Styrian razors, or perhaps *Merikanis, i.e.* pieces of bad American cotton goods of a certain size.

The conditions of trade in ancient Africa were very similar; under the New Empire at any rate a copper piece of one uten, *i.e.* of 91 grammes, was in use as a measure of value. This copper piece was in the form of a spiral wire ⟹ ⟹, and the weight was so firmly established that a wire of this kind served in writing as a sign for the uten. The reader will see incidentally from a bill of goods given above (p. 123), how this copper weight was used in the reckoning of payments. We will give another example, which shows us how an account was settled in buying an ox. In the latter case 119 uten of copper were to be paid up in all—111 uten for the animal itself, the remainder in presents and similar expenses—but of these 119 uten not one metal uten really changed hands. A stick (?) with inlaid work was substituted for 25 uten, and another of less elaborate design for 12 uten, 11 jars of honey for 11 uten, and so on.[1] We may observe that a few of these legal tenders recur in various reckonings, for instance certain sorts of sticks, and, if I rightly understand, certain kinds of paper also. The meanings of most of the terms used in the various accounts are unfortunately unknown to us, and therefore we must forgo trying to solve the interesting problem as to the relative values of the articles in greatest request. I am able however to give one instance: in the text quoted above, whilst an ox is said to be worth 111 uten, with additional expenses bringing it up altogether to 119 uten, an ostracon at Berlin[2] gives the value of a donkey as 40 uten. The relative value therefore of an ox and a donkey was as three to one.

We see by the important contracts of Ḥepd'efae', which we have had occasion to cite several times, that it was possible to carry on complicated commercial transactions with these primitive conditions of payment. This prince, who ruled in Siut under the Middle Empire, desired that for all future time the priests of his nome, with of course indemnification for cost,

[1] Inscr. in the hier. char., T. 15.

[2] Berlin, 8241. A comparatively good donkey may be purchased in Egypt at the present day for about 80 francs.

should present certain small offerings to his *ka*. Under complicated conditions he made over a certain fund to the temple, the yearly interest of which would cover the really small cost of these loaves and lamp-wicks: the endowments for masses in the Middle Ages and also at the present day present examples of a corresponding custom. Ḥepd'efae' had recourse to a rather peculiar procedure.[1] On one hand he ceded parts of his fields, thus, *e.g.*, he gave a piece of land to a priest of Anubis for the yearly supply of three wicks. On the other hand he bequeathed parts of his revenues, the first-fruits of his harvest, or the feet of the legs of the bull which belonged to him and his successors out of the sacrifices; but above all he preferred to pay with the revenues which he drew as member of a priestly family from the emoluments of the 'Epuat temple, the so-called "days of the temple." These daily rations, however, which consisted of provisions of all kinds, could not be received by people who lived at a distance from the temple; he was therefore obliged, if he wished to use them as payment for these people, to have recourse to a system of exchange; thus he gave up 22 "days of the temple" to his colleagues in exchange for a yearly supply of 2200 loaves and 22 jugs of beer to be given to those persons whom he really wanted to pay. In this way he exchanged those revenues of the temple, that were unsuitable to serve as payments, into bread and beer, which he could hand over to any one.

Though the home trade in Egypt never apparently flourished to any great extent, yet commerce with foreign countries seems to have been carried on at times with brisk activity. Nevertheless, as far as we know, Egypt always required to possess a special political position in order to bring her for a time into active intercourse with the neighbouring countries; an outside impulse of this kind being alone capable of overcoming the natural barriers—the rapids, the deserts, and the currents of the sea—which divide the valley of the Nile from all other countries. In the following pages we shall describe the development of these peaceful relations between Egypt and the neighbouring states, and the effect they exercised on the inhabitants of the Nile valley.

The country most accessible from Egypt is Nubia, but owing to the unproductive nature of the soil, it was only in late times, under the influence of Egyptian government, that this country attained a certain standard of civilisation. The northern part of Nubia was inhabited by a dark brown race, the ancestors of the present Nubians; the Egyptians classed them, however, with all the southern barbarians, as *Neḥes* or *negroes*. The natural political boundary between Egypt and Nubia was the first cataract. Here the island of Elephantine became the place of mart, where the Nubians exchanged the productions of their own country, and the goods that they had obtained from tribes further to the south, for Egyptian products. Panther skins, monkeys, ebony, but above all ivory, were brought here to be imported into Egypt. Even the names of the two places at the frontier, 'Abu (Elephantine) and *Suênet* (Syene), which

[1] See my revision of this inscription, Ä. Z., 1882, p. 159 ff.

signify *ivory island* and *commerce*, bear witness to the importance of this ancient trade.[1]

There is no doubt that Egypt exercised a certain supremacy over those tribes living next to her frontier. Even under King Pepy, the negro countries of 'Ert'et, Med'a, 'Emam, Uauat, Kaau (?), and Tat'e'am were obliged to reinforce the Egyptian army with mercenaries. Under Merenrê', also the successor of Pepy, the princes of the countries 'Ert'et, Uauat, 'Emam, and Med'a brought supplies of acacia wood to Elephantine for Egyptian shipbuilding. On the other hand, the same inscription which gives us this account, expressly emphasises the fact as really extraordinary that a large expedition sent by Merenrê' to the quarries of Syene was escorted by *one* warship only—the Egyptians evidently did not feel quite safe from attacks at the frontier.[2] Moreover, Elephantine itself was originally in the possession of Nubian princes, though even in early times they naturalised themselves as Egyptian officials and vassals of the Pharaohs; the most ancient of their tombs, belonging perhaps to the 6th dynasty, shows that the governor of that time was a dark brown Nubian, though his court seems to have been purely Egyptian.

The mighty kings of the 12th dynasty penetrated farther into Nubia, and completely opened out the northern part of that country to Egyptian civilisation. Usertsen I. subjected the south as far as the "ends of the earth," doubtless with the principal object of gaining access to the gold mines of the Nubian desert; and under his reign we hear for the first time of the "miserable Cush," *i.e.* of the southern part of Nubia.[3] Nevertheless, it was only the northernmost part of his conquest, the country of Uauat, that he was able to retain and to colonise, or as the Egyptians said, to provide with *monuments*;[4] his great-grandson, Usertsen III., was the first to achieve more. The latter extended his "southern frontier" as far as the modern Semneh, and boasted that "he had pushed forward his boundaries further than those of his fathers, and had added an increase to that which he had inherited."[5] In the eighth year of his reign he established the frontier stone there, "so that no negro might pass it, neither by water nor by land, neither with boats nor with herds of the negro." Those negroes only who came as ambassadors, and those who were travelling to the market of 'Eqen (this must have been the frontier station) were excepted, and free passage was allowed to them, though not on their own boats.[6]

Whilst the king was thus arranging for peaceful frontier relations, his sovereignty over this part of the country was again threatened. Eight

[1] *Sunt* is evidently identical with the word used in direct reference to this frontier trade (L. D., ii. 136 i) *sunt*, which still exists in the Coptic as **σουεν**, *value*.

[2] Ä. Z., 1882, pp. 12, 25.

[3] L. D., ii. 122.

[4] Thus L. D., ii. 123 e, ib. 151 c (named after Usertsen III.). Under the New Empire, in the inscriptions mentioned below from the tomb of Ḥuy. It is probable that the word is identical with , but this is not certain, owing to the constant variations in the way the word is written.

[5] L. D., 136 h.

[6] L. D., ii. 136 i; *ḥrt* is the word for desert-travelling.

years later the Pharaoh was obliged to take the field, and the solemn way in which, on the newly-erected frontier stones, he proclaims his triumph to posterity, shows sufficiently that he was himself conscious that it was only now with his second victory that he really sealed his conquest. He conjures his successors in the most impressive way not to let slip his conquered possessions. He says: "He of my sons who shall maintain this frontier stone which my Majesty has erected, he is in truth my son, and his children shall be my children; he resembles that son who protected his father (*i.e.* the Horus), and who maintained the frontiers of him who begat him. But he who lets the stone be destroyed, and will not fight for it, he is not my son, and his children have no part in me."[1] The colony which he established at this frontier was not only provided with a fortress but also with a temple, and it is a sign of his wise policy that this king dedicated the latter in the first place to Dedun, a Nubian god, and only in the second place to Chnum the Egyptian god. During the few next generations the new Egyptian province remained intact, and the successors of the conqueror were able to mark the height of the Nile during the inundation on the rocks of Semneh, the frontier of their kingdom.[2] They even penetrated further to the south, and a King Sebekḥôtep of thc 13th dynasty erected a statue to himself on the island of Argo, more than 360 miles to the south of Egypt.[3]

During the troublous times of the Hyksos rule, Nubia was apparently lost to Egypt, for the first two kings of the New Empire seem to have been obliged to fight close to the Egyptian frontier. Thothmes I., however, carried his arms nearly as far as King Sebekḥôtep had previously, and one of his immediate successors conquered Napata (the present Gebel Barkal), 540 miles up the Nile from Syene. From this time Nubia, or, as it was called in Egyptian, Cush, remained for 500 years under Egyptian rule, and though meanwhile there were some petty wars in that country, yet these really consisted merely of skirmishes with the desert Beduins, or fights with the frontier tribes of the south; the whole of the long valley from Syene to beyond Gebel Barkal was in the undisputed possession of the Pharaohs. At the same time Nubia never became an integral part of the Egyptian kingdom, it was always governed by viceroys, who bore the titles of the "royal son of Ethiopia," and "the superintendent of the southern countries" (or "of the gold countries"). This surprises us the less when we remember that the new subjects of the Pharaoh really possessed no civilisation of their own.

The southernmost tribes, the subjection of whom is pictured in the battle scenes, are represented by the Egyptian artists as barbarians, almost nude, and with long angular limbs very much like monkeys. Originally the northern tribes scarcely possessed a higher status; they soon gained, however, an outward civilisation, at any rate under the Egyptian government. In a picture of the time of Thothmes III. most of the negroes who are bringing tribute are still dressed in short skirts of skin,

[1] L. D., ii. 136 h. [2] L. D., ii. 139, 151, 152. [3] L. D., ii. 151 i.

two only wear Egyptian linen skirts like those formerly worn in Egypt by the peasantry.[1] A hundred years later a complete change had taken place in this respect, as we see by the representation bequeathed to us in his tomb by Ḥuy, the governor of Ethiopia under King Tuet'anchamun.[2] It represents the solemn ceremony when Ḥuy "came out of Ethiopia with this beautiful tribute, the choicest of all the southern countries," and brought it, together with the bearers thereof, the "great men of Ethiopia," to present to the king. There are here more than forty great men of Nubia (who like their modern descendants are partly brown and partly black); four only wear the old skin skirt of their forefathers, and even they have beautified it with a front piece of white material—all the others wear Egyptian garments, and indeed of the most fashionable kind. Many of them have even laid aside the old coiffure, in which the hair

NEGRO PRISONERS WITH THEIR WIVES AND CHILDREN.
They are being registered by a scribe (Thebes, after W., i. 270).

stood off from the head on all sides like a great roof, as well as the ostrich feather, the national head-ornament; they have let their woolly hair grow, and dressed it, as far as possible, in Egyptian fashion. A few have also given up the heavy national earrings and armlets, and replaced them by Egyptian ornaments. If we did not recognise by the colour of the skin, the woolly hair, and the negro features to which nationality these great men belonged, we might from their appearance almost mistake them for distinguished courtiers of the Pharaoh. One of these Nubian ladies is even driving in a carriage built exactly after the pattern of the Egypto-Syrian *merkobt;* yet strange to say she has substituted a team of dwarf oxen for the usual horses.

Amongst the presents that these *great men* are bringing, the show-pieces are of particular interest; the one in our illustration represents a table covered with panther-skins and woven material; upon the table is represented a Nubian landscape. The tall conical thatched huts, the giraffes, the dôm-palms with the monkeys playing in the boughs—all this represents a scene, the like of which can still be seen on the Upper Nile.

[1] W., i. pl. ii. b.

[2] L. D., iii. 116-118.

This village evidently belongs to one of the brown tribes of the north, for whilst these brown folk are depicted kneeling adoring the Pharaoh, the black negroes lie pitiably on the ground, or are obliged to allow their heads to be used as decoration for the huts.

It may fairly be questioned whether in these show-pieces brought from Nubia we really have specimens of native Nubian art. As a matter of fact, both here and in other places[1] we find that the tribes from the south generally brought as presents to the Pharaoh the natural products of their country, such as gold—in rings, bars, and bags,—precious stones, ivory, panther-skins, ostrich-feathers and ostrich-eggs, monkeys, panthers, giraffes,

SHOW-PIECE OF THE NUBIAN TRIBUTE.
The lower part, consisting of a table covered with skins, etc., is left out here (after L.D., iii. 118).

dogs, and cattle. At most we may regard the decoration of the cattle, the human heads and hands that are stuck on the points of the horns, and perhaps even the entire landscape that one of them bears on his head, as true products of the Nubian art industry.[2] The other works of art carried by the negro princes under the escort of Ḥuy, the golden carriages, the pretty ebony furniture, and the splendid metal vases, are evidently Nubian only as far as the material is concerned. In fact, the texts rarely, if ever, speak of the manufactures of those tribes,[3] whilst those of the Syrians are frequently mentioned; the Egypt of the New Empire indeed was evidently inundated with the industrial arts of the latter people.

The Nubian barbarians were not content however with imitating the clothing only of their Egyptian lords, they also adopted what was more

[1] W., i. pl. ii. b.

[2] Nevertheless an example of similar decoration is also found in the case of a sacrificial animal in an Egyptian temple (L. D., iii. 94).

[3] An exception An., 4, 2, 126 (=Koller, 3, 1), where a ship's cable or something similar is mentioned as the "work of Cush."

important, their religion, and perhaps also their language and writing.[1] When Usertsen III. founded a temple in his frontier fortress, it is true that he had the wisdom to install the Nubian god Dedun as principal divinity, but the worship established there was appointed in pure Egyptian fashion, and the barbarian god was simply received into the Egyptian pantheon. The rulers of the 18th dynasty again took up the work of their great ancestors. At Kumneh, opposite Semneh, where Usertsen III. had already built a small temple to the god Chnum and to himself,[2] Thothmes I. and Thothmes II. enlarged the temple, and the third king of this name finished it.[3] The latter ruler then restored also the temple of Semneh, and on the proposal of the governor of Nubia he re-established the endowment of corn, clothes, and cattle, which Usertsen III. had formerly founded for the festival days of that temple.[4] Further north at Amada he built a temple to Harmachis,[5] whilst the governor Neḥy caused a grotto temple to be excavated at Ellesieh to the Horus gods of northern Nubia.[6] Other buildings were erected by the same monarch further to the south, at Sai, at Gebel Doshe, and at other places. The custom introduced by Usertsen III. of giving to the barbarians the Pharaoh himself as the god of their country was followed afterwards by Amenḥôtep III., who built a temple to himself at Soleb, and another to his consort at Sedeinqa. Under the 18th dynasty the great Egyptian gods were also provided with their own sanctuaries in Nubia—thus, for instance, under Tuet‘anchamun, the town of Napata was called after the temple of Karnak, the "throne of the two countries."[7] Ramses II. was the first, however, who went systematically to work; at Abu Simbel, Gerf Ḥusên, Wadi Sebu‘, and at Derr, he excavated immense rock temples for Amon, Ptaḥ, and Rê‘, the great gods of Thebes, Memphis, and Heliopolis. These sanctuaries, the first of which was one of the grandest ever created by Egyptian skill, prove that at that time Nubia was essentially an Egyptian province, and as such the final consecration was given to the country by providing it with imitations of the chief religious cities of Egypt. In fact, a few centuries later and the *miserable Cush* of former times had become more Egyptian than Egypt herself, and maintained that the orthodoxy of her religion was even purer than that of the home of her gods, which was distracted by Semitic and Libyan influences.

The further this Egyptian influence spread, the more the administration of Nubia lost its individual character, though she retained her viceroyalty —which was administered as formerly by a virtually independent[8] "royal son of Ethiopia."[9] At various times we obtain a glimpse into the working

[1] It is doubtful at what period the Egyptian became the written language of Nubia, whether under the New Empire or only after its separation from Egypt.

[2] L. D., ii. 136 d, f, g.

[3] L. D., iii. 59 a.

[4] L. D., iii. 55 a.

[5] L. D., iii. 45 a, c.

[6] L. D., iii. 46.

[7] Unpublished inscription in the tomb of Ḥuy.

[8] For instance these governors even erected temples and allowed themselves to be represented in them (L. D., iii. 46, 47, 56, 178).

[9] For instance towards the end of the 20th dynasty. Cp. the interesting royal letter of recommendation for an official sent to Nubia; Tur., 66-67.

of this administration, and each time it seems to have assumed a different form. Towards the end of the 18th dynasty our old friend Ḥuy was appointed governor of Ethiopia by King Tuetʿanchamun.[1] The solemn ceremony of the appointment took place in the temple of Amon at Thebes ("Amon received him," so it is said), and the treasurer delivered to him as the symbol of his rank the "golden seal-ring of his office." His jurisdiction was to extend from the town of Nechen to the town of the "Throne of the two countries," or, as the latter was also called, the country of Q̣er, *i.e.* from El Kab to Napata on Gebel Barkal.[2] Now when Ḥuy went home to his province, all the highest officials there received him, in particular the "deputy governor of Ethiopia," and the "superintendent of oxen" in this province; also the princes of the two Egyptian settlements, "Shining in truth" (*i.e.* Soleb) and "Inclosure of the gods," as well as the "deputy governor" of the latter and two officiating priests of that place. Under these Egyptian officials however there still ruled—even in northern Nubia—native petty princes as Egyptian vassals, though they may have had no more power than the Indian Maharajahs of the present day under the English sovereignty. One of them, the prince of M'eʿam, must have been considered a man of special merit, for he bore the epithet of the "good ruler."[3]

A few generations later we find the "royal son of Cush" surrounded by quite a different class of officials, by *scribes*, *scribes of the soldiers*, *scribes of the granaries*, etc.;[4] there is no further question of colonies or *monuments*, but rather of *towns*, which are subject to the "superintendent of the towns of Cush."[5] What is perhaps still more significant, is that Nubia held her own court of justice; thus the governor under Ramses II. styles himself "the superintendent of the great house" (*i.e.* of the court of justice, see pp. 87, 138) "in the house of truth, and the chief judge of northern Nubia."[6]

An interesting tomb at Ạnibe, not far from Derr, shows us the state of Nubia towards the end of the 20th dynasty. Pennut, the official who was buried there, was the "deputy governor" of the town of M'eʿam. His sons had appointments in the home government, and his daughters served as *singers* in the temples of the town. He himself was a deserving and loyal official; he had reduced the gold districts of the Nubian deserts to a state of security, and "had subjected the negro races (?) of the country of 'Ekayte, and had led them as captives before the Pharaoh." Moreover he had caused a statue of the king, half as large as life, to be erected for his district, representing the ruler with the ancient insignia—the royal helmet on his head, and two sceptres in his hands. He had

[1] All that follows is from the unpublished representations in the tomb of this man.

[2] By Nechen are we to understand the well-known town of El Kab in Upper Egypt, or a Nubian town of the same name?

[3] L. D., iii. 117.

[4] L. D., iii. 184 d.

[5] Mar. Cat. d'Ab., 1169.

[6] L. D., iii. 174 c. If the titles are complete (a break follows) the court of justice was only appointed for the northern and most civilised part of the country.

also settled great gifts of land on this statue, as well as on two similar ones in the possession of the priest Amenemopet and the deputy governor Mery, in order that offerings might be brought to them to the end of time. The king honoured him with a costly present as a reward for this excellent conduct: he sent him two silver ointment bowls, which were filled with costly Qam'ey ointment.[1] This town of M'e'am, where everything was so very Egyptian, was most probably (as Brugsch conjectures) the identical town M'e'am that was ruled two or three centuries earlier by its own Nubian *good prince*.

We see that in Nubia Egypt really fulfilled a mission and by degrees civilised a barbarian country. This is however, as far as we know, the only quarter where the Egyptians succeeded in such an attempt; the other races of lower civilisation, with whom they came in contact, were either nomadic tribes or were so remote from Egypt that it was quite impossible to develop really close relations. This was particularly the case with the incense countries of the Red Sea, to the consideration of which we now turn.

The two countries, the *Divine Land* and the country of Punt,[2] were considered of old by the Egyptians as the original source of incense and other precious things. A definite idea, however, is scarcely to be attached to the name of either country; they were general terms,—terms such as are still created by commerce, *e.g.* the word *Levant* of modern times.

The Divine Land signified originally only the East, where God, *i.e.* Rê', appeared daily; in common parlance the term was applied probably to the mountainous desert between the Nile and the Red Sea,[3] the peninsula of Sinai,[4] and also doubtless to the northern and central part of Arabia. Punt, on the other hand, evidently signified the more tropical coast lands of the Red Sea, the south of Arabia, and the Somali coast.

There is no doubt that the Egyptians of very early times were in communication with the Divine Land; there, in fact, lay the quarries of Ḥammamât, and through that country the way led to the Red Sea, and therefore to the mines of Sinai,[5] and to the incense countries. Doubtless ever since the time of Snefru, the "treasurers of the god," and their subordinate officials,[6] travelled along this road, and indeed in all probability by almost the same route as is now taken by the caravans of modern times—the route of Qoṣêr. In the course of centuries the starting and arrival points alone seem to have been somewhat changed. In the early

[1] L. D., iii. 229 ff.

[2] The name Punt is not a one-syllabled word (this would be written Pnt), but a word of two syllables containing the consonants p, w, n, together with the feminine ending t. Nothing is known about the vowels of the word.

[3] Cp. Ä. Z., 1882, 205. Also L. D., ii. 149 d; L. D., iii. 223 c, where Ḥammamât is expressly stated to be situate in the Divine Land.

[4] L. D., iii. 29 a.

[5] The St. Petersburg tale expressly states that the quarries were reached by ship; Dümichen also, in his History, has proved from the later religious geography that such was the ancient idea.

[6] The captains [hieroglyphs] belong to this class: L. D., ii. 115 b, f, m, 116 a.

ages, and even in Greek times, travellers started from Coptos; in the Middle Ages from the neighbouring town of Quṣ, while at the present day Keneh has become the starting-point of these caravans. Further, though the sea is now reached at the harbour of Qoṣêr, in Greek times the *white haven* was the goal of the journey, and in old times (at any rate for a time) it was situate in the Wadi Gasûs, somewhat to the north of Qoṣêr, at a place called Sauu. The Egyptians built a fortress there to protect this important point from the barbarians; they also erected a small temple where travellers might commend themselves to the protection of the mighty protector of the deserts of the Divine Land, the god Min of Coptos.[1]

Two remarkable pieces of information touching events in the Divine Land have come down to us from the time of the 11th dynasty. Under the same King Mentuḥôtep, who opened a well in Ḥammamât, or "bored for water in those mountains, which had before been impassable for men," and who thus "opened out the way for travelling,"[2] the officer Se'anch went to Ḥammamât and provided it "with all the green plants of Upper Egypt." He relates further: "I transformed its valleys into gardens of herbs and its heights into tanks of water, and provided it with children throughout its whole extent, southwards to the country of Ta'au, and northwards to the town of Men'at Chufu. I repaired to the sea and hunted people and hunted cattle, and I came to this region with sixty full-grown people and seventy of their young children at a single time."[3] Thus in order to supply the newly-established well-station with inhabitants, a raid had been made upon the poor Beduins of the mountains, the Troglodytes of the Greek travellers.

No less interesting is the inscription, belonging to the time of the somewhat later King Se'anchkerê', which the "chief treasurer Ḥenu the commander in the desert, the chief in the mountains, satisfying the two Egypts, the much feared and zealously loved," has engraved in Ḥammamât. It relates as follows: "His Majesty commissioned me to fit out ships for Punt, in order to fetch fresh incense from the princes, the chiefs of the red country,[4] for the fear of him pursues the barbarians. Behold, as I marched out of the town of Coptos on the way that his Majesty had commanded me, I had troops from the south countries with me, who prepared the way before me, and subjected all that were adversely disposed towards the king. Thus I marched out with an army of 3000 men." There were all manner of artisans also who followed the soldiers. The route of the journey was through various places unknown to us, and everything was so well arranged that Ḥenu was able to give to each of his men two jugs of water and twenty cakes of bread daily. Furthermore, he dug two deep wells in the country of 'Edahet, and a

[1] Ä. Z., 1882, p. 203.
[2] L. D., iii. 140 d; the expression is taken from an inscription of the New Empire.
[3] L. D., ii. 149 g.
[4] The "red country" is any foreign country in contradistinction to the "black," *i.e.* Egypt.

third in the country of 'Eaheteb. He relates also: "I reached the sea, and I built this ship, and I equipped it entirely and prepared a great sacrifice for it of calves, oxen, and gazelles. But when I had returned from the sea and had fulfilled everything that his Majesty had commanded me, I brought him all the products that I had found in the districts of the Divine Land." Ḥenu, not content with what he had already accomplished on this journey, made his way back by the stone quarries of Ḥammamât, and "brought blocks of stone for colossi and statues of the temple. Nothing of like importance had taken place under former kings, and never had the like been carried out by any relative of the king that had been sent out since the time of God. I, however," continues Ḥenu, "have done this for the Majesty of my lord, because he loves me so much and because he has allotted to me the first place in his palace before all the great men of this country. . . . I am indeed his beloved servant who does everything that he commands day by day."[1]

As we see, Ḥenu did not go himself to Punt. He marched with his men from Coptos to the Red Sea; there he equipped a ship, and assured to her a lucky voyage by the sacrifices which he offered to the gods. Unfortunately we learn nothing about this voyage, though the fact alone that the Egyptians of the 11th dynasty made voyages to Punt is of importance. Were it not for this inscription of Ḥenu, and another of the chief-treasurer Chentchetuêr, who under Amenemḥêt II. "returned happily from Punt—his soldiers were with him, hale and hearty, and his ships landed at Sauu,"[2]—we might doubt whether the products of the incense countries did not make their way into the Nile valley solely by means of the carrying trade of Arabia. These products had, in fact, been long familiar to the Egyptians; even under the Old Empire incense and myrrh were necessary requisites for all religious services, and we even meet with a native of the incense countries, the negro Ḥert'es'e, amongst the servants of one of the sons of King Chufu.[3] Nevertheless many centuries later the country of Punt was still considered by the Egyptian people to be a semi-mythical fairyland.

The latter conception is not without general interest, for similar ideas are found in all parts of the world; every primitive people imagines that the distant countries, from which precious things are brought by commerce, are fabulous realms inhabited by wonderful creatures. The primitive man finds it difficult to realise that these strange rare spices are the fruit of ordinary plants, the cultivation and harvest of which costs as much trouble as the cultivation and harvest of his native fruits. It is as incomprehensible to him also that precious stones are essentially the same as the pebbles that he picks up out of his fields. How could they then be so rare and so valuable? With his tendency to love the marvellous,

[1] L. D., ii. 150 a. For the correct reading of the word *uad'uêr*=sea, I am indebted to a verbal communication from Golenischeff.

[2] Ä. Z., 1882, p. 203.

[3] L. D., ii. 23. The coiffure shows that this *negro* belonged to the *negroes of Punt*.

and his disinclination to common sense, man allows his imagination to weave tales about distant countries—tales which are much alike in all folk-lore.

Ants or griffins may seek for gold in the desert, gigantic birds may collect precious stones in the nests they have built high up in the mighty mountains, while even ivory cannot possibly be obtained from the prosaic elephant, it must be the horn of the noble unicorn. The spices and essences must come from wonderful islands lying far away in the ocean; there the sailors find them at certain times lying on the strand, guarded only by spirits or by snakes. The air is so heavy with the fragrance that they emit, that it is necessary to burn asafoetida and goat's hair to counteract the excess of sweet scents.[1]

The wondrous traveller's tale contained in a St. Petersburg papyrus of the Middle Empire shows that for a long time the Egyptian people cherished similar ideas about the incense countries. "I was travelling to the mines of the Pharaoh," relates some treasurer, "and I had put to sea in a ship which was 150 cubits long and 40 cubits broad, and was manned by 150 of the choicest Egyptian sailors, who knew both the sky and the earth, and in whom the heart was wiser than that of a lion.

"They had said that the wind would not be bad, that, indeed, it might be quite calm; but when we were on the sea there arose a gale, and scarcely did we near the land when the wind rose, and the waves became 8 cubits high. I alone, I seized a piece of wood; all the others who were in the ship perished without exception. A wave washed me on to an island after I had spent three days alone (in the sea) with my heart together alone. Then I lay down in a thicket, and it became dark before my eyes (?). At last I set out to seek for some food for my mouth. There I found figs and grapes, all manner of plants and fruits,[2] all kinds of melons, fish, and birds. Nothing was wanting. Then I ate till I was satisfied; and what I had taken that was too much for me, I laid down for myself on the ground. Then I made a pit, lighted a fire, and offered a burnt sacrifice to the gods.

"Suddenly I heard a noise of thunder, which I thought to be the roar of a wave; the trees trembled and the earth shook. I raised my face and saw that it was a snake approaching; he was 30 cubits in length, and his beard was more than 2 cubits long. His limbs were inlaid with gold, and his colour was like real lapis-lazuli. He rolled forwards and opened his mouth; I threw myself down before him, and he spake: 'Who has brought thee hither? who has brought thee hither, little one? who has brought thee hither? If thou dost not tell me immediately who brought thee hither, then I will show thee who thou art!' . . .

"Then he took me in his mouth, carried me to his lair, and laid me down without doing me any harm: I remained unhurt, and nothing

[1] Some of the ancient literature treating of the incense countries corresponds in a striking way with the Egyptian legend which is related here.

[2] In the original there are specific names of plants and fruits.

happened to me. Then he opened his mouth towards me, I threw myself down before him and he spake: 'Who has brought thee hither? who has brought thee hither, little one? who has brought thee to this island, which is situate in the sea, and whose shore is surrounded by the waves?' Then I answered him, bowing myself before him with my arms by my sides: 'I had by command of the Pharaoh embarked for the quarries on a ship 150 cubits long and 40 cubits broad, that was manned by 150 of the best Egyptian sailors, who had knowledge of both heaven and earth, and in whom the heart was wiser than that of a lion. They emulated each other in wisdom of heart, and in strength of arm, and I was indeed their equal. They had said that the wind would not be bad, and that it might be quite calm; but when we were on the sea, there arose a gale, and scarcely had we neared the land, when the wind rose and the waves became 8 cubits high. I alone, I seized a piece of wood; all the others who were in the ship perished without exception during those three days. Here I am now at thy dwelling-place, for a wave has washed me on to this island.'

"Then he said to me, 'Fear thou not, fear thou not, little one, and let not thy face be anxious. For if thou hast reached me, then it is God who has preserved thy life. He has brought thee to this spirit-island, where nothing is wanting, and which is plenteous in all good things. Behold, thou wilt remain here one month after another, till thou hast spent four months on this island. Then a ship will come with sailors out of thy country, and thou wilt be able to return with them into thy country. Thou shalt die in thy native land. Conversation is a joy, it helps us to while away sad times; I will therefore relate to thee what is on this island. I live here with my brothers and my children, surrounded by them; we are seventy-five snakes with the children and the domestics, and another maiden. . . .[1] If thou art strong and hast a patient spirit, then shalt thou press thy children to thy heart and embrace thy wife; thou shalt again see thy home, which is of all things the best, and shalt return to thy country and live with thy friends.'

"Then I bowed myself down and threw myself on the ground before him, and spake; 'I will give thee this answer: I will tell the Pharaoh of thee; I will describe to him how great thou art, and will cause to be brought to thee the sacred oil *Ab*, and frankincense, and cassia, and incense, such as is set aside for the temple use, and with which all the gods are honoured. Then I will relate to him what I have experienced, and thanks shall be rendered to thee before the whole country. I will slay donkeys as offerings to thee; I will pluck geese for thee, and will cause ships to be brought to thee with all the treasures of Egypt, as one should do for a god, who is favourable to mankind in a foreign land that is unknown to the people.'

"Then he laughed at my speech, because of what he thought of it, and said: 'In truth thou art not rich in myrrh, for all that is only common incense. I, however, the prince of the land of Punt, I

[1] The end of this narrative is very obscure.

possess myrrh. The oil *ḥeken* alone, which thou shalt cause to be brought to me, is rare on this island. But (trouble not thyself to send it to me, for) as soon as thou shalt have departed from this place, thou shalt never see this island again: it will be changed into water.'

"And behold when the ship came as he had prophesied, I climbed up into a high tree, in order to see who should be therein. Then I went to tell him, but he knew it already. Then he said to me: 'Return home in peace, little one; mayest thou see thy children again, and leave behind thee a good name in thy city; this is my desire for thee.'

"Then I bowed myself before him with my arms by my sides, and he gave me presents of myrrh, of the oil *ḥeken*, of frankincense and cassia, of the woods *teshepes* and *sha'as*, of panther-skins (?), of *merery* wood, of much common incense, of elephants' teeth, of greyhounds, of the *Guf* monkeys and the *Kiu* monkeys, and of all manner of precious things. I caused all to be taken on board the ship that had arrived, and I thanked him, whilst I threw myself down before him. Then he said to me: 'Behold, after two months thou shalt arrive in thine own country, and shalt press thy children to thy heart, and shalt (sometime) rest safely in thy tomb.'

"Then I descended to the shore to the ship and called the sailors. And on the shore I thanked the lord of this island and all who lived upon it. When, after spending two months on the return journey, as he had said, we reached the residence of the Pharaoh, we betook ourselves to the palace. I entered in to the Pharaoh, and delivered to him the presents which I had brought home from that island. Then he thanked me before the face of the whole country."[1]

Thus even to the Egyptians of the Middle Empire the incense countries appeared to be fabulous realms. A few centuries later and this mist of romance cleared away; even the common people could no longer believe the country of Punt to be an island inhabited by snakes, after Queen Chnemtamun had caused it to be represented in her great temple, with its inhabitants, its villages, its plants and its animals.

These representations of the temple of Dêr el Baḥri belong to that remarkable period when the Egyptians, freed from the yoke of years of foreign rule, began to feel themselves a power in the world. It was as if the veil which concealed the world had fallen from their eyes; the Pharaohs carried their conquering arms as far as the Euphrates and the Blue Nile, and Egypt became the central point of anterior Asia and of East Africa. Then the Egyptians called to mind also the ancient marvellous countries of the Red Sea; and the mighty Queen Chnemtamun sent out an expedition to investigate them.[2] Or, as it is expressed in official Egyptian

[1] I only know this singular narrative from the translation, which Golenischeff the discoverer has given in the Transactions of the Oriental Congress of Berlin. In the second narrative of the storm I have transposed a sentence which appeared to me to be in a wrong place. It is much to be hoped that this important text may soon be published.

[2] For the very remarkable pictures representing this expedition, see Düm. Hist. Inschr., ii. pl. 1-3, 8-18. (The same repeated Düm. Flotte; a summary is given by Mariette, Dêr el Baḥri.)

style: "Amon of Thebes, the lord of gods," suggested this thought to her "because he held this ruler so dear—dearer than any other king who had ever been in this country."

In one of the harbours of the Red Sea lies the fleet, which the soldiers of her Majesty are to conduct into that distant country; the stately vessels are about 65 feet in length, and they are provided with thirty rowers and with gigantic sails, which stand out like wings beyond both sides of the ships. The great jars, which contain the provisions, are being conveyed on board by a rowing boat; on the shore however, near the trees to which the ships are tied, a sacrifice is being offered to the goddess "Ḥatḥôr, the lady of Punt," that "she may send the wind." Then the sails are hoisted up, the sailors climb on the yards to make fast the last ropes, the rowers dip their long oars in the water, and from the wooden partitions in the bows, in which the two captains stand, resounds the command *to larboard.* The ships begin to move, and thus "the royal soldiers voyage on the sea, they begin their beautiful journey to the Divine Land, and voyage happily to Punt."

We do not learn how long the voyage lasted; if we judge by the time which the Arabs of to-day take for their voyages in the Red Sea, we may perhaps conclude that the fleet spent a month at sea before it sighted the shores of the wonder-land they sought.

The aspect of Punt, with the luxuriant tropical vegetation, did not fail to produce its effect upon the inhabitants of the homely valley of the Nile; but they seem to have regarded the natives as barbarians of the lowest type. Close to the shore, hidden amongst great trees and curious gigantic plants, are the wretched little villages, consisting of small semi-conical huts, built on piles to protect them from the enemy and from wild animals, a ladder being the only means by which it is possible to reach the hole which serves for a door. Amongst the houses lie small short-horned cows, and the donkeys which the people of Punt employ as beasts of burden or for riding. The clothing also of the natives bears witness to no high civilisation, for even at the time of Queen Chnemtamun the people of Punt still wear the same skirt, plait their hair into the same pigtail, and wear the same pointed beard as was worn in the incense countries in the ancient times of King Chufu.[1] More than a thousand years had therefore elapsed without any essential change having taken place in the costume of the people of Punt—a lack of initiative only possible in the case of primitive nations. The inhabitants of the village advance as suppliants to meet the Egyptians as they disembark; the latter regard them with little respect, and especially make merry over the wife of the chief. In fact this lady has nothing very aesthetic in her appearance, for she is suffering from a state of corpulence due to disease, such as is still common amongst the women of the interior of Africa. The shape of her legs, of her breasts, and above all of her back, is such as to awaken disgust, and her clothing—a wretched, short yellow shirt and a

[1] Cp. the picture cited above, L. D., ii. 23.

thick collar—does not help to make her look more pleasing. This *princess* is so stout that she is unable to walk, and the artist, who has evidently enjoyed perpetuating her on the temple walls of Dêr el Baḥri, has not failed therefore to represent behind her husband a donkey with a saddle, the "donkey which carries his wife."

The "treasures of the land of Punt" are obtained from these barbarians, the natives heap up incense before the "royal ambassador" and his soldiers, and also lead forward monkeys and panthers—the Egyptians also have put up a table on the beach, which is covered with things to rejoice the heart of a native of Punt, such as daggers and battleaxes, and gay necklets. When the bargains have been concluded to the satisfaction of both sides, the "great men of this land" are conducted into the "tent of the royal ambassador, who presents them with bread, beer, wine, meat, fruits, and all the good things of Egypt, according to the command of the august court."

Thus we have here a true instance of barter and exchange, such as is still practised between the negroes and Europeans; but the official Egyptian report will not confess to such a fact. How could the Pharaoh buy anything from a barbarian people, he [she][1] "to whom all countries bring their gifts," that he by his favour "might allow them to breathe the breath of life"? In the legal style adopted by the Egyptians therefore, the incense that has been acquired by trade is called "the tribute of the princes of Punt," and the weapons the Egyptians paid for it are characterised as an offering laid there for the goddess Ḥatḥôr, the lady of Punt.

Happily this official conception is purely theoretical; as a matter of fact trade goes on briskly; on the planks leading to the ships the carriers pass ceaselessly to and fro; and "the ships are laden very high with the treasures of the land of Punt, and all the beautiful plants of the Divine Land; with heaps of incense; with great myrrh trees; with ebony, together with pure ivory; with white gold from the country Amu; with sweet-scented woods; with all manner of incense and eye pigments; with baboons, monkeys, and greyhounds; with skins of the panther of the south; with slaves and their children; never has the like been brought to any king whatsoever since the beginning of time."

A superintendent causes all these heterogeneous articles to be carefully piled up on the ship, where the heap reaches nearly as high as the lower yard. The monkeys are allowed, nevertheless, to run about freely; during the homeward journey they enjoy clambering about on the strong sail that extends above the ship; one however seems to prefer to squat by the side of the captain, where with comical gravity he repeats his worship's gestures of command, doubtless to the ever-renewed delight of the sailors. When "the soldiers of the lord of the two countries have voyaged home in peace, and travelled to Thebes with joy," their arrival there is the occasion of quite a triumphal pageant. With green boughs in their hands, they enter the town in festive procession and bring their gifts to their lady ruler;

[1] The masculine is used for Queen Chnemtamun.

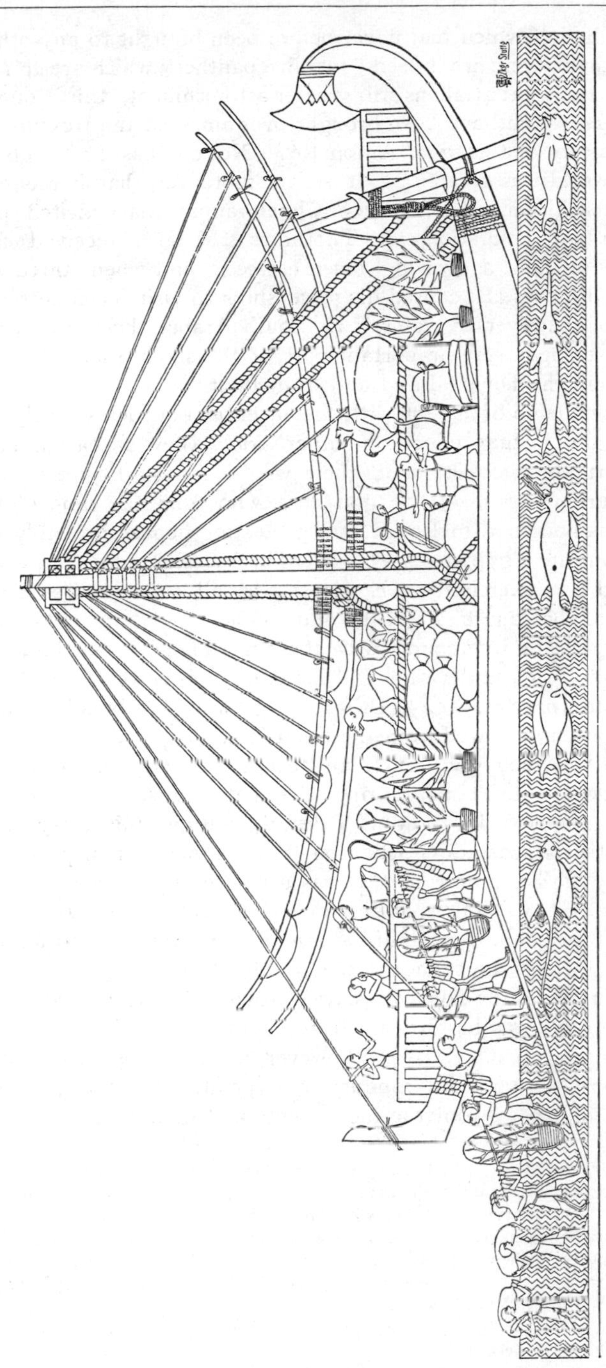

FROM THE PICTURES OF THE EXPEDITION OF QUEEN CHNEMTAMUN.

The lacing of a ship (after Düm. Flotte, pl. 2).

gifts, "the like of which had never before been brought to any other king." Amongst them, there are indeed "two live panthers, which are to follow her majesty"; and what awakens still greater astonishment, "thirty-one growing incense trees, which have been brought over amongst the treasures of Punt for the majesty of this god, Amon Rê‘. No one has ever seen the like since the world was created." It seems, moreover, that it was especially this latter achievement of Queen Chnemtamun that excited particular admiration and emulation, for Thothmes III. also received from the inhabitants of Punt a growing incense tree;[1] and when, three centuries later, King Ramses III. caused his great ships to visit the countries of "the great sea of the reversed water,"[2] *i.e.* South Arabia, these trees were again considered to be a very important part of the spoil[3] that the expedition brought from the Divine Land and from Punt.[4]

The commerce of Egypt with the incense countries scarcely seems to have left any lasting effect on either side; a few barbarian names for various sorts of incense made their way into the Egyptian language, and the curious figure of the god Besa, who from the time of the New Empire was honoured in Egypt as a protecting genius, probably owed his introduction into Egypt to this trade. The influence which these countries of the Red Sea exercised on Egypt was at all events quite insignificant compared to that due to Palestine and Syria.

A trace of the intercourse with these neighbouring northern countries can be found even under the Old Empire; for as we have seen in the ninth chapter (p. 188), even at this early age, a kind of bread was employed which had been borrowed from the Semitic nations. The story of Sinuhe (see p. 370), which gives such an accurate description of Beduin life, presupposes the existence during the 12th dynasty period of active intercourse between Egypt and Palestine. From this story we gather that Egyptian ambassadors, when on their journeys, often passed through the country of Tenu, and that it was usual for Egyptians to reside with the princes of that land, doubtless on account of trade. In fact, we are told that at this time Egyptian *weapon-makers* travelled into foreign parts with their wares;[5] the stelae of the Middle Empire also often represent Semitic damsels as the favourite slaves, proving that at any rate one article of Semitic origin was highly valued in Egypt.[6]

The northern countries were however first really opened up under the New Empire, through the conquering expeditions of the great kings of the 18th dynasty. From the monuments and writings of this period, we

[1] W., i. pl. 2 a.

[2] *Yum ‘a n mu qd.* As in L. D., iii. 5 a, the Euphrates is designated as the *mu qd*, the great sea in the latter expression must signify the Persian Gulf, and as Punt is expressly named as the goal of the journey, South Arabia must certainly be here indicated. Of course, the assertion of the king may be somewhat exaggerated; it is not possible that he can have penetrated far into the Persian Gulf, as the only results he brought back were incense and such-like substances.

[3] Harr., i. 7, 7.

[4] The expedition is described shortly: Harr., i. 77, 8 ff.

[5] Sall., 2, 7, 4-6=An., 7, 2, 6-8.

[6] Mar. Cat. d'Ab., 690.697.699, Louvre, C. 170. They bear of course Egyptian names, often in fact those of their masters.

obtain a view of anterior Asia which in many particulars may indeed be incomplete and obscure, but which is of priceless value for history.

The country of Charu, which extended from the Egyptian frontier fortress of T'aru to the town of 'Eupa, was divided into several distinct parts. The southern division, "the upper Ret'enu," corresponding probably to our Palestine, was divided into two districts, of which the southern was called Ken'ana (Canaan), the northern 'Emur, the country of the Amorites. By "the lower Ret'enu," was understood the low plain of Syria. Phoenicia bore the name of *Keft*, while the inhabitants were called *Fenech*. The above-named territories were split up into small feeble townships, which had no political significance as regards Egypt; but in northern Syria, at any rate for a time, the Pharaohs were opposed by powerful states, especially by the nation of the Cheta, of which we have spoken above (p. 47), also by that of Qede and others. To the north-east, where the Egyptians came across the Assyrian civilisation, the state of Naharena on the Euphrates was usually their furthermost limit. Beyond that point, they traded indeed with Sangar, *i.e.* the mountainous country between the Euphrates and the Tigris, now called Sindjar; with Assyria itself, however, the Pharaohs never seem to have come into contact, and in the same way Babylonia also appears to have been entirely unknown to them. Even the Euphrates was never known to the Egyptians by any fixed name; they called it the "water of Naharena," or, struck by the direction of its stream, which of course appeared most unnatural to the dwellers on the Nile, they spoke of it as that "reversed water, on which one voyages to the northward in going up-stream."[1] The names of places that have come down to us belonging to this part of the world, and especially to its southern division, may be counted by hundreds. Most of them are quite unrecognisable by us, though fortunately we are able to pick out some of the names of the famous cities of Syria. Thus we read of Damascus and Beyrout, of Byblos and of Tyre, "the city in the sea to which water is brought by ship";[2] the neighbouring cities of Gaza and Joppa are also often mentioned by the Egyptians.

It would be very interesting to know whether the Egyptian communications extended also further to the westward, especially to the Greek islands, or whether the ships which Ramses II. and Ramses III. sent out to sea to "bring back the gifts of the countries,"[3] always coasted along the Syrian shore only. We might almost assume that the latter was the case, for the western countries are always spoken of in general terms, such as "the islands of the sea," etc. Cyprus alone, which lies close to countries that were well known to the Egyptians, bears a definite name.

In the following chapter, we shall consider the political and military relations of Egypt with these northern countries; in this place however we have only to describe the effect produced on the two countries by the commercial relations that existed between them. Under the New Empire

[1] L. D., iii. 5 a. It is not possible to reproduce the pun in our translation. The name the "reversed water" is also found Harr., i. 77, 8. [2] See p. 382. [3] Sall., 3, 2, 10.

a brisk trade sprang up,[1] and near the old frontiers of Egypt there was so much traffic to and fro, that for a time at least it interfered with the centre of gravity of the country.[2] As regards civilisation, the east of the Delta was then as it is even now, decidedly behind the rest of the country. Nevertheless at this time this part of Egypt stepped into the foreground of political life; new towns arose, and for a time even the seat of government was transferred hither from the great city of Thebes.

The number of Syrian products imported into Egypt during this period was immense. If we were to judge of these imports by the pictures in the Egyptian tombs alone,[3] we should obtain very false ideas; these pictures seem to imply that the Egyptians had no need of any of the *works* of these northern nations, except those that are constantly repeated in the representations—splendid silver and gold vessels, precious stones, horses, and a few rare animals such as bears and elephants. But fortunately we learn the true state of things from the literature of the 19th and 20th dynasties;[4] and when we come to consider this literature, we almost feel inclined to maintain that really there was scarcely anything that the Egyptians of this period did not import from Syria. This fact is very significant, it implies that the civilisation of the Ret'enu must have reached a very high standard to gain such a pre-eminence, notwithstanding the high development of the industrial arts in Egypt.

Amongst the imports were the following:—

Ships: the *t'arut'e;*

Carriages: the *merkabut'e*, together with their manifold accessories, and the *'agolt'e;*

Weapons: the sword *ḥurpu* (חרב), the lance (?) *merḥu*, the quiver *'espat'e* (אשפה);

Sticks: the *shabud* (שבט) and the *puga;*

Musical instruments: the lyre *ken'en'euru* (כנור), the flutes *uad''a* and *uar;*

Vessels, etc.: the *mend'eqet'e* (מנצקה?) for beer, the *yenra* of silver, the sack, (?) *techbusat'e;*

Liquids: the drinks *cheuaua*, *yenbu*, *qad'auar*, the *nekfet'er* of Sangar, the beer of Qede, the wine of Charu, and "much oil of the harbour";

Bread, such as that of *t'urut'e* (סלת); other kinds of bread, Kamḥu (קמח), 'Ebashtu and Kerashtu; Arupusa bread and "various Syrian breads";

Incense: *qadarut'e* (קטרות);

[1] It is interesting to note in connection with the development of the trade by sea, that according to An., 4, 3, 10, the rich man there spoken of possesses his own ship, to bring his treasures from Syria.

[2] Cp. concerning the frontier trade of this time, the following chapter, pp. 537, 538.

[3] L. D., iii. 115, 116, 127 b: W., i. pl. 2 a, b. Ros. Mon. civ., 58. Also an unpublished tomb at Dra-abulnega.

[4] The foreign products may often be recognised by their foreign names (which moreover are not all of them Semitic); there are however certain articles, which though doubtless imports (as cattle, beer, wine), do not bear foreign names. The meaning of the barbarian terms is as yet to a great extent unknown.

Fish: the *'ebary* and the *hauana;*
Cattle: horses from Sangar, cows from 'Ersa, bulls (*'ebary*) from Cheta, etc.[1]

Buildings, etc., such as by their nature could not be imported, were imitated. *Mekt'er* (מגדל) were erected as castles, the temple walls were provided with *'art'e* and *t'akar, i.e.* probably with battlements and bays; they talked of buildings called *men'at'e,* and locked up prisoners in a *sha'ar,*[2] and so on.

We have seen that with the products of the northern countries, their foreign names were also imported; and as it always happens, when an older civilisation is overpowered by a younger one, a very great number of other words were also adopted from the Semitic without any reasonable ground. A scribe was called *t'upar* (ספר), a house, *bpayt'e* (בית), the tank, *barkat'e* (ברכה), the sea, *yum* (ים), and the river, *necher* (נחל); "to say" was translated by *'anne* (Arab. *ranna*), "to evade" by *sauababa* (סובב), "to rest" by *sharam* (שלם), and "provision" by *sharmat'e,* showing that at this time the Egyptian language reinforced itself considerably with Semitic words, in the same way as a thousand years later with Greek ones. On the other hand, we cannot deny that in these old times it was chiefly the educated classes who affected these foreign words in their talk, for whilst the poems and letters of the scribes are crowded with foreign words, they are rarely to be found in the folk-lore; and in fact in Coptic, which is a development from the language of the lower classes, they are, comparatively speaking, poorly represented.

The subservience into which the civilisation of the New Empire had fallen, with regard to that of these northern countries, is also clearly seen by the manner in which the Egyptians borrowed in the domain of religion; they admitted Syrian divinities, such as Ba'al, Astarte, 'Anat, into their official religion.

This semiticising of the Egyptian kingdom, if we may so express it, would scarcely have been carried so far, had not a large immigration of northern barbarians taken place after the close of the 18th dynasty. This immigration was indeed started in the first place by the importation of slaves, in consequence partly of the military expeditions of the Pharaohs, but chiefly as the result of trade. Slaves from Charu, from Canaan, from Karka, and from other places, are frequently mentioned under the New Empire, and as we have seen in the sixth chapter (p. 105 f.), many of these slaves attained positions of high honour. It was natural that they should then prefer to naturalise themselves as Egyptians; they did this so effectually that by the second generation all trace of barbarian descent seems often to have disappeared. Who, for instance, would suspect that Mery-Rê' (beloved of Rê), the weapon-bearer of Thothmes

[1] The examples given are taken at random, chiefly from An. 3 and An. 4; they might be multiplied tenfold from these and other texts. What remains is expressed in known and unknown languages, and still awaits a careful investigation.

[2] Harr., i. 4, 2; Harr., 500, 8, 7; Amh., 4, 3.

III., and his brother, the priest User-Min (Min is strong), were the sons of a barbarian, the judge Pa-'Emer'eu (the Amorite) and of his wife Karuna?[1] These two Syrians were moreover brought up at the court of the king, for Mery-Rê' relates that "since his birth" he had been "honoured."

On the other hand, we cannot help observing that in spite of everything, the people of the Pharaohs were conscious of possessing a somewhat higher status than their northern neighbours; we find, for instance, that in their art they always represented the barbarians in a semi-comical fashion. The spirit of caricature is shown in the manner in which Egyptian artists depict the Syrians bearing tribute; they are represented with short bulging figures, crooked noses, and pointed beards;[2] their clothing also is calculated to form a very marked contrast to the full white dresses of the Egyptians. The narrow richly-embroidered purple robes in which blue and red layers alternated, the yellow under-garments with the narrow sleeves and tight breeches, evidently did not delight the Egyptian eye.[3] On the other hand, the Egyptians obviously rather admired the Cheta and the nations resembling them, with their long plain dresses and their beardless faces.[4]

A SYRIAN OF THE CLOSE OF THE 18TH DYNASTY. The different layers of the dress are alternately blue and red, also the embroidery. The sleeves are yellow (after L.D., iii. 116).

If for a time the ancient civilisation of Egypt became subservient to that of Syria, we are tempted to inquire whether and how far this influence was reciprocal. This question can only be answered with any certainty when the Syrian monuments have been far more accurately examined than they have been as yet. Many facts however seem to indicate conclusively that the Syrians received almost as much as they gave, and that in their manners and customs they experienced a strong Egyptian influence.[5] In Palestine particularly, where the authority of the Pharaohs was for a long time uncontested, and where there were Egyptian towns with Egyptian temples,[6] we may expect to find traces of this influence. As

[1] Mar. Cat. d'Ab., 1055. Many similar examples.

[2] Cp. amongst many similar passages, e.g. L. D., iii. 156, in which the prince plucks the captives by the beard.

[3] The Phoenicians were more simply dressed (W., i. pl. 2 a), but their skirts with the coloured embroidery and fringes also look quite un-Egyptian.

[4] Costume of the Cheta: L. D., iii. 154, 157, 158, 164, 165. Somewhat different: ib. 196. Peculiar: Ros. Mon. Stor., 103, one has the head shorn with the exception of a pig-tail. Cp. also the "northern people," W., i. pl. 2 b, in long white garments.

[5] The Egyptian influence was doubtless most felt in Syria, in Phoenicia, and the other Mediterranean countries at the time of the 26th dynasty.

[6] Thothmes III. built a "monument" (*mnnu*, the same word that is employed in speaking of the older Nubian colonies), in Ret enu: L. D., iii. 30 b, 1. Merenptaḥ built a town in 'Emur (An., 3, 5 Rs.). Ramses III. built a temple to Amon in Canaan (Harr., i. 9, 1 ff.).

regards the language, we find Egyptian words employed ; *e.g.* for *box* (תבת), for the *lily* (שושן), for a *measure* (הין), for *wretched*, (אביון), etc. ; and in these examples of borrowed words we find a proof that the Egyptians did not fail to exercise a certain ascendency at any rate over those countries in their immediate neighbourhood.

A HIPPOPOTAMUS IS SEATED IN A TREE, TO WHICH A BIRD IS MOUNTING BY A LADDER (after Leps., Ausw. 23).

THE KING OF THE MICE, STANDING ON HIS BATTLE CHARIOT, DRAWN BY DOGS, IS BESIEGING THE CATS' FORTRESS. Parody of Egyptian battle-pictures. (From the Turin satirical papyrus, after the restoration by Lepsius, Auswahl, Pl. 23).

CHAPTER XX

WAR

EGYPT, says Strabo, from the beginning of time has as a rule been a peaceful country, for she not only suffices for herself, but she is also very inaccessible to foreigners. On the north she is bounded by the harbourless shore of the Egyptian Sea, on the east and west by the Libyan deserts and the Arabian mountains. To the south moreover, the other side of her frontier is occupied by the Troglodytes, the Blemmyes, the Nubians and Megabares (*i.e.* the Ethiopians above Syene) ; these nomadic tribes are neither numerous nor warlike, as they have been considered by earlier writers, who thus thought of them because they often waylaid and robbed the unwary. Finally, the Ethiopians in the south, as far as Meroe, are neither numerous nor united ; they inhabit the long narrow winding valley of the river, which affords few facilities for war and but a scanty livelihood. That this state of affairs exists even at the present day, is proved by the fact that the Romans guard the country (here) with three cohorts, and these cohorts are not even complete in number, and yet when the Ethiopians ventured to attack them, they (only) endangered their own country. The other troops stationed in Egypt are, comparatively speaking, not even as strong, yet the Romans have not once been obliged to combine their forces, for the Egyptians, though they are so numerous, are neither warlike themselves, nor are the nations around.

This description of the military condition of Egypt, which Strabo has thus sketched out as the result of his own observation during the Graeco-Roman time, is only too true of the Egypt of the Middle Ages and of modern times ; indeed, scarcely any other nation can be said to be so unwarlike as the fellahin. In a revolt, they may obtain a momentary triumph, but at the first serious rebuff, they submit in the most pitiable fashion. In great wars they fully develop but *one* quality, swiftness in running away. Whenever and wherever an army of the Egyptian government has had any success in war, that army consisted in great measure of foreign mercenaries. The Egyptian wars of the Middle Ages were carried on by

Kurds and Turks; Mohammed Ali and his powerful adopted son owed their conquests to Albanian troops; and in the last English war it was the negroes who held their own so heroically against the English at Tell el Kebir, whilst the flight of the fellah regiments was the most disgraceful scene that modern history has ever recorded.

As far as we know, the Egyptians of ancient times were no greater heroes than their descendants, and this is in no way surprising, for the natural conditions which effectually prevented the growth of the warlike spirit in this nation are common to all time. Ancient Egypt was also encircled by deserts, and her boundaries were threatened only by wretched negroes and nomadic tribes, the oft-mentioned *nine bows*. These desert tribes, whose attacks consisted, then as now, in the stealing of cattle and the plundering of caravans, were the traditional enemies of Egypt; and the fact that the kings styled themselves the "vanquishers of the nine bows," shows plainly how little real opposition the Egyptians encountered. It was impossible that wars with these Beduins should make the nation mighty in war, and the same may be said of the civil wars. In fact, there was nothing whatever in the countries round Egypt that could incite a nation to conquest, for neither the deserts of Nubia nor the arid land of Palestine could appear very attractive to those who called the fertile soil of the Nile valley their own.

Hence it happens that neither war nor soldiers played the same part in Egypt of old as they do in the history of other ancient nations. Once only, under the New Empire, did Egypt become a military power, but this sudden outburst of a warlike spirit was of very short duration, and ended characteristically by the barbarian mercenaries becoming the lords of the country.

Under these circumstances, it cannot surprise us that in the Egypt of early times we find no national army. Each nome under the Ancient Empire had its own armoury, the *battle-house*,[1] as well as its own militia, which was under the command of the nomarch. To this we must add the contingent supplied by the estates of the great temples:[2] the soldiers of the treasury department;[3] the mercenaries of the friendly chiefs of northern Nubia, and other companies, which altogether might certainly form a considerable number of troops, but could scarcely be considered a united army. This defect is clearly recognisable in the one description of a great war which has come down to us from the time of the Old Empire. Under King Pepy, "the Asiatics who live on the sand," *i.e.* probably the Beduins of the south of Palestine, had undertaken one of their usual predatory expeditions against the Delta, with the object of settling with their herds in the beautiful fertile country of that district, as the Libyan and Semitic nomads have often succeeded in doing in later times. In this case they

[1] With nomarchs: R. J. H., 81—Mar. Mast., 214 ff. With chief judges: L. D., ii. 75. Mar. Mast., 228 ff.

[2] The high priest of Heliopolis styles himself the "commander of the troops"; Mar. mon. div., 18.

[3] L. D., ii. 100 b. Mar. Mast., 162.188 f.

were too numerous to be driven out by the usual methods, Pepy therefore determined to call together all the sinews of war that were at his command. He commissioned neither nomarch nor treasurer with the organisation and direction of this army, though these officials had always formerly been styled the "superintendents of the soldiers"; but he chose Un'e, a favourite chief judge, who enjoyed his special confidence. Evidently in spite of their military rank the treasurers and nomarchs had had no actual experience of a real war; they might have led the troops against a rebellious tribe in Nubia or against the robber Troglodytes of the Arabian desert, but they were not equal to an undertaking on a large scale, and a trustworthy energetic man like Un'e was more adapted for the work. Un'e fully justified the confidence of his master, as is seen by the account he himself gives in his tomb.[1]

"His Majesty made war against the Asiatic Beduins and brought a great army together of many tens of thousands from the whole of the south, from Elephantine upwards, and northwards from the bifurcation (?) of the Nile, from the north country, from the temple estates (?), from the fortress (?), and from the interior of the fortresses (?), from the negro countries of 'E'rt'et, Med'a, 'Emam, Uauat, Kaau, and Tat'e'am. His Majesty sent me at the head of this army. There stood the princes; there stood the chief treasurers; there stood the nearest friends of the palace; there stood the governors and the town-princes of the south and of the north, the friends and superintendents of the gold, the superintendents of the prophets of the south and of the north country, and the superintendents of the temple property—at the head of a troop of the south and of the north country, of the towns and districts over which they ruled, and of the negroes of those countries. It was I, indeed, who led them, though my rank was only that of a superintendent of the garden (?) of the Pharaoh."[2]

When all these small contingents had been united into one army, a new difficulty presented itself, the difficulty of provisioning these "many tens of thousands." The problem was solved in a very easy manner: "each one carried as much with him as another; some of them stole the dough and the sandals from the traveller; some of them took the bread from each village, some of them took the goats from everybody." Unfortunately we cannot quite make out what Un'e thought of these proceedings; probably they rejoiced his heart. After he had led the army on the *north island* to the *gate of Yḥotep*, and had once more reviewed it at this place, he began the war, which he thus describes in poetical fashion:

"This army fared happily and cut to pieces the country of the Beduins.
This army fared happily and destroyed the country of the Beduins.
This army fared happily and overthrew their castles.

[1] Inscription of Un'e: Ä. Z., 1882, 12 ff.

[2] In a preceding chapter (p. 87), and in many places, I have construed this title otherwise in concurrence with Brugsch; I now make the suggestion, however, that the *chnt* in this title has really nothing to do with *chnt*, "existing in front, Nubian," but simply signifies *garden*, or something similar.

This army fared happily and cut down their fig-trees and their vines.
This army fared happily and slew troops there, even many tens of thousands.
This army fared happily and brought back many captives, even a great multitude."

Thus the great war was brought to a close; but four times again there arose disturbances amongst the Beduins, and each time Un'e was again sent out, "in order to march through the country of the Beduins with these troops." A war broke out also "in the north of the country of the Beduins," to which Un'e "went with these troops in ships"; in this war also "he beat them all and slew them."

It is evident that the disintegration of the state, which ensued towards the close of the Old Empire, could not be conducive to the formation of a national army. Under the 12th dynasty, as in earlier times, each nomarch had his own small army, commanded by a "superintendent of the soldiers," as his deputy. As a fact, there was rarely anything important for these troops to do, and therefore in times of peace this officer assisted in the superintendence of the fields,[1] whilst the greater number of the men were probably only called out in case of need. Doubtless they were most unwilling to serve, and when the "scribe of the soldiers" appeared in the nome, in order to "choose out fine young men,"[2] the grief of the people was probably as heartrending as it has been of late times, when the men were called out for the corvée. As a matter of fact, the service the government required of these soldiers was not as a rule of a very warlike nature; frequently it might be to escort an expedition to the mines and quarries of the desert.[3] Even in these expeditions, the soldiers were evidently often employed as workmen to drag the blocks of stone; their labour was of course very inexpensive to the state. To quote but one instance, how else can we explain the fact that an official in charge of the mines at Ḥammamât had 2000 soldiers[4] with him in addition to his stone-masons? it was impossible that so many could be required to protect eighty workmen from the Beduins. Now and then, of course, the troops of the nomes had to fight in earnest; thus Ameny, the oft-mentioned nomarch of Beni Hasan under Usertsen I., accompanied the king with his troops to Cush, he "followed his master as he voyaged up-stream in order to overthrow his enemies amongst the foreign nations; he went indeed as the son of the prince, the chief treasurer, the great superintendent of the soldiers of the Nome of the Gazelle, as substitute for his aged father. When His Majesty now returned home in peace, after he had subdued his enemies in the miserable land of Ethiopia, he also followed him and took great care that none of his soldiers were lost."

It is characteristic of this war-report that Ameny does not recount any victory won, but only tells of *tribute* raised, *i.e.* of spoil carried off. These wars were in fact merely predatory expeditions, and even the great

[1] L. D., ii. 127 (he is the third officer of the nome, L. D., ii. 131).
[2] Stele, 1198, at Berlin, of the 12th dynasty.
[3] In particular the report: L. D., ii. 122, officers at the mines: L. D., ii. 138 a, 149 g.
[4] L. D., 138 c.

victory gained by Usertsen III. over the Nubians eighty or ninety years later, and commemorated by him in a monument at Semneh, was of no greater importance, for thus the king himself describes it:[1] "I have carried off their women, and captured their men, for I (?) marched to their well; I slew their oxen, cut down their corn and set fire to it." Yet this razzia was considered such a mighty deed that the king considered it necessary to swear by his fathers that he was saying the truth and not exaggerating.

It stands to reason that wars of this kind were not calculated to increase the valour of the soldiers, especially when in the intervals of peace the men were employed in manual labour. It seems that the kings of the 12th dynasty, realising that their troops lacked efficiency, formed a standing bodyguard, which they employed specially for the subjection and defence of Nubia. These are the "retainers of the monarch," who are often mentioned at this period and evidently constituted a corps of élite.[2]

SOLDIERS UNDER THE MIDDLE EMPIRE PERFORMING THEIR WAR-DANCES. (Beni Hasan; after Ros. M. C., 117.)

We do not know much of the equipment of the soldiers of the Middle Empire. The common soldiers of that time, like those of the Old Empire, carried a large bow; as a badge they generally wore on their heads one or two ostrich feathers, which according to Egyptian ideas signified victory;[3] they wound a narrow band round the upper part of their body,—this evidently represented a coat of mail.[4] Other companies of troops were armed with a great shield and a spear,[5] or with a small shield, over which a skin was stretched, and a battle-axe; others again carried no shield, but bore a large axe and a lance, or perhaps indeed only a sling.[6]

SOLDIER OF THE MIDDLE EMPIRE. (Tomb at Siut, after W., i. 202.)

It is a remarkable fact that under the Middle Empire the Egyptians took great trouble to fortify against the barbarians those weak points which occurred in the natural bulwarks of Egypt,

[1] L. D., ii. 136 h.

[2] *Shmsu* (cp. p. 103), Mar. Cat. d'Ab., 634, 649, 699, 744. In the Nubian inscriptions, L. D., ii. 136, e, g, 138 g, 144 i, k. Officers of this corps, Mar. Cat. d'Ab., 664; L. D., ii. 136 g, 138 a, g, 144 k. Cp. also Mar. Cat. d'Ab., 667.

[3] Mar. Abyd., i. p. 49.

[4] Clearly recognisable in the accompanying illustration, which is taken from a picture of the time of the Middle Empire. That the soldiers of the Old Empire were dressed in like fashion is shown by the usual hieroglyphs in the inscriptions of this period; the feathers indeed seem to be wanting, but the ends of the bands may be recognised behind the skirt.

[5] W., i. 202.

[6] The three latter at Beni Hasan: Ros. M. C., 117, 118, 119.

FORTRESS OF SEMNEH. Restored by Chipiez. On the opposite bank is the smaller fortress of Kumneh.

and which they called "the gates of the barbarians."[1] At the Nubian frontier, where the fortress of Assuan now stands, was the "southern gate," which was sometimes placed under the "superintendent of the South,"[2] and sometimes under the nomarch of Thebes.[3] There was also a particularly weak point in the east of the Delta, where the long valley of the old Land of Goshen, the present Wadi Tumilat, led straight from the heart of the Delta to a break in the chain of the Bitter Lakes. The importance of this place from a strategic point of view has been shown of late years in the military operations of the English in Egypt. Under the Middle Empire, if not earlier, a great fortress was built here, the "wall of the monarch, which is erected to keep off the Asiatics"; it was garrisoned, and from the top men were always on the look-out for the enemy.[4]

The ruin of one of these fortresses of the Middle Empire gives us a good idea of the plan on which they were built. Usertsen III. blockaded the right bank of the river at Semneh in Nubia with a great fortress, of which such large portions still remain, that in the restoration here given from Chipiez, nothing essential has been supplied by fancy.[5] This immense brick building, with its many projecting corners and its irregular ground-plan, is surrounded on the outside by a wall. Chipiez has explained in the most interesting way the curious change of direction in the line of the slope of the outer wall; the object was to render the planting of scaling ladders more difficult. To reach the parapet of a wall built with this change of angle, it is necessary to have much longer ladders than for a perpendicular wall of the same height. In a tomb at Beni Hasan there is also a representation of a fortress of the Middle Empire, with a similar change of angle in the wall. On one of the walls of this fortress may be seen a tower that is only about 15 ft. high, and that has two closed doors at the foot. It is interesting that in this representation we have also a scene of the siege of the fortress. The besiegers advance under cover of a penthouse, they are driving a long battering-ram against the wall, and are sending a storm of arrows against the defenders. The besieged stand protected by a parapet about 3 feet high, or they lie in small balconies that project obliquely, so as to enable them to pour down arrows and stones on the enemy.[6]

I have already remarked that in contradistinction to other periods of Egyptian history, the character of the New Empire was warlike. The army had been trained in the war against the Hyksos, and the nobles had imbibed a taste for fighting; the political conditions also of the neighbouring northern countries at that time were such that they could not just then make any very serious opposition; consequently the Egyptians began to act on the offensive in Syria. At the same time it was a very different thing to carry on war with the civilised Syrians instead of with the semi-savage

[1] Br. Wb. Suppl., 184; Br. Dict. Géogr., 1288 ff. [2] L. D., ii. 113 h-k.
[3] Mar. mon. div., 50. [4] Berlin Pap., 22 Z, 17 ff. Ä. Z., 1876, 110.
[5] This fortress may indeed have been built by Thothmes III.
[6] Ros. M. C., 118. Wilk., i. 242. The plan of the buildings in front is somewhat uncertain.

Nubians or Beduins, and in place of the old raids for the capture of slaves, the driving off of cattle, and the devastation of fields, we find regular warfare. The science of strategy was now studied, and Thothmes III. tells us the story of his great expedition in full detail; for instance, where his forefathers would have used high-flown language about the annihilation of the barbarians, he speaks of the various routes that lead over Mount Carmel. The tone of the tomb-inscriptions of these kings seems to us most un-Egyptian and strange,—they speak of war, not as a necessary evil, but as the highest good for the country. In the official reports of this period, which enumerate the military expeditions of these kings, the "first expedition" is spoken of before a second has taken place,[1] as if there were no doubt that each monarch would take the field several times.

Amongst the kings of the 19th dynasty this view had become such an accepted fact, that delight in fighting was considered as great a virtue in a ruler as reverence for Amon. When it was announced to the king that the "chiefs of the tribes of the Beduins" had banded themselves together to despise the "laws of the palace, his Majesty then rejoiced thereat. For the good god exults when he begins the fight, he is joyful when he has to cross the frontier, and is content when he sees blood. He cuts off the heads of his enemies, and an hour of fighting gives him more delight than a day of pleasure."[2] The Pharaoh in person now commanded in battle, and the temple pictures continually represent him in the thickest of the fight. Like his soldiers, he lays aside all his clothing, even to his girdle and the front flap of his skirt;[3] in a leathern case in his chariot he has his short darts, which he hurls against the enemy, while from his great bow he sends out arrow after arrow amongst them. He even takes part in the hand-to-hand fight, and his dagger and sickle-shaped sword are close at hand.[4] In fact, if we may trust these representations of battle scenes, the king was indeed the only warrior who, with the reins of his horses tied round his body, and without even a chariot-driver, broke through the ranks of the enemy; we may surmise however that this was but a flattering exaggeration on the part of the sculptor in which even the poets scarcely ventured to join.[5]

It is well known that the military expeditions of the kings of the 19th dynasty had no very great results. Yet we must not therefore conclude that they were less warlike than the monarchs of the 18th dynasty, for they had a more difficult part to play than their predecessors; instead of the separate small states and towns of Syria, they found the mighty kingdom of the Cheta arrayed against them (cp. pp. 47 ff., 392 ff.). How the war was carried on with this nation is well illustrated by the history of one great battle of which we have unusually full details: this battle was fought by Ramses II. in the fifth year of his reign, in his second expedition against the king of the Cheta.

[1] L. D., iii. 65 a. [2] L. D., iii. 128 a. [3] L. D., iii. 127, 130 a, b.
[4] L. D., iii. 127 a, 128 a. [5] Sall., 3, 5, 3 ff.

Both kingdoms had called out all their forces for the war; the "miserable prince of the Cheta" had summoned all his vassals and confederates from "the ends of the sea,"[1] he had also looked carefully after his coffers for the war, for he "had left no silver nor gold behind him in his country, he had despoiled everything in order to take all with him."[2] Slowly the Egyptian army moved forward, in four divisions; in advance came the king with his bodyguard; at some distance behind him marched the *first army*, that of Amon; the army of Rê' was to the westward, that of Ptaḥ and that of Sutech were some way behind.[3] Thus without any opposition, and without meeting the Cheta, they reached the valley of the Orontes in North Syria, and on the 9th Epiphi they pitched the royal camp to the south of the town of Kadesh.[4] Early in the morning they decamped and moved further northwards. "When now his Majesty had come to the region south of the town of Shabtun, two Beduins came and said to his Majesty: 'Our brothers who, as chiefs of the tribe, are with the prince of the Cheta, have sent us to his Majesty to announce that we wish to submit to the Pharaoh, and to break with the prince of the Cheta. The prince of the Cheta is now in the country of Charbu to the north of Tunep, and is in such great fear of the Pharaoh that he dare not move southwards.'

"But in that which these two Beduins had said to his Majesty, they had lied; the prince of the Cheta had sent them out to seek out and discover where his Majesty then was, in order that the army of his Majesty might not take him by surprise." The Egyptians were soon to learn the truth, for the large army of the enemy lay in wait in the immediate vicinity, close to Kadesh. In fact, "there came two spies who were in the service of his Majesty, and brought with them two spies of the prince of the Cheta. They were led into the presence of the king, and his Majesty asked them, Who are you?' When they had answered that they belonged to the prince of the Cheta and had been sent out by him to seek out and discover where his Majesty might be, then his Majesty asked them: 'Where then is he, the prince of the Cheta? I heard that he was in the country of Charbu.' 'Behold,' they answered, 'the prince of the Cheta has many people with him, that he has victoriously brought with him from all the countries belonging to the territory of the country of the Cheta, and of the country of Naharena, and of the whole Qede country. They are armed, they have infantry, and chariots, and weapons, and are more in number than the sand of the sea. Behold, they are in fighting order hidden behind the town of Kadesh.' Then his Majesty ordered the princes to be called into his presence, that they might hear everything that these two spies of the prince of the Cheta had spoken before the king; he then said to them: 'Now ye see what sort of folk the superintendents of the peasantry and the chiefs of the countries of the Pharaoh are! They have stood there daily and said to the Pharaoh that the prince of the Cheta remained in the country of Charbu, having

[1] Pap. Raifet, 5. [2] Pap. Raifet, 7 ff. [3] Pap. Raifet, 9 ff.

[4] The following after the text: L. D., iii. 153=ib. 187=Ros. Mon. Stor., 100 ff.

fled before his Majesty. Thus ye came and said day by day. And now, behold, I have just heard from these two spies of the prince of the Cheta, that the prince of the Cheta has come accompanied by much people, with men and horses in number as the sand of the sea, and is behind Kadesh. Thus it is told to me, and the superintendents of the peasantry, and the chiefs to whom the country of the Pharaoh is entrusted, have not been able to give me this information.'

"Then answered the princes who stood in the presence of his Majesty: 'It is a great crime that the superintendents of the peasantry and the chiefs of the Pharaoh have committed, in that they have not shown where the prince of the Cheta lay, though they brought their reports daily to his Majesty.' Then his Majesty ordered the governor to summon in the greatest haste the soldiers of his Majesty, who were marching southwards from Shabtun, and to bring them to his Majesty."

But it was already too late: "Whilst his Majesty sat there and spake with the princes, the prince of the Cheta had advanced with his infantry and his chariot force, as well as with much people who accompanied him, and had crossed the canal of Kadesh on the south side. They came into contact with the soldiers of his Majesty, who were marching along ignorant of everything; the infantry and the chariot force of his Majesty were disheartened before them, as they advanced northwards to the help of his Majesty.

"Thus the army of the prince of the Cheta surrounded the servants of his Majesty who were with him. But when his Majesty saw them, he became as a lion against them, like the god Mont, the lord of Thebes. He seized his attire for the fight, he put on his armour, he was like unto Ba'al when he is angry. Then he hastened to his horses and stormed forwards—he quite alone. Then he broke through the ranks of the army of the prince of the Cheta and of the many confederate nations. His Majesty was like the god Sutech, the glorious, when he cut them down and slew them. His Majesty made havoc of them and threw them one after the other into the waters of the Orontes."

"'I have defied all nations'," the Pharaoh could boast; "when I was alone, and my infantry and my chariot force had forsaken me; not one of them stood still or returned! I swear however that as truly as Rê' loves me, and as truly as Atum rewards me, I myself truly did all that I have said, in the sight of my infantry and of my chariot force."

The account that the inscriptions give us of this battle is confirmed by the great series of pictures on the pylons of the funerary temple of Ramses II. We see there how the two captured spies of the prince of the Cheta are induced by a merciless bastinado to betray their secret, and how the king, seated on "his golden throne," after hearing the fatal news, wastes his time by demonstrating to his princes the uselessness of his own officers.[1]

Next we see how the soldiers of the "first army of Amon" pitch their

[1] L. D., iii. 153.

camp;[1] the shields are placed side by side so as to construct a great four-cornered enclosure. One entrance only is left, and this is fortified with barricades and is defended by four divisions of infantry. In the middle of the camp a large square space indicates the position of the royal tent; the smaller tents of the officers surround it. The wide space between these tents and the outer enclosure serves as a camping-ground for the common soldiers and for the cattle, and here we see a series of life-like scenes, in the representation of which the Egyptian artist has evidently taken great delight. In one corner stand the rows of war-chariots; the horses are unharnessed and paw the ground contentedly, while they receive their food. Close by are posted the two-wheeled baggage cars; the oxen are looking round at the food, and do

OX AND BAGGAGE TRUCK IN CAMP.
(After L. D., iii. 155.)

CAMP SCENE. To the right are the shields which are placed round the camp (after L. D., iii. 154).

not appear to trouble themselves about the king's big tame lion, which has lain down near them wearied out. The most characteristic animal in the camp, however, is the donkey with his double panniers, in which he has to carry the heavy sacks and jars of provisions. We meet with him here, there, and everywhere, in all manner of positions; for instance, he drops on his knee indignantly, as if he could carry his panniers no longer; he prances about when the soldiers want to lade him with the sacks; he lies down and brays, or he takes his ease rolling in the dust near his load. The boys also, whose business it is to fasten up the donkeys to pegs, contribute to the general liveliness of the camp; in more than one place they have begun to quarrel about their work, and in their anger they beat each other with the pegs. Other boys belonging to the camp have to hang the baggage on posts, or to bring food for the soldiers, or to fetch the skins of water. These boys insist upon quarrelling too; the skins are thrown down, and they use their fists freely.

In contrast to these scenes of daily life in the camp, we have on the other hand a representation of the wild confusion of battle.[2] Close to the bank of the Orontes is the royal chariot, in which the king stands drawn

[1] L. D., iii. 153, 154. [2] The following after the great pictures: L. D., iii. 157-161, ib. 164-165.

up to his full height; behind and on each side the chariots of the Cheta surround him, while many more are crossing the stream. The Egyptian chariots are indeed in the rear of the king, but in order to come to his help they would have first to force a way through the chariots of the Cheta. In the meantime, the Pharaoh fights by himself, and pours down such a frightful rain of arrows on the enemy that they fly in wild confusion. Hit by the arrows, their horses take fright, dash the chariots to pieces, and throw out the warriors, or they get loose and breaking through their own ranks, spread confusion everywhere. The dead and the wounded Cheta fall one upon another; those who escape the arrows of the king throw themselves into the Orontes and try to swim across to Kadesh, which is seen on the opposite bank surrounded by walls and trenches. All do not succeed in making their way through this confusion of horses and men, and in swimming the stream; thus we see the soldiers pulling out the body of the prince of Charbu from the water. Cherpaser, the "scribe of letters" of the prince of the Cheta, was also drowned; T'ergannasa and Pays his chariot-drivers were shot, as were also T'e'edura, the chief of his bodyguard, Kamayt'a the commander of the corps of élite, 'Aagem, a chief of the mercenaries, and several other men of rank; Met'arema, the brother of the prince of the Cheta, fell before he could reach the stream to save himself.

Whilst the Pharaoh thus slays the Cheta, the prince of the latter people stands watching the battle from the corner between Kadesh and the Orontes in the midst of a mighty square of 8000 foot soldiers of the élite of his troops; "he does not come out to fight, because he is afraid before his Majesty, since he has seen his Majesty." When he sees that the battle is lost, he says in admiration: "He is as Sutech the glorious, Ba'al lives in his body."

It would not do for us, the sceptics of the modern world, to doubt the fact that the prince of the Cheta acknowledged to be true; Ramses II. was no doubt cut off from the body of his troops, and made a stand against an overwhelmingly superior force until the legion of Amon came up and won the battle. However great the loss might be however, that he inflicted on the army of the Cheta, yet the famous fight of Kadesh was not really a decisive victory. The war was carried on afterwards for many years, and indeed with varying success, for we find the Pharaoh fighting, sometimes in the country of the Cheta, and sometimes close to his own frontier.

The incidents recorded in these later wars of Ramses II. are chiefly the storming of those great castles, which seem to have been situate close to each town in Syria and Palestine. These castles have always essentially the same form; through the strong gates entrance is obtained to the broad lower story, which is crowned with battlements above, and provided on each side with four widely-projecting balconies; above this story is a second narrower one with similar balconies, and barred windows. Several pictures represent the storming of these fortresses. For instance,

STORMING OF DAPURU, THE FORTRESS OF THE CHETA (after L. D., iii. 166).

there is the "miserable town of 'Esqaruna," *i.e.* Ascalon, the citadel of which is built on a hill. Its strong position however does not save it; the Egyptian soldiery force their way through the enemy to the walls, they burst open the gates with axes, they plant mighty scaling-ladders against the walls, and ascend, with their shields on their backs and their daggers drawn, to the first story. The inhabitants, who with their wives and children have taken refuge in the upper floor, seeing their destruction approach, are in despair; some try to let down the women and children over the wall, others crave the king's mercy, raising their hands in supplication.[1]

The storming by Ramses II. of *Dapuru* (or some such name signifying the fortress of the Cheta), which is represented in our illustration, was on a larger scale, and a more difficult affair. This fortress, as we see, deviates somewhat from the ordinary style of building. Below, a battlemented wall surrounds an immense lower building, which supports four towers, the largest of which has windows and balconies. Above the towers is seen the standard of the town, a great shield pierced through with arrows. Outside, on the field of battle, the king fights the Cheta, who have hastened to the relief of the fortress; while under the conduct of his sons a systematic attack is made on the town. In order to protect themselves from the shower of stones and arrows that the besieged pour down from above, the Egyptian soldiers advance under cover of pent-houses, which are pushed forward with poles. Then ensues the actual storming of the castle by means of scaling-ladders, and again we find that it is two of the princes who, with almost incredible boldness, are climbing up the rungs of the scaling-ladders. Then we see the course of events round the fortress: some of the besieged let themselves down over the wall, more than one being killed in this attempt to escape; others bring tribute to the victors, and "say, whilst they adore the good god, 'Give us the breath of life, thou good ruler; we lie under the soles of thy feet.'"

After this success the good god returns home from the campaign, with "very great booty, the like of which had never been seen before,"[2] and the "living captives, which his hand had spared";[3] at the frontier canal, at the fortress T'aru, the great prophets and the princes of the south and of the north await him with their greeting. The priests have placed themselves on the right, and present to him, as if they were presenting an offering, large bouquets of flowers; on the left, their hands raised in supplication, stand the high officials, with the bald-headed governor at their head. "Welcome," they say, "from the countries that thou hast subdued; thy cause has conquered, and thine enemies are subject to thee. Thou shalt be king as long as Rê' rules in heaven, and shalt renew thy courage. Thou lord of the people of the nine bows! Rê' makes fast thy frontiers, and spreads out his arms as a protection behind thee. Thine axe strikes the heart of all countries, and their princes fall before thy sword."[4]

1 L. D., iii. 145 c.
2 L. D., iii. 128 b.
3 L. D., iii. 128 a.
4 L. D., iii. 128 b.

The common people also take part in these rejoicings: "the young people of the triumphal town put on festive garments every day and (pour) pleasant oil on their heads, on their new coiffures; they stand at their doors, bouquets in their hands, *Uad'et* flowers from the temple of Ḥatḥôr, and *Meḥet* flowers from the tank; on the day when Ramses II. makes his entry, the god of war of the two countries, on the morning of the *Kaḥerka* festival. Every one joins with his neighbour and recites his adoration."[1]

The facts that the actual results of the war were small, and that though Ramses II. herewith closed two decades of the campaign, the enemy was yet acknowledged as an equal, seem not to have interfered with this celebration of the victory. We learn that in the 21st year, on the 22nd of Tybi, when the king repaired to the town, the *house of Ramses*, Tartesebu and Ramses, the Cheta ambassadors, were conducted into his presence, in order to "sue for peace from the Majesty of Ramses, the bull of the princes, who places his boundaries in every country where he will." As a matter of fact however, they were merely the bearers of the following document,[2] concerning the peace which had already been concluded, a document which in no way reads like an enemy suing for peace:

"The treaty, which Chetasar, the great prince of the Cheta, the strong, the son of Marsar, the great prince of the Cheta, the strong, the grandson of Saparuru, the great prince of the Cheta, the strong, has addressed on a silver tablet to Ramses II., the great monarch of Egypt, the strong, the grandson of Ramses I., the great monarch of Egypt, the strong—the beautiful treaty of peace and alliance which gives peace . . . eternally.

"In the beginning from all eternity, the relationship between the great monarch of Egypt and the great prince of the Cheta was such that the gods did not allow hostilities to arise between them, (but they were) in alliance. But in the time of my brother Mut'enr, the great prince of the Cheta, he made war with (Ramses II.) the great monarch of Egypt. But now from the present time, behold Chetasar the great prince of the Cheta stands in an alliance, which shall cause the relationship that Rê' and Sutech have made between the country of Egypt and the country of the Cheta to endure, so that no enmity may arise between them for ever. Behold, Chetasar the great prince of the Cheta has allied himself by a treaty with Ramses II. the great monarch of Egypt, that a beautiful peace and a beautiful alliance may proceed therefrom between us for ever, since he allies himself with me and he is in peace with me, since I ally myself with him and I am in peace with him.

"Since the death of my brother Mut'enr, the great prince of the Cheta, Chetasar has sat on the throne of his fathers as the great prince of the Cheta, behold, I together with Ramses II. the great monarch of Egypt have wished: that (we might re-establish) the peace, and the alliance; that they may be better than the former peace and the former alliance; that the relationship (?) between the great prince of the Cheta and Ramses II.

[1] An., 3, 3, 2 ff.

[2] L. D., iii. 146.

the great monarch of Egypt may be a beautiful peace and a beautiful alliance; that the children's children of the great prince of the Cheta may remain in a beautiful peace and a beautiful alliance with the children's children of Ramses II. the great monarch of Egypt, so that they may be in alliance as we are, and in peace as we are; that the whole country of Egypt may be for ever in peace and alliance with the whole country of the Cheta; that no hostilities may arise between them for ever; that the great prince of the Cheta may not ever invade the country of Egypt to carry anything out of it; that Ramses II. may not ever invade the country of the Cheta to carry anything out of it.

"The treaty of equality (?) that existed in the days of Saparuru, the great prince of the Cheta, as well as the treaty of equality (?) that existed in the days of my father Marsar, the great prince of the Cheta: I am bound by it, behold, Ramses II. the great monarch of Egypt is bound by it; we together from this day forward, we are bound by it, and we stand together in a treaty of equality (?).

"If another enemy should come into the countries of Ramses II., the great monarch of Egypt, and if the latter should write to the great prince of the Cheta: 'Come with me as reinforcement against him,' then shall the great prince of the Cheta come to him as reinforcement, and may the great prince of the Cheta slay his enemy. But if the great prince of the Cheta does not wish to come (himself), then he shall send his infantry and his cavalry to slay his enemy.

"When Ramses II. the great monarch of Egypt is furious against foreign (?) subjects, who have committed a crime (?) against him, and he goes to slay them, then shall the great prince of the Cheta (assist) him."

There then follow the corresponding clauses about the help that Ramses II. on his side guarantees to give to the prince of the Cheta in case of war. The treaty next goes on to speak of another point, a most important one in oriental states, the provisions for the treatment of subjects on either side who might prefer to exchange the yoke of their own ruler for that of his enemy.

"If (inhabitants) of the countries of Ramses II. the great monarch of Egypt (emigrate) and come to the great prince of the Cheta, then shall the great prince of the Cheta refuse to receive them, but the great prince of the Cheta shall cause them to be brought back to Ramses II. the great monarch of Egypt.

"(If servants have escaped from Egypt, and it has been) notified, and they come to the country of the Cheta, in order to take service with another, they shall not be allowed to remain in the country of the Cheta, but they shall be brought back to Ramses II. the great monarch of Egypt."

The analogous clauses regarding the surrendering by the Egyptians of the subjects and servants of the prince of the Cheta close the treaty proper, and then follow the customary concluding formulae, placing the compact under the protection of the gods. "A thousand divinities of the male divinities and of the female divinities of the gods of the country of the Cheta, together with a thousand divinities of the male divinities and of the female divinities of the country of Egypt," are the witnesses of all "that stands on this silver tablet." All the divinities of the various Cheta towns that are named Sutech, those named Astarte of the country of the Cheta and all the nameless gods "of the mountains and the streams of the country of the Cheta" on one side, and "Amon, Rê', and Sutech, and the male divinities and the female divinities of the mountains and the streams of the country of Egypt" on the other side, are invoked as sureties. "Whosoever shall not keep the words that stand on this silver tablet regarding the country of the Cheta and regarding the country of Egypt, may the thousand gods of the country of the Cheta and the thousand gods of the country of Egypt pursue him, his house, and his people (?), and his servants." But he who shall keep to them, him shall the same gods guard.

Finally, but added only as a supplement to the treaty, is another proviso, which, though not of wide-reaching importance, is very characteristic of the relations that had hitherto existed between the two great kingdoms. During the war many of the Cheta had gone over to the Egyptians, and many Egyptians had gone over to the Cheta—for instance, we meet with one of the Cheta named Ramses,—these had of course been received with open arms by the enemy. Now after the peace the question arose as to what should be done with these deserters, and how the two powers could disembarrass themselves of them in a fitting manner. The agreement which they came to on the subject runs thus: "If men have fled from the country of Egypt, if it be one man or two men or three men, and have come to the great prince of the Cheta, then shall the great prince of the Cheta take them into custody and cause them to be brought back to Ramses II. the great monarch of Egypt. But with regard to him who is brought back to Ramses II. the great monarch of Egypt, his crime shall not be brought up against him, neither shall his house nor his wives nor his children be (destroyed), neither shall his mother be slain, and he shall not be (punished) neither in his eyes nor in his mouth nor in his feet; and no crime whatever shall be brought up against him." The same clause was enacted for the Cheta who had gone over to the Pharaoh.

This remarkable document, which gives us a glimpse behind the scenes, shows us at the same time the true facts hidden beneath the bombastic phrases of the inscriptions, and marks at once a new departure in Egyptian politics—Egypt acknowledging the Cheta as an equal power, with whom she had to share the supremacy in Palestine. This friendly relationship was an enduring one; Ramses II. married a daughter of the king of the Cheta, and when on one occasion the latter came to Egypt to visit his son-in-law, the Pharaoh caused him to be represented as a prince by his side in the temple of Abu Simbel. It was indeed an unheard-of thing that a barbarian prince, a "miserable chief," according to the customary expression, should be represented on a public monument as the associate of the Pharaoh; this was, as it were, an earnest of the new era that was approaching for Egypt. Not long after the death of Ramses II. the dominion of a Syrian inaugurated an epoch of foreign rule in Egypt, which, with certain intervals of longer or shorter duration, has lasted on to the present day. It therefore sounds rather comical to us when in the usual way a loyal court-poet interprets the visit of the king of the Cheta as a sign of the might of the Pharaoh:—

"The great prince of the Cheta writes to the prince of Qede:

> 'Prepare thyself, that we may hasten to Egypt.
> What the divine spirit says, that happens.
> We wish to flatter Ramses II., that he
> May give us after his pleasure;
> For every country depends upon his favour
> And Cheta in . . . ;
> If the gods do not accept his offering,
> Then is there no rain to be seen.
> Let us honour (?) Ramses II.,
> The bull who loves valour.'"[1]

The immediate and natural consequence of these years of peace was an increase of intercourse between the two countries; in fact, the friendship of the Pharaoh towards the prince of the Cheta went so far that he even sent to the latter ships of corn, when his country was suffering from a period of great calamity.[2] In spite of these friendly relations, the north-east frontier of Egypt was still carefully guarded by soldiers, for though Egypt might now be in the peaceful possession of the south of Palestine, yet the latter contained so many nomadic elements, that, even under the strictest rule, the tribes could not entirely be restrained from their predatory habits.

The line of fortifications which was intended to keep back these Beduins of the Delta, is met with as early as the time of the Middle Empire, and is still standing. It consisted of a wall strengthened by small towers, or according to the Semitic word, *migdols;* this formed an *obstruction* which the slaves who tried to escape from Egypt,[3] and the Beduins who wanted to pasture their cattle on the fields of the Delta, found difficult to pass.[4] At this time we also meet with a defensive work of another kind, namely a broad canal, which presumably connected the lakes of the isthmus together. At the point where a bridge crossed this canal were strong fortresses on both sides; all the various well-stations of the desert route on the Syrian side were also provided with small forts.[5] The great fortress which defended this bridge was the "fortress of T'aru," which is so often mentioned as the starting-point of the military expeditions.

This frontier was most strictly watched. Captains of the mercenaries

[1] An., 4, 6, 7 ff. The accepted interpretation of this line cannot strictly be proved, but seems probable.

[2] Mar. Karn., 53, 24.

[3] An., 5, 19, 2 ff.

[4] An., 6, 4, 13 ff.

[5] L. D., iii. 128=Ros. Mon. Stor., 50, 51; Br. Dict. Géo., 645.

with the divisions under their command garrisoned the fortresses and the wells, and nobody might pass without giving his name, his position and the object of his journey, and producing the letters he bore. For our knowledge of these facts we are entirely indebted to the young scribe Paebpasa, who lived under Merenptaḥ, and was a pupil of Amenemopet, the chief charioteer. He seems to have been stationed in the fortress T'aru, and to have had to keep an account of those who went out or in, and to inform the authorities. For several days he entered the necessary information on this subject on the first piece of good paper that he chanced upon, the back of his school copy-book; and it is in this copy-book that they have been preserved to us.[1] I need not say that these scribbles are of infinitely more importance to us than all that is contained on the other side of the pages of the copy-book; unfortunately they are scarcely legible in places. The following are some of the notes made by Paebpasa:

"In the 3rd year, on the 15th of Pachon.

There went out the servant of Ba'al, son of D'apur of Gaza, who had two separate letters to take with him to Syria, (namely to) Cha'y the superintendent of the peasantry, 1 letter;

(to) Ba'al the prince of Tyre, 1 letter.

"In the 3rd year, on the 17th (?) of Pachon.

There came one here, from the well of Merenptaḥ, situate in the mountainous country, to the captain of the mercenaries, in order to hold an inspection (?) in the fortress, which is in T'aru.

"In the 3rd year, on the . . . Pachon.

There ascended hither the servant Dḥoute, son of T'akarumu of Gaqaty.

Dut'eu the . . ., the son of Shamba'al, likewise.

Sutechmes, son of 'Aperdgar, likewise, who had with him to the royal residence (to) Cha'y, (the) superintendent of the peasantry, 1 letter.

"In the 3rd year, on the . . . Pachon.

The servant Nechtamon, son of T'ar, from the castle of Merenptaḥ, who is to arrive at (?) D'arrum, who has with him for Syria two separate letters:

(to) Penamun, (the) superintendent of the peasantry, 1 letter;

(to) Ramses, (the) estate superintendent of this town, 1 letter.

There ascended the captain of the stable, Pamerchetmu, son of Any, from the town of Merenptaḥ, which lies in the nome of 'Emur, who has with him (to the) royal residence two separate letters;

(to) Pa . . . mḥeb,[2] (the) superintendent of the peasantry, 1 letter;

(to) Para'mḥeb, (the) deputy, 1 letter," etc.

We see what a number of Egyptian officials must have formerly resided in Syria, or *ascended* thither from the lower-lying country of Egypt; the "superintendents of the peasantry," who are mentioned here and in other places[3] as living in Palestine, had, as Brugsch has doubtless rightly

[1] An., 3, 4-6 R. There is much that cannot be read, especially in the names.

[2] The scribe did not exactly know what the name was, and therefore left the middle blank. As it stands now, it signifies: *the . . . at the feast.*

[3] L. D., iii. 187 d, 24; cp. also ib. c. 2, and d. 27; where they are called "superintendents of the countries."

concluded,[1] the administration of colonies of Egyptian workmen. We learn from our text that there belonged also a *town* to these colonies, and perhaps it may have been the same as that in which the court formerly resided.

Whilst the frontiers were thus carefully watched on account of their own Semitic subjects, the Egyptians were threatened by a much more serious danger from quite another quarter. This danger was due in part to the old enemies of Egypt, such as the various tribes of Libyans, with whom Amenemḥ'êt I. and other kings had fought; in part to new hostile neighbours, such as the Shardana, the Shakarusha, the Tarusha, etc., by which names the people were known, who came from the coasts of the Mediterranean to invade the valley of the Nile. It seems that Sety I. had already come in contact with them, for amongst the Egyptian troops, at the beginning of the reign of his son we meet with Shardana, of whom it is expressly stated that they had originally been captives. In the meantime these pirate races, who "marched fighting through the country in order daily to fill their mouths,"[2] and who, if I rightly understand, had already made an incursion into Syria and into the kingdom of the Cheta,[3] took service with the Libyan prince Mar'eayu, who with their help now undertook a great predatory expedition. They descended upon the western frontier of Egypt, which from early times had been left as pasture land to the Libyan races of the Teḥen; this part of the country, however, really belonged to Egypt, and, like Syria and Nubia, had been occupied by *monuments*, *i.e.* colonies.[4] Thence they penetrated into the Delta, plundering as they advanced, and even threatened Heliopolis; at the same time they also invaded the oases. The danger was most serious, for these races were well armed, and (if we may judge from the number of killed and wounded) might be reckoned by tens of thousands. The gods, however, took Egypt under their protection, and the god Ptaḥ appeared to the king Merenptaḥ in a dream, and promised him the victory. In fact, after a fight of six hours, his troops succeeded in gaining a splendid victory, a victory so glorious that Mar'eayu, the Libyan prince, did not await the issue, but fled from the field, leaving behind his sandals and his quiver. The whole camp, with all the treasure as well as all the family of the prince, fell into the hands of the Egyptians. The camp was burnt after being plundered by the soldiers; in it there were found of metal vessels alone 3174, while 9376 captives completed the sum of the spoil. In order to prove to the people at home the number of the dead, they cut off certain portions from the fallen, *e.g.* the hands in the case of the Aqayuasha, who practised circumcision,[5] they then laded the donkeys with this booty. Gladly would they also have taken the fugitive Mar'eayu, and the Pharaoh sent officers, "who were on horses," after him and the other fugitives. These mounted officers however were not able to overtake him, and

[1] Br. Wb. Suppl. p. v. [hieroglyphs].

[2] Mar. Karn., 53, 22.

[3] Mar. Karn., 53, 24.

[4] Mar. Karn., 52, 19, 54, 41.

[5] This is the only passage from which we gather that the Egyptians attached any importance to their custom of circumcision.

"under cover of night" he escaped. Notwithstanding his escape, his power was completely broken; he had not fulfilled the promises with which he had enticed his people to the war; "all his words had turned back on his own head," and he "had become an enemy to his own army." It was not even known, as the commander of the "monuments of the west" added to this report, whether indeed he still lived, and the people resolved to set up one of his brothers in his place.[1]

Thus for a time the imminent danger which threatened Egypt from the Libyans was turned aside; it was not however permanently averted. The next king of whose great deeds we have any record, Ramses III., had again twice to fight against the Libyans, and as the number of the bloody trophies above mentioned reached in one case the sum of 12,535, there must have been a fight of the most serious importance. At this time the Libyans had evidently some pressing need for enlarging their borders, for apart from this attempt to penetrate into Egypt by force, they entered the service of the Pharaohs as mercenaries in such great numbers that, two centuries later, they were able as the ruling class to take possession of the Nile country.

In these later wars, moreover, the Libyans appear alone on the scene, though the Egyptians had still to face troubles arising from those nations of the sea who had fought with them in the time of Merenptaḥ. For centuries there was manifestly a continuous movement of tribes eastward, and the most dangerous shock of this tribal migration seems to have been felt in Egypt under Ramses III. In addition to their old enemies the Shardana, the T'eursha, and the Shakarusha, fresh ones now appear on the scene, namely, the Purasat'e, the T'akekar, the Da'en'euna, and the Uashash; thus in the great migrations of our history also, one people has always dragged along another. From the north they penetrated into Syria, partly by land in carts drawn by oxen, partly by sea in their ships, which seem to have been little inferior to those of Egypt. The Syrian kingdom was not able to stand the stress of this invasion; Qede, Cheta, and Palestine were subdued by the barbarians. But just as in later ages, after anterior Asia had fallen a victim to the power of the Scythians, this same power was afterwards broken in Egypt, so in these old times also, the force of this tribal migration was crippled at the Egyptian frontier. When the people endeavoured to enter the mouth of the Nile by sea, Ramses III. attacked them with his war-ships and his foot-soldiers, and won the most complete victory. Though the empty phrases of the inscriptions teach us very little about the particulars of this naval battle, yet we are able to form a general idea of it from the accompanying illustration. The ships on both sides—we can recognise the Egyptian by the lion-heads in the bows—have reefed their sails in order not to interfere with the men who are fighting; the basket at the masthead also has been removed to make

[1] The report, Mar. Karn., 52 ff., consists only of half lines, the details are therefore very difficult to understand. I see nothing in it to imply that these tribes already occupied the Delta before the war.

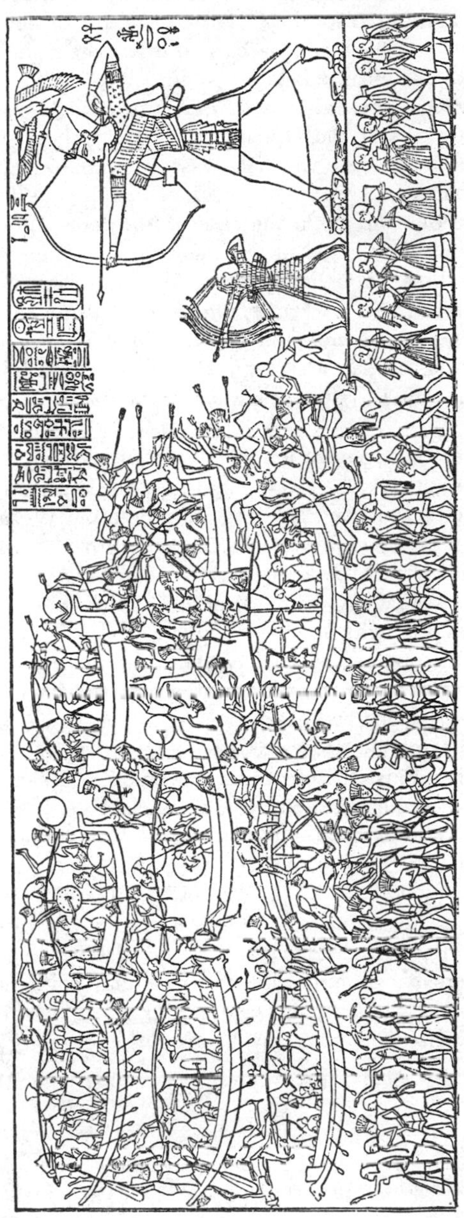

THE BATTLE WITH THE MARITIME NATIONS. To the right on the shore are Ramses III. and his soldiers. The king is standing on the corpses of the enemy; above him, protecting him, is the goddess of the north in the form of a vulture. Below are officers with the prisoners who are being bound and led away (after Ros. Mon. Stor., 131).

room for a slinger. The Egyptians understand how to pull round the ships of the enemy with their grappling irons, so as to bring them to close quarters; in fighting also they have the better of their opponents, for they all carry bows, whilst the barbarians with their short swords can only fight in a hand-to-hand medley.

This battle is almost the only naval engagement in Egyptian history; for though in the wars with the Hyksos we certainly hear of fighting on the water, yet in the latter case the Nile was the scene of action.[1] From the account of this battle, we learn that on the ships of war the subordinate officer bore the title of *u'au,* as in the case of the foot-soldiers, while the highest rank that an officer could attain was that of "chief of the ships," *i.e.* admiral. The ships had their individual names, as *Battle Animal,* or *Glorious in Memphis.* The *ship of Pharaoh* is also called *Beloved of Amon,* and as the *standard-bearer* and the *u'au* of the latter ship are often mentioned,[2] it must have been a ship of war. As a rule however, as far as we know, the army in Egypt was always of far more importance than the navy.

We know little of the organisation of the troops with which the kings of the 18th dynasty undertook their campaigns, for the inscriptions generally speak of *soldiers* merely without entering into detail. We are far better informed as to the military conditions under the 19th and 20th dynasties, though even here much still requires elucidation.

As we have seen, the army of the Middle Empire consisted essentially of companies of militia, which were supplied in times of need by the princes of the various nomes; it is uncertain how far this old institution was retained under the entirely new conditions of the New Empire. At any rate, in the inscriptions, we hear no more of what we might almost call the private armies of the nomes, and with regard to the soldiers of the temple estates, which existed afterwards as before,[3] I can scarcely say whether they were more than a body of police which had to keep order in the sanctuary and on the estates of the god. The great wars of the New Empire at all events were carried on with a state army, of which only the smaller part was raised in Egypt,[4] while the larger part was recruited from foreign mercenaries. This was the case at any rate under the 19th dynasty; for instance, a small army of this time consisted of 3100 barbarian mercenaries, and only 1900 regular soldiers.[5] Of these regular soldiers also one part only had really the right to be called Egyptian troops in the old sense, the company bearing the old original name of soldiers, . On the other hand, the soldiers called the *Na'aruna* were

[1] L.D., iii. 12 d.

[2] Liebl., 208, 716, 763, 916. Two other ships, ditto, 591, 667.

[3] Concerning the temple soldiers of the N. E., see p. 304. That the great sanctuaries had their soldiers even under the Old Empire, we see from the titles of the high priests, as Mar. mon. div., 18, and other examples.

[4] In L.D., iii. 219, it is worthy of notice, that after the regular soldiers, mention is made of "200 officers of the squadron of the fishers of the state"; this seems to imply that the fisher-serfs formed a military company.

[5] An., 1, 17, 2 ff.

(as their Semitic name derived from נער *youth* probably implies[1]) a new organisation formed after foreign fashion, and the oft-mentioned *Pidt*, the *bow-company*, seem to have been a barbarian corps. With great probability it has been suggested that their curious appellation *bow* indicates that they were recruited from the *nine bows, i.e.* from the neighbouring barbarian tribes.[2] As a fact, we learn from an inscription of the 20th dynasty, that in the transport of stone, for instance, the barbarians called ‘Apur belonged to the "bow of the ‘Anuti barbarians."[3] It is therefore usually considered that the term *bows* signifies auxiliary forces, and this interpretation of the word is retained in this book. These *bow-troops* were commanded by *chiefs*, men of rank and education, from whose correspondence one or two letters have been preserved. A chief of one of these auxiliary companies commanded in Ethiopia;[4] others occupied the frontier fortresses in the east of the Delta,[5] and the well-stations of southern Palestine;[6] it is a fact therefore that we meet with them on foreign soil, and consequently they have a right to bear the title "superintendent of the barbarian country";[7] though at the same time a similar officer seems also to have resided in Heliopolis.[8]

It is possible that the corps of the Mad'ay were reckoned originally amongst these *bow-troops*. These men belonged to the Nubian race of the Med'a, who even under the Old Empire (see p. 522) sometimes served in the Egyptian army and as it appears were celebrated in old times as desert hunters.[9] Under the New Empire however they were formed into a military corps that answered in many respects to our constables and police, and were employed in various ways by the government. At all events they were under *chiefs*,[10] and their commander was the "prince of Mad'ay."[11] It is not now known from which tribes they were recruited under the New Empire, for it is but seldom that one of them bears a native name like Bekuarenra;[12] most of them adopted good old Egyptian names such as *Nechtset*,[13] *Set is victorious;* or *'Enḥernacht*,[14] *'Enḥor is victorious,* and similar names bearing a warlike character. But in spite of thus outwardly naturalising themselves as Egyptians, yet in the eyes of the pure-bred natives of the Nile Valley they were still homeless barbarians; for instance, a "deputy of the soldiers" writes contemptuously to the "prince of the Mad'ay: ‘Thou art a child of a bond-servant, thou art no prince at all; thou hast immigrated from some other place, in order to resort hither.’"[15] In another case moreover, one of these princes is also invested with other high military dignities.[16] The Egyptian officials were

[1] This explanation *youths* is rendered probable by the passage Mar. Karn., 54, 45, where the opposite appears to be *old men*. Under Ramses II. there was a *na‘aruna* (the word is used as if it were a collective noun, cp. נערון) in 'Emur: L.D., iii. 187 e.

[2] The signification *archers* is inadmissible, as these are called [hieroglyph], a quite different term.

[3] L.D., iii. 219.
[4] P. j. T., 5, 3.
[5] An., 3, 6, R.
[6] An., 5, 11, 7 ff.
[7] An., 5, 11, 7.
[8] An., 1, 10, 1.
[9] *Md'a* really signifies hunter: see Br. Wb. Suppl., 594.
[10] Abb., 1, 7, 10 b.
[11] An., 5, 25, 2.
[12] Abb., 1, 10 a.
[13] Turin, 16.
[14] An., 5, 25, 3.
[15] An., 5, 26, 5.
[16] L. D., iii. 138 n.

accustomed as a rule to speak ill of the Mad'ay "with their many commands,"[1] and without mincing matters, the above-mentioned Nechtset compares one of them to "that enemy of Rê‘,"[2] or as we should say, to the devil. We may further remark that in later times the Mad'ay must have played a still more important part in the state, for their name in the form of the word *Matoi* finally became the general term for soldiers, and was still in use amongst the Egyptians of Christian times.

To these original barbaric elements of the Egyptian army we must add under the 19th dynasty the oft-named Shardana, Qahaq and Mashauasha,[3] tribes of the conquered Libyans and sea-folk, who, like the Turkish tribes of the Middle Ages, entered the service of the Pharaohs under their own *chiefs*, and like them also finally became the ruling power in the state. That they were employed in considerable numbers is shown by the corps of 5000 men we have already mentioned, which contained 520 Shardana, 1620 Qahaq, and 880 Mashauasha and negroes. The battles also which Merenptaḥ and Ramses III. fought with these same tribes and their allies were doubtless fought chiefly by the help of these barbarian mercenaries. In the periods with which we are concerned, these troops of savages were always expressly kept separate from the regular army;[4] they remained in distinct *tribes*, for Ramses III. calls the commanders, whom he set over the barbarians in his service, the "chiefs of the auxiliary troops, and the chiefs of the tribes."[5]

The usual division of the army was into *squadrons*; as to the size of each squadron I really have nothing conclusive to say, though we know a few of their names. Thus under the 18th dynasty we meet with the *squadron of Amon*,[6] a squadron styled the *beauty of the sun-disk*,[7] and the *squadron of the Pharaoh*.[8] Under the kings of the 19th dynasty the regiments were called by even more high-sounding names; a regiment of auxiliary troops that was stationed in the country of D'apur, was called *the squadron shining as the sun-disk*,[9] and a regiment under Sety I. bore the name of *Amon protects his soldiers*.[10] In time of war larger bodies of troops were formed from these squadrons; Ramses II., for instance, had four such bodies of troops with him on his second campaign, which he named after the four great gods of the country, the armies of Amon, of Rê‘, of Ptaḥ, and of Sutech,[11] or rather, if we quote the full names, "the first army of Amon, who gives victory to Ramses II." etc.[12]

Doubtless a military eye would have easily distinguished the various

[1] An., 5, 26, 5.
[2] Tur., 16, 2.
[3] An., 1, 17, 2 ff.; Harr., 76, 5.
[4] E.g. Harr., 76, 5.
[5] Harr., 77, 5.
[6] Mar. Cat. d'Ab., 1063, 1076.
[7] Mar. Cat. d'Ab., 1062, 1070.
[8] Mar. Cat. d'Ab., 1087.
[9] Ä. Z., 1881, p. 119.
[10] Mar. Cat. d'Ab., 1137.
[11] Raifet, 10.
[12] L. D., iii. 155. With regard to these armies named after the gods, they are not identical with the troops supplied by the temples of those gods. In the first place, the relative wealth of the temples varied so considerably that the size of the various corps would also consequently be very disproportionate; and further, if we were to accept this conclusion, the king would have no military force of his own with him.

divisions of the Egyptian army by their clothing and by their arms; meanwhile we cannot attain to this knowledge, and we must content ourselves with noticing a few especially striking points in the outward appearance of the soldiers.

As it is necessary for a soldier to be able to move easily and quickly, the Egyptian soldiers as a rule wore nothing but a short skirt, which was still further shortened in front to allow of a rapid stride. This costume however afforded no protection at all to the lower part of the body,

WADDED COAT OF MAIL WITH EMBROIDERY.
(Tomb of Ramses III. After W., i. 220.)

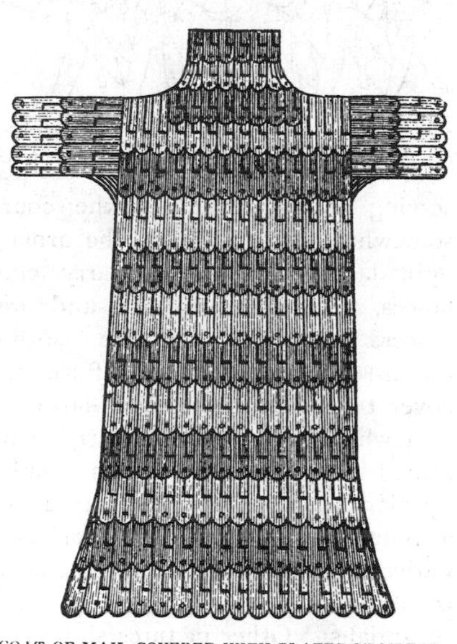

COAT OF MAIL COVERED WITH PLATES OF METAL.
(Tomb of Ramses III. After W., 221.)

which was therefore covered by a special three-cornered or heart-shaped lappet, fastened on in front, and probably made of leather.[1] It appears that Ramses II., if the chance pictures we possess do not mislead us, introduced a great change into this conventional costume, for his warriors no longer wear this lappet to their skirt, but are mail-clad in a thick cap, and a close-fitting upper dress.[2] This helmet and coat of mail, however, did not consist of metal, they were made more probably, as many of the pictures seem to show, of thickly-wadded material, such as is worn even now in the Sudan and forms an excellent protection. In rare instances they may have been covered with metal plates. Under Ramses II. the high officers and especially the charioteers certainly wear a special costume, viz. a long skirt, an upper dress, and over that a short leathern coat of

[1] L. D., iii. 94, 97 e, 117, 121 a. Does the central flap of the ancient Shend'ot correspond with this piece? and is the Shend'ot possibly the original war-costume of the kings?

[2] L. D., iii. 154, 156, 168: particularly clear and somewhat dissimilar: L. D., iii. 214.

mail covering the breast, back, and thighs.[1] Later they seem to have returned again to the old war costume with the heart-shaped lappet in front.[2]

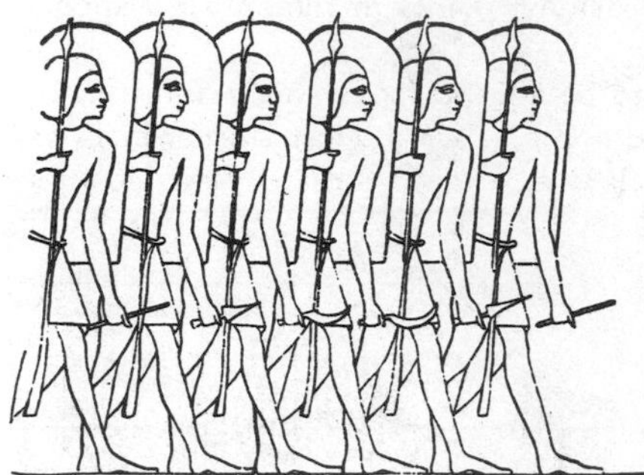

INFANTRY OF RAMSES II. (after L.D., iii. 155).

The accompanying picture, which shows the foot soldiery of *the first army* on the march, illustrates the equipment of the troops under Ramses II. They are armed with lances, and alternately also with daggers or sickle-shaped swords, while every fifth man, probably a subordinate officer, carries a short wand. They have hung their heavy shields over their backs during the march.

The pictures of the troops serving as bodyguard at the court of King Chuen'eten belong to a somewhat earlier date.[3] The arms of this corps consist of a shield and light lance; the officers carry clubs. Another company carry heavy lances, an axe, and a shield, and are commanded by officers with sticks; they are also distinguished from the first corps by their coiffure, which is made to cover their ears;[4] the front flap of their skirt is also somewhat narrower. Similarly attired is a company armed with a sort of threshing flail, and commanded by men bearing clubs. We are also able to recognise a troop of auxiliaries of this period—Syrians in their native costume armed with long lances; a short dagger is stuck in the girdle; they are commanded by Egyptians. Other pictures show us negro companies serving under the same king and armed with bows and arrows.[5] These various regiments are of course accompanied by the standard-bearers, so often mentioned in the inscriptions; representations of a few of the various standards are given in the accompanying illustration.[6] As we see, some of these standards are in the form of fans, while others consist only of single ostrich feathers, which as we have already observed were a symbol of victory.

SOLDIER OF THE TIME OF THE CLOSE OF THE 18TH DYNASTY (after L. D., iii. 121 b).

Entirely distinct from the kind of troops we have already mentioned were those whom we may style the fashionable force under the New Empire, namely, the *tent-ḥtor*, the *horse-estate*, *i.e.* the chariot force. In every respect they played the part of our cavalry. As we have already seen in the preceding chapter, the chariot in Egypt was of

[1] L. D., iii. 153, 187 c. [2] L. D., iii. 231. Ros. Mon. Stor., 124.
[3] L. D., iii. 92; in part also the same troops: L. D., iii. 121 b.
[4] May not this possibly represent a helmet?
[5] L. D., iii. 97, 104. [6] L. D., iii. 92. In part the same: ib. 104, 105.

foreign origin, and perhaps for that very reason it stood in very high favour with the Egyptians, both in times of peace and of war.

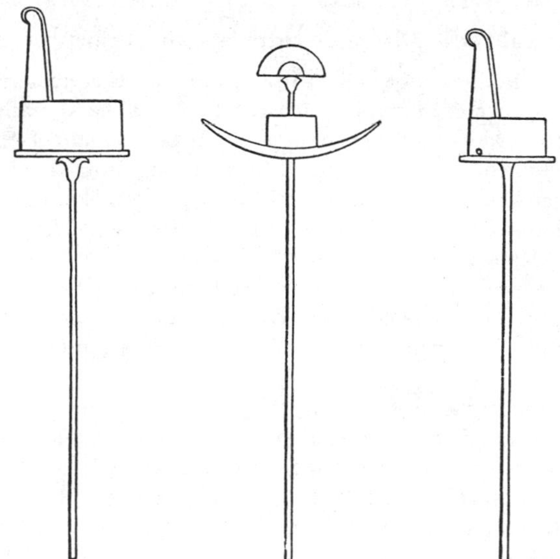

STANDARDS OF THE TROOPS OF CHUEN'ETEN (after L. D., iii. 92).

The chariot soldiers stood two abreast on the chariot. One fought from the chariot with his bow and arrows [1] or with his darts, which were

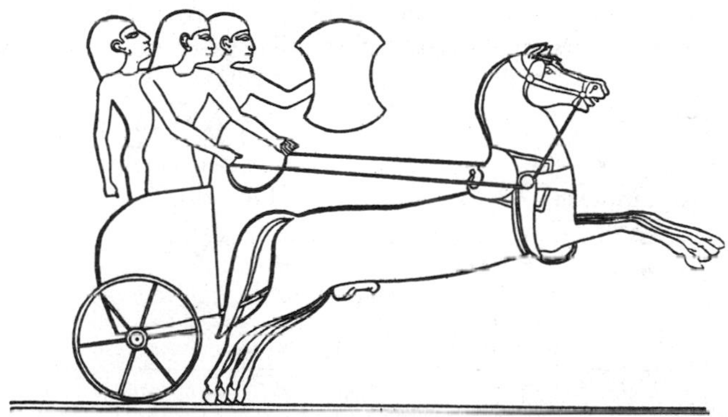

WAR-CHARIOT OF THE CHETA (after L. D., iii. 158).

conveniently at hand, stuck into two quivers on the edge of the chariot; the other drove the horses, which were sometimes protected by wadded coats.[2] To the surprise of the Egyptians the Cheta drove in a different fashion;[3] they manned their chariots with three soldiers; that is to

[1] L. D., iii. 160. [2] L. D., iii. 165. [3] Sall., 3, 1, 1.

say, they added a shield-bearer, who had to protect the other two with his shield, whilst the Egyptian chariot-soldier had to cover himself with his own shield.[1] The barracks for the chariot force were the *'eh* [hieroglyphs], the royal *stables*,[2] large departments with "chiefs of the stables,"[3] and "scribes," who had not only to take care of the horses, but also to look after many other matters, which to our ideas have really very little to do with the army. For instance, the scribe of one of these stables in writing to his chief, after he has informed him how it fared with the horses, continues: "I have attended to what my lord wrote to me: 'Give provision to the soldiers and to the 'Aperu, who are dragging the altar of Rê' of Ramses to Memphis.'"[4] We see that in times of peace the division of the chariot force was employed on the public works just as much as that of the foot soldiery. We have already mentioned (p. 330) the "stable of the causing to become," *i.e.* in Egyptian parlance, of education.[5]

Amongst the highest officers of this force were the royal charioteers, or, according to the foreign term usually employed, the Kat'ana.[6] These were, at any rate some of them,[7] distinguished, well-educated men of high rank, and Ramses II. as well as Ramses III. availed themselves of the services of their own sons as "chief charioteers of his Majesty, and superintendents of the horses."[8] Amenemopet, another "chief charioteer," a number of whose letters have been preserved, styles himself in them a "royal ambassador to all countries, the governor of foreign countries and peoples";[9] he was therefore not only a general but also a diplomatist. He was a man of scholarly education, and doubtless in his heart he felt contempt for his lower more practical military appointment. Otherwise we can scarcely understand why amongst other wise letters and specimen passages of poetry he should make his pupil Paebpasa write out a warning against the "unhappy position of officer [hieroglyphs] of the chariot-force."[10] As a boy the poor fellow referred to here was placed through the good offices of his grandfather in the *stable* of the king:—

"He hastens to lay hold of the horses
In the stable before his Majesty.
He receives beautiful horses,
And rejoices and exults,
And returns with them to his town."

[1] L. D., iii. 155, 160.

[2] An., 3, 5, Rs.; An., 3, 6, 4; Leyden, 349.

[3] Mar. Cat. d'Ab., 1162, as a relative of a commander of the auxiliary troops. Another is at the same time Kat'ana and governor of Nubia, L. D., iii. 138 n.

[4] Leyden, 349; cp. also L. D., iii. 219, the "chiefs of the stables of the court" at Ḥammamât.

[5] Inscription of Bekenchons, l. 3. For the interpretation of *sochpr* by *education*, cp. amongst other passages, l. 4 of the same inscription.

[6] That the Kat'ana signified originally only the driver of a favourite carriage, we see from L. D., iii. 10 a, bis.

[7] L. D., iii. 219, "a Kat'ana of the court" amongst the highest officers, and "fifty Kat'ana of the horse estate," mentioned after "the twenty chiefs of the stable of the court."

[8] Ä. Z., 1883, p. 61.

[9] An., 3, 1, 9 ff. = An., 3, 7, 11.

[10] An., 3, 6, 3 ff.

He cannot bear the life at home however, so he gives his property into the charge of his grandfather, and drives away in his chariot. Therewith all manner of ill-luck happens to him, and when at last the review of the troops takes place, his misfortunes reach their climax:—

"He is bastinadoed on the ground,
Bastinadoed with a hundred stripes."

Still less indeed must Paebpasa think of becoming an "officer of the foot soldiery," [hieroglyphs], whose fate is even far worse. In order to warn him of the evils of the latter profession, Amenemopet propounds the following poem to him, a poem that is also to be found in the school literature of that period:—[1]

"Oh what does it mean that thou sayest:
'The officer has a better lot than the scribe?'
Come let me relate to thee of the fate of the officer, so full of trouble.
He is brought as a child into the barracks (?) to be shut up (?) there.
A blow, that . . . he receives in his belly,
A blow, that cuts open, he receives on his eyebrows,
And his head is split open by a wound!
They lay him down and beat upon him as upon a book,
He is broken by flogging.
Come let me relate to thee how he travels to Syria,
How he marches in the upland country.
His food and his water he has to carry on his arm,
Laden like a donkey;
This makes his neck stiff like that of a donkey,
And the bones of his back break.
He drinks dirty water . . .
If he arrives in face of the enemy,
He is like a bird in a snare.
If he arrives at his home in Egypt,
He is like wood, that the worms eat.
He is ill, and must lie down.
They have to bring him home on the donkey,
Whilst his clothes are stolen, and his servants run away.
Therefore, O scribe,
Reverse thine opinion about the happiness of the scribe and of the officer."

As we have said, this contempt affected by a higher officer for the position of his subordinate is apparently explained by the fact that a learned education was always required for the higher appointments. In truth, amongst the highest officers,[2] we always meet with "scribes of the army"; and when we consider that it was a "royal scribe of the command of the army,"[3] and another officer,[4] who entered into the

[1] An., 4, 9, 4 ff. = An., 3, 5, 5 ff. A similar poem of like import: Ä. Z., 1880, p. 96.

[2] The most important source for ascertaining the rank of the various officers is the inscription: L.D., iii. 219, which evidently gives the officers and officials named therein in their order of rank.

[3] An., 1, 2, 3.

[4] Ib. 1, 8. I know not what is meant by the [hieroglyphs]. Cp. the [hieroglyphs] L.D., iii. 219, which might nevertheless be also construed *snne*.

above-mentioned controversy about a fine style of writing (see p. 380), we see at once that these officers felt themselves to be the representatives of classical education. There were moreover many different degrees in this rank of scribe: some scribes were only attached to a certain company,[1] while others were certainly eligible for the highest commands in the whole army, as *e.g.* the "superintendent of the soldiers, and scribe of the army."[2] The latter indeed might do the work of deputy for the distinguished "representative of the army" (often termed *representative* alone for short), a man who, at any rate in one case, took precedence even of the high "charioteer of the court."[3]

This scholarly education of the officers does not seem to have been prejudicial to the performance of their practical duties; in times of peace both in the earlier and later periods they were employed in all manner of engineering works, such as the transport of stone,[4] or the organisation of irrigation canals.[5] These duties were not felt to be in any way derogatory for the high officers:

> "The superintendent of the army, the chief of the bow-troops, the Saket, who stands before them,
> the standard-bearer, the representative,
> the scribe of the army, the commander of the peasantry—
> they go in and go out
> in the courts of the king's house,"

whilst the poor subordinate, the inferior officer, the *u'au*, is compared to a laden donkey. For "he must work till the sun sets," and at night he cannot sleep for hunger: "he is dead while he yet lives."[6]

Thus according to Egyptian ideas, even in the profession of arms, a good education was the only thing that could bring men happiness and success.

[1] Mar. Cat. d'Ab., 1137. Cp. also L.D., iii. 219, where in addition to two specially mentioned scribes of the army ("scribe of the Sḥu" and "scribe deputy"), twenty are named together without any title.

[2] Inscr. in the hier. char., 29. Also the "royal scribe and superintendent of the soldiers." An., 5, 21, 8; frequently also merely "superintendent of the soldiers," and doubtless also often simply "royal scribe."

[3] L. D., iii. 219. An., 5, 23, 7 ff. Leyden, 348, 7. An., 3, 5, Rs., etc.

[4] L. D., iii. 219. An., 1, 15, 3. An., 5, 23, 7 ff. Leyden, 348, 7.

[5] An., 5, 21, 8 ff.

[6] Ä. Z., 1880, 96. The explanation I gave there now seems to me to be erroneous. It is uncertain whether in the poetical list here given of the officers superior to the *u'au*, they are really in order of rank.

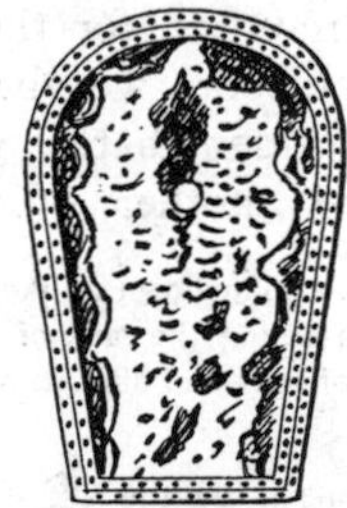

SHIELD COVERED WITH FUR (after W., i. 198).

INDEX

TABLE OF PASSAGES QUOTED FROM LEPSIUS, "DENKMÄLER," AND FROM THE "SELECT PAPYRI."

LEPSIUS, DENKMÄLER

Part III.

SELECT PAPYRI OF THE BRITISH MUSEUM

A CATALOGUE OF SELECTED DOVER BOOKS IN ALL FIELDS OF INTEREST

A CATALOGUE OF SELECTED DOVER BOOKS IN ALL FIELDS OF INTEREST

AUSTRIAN COOKING AND BAKING, Gretel Beer. Authentic thick soups, wiener schnitzel, veal goulash, more, plus dumplings, puff pastries, nut cakes, sacher tortes, other great Austrian desserts. 224pp. USO 23220-4 Pa. $2.50

CHEESES OF THE WORLD, U.S.D.A. Dictionary of cheeses containing descriptions of over 400 varieties of cheese from common Cheddar to exotic Surati. Up to two pages are given to important cheeses like Camembert, Cottage, Edam, etc. 151pp. 22831-2 Pa. $1.50

TRITTON'S GUIDE TO BETTER WINE AND BEER MAKING FOR BEGINNERS, S.M. Tritton. All you need to know to make family-sized quantities of over 100 types of grape, fruit, herb, vegetable wines; plus beers, mead, cider, more. 11 illustrations. 157pp. USO 22528-3 Pa. $2.25

DECORATIVE LABELS FOR HOME CANNING, PRESERVING, AND OTHER HOUSEHOLD AND GIFT USES, Theodore Menten. 128 gummed, perforated labels, beautifully printed in 2 colors. 12 versions in traditional, Art Nouveau, Art Deco styles. Adhere to metal, glass, wood, most plastics. 24pp. 8¼ x 11. 23219-0 Pa. $2.00

FIVE ACRES AND INDEPENDENCE, Maurice G. Kains. Great back-to-the-land classic explains basics of self-sufficient farming: economics, plants, crops, animals, orchards, soils, land selection, host of other necessary things. Do not confuse with skimpy faddist literature; Kains was one of America's greatest agriculturalists. 95 illustrations. 397pp. 20974-1 Pa. $3.00

GROWING VEGETABLES IN THE HOME GARDEN, U.S. Dept. of Agriculture. Basic information on site, soil conditions, selection of vegetables, planting, cultivation, gathering. Up-to-date, concise, authoritative. Covers 60 vegetables. 30 illustrations. 123pp. 23167-4 Pa. $1.35

FRUITS FOR THE HOME GARDEN, Dr. U.P. Hedrick. A chapter covering each type of garden fruit, advice on plant care, soils, grafting, pruning, sprays, transplanting, and much more! Very full. 53 illustrations. 175pp. 22944-0 Pa. $2.50

GARDENING ON SANDY SOIL IN NORTH TEMPERATE AREAS, Christine Kelway. Is your soil too light, too sandy? Improve your soil, select plants that survive under such conditions. Both vegetables and flowers. 42 photos. 148pp. USO 23199-2 Pa. $2.50

THE FRAGRANT GARDEN: A BOOK ABOUT SWEET SCENTED FLOWERS AND LEAVES, Louise Beebe Wilder. Fullest, best book on growing plants for their fragrances. Descriptions of hundreds of plants, both well-known and overlooked. 407pp. 23071-6 Pa. $4.00

EASY GARDENING WITH DROUGHT-RESISTANT PLANTS, Arno and Irene Nehrling. Authoritative guide to gardening with plants that require a minimum of water: seashore, desert, and rock gardens; house plants; annuals and perennials; much more. 190 illustrations. 320pp. 23230-1 Pa. $3.50

THE ART DECO STYLE, ed. by Theodore Menten. Furniture, jewelry, metalwork, ceramics, fabrics, lighting fixtures, interior decors, exteriors, graphics from pure French sources. Best sampling around. Over 400 photographs. 183pp. 8³/₈ x 11¼.
22824-X Pa. $4.00

THE GENTLEMAN AND CABINET MAKER'S DIRECTOR, Thomas Chippendale. Full reprint, 1762 style book, most influential of all time; chairs, tables, sofas, mirrors, cabinets, etc. 200 plates, plus 24 photographs of surviving pieces. 249pp. 9⁷/₈ x 12¾.
21601-2 Pa. $6.00

PINE FURNITURE OF EARLY NEW ENGLAND, Russell H. Kettell. Basic book. Thorough historical text, plus 200 illustrations of boxes, highboys, candlesticks, desks, etc. 477pp. 7⁷/₈ x 10¾.
20145-7 Clothbd. $12.50

ORIENTAL RUGS, ANTIQUE AND MODERN, Walter A. Hawley. Persia, Turkey, Caucasus, Central Asia, China, other traditions. Best general survey of all aspects: styles and periods, manufacture, uses, symbols and their interpretation, and identification. 96 illustrations, 11 in color. 320pp. 6¹/₈ x 9¼.
22366-3 Pa. $5.00

DECORATIVE ANTIQUE IRONWORK, Henry R. d'Allemagne. Photographs of 4500 iron artifacts from world's finest collection, Rouen. Hinges, locks, candelabra, weapons, lighting devices, clocks, tools, from Roman times to mid-19th century. Nothing else comparable to it. 420pp. 9 x 12.
22082-6 Pa. $8.50

THE COMPLETE BOOK OF DOLL MAKING AND COLLECTING, Catherine Christopher. Instructions, patterns for dozens of dolls, from rag doll on up to elaborate, historically accurate figures. Mould faces, sew clothing, make doll houses, etc. Also collecting information. Many illustrations. 288pp. 6 x 9.
22066-4 Pa. $3.00

ANTIQUE PAPER DOLLS: 1915-1920, edited by Arnold Arnold. 7 antique cut-out dolls and 24 costumes from 1915-1920, selected by Arnold Arnold from his collection of rare children's books and entertainments, all in full color. 32pp. 9¼ x 12¼.
23176-3 Pa. $2.00

ANTIQUE PAPER DOLLS: THE EDWARDIAN ERA, Epinal. Full-color reproductions of two historic series of paper dolls that show clothing styles in 1908 and at the beginning of the First World War. 8 two-sided, stand-up dolls and 32 complete, two-sided costumes. Full instructions for assembling included. 32pp. 9¼ x 12¼.
23175-5 Pa. $2.00

A HISTORY OF COSTUME, Carl Köhler, Emma von Sichardt. Egypt, Babylon, Greece up through 19th century Europe; based on surviving pieces, art works, etc. Full text and 595 illustrations, including many clear, measured patterns for reproducing historic costume. Practical. 464pp.
21030-8 Pa. $4.00

EARLY AMERICAN LOCOMOTIVES, John H. White, Jr. Finest locomotive engravings from late 19th century: historical (1804-1874), main-line (after 1870), special, foreign, etc. 147 plates. 200pp. 11³/₈ x 8¼.
22772-3 Pa. $3.50

HOUDINI ON MAGIC, Harold Houdini. Edited by Walter Gibson, Morris N. Young. How he escaped; exposés of fake spiritualists; instructions for eye-catching tricks; other fascinating material by and about greatest magician. 155 illustrations. 280pp. 20384-0 Pa. $2.75

HANDBOOK OF THE NUTRITIONAL CONTENTS OF FOOD, U.S. Dept. of Agriculture. Largest, most detailed source of food nutrition information ever prepared. Two mammoth tables: one measuring nutrients in 100 grams of edible portion; the other, in edible portion of 1 pound as purchased. Originally titled Composition of Foods. 190pp. 9 x 12. 21342-0 Pa. $4.00

COMPLETE GUIDE TO HOME CANNING, PRESERVING AND FREEZING, U.S. Dept. of Agriculture. Seven basic manuals with full instructions for jams and jellies; pickles and relishes; canning fruits, vegetables, meat; freezing anything. Really good recipes, exact instructions for optimal results. Save a fortune in food. 156 illustrations. 214pp. 6⅛ x 9¼. 22911-4 Pa. $2.50

THE BREAD TRAY, Louis P. De Gouy. Nearly every bread the cook could buy or make: bread sticks of Italy, fruit breads of Greece, glazed rolls of Vienna, everything from corn pone to croissants. Over 500 recipes altogether. including buns, rolls, muffins, scones, and more. 463pp. 23000-7 Pa. $3.50

CREATIVE HAMBURGER COOKERY, Louis P. De Gouy. 182 unusual recipes for casseroles, meat loaves and hamburgers that turn inexpensive ground meat into memorable main dishes: Arizona chili burgers, burger tamale pie, burger stew, burger corn loaf, burger wine loaf, and more. 120pp. 23001-5 Pa. $1.75

LONG ISLAND SEAFOOD COOKBOOK, J. George Frederick and Jean Joyce. Probably the best American seafood cookbook. Hundreds of recipes. 40 gourmet sauces, 123 recipes using oysters alone! All varieties of fish and seafood amply represented. 324pp. 22677-8 Pa. $3.50

THE EPICUREAN: A COMPLETE TREATISE OF ANALYTICAL AND PRACTICAL STUDIES IN THE CULINARY ART, Charles Ranhofer. Great modern classic. 3,500 recipes from master chef of Delmonico's, turn-of-the-century America's best restaurant. Also explained, many techniques known only to professional chefs. 775 illustrations. 1183pp. 6⅝ x 10. 22680-8 Clothbd. $22.50

THE AMERICAN WINE COOK BOOK, Ted Hatch. Over 700 recipes: old favorites livened up with wine plus many more: Czech fish soup, quince soup, sauce Perigueux, shrimp shortcake, filets Stroganoff, cordon bleu goulash, jambonneau, wine fruit cake, more. 314pp. 22796-0 Pa. $2.50

DELICIOUS VEGETARIAN COOKING, Ivan Baker. Close to 500 delicious and varied recipes: soups, main course dishes (pea, bean, lentil, cheese, vegetable, pasta, and egg dishes), savories, stews, whole-wheat breads and cakes, more. 168pp. USO 22834-7 Pa. $1.75

SLEEPING BEAUTY, illustrated by Arthur Rackham. Perhaps the fullest, most delightful version ever, told by C.S. Evans. Rackham's best work. 49 illustrations. 110pp. 7⅞ x 10¾. 22756-1 Pa. $2.00

THE WONDERFUL WIZARD OF OZ, L. Frank Baum. Facsimile in full color of America's finest children's classic. Introduction by Martin Gardner. 143 illustrations by W.W. Denslow. 267pp. 20691-2 Pa. **$3.00**

GOOPS AND HOW TO BE THEM, Gelett Burgess. Classic tongue-in-cheek masquerading as etiquette book. 87 verses, 170 cartoons as Goops demonstrate virtues of table manners, neatness, courtesy, more. 88pp. 6½ x 9¼. 22233-0 Pa. **$2.00**

THE BROWNIES, THEIR BOOK, Palmer Cox. Small as mice, cunning as foxes, exuberant, mischievous, Brownies go to zoo, toy shop, seashore, circus, more. 24 verse adventures. 266 illustrations. 144pp. 6⅝ x 9¼. 21265-3 Pa. **$2.50**

BILLY WHISKERS: THE AUTOBIOGRAPHY OF A GOAT, Frances Trego Montgomery. Escapades of that rambunctious goat. Favorite from turn of the century America. 24 illustrations. 259pp. 22345-0 Pa. $2.75

THE ROCKET BOOK, Peter Newell. Fritz, janitor's kid, sets off rocket in basement of apartment house; an ingenious hole punched through every page traces course of rocket. 22 duotone drawings, verses. 48pp. 6⅞ x 8⅜. 22044-3 Pa. $1.50

PECK'S BAD BOY AND HIS PA, George W. Peck. Complete double-volume of great American childhood classic. Hennery's ingenious pranks against outraged pomposity of pa and the grocery man. 97 illustrations. Introduction by E.F. Bleiler. 347pp. 20497-9 Pa. $2.50

THE TALE OF PETER RABBIT, Beatrix Potter. The inimitable Peter's terrifying adventure in Mr. McGregor's garden, with all 27 wonderful, full-color Potter illustrations. 55pp. 4¼ x 5½. USO 22827-4 Pa. $1.00

THE TALE OF MRS. TIGGY-WINKLE, Beatrix Potter. Your child will love this story about a very special hedgehog and all 27 wonderful, full-color Potter illustrations. 57pp. 4¼ x 5½. USO 20546-0 Pa. $1.00

THE TALE OF BENJAMIN BUNNY, Beatrix Potter. Peter Rabbit's cousin coaxes him back into Mr. McGregor's garden for a whole new set of adventures. A favorite with children. All 27 full-color illustrations. 59pp. 4¼ x 5½. USO 21102-9 Pa. $1.00

THE MERRY ADVENTURES OF ROBIN HOOD, Howard Pyle. Facsimile of original (1883) edition, finest modern version of English outlaw's adventures. 23 illustrations by Pyle. 296pp. 6½ x 9¼. 22043-5 Pa. **$4.00**

TWO LITTLE SAVAGES, Ernest Thompson Seton. Adventures of two boys who lived as Indians; explaining Indian ways, woodlore, pioneer methods. 293 illustrations. 286pp. 20985-7 Pa. $3.00

THE RED FAIRY BOOK, Andrew Lang. Lang's color fairy books have long been children's favorites. This volume includes Rapunzel, Jack and the Bean-stalk and 35 other stories, familiar and unfamiliar. 4 plates, 93 illustrations x + 367pp.
21673-X Paperbound **$3.00**

THE BLUE FAIRY BOOK, Andrew Lang. Lang's tales come from all countries and all times. Here are 37 tales from Grimm, the Arabian Nights, Greek Mythology, and other fascinating sources. 8 plates, 130 illustrations. xi + 390pp.
21437-0 Paperbound **$3.50**

HOUSEHOLD STORIES BY THE BROTHERS GRIMM. Classic English-language edition of the well-known tales — Rumpelstiltskin, Snow White, Hansel and Gretel, The Twelve Brothers, Faithful John, Rapunzel, Tom Thumb (52 stories in all). Translated into simple, straightforward English by Lucy Crane. Ornamented with headpieces, vignettes, elaborate decorative initials and a dozen full-page illustrations by Walter Crane. x + 269pp. 21080-4 Paperbound **$3.00**

THE MERRY ADVENTURES OF ROBIN HOOD, Howard Pyle. The finest modern versions of the traditional ballads and tales about the great English outlaw. Howard Pyle's complete prose version, with every word, every illustration of the first edition. Do not confuse this facsimile of the original (1883) with modern editions that change text or illustrations. 23 plates plus many page decorations. xxii + 296pp.
22043-5 Paperbound **$4.00**

THE STORY OF KING ARTHUR AND HIS KNIGHTS, Howard Pyle. The finest children's version of the life of King Arthur; brilliantly retold by Pyle, with 48 of his most imaginative illustrations. xviii + 313pp. $6\frac{1}{8}$ x $9\frac{1}{4}$.
21445-1 Paperbound **$3.50**

THE WONDERFUL WIZARD OF OZ, L. Frank Baum. America's finest children's book in facsimile of first edition with all Denslow illustrations in full color. The edition a child should have. Introduction by Martin Gardner. 23 color plates, scores of drawings. iv + 267pp. 20691-2 Paperbound **$3.00**

THE MARVELOUS LAND OF OZ, L. Frank Baum. The second Oz book, every bit as imaginative as the Wizard. The hero is a boy named Tip, but the Scarecrow and the Tin Woodman are back, as is the Oz magic. 16 color plates, 120 drawings by John R. Neill. 287pp. 20692-0 Paperbound **$3.00**

THE MAGICAL MONARCH OF MO, L. Frank Baum. Remarkable adventures in a land even stranger than Oz. The best of Baum's books not in the Oz series. 15 color plates and dozens of drawings by Frank Verbeck. xviii + 237pp.
21892-9 Paperbound **$2.95**

THE BAD CHILD'S BOOK OF BEASTS, MORE BEASTS FOR WORSE CHILDREN, A MORAL ALPHABET, Hilaire Belloc. Three complete humor classics in one volume. Be kind to the frog, and do not call him names . . . and 28 other whimsical animals. Familiar favorites and some not so well known. Illustrated by Basil Blackwell. 156pp. (USO) 20749-8 Paperbound **$2.00**

EAST O' THE SUN AND WEST O' THE MOON, George W. Dasent. Considered the best of all translations of these Norwegian folk tales, this collection has been enjoyed by generations of children (and folklorists too). Includes True and Untrue, Why the Sea is Salt, East O' the Sun and West O' the Moon, Why the Bear is Stumpy-Tailed, Boots and the Troll, The Cock and the Hen, Rich Peter the Pedlar, and 52 more. The only edition with all 59 tales. 77 illustrations by Erik Werenskiold and Theodor Kittelsen. xv + 418pp. 22521-6 Paperbound **$4.00**

GOOPS AND HOW TO BE THEM, Gelett Burgess. Classic of tongue-in-cheek humor, masquerading as etiquette book. 87 verses, twice as many cartoons, show mischievous Goops as they demonstrate to children virtues of table manners, neatness, courtesy, etc. Favorite for generations. viii + 88pp. 6½ x 9¼. 22233-0 Paperbound **$2.00**

ALICE'S ADVENTURES UNDER GROUND, Lewis Carroll. The first version, quite different from the final *Alice in Wonderland,* printed out by Carroll himself with his own illustrations. Complete facsimile of the "million dollar" manuscript Carroll gave to Alice Liddell in 1864. Introduction by Martin Gardner. viii + 96pp. Title and dedication pages in color. 21482-6 Paperbound **$1.50**

THE BROWNIES, THEIR BOOK, Palmer Cox. Small as mice, cunning as foxes, exuberant and full of mischief, the Brownies go to the zoo, toy shop, seashore, circus, etc., in 24 verse adventures and 266 illustrations. Long a favorite, since their first appearance in St. Nicholas Magazine. xi + 144pp. 6⅝ x 9¼. 21265-3 Paperbound **$2.50**

SONGS OF CHILDHOOD, Walter De La Mare. Published (under the pseudonym Walter Ramal) when De La Mare was only 29, this charming collection has long been a favorite children's book. A facsimile of the first edition in paper, the 47 poems capture the simplicity of the nursery rhyme and the ballad, including such lyrics as I Met Eve, Tartary, The Silver Penny. vii + 106pp. (USO) 21972-0 Paperbound **$2.00**

THE COMPLETE NONSENSE OF EDWARD LEAR, Edward Lear. The finest 19th-century humorist-cartoonist in full: all nonsense limericks, zany alphabets, Owl and Pussycat, songs, nonsense botany, and more than 500 illustrations by Lear himself. Edited by Holbrook Jackson. xxix + 287pp. (USO) 20167-8 Paperbound **$3.00**

BILLY WHISKERS: THE AUTOBIOGRAPHY OF A GOAT, Frances Trego Montgomery. A favorite of children since the early 20th century, here are the escapades of that rambunctious, irresistible and mischievous goat—Billy Whiskers. Much in the spirit of *Peck's Bad Boy,* this is a book that children never tire of reading or hearing. All the original familiar illustrations by W. H. Fry are included: 6 color plates, 18 black and white drawings. 159pp. 22345-0 Paperbound **$2.75**

MOTHER GOOSE MELODIES. Faithful republication of the fabulously rare Munroe and Francis "copyright 1833" Boston edition—the most important Mother Goose collection, usually referred to as the "original." Familiar rhymes plus many rare ones, with wonderful old woodcut illustrations. Edited by E. F. Bleiler. 128pp. 4½ x 6⅜. 22577-1 Paperbound **$1.50**

AGAINST THE GRAIN (A REBOURS), Joris K. Huysmans. Filled with weird images, evidences of a bizarre imagination, exotic experiments with hallucinatory drugs, rich tastes and smells and the diversions of its sybarite hero Duc Jean des Esseintes, this classic novel pushed 19th-century literary decadence to its limits. Full unabridged edition. Do not confuse this with abridged editions generally sold. Introduction by Havelock Ellis. xlix + 206pp. 22190-3 Paperbound **$2.50**

VARIORUM SHAKESPEARE: HAMLET. Edited by Horace H. Furness; a landmark of American scholarship. Exhaustive footnotes and appendices treat all doubtful words and phrases, as well as suggested critical emendations throughout the play's history. First volume contains editor's own text, collated with all Quartos and Folios. Second volume contains full first Quarto, translations of Shakespeare's sources (Belleforest, and Saxo Grammaticus), Der Bestrafte Brudermord, and many essays on critical and historical points of interest by major authorities of past and present. Includes details of staging and costuming over the years. By far the best edition available for serious students of Shakespeare. Total of xx + 905pp. 21004-9, 21005-7, 2 volumes, Paperbound **$11.00**

A LIFE OF WILLIAM SHAKESPEARE, Sir Sidney Lee. This is the standard life of Shakespeare, summarizing everything known about Shakespeare and his plays. Incredibly rich in material, broad in coverage, clear and judicious, it has served thousands as the best introduction to Shakespeare. 1931 edition. 9 plates. xxix + 792pp. 21967-4 Paperbound $4.50

MASTERS OF THE DRAMA, John Gassner. Most comprehensive history of the drama in print, covering every tradition from Greeks to modern Europe and America, including India, Far East, etc. Covers more than 800 dramatists, 2000 plays, with biographical material, plot summaries, theatre history, criticism, etc. "Best of its kind in English," *New Republic*. 77 illustrations. xxii + 890pp. 20100-7 Clothbound **$10.00**

THE EVOLUTION OF THE ENGLISH LANGUAGE, George McKnight. The growth of English, from the 14th century to the present. Unusual, non-technical account presents basic information in very interesting form: sound shifts, change in grammar and syntax, vocabulary growth, similar topics. Abundantly illustrated with quotations. Formerly *Modern English in the Making*. xii + 590pp. 21932-1 Paperbound **$4.00**

AN ETYMOLOGICAL DICTIONARY OF MODERN ENGLISH, Ernest Weekley. Fullest, richest work of its sort, by foremost British lexicographer. Detailed word histories, including many colloquial and archaic words; extensive quotations. Do not confuse this with the Concise Etymological Dictionary, which is much abridged. Total of xxvii + 830pp. 6½ x 9¼. 21873-2, 21874-0 Two volumes, Paperbound **$10.00**

FLATLAND: A ROMANCE OF MANY DIMENSIONS, E. A. Abbott. Classic of science-fiction explores ramifications of life in a two-dimensional world, and what happens when a three-dimensional being intrudes. Amusing reading, but also useful as introduction to thought about hyperspace. Introduction by Banesh Hoffmann. 16 illustrations. xx + 103pp. 20001-9 Paperbound **$1.50**

DECORATIVE ALPHABETS AND INITIALS, edited by Alexander Nesbitt. 91 complete alphabets (medieval to modern), 3924 decorative initials, including Victorian novelty and Art Nouveau. 192pp. 7¾ x 10¾. 20544-4 Pa. $4.00

CALLIGRAPHY, Arthur Baker. Over 100 original alphabets from the hand of our greatest living calligrapher: simple, bold, fine-line, richly ornamented, etc. —all strikingly original and different, a fusion of many influences and styles. 155pp. 11⅜ x 8¼. 22895-9 Pa. $4.50

MONOGRAMS AND ALPHABETIC DEVICES, edited by Hayward and Blanche Cirker. Over 2500 combinations, names, crests in very varied styles: script engraving, ornate Victorian, simple Roman, and many others. 226pp. 8⅛ x 11. 22330-2 Pa. $5.00

THE BOOK OF SIGNS, Rudolf Koch. Famed German type designer renders 493 symbols: religious, alchemical, imperial, runes, property marks, etc. Timeless. 104pp. 6⅛ x 9¼. 20162-7 Pa. $1.75

200 DECORATIVE TITLE PAGES, edited by Alexander Nesbitt. 1478 to late 1920's. Baskerville, Dürer, Beardsley, W. Morris, Pyle, many others in most varied techniques. For posters, programs, other uses. 222pp. 8⅜ x 11¼. 21264-5 Pa. $5.00

DICTIONARY OF AMERICAN PORTRAITS, edited by Hayward and Blanche Cirker. 4000 important Americans, earliest times to 1905, mostly in clear line. Politicians, writers, soldiers, scientists, inventors, industrialists, Indians, Blacks, women, outlaws, etc. Identificatory information. 756pp. 9¼ x 12¾. 21823-6 Clothbd. $30.00

ART FORMS IN NATURE, Ernst Haeckel. Multitude of strangely beautiful natural forms: Radiolaria, Foraminifera, jellyfishes, fungi, turtles, bats, etc. All 100 plates of the 19th century evolutionist's Kunstformen der Natur (1904). 100pp. 9⅜ x 12¼. 22987-4 Pa. $4.00

DECOUPAGE: THE BIG PICTURE SOURCEBOOK, Eleanor Rawlings. Make hundreds of beautiful objects, over 550 florals, animals, letters, shells, period costumes, frames, etc. selected by foremost practitioner. Printed on one side of page. 8 color plates. Instructions. 176pp. 9 3/16 x 12¼. 23182-8 Pa. $5.00

AMERICAN FOLK DECORATION, Jean Lipman, Eve Meulendyke. Thorough coverage of all aspects of wood, tin, leather, paper, cloth decoration — scapes, humans, trees, flowers, geometrics — and how to make them. Full instructions. 233 illustrations, 5 in color. 163pp. 8⅜ x 11¼. 22217-9 Pa. $3.95

WHITTLING AND WOODCARVING, E.J. Tangerman. Best book on market; clear, full. If you can cut a potato, you can carve toys, puzzles, chains, caricatures, masks, patterns, frames, decorate surfaces, etc. Also covers serious wood sculpture. Over 200 photos. 293pp. 20965-2 Pa. $3.00

HOW TO SOLVE CHESS PROBLEMS, Kenneth S. Howard. Practical suggestions on problem solving for very beginners. 58 two-move problems, 46 3-movers, 8 4-movers for practice, plus hints. 171pp. 20748-X Pa. $2.00

A GUIDE TO FAIRY CHESS, Anthony Dickins. 3-D chess, 4-D chess, chess on a cylindrical board, reflecting pieces that bounce off edges, cooperative chess, retrograde chess, maximummers, much more. Most based on work of great Dawson. Full handbook, 100 problems. 66pp. 7⅞ x 10¾. 22687-5 Pa. $2.00

WIN AT BACKGAMMON, Millard Hopper. Best opening moves, running game, blocking game, back game, tables of odds, etc. Hopper makes the game clear enough for anyone to play, and win. 43 diagrams. 111pp. 22894-0 Pa. $1.50

BIDDING A BRIDGE HAND, Terence Reese. Master player "thinks out loud" the binding of 75 hands that defy point count systems. Organized by bidding problem—no-fit situations, overbidding, underbidding, cueing your defense, etc. 254pp. EBE 22830-4 Pa. $3.00

THE PRECISION BIDDING SYSTEM IN BRIDGE, C.C. Wei, edited by Alan Truscott. Inventor of precision bidding presents average hands and hands from actual play, including games from 1969 Bermuda Bowl where system emerged. 114 exercises. 116pp. 21171-1 Pa. $1.75

LEARN MAGIC, Henry Hay. 20 simple, easy-to-follow lessons on magic for the new magician: illusions, card tricks, silks, sleights of hand, coin manipulations, escapes, and more —all with a minimum amount of equipment. Final chapter explains the great stage illusions. 92 illustrations. 285pp. 21238-6 Pa. $2.95

THE NEW MAGICIAN'S MANUAL, Walter B. Gibson. Step-by-step instructions and clear illustrations guide the novice in mastering 36 tricks; much equipment supplied on 16 pages of cut-out materials. 36 additional tricks. 64 illustrations. 159pp. 6⅝ x 10. 23113-5 Pa. $3.00

PROFESSIONAL MAGIC FOR AMATEURS, Walter B. Gibson. 50 easy, effective tricks used by professionals —cards, string, tumblers, handkerchiefs, mental magic, etc. 63 illustrations. 223pp. 23012-0 Pa. $2.50

CARD MANIPULATIONS, Jean Hugard. Very rich collection of manipulations; has taught thousands of fine magicians tricks that are really workable, eye-catching. Easily followed, serious work. Over 200 illustrations. 163pp. 20539-8 Pa. $2.00

ABBOTT'S ENCYCLOPEDIA OF ROPE TRICKS FOR MAGICIANS, Stewart James. Complete reference book for amateur and professional magicians containing more than 150 tricks involving knots, penetrations, cut and restored rope, etc. 510 illustrations. Reprint of 3rd edition. 400pp. 23206-9 Pa. $3.50

THE SECRETS OF HOUDINI, J.C. Cannell. Classic study of Houdini's incredible magic, exposing closely-kept professional secrets and revealing, in general terms, the whole art of stage magic. 67 illustrations. 279pp. 22913-0 Pa. $2.50

VISUAL ILLUSIONS: THEIR CAUSES, CHARACTERISTICS, AND APPLICATIONS, Matthew Luckiesh. Thorough description and discussion of optical illusion, geometric and perspective, particularly; size and shape distortions, illusions of color, of motion; natural illusions; use of illusion in art and magic, industry, etc. Most useful today with op art, also for classical art. Scores of effects illustrated. Introduction by William H. Ittleson. 100 illustrations. xxi + 252pp.
21530-X Paperbound **$2.50**

A HANDBOOK OF ANATOMY FOR ART STUDENTS, Arthur Thomson. Thorough, virtually exhaustive coverage of skeletal structure, musculature, etc. Full text, supplemented by anatomical diagrams and drawings and by photographs of undraped figures. Unique in its comparison of male and female forms, pointing out differences of contour, texture, form. 211 figures, 40 drawings, 86 photographs. xx + 459pp. 5⅜ x 8⅜.
21163-0 Paperbound **$5.00**

150 MASTERPIECES OF DRAWING, Selected by Anthony Toney. Full page reproductions of drawings from the early 16th to the end of the 18th century, all beautifully reproduced: Rembrandt, Michelangelo, Dürer, Fragonard, Urs, Graf, Wouwerman, many others. First-rate browsing book, model book for artists. xviii + 150pp. 8⅜ x 11¼.
21032-4 Paperbound **$4.00**

THE LATER WORK OF AUBREY BEARDSLEY, Aubrey Beardsley. Exotic, erotic, ironic masterpieces in full maturity: Comedy Ballet, Venus and Tannhauser, Pierrot, Lysistrata, Rape of the Lock, Savoy material, Ali Baba, Volpone, etc. This material revolutionized the art world, and is still powerful, fresh, brilliant. With *The Early Work,* all Beardsley's finest work. 174 plates, 2 in color. xiv + 176pp. 8⅛ x 11.
21817-1 Paperbound **$4.00**

DRAWINGS OF REMBRANDT, Rembrandt van Rijn. Complete reproduction of fabulously rare edition by Lippmann and Hofstede de Groot, completely reedited, updated, improved by Prof. Seymour Slive, Fogg Museum. Portraits, Biblical sketches, landscapes, Oriental types, nudes, episodes from classical mythology—All Rembrandt's fertile genius. Also selection of drawings by his pupils and followers. "Stunning volumes," *Saturday Review.* 550 illustrations. lxxviii + 552pp. 9⅛ x 12¼.
21485-0, 21486-9 Two volumes, Paperbound **$12.00**

THE DISASTERS OF WAR, Francisco Goya. One of the masterpieces of Western civilization—83 etchings that record Goya's shattering, bitter reaction to the Napoleonic war that swept through Spain after the insurrection of 1808 and to war in general. Reprint of the first edition, with three additional plates from Boston's Museum of Fine Arts. All plates facsimile size. Introduction by Philip Hofer, Fogg Museum. v + 97pp. 9⅜ x 8¼.
21872-4 Paperbound **$3.00**

GRAPHIC WORKS OF ODILON REDON. Largest collection of Redon's graphic works ever assembled: 172 lithographs, 28 etchings and engravings, 9 drawings. These include some of his most famous works. All the plates from *Odilon Redon: oeuvre graphique complet,* plus additional plates. New introduction and caption translations by Alfred Werner. 209 illustrations. xxvii + 209pp. 9⅛ x 12¼.
21966-8 Paperbound **$6.00**

THE MAGIC MOVING PICTURE BOOK, Bliss, Sands & Co. The pictures in this book move! Volcanoes erupt, a house burns, a serpentine dancer wiggles her way through a number. By using a specially ruled acetate screen provided, you can obtain these and 15 other startling effects. Originally "The Motograph Moving Picture Book." 32pp. 8¼ x 11. 23224-7 Pa. $1.75

STRING FIGURES AND HOW TO MAKE THEM, Caroline F. Jayne. Fullest, clearest instructions on string figures from around world: Eskimo, Navajo, Lapp, Europe, more. Cats cradle, moving spear, lightning, stars. Introduction by A.C. Haddon. 950 illustrations. 407pp. 20152-X Pa. $3.50

PAPER FOLDING FOR BEGINNERS, William D. Murray and Francis J. Rigney. Clearest book on market for making origami sail boats, roosters, frogs that move legs, cups, bonbon boxes. 40 projects. More than 275 illustrations. Photographs. 94pp. 20713-7 Pa. $1.25

INDIAN SIGN LANGUAGE, William Tomkins. Over 525 signs developed by Sioux, Blackfoot, Cheyenne, Arapahoe and other tribes. Written instructions and diagrams: how to make words, construct sentences. Also 290 pictographs of Sioux and Ojibway tribes. 111pp. 6⅛ x 9¼. 22029-X Pa. $1.50

BOOMERANGS: HOW TO MAKE AND THROW THEM, Bernard S. Mason. Easy to make and throw, dozens of designs: cross-stick, pinwheel, boomabird, tumblestick, Australian curved stick boomerang. Complete throwing instructions. All safe. 99pp. 23028-7 Pa. $1.75

25 KITES THAT FLY, Leslie Hunt. Full, easy to follow instructions for kites made from inexpensive materials. Many novelties. Reeling, raising, designing your own. 70 illustrations. 110pp. 22550-X Pa. $1.25

TRICKS AND GAMES ON THE POOL TABLE, Fred Herrmann. 79 tricks and games, some solitaires, some for 2 or more players, some competitive; mystifying shots and throws, unusual carom, tricks involving cork, coins, a hat, more. 77 figures. 95pp. 21814-7 Pa. $1.25

WOODCRAFT AND CAMPING, Bernard S. Mason. How to make a quick emergency shelter, select woods that will burn immediately, make do with limited supplies, etc. Also making many things out of wood, rawhide, bark, at camp. Formerly titled Woodcraft. 295 illustrations. 580pp. 21951-8 Pa. $4.00

AN INTRODUCTION TO CHESS MOVES AND TACTICS SIMPLY EXPLAINED, Leonard Barden. Informal intermediate introduction: reasons for moves, tactics, openings, traps, positional play, endgame. Isolates patterns. 102pp. USO 21210-6 Pa. $1.35

LASKER'S MANUAL OF CHESS, Dr. Emanuel Lasker. Great world champion offers very thorough coverage of all aspects of chess. Combinations, position play, openings, endgame, aesthetics of chess, philosophy of struggle, much more. Filled with analyzed games. 390pp. 20640-8 Pa. $4.00